ALLIANCE *and* ILLUSION

ALLIANCE *and* ILLUSION

CANADA AND THE WORLD, 1945-1984

Robert Bothwell

UBCPress·Vancouver·Toronto

16 15 14 13 12 11 10 09 08 07   5 4 3 2 1

Printed in Canada on acid-free paper.

LIBRARY AND ARCHIVES CANADA CATALOGUING IN PUBLICATION

Bothwell, Robert, 1944-
    Alliance and illusion : Canada and the world, 1945-1984 / Robert Bothwell.

Includes bibliographical references and index.
ISBN 978-0-7748-1368-6

    1. Canada – Foreign relations – 1945- . 2. Canada – Politics and government – 1935- . 3. Cold War. I. Title.

FC242.B675 2007   327.71009'045   C2006-906278-1

Canadä

UBC Press gratefully acknowledges the financial support for our publishing program of the Government of Canada through the Book Publishing Industry Development Program (BPIDP), and of the Canada Council for the Arts, and the British Columbia Arts Council.

This book has been published with the help of a grant from the Canadian Federation for the Humanities and Social Sciences, through the Aid to Scholarly Publications Programme, using funds provided by the Social Sciences and Humanities Research Council of Canada.

Printed and bound in Canada by Friesens
Typeset in Minion by Artegraphica Design Co. Ltd.
Copy editor: Barbara Tessman
Proofreader: Gail Copeland
Indexer: Noeline Bridge

UBC Press
The University of British Columbia
2029 West Mall
Vancouver, BC V6T 1Z2
604-822-5959 / Fax: 604-822-6083
www.ubcpress.ca

For my mentor, colleague, and friend, Robert Craig Brown

CONTENTS

ACKNOWLEDGMENTS

This book has evolved over many years, and the number of people and institutions who should be thanked is legion. First is my wife, Gail, who has put up with the many mood swings that producing such an opus seems to entail. Then there are the undergraduate students in my various courses, who have over the years heard and read much of the book.

As the book progressed it was generously supported from a variety of sources. The Social Sciences and Humanities Research Council of Canada funded an earlier conception, centred on Canada and the Vietnam War, in the late 1990s. The University of Toronto granted me a Connaught Research Fellowship in 1997, in conjunction with the same earlier version of this project. In 1997-1998, I had the privilege of a fellowship at the Woodrow Wilson Center in Washington, crucial for researching the many Canadian-American sections of the book. At a later stage the Donner Canadian Foundation came to the rescue with a grant to finish up my research in the United States. Finally, as the holder of the May Gluskin Chair in Canadian History at the University of Toronto, I have benefited from its enlightened endowment, which has allowed me to spend the past few years writing and *not* filling out forms begging for grants.

Many friends have assisted with the conception and evolution of this work. The late Bill and Louise Armstrong, veterans of the US Foreign Service specializing in Canada, were free with advice and hospitality in Washington. Tom Delworth, former political director of the Department of External Affairs and former Canadian ambassador in Bonn, read various chapters and tried to save me from error. Allan Gotlieb, former undersecretary for external affairs and former ambassador in Washington, read the whole manuscript and was generous with his time and comments. Tom Nichols, a political scientist with a salutary hatred of jargon, helped me with the cultural context of the early 1980s – especially the relationship between popular music and the various "peace" campaigns of the early 1980s. John English, Norman Hillmer, Doug Owram, and Margaret MacMillan all read the manuscript in whole or in part, and assisted greatly with their comments.

I have likewise been fortunate in a succession of research assistants: Alison Meek, Trish McMahon, Kathleen Rasmussen, Rutha Astravas, Mike Morgan, Maria Banda, Yasemin Akcakir, Colum Grove-White, and Sadia Rafiquddin have contributed immeasurably to the research from its first stages to the last desperate scramble. My assistant in the International Relations Program at Trinity College, Marilyn Laville, helped save me from a natural propensity to double-book my days, and sped the manuscript to the publisher.

The publisher, UBC Press, has been endearingly forbearing as the manuscript slowly – very slowly – became a book. Emily Andrew had faith in the project and ensured that it would, eventually, appear. Camilla Blakeley did yeoman service managing the transformation of the manuscript, despite apparently endless and always complicated computer glitches. I very much appreciate Barbara Tessman's stringent editing and Noeline Bridge's comprehensive indexing. The result greatly strengthens the book.

CHRONOLOGY

1944

1-22 July   Canada attends the Bretton Woods conference, which establishes the bases for the International Monetary Fund and the eventual World Bank.

Aug.-Sept.   Dumbarton Oaks conference, between the United States, the UK, and the USSR, agrees on a draft charter for the United Nations.

1945

25 Apr.-26 June   Canada attends the San Francisco conference, which drafts the final version of the UN charter. Fifty-one nations, including Canada, become members.

5 May   Canadian General Charles Foulkes accepts the surrender of German troops in the Netherlands.

8 May   War in Europe ends with a general German surrender.

11 June   Prime Minister Mackenzie King's Liberal Party wins a narrow majority in a general election.

6 and 9 Aug.   Two atomic bombs are dropped on Japan.

2 Sept.   The Japanese Empire surrenders to the allies.

5 Sept.   Igor Gouzenko brings to Canadian authorities evidence of a Soviet spy ring in Canada.

1946

10 Jan.   The first session of the United Nations opens in London.

2 Mar.   The British government accepts the terms of a Canadian loan of $1.25 billion.

5 Mar.   Winston Churchill makes his "iron curtain" speech at Fulton, Missouri.

15 July   A royal commission reports on the Gouzenko spy ring.

29 July-15 Oct.   Canada attends the Paris peace conference, which drafts treaties with Germany's allies. The treaties take effect in January 1947.

1 Aug.   The Anglo-Canadian wheat contract is signed.

4 Sept.   Louis St. Laurent becomes external affairs minister.

1947

13 Jan.   St. Laurent delivers the Gray Lecture at the University of Toronto.

June-Sept.   In discussions in Paris a vast American aid program for Europe (the Marshall Plan) is formulated.

1948

1 Jan.   Canada and twenty-two other countries sign the General Agreement on Tariffs and Trade (GATT) in Geneva.

25 Feb.   A Communist coup takes place in Czechoslovakia.

Mar.   Secret Canada-US-UK discussions take place about a North Atlantic security pact.

July   Seven-power talks open in Washington to draft an agreement for a North Atlantic pact.

24 July   The Berlin blockade begins.

10 Sept.   Lester B. Pearson becomes external affairs minister.

15 Nov.   Mackenzie King resigns and Louis St. Laurent becomes prime minister.

1949

4 Apr.   Canada signs the North Atlantic Treaty, becoming a founding member of the North Atlantic Treaty Organisation (NATO).

12 May   The Berlin blockade ends.

27 June   St. Laurent's Liberals win a sweeping majority in a general election.

1950

25 June   North Korea invades South Korea.

19 Dec.   Canadian troops arrive in Korea.

1951

10 Apr.   Pearson creates a stir with a speech on Canadian-American relations.

Oct.-Nov.   Canadian troops sent to Europe to serve with NATO.

1953

27 July   An armistice ends fighting in the Korean War.

10 Aug.   St. Laurent and the Liberals win another large majority in a general election.

1954

Apr.-July   Canada attends a conference on Korea in Geneva; subsequently, Canada agrees to become a member of the International Commission on Security and Control in Indochina, to oversee the agreements that had ended the Indochina War (1946-1954).

1956

May-June   The pipeline debate takes place in the House of Commons.

26 July   Egypt nationalizes the Suez Canal, beginning the Suez Crisis.

29 Oct.   Israeli invasion of Egypt begins concerted action agreed with the French and British governments to seize the Suez Canal.

4 Nov.   The UN General Assembly adopts Pearson's proposal for the creation of a United Nations Emergency Force (UNEF) in the Sinai.

1957

10 June   The Progressive Conservatives under John Diefenbaker win a plurality of House of Commons seats in a general election.

22 June   Diefenbaker becomes prime minister and minister of external affairs.

1 Aug.   Canada and the United States establish the North American Air Defense Command (NORAD).

13 Sept.   Sidney Smith becomes external affairs minister.

1958

31 Mar.   Diefenbaker's Progressive Conservatives win a huge majority in a general election.

1959

4 June   Howard Green becomes external affairs minister.

1961

17 Jan.   Diefenbaker and Eisenhower sign the Columbia River treaty.

Mar.   At a Commonwealth conference in London, Diefenbaker reiterates Canada's opposition to that country's racial policy; South Africa leaves the Commonwealth.

13 Aug.   East Germany erects the Berlin Wall.

1962

18 June — In a general election, Diefenbaker scrapes by with a minority government.

22 Oct. — US president Kennedy announces a blockade of Cuba to force the removal of Soviet missiles installed there.

1963

5 Feb. — The opposition parties defeat the Progressive Conservative minority government over nuclear weapons.

8 Apr. — Lester Pearson's Liberals win 128 out of 265 seats in a general election.

22 Apr. — Paul Martin becomes external affairs minister in the new Pearson minority Liberal government.

5 Aug. — The Limited Test Ban Treaty is signed in Moscow.

8 Aug. — Canada signs Limited Test Ban Treaty.

1964-1967 — The "Kennedy Round" of GATT negotiations is undertaken.

1965

16 Jan. — Pearson and US president Johnson sign the Auto Pact establishing (mostly) free trade in automobiles and auto parts between the two countries.

8 Nov. — Pearson wins another minority in a general election.

1967

June — The Six-Day War between Israel and its Arab neighbours results in Israeli occupation of the Sinai, the West Bank, and the Golan Heights. Canadian troops in UNEF are singled out for rapid expulsion by Egypt in a prelude to the war.

24 July — French president de Gaulle proclaims, "Vive le Québec libre" in a speech in Montreal.

13-14 Dec. — NATO issues the Harmel Report.

1968

20 Apr. — Mitchell Sharp becomes external affairs minister.

25 June — A general election gives Pierre Trudeau and his Liberal Party a clear majority in the House of Commons.

1971

Aug.   President Nixon announces unilateral American trade measures; acrimonious but fruitless discussions with Canada follow.

1972

15 Apr.   Nixon and Trudeau sign the Great Lakes Water Quality Agreement.

Oct.   The government announces a "Third Option" policy of economic diversification.

30 Oct.   A general election returns a weak Liberal minority government.

1973-1979 The "Tokyo Round" of GATT negotiations are undertaken.

1973

Jan.   As a result of the Paris accords ending the Vietnam War, Canada becomes a member of an International Commission for Control and Supervision (ICCS) in Vietnam.

29 May   Canada announces its withdrawal from the ICCS.

Oct.   War is renewed between Israel and its Arab neighbours. An Arab oil boycott of countries friendly to Israel exacerbates a sharp oil price rise.

1974

8 July   A general election returns a Liberal majority government.

8 Aug.   Allan MacEachen becomes external affairs minister.

1976

14 Sept.   Donald Jamieson becomes external affairs minister.

1978

22 Nov.   The Great Lakes Water Quality Agreement is renewed and expanded.

1979

Jan.   A revolution in Iran panics international petroleum markets, causing oil prices to spike.

22 May   Joe Clark's Progressive Conservatives win a plurality of House of Commons seats in a general election.

4 June   Flora MacDonald becomes external affairs minister.

1980

18 Feb.	Trudeau's Liberals win back a majority in the House of Commons.
3 Mar.	Mark MacGuigan becomes external affairs minister.
20 May	Trudeau and his federalist allies decisively defeat the Quebec separatists in a provincial referendum.
28 Oct.	The government announces the National Energy Program (NEP).

1981

13 Oct.	Talks in Ottawa fail to resolve Canadian-American differences over the NEP.

1982

10 Sept.	Allan MacEachen becomes external affairs minister for the second time.

1983

31 Aug.	Trudeau government seeks sectoral free trade with the United States.

1984

30 June	Jean Chrétien becomes external affairs minister in John Turner's government.
17 Sept.	Turner government resigns.

ALLIANCE *and* ILLUSION

INTRODUCTION

Canada, an old saw goes, is a country with too little history and too much geography. Readers of this book may be tempted to think otherwise. And yet this book covers only a fragment of Canada's human history, the history of Canadian foreign affairs in the period since 1945, more specifically from the beginning of the Cold War to the end of the Trudeau era in 1984.

Canada has a history that is political, economic, military, social, and intellectual. But it has its roots in geography. Canada is of course a vast land, spreading more than 3,000 miles from coast to coast. At almost 10 million square kilometres, Canada is the second-largest political jurisdiction on earth. It is also one of the emptiest. With 32 million people in 2005, Canada is middling in numbers, but 90 percent of those millions snuggle within 250 kilometres of the US border, leaving most of the country empty, if not untouched. The notion of Canada as a northern country is thus true only in part – some might say in very small part. Fragmented on its north-south axis, Canada is also fragmented east-west, with its major regions – British Columbia, the Prairies, central Canada, and the Atlantic provinces – divided from each other by stretches of scenic rock and lakes.

Canada is also fragmented historically. Waves of occupation in both historic and prehistoric times left layers of language and cultures on the geography. Clashes of cultures produced wars that spilled across the divide between prehistory and history and that marked the contacts between Aboriginal North Americans and the European settlers who flooded the land in the wake of explorers and empires. Canada began to take its modern shape only in the aftermath of a series of wars in the middle of the eighteenth century that left the British briefly in occupation of most of the continent.

And so Canada was, to begin with, a fragment of the British Empire. Its design, its boundaries, even its ethnic makeup suited imperial purposes and tied Canada not only to the imperial motherland, Great Britain, but to the former British (and English-speaking) colonies to the south. Canada enjoyed a symbiotic relationship with both Great Britain and the United States. Some Canadians doubted that Canada, by itself, was a complete nation. Others saw the country suspended between two poles, the great republic to the south and the imperial British mother across the Atlantic. An uncertain national identity has been, and remains, a major theme of Canadian history and has been reflected in Canada's foreign relations.

The fortunes of war had left the British Empire in North America with two main ethnic groups – people from the British Isles and those from France. The latter, who were left over from the collapse of an even earlier empire, were concentrated in Quebec. Unlike both Great Britain and the United States, Canada was a compromise between two languages, and its politics therefore had an extra complication that reflected Canada's binational fact.

In 1945 Canada had only recently become a sovereign state, and it had taken Canadians some time and considerable mental effort to get used to the fact. As a recent former colony, Canada prized the acquisition of sovereignty even as it explored what sovereignty might, in fact, mean. Not surprisingly, Canadian governments in 1945 and after kept a jealous eye on Canada's independence and worried endlessly over any hint that this independence might be compromised or overridden.

If Canada was an independent country, it was also a minor country. That had not mattered a great deal before 1939 or even during the war. Canada was part of the British Empire – part ally and part subordinate imperial associate. Relations were primarily with the imperial centre, Great Britain; association with other parts of the empire like Australia or India mattered much less, if at all. Imperial relationships were primarily bilateral relationships. There was also a bilateral relationship with the United States, though without the benefit of a constitutional linkage. Nevertheless, similarity and proximity, not to mention economic ties, counted for much in maintaining links between Canada and its southern neighbour.

The character of a relationship is also important. English Canadians prized their affinity for and resemblance to other English-speaking nations, especially Great Britain and the United States. In 1945 a Canadian historian published a book on the subject of Canada's relationships with its two larger partners – *The North Atlantic Triangle*.[1] Two sides of the triangle were larger, older, and more important than Canada, but Canadians believed that there was still a place in Anglo-Saxon geometry for their country, and they liked the British and Americans to understand that Canada was close to them politically, perhaps even that Canada was their best friend. In return, Canadians expected to be noticed, to be thanked. If Canada was expected to contribute to some common enterprise, Canadians expected to be asked first. In some senses, Canadians had two identities – national and collective, neither complete without the other.

This dual identity was a legacy from Canada's colonial past. Canadians were local and imperial, Canadian and British, with a strong American accent. Being British meant that Canadians had rights as well as duties to Britain and the empire. The most important right was to be asked. Not to be asked was to be taken for granted. Canada's history in the British Empire was rife with moments when the imperial government had assumed rather than asked for Canadian assistance. Sometimes the Canadian government had made the best of it and gone along, as the government of Wilfrid Laurier had in an imperial war in South Africa in 1899. Sometimes Ottawa had refused to cooperate, as when the British asked for Canadian troops to reinforce a British garrison in Turkey in 1922, in what Prime Minister Mackenzie King considered to be a minor and pointless adventure.

On larger questions, however, Canadian and British interests were assumed by English Canadians, especially, to be much the same. As Mackenzie King put it in 1923, "if the great and clear call of duty comes," Canada would be at Britain's side.[2] This proved to be the case in 1939, and throughout the war that followed the Canadian government generally (if sometimes grudgingly) accepted Britain's lead. Canada needed to be in an alliance, and it needed and accepted the direction of its senior partner, the British. But the Canadians were not alone in the empire with the British, and by the 1940s a system of regular consultation among its component parts had come to exist. The empire, in other words, was not simply a bilateral Anglo-Canadian axis, but a multilateral alliance, in form and in effect.

If Canadian relations with Great Britain had some of the characteristics of a formal alliance, and had accumulated a practical history that guided the British and Canadian governments in their contacts, the same was not quite true of relations with the United States. Canadian relations with its southern neighbour were much broader than with Britain. Fads, fashions, opinions, ideologies, and organizations had a habit of slopping over the border. The United States was not thousands of miles away, but right next door. Canadians and Americans could walk right across the line. Individual Canadians and Americans were hard to tell apart – this was true even of French Canadians, if one inquired on both sides of the borders between Canada and adjacent parts of New England, where French Canadians were plentiful.

Canadians looking south – at least as far south as the Ohio River, the frontier between North and South – could see themselves in the patterns and assumptions of US daily life. The Americans were more plentiful and more various, and richer too, but from highway signs to architecture to comic strips there was a marked resemblance. If official Canada resembled Great Britain, unofficial Canada, the English-speaking part, looked like the United States.

In the interwar years Canadians endlessly debated whether they were more British or American. (As a later, 1957, musical put it, this left them no time to be themselves.[3]) Of course, the reality was that they were distinct from both, but it was useful for Canadians to be able to use their imperial connection to distance themselves from the Americans, and their physical and cultural proximity to the Americans to distance themselves from Great Britain.

The connections to, rather than the distinctions from, both countries were reinforced during the crisis of the Second World War. Just before the war, in 1938, Mackenzie King and the American president, Franklin D. Roosevelt, exchanged public promises of military support in case of foreign invasion, and this was supplemented in 1940 by the establishment of a joint military board to oversee the common defence. Most of Canada's military activity during the war took place far from Canadian shores, and under British command. Canada reflexively accepted that in a world war Canada's task was to follow rather than lead.

This pattern of following a greater power's lead continued after 1945, although the United States took on the part previously played by Great Britain. The dramatic circumstances of the Cold War – the onset of the confrontation with communism – allowed the recent past to be submerged and almost forgotten. The Cold War defined intellectual and political currency, and for more than forty years all things were new under the sun. In his own lifetime Mackenzie King became an anachronism, an embarrassing remnant of the colonial past in which the true colonial used autonomy to escape the responsibilities that fell on the older, larger relatives. Yet when the occasion arose, as it was bound to do, his successors from St Laurent to Trudeau mimicked his behaviour as, largely unconsciously, they followed his policies. Over Suez in 1956, nuclear warheads in 1963, Vietnam in the 1960s, NATO garrisons in 1969, energy supplies in the 1970s and 1980s, Canadian governments declined to follow where their more senior allies wished them to go.

Older patterns therefore persisted. Canadians had a collective identification with their allies that saw the country into – and eventually through – the Cold War. In return, they expected that their allies, meaning mostly the Americans, would not tread indelicately on Canadian toes. Most of the time, the allies obliged.

Foreign relations are, of course, reciprocal. Great Britain and the United States usually kept their powder dry in dealings with Canada. All things considered, there were remarkably few explosions in British and American relations with Canada over time, although, as the British link dwindled, the British appreciation for the consequences of bad manners or antagonistic policies dwindled too, as Canadian governments under Diefenbaker, Trudeau, and Mulroney learned to their surprise and cost.

As David Haglund has observed, the notion of a what a "triangle" was or what it did could change over time. The North Atlantic Triangle differentiated as well as unified its participants. If one side of the triangle grew too large or too pressing, there was always the other for some counterbalance. Great Britain came to exchange Canada, and the rest of the Commonwealth, for Europe. "Europe" thus became a surrogate part of the triangle, but without ever fully supplanting Britain. From at least the 1950s on, Canadian governments talked of Europe rather than Britain and proclaimed an "Atlantic" destiny. (This concept was inevitably labelled "Atlanticism."[4]) Some Canadians, in but also outside government, invoked worlds beyond Europe – sometimes Japan, or "the Pacific," or the Third World, seeking to substitute one form of collective identification, historical and traditional, for another. The most notable example of these tendencies occurred in the 1970s, when the Trudeau government sought a "Third Option," attempting to balance close relations with the United States with significant relations with Europe and Japan. In the 1970s and 1980s other Canadians sought to pursue the underdeveloped world, attempting to match Canada's long-term interest in correcting global imbalances and disharmonies with a short-term rapprochement with countries that most Canadians found strange and sometimes even repugnant. As a result, Canadian foreign relations became more diffuse, sometimes in a predominantly Cold War context, sometimes not.

Economics mirrored politics throughout the Cold War. Considerable time could be spent debating whether economics or politics came first in the development of Canada's foreign relations or the elaboration of Canadian foreign policy. It is sufficient to observe that in both politics and economics, cultural similarities continued to count. American investors, like earlier generations of British investors, found Canada culturally compatible and institutionally familiar; like British investors, they were sometimes disappointed in the return on their money. Canadian investors returned the compliment, though on a lesser scale and perhaps with greater profit, when it came to the United States. As far as trade was concerned, Canada was and remained throughout the forty-five years of the Cold War the United States' leading trade partner. It was an inescapable and sometimes useful fact, for the Americans noticed economic Canada even when political Canada dipped beneath the horizon of American policy.[5]

Another consideration in the development of Canadian foreign policy is the moralism that sometimes suffused Canada's approach after 1945. It may have been merely the consequence of a Canadian search for distinctiveness, but it may also have derived from a well-established moralizing tradition common to most countries in Western culture but especially obvious in the English-speaking world – and resented outside. The moralizing Briton or American is a stock figure in non-Anglo-Saxon complaints about the "hypocrisy" of the foreign policy of these two countries. It is no surprise that Canada too contributed to the genre, most notoriously when Senator Raoul Dandurand, a member of Mackenzie King's Cabinet, called attention in a speech at the League of Nations to the superiority of Canada's North American location, "a fireproof house," far from the "inflammable materials" piled around Europe.

Norman Hillmer has used the term "moral superpower" to describe some Canadians' self-conception. As he notes, it is not unique to Canada – indeed it was applied first to Sweden, which throughout the Cold War was ostentatiously neutral, standing between but apart from the contending international blocs – in public at least.[6] Canada was part of one of the blocs, but despite that fact it from time to time irritated its more "realistic" allies – France over Algeria, Britain over Suez and later over South Africa, and the United States over Vietnam.

Sometimes Canadians invoked – incredibly but honestly – their country's lack of a colonial past to justify a special mission to commune with the Third World. In their defence, Canadian politicians and diplomats claimed enlightened self-interest – the need for Canada and for the West in general to be a trusted "honest broker." This idea sometimes prevailed over the shorter-term advantages of alliance solidarity, though not always. Disappointment only fed the appetite of the supporters of the "honest broker" or "helpful fixer" role and helped confuse the notion of Canada as a "middle power," another defining phrase much used to describe Canada's "special" place in the world.[7]

No account of Canadian foreign relations is complete without reference to the requirements of Canada's domestic situation. Foreign policy almost tore the country apart along linguistic lines – in war in 1917 and 1944, and possibly again in peace during the 1960s and 1970s. On imperial issues French Canada had different views from English Canada. Of course, English and French Canadians also differed among themselves as to what policies their common country should follow.

The Cold War was for a time a useful sedative for Canadian internal quarrels: it was one issue where the elites of English and French Canada could and did agree. Nevertheless, the directors of Canadian foreign policy could never entirely forget that French-speaking citizens might well have different impressions than their English-speaking counterparts of the bona fides of the federal government in managing relations with France or French Africa. From that considerable difficulty there flowed such policies as the anxious recruitment of bilingual staff and the pursuit of a French-speaking commonwealth – la Francophonie – in the 1970s. Indeed for periods in the 1970s, 1980s, and 1990s Canadian foreign policy, like all other policies of the central government, had to pass political scrutiny in terms of its potential impact of the larger question of whether Quebec would or would not remain in Canada and, by extension, whether Canada would continue to exist. In the quest for friends and allies, even some of the government's most cherished priorities – nationalist policies designed to ward off American investment, for example – suddenly became unimportant.

Canadian foreign relations, as contemplated in the pages that follow, cannot be neatly compartmentalized or categorized. They have been the creature of internal as well as external circumstance. They have been shaped by the peculiarities of the Canadian national character in both its English and French versions. They have not been the product of Canadian circumstance alone, but of much larger international trends. They are the product of economics as well as politics – world economic trends and American and British politics in addition to the Canadian variety. And in the end they return to geography and society.

CONSTRUCTION
AND RECONSTRUCTION:
CANADA IN 1945

1

In 1945 Canadians celebrated victory in war. The Second World War did not officially come to an end until 2 September, when the allied powers, including Canada, accepted Japan's surrender on board an American battleship in Tokyo Bay, but as far as most Canadians were concerned the real war finished in Europe in May with the surrender of Germany.

In May – as they would later in September – crowds surged onto Parliament Hill in Ottawa and main streets across the country. Citizens clustered around their radios for the latest news: Hitler was dead, and the occupied countries of Europe liberated. It was Germany's turn to be defeated, devastated, and occupied. Over the air waves Prime Minister Mackenzie King gave thanks in English and Justice Minister Louis St Laurent did the same in French.

There was much to be thankful for. Nazi Germany proved to be worse in fact than the propagandists had imagined. The toll of Nazi atrocities mounted as allied troops discovered and entered German death camps: the evil nature of the Nazi government and the providential nature of its defeat could no longer be doubted. Canadian casualties during the last eleven months of the war had been heavy, but over six years the military dead numbered only 42,000. This out of armed forces that had enlisted over a million men and women – one in twelve Canadians. Now the troops would be coming home.

Superficially, Canada looked much the same as it had in 1939: civilian society had lived on its existing resources for most of the war, repairing rather than replacing, doubling up in scarce accommodations, stretching the civilian economy to make room for military supplies. It was a worn and weary Canada that met the eye of the visitor; yet the appearance was deceptive. Statistics showed a growing economy – up 50 percent over 1939. More people were working than ever before. Canadians were making more money than in 1939, though they were spending less, for there was not very much to spend it on. Canadians also paid more taxes than in 1939, more than Americans did and almost as much as the beleaguered British. In terms of gross national product, as far as such things could be measured in the chaotic conditions of 1945, Canada ranked fifth or sixth in the world – $11,863,000,000 in the dollars of the day, or not quite $1,000 per person. Such wealth helped pay for a navy of 362 ships of all kinds, an army of 750,000 troops, and an air force of 1,000 or more aircraft.[1]

It was a real, though temporary, eminence. No one thought that Canada's hundreds of thousands of military could possibly be permanent. Factories producing military supplies were already being converted to peacetime production. Within a few months of the end of the war, unused aircraft were being incinerated, while ships were mothballed or, if possible, sold off. The troops were coming home as fast as shipping could be found and, on arrival, were demobilized and handed a package of veterans' benefits. Soldiers who had been fighting in the Netherlands in May could find themselves enrolled in university by September. Many more were to follow.

For the first time in six years, Canada's priorities were domestic. Foreign events continued to fascinate readers of newspapers and viewers of newsreels, but after May 1945, and certainly after the Japanese surrender, they were no longer a life-and-death issue for Canadians. Citizens instead worried about "security," defined as security of income and security of employment – issues that looked back to the economic depression of the 1930s, when both commodities were in short supply. There was enough to keep Canada preoccupied with domestic affairs, starting with a national election in June. By a narrow margin and with only 41 percent of the votes, the existing, wartime government remained in office.

Politics and the Prime Minister

Prime Minister William Lyon Mackenzie King may have been the most successful politician ever to hold the office in Canada. Certainly he held it the longest – twenty-two years, spread over three decades, before he quit in November 1948. In 1945 King was seventy, with a political life that stretched back to 1908, when he had first won a seat in Parliament. He was a Liberal by conviction and heredity, the descendant of an unsuccessful liberal revolutionary of the 1830s. Revolutionary fires burned low in Mackenzie King: he far preferred the orderly, almost dull rhythm of Canadian politics. But he used politics to express liberal themes that would have been familiar anywhere in the English-speaking world. He championed self-determination, favoured lower tariffs and open economies, and hesitated in the face of too much or too forceful government intervention in society. He deplored tyranny abroad, while seeking signs that such tyranny was not so dark or so deep as to make war or the use of force inevitable.[2]

King feared war and disliked force; by the same token, he loved order and orderly procedures. In 1935 he used the slogan "King or Chaos" to defeat his Conservative rival, R.B. Bennett; it was a juxtaposition that appealed to King and may have actually defined his domestic policies. He did not want to overturn society or the social order, though he hoped, by stages, to ameliorate them. Radical, violent change was for romantics, and, as far as domestic politics was concerned, King despised romanticism and drama. (He was far from despising them in the private realm, as his collection of ruins at his Kingsmere estate made clear.)

King applied the same caution to foreign affairs. Born into late Victorian Canada at a time when his country was little more than a large and almost vacant colony of the British Empire, he viewed foreign affairs through the same prism as his mentor, the turn-of-the-century prime minister, Sir Wilfrid Laurier – that is, as a dangerous nuisance. Yet, unlike Laurier, King understood the balance of international force in the first part of the twentieth century. Canadian politics taught him a second lesson, that English Canadians were firmly attached to the British Empire and, if pushed to make a choice, would opt to remain in the empire and to sustain it in war. He understood that French Canadians did not feel the same way, but they were a minority in Canada – a bit less than a third of the population, in the census of 1941. During the First World War, English-Canadian fervour and French-Canadian reluctance had imperilled Canada's political structure, causing King to place an even higher value on "national unity" and to view foreign affairs with even greater suspicion. During the 1920s he sought and achieved a greater formal distance between Canada and Great Britain, shoring up his country's position as an independent but still loyal part of the British Empire. King promised Britain that, in a crisis, Canada would be at its side. And it was: indeed, in recognition of the fact, King entitled a volume of his wartime speeches *At Britain's Side*. He knew his English-speaking compatriots would understand and approve.

Then there was the United States. Friendly and familiar, but at the same time foreign, the United States could not be ignored. The great republic had been, ever since 1776, an example and a reproach to Canadians. They had sometimes flowed over a border that was usually wide open to citizens of either country. Rather less often, Americans repaid the compliment. The Canadian standard of living was, after all, less than theirs, and their own country was so large and various that it made Canada seem small, or irrelevant, or invisible. Yet there were many similarities between the two nations. Canadians spoke with something approaching American, not British, accents, and an American accent was more easily accepted than a British one in Canada. American styles and fads usually found a ready echo in Canada, and Canadians and Americans assumed that a similarity of geography led to a similarity of interest – in everything but politics.

Politics had, however, made the difference. In 1911 the Canadian electorate had repudiated the Liberal government of Sir Wilfrid Laurier – and with it his youngest minister, Mackenzie King, who had lost his seat in the House of Commons – over the issue of relations with the United States. Laurier had signed a trade agreement with the Americans, mightily offending Canadian economic nationalists and the many interests who benefited, or thought they benefited, from a high Canadian tariff wall. King never forgot – nor for that matter did those Americans who had watched the election unfold. The rhetoric employed by the Conservative opposition during the election was extreme, but they found the results politically gratifying. If Laurier won and let down Canada's tariffs, Canadian society would be undermined – rampant divorce, political corruption, and finally outright annexation would follow. Enough Canadians seem to have believed it. It was a warning of what might happen should a Canadian government appear to get too close to the United States.

King, who had lived some years as a student in the United States and had a Harvard PhD, once told an American diplomat that in Canada he was known as "the American" and that consequently he had to watch his step, politically speaking. King may have understood the United States better than any other Canadian politician in his generation, and at bottom he had few doubts about American political values. He and the American president Franklin D. Roosevelt, whose time in office overlapped to a large extent with King's hold on power in the 1930s and during the war, shared much the same political culture and many of the same attitudes about the world; King moved easily in Roosevelt's shadow.

King understood that the United States had become steadily more powerful, economically and militarily, throughout his lifetime. British power, on the other hand, had gradually faded until in February 1941, in the middle of the war, the Canadian prime minister confided to his diary the latest news, that Great Britain was "a bankrupt country." Great Britain did not go bankrupt, of course: American aid and Canadian credits helped sustain it through the war, but the fact was that the British unaided could no longer maintain their position in the world.

For the duration of the war, the Canadian government did whatever it could to help. By 1945 it had provided Britain with over $3 billion in gifts and loans. Canada assisted on programs like air training and housed the British atomic bomb project – operations that could not be accommodated in the narrow and exposed British Isles. Militarily, Canadian soldiers, sailors, and aircrew, wearing British uniforms with a "Canada" patch on the shoulder, served under ultimate British command. Their presence as part of Britain's armed forces enhanced British military and diplomatic standing, at least for the duration of the war. In the eyes of English-speaking Canadians, it added to Canada's own importance and standing, which was inextricably – to French Canadians, inexplicably – bound up in the fortunes of the British Empire.

Politically, the Canadian government did not seek to intervene in high policy during the war, which, King understood, must be shared between his two senior partners, the British prime minister, Winston Churchill, and the American president, Franklin D. Roosevelt. Useful and impressive as Canada's contribution to the war effort was, it was dwarfed in most categories by that of the British and Americans. Yet Roosevelt and Churchill scrupulously cultivated King's own political interest, making it symbolically clear in photos, newsreels, and newspapers that he was an esteemed colleague. Practically, however, King limited any demands he might have on his allies to Canadian interests, strictly defined. He did not attempt to pronounce on bombing Germany or invading Italy or any of the other great strategic issues that Roosevelt and Churchill considered to be their province, and theirs alone.

The results could be both positive and negative. On the positive side, King hosted two Anglo-American conferences in Quebec City in 1943 and 1944, and appeared at social functions and in photos with Roosevelt and Churchill. He then retired from the scene and busied himself being a good host. The photos lingered and could be reproduced whenever the opposition questioned King's proximity to the councils of the great. Liberal propaganda praised King as a great international statesman, based on his acquaintance with Churchill and Roosevelt. There was, after all, irrefutable photographic evidence of their many meetings. Some Canadians surmised that King could not have said very much to his senior partners, and, on the great issues of the direction of the war, they would have been right. But that was not what most Canadians saw, or expected. They wanted to know that their leader got along with the Americans and the British.

After the war the prime minister learned that a Canadian carillon in a park on the Niagara River was to be dedicated to "Our great wartime leaders," Roosevelt and Churchill, and not to King himself. The prime minister's protests were unavailing. It was the paradox of Canada's position, King might have reflected: Canada's representatives must be seen by Canadians, but not heard by their allies, at great international events.

Nor did King protest when the charmed circle of the allied supreme command expanded to admit the Soviet Union. In 1941 Hitler attacked the USSR, his erstwhile ally. It was a fatal mistake. The Soviet Union and its leader, Joseph Stalin, were crucial to the Allied victory; without the Red Army and its stunning victories over the Nazis, the war might never have been won or might have lasted years longer. Yet the Soviet Union was not merely an ally, but the headquarters of international communism, the only country with a communist regime before and during the war. As such, it was a focus of hope and admiration for Canadian and other communists around the world.

Communist cooperation smoothed labour relations through communist-leaning unions (a minority of the trade union movement), and the communists did not hesitate to cooperate politically. Politically, however, the Canadian Communist Party had little to offer to the citizenry, and soon it would have even less.

Relations with the Soviet Union were relatively less important and more distant than relations with Great Britain and the United States. Canada had not been represented in Moscow before the war, and it was only in 1943 that a Canadian mission was sent to the Soviet Union. King had no personal history with Stalin as he did with Roosevelt and Churchill, nor did any issues arise that demanded his intervention. The Soviets for their part found Canada a minor convenience, good for munitions and credits, but little better than a pawn in the global competition between the two principal capitalist states, the United States and Great Britain.[3] There was objectively no need for King to pay attention to the Soviet Union, nor, until 1945, did he. Even in relations with the British and Americans, King husbanded his energies, leaving the details, even important details, to his subordinates.

THE DEPARTMENT

In 1939 Mackenzie King carefully manoeuvred a declaration of war through the Canadian Parliament, thereby asserting Canada's autonomy as a self-governing component of the British Empire. He did not mean by that action to engage Parliament seriously in the oversight of foreign affairs. In Parliament, the majority ruled, and the majority in the Parliaments elected in 1935 and 1940 – and 1945 for that matter – was Liberal. The majority followed its leader, and the Cabinet chosen by the leader. The Cabinet, led by the prime minister, governed the House of Commons, not the other way round. The Canadian party system made no allowance for personal idiosyncrasies on the part of ordinary members of Parliament. Party loyalty was highly prized and sometimes rewarded; disloyalty was almost invariably punished.

Nor was the Mackenzie King Cabinet an assembly of equals. King was very much the senior minister, and after 1940 his authority, reinforced by a smashing election victory, was essentially unchallenged. He was not only prime minister but secretary of state for external affairs, so he combined oversight with departmental and policy responsibility in that area. Admittedly, foreign affairs spilled over into the responsibilities of other ministers, especially the minister of finance and the minister of munitions and supply; yet even in those cases it was the prime minister who determined the shape of things and modified policy according to his judgment of the political scene. But King was a careful leader: he tried to anticipate his ministers' preferences and policies, especially if they impinged on the overriding issue of national unity. English and French Canada had a tendency to wander off in different political directions. It was King's job to prevent this, and thereby to preserve the country. Twice during the war King averted

– or, if he did not avert, skilfully managed – major political clashes between English and French Canada over the issue of conscription for overseas military service. To his colleagues' amazement, he was successful, and his success made him seem even more essential to the future of the Cabinet and the Liberal Party.

Technically, responsibility for the conduct of international relations lay with the Department of External Affairs, Canada's foreign office. In fact, "the Department," as it liked to call itself, handled mostly political affairs rather than economic foreign policy, and it was far from autonomous. King kept a close eye on "his" department from an office just down the hall in the East Block of the Parliament Buildings.

The department only slightly predated King. Established in 1909, it was designed to be a large filing bureau, to bring order to the chaotic state of Canadian relations with the outside world, especially the United States. In 1912 External Affairs was brought directly under the prime minister, and there it had stayed through governments Liberal and Conservative. King had expanded the department during the 1920s and professionalized it, appointing a university professor as undersecretary (deputy minister) and, through him, a staff of diplomats. Because the prime minister's own office was tiny, King and his predecessors drew on External Affairs for advice and help, sometimes on problems quite unrelated to foreign policy.

The department was closely modelled on its British and American counterparts. For officers, it hired male university graduates, often if not usually with advanced degrees taken abroad – people who might otherwise have become university professors. Educated in Great Britain or the United States, they usually had British or American friends and made new friends easily among their British and American colleagues. In terms of general culture and liberal politics, they were not very different from other Anglo-American diplomats aside from the national obligations their respective posts imposed.

Because diplomatic pay scales were generous, certainly as compared to those at universities, and because diplomacy promised a life and career out of the Canadian norm, its intake was, on average, highly qualified and highly intelligent.[4] There were indeed foreign postings – London, Washington, and Paris to begin with, Tokyo and The Hague later, and during the war the Soviet Union, Australia, South Africa, New Zealand, and much of Latin America. Young anglophones joined, and so did a limited number of francophones. More than other departments in Ottawa, External Affairs had some bilingual potential.

The department's first undersecretary lasted fifteen years in the job, and the second seventeen, until he died from overwork in 1941. The third, Norman Robertson, was blessed with youth and stamina, and an ability alternately to shrug off and to satisfy Mackenzie King's carping demands.[5] During the 1920s and 1930s King had kept External Affairs on a very short leash, instructing his delegates to say nothing if possible, and very little if not. One Canadian diplomat, Hume Wrong, fantasized that the perfect Canadian representative would not really exist – business cards, an office, and luggage would suffice.

Robertson changed things. The greater powers, he believed, were used to having things their own way but were sometimes unprepared in discussions or conferences, or disagreed among themselves. Robertson permitted his clever young men to prepare for conferences, preparing positions and proposals as if they indeed represented great powers. At an aviation conference in Chicago in 1944, to take one particularly influential example, the Canadians were ready with demands for autonomy and the rights of smaller countries (music to King's ears, if he ever heard it) but also with practical proposals and a draft treaty. The Chicago conference became a model for future Canadian efforts. As the war drew to a close, Canadian civil servants prepared position papers and proposals for a future international organization designed to replace the moribund League of Nations. The Canadians might not prevail in international discussions weighted heavily in favour of the great powers, but they would not fail from ignorance or lack of preparation. The department was happy to compare itself – and Canada – to other, less prepared, less favoured, less competent nations. Professionalism, according to the professionals, was one of the attributes that made Canada a "middle power."[6]

Mackenzie King had always feared the intrusion of the great powers' priorities in Canadian politics. Canadians were prone to look abroad for their opinions, and sometimes their allegiances too. He knew it was unavoidable; the outbreak of the Second World War and Canada's prompt participation in it had proven that proposition. At least Canada should be able to offer its consent, as it had when it declared war on its own in 1939, rather than simply accepting the British declaration of war on Germany. Nevertheless Canadian politicians and civil servants were painfully aware that Canada's role in the war was simply to produce soldiers, munitions, and other supplies, without any say in how they would be used or any voice in the larger Allied strategies that would consume them. They may have suspected – public opinion polls would have told them so – that Canadians expected and wanted little more than to be useful, and to be appreciated.

This public complacency was not an easy proposition for Ottawa to swallow. National self-determination, if not self-respect, demanded something more; but political realism and practicality suggested the contrary. The country was doing very well out of the war, and Canadians were pleased with the way the government was handling it – including the apparently trouble-free relations with Canada's principal allies.

King's staff provided a formula for Canadian participation in an international system that was largely beyond Ottawa's control and even influence. A British political scientist, David Mitrany,[7] had come up with the notion that nations should take on international roles for which they were best suited and should enjoy influence proportionate to their contributions. Application of this principle would allow international cooperation to function most effectively. This doctrine Mitrany called the functional principle or functionalism.[8] King, heavily scripted by his staff, expounded the functional principle in Parliament in 1943. Armed with this principle, the Canadian government justified its elaborate preparation for the uncertainties of peace. Canada's busyness, King told the House of Commons, "arose from our recognition of the needs of humanity."[9] Functionalism also contributed to Canada's self-image as a middle power. But would anyone listen when Canada spoke?

The Second World War made it apparent that the international system, as it existed before 1939, had failed. It had to be replaced, presumably by something better and more reliable – a higher internationalism. Yet there was a contradiction at the heart of this diagnosis: between international cooperation and sovereignty, with its attendant nationalism. Unbridled nationalism, in the form of Nazism or Fascism or Japanese imperialism, had spun out of control in the 1930s. At great cost, other nations had combined to defeat the aggression. Clearly cooperation among nations, concerted international action, was necessary for victory. The label given the wartime Grand Alliance – the United Nations – conveyed the idea. It was nevertheless a difficult idea, for how could sovereign nations be genuinely united for very long?

In Allied capitals, planners got busy. Those who did the planning had, almost invariably, experience with the failures of the 1930s either as participants or as close observers. Sometimes these planners – intellectuals, diplomats, and other civil servants – knew each other, from university or conferences or diplomatic assignment in the bad old days of the 1930s. And perhaps, left to themselves and equipped with unlimited authority, they might have devised a more perfect world. But serving as they did their various national and sovereign governments, they were bound to come up with proposals that respected national sovereignty and closely mirrored the international institutions of the interwar period.

The Canadian government was no exception. King might rhetorically embrace the service of humanity, but he knew that it was his task to represent only the Canadian section thereof. King and his Liberals and most other Canadians accepted the international state system as it was. They were devoted to the principle of Canadian autonomy and refused to contemplate any arrangements that would treat their country as less than formally equal to every other independent state. The prewar League of Nations (King sarcastically called it "the League of Notions") had failed, in the Canadian prime minister's view, because it had tried to do too much, not because it had tried to do too little. The league had had too few members, with the absence of the United States and most of the Americas, as well as, from time to time, Germany, Italy, Japan, and the Soviet Union. Yet the League had its good points too, one of them being the sovereign equality of all its members. On this point there was no division between the prime minister and his colleagues, political and diplomatic: national sovereignty should be the foundation of any future international organization. Canada was interested in new institutions for the world, not a new world altogether.

Creating the United Nations

Ironically, the model for the United Nations was the institution it was intended to replace, the League of Nations. Indeed, the League was not even dead, merely dormant, its organs scattered between Switzerland and the United States, although the old institution stimulated so many negative memories that it seemed best that it be decently buried as soon as possible. Yet the designers of the League had created a practical institution. All its members belonged to its assembly, which before 1939 had met once a year in Geneva in a symbolic affirmation of their sovereign equality. Sovereignty and autonomy were the basis of the League, not its antithesis. The Canadian government had no quarrel with this, nor did any other sovereign government. Supervising the day-to-day business of the League was a council comprising the more important members, which had permanent status, plus a number of other states elected for fixed terms by the assembly. This model reflected the balance of power among League members and gave those states with enlarged responsibilities a suitably enlarged status. If the assembly was the League's soul, the council was its brain and, it was hoped, its muscle.

The greater Allied powers – the United States, Great Britain, and the Soviet Union – agreed among themselves to try to design a postwar international security organization. Meeting in the summer of 1944 at Dumbarton Oaks, an estate in Washington DC, they concocted a plan for a world organization that bore a marked resemblance to the League of Nations. Canadian diplomats hung about on the fringes of the conference, gleaning titbits to send home for the preparation of an eventual Canadian response. There would be a general assembly, and a council that would include the great powers – Britain, France, the United States, the Soviet Union, and China – on a permanent basis. The great powers would each have a veto over United Nations actions; without such a guarantee that their interests would be protected, neither the United States nor the Soviet Union would have joined. The veto was in effect an antidote to the fragmentary and incomplete membership of the League of Nations, which the United States had never joined. Protected by the veto from infringements on its absolute sovereignty, the United States would join the United Nations.

From a Canadian point of view, a universal United Nations organization was highly desirable.[10] If the price was the veto, so be it: "Better to take the organization we can get," Robertson noted in the spring of 1945, than to make "perfectionist speeches" in favour of universal equality.[11] There were other things to be thankful for as well. The UN would be a single, worldwide body rather than a loose confederation of regional assemblies, each dominated by its respective great power. For Canada, struggling to establish an identity and interests distinct from both Great Britain and the United States, this development was highly desirable.

Equally fortunate from the Canadian government's point of view was Franklin Roosevelt's decision to abandon his inclination to give Brazil privileged status in the new organization. Canadians might just swallow an unequal organization constructed along traditional lines, with the customary great powers; they would choke on rewarding Brazil. It was a country with a larger population than Canada, true, but with a smaller economy, and a much smaller participation in the war that was entering its final months. Brazil was also on the fringes of the world, as most Canadians saw it, unfamiliar and exceedingly distant to all but a few Canadian investors. Latin America, Brazil included, was a caricature of democracy, governed more by dictators than by civilian politicians, its societies remote and incomprehensible.

Mackenzie King, while conceding the form of the United Nations, hoped that it would act differently from the old League. In this respect, he had to some extent changed his opinion. Back in the 1930s he had identified the problem of the League not as its unwillingness to use force, but as its predisposition to "coercion, sanctions, etc." The war modified his views, to the point where he conceded that force might be used as "the ultimate sanction," but he remained sceptical as to how, or whether, the United Nations could be persuaded to apply it.[12]

Before such items could be worked out, the United Nations had to be founded. The great powers scheduled a conference in San Francisco for April 1945. Organized by the United States, it proved to be the first challenge to Harry Truman, who succeeded to the presidency on the death of Roosevelt just as the conference was convening. King decided he must personally represent Canada, and he headed for San Francisco at the head of a large delegation. The UN was not the only item on his agenda: the mandate of the Canadian Parliament was about to expire and, rather than extend it, as the constitution allowed, King decided to face the electorate in June.[13] King knew that his conspicuous presence at the conference would reinforce his carefully cultivated image at home as an international statesman – the only one Canada had. On the other hand, he carefully balanced the Canadian delegation, taking the leading French Canadian in the Cabinet, Louis St Laurent, minister of justice, as his second in command, as well as representatives of the opposition parties in the House of Commons.

The Canadian delegation had two principal objectives. John Holmes summarized one as "no taxation without representation," while the other sought preference in representation for countries that, like Canada, could afford to participate in a broad range of United Nations activities.[14] These two points were a projection of the functional principle. The Canadians also had another objective, expressed as a matter of tactics:

the Canadian delegation would be determined rather than loud in the pursuit of its goals. It would get what it could, but not at the price of offending the great powers, meaning the Americans and the British.

As a result, the Canadians played to what they saw as their strengths – professional caution and an understanding of the process of international conferences. As a prerequisite for what was to follow, the Canadians sought the smooth functioning of the conference. Then they took care of Canada's own desiderata. They secured an amendment (article 43) to the draft Charter of the United Nations that allowed members whose forces were being demanded for UN use to participate in the decision to use them. The Canadian delegation also secured a reference to proper qualifications for non-permanent members of the future Security Council that would take the place of the League of Nations Council (article 23). On regionalism, the Latin Americans prevailed, inserting references to regional security agencies (articles 51 and 53). The Canadians, though distinctly unenthusiastic, acquiesced.

The Canadian delegation avoided becoming involved in an Australian campaign against the great power veto. The noise made by the Australians was, the Canadians believed, at best pointless and at worst upsetting to the fragile agreement among the great powers on the structure and nature of the United Nations. With a certain sense of superiority, the Canadians intervened with the Australians, and between the Australians and the distinctly irritated British and American delegations. They could take comfort in the fact that the Australian objections were futile: the veto sailed through. Pragmatism, not idealism, ruled at San Francisco.

Human rights were not so much a casualty of the San Francisco conference as a simple non-event. The United Nations was a coalition of sovereign states, consulting and combining for specific and limited purposes. Interference in domestic affairs from a notional world body was not welcomed by anyone, and Canada was no exception. The United Nations' job was to prevent war, not meddle in its members' affairs, a point King explicitly made to his delegation. Subjects such as human rights, immigration, and education in Canada were nobody's business outside the country. Not all members of the delegation agreed with the prime minister, but they knew better than to contradict him.[15]

The founders of the UN broadly agreed on the desirability of human rights and the possibility of human betterment. That was so even though three of the great powers, Great Britain, France, and the United States, maintained formal colonial empires while the other two, the Soviet Union and China, vigorously suppressed the claims to independence of various nationalities inside their boundaries. The United States, it was true, soon gave up its largest colony, the Philippines, in 1946, while the British granted independence to India and Pakistan in 1947. Many, perhaps most, Americans did not think of their country as an imperial power but as the world's prime example of a successful former colony; it was a sentiment that Canadians broadly shared. "Politicians and officials in Ottawa did believe in the liberating force of self-government," as the Canadian diplomat John Holmes put it, and were not shy about sharing their views with the representatives of the remaining imperial powers, especially the British and French. This Canadian "smugness" (Holmes's word again) would prove a constant irritant in relations with those powers at the UN until, in the 1960s, they granted independence to almost all of their remaining colonies.[16] The same anti-colonial smugness played well in other quarters, especially among representatives of the most recently independent countries. It would be a mitigating factor in the generally harmonious relations between Canada and the other liberal democracies of Western Europe; in a slightly different form it would even affect relations with the United States.

The United Nations was only a part, though an important part, of Canada's world in 1945. In the spring and summer of 1945, most Canadians, like their prime minister, looked inward, picking up their lives where they had dropped them in 1939. In voting for the Liberals in the 1945 election, Canadians accepted a political agenda that promised security – job security, economic security – through an active, but not too active, government. Facing in, King's fellow citizens cast occasional glances over their shoulders at a world too uncertain to be as orderly or safely predictable as their life at home promised to be. Craving security at home, Canadians knew it must be associated with security abroad, and security abroad must involve a common effort – in other words, collective security.[17]

LIFE BEYOND GOVERNMENTS

Of course, not every Canadian was interested in international affairs. Those who were might be said to have an interest or interests that frequently went beyond the national aspirations of the Canadian government.[18] That the Canadian government should further their interests was both acceptable and desirable, but the world they sought was more than a loose association of states.

Canada's churches were transnational in origin and practice and were highly predisposed to associations and activities that went beyond mere nationality. That had always been so, as far back as the seventeenth century. By the nineteenth century the churches were active in sending missionaries abroad and in raising funds to support them and their missions. As the connection between state and church disappeared, the churches were free to do what they pleased in foreign parts – in effect, to conduct their own foreign policies and to construct a world view separate from that of the secular society at home.[19]

Clergy as well as lawyers, doctors, and other professionals either belonged to international bodies or participated as individuals in transnational activities. The international interests of business had always been recognized, even in colonial Canada in the nineteenth century. Groups with similar interests began to communicate and confer. The Canadian Red Cross Society (incorporated in 1909) belonged to the International Committee of the Red Cross, founded in 1863 and headquartered in neutral Switzerland. The Canadian Olympic Committee was part of the international Olympic movement, promoting peaceable competition in sports. The National Council of Women belonged to the International Council of Women, founded in 1888. Between the First and Second World Wars there had been a League of Nations Society, in furtherance of the aims and purposes of the League.[20] After the Second World War, there would be a Canadian United Nations Association (founded in 1946), in support of the League's successor. There was also a Canadian Institute of International Affairs (CIIA), founded in 1928, with links to other international institutes and foreign affairs councils. An elite group, it brought together business and academics (and, eventually, a number of retired diplomats). The Department of External Affairs paid close attention to the CIIA and sometimes used it as a sounding board for its ideas.

Internationally minded Canadians were a point of contact, and a point of reference, for Canadian politicians and diplomats as they tried to secure a place for Canada in the postwar world. Human rights were a natural concern for such individuals, and for similarly minded individuals elsewhere, but they were not the only issue they wished their government, and other governments, to confront. The influence of the internationalists in Canada, in their various societies and leagues and associations, was seldom concentrated, and, on any given issue, and at any given time, their impact on government and diplomacy might be negligible. But as a species, and as individuals who were often leaders or at least notables in their communities, they had an impact that could be very great. Governments might find them a nuisance, but they ignored them at their peril. In the short term, internationally minded people were an electoral force to be reckoned with. In the longer term, if national governments, individually or collectively, were found insufficient or, worse, obstructive, they might be replaced. In 1945 there was as yet no word to describe the phenomenon, but as Akira Iriye writes, "Globalization, as a state of mind and as an international expression, was dawning."[21]

IN 1945 CANADIANS DID NOT EXPECT OR SEEK a radical revision of domestic politics or international relations. The two items were connected. The war had been won by a massive mobilization of national resources, by the cooperation of various social groups, and by collective sacrifice. The English-speaking democracies, especially Great Britain and the United States, the nations closest to Canada, shared what was broadly the same experience. Under government direction, it had proved possible to secure full employment, a rise in living standards, and a modernization of industry. Yet these changes were accomplished without doing violence to Canada's parliamentary political system and without changing the private ownership or control of most of the economy. All of Canada's political parties agreed that a proper balance had been achieved; and when they looked abroad they saw their experience repeated and confirmed in Great Britain and the United States.

Canadians expected the same kind of incremental change in foreign relations. They plumped for the familiar: the international system as they knew it had gone wrong in the 1930s, but it had been fixed rather than transformed by the war. Canadians' world was a familiar one – the world of 1945 was not all that distant from the world of 1939. Identifying closely with the British and Americans, Canadians found it natural that their government should pursue policies similar to those of their senior allies and expected that British and American policies would be broadly appropriate for Canada too.

REAL PROSPERITY
AND
ILLUSORY DIPLOMACY

2

Canada joined in the Second World War in defiance of economics. No one was more surprised than the Canadian government's experts when economic collapse did not follow. Success in war depended on a successful economic performance. And the economy exceeded expectations. There was essentially no unemployment. The living standards of the poorest Canadians improved substantially, despite heavy taxation and material shortages.[1] Would it last?

TRADE AND SECURITY

Economics, not politics, was the focus of Canadian foreign policy at the end of the Second World War. In 1941 the American president, Franklin D. Roosevelt, caught the public imagination when he spoke of "four freedoms" as the basis of a civilized international society.[2] The four freedoms were freedom of speech and religion and freedom from want and fear. In terms of Canadian priorities, freedom from want had precedence over freedom from fear. This was not because Canadians were indifferent to military or ideological threats from abroad, but because they believed that those threats had just been disposed of, and that it was time to pick up life – but not where it had been left in 1939.

The world of 1939, the last year of peace, was an unpleasant memory. Canada had been beginning to show signs of lifting out of the Great Depression – unemployment rates were down to 11 percent – but exports were only 29 percent of what they would be in 1945. That their economy was bigger than it had been before the war, most Canadians knew; but 1945 was also better. The war had changed many things. Most important, Canadians in 1945 enjoyed new forms of institutionalized protection. There was, for the first time, a limited form of income security against job loss: unemployment insurance had arrived, via a constitutional amendment in 1941. The large industries of the war encouraged unionization, and so the workforce by 1945 was 24 percent unionized, up from 17 percent before the war.

The trade unions were not a force for political radicalism or socialism, nor were they the vanguard of the revolution. Unionized or not, labour had placed its trust in the government's promise, during the 1945 election campaign, of full employment, and it was on this issue that the government would stand or fall in the years ahead. On that political foundation, Canada faced the postwar era with a liberal and basically free-enterprise political consensus – albeit one modified by government responsibility and economic intelligence and planning. Full employment by itself was not a prospect that enchanted most ministers or, for that matter, most professional economists. They believed that employment depended on trade, and trade on markets. Try as they might, they could not see where Canada could sell enough goods in the years to come to sustain its economy. Unemployment, not full employment, was the likely prospect.

The prospect of trying to engineer continued full employment did not discourage C.D. Howe. Howe was in 1945 minister of reconstruction and of munitions and supply. The job of producing munitions was effectively over; as Howe saw it, his task was to convert war industry to peacetime production with as little downtime as possible. The veterans were returning home by the hundreds of thousands in the fall of 1945; with every boatload landing in Halifax or Quebec City, the urgency of finding jobs grew.

Howe was no trained economist. But part of his job during the war had been enforcing scarcity and sacrifice on the home front – postponing repairs, forbidding new construction if not for war purposes, and so forth. Canadians, with little to spend their money on, saved, and the government encouraged them with a variety of ingenious and patriotic schemes. The end of the war removed the psychological prop that kept Howe's system of rationing and controls upright. As a sign that an era had ended, Howe removed gasoline rationing simultaneously with the Japanese surrender. He suspected that this was but the beginning and that demand for gas would be followed by demand for refrigerators, washing machines, housing, and, eventually, such new consumer desirables as televisions.

Howe's colleagues, as well as Canada's senior economic civil servants, sometimes thought that "the minister of everything" was both ignorant and foolhardy. In terms of economic theory, ignorant he was; but he was never foolhardy. He knew there had to be demand, and he was aware of the dollars piled up in war bonds and savings accounts. There would, he thought, be a market, as long as the government got out of the way; and through the winter of 1945-1946 he did just that, removing control after control. All this would have an important effect, but it was incremental, not dramatic. In terms of policy and publicity, Howe's was merely the second string to the government's economic bow. What attracted most attention was trade, and what to do about it.

Canada had a long tradition of dramatically high tariffs. They were installed in the early nineteenth century as a matter of necessity – they were the major source of government revenue. In the middle of the nineteenth century creative colonial politicians added to the revenue tariff the considerations of protection and encouragement for domestic manufacturing. Tariffs became a matter of contention: farmers and resource producers generally knew that tariffs did little to protect their products, while they were forced to buy protected Canadian goods at high (but authentically Canadian) prices. But manufacturers and, equally important, their workers regarded tariffs as an essential prop of economic life.

Parties defined themselves in terms of their view of the tariff. Mackenzie King's Liberals inherited a reputation as a low-tariff party, while the Conservatives (renamed Progressive Conservatives in 1942) were supposed to believe in higher tariffs. The Conservatives were correctly viewed as the party of (most of) the business community, which in the 1945 election contributed lavishly to their failed campaign.[3] Thus, if the Liberals faltered in their defence of the Canadian tariff there was an alternative party, one that the business beneficiaries of the tariff in fact preferred.

The Liberals', and King's, reputation as pro-American also counted in the politics of tariffs and trade. Since the 1890s Canada had offered a "preference" (a lower tariff rate) to goods from Great Britain and the empire. This "imperial preference" was calculated to be lower even than the rate offered to countries with which Canada had trade treaties that offered "most favoured nation" rates. (There was an even higher, "general," rate for countries without treaties and without British status.) Intra-imperial tariffs had been regulated in the Ottawa Agreements of 1932, in which British countries exchanged tariff concessions and systematized the imperial preference.

The Ottawa Agreements probably did increase trade within the empire, and certain sectors of the Canadian economy (automobiles, for example) benefited from imperial preference in the 1930s. Their most important effect was on a non-British country excluded from the benefits of imperial preference. The United States government took a dim view of this British preferential system, although after 1933 it agreed that high American tariffs had invited retaliation. The Democratic administration of Franklin D. Roosevelt through his secretary of state, Cordell Hull (1933-1944), undertook to negotiate away imperial preference, offering in return a much revised American policy towards tariffs and trade. Roosevelt and Hull secured passage of the Reciprocal Trade Agreements Act of 1934 (RTA), perhaps the most important single piece of legislation in American trade history. The RTA took tariff making out of the hands of Congress, where it had resided since the foundation of the American government in 1789. (As a result of Congressional deadlock or obstruction, the United States had ratified precisely three trade treaties between 1789 and 1934.) Instead, the administration or executive was authorized to offer a reduction of 50 percent in US tariffs, on a per-product basis, in return for equivalent concessions by a foreign government.[4]

The RTA bore fruit: the next year the Canadian government, headed by the Conservative R.B. Bennett, negotiated a reciprocity agreement with the United States, moderately lowering tariffs. As his first international act, Mackenzie King signed the agreement after the 1935 election that repudiated the Conservatives and brought the Liberals back to power. Another trade agreement followed in 1938, part of a tripartite deal involving Great Britain and the United States. The experience of the 1938 agreement indicated that Canada had to keep a wary eye on Anglo-American negotiations that might lead to British concessions to the Americans: such concessions could well reduce the preferential advantage Canada held in the British market. When war began, the Ottawa Agreements remained essentially intact.

It soon became clear that British and Canadian economic survival in the war necessitated aid from the United States. The Americans devised Lend-Lease, which supplied necessary materials to Great Britain and other allies free of charge – that is, free of payment in money. As part of the deal, the United States insisted on trade negotiations, with an eye to abolishing the imperial preference system. For a variety of reasons, these grand negotiations never took place, and official action on trade was postponed until after the war.[5]

Canada refused to take advantage of Lend-Lease, though it did benefit from British purchases in the United States under the Lend-Lease system. Instead, Canada had its own arrangements with the United States under the Hyde Park Agreement of 1941, exchanging war supplies with the Americans while piling up a considerable surplus of US dollars.[6] Canada gave large amounts of supplies and US dollars to the British and other allies on its own account, thereby accruing a certain amount of prestige in Washington, where officials appreciated the fact that the United States was not alone as a provider of aid among the Allies. As the war drew to a close, so did Allied aid programs, including Lend-Lease. The Canadians spent the last months of the war attempting to work out, with the British, what might happen next. The Canadians needed British trade, for without their traditional surplus in that market there would not be enough money to pay for American imports. As Louis Rasminsky, a Canadian financial official, put it, Canada would be "ground between the upper and nether millstones."[7]

Neither side was in a good position – the Canadians anxious to sell and the British unable to buy – but because the exchanges among British and Canadian officials were of a high intellectual calibre they have attracted the attention of historians. (The chief negotiator on the British side was the famous economist John Maynard Keynes, by then Lord Keynes, and several of the Canadian negotiators were products of his seminars at Cambridge University before the war.)[8] The discussions were cordial, and, in the opinion of Kathleen Rasmussen, "the Cambridge talks were a success."[9] The Canadian and British officials hoped for the broadest possible negotiations after the war, with all sides putting their tariffs on the table, prepared to trade across-the-board tariff cuts. But Canada and the United Kingdom were smaller players. Both depended on their ability to sell and buy in the United States; apart, they could hope to do little, as Anglo-Canadian negotiations proved.

What would the Americans do? President Roosevelt was, in principle, a free trader, but he was also deeply suspicious of European wiles, including those of the British.[10] He was willing to seek improvements to the world economic system, starting with discussions over money. In July 1944 delegates from Allied nations, including the Soviet Union, convened in a resort in New Hampshire, Bretton Woods. The main powers present were Great Britain and the United States, and the principal discussions were between Lord Keynes and the undersecretary of the US Treasury, Harry Dexter White. The Canadians, who knew both sides well, tried to act as intermediaries and facilitators; they dreaded above all Anglo-American disagreement.

The British could not afford to disagree, and so the conference reached an accord on what were basically American terms. Bretton Woods created the International Monetary Fund (IMF), which would attempt to maintain a stable exchange value among currencies while providing short-term help to countries whose currency exchange rates came under pressure. All members of the IMF agreed to keep their currencies at a constant value, measured in American dollars. The IMF was founded on the American dollar, and American dollars could be bought and sold for a fixed price in gold. But the Americans did not donate as many dollars to the fund as Keynes would have liked. There were certainly not enough dollars to bail out the British – or probably any other significant trading nation. They could not, therefore, afford to exchange their currency, the pound sterling, freely – to make it "convertible," in the language of the market. Convertibility therefore remained an issue in British trade policy.

Bretton Woods also spawned the International Bank for Reconstruction and Development (IBRD), later known as the World Bank. The IBRD's task was to provide long-term assistance to countries, in contrast to the short-term aid of the IMF. In effect, the IMF was for those countries with developed economies and large trading interests; the IBRD was supposed to help out countries with structural problems in their economies.

Neither the IMF nor the IBRD began to function immediately. It took time to ratify the agreements and to collect the resources to start them up. As a result, for the first few years after the war, crucial international economic negotiations took place as before, in ad hoc meetings of governments. The effects of this will be seen below.

After money came tariffs. Roosevelt sponsored a renewal of the RTA in 1945, but he was not around to see it passed. That fell to his successor, Harry Truman, in the summer of 1945. The Canadians, and some of their friends among the American bureaucracy, had hoped for a simplified across-the-board exchange of tariff cuts. But for Congress that was too much. The American legislature did not trust its trading partners not to take advantage of the Truman administration – and to be fair, it did not trust the administration either. Truman would likely need the votes of key producers, who might become unsettled if they thought their interests would not be specifically protected. There would be negotiations later, looking to the creation of an international organization to regulate trade; perhaps by that point the Truman administration would have found its sea legs.[11] What critics forgot, then and later, was that a worse outcome was always possible – a return to the protectionism of the 1920s and earlier. The Truman administration and its Congressional allies had kept a liberalized vision of trade alive, even if its horizon was cluttered with special interests.[12]

Meanwhile, the war ended. Lend-Lease, on which the British depended for a great deal besides military supplies, also ended. Canada's exports to Britain, consisting mostly of war or war-related supplies, stalled. This was a serious matter: in 1944 Canada exported almost $1.2 billion worth of goods to Britain, and in 1945 $948 million. The 1944 figure represented a third of Canadian exports and 10 percent of the country's gross domestic product. But with war finance arrangements terminated, the British could afford to buy no more and would be forced to live on their own resources – what Keynes in a memorable phrase called "starvation corner."

To avoid this unpleasant outcome, the British government sent emissaries to North America, first to the United States in November 1945 and then to Canada in February 1946. They asked for a multi-billion-dollar, interest-free loan. British needs were large, even by American standards. To supply them required not just dollars but President Truman's political credit, and that credit did not extend very far.

Canadian officials estimated that a loan to the British would have to be in the range of $10-12 billion. Of that, Canada could afford to lend $1.2 billion. But the United States offered only $3.75 billion, at an interest rate of 2 percent.[13] In return the British were to make the pound convertible and free of government restrictions a year after the agreement took effect – that is, by the summer of 1947. There was grave doubt that the British could do it, but, desperate for cash, they had to pretend they could.

The American terms were, of course, known when the British came to Ottawa. The Canadians offered their $1.25 billion (in US dollars), which, given the size of Canada's population and of the Canadian economy, should have matched a US loan of $15 billion. The loan was equivalent to 10 percent of Canada's GDP for 1946, a staggering amount. Despite the size of the Canadian offer, the negotiations did not go entirely smoothly: the Canadians took offence at what they took to be the imperious attitude of the British negotiators, and the British thought that Canadian insistence on interest equivalent to that on the American loan – 2 percent – was ungenerous.

The insistence on interest was a political precondition for the Canadian negotiators. The King government had a majority in the House of Commons, but it was slim. Half the Liberal caucus came from Quebec, and the attitude of French-Canadian ministers and MPs was important. The most important minister from Quebec was Louis St Laurent, minister of justice. Recruited to politics at an advanced age, fifty-nine, by Mackenzie King in 1941, St Laurent had impressed his leader and his colleagues with his moderation and intelligence. His steadfast support of Canadian unity was crucial to the resolution of the conscription issue in 1944, and to Liberal success in Quebec in the 1945 election. Symbolically and practically, St Laurent's presence gave French Canada a place at the international table, acting as a restraint on the English Canadians and a guarantee that French-Canadian values and interests were not forgotten.

King placed St Laurent on the negotiating team for the British loan. As a lawyer and as justice minister, St Laurent had never had to deal with questions of trade and finance. He was quick to learn, intrigued by the notion that, by lending money to the British, Canada was acting, not in the British interest, but in its own self-interest. The British could not buy Canadian goods without Canadian money, and unless existing trade channels were maintained, perhaps they never would.

St Laurent had difficulty explaining the notion to some of the fiercer Liberal MPs from Quebec. "Avez-vous été élu député de l'Angleterre ou du Canada?" one of them demanded. But party discipline held – only a handful of French-Canadian MPs, all nationalists, voted against. The loan sailed through, a triumph of optimism over foreboding.

A few months later there was another burst of optimism. This time the initiative was Canadian, but domestic politics were equally involved. Wheat farmers on the Prairies were nervous about a future without the guaranteed markets of wartime. They pressed for a framework that would give them regular and predictable revenues from their production. Great Britain was the obvious market, the traditional destination of bounteous Canadian harvests. Why not tie up the British market with a wheat contract?

The marketing of Canadian grain was a government monopoly and had been since the closure of the Winnipeg Grain Exchange in 1943. In Great Britain food imports were controlled by government, which had to authorize the spending of scarce foreign exchange for the purpose. Government-to-government negotiations began, spurred on, on the Canadian side, by the minister of agriculture, Saskatchewan's Jimmy Gardiner. Gardiner was a political warhorse, a veteran of every political fight back to the early 1900s. In some ways Gardiner's view of the world had not changed since 1914: for him the British Empire was still Canada's natural economic partner and spiritual home.

Gardiner understood well enough the demands of his prairie constituency – the farmers wanted security equivalent to union contracts in the eastern cities.[14] For prairie Canadians, Canada's system of protective tariffs was something that worked to their perpetual disadvantage: obtaining guaranteed prices for farm products would counterbalance that insistent grievance. Regular British purchases would meet that need. The Canadians set out to get a contract for four or five years.

But at what price? If the 1930s were any guide, the prospects were dismal. The war was an aberration, and with the war over, the price of wheat would, and should, fall. British negotiators naturally thought this was a reasonable assumption. Canadian and British negotiators concluded that $1.55 a bushel was a good price to start with. That price would then drift downwards until in the fourth year of the contract, 1949-1950, it reached $1 a bushel. Gardiner, in tune with the pessimistic economic forecasts of the day, believed prices would drop. In case they did not, he negotiated a further clause that bound the British to "have regard to" any difference between the world price of wheat and the price they were bound to pay under the contract.[15]

Unfortunately, "have regard to" had no legal meaning. If prices rose, the British could "have regard to" the money they would not have to pay and congratulate themselves. They had occasion to do this, since prices rose and the British nevertheless paid the $1 a bushel that Gardiner had negotiated. The wheat contract, initially hailed as an example of agricultural statesmanship, proved to be a political disaster as prairie farmers became converts to market value. The Canadian government had taken a gamble on wheat futures and lost.

Together, the loan and the wheat contract represented a sizeable commitment to the economic reconstruction of Great Britain. But Britain was not the only country in need. Between 1945 and 1948, Canada doled out $234.7 million in export credits to France, $113 million to the Netherlands,[16] and $66 million to Belgium; other aid recipients included Norway ($23.3 million), China ($51 million), Czechoslovakia ($16.4 million), and the Soviet Union ($11.7 million). Those agreements were bilateral: other funds – $34 million in 1945 – flowed through the United Nations Relief and Rehabilitation Agency (UNRRA), in which a variety of Canadians served.[17] There was also "military relief," $71 million in 1944-1945.

The figures for Canadian aid were impressive, especially when measured against GNP. They were impressive too because the national government was trying to bring its expenditures down and, with them, wartime rates of taxation. In this, they were succeeding: expenditure dropped from $5.7 billion in 1945 to $3.4 billion in 1946 and $3.1 billion in 1947.[18] The government was removing controls on what Canadians could buy and combating inflation by reigning the exchange rate of the Canadian dollar to parity with the US dollar in 1946. Canadians responded by going on a spending spree for American goods: during 1946-1947 imports from the United States soared, and the

Canadian exchange reserves drained away. It was not easy to find the foreign exchange to finance credits for Europe.

The biggest drain was the British loan, with $960 million drawn by the end of 1947. It propped up British purchases in Canada ($600 million in 1946); export credits did the same for sales to the rest of Europe ($335 million). Together, these items accounted for 40 percent of the value of Canadian exports. Money flowed out to the United States and to Europe but, except for American investment and purchases in Canada, not enough of the American kind to buy oranges in Florida or machinery in Pennsylvania. Canadian foreign exchange reserves fell from $1.6 billion early in 1946 to $500 million in November 1947.

Something had to give. The Canadians begged the British to slow down their withdrawals from the loan, but that by itself was not enough. Within a measurable future the Canadian government would run out of American dollars to finance Canadian purchases in the United States. The British and other European governments had the same problem, a shortage of American dollars, and could not help. They were happy to buy Canadian products, but only if the Canadians gave them the hard currency – Canadian or American dollars – to do so. The IMF, set up for precisely this kind of difficulty, was not fully functioning. At this rate, Canadian dollars would not be "hard" much longer.

In the summer of 1947 Canadian officials delicately let their American counterparts know that Canada might soon be facing a foreign exchange crisis. Canada would need sympathy and help in roughly equal amounts – sympathy because the government was thinking of placing severe restrictions on what Canadians could buy in the United States, and help in the form of a loan to plug the hole in Canada's foreign exchange reserves. The Americans agreed: Canada was important to them, practically and symbolically. If even Canada, the country closest to the United States politically and economically, crumbled, Americans would feel the consequences. And Canada was Canada. "I am authorized," an American official stated in 1945, "to take the position for the State Department that to treat Canada like any other foreign Government would be contrary to our policy. It is their view that the Canadian economy should be treated as nearly as possible like our own in peacetime as well as in war, based always on mutual reciprocity."[19]

GATT AND FREE TRADE

Could Canada's sovereign identity be preserved when the foundations of Canadian trade were shifting away from Great Britain and towards the United States? For this question there were two answers, one conscious and to a large degree intentional, the other undirected and structural. Historians have paid a great deal of attention to the first, or policy, answer. As we will see, postwar negotiations on free trade between the

United States and Canada were supplemented by broader international negotiations that resulted in the General Agreement on Tariffs and Trade (GATT) and the establishment of the International Trade Organization (ITO).

Both the GATT and the proposed free trade pact represented a substantial change in Canadian policy. Although only the GATT was formally drafted and subsequently ratified, the two events signalled that the economic link to Great Britain was no longer Canada's major trade connection. The link had already been seriously weakened. The loan and the wheat deal of 1946 represented artificial resuscitation on a patient – the political-economic connection with Great Britain – already terminal if not quite at the point of death. A third of all British imports from Canada in 1946 was wheat or flour, in tribute to the wheat agreement. What would happen when that agreement came to an end?

The Americans were already dominant when it came to imports. "For many years the United States [has] been the principal source of Canadian imports," the government's statisticians observed in 1947, and the war had only aggravated that situation.[20] Closer to Canada, better suited to Canadian tastes, American products dominated Canadian consumption. The British were unable, for a variety of reasons, to increase their exports to Canada, or even maintain them: in areas where the British had once been strong the Americans had taken their place.

Canadian policy in 1945 and 1946 sought to restore and enhance prewar patterns of trade. The reasons for this were historical and political: Canada had always had a large trade with Great Britain, and such trade reinforced links with the British Empire and the British monarchy, while strengthening Canada's political separation from the United States. It had always been so. As the *Canada Year Book*, the government's annual summary of Canadian facts and statistics, intoned, a combination of the United States and the United Kingdom had "dominated Canadian trade since exports and imports ... were first recorded."[21] It was a wrench to conclude that this history was coming to an end, or had ended. Where trade was concerned, policy merely ratified reality: it gently closed the door and turned out the lights.

For the longer term, the Canadian, British, and American governments hoped to create an international agency, the International Trade Organization, to establish and enforce a multilateral system of tariff reductions and commercial rules. Planning for such an organization began during the war and continued inside an eighteen-nation group in 1946 and 1947. A preliminary meeting convened at Geneva in the summer of 1947. The American government suggested two things: turning part of the draft charter of the ITO into a General Agreement on Tariffs and Trade, and negotiating a complex of tariff reductions. The Americans, whose large and rich home market offered the best and sometimes the only hope for trade expansion for other trading countries, got the conference they desired.

The Geneva conference produced 123 agreements and affected 45,000 items in the tariff schedules of 23 countries. Participants agreed to allow "principal suppliers" of a given commodity to handle the negotiations affecting that product. The Americans had most to offer and, in the end, most to give: their tariff fell by 35 percent on the average, matched by concessions from other countries deemed to be equivalent.

For the Canadian delegation, the main object was the success of the conference as a whole and the negotiating system of principal suppliers that it established. Bringing tariff diplomacy into a multilateral forum played to the strengths of a Canadian delegation experienced in both the theory and practice of trade agreements. But all the multilateral success in the world could not conceal that the most practical and effective result of the conference was a bilateral agreement with the United States that built upon the existing 1935 and 1938 agreements. Overall, Canada made 600 reductions in existing tariff rates and "bound" (agreed not to increase) 500 others.

For the Canadian government the most politically sensitive part of the Geneva negotiation involved imperial preferences. The Americans wanted to get rid of them; the British did not. If the preferences were abolished it would be a clear sign that the new trading system was truly a creature of American desires and American policy – a highly negative symbol with potentially volatile political results in London, Ottawa, and elsewhere. The American delegation finally gave way on the issue, settling for "binding" the preferences: no new preferences could be created, and existing preferences could only be maintained, reduced, or abolished. The GATT also stipulated rules for the treatment of foreign investment, demanding "national" treatment for foreign investors – that is, foreign investors, once admitted, would live by the same rules as their domestic counterparts. Discrimination at the border – segregating parts of the economy for citizens only – was not prohibited. All these were innovations, and promising, but their effect lay in the future.

When the government brought the GATT before the House of Commons in December 1947 it met intense criticism from the opposition. Ratification would be slow and painful, so the government implemented the GATT by order-in-council effective 1 January 1948.

The principle of an international trade regime really worried only the occasional crank. It was the frozen imperial preference that bothered some members of the Conservative opposition. Surely Canada was betraying its heritage, turning its back on Britain, they argued. Was this not another sign of the Liberal tendency to appease the United States? Fortunately for Mackenzie King, Parliament considered the GATT in isolation. Nobody knew that the Liberal government had pursued another set of negotiations with the United States, and King was determined to keep them a deep secret.

These negotiations went back to the summer of 1947, when a Canadian official visiting Washington suggested that an American loan, to tide the Canadians over until better days, would not be amiss. This was followed by a much more serious visit from the deputy minister of finance, Clifford Clark, in September. Clark met with the usual galaxy of American officials, including Paul Nitze of the Policy Planning staff in the State Department. "Mr. Paul Nitze was sympathetic, understanding, constructive and able – much the ablest of the group," Clark reported.[22]

It was in this context that the US granted a loan to Canada in the fall of 1947. Yet the Canadian economy was fundamentally sound, in the opinion of Clark and most of his colleagues. To Clark, Canada's problem differed from Europe's, where lack of enterprise and flagging production would have to be remedied before economic equilibrium could be restored.

The American response was divided. The Canadian desk officer at the State Department pointed out that "a great many American tourists had been up in Canada during the summer and that what they saw was full employment, high prosperity, everybody eating juicy steaks and living on a high North American standard." Clark left with his audience only partly convinced, but with at least some allies in the American capital.[23]

Clark recruited one key ally, Nitze, who took the lead in devising a constructive American response to the Canadian problem. The Americans would furnish a loan, $300 million from Washington's Export-Import Bank, consideration for Canadian purchases using Marshall Plan funds, and consent to Canadian-imposed special trade restrictions aimed at American goods alone.[24]

The restrictions were announced to the public on 17 November in a radio speech by the finance minister, following immediately after the happy announcement, by the prime minister, of agreement on the GATT. The public swallowed the pill with remarkable equanimity. Controlling private expenditures of US dollars was easier in 1947 than later: Canadians had neither money nor opportunity for mass migrations to Florida in 1947-1948, and there were few expatriates living abroad on Canadian pensions.

With high employment, declining taxes, budgetary surpluses, and rising production, Canadians did not believe that they were hard done by, or that their governmental system had failed. Douglas Abbott, the finance minister, gave a radio speech, but he did not announce that Canada was once again, and on another front, engaged in discussions with the United States about tariffs and trade. In 1947, confronted by an incurable shortage of American dollars, Canadian officials began to talk about a North American free trade area with their American counterparts.

The free trade negotiations of 1947-1948 would have surprised most Canadians, had they known of them. It was obvious that there was a problem, but if Canada was short of US dollars, so was the rest of the world; an American dollar shortage seemed perpetual, a fixed condition of economics.

The exchange rate crisis of 1947 was a predicament known mostly to professionals. It alarmed currency managers, economists, certain politicians, and a couple of diplomats. It filtered into the newspapers from time to time, but as an episode in foreign relations it was remarkably self-contained, with almost no outside, non-governmental, input. Public opinion in an active sense was absent from the issue after November 1947, but potential public opinion – how the politicians thought the public might react – was crucial to what followed.

The interpretation of public opinion varied. To the American embassy in Ottawa, public opinion "had reached probably an all time high in favoring a closer integration of the economies of Canada and the United States." The American ambassador reported on 29 October that "economic union between the two countries is taken as a natural parallel development with intimate military ties existing since early in the late war and close political collaboration as now manifest at the UN." Ray Atherton, the ambassador, realized that this interest in closer economic ties with the United States was not a first choice. Given the failure to re-establish a "multilateral" trading system based on "the Atlantic Triangle" of the United States, Canada, and Great Britain, "Canada today more than ever before appears ready to accept virtual economic union with the United States as a necessary substitute." Atherton based his assessment on newspaper gleanings and, apparently, official conversations, using the former to confirm the latter.[25]

Some of his official contacts meanwhile showed up in Washington. Hector MacKinnon, chairman of the Canadian Tariff Board, and John Deutsch, a senior official in the Canadian Finance Department, called on Clair Wilcox and Nitze, senior economic specialists in the State Department. They reviewed Canada's emergency economic program, then pending, but then added something quite new. "The Canadian Cabinet," they reported, "[had] authorized [MacKinnon] to explore with United States officials the possibility of concluding a comprehensive agreement, including, wherever possible, the complete elimination of duties." Such a comprehensive package ("a major readjustment") would require Congressional approval. That was obvious enough, and the American negotiators said they would discuss with their superiors what to do next.[26]

Matters were not as they seemed. The Canadian Cabinet as a whole had not been consulted. Some ministers knew, including Mackenzie King. It was not the politicians who did the negotiating but the senior officials. MacKinnon and Deutsch were responsible and experienced – indeed, they had just completed negotiating the GATT. In Washington, their task was to discover, in the strictest secrecy, what terms the Americans might agree to. Had Canadians known of the avenues being explored, the American ambassador's assessment of the public mood may have changed.

Nor was it easy to gauge the mood on the American side. Officials liked the idea, although most, like Jack Hickerson, were cautious. (Hickerson was the American diplomat with the longest experience of Canada, which equipped him with a profound respect for the dangers of provoking Canadian nationalist sentiments.) The upper political levels of the administration were not informed; it was mostly civil servants who were engaged on the American side. As for the Republican Congress, the Democratic Truman administration was not perhaps the best judge. There was only one guarantee of success for any bold foreign policy initiative – to raise the spectre of security and to suggest that vital American interests were in danger. At the end of 1947, in the case of Canada, that was too much for most Americans to swallow.

Political events outside North America could drive North America in upon itself. Under those circumstances, economic union or political union with Canada might be a possibility. Nothing negotiators in Washington could devise could make a difference in that kind of situation. On its own merits, however, Canadian-American free trade, or customs union, or economic union, would not fly.

The alternative to this negotiation, on the Canadian side, was an unending regime of restrictions, quotas, and controls, and less affluence. John Deutsch of the Finance Department put the alternatives succinctly: "a relative[ly] free enterprise world with the highest existing standard of living and a government controlled world with a lower standard of living. Which we did not want."[27]

The Canadian negotiators travelling to Washington in the winter of 1948 became increasingly intrigued with the notion of free trade as an elegant and feasible solution to Canada's apparently chronic economic problems. The American side of the negotiating team was experienced, friendly, and increasingly enthusiastic as the talks progressed. If the tariff barrier were abandoned, would it not be a first step to a broader merger of interests and eventually of sovereignty?[28] Perhaps coincidentally, even *Life* magazine, the exceedingly popular American illustrated weekly, much read in Canada, took up the cause: Canadians, *Life* wrote, "need complete and permanent economic union with the US. The US needs this too, and so does the future of a healthy world."[29] *Life* did not mention sovereignty; it did not need to.

Life's happy vision also occurred to Mackenzie King, and it troubled him. The uncertain world of 1948 was light years away from the comfortable imperial certainties of his Victorian childhood. He recalled that as a young politician he had been swept from office in the 1911 general election in a wave of anti-Americanism. Sentiment and prudence were now reinforced by superstition. Hearing the news from Washington, King wandered into his library to think. He absent-mindedly plucked from the shelf a thirty-year-old book, *Studies in Colonial Nationalism*, by Richard Jebb. Jebb examined the progress of Britain's colonies, including Canada, towards autonomy and independence. Independence, King believed, was his true life's work. If as his last public act he took Canada irretrievably into the American economic orbit, King decided his cause and his reputation would be lost.

King decided to abandon the free trade negotiations. They were, he thought, wrong in principle, and they would prove politically disastrous. He knew that ending the negotiations did nothing for Canada's balance of payments or its shortage of American dollars. And yet there might be another way to address these problems. At that very moment, another negotiation was beginning with the Americans, this time for a comprehensive security pact. These negotiations included the British. Why not add an economic dimension to the security discussions, and conclude with the best of all possible outcomes – a political-economic security instrument that brought Canada, the United States, and Great Britain together in happy concord? Not even the most blinkered Canadian Tory could object. Thus, 1948 would not be the year of American free trade after all: if King had his way, it would set off an explosion of Anglo-American-Canadian economic harmony. Of course, that agenda item would have to wait until security was satisfied, and wait too for the Western Europeans to catch up and sign on.

❦

BETWEEN 1945 AND 1948 THE CANADIAN GOVERNMENT MANOEUVRED, at considerable expense and political cost, to shore up the Canadian economy by promoting trade and other forms of economic linkage with Great Britain and Western Europe. It did not forget the United States, but that was an area where it had no special policy except to go with the flow. The flow was well channelled. The United States provided goods that Canadians would buy, in styles that suited Canadian homes, farms, and factories. Canadians also knew that if they ordered something it would come, whether it was a machine tool or a refrigerator. At the same time, Canadian exports needed no special negotiation and no government permission. The purchase price would not sit in a blocked account overseas, waiting for exchange control to end, but would be immediately convertible.

Imports and exports were obviously extremely important to the Canadian economy in the postwar years. But they were not as important as the pessimists predicted. Prosperity turned on trade, true, but also on the pace of domestic investment and consumer demand. The careful civil servants of 1945 were doing their job by being prudent and devising plans to meet a worst-case scenario that never came to pass.

In one very large sense Canadian postwar economic policy was a dead end. For reasons of politics and history, the Canadian government attempted to reinvent Europe and particularly Great Britain using the model of the 1930s. Canada invested almost $2.5 billion in loans and credits to Great Britain and the rest of Europe. These sums were useful to their recipients and in the short term to Canadian exporters. They propped up Canadian overseas exports in 1946 and 1947, though not at the levels of

1945 or earlier. But they did not recreate a pattern of trade with Europe that time and circumstance had made obsolete. The British loan drained Canadian foreign exchange reserves and helped bring on the exchange crisis of 1947.

Something else would be needed. Whatever that was, it would be more than Canada could afford. In terms of aid, Canada had shot its bolt between 1945 and 1947. Leadership would have to come from the United States. But that would become a political question, with a different answer.

REALIGNING
CANADIAN FOREIGN POLICY,
1945-1947

3

Between 1945 and 1947 Canada had many adjustments to make. But the main adjustment was curiously traditional, responding to a situation that had existed ever since Canada took a distinct form, back in the eighteenth century, with the clash between the revolutionary American republic and the British Empire. Canadians had plumped for Britain – some more consciously or willingly than others – and, in the hundred and fifty years that followed, Canadian politics and economics revolved around that fundamental fact. Thus, it was an old issue that dominated Canadian policy in 1945 and after. The circumstances were, however, unprecedented.

Great Britain was declining, economically and politically, while the United States enjoyed unprecedented prosperity and power. How far that process would go, and how long it would last, were open questions.[1] In 1947 the British withdrew from India and Pakistan, winding up two centuries of domination in the Indian subcontinent.[2] In 1948 the British pulled out of Ceylon, Burma, and Palestine; meanwhile the Irish formally withdrew from the Commonwealth, as did the Burmese. Simultaneously the British decided to withdraw troops and aid from Greece and Turkey, a decision they announced to the Americans in February 1947.

There was a modest fig leaf attached to the process. As the British Cabinet put it in December 1946, while contemplating the process of imperial contraction, "withdrawal need not appear to be forced upon us by our weakness nor to be the first step in the dissolution of the Empire." But withdrawal from India *had* been forced upon the British, and leaving India was the first big step in dissolving the empire.[3] In politics, as in punditry, appearance is (almost) all, and rhetoric cast a befuddling fog over the harsher aspects of reality not just in Britain, but in Canada and other parts of the Commonwealth. The very idea of a Commonwealth was an essential ingredient of the fog. The British Empire was not gone, but had ascended. What had been forced was now free.

A freer but weaker Britain was not suddenly irrelevant to a freer but stronger Canada. The weak, however, interpret their interests more narrowly than the strong, while the strong (or, in the case of Canada, the recently and temporarily strong) are obliged to be more generous in their actions than they might wish to be. Britain was for Canadians more than a land of Shakespeare, castles, and ancestors. It was also a laboratory for social experiment. The British government, Labour since 1945, had an ambitious and expensive program at home, nationalizing coal, steel, and rail, and establishing a socialized National Health scheme. These programs were admired by some in Canada, where British policy was an omen of what might happen at home. The scale and uniqueness of the British social-economic experiment concentrated British minds and made the British government more rather than less nationalistic, determined to pursue its own course, by insulating Great Britain from Europe while reducing its engagement in the empire and Commonwealth.

The Commonwealth as a tonic for fading British energies floundered and finally faded. It was the United States, not the disparate and intractable Commonwealth, that held the key to Britain's survival, militarily and financially. Britain remained a formidable military power, but the power was receding. It was for the Canadian government to weigh what this decline meant in a world where Canada had no counterbalance to the United States.

The first indication of what it might mean, in theory and practice, came in the area of atomic weapons.

THE SHADOW OF THE BOMB

If any single action brought the Second World War to a close, it was the dropping of an American atomic bomb on the Japanese city of Hiroshima on 6 August 1945. Within ten days the Japanese government surrendered, and within a month Allied, mostly American, troops landed in Japan.

Very few Allied officials had known that such a bomb existed, and even fewer knew that one would be used. The American president knew, of course, but not most of his Cabinet. The British prime minister knew too, for the development of the bomb was in large part a British idea, and British scientists participated in the search for a usable atomic weapon. Mackenzie King and his minister of munitions and supply, C.D. Howe, were also in on the secret. Canada created and paid for a joint atomic laboratory with the British during the war and mined and refined uranium for the bomb project.[4] This laboratory, located until 1945 in Montreal, started up a tiny atomic reactor in the isolated hamlet of Chalk River, northwest of Ottawa, in September 1945. Because of Canada's nuclear role, Howe became a member of the Allied Combined Policy Committee that watched over the atomic bomb.

On 6 August Howe, sitting in a federal-provincial conference in Ottawa, got word of the Hiroshima bomb in a note from Malcolm MacDonald, the British high commissioner. "The thing has gone off," MacDonald wrote. The atomic bomb was a secret no longer. President Harry Truman broadcast the fact in an address to the American people. In the fall of 1945 the Americans published a best-selling book on the building of the bomb. The scientists of the Montreal laboratory gave well-attended public lectures to explain the scientific achievement. Most public comment was relieved, if not admiring. Canada was a partner, though a junior partner, in the great scientific event that had ended the war.[5]

Not everybody was reassured. "HAVOC" was the headline in the *Regina Leader-Post*. The bomb was a nightmare come true. Scientists had concocted the ultimate dreadful weapon. The world would never be the same. Through fiction and film, Canadians knew about such things – *Frankenstein* was a staple of western culture, a story in which a well-intentioned scientist defied nature and created a monster.[6] The dread of a horrific future transferred itself to the present, for while the war had come to an end, the threat of the bomb had just started.

Mackenzie King was both proud and uneasy. His first reaction to the possibility of an atomic bomb was "absolute horror and panic," according to a British witness. King had provided Canadian land, money, uranium ore, scientists, and engineers. In return he got the secret of the atom. "How strange it is," King told his diary in October 1945, "that I should find myself at the very centre of this problem, through Canada possessing uranium, having contributed to the production of the bomb, being recognized as one of the three countries to hold most of the secrets."[7]

Postwar Fissures

By October 1945 King knew that "the very centre of this problem" meant that Canada had to play a larger and unwelcome role in relations among the great powers. The wartime alliance, always uneasy, was under strain in the summer and fall of 1945. The Soviet Union and the Western powers had been forced together only by the menace of Nazi Germany. They differed on a wide variety of issues: what kind of government should be imposed on the states of Central and Eastern Europe, under Soviet occupation; whether American aid to the Allies should continue; and whether the United States should be the sole manager of the secret of the atomic bomb.

These were important concerns, but they masked another worry: the Soviet Union was a revolutionary and anti-capitalist state. All power in the Soviet Union was concentrated in the hands of the Communist Party and its leader, Joseph Stalin. Every Western country had its own Communist Party, whose objective was to overturn the established order and replace it with the dictatorship of the proletariat. Many Western Communists, including Canadians, took subsidies from Moscow and did their best to serve Soviet interests. Indeed, Stalin had converted their leadership into Soviet puppets. He guarded Soviet interests first, sacrificing the political credibility of his allies in the West by showing them to be no more than parrots of Soviet policy and doctrine.

One practical way of assisting the Soviet Union was keeping it informed of capitalist secrets. The atomic partners were not sharing their secrets with the Soviet Union. Soviet scientists had deduced that the absence of references to nuclear physics in Western scientific journals must mean that the British and Americans were attempting to develop atomic bombs, so naturally Soviet intelligence searched for information on the subject. Meanwhile, Stalin authorized a Soviet bomb project in 1943 and awaited results. He commented in August 1945 that "Hiroshima has shaken the whole world. The balance has been destroyed." To restore the balance, Stalin devoted all possible resources to building a Soviet bomb within five years.[8]

The first inkling of active Soviet interest came in Ottawa. In September 1945 a junior intelligence officer in the Soviet embassy, Igor Gouzenko, decided to remain in Canada with his family rather than return to Moscow. He told Canadian authorities of Soviet espionage in their country and had the documents to prove it. The notion of Soviet spies astounded Mackenzie King, who instantly feared that Canada might become the centre of a new and unwelcome international incident. Learning that Gouzenko was threatening suicide unless the Canadians took him in, King speculated that this might be a useful solution. Gouzenko's documents could be copied and returned to the Soviet embassy, and Gouzenko would no longer be an issue.

Fortunately, this crass idea was not put into effect. Gouzenko, his family, and his documents were safe in Canadian custody. Preliminary examination revealed not one but two Soviet spy rings in Canada, both staffed by personnel from the Soviet embassy and by Canadian and British scientists, military officers, and civil servants.

Investigations continued in secret while King scurried off to tell the Americans and the British what had occurred. He informed his allies, including a very sceptical Dean Acheson, the American undersecretary of state, and British prime minister Clement Attlee.[9] They were not as impressed as he might have wished at the time.[10] He continued to worry about Soviet reactions, hoping that the Russians would not blame *him*, or Canada, for damaging East-West relations and that the Gouzenko affair was not the damning indictment of Soviet society or intentions some of his advisers believed it to be.[11]

The Soviet government was undecided in 1945 as to what to expect from the West. Assessments by senior Soviet diplomats – more senior and more important than those stationed in Ottawa – suggested that the war would be followed by a period of stability, during which there were "no grounds to expect that relations between the USSR on one hand and the USA and England on the other, would be bad." To Andrei Gromyko, ambassador in Washington, writing in June 1944, "the necessary conditions are clearly present for a continuation of cooperation between our two countries in the post-war period." Another senior official argued there was hope for an Anglo-Soviet condominium in Europe, and for stable, not hostile, relations with the United States.[12]

Such an outcome would not have displeased Mackenzie King, or his ministers, or most of his officials.[13] But the effect of the Gouzenko affair was to make cooperation seem less likely; it stimulated an appetite for analysis of the Soviet Union, in the hope of better predicting Soviet actions. But alternatives to friendship were not precluded – not yet. These would eventually be judged in a new and harsher light.

For a few months King contemplated the Gouzenko revelations in secret. Public opinion was uncertain. During the war Ottawa stimulated friendship with its Soviet ally, painting Stalin's Russia in terms that were little short of fantastic. The Canadian ambassador in Moscow at the time, Dana Wilgress, warned that after the war there would be "a reaction against excessive adulation," when it was discovered that the Soviets were "as totalitarian as the Germans."[14] Sure enough, with the end of the war, Canadian anti-communism resurfaced, first in a provincial election in Ontario in June 1945. Mistrust for the Soviet Union appeared in secret opinion polls conducted for Ottawa. They showed that Canadians – even more than Americans – hesitated to trust the Soviets, and that such a perspective was "stiffening."[15]

Events in the fall of 1945 did little to improve matters. The foreign ministers of the great powers (grandly titled the Council of Foreign Ministers, CFM) met in London, and disagreed. The new United Nations also met in London, and disagreed. The lines of conflict were not absolutely clear – at the CFM the Soviets made an attempt to play on American prejudices against the British, stoking British fears and inspiring the British to contemplate how they might again get the Americans on their side. Meanwhile, British ministers and generals told a visiting Mackenzie King how perilous the international situation was. King was impressed, but not so impressed that he did not consent to what was a last attempt to negotiate with the Soviets on international control over atomic weapons. This he did at a conference in Washington in November with President Harry Truman and Prime Minister Clement Attlee. They agreed to launch a negotiation using the new United Nations as a forum. The UN duly established the United Nations Atomic Energy Commission (UNAEC). It debuted in hope and optimism in the spring of 1946 but expired in bitterness and recrimination in May 1948. UNAEC did not resolve confrontation but rather enhanced it by giving the differences and mistrust among the great powers a public forum. The Americans demanded effective oversight of any nation's capacity to make nuclear weapons, including uranium mines and refineries, items which would affect Canada. The Soviets, on the other hand, demanded a level negotiating field, meaning the immediate abolition of all existing atomic weapons, an American monopoly. The Canadians trudged a middle road, attempting to build an agreement on a foundation of details; but even with that method there was no agreement.[16]

King gradually came to grips with the problem of the Soviet Union. Wilgress, his ambassador in Moscow, explained the problem in a series of dispatches in the fall of 1945. The external affairs undersecretary, Norman Robertson, sent the prime minister a summary. According to Robertson, "Mr. Wilgress develops the thesis that a privileged class has emerged in the Soviet Union," meaning that the Soviet Union was in no sense a democracy operating on normal political lines. The Soviet leadership would do anything to protect its privileged position, which in practice meant that it was "fearful of the possibility of attack from abroad" and "obsessed with problems of security." The leadership would search for more security, but it would not deliberately seek war. "On the whole," Wilgress concluded, "the interests of the Soviet privileged class are bound up with the maintenance of a long period of peace."[17]

At this point Winston Churchill, retired as prime minister by the British electorate in July 1945, came to North America. On 4 March 1946, on a stage with a beaming President Truman sitting behind him, Churchill appealed for English-speaking solidarity against the Soviet menace. There was, claimed Churchill, a community of values and of interests that stretched across the Atlantic and around the world but did not include the Soviet Union. Whereas the United States and the British Commonwealth were natural allies, the English-speaking powers and the Soviet Union were inevitable antagonists. In the most famous phrase of his speech, Churchill declaimed, "From Stettin in the Baltic to Trieste in the Adriatic, an Iron Curtain has descended across the continent." This was bad enough, but elsewhere there were "Communist fifth columns" – an image straight from the anti-fascist struggles of the Second World War.[18]

Mackenzie King knew of the speech, and the Canadian ambassador in Washington, Lester Pearson, had read and commented on it. King was approving when he heard Churchill over the radio. "It was the most courageous speech I have ever listened to, considering what we know of Russia's behaviour in Europe and in Asia since the war and what has been disclosed here in Ottawa, much of which is not yet public." It was "in every way opportune."[19] King phoned Churchill to congratulate him. Finding him with Truman, he repeated for the president his most salient conclusion: "I felt we must all work together naming the US, the UK, Canada and other parts, to see that our position was made secure." Truman said little in response; Churchill's grand project may have been too much to contemplate or comment upon.[20]

"Iron Curtain" is the kind of phrase that lasts. As important was Churchill's call for Anglo-American solidarity. There, Truman paused for thought – the idea of a close identity of interests with the British was not easily saleable, even in the face of an Iron Curtain. King had no such worries. He worshipped the idea of trans-Atlantic harmony. It was axiomatic: Canada did best when its closest allies and largest trading partners were at peace with each other. The universe looked best when viewed through a triangular lens.

Another phrase was coming into use: the "Cold War" was apparently coined by the British author George Orwell in October 1945 to describe a strategic stalemate between two (or more) "unconquerable" powers. The term was picked up by the American journalist Walter Lippmann in 1947, and for the next forty years described what seemed to be a permanent reality of international affairs, a standoff between the Soviet Union and its (generally unwilling) allies, and the rather more willing Western coalition led by the United States. The West recognized the Soviet Union, accurately enough, as a tyranny and its political system as totalitarian. In 1946-1947 most of the news from abroad seemed to underline the Soviet threat.

Sometimes the news was not from abroad. In mid-February 1946 news of the Gouzenko spy rings finally broke. The leak came from Washington, just in time to bolster the impact of Churchill's speech. In Canada and Great Britain arrests followed, and a Canadian royal commission opened hearings into the affair.[21]

Meanwhile, atomic research in Canada proceeded. (One of the scientists still at Chalk River in 1946, Bruno Pontecorvo, later caused a sensation by fleeing from Great Britain to the Soviet Union with all the secrets his brain could accommodate. Pontecorvo was not on Gouzenko's list, though his left leanings were well known.) Given the Canadian government's prompt action in response to the Gouzenko revelations, and the relatively minor level of Canadian atomic research, the Americans did not seriously question Canadian security. The real issue was what the British government, Canada's partner, intended to do. This was not really a security question, though it might have become one had the British decided to continue their wartime atomic partnership with Canada.

Great Britain consulted its own interests. It brought the major part of the Canadian laboratory – British in its direction and in most of its scientific and engineering components – back to England, to a site outside Oxford. At the same time the British decided to build their own nuclear weapon, with or without American cooperation. The Canadian government learned of all this through the newspapers, which did not impress either Mackenzie King or the responsible minister, C.D. Howe. Up to that point it was possible that the momentum of the wartime project and the continuing research it bequeathed could have kept the Canadians and the British together as atomic partners.

The abrupt and unilateral British decision caused the Canadians to think more fondly of the United States. Howe anticipated this in August 1945, when he said he was "glad ... that the US and Canadian partnership [would] continue."[22]

It took time to build a British laboratory, and the Anglo-Canadian project decoupled very slowly. Howe reluctantly hired a new British scientist, W.B. Lewis, to direct the Chalk River laboratory and oversee the completion of its first large reactor, called NRX, in 1947. NRX, for National Research Experimental, was designed during the war to be a plutonium factory, plutonium being a useful fuel for a nuclear weapon. In 1947 and for some time thereafter, the Canadians had at the back of their minds the possibility that Chalk River might become a centre for plutonium production for British and American weapons. But they declined to support British weapons research directly and rebuffed British suggestions of a joint approach to the Americans, fearing it might imperil Canada's close relations with the United States.

The Canadian government never seriously considered building its own nuclear weapons. The cost was too great, and such a project demanded more scientists, engineers, and technicians than Canada could provide. C.D. Howe casually announced the fact in the course of a debate in the House of Commons. To Howe, it was a statement of the obvious: Canada could not afford nuclear weapons, and its close relationship with the United States meant it did not need them. Yet, Howe did not renounce nuclear weapons, assuming that Canada could and would be defended by American weaponry.[23]

The Canadian government cooperated in procuring uranium for weapons production at the American Atomic Energy Commission (AEC) and hoped to produce plutonium as well. Uranium sales became a substantial item in Canada's export trade during the 1950s, and the bonanza continued until the mid-1960s, when American uranium purchases from Canada were finally terminated. By good fortune, NRX was designed as an efficient producer of isotopes, which meant that Canada became a major source of nuclear materials for medicine and other technologies, and remains so. From the mid-1940s to the mid-1960s, nuclear resources and technology constituted a significant item in Canada's Cold War diplomacy, and in the balance of relations with the United States. Ironically, for a project that was British in origin, nuclear technology marked a significant break – also British in origin – in Canada's relations with Great Britain.

RECONCEIVING FOREIGN POLICY
Canada's foreign policy decisions regarding Great Britain entailed a series of steps that the Mackenzie King government took reluctantly, modestly, and without alarming the Canadian public. Because Canadian politics were placid and its government long-lived and competent, Canada appeared from the outside to be strong. Because the Canadian

economy was booming, and unemployment negligible, the dominion's strength was rated relatively high. The government was not averse to tapping that strength on its own terms, even when those terms were exceedingly generous, as with the British loan of 1946. It reacted badly when Canadian consent was assumed, as with the Anglo-Canadian atomic project. The same consideration applied to the question of a Canadian contribution to the British occupation of Germany.

The occupation of Germany was agreed among the great powers before the end of the war. After the war it appeared to the British that they could act most effectively as a great power, and match the contributions of the Soviets and the Americans, if they used troops from the dominions, particularly Canada, whose troops were already on the ground, awaiting transport back to North America. A first appeal by the Attlee government, based on imperial solidarity, fell on stony ground. A second, based on duty to the United Nations, got more sympathetic consideration, but eventually, in February 1946, it too was refused. The Canadians lectured that they would not take on "responsibilities arising out of commitments or decisions in which we had no part as a separate state."[24]

Mackenzie King hoped to make a stronger impression on international opinion when he arrived in Paris for a peace conference in the spring of 1946. He was the senior statesman on the Western side, surpassing even Stalin in longevity in office. But King was not up to the job of reinforcing Canadian interests or reconciling the erstwhile allies, who disagreed among themselves, mostly about what should be done with Germany. When he got his chance to address the conference, King emitted a lengthy and painful drone of words. At a reception the prime minister spotted V.M. Molotov, the Soviet foreign minister, and fruitlessly followed him around the room, hoping to repair the fissure opened by the Gouzenko affair. Molotov prudently stayed out of reach, and the breach remained unbridged.[25]

It was just as well. King could say or do little that would alleviate tension between communism and capitalism or between Canada and the Soviet Union. When the royal commission reported on the Gouzenko affair, its revelations and blunt conclusions widened the gulf between East and West. Stalin and his sympathizers, the commission asserted, would stop at nothing to have their way. King's efforts to alleviate tension, murmuring in Parliament about a visit to Moscow, were gently discouraged by his staff. Instead, in an international forum the Soviet foreign minister, Andrei Vishinsky, unleashed a verbal attack on Canada. Outside the Canadian embassy in Moscow, a doubled set of guards paced; at Soviet receptions the Canadian ambassador was shunned. He did not have to endure such treatment for long; in a sign of disapproval Ambassador Wilgress was withdrawn. From 1946 until the death of Stalin in 1953 Canada was represented in Moscow by a succession of junior diplomats.[26]

A New Canadian Policy

In defining external policy, Canada relied on its British connection intellectually and came to accept the British view of things, which in 1945-1947 involved a crisis so great that it forced decisions. The crisis that shaped Canadian foreign relations for the next forty years began in the British Treasury towards the end of 1946. It was closely related to the problems Canada was facing – a shortage of hard currency and a serious trade deficit – but it was complicated by Britain's worldwide commitments, maintaining armies from Palestine to Vietnam, shoring up the empire, and occupying Germany.

Worse still, there was a long-term difficulty. Britain's ability to trade had deteriorated in the face of foreign competition and import substitution by other countries during the war. "We are facing," in the opinion of the British Foreign Office, "a diminution of our economic strength which may be of long duration." "The hard fact" was that Britain could no longer do what it might wish to do in foreign policy, not merely on peripheral issues, but on subjects or in areas that were crucial to British interests.[27] Yet these crucial interests must somehow be served, and this would mean that Britain had to become the "junior partner" of the United States and work towards harmonizing the political objectives of the two countries. As the Foreign Office told the Cabinet, "Only if we were to find ourselves alone with our political objectives widely divergent from those of the United States would our financial nakedness be fully apparent to the world."[28]

A calamitous winter underlined British weakness. Blizzards shut down transportation. Bitter cold froze coal production and the industry it fuelled – down by 25 percent from January to February 1947. (It was effectively the West's first energy crisis – but not its last.[29]) Everything – imperial grandeur, defence commitments, centuries of policy – would have to be scrutinized and those things deemed expendable broken up and tossed into the furnace of financial necessity.

The Cabinet did not abandon everything. The British occupation of Germany, a financial drain that some likened to paying reparations to the defeated Germans, carried on. But aid to Greece (£15 million, or roughly $65 million) would have to go. The British occupation of Palestine, held in the face of a Jewish-Arab civil war, would also have to cease, though under the veil of United Nations authority. India, another theatre of civil conflict, would be granted independence, whether or not its political leaders were ready for it.[30]

In Europe the British hoped that the Americans could pick up the tab. In Germany the British government decided to offload occupation costs as far as possible, meanwhile drafting terms and conditions that effectively precluded cooperation with the Russians.[31] It was in Greece that British need provided American opportunity, and the Americans seized it. The United States announced that it would aid Greece and Turkey, indeed any nation threatened by communism. British aid to Greece would end 31 March

1947. Truman delivered a speech to Congress on 12 March. He tried hard to set the right tone, and that tone was close to panic. The resulting combination of alarmist verbiage and anti-communist strategy was dubbed the "Truman Doctrine." Its creators hoped that, like the nineteenth-century Monroe Doctrine, it would define American foreign policy.

On 5 June, the American secretary of state, General George Marshall, proposed a program of financial aid to Europe, to be granted by the United States on submission of a European economic plan. Such a plan must be cooperative and must be agreed upon by the Europeans themselves. International in scope, it would be open to all European countries, including the Soviet Union, which sent a delegation under foreign minister V.M. Molotov to a European conference in Paris in July to consider a response to the American offer. But, in retrospect, the result seems to have been foreordained. The Americans were not about to drop money over the Iron Curtain to be used according to the mysterious ways and peculiar customs of the Soviet government.

The western Europeans, more open in their politics though sometimes equally mysterious in their ways, took the money, which was duly authorized by Congress in March 1948 after lengthy debate. The American creation, properly called the European Recovery Program, became known as the Marshall Plan, after its sponsor; it was administered by the Economic Co-operation Administration, and headquartered in Paris.

These two political acts, the Truman Doctrine and the Marshall Plan, defined the division of Europe and set the United States and the Western Europeans in collaborative motion. The British had, for the last time, been the catalysts of a great revolution in international affairs. The British collapse and the American and European response had not depended on Canada. As the events of early 1947 unfolded, however, Canada could not help but be involved.

Canada, American undersecretary of state Dean Acheson reported to his president, was "generally sympathetic" to the Truman Doctrine. But Canadians faced economic difficulties and remained concerned about their "position in a war between the great powers."[32] Generally, the Mackenzie King government was constrained by Canadians' political and economic expectations. As the government knew, these expectations were to some extent contradictory. On the one hand, in the face of communism, Canadian opinion was remarkably united. Gouzenko, Soviet behaviour in Eastern Europe, anti-communist political traditions, all led Canadians – both English and French speaking – to be deeply suspicious about Soviet behaviour. Recent history also suggested, and for many Canadians demonstrated conclusively, that Europe's future and Canada's were inextricably linked, economically and politically.

Until 1947 Canada enjoyed the luxury of exempting itself from British policy, knowing that for the most part the British would still be there, standing between North America and a potentially dangerous and certainly unreliable Europe. That in turn allowed Canadians to proclaim a policy of no automatic commitments. Such a policy, King hoped, might restrain a headstrong Britain. Now it appeared that such restraint was no longer needed.

Where would Canada stand? One answer came in response to an invitation asking the secretary of state for external affairs, Louis St Laurent, to inaugurate a lecture series at the University of Toronto. The Gray Lecture, named in honour of two graduates, brothers killed during the Second World War, was intended to promote better English-French relations in Canada. St Laurent took the occasion to define a Canadian foreign policy that would, he hoped, contribute to national unity.

National unity was the first principle St Laurent enunciated for Canadian foreign policy: "No policy can be regarded as wise which divides the people whose effort and resources must put it into effect." This applied not merely to French-English relations but to regional differences: "A disunited Canada will be a powerless one." The second consideration was "political liberty," a Canadian characteristic, inherited from Western Europe, but applicable to international affairs in general: "Stability is lacking where consent is absent." Third was the "rule of law," again with both a domestic and an international dimension. Targeting those who believed in the "spurious efficiency" of totalitarianism, St Laurent recalled the awful consequences that flowed from government above or beyond the law. With Auschwitz and Buchenwald a recent memory, this argument had particular salience.

All Canadians, the minister continued, enjoyed a common heritage and values: these values permitted the pursuit of an active and united policy in foreign affairs. He concluded by pledging an active role for Canada in international affairs, while reviewing Canada's good relations with the British Commonwealth, the United States, and France. The United States received special mention: Canada was ready "to accept our responsibility as a North American nation in enterprises which are for the welfare of this continent." But at the same time, there was no thought "that this continent could live unto itself." St Laurent did not mention the Soviet Union, but perhaps he did not have to.[33]

The sequence of St Laurent's argument was significant; it was also one that his audience would not have questioned. Canada would take a prominent role in the world. But whether political or economic, St Laurent's condition, that national unity must be maintained, implied or recalled the fragility of the Canadian political economy.

In the summer of 1947 economics came first.[34] There was a steady drain of Canadian foreign exchange reserves, and export earnings and other receipts were not enough to replenish them. It reminded Canadian officials and politicians that Canada was a small country facing a large world. The size of its population meant that Canada by itself could never make a decisive difference. It must act in combination or be resigned to ineffectiveness. Canada and Europe and Britain were on parallel tracks in the winter of 1947, each fearing, and half believing, that the tracks led into the abyss. Only the timetable was uncertain; as it happened, the British were considerably ahead of the Canadians.

At the end of May 1947 Canadian and American officials met in Washington. Ambassador Hume Wrong, appointed the previous fall, attended. The problem was the worrisome Canadian balance of payments, set against the state of Western Europe, "There is no satisfactory solution for Canada," wrote Wrong, "so long as the United Kingdom and Western Europe are in difficult straits." A comprehensive solution was necessary, and that could come only from the Americans.[35] If the dollar shortage could not be solved, if the economic situation remained "difficult," each country would have to seek its own salvation by restricting trade and strictly controlling exchanges. American exports would fall. Multilateral trade talks, scheduled for Geneva in the hope of establishing an International Trade Organization, would prove abortive.

The Canadian government, unlike the American, did not intend to formulate plans or raise more money for Europe. But when Secretary Marshall proposed his plan for European recovery in a speech on 5 June, the Canadians applauded and hoped for the best. The best, paradoxically, was more bad news from Europe, which, Ambassador Wrong noted, "may be helpful in this connection."[36] A truly grave crisis in Europe could so unsettle the Americans that they would take a bolder and more generous approach to their most secure ally, Canada.

As the summer of 1947 dragged on, new worries surfaced. The first was the long-anticipated British foreign exchange crisis. In July 1947, as promised, the British government moved the pound sterling to convertibility against the US dollar and, by extension, the Canadian dollar. The result was a run on the pound, panic in financial markets, and, on 20 August, suspension of British convertibility.[37] The sense of economic crisis abroad, and the lack of one at home, was the background for what came next. News from Europe – of strikes in France, misery in Germany, a Communist takeover in Romania and another in Poland – captured the imagination in the fall of 1947. Shrinking Western influence, slow recoveries, dawdling in the American Congress over Marshall Plan aid: these events prepared Canadians for a crisis in Europe. Compared to that, economic relations with the United States, exchange rates, and import restrictions seemed unimportant. But the news from Europe did suggest the possibility of an isolated North America in a sea of communism. That perception, coupled with knowledge inside government of how serious the foreign exchange crisis of 1947 actually was, led directly to the government's next foreign policy initiative on the economic front, the negotiations with the United States over free trade. Paradoxically it also helped to account for the failure of free trade when, in March 1948, discussions began on what the American undersecretary of defense, Robert Lovett, called "a defense agreement."

GREAT BRITAIN'S DECISION TO CONCENTRATE its resources closer to home but to maintain as far as possible its position as a great power forced a redefinition in Canada's approach to the outside world. Ironically, there were great similarities in the two countries' priorities, and the only way of realizing them was to rely on the United States. The United States was thus a common focus for Canada and Great Britain, as it was for all liberal and democratic societies that hoped to preserve themselves in the face of totalitarian threats and temptations after 1945.

Canadians accepted that they were poorer and had fewer opportunities than Americans. That was to be expected – or remedied by emigration to the United States, the US border being open to incoming Canadians. In contrast, Great Britain's position, a state of political decline and apparently constant economic crisis, was a novelty.

The British conundrum affected the psychological relationship not only between Canada and Britain but also between Canada and the United States and Britain, and even between Canada and the rest of the world. Canadians were used to seeing themselves and their country as requiring help – "demandeurs" in diplomatic terms. Help, protection, and leadership came from Britain. They always had. Suddenly, they were no longer there.

The issue of the atomic bomb, symbol of American power and reminder of American unilateralism, showed what might happen. Accordingly the Canadians and the British exerted themselves to shore up American trust, all the while arguing that they too had something to contribute to the common security. The two countries shared a crucial interest in an orderly, liberal, and democratic world, and because they could not manage it by themselves, they had to induce the Americans to do it, with them but also for them.

The Canadians and British were fortunate in their American interlocutors. The US government responded imaginatively and generously through the agency of the Marshall Plan, to Europe's (and Britain's) political needs and economic requirements. The Americans accepted a world role, and in much the way the Canadians hoped they would. Canada responded no less imaginatively, adjusting its political compass to a longer term engagement. Through External Affairs Minister Louis St Laurent, the government affirmed that it would not retreat from international affairs or shrink from a broad interpretation of Canada's interests. The desirability of a stable and liberal international system linked all democracies, just as its opposite, Stalin's Soviet Union, repelled them.

DIVIDING THE WORLD,
1947-1949

The division of the world into two camps, one led by the United States, mostly democratic and universally anti-communist, and one led by the Soviet Union, practising Marxism and opposed to the United States and its allies, occurred definitively between 1947 and 1949. Each side felt menaced by the other, yet neither was willing or ready to go to war. Economically, the Soviet Union was not ready for war and had to await the reconstruction of industry and transportation, although it maintained a very large army parked in the centre of Europe. Militarily, the Western countries were unprepared and uncoordinated, although economically they were in far better shape than the Soviet Union. More important, they were politically unwilling to contemplate another war: only a tiny minority in any Western country was actually willing to advise or seek the destruction of the Soviet Union in what would presumably have been an atomic conflict. For the first time, but not the last, the awesome power of the atom acted as a constraint rather than as a spur on Western politicians.

There was never any question that Canada would be an active member of the Western camp. Yet in 1947 it was unclear how, or if, that camp would be organized and led. The experience of the first postwar years showed that the British were not up to the task. The only conceivable alternative was the United States, rich and potentially powerful, but as yet uncertain of its new role. The United States must exercise leadership, but Canadians hoped for leadership of the right kind – firm without being domineering, and directed, as Canada preferred, toward Europe. Throughout 1947 the Canadian government debated what could or should be done, first defining its own interests, then deciding where those fit in the developing Cold War and deciding how best to express them. Canada, Louis St Laurent announced in the Gray Lecture of January 1947, would not turn its back on Europe. And Canada, with misgivings inside the government, would accept American leadership.

THE CANADIAN DILEMMA

In March 1948, towards the end of the abortive free trade negotiations between Canada and the United States, the American undersecretary of state, Robert Lovett raised the possibility of a bilateral defence agreement. Such an agreement involved diplomacy on the grand scale. It was the political parallel to and the logical consequence of the Marshall Plan. And it was an unsought, unformulated, but deeply desired item on Canada's international agenda.

There was a link between the small-scale bilateralism of the economic negotiations and the much larger defence agreement, although it was not the one that Mackenzie King sought. The 1947-1948 trade negotiations indicated that Canada had importance for the United States. The importance was political and symbolic, although it was sometimes expressed in strategic terms and always in the belief that a sound polity was based on a firm economy. The negotiations reflected the belief that the United States and Canada were linked not just geographically, but also in time and spirit. This conception was less defined than reiterated. Perhaps the columnist Walter Lippmann put it best when he described in 1947 what made him nervous about an alliance, and allies. An American alliance, he wrote, meant "that we must stake our own security and the peace of the world upon satellites, puppets, clients, agents about whom we can know very little."[1] (Lippmann would probably not have extended the argument to Canada, which Americans assumed was so familiar that it hardly mattered that they knew "very little" about it.) There was no question that American security was linked with that of Canada. Time and again, in the negotiations of 1948, the United States *and Canada* were bracketed together in the minds and words of both Europeans and Americans.

The defence agreement sprang from the need for defence and the lack of credible international provision for security. The Canadian government could see, well enough, that the United Nations would not serve the purpose. Nor was there any idea that Canada by itself could defend its own territory. Some Canadian diplomats believed, at first, that tradition would reassert itself, that Canada in some future conflict would be motivated by an interest separately defined from that of the United States;[2] on the political level that was tacitly conceded not to be the case.

The early postwar years saw the Canadian and American governments struggling to establish what their common defence interests might be. Canada's geographical situation on the air (or bombing) routes from Eurasia to North America linked the two countries' defence concerns. But was bombing an immediate problem? An invasion from the north, across the polar icecap, was highly improbable. Landings on the East Coast were also unlikely. While there might be air attacks at some future point, they too were not thought to be imminent.

Early discussions between the two countries were held in the forum of the Permanent Joint Board on Defence (PJBD); their significance lies in their inconclusiveness. The Americans were divided and undecided, caught in a sea of confusion over their own defence plans, while the Canadians had no idea which American initiative they should take seriously. (According to the minister of national defence, Brooke Claxton, "The plans included what would have to be done to meet the shock of an immediate world war. There was even a 'Black Plan' on what should be done if Europe and Britain were overrun."[3]) In the event, the question resolved itself largely on civilian-military lines: "All defence plans must be regarded as somewhat utopian," a group of Canadian and American officials concluded, "and as goals to be attained in the event of an emergency." The emergency, according to the Americans, was not yet on the horizon. Mackenzie King said as much to the House of Commons in an unusually candid comment: "There has been talk of Maginot Lines, of large scale projects, all of which is unwarranted, and much of which is fantastic."[4]

There were other aspects to these early discussions that were not so fantastic. There was little doubt on either side that defence preparedness was not merely useful but essential. If there were to be a future war, it would probably be much like the Second World War, and it would be fought in Europe. And in such a war, the enemy would be coloured Red. Defence was therefore cast in familiar terms: the past was prologue to the future, and the present was prisoner to the past – especially the recent past. That past included a strong Commonwealth element; as of 1946 or 1947 no Canadian official, least of all the prime minister, was willing to let that go by the boards. The best defence, King thought, was a transatlantic, triangular arrangement, Canadian, American, and British. If the wars of the future occurred in Europe, that was natural, and if they resembled the Second World War, that was more natural still. King was also thinking of other, distant, wars – in 1776 and 1812 – that had separated Canada from the United States.

But the enemy and the times were different. The Americans were allies. The Russians had been allies too, though only recently. Fortunately, the Soviet Union had not managed to sweep up to the English Channel, like the Germans, or blockade the Mediterranean. The Soviet threat to Canada's Arctic, or to North America in general, was remote. The USSR did not have the atomic bomb or the bombers or rockets that could deliver it. The country had been devastated by the war; its armies squatted uneasily atop an assortment of mostly hostile peoples in Eastern Europe. All this the Canadian embassy in Moscow had at one time or another duly reported to Ottawa.

But the Soviet Union, as Ambassador Wilgress also reported, was a society different from Canada. It was not a democracy. It had few internal balances and controls, apart from the self-interest of the Soviet privileged class. Democracies were, to Canadians, rather reassuring factors in international politics. Would a democracy go to war against another one? Surely not, or only in cases of the gravest misunderstanding. It was too bad that the United Nations was not made up solely of democracies. Yet democracies were such slow, imperfect creatures, especially when set against the secrecy and swiftness of totalitarian societies like Nazi Germany or Stalinoid Russia – or so some believed. St Laurent went out of his way to warn of the "spurious efficiency" of totalitarianism – surely a sign that this point of view was familiar and perhaps widely held.

The intentions of the Soviet Union, being neither apparent nor, certainly, transparent, had to be deduced from existing evidence. But *what* evidence? This question bedevilled Canadian officials and politicians through 1946 and 1947. And once a diagnosis was arrived at, which medicine should be selected? The attending physicians ranged from Cabinet ministers to bureaucrats. The final decision rested on the Cabinet table; but while ministers disposed, subordinates might impose details, and sometimes large policy. After years of personal contact and friendship in Ottawa's small society, ministers and officials sometimes overlapped. At the top, the minister of external affairs had defined Canadian foreign policy in essentially ideological terms in his Gray Lecture of January 1947, but his speech had after all been drafted by his senior officials.

Two steps forward, with St Laurent and the Gray lecture; one step back, with Mackenzie King the old leader and prime minister. St Laurent had lofty ambitions for his country and its foreign policy, but he did not forget to add that an effective foreign policy had to be founded on Canadian unity. St Laurent might be the new man, the future leader, but he was also only eight years younger than Mackenzie King, and like King he had been raised in a country that was used to seeing itself as a nation in the making, economically undeveloped and psychologically dependent. Canada might be rich and vast in territory, but it was also small, fragile, not to be lightly deflected from the path of internal development. Canada had done a great deal during the war; but now its government wanted to pause for breath.

There was another respect in which King and St Laurent brought traditional Canadian concerns into postwar policy. They were both Canadian nationalists, which meant that they were both suspicious of British wiles and machinations. In 1946, when the British tried to plan for a Commonwealth defence policy, King and St Laurent took the view that this was just imperial centralization in a new guise. In June 1948, when the British prepared to airlift supplies into blockaded Berlin, they made the mistake of publicly soliciting imperial assistance; inevitably this put pressure on Canada and was badly viewed in Ottawa. Mainly for that reason, the King government declined aid.[5]

Experience with the British loan had taught Canada caution. Canadian resources were limited; for a new commitment, there would have to be a new framework, maybe even a new international system.

Fortunately the Department of External Affairs had a visionary in residence. Escott Reid, an assistant undersecretary who later styled himself a "radical mandarin," specialized in the application of thought to problems, or so he believed; some of his colleagues considered that he helped create the problems in the first place. He had for some time[6] been contemplating the problem of Russia, its obstructionism, its self-centredness, its unpredictability.[7] What could be learned, and what could be deduced, about this distant tyranny? And what could be expected of the United States in response? In answering these questions, he had access to "The Sources of Soviet Conduct," an essay by "X," more formally George Kennan of the US State Department and recently of the American embassy in Moscow. Kennan argued that Soviet obstruction and intransigence were not the result of Western policy but inherent in the nature of the Soviet regime. The West had little to hope for from the Soviet Union, in the foreseeable future. The only proper response was "containment," coupled with infinite patience. There would be no shooting war but neither a satisfactory peace based on mutual respect or shared interests.

Kennan was generally favourably regarded in Ottawa; his opinions, in the summer of 1947, seemed not only sensible but timely, and in Canada they helped spark an extended discussion among the government's foreign policy advisers – a discussion led, naturally, by Reid.[8] Reid's nervous energy encouraged him in the summer of 1947 to draft a paper that defined Canadian foreign interests, as he saw them. Like Kennan, he would deal with Soviet conduct; like Kennan, he would also scrutinize American behaviour with an eye to the proper Canadian response. What may have started as a commentary on Kennan became instead the first major Canadian attempt to come to grips with the Cold War. On 30 August Reid forwarded his product to St Laurent and the department's most senior diplomats.

"The United States and the Soviet Union" considered the existing international crisis and contemplated whether it was likely to lead to war.[9] There was nothing original about "the source of the conflict" – namely, the Soviet Union's "governing class," much as described by Wilgress back in November 1945. The rulers of the USSR wished to maintain their privileges, and that made them fearful of anything that might undermine their position – whether armed attack or the penetration of Western ideas.[10] There was, opined Reid, nothing to expect from the Soviet Union in terms of a mutually satisfactory settlement in Europe. There would probably be no agreement over Germany, and both East and West would probably acquiesce in the division of the country into Communist and non-Communist zones.

Reid also argued that the United States had its own aspirations, and its own anxiety about the need to shore up capitalist society through the maintenance and "expansion" of its "defence area." Almost inevitably, there would be conflict in the borderlands between the two systems, from Korea to Finland. The Soviet Union would seek to disrupt the formation, actual or potential, of an alliance among the Western powers directed against itself. According to Reid, there was already a "hard core of the Western alliance" – the United States, the British Commonwealth, and the Benelux countries (though not, significantly, France, presumably because of that country's disrupted politics). But, noted Reid, the "hard core" was not hard enough; each of those countries contained within its borders "a dissident minority" who might be "saboteurs and even rebels." But direct attack from the Soviet Union, "a Soviet-American war," was unlikely in the short or medium term. Instead, there would be a nibbling away and a softening up, culminating in the encirclement of North America. Such a process, calculated and controllable by Moscow, reduced the chance of accidental war and might permit the Russians to distance themselves from trouble and possibly to disavow proxy attacks through one or another of their "satellites."

In Reid's opinion, the danger of war came, in the shorter term, from the United States, where "panic" might set in if the Soviet Union increased steadily in power and thus became a more credible threat. That might happen when the Soviet Union, as it must, cracked the "atomic secret" and exploded its own nuclear bomb. Above all the West had to keep calm. Western policy must act to shore up the economies of Western Europe, as the Marshall Plan proposed. Without explicitly saying so, Reid drew on the lessons of appeasement in the 1930s. Appeasement had ended in war of course, but it had also ended in the acceptance that there was no alternative but war – it had produced virtual unanimity in public opinion. Now, in these crucial postwar years, liberal or left opinion, "soft" on issues of war and peace, would be crucial in securing an effective reaction to the expansion of Soviet power.

Despite its threat, the Soviet Union must be fairly treated – a stretch in the conditions of 1947, but a useful prescription nevertheless. There must be "firmness" without "rudeness." And there must be strength and therefore unity among the Western powers. That meant following the American lead. "In the event of war," Reid observed, "we shall have no freedom of action in any matter which the United States considers essential." That was not quite the case in time of peace, but Canadian freedom even then would be "limited." In case of conflict or disagreement between the Canadian and American governments, it was entirely possible that some Canadians would take the American point of view, and some Americans, whether they knew it or not, the Canadian. The "similarities" between the two peoples would make this so. Canadian foreign policy, where it touched upon the United States, would never be entirely "foreign" – and vice versa.

At the same time, Reid stressed that it was in Canada's interest to maintain a friendly but critical distance from the United States. A distinctive Canadian perspective was natural and desirable, even from the American point of view, for the United States did not need or require complacent satellites. Reid accepted that disagreements, if and when they occurred, should be expressed quietly, so as to avoid comforting the enemy with the spectacle of Western discord.

Reid knew that his was no short-term prescription. Hope, if hope there was, lay in the long term. The best hope lay, paradoxically, in the Soviet elite. Perhaps they were already "tired in mind, body and spirit by thirty long years of relentless, revolutionary drive." In ten or twenty years more, their "Messianic" drive would dwindle. Nor would the West be unaffected: over time, the two societies, symbiotically linked in "an uneasy peace," might come to resemble each other sufficiently to preclude the possibility of war, or at any rate a war based on profound divergences. Whether such a confluence was a good or bad thing, Reid did not say. It was, at any rate, better than the alternative of another world war.

Reid had invited his colleagues' views on his paper. Some were positive, some negative, and some merely silly. The decline of Britain was noted, and regretted. The further east the Canadian reader was located, the more pessimistic the reaction. Communism was a dynamic, restless force according to R.M. Macdonnell, the Canadian minister in Prague; uncontrollable and unpredictable, it would seek to expand wherever it could. The United States, which Reid had placed in a kind of balance with the Soviet Union, was in reality a much more benign force in international affairs, Macdonnell argued. With Canada, the United States would rely on "friendly discussion" rather than "insistence," which, given the positive nature of Canadian public opinion, would be counterproductive.[11] From Moscow, the chargé d'affaires, R.A.D. Ford, was pessimistic. "At the present time the Soviet system does not seem to give any indication of either mellowing or collapsing. So far as one can see, Stalin is at the peak of his power," he wrote, and even if Stalin were to die there was no great reason to expect an improvement in Soviet conduct – that was "wishful thinking."[12]

Elsewhere in Europe, Charles Ritchie, counsellor in Paris, raised the British factor. Canada needed "a more balanced equilibrium," which only the restoration of British power and influence could achieve. A Western world dependent on the United States "is neither healthy for the countries concerned nor for the United States." Ritchie too found Reid's conclusion that the Soviet Union was on the verge of "mellowing" curious and unconvincing.[13] To R.A. MacKay, who headed the Second Political Division (which handled the Commonwealth and Europe) in the department in Ottawa, the best policy for Canada seemed to be to closely control its inevitable alliance with the United States, while encouraging the revival of Great Britain and Western Europe. That must mean the modification of Canada's traditional mistrust of the mother country, and the reinforcement of the Commonwealth.[14] This Commonwealth approach was a great deal to ask of Mackenzie King and even some younger Liberals: too much in some cases, as time would show.

Finally, Hume Wrong, ambassador in Washington, weighed in with an original essay. In his opinion, Reid had rated the quality of Soviet policy too highly; on the contrary, it was both domineering and blundering – fortunately, because Soviet blunders stimulated a desirable American reaction. And Reid had fallen into the trap of misreading the United States (through a "supercilious" approach), and underestimating American foreign policy. Soviet blundering was admittedly not a firm or reliable foundation for American policy, and it was "an unhappy fact that the major incentive for the United States to assume its world responsibilities is dislike of Russia and Communism." On the other hand, American reactions ought not to be exaggerated: unlike Reid, Wrong discounted the appeal of "preventive war" in American thinking about the Soviet Union.[15]

What, then, was shaping American policy? Its broad principles, as the administration defined them, were unexceptionable and indeed admirable. Reviving the world economy, securing free institutions, and containing communism all deserved support. The devil was, however, in the details. Wrong warned of a proclivity in Congress to use American economic power as a lever to interfere in the internal affairs of recipients of American aid. There were outbursts of belligerence and other "unfortunate tendencies." Indeed, the necessity under the American constitution to appease Congress "tends to debase the framing and execution of foreign policy." That was undoubtedly why George Kennan had warned American allies to "remain at all times cool and collected" when dealing with the US government. Canadians must never forget that it was the Soviet Union "whose ignorant and short-sighted leadership" had produced the current crisis in international affairs, what Walter Lippmann had recently dubbed "the Cold War" in a series of newspaper articles.[16] Lippmann was right about one thing: the true interest of the United States lay among "the nations of the Atlantic community," and it must somehow shape its foreign policy to meet the needs of its natural allies. How that could be, Wrong did not venture to say.

Negotiating a North Atlantic Treaty

It was already plain that the United Nations did not suffice as a tool to prevent international conflict. In 1946 the UN moved from London to Paris and finally to New York, its permanent home. Because the building to house the UN was not yet constructed, the organization located itself in an abandoned munitions plant at Lake Success, in suburban Long Island. From there, observers were treated to the spectacle of disagreement between East and West. The veto, it became clear, was more than theoretical. With the United States and its friends overwhelmingly dominant in the organs of the world organization, the Soviets found it necessary to wield the veto repeatedly. (Between 1945 and 1955 the veto was used seventy-eight times, seventy-five of them by the Soviet Union.)

Canadian diplomats were disappointed. In a position paper for the minister of external affairs, St Laurent, the department regretted "the action by certain delegations to the United Nations to impede proceedings and to nullify the effectiveness of the organization." Of course, St Laurent was reminded, Canada had never liked the veto power and would continue to argue for its modification if not abolition. Meanwhile, Canada should stick to damage control.[17] However successful that might be, it was a far cry from the collective reassurance and even collective security that the UN was supposed to provide.

There appeared to be three alternatives. First, the paralysis of the UN and its organs could be relieved by amputation of the veto. That was extremely unlikely, and would probably precipitate the departure of the Soviet Union. Second, there was the possibility of improving the United Nations by removing the Soviet Union and with it the Soviet veto. Third, there was the possibility of creating a new security organization, using the broad terms of article 51 of the UN Charter as cover. Article 51 permitted "regional" security organizations and had been intended to cover such entities as the Pan-American Union. By giving "region" a cultural and economic dimension, it was possible to argue that the North Atlantic, instead of dividing the European region from North America, actually united it. In his Gray Lecture, St Laurent had already stressed that Western Europe and North America were a community in spirit. But could they be a community in practice?

In a test of public reaction, Escott Reid gave a speech at the Canadian Institute of Public Affairs in August 1947 that suggested how a regional security organization might be created, and possibly supplemented by expanding the powers of such organs as the World Bank or UNESCO. There was no need to ask the Soviet Union to join any collective organization.[18] In a speech at the United Nations in September, St Laurent said much the same thing.

But the Canadians were not setting the agenda of international affairs in 1947-1948. Reid's and St Laurent's speeches interested specialists in the United States and Great Britain, but not people generally. The focus of attention in 1947 was the Marshall Plan, the European response, and the fate of Germany. On all these topics the former allies continued to disagree. In the fall of 1947, the Council of Foreign Ministers (CFM) met in London in pursuit of an agreement on Germany. They did not find it, and adjourned.

Mackenzie King was in London as the foreign ministers staggered through their meetings. (He was attending the wedding of the king's elder daughter, Princess Elizabeth.) As usual, the British briefed King on the course of events. The situation in Europe was alarming. France was "honeycombed" by Communists. Italy confronted the danger of civil war. In Romania "hundreds of thousands of the middle classes had been ruthlessly murdered."[19] The Russians might at any time block allied access to the western sectors of Berlin, risking "conflict" and possibly war.

War so soon? King was surprised. Had it not been predicted that the USSR would take at least five years to recover from the devastation of the war? That was so, Foreign Secretary Ernest Bevin responded. But he quickly added that a decision to go to war was not rational.

King was strongly influenced if not entirely convinced. Returning home, he alarmed his colleagues by ruminating on the possibility of a "conflict coming on immediately between Russia and the other nations."[20] Such sentiments were accompanied by a noticeable softening in his attitude towards the British in a dispute over food supply. It was not the time for a break with Great Britain, he told his colleagues: Canada's terms were lightened at the prime minister's insistence, and the British accepted them.[21] King had come to believe that war might break out at any moment, even in response to trivial irritants.

Trouble was anticipated, and it came. The collapse of the CFM in London in December 1947 was a signal. In response, British foreign secretary Ernest Bevin told the "respected and influential" Canadian high commissioner, Norman Robertson, that it was time for the Western powers to contemplate some kind of union – a federation or an alliance. Bevin was, according to an American observer, "really bringing the Canadians in from the outset to establish the transatlantic linkage to North America."[22]

At the end of December, the Communists consolidated their control over Romania, expelling the king. In February 1948, after a prolonged crisis, the Communists in Czechoslovakia outmanoeuvred their democratic opponents, leaving only foreign minister Jan Masaryk and an isolated president Beneš as symbols of democracy. Murder removed the one, early in March, and retirement the other, in June. The Communist seizure of power was accomplished without Soviet troops but under threat of civil war from an armed "workers' militia."

The Czech coup d'état had a profound effect throughout Western Europe. Mackenzie King, who knew and liked Masaryk, was deeply moved by the news of his death, which the Communists claimed was a suicide. Whether that was true or not, King reflected, "it has proven there can be no collaboration with Communists."[23]

On 11 March 1948 King heard from the British prime minister, Clement Attlee, who proposed a conference with the Americans to work out the "collective security" (King's phrase) of the North Atlantic area in response to the further expansion of Communist power. That afternoon, King, meeting with the British high commissioner, Undersecretary Lester B. Pearson, and External Affairs Minister Louis St Laurent, agreed that something must be done. "If we did not join in at once with the United Kingdom and the United States in seeking to arrange a situation that might help to preserve peace, we would certainly be destroyed in no time."[24] A transatlantic arrangement was plainly in the mind of the British government, despite the simultaneous conclusion of a new European alliance, the Brussels Pact, on 17 March. That pact linked Great Britain, France, and the Benelux countries in a Western European Union (WEU). The WEU was tacitly regarded as insufficient right from the beginning, even though it proved to be an enduring alliance. Perhaps because little was expected of the WEU, it did not disappoint.

The real action was secret tripartite British-American-Canadian talks, in early March at the Pentagon in Washington, with Pearson leading the Canadian delegation. From the first, Pearson wanted an alliance that would "rally the spiritual as well as the military and economic resources of Western Christendom against Soviet totalitarianism." Using a phrase popular at the time, Pearson spoke of securing "an overwhelming preponderance of force" over the Soviet Union; but the force would derive much of its strength by attracting the "apathetic, fearful or doubtful."[25]

Pearson believed that the crisis confronting the West was so great and terrible that the endangered Western nations must agree to submerge their differences in a shared necessity. These ideas were not uncommon at the time. A collective defence expressed not just a general perception of threat, but a true community – the Atlantic Community, as it came to be called. As one NATO historian later put it, "A community, by nature, is organic: it is a growing and evolving body of people leading a common life under some form of shared social and political organization."[26] Not everyone agreed, even in Canada. In Ottawa, Escott Reid agreed. In Washington, Pearson's old friend, Ambassador Hume Wrong, was more sceptical, even if, obedient to his instructions, he busied himself to achieve through diplomacy the spiritual as well as military alliance of the West.

To himself, Pearson may have exaggerated the dangers the West faced; to others, he exaggerated the opportunity for united thought and action. Not for the last time, Pearson's sense of opportunity overreached itself; but on the way it guided him to seek and help achieve an alliance that would bind the United States, formally, to come to the defence of Western Europe, and that would keep the Americans engaged for the indefinite future.[27] That alliance was Pearson's vital minimum goal. While keeping his eyes fixed on the heavenly city of spiritual union, he kept his feet firmly planted in the politics of the American Congress. Pearson and many of his colleagues – and many Americans too – were deeply sceptical of the wisdom of the US constitution and the political capacity of the American Congress. To overcome constitutional obstacles and political inanity was a challenge that could not be avoided. But Congress set the timetable for the Truman administration's halting progress toward NATO: negotiation would last for over a year.

The first stage, negotiations among Canada, Great Britain, and the United States, lasted eleven days, from 22 March through 1 April, and produced an agreement that the United States would invite thirteen other countries to negotiate a collective defence agreement covering the North Atlantic "region."[28] In the meantime, the United States would announce that it would treat an attack on any member, present or future, of the Brussels Pact as an attack on itself.[29]

There were some odd features about the Pentagon talks. First, while pains were taken to keep the talks secret – Canadian generals wore civilian clothes, and the whole delegation slipped into the vast Pentagon building via an underground parking lot and a kitchen door – they were secret only in the West. A prominent member of the British delegation, Donald Maclean, was a Soviet agent and presumably lost no time in conveying a sense of events to Moscow. Second, while the American delegation was strongly in favour of an Atlantic alliance, other officials in and out of the State Department found the notion of a formal alliance strange if not obnoxious. The Canadian delegation, which included Pearson and Wrong, was pleased by the results of the conference. They reported back to Ottawa that an alliance was virtually certain, possibly by the end of May.

That did not happen. A furious debate began inside the State Department. On one side were the two principal advocates of an Atlantic pact, John D. (Jack) Hickerson and Theodore Achilles; on the other were the head of policy planning, George Kennan, and the department "counselor," Charles (Chip) Bohlen. Kennan did not want an alliance at all. He preferred a joint US-Canadian security guarantee to Europe, which would organize its defence within the framework of the Western European Union. This idea was called a "dumbbell" – a reference to the two heavy weights at either end of a connecting shaft. The security guarantee would be unilateral or (if Canada were involved) bilateral, without negotiation with the British or other Europeans.

Kennan's dumbbell did not appeal to either the Canadians or the British. Wrong patiently explained to Kennan that Canada preferred to be "part of a larger whole" rather than isolated in a lopsided "partnership" with the United States. In any case, Canada had to consider its relationship with the British. "An Atlantic pact would go a long way towards curing Canada's split personality in defence matters by bringing the US, the UK and Canada into a regular partnership."[30]

Kennan was partly convinced. The British made their objections known to him, while a statement by External Affairs Minister St Laurent in the House of Commons on 29 April publicly reiterated Canada's preference. If the United States persisted in dragging its feet, or in preferring a unilateral guarantee, it would "place [itself] in the position of being the obstacle to further progress toward the political union of the western democracies." A Western security pact would create "a dynamic counter-attraction to Communism."

Muting Kennan was only part – and probably the less important part – of the battle to get North Atlantic treaty talks underway. The real struggle was in Congress, and that body was controlled by the opposition Republicans, who had every hope of displacing Democratic president Harry Truman in the general elections due in November 1948. Fortunately, the Republican chairman of the Senate Foreign Relations Committee, Arthur Vandenberg of Michigan, was convinced that action was needed; equally fortunate was Stalin's timely blockade of access by land to the western sectors of the jointly occupied city of Berlin. Vandenberg secured passage of a resolution (called thereafter the Vandenberg Resolution) that proposed "progressive development of regional and other collective arrangements" and "the association of the United States by constitutional process with such regional and other collective arrangements." The resolution passed the Senate on 11 June. The words were vague, but the idea was clear enough: Truman had a green light to proceed, cautiously, with "development" of an alliance and "association" that included the United States – always subject to the scrutiny of the US Senate.

Meanwhile, on 24 June Soviet authorities halted all allied land traffic into Berlin, the next step in strangling the western sectors of the city, and cut off electricity supplies to West Berlin from the Soviet sector. West Berlin's two million people and its allied garrison were isolated. The Soviet goal appeared to be to make the Western powers' position in the divided and isolated city untenable and to force them to be more accommodating to Soviet objectives in Germany as a whole.

The "Berlin Blockade" dominated news headlines in the West through the summer of 1948. At first it seemed that the city must fall, and that the allies must ignominiously withdraw. That at least was what the Canadian government expected. Writing on 22 July to Prime Minister King, Pearson predicted that the Western allies would have to agree to hold new great power talks on Germany. Such talks, he suggested, would "at best result in the Western Allies remaining in Berlin by a new agreement [and] at worst they may create a situation, which certainly does not exist at present, where it would be possible for Berlin to be abandoned with results which, while unpleasant, will not be fatal."[31]

Berlin was not abandoned. Instead, the Western allies began to airlift in supplies, feeding and heating the western zones through the fall and winter of 1948-1949. For the West, the blockade came to symbolize the brutality and menace of Soviet foreign policy. Western diplomats and commentators had only to refer to Berlin to evoke a graphic example of why a united Western policy towards the Soviet Union was necessary, and how it could succeed.[32]

On 6 July the ambassadors of the United Kingdom, Canada, France, the Netherlands, Belgium, and Luxembourg met in Washington under the chairmanship of the American undersecretary of state, Robert Lovett. They had to consider how the Vandenberg Resolution might be applied to the question of Western security.

The Canadian position in these discussions was already familiar. Ottawa wanted a multilateral alliance that was as stable and long-lasting as possible. The Canadians defined the mutual interest of the Western powers in terms that evoked St Laurent's Gray Lecture and his 29 April statement in the House of Commons. They wanted more than a military alliance, believing, as they told the ambassadors' committee, that non-military cooperation "would contribute directly to general security." This was "the dynamic counter-attraction" St Laurent had mentioned, "of a free, prosperous and progressive society ... [with] a preponderance of moral, economic and military force."[33]

The discussions did not go entirely smoothly. The ambassadors met in the heat of a Washington summer, without air conditioning. The French position was intensely self-interested, and the French ambassador difficult; irritation between the Americans and the French could barely be contained. The most important point was gained early on: the Canadians and the Europeans prevailed on the American participants to accept that only a treaty, and not a unilateral guarantee, would do. Much of the credit goes to Hickerson and Achilles, who handled most of the busy work (in a "working group") on the American side. It was a situation the Canadians found convenient and comfortable, as their views were closer to those of Hickerson and Achilles than to those of Kennan and Bohlen, let alone the politicians of the Senate. The principal Canadian participant – and after the two Americans and the British representative, Derick Hoyer-Millar, the most active diplomat in the talks – was Thomas (Tommy) Stone, the second-in-command at the Canadian embassy. (The least active participant was the minister from Luxembourg, who dozed peacefully through most of the proceedings.)

There was no question that the principal feature of any treaty was the establishment of a political-military link among the North Atlantic nations, however that category might be defined. How much farther should the treaty go, in the interest of creating a stable connection among its signatories? The Canadians, as became apparent later, were the most anxious to emphasize the cultural and ideological basis of North Atlantic unity. The British were the least interested in this proposition and quietly set out to block or sidetrack this Canadian concern.[34]

In terms of national positions, the French were the most difficult, the Americans the most elusive. The French problem was solved circuitously, by emergency aid to the French army from the Pentagon and by a change in government and ministers in Paris. The American problem was different. The American representatives did not conceal that they spoke for only part of the government. They wanted a treaty but admitted that they did not know whether it would pass Congressional muster. Certainly what they had was the basis for a treaty, but as yet the president had not given any instructions to negotiate one. The summer talks, like those at the Pentagon in March, were only exploratory.

The power of the Senate to reject executive treaties was in everyone's mind, a continual constraint on the American representatives. There was also the presumption that the Truman administration would not be in office much longer: Truman was apparently engaged in a losing fight for re-election, with the polls and the pundits agreeing that the next administration in Washington would be Republican. The ambassadors concluded their work in early September; the US election was on 2 November. Until then, nothing more could be done.

Against all predictions to the contrary, Truman was re-elected. The Democrats won not only the presidency but also Congress, which meant that Senator Vandenberg was no longer chairman of the Senate Foreign Relations Committee. That job fell to a political hack from Texas, Tom Connally, who over the next few years would prove that he was not up to the task. The first challenge facing Truman was the resignation of the secretary of state, General Marshall, as a result of illness. As his replacement, Truman appointed the elegant and intelligent Dean Acheson, a man with long and creditable experience in the State Department. Acheson did not suffer fools gladly, and it showed in his relations both with the mediocre Connally and with Congress in general. Acheson took office on Truman's inauguration on 20 January 1949; until then affairs were handled by Marshall's undersecretary, Robert Lovett.

There was a change of personnel in Canada as well. Mackenzie King was due to retire, though no one quite knew when. A Liberal convention in August selected External Affairs Minister Louis St Laurent as Liberal leader. While he awaited King's departure as prime minister, St Laurent was parked in the post of minister of justice, and King, with St Laurent's enthusiastic concurrence, selected Undersecretary Lester B. Pearson as the new minister of external affairs. King eventually retired on 15 November, giving way to a new team, among whom were those who would supervise the final stages of the North Atlantic treaty negotiations.

Truman gave a North Atlantic treaty pride of place in his new administration, and formal negotiations began. The committee of ambassadors resumed discussions on 10 December with the object of securing "a workable paper" that the president could use to consult with Congress. Matters moved swiftly, "with crucial input ... from the Canadians."[35] Indeed, in these discussions Hume Wrong's precise and forceful personality showed to best advantage – he had the brains and the temperament to advance the discussions, driving the woollier minded Europeans before him.

Many questions remained unresolved. The purpose of the proposed security organization, Wrong stated, should be collective defence, and the terms should be as binding as possible. It should expand to include Ireland, Iceland, Denmark, Sweden, and Iceland; as for Italy, Wrong expressed no enthusiasm but tacitly recognized that its champions might prevail. He repeated the Canadian position, by then well known, that there should be "some general provision which would encourage economic and social collaboration between the members."[36] Finally, he proposed that the alliance should have some organizational form – a "political organ" analogous to the secretariat established under the Brussels Treaty for the European Union. This organ ought to be a council of foreign ministers, with supporting staff. Finally, the ambassadors should set a deadline for the signature of the treaty – perhaps the end of January.

Some of Wrong's desires were met in a draft treaty dated 24 December. A provision for "general welfare" was included in article 2, which encouraged "collaboration in the cultural, social and economic fields." Its form was weak, and its scope doubtful, but it was there. The crucial provision was article 5, which provided that the signatories to the treaty "agree that an armed attack against one or more of them ... shall be considered an attack against them all." The members would then take military or other action to restore the peace of the North Atlantic area. While the Americans at the table thought the wording of this article was satisfactory, they warned their partners that the Senate's reaction remained to be seen. The question of membership remained unsettled.

So matters stood when Truman was inaugurated on 20 January. He included in his inaugural address a commitment to send a North Atlantic Treaty to the Senate; such a treaty would make it clear that a military threat to American national security would be met "with overwhelming force." It was up to Acheson to get the treaty through the Senate. Initially, he fumbled. The senators he consulted, including Connally, did not like the wording of the treaty, especially its keystone, article 5. It had to be watered down, to protect the powers of the Senate: in effect, there must be no automatic American response. Discouraged, Acheson conveyed his disappointment to the ambassadors' committee, lecturing them on what could and could not be done under the American political system. The American commitment would have to be reviewed.

It took Truman to sort out the mess, put pressure on the Senate, and bring the treaty back to where it had been before Acheson took office. St Laurent, on a visit to Washington, pressed Truman on the matter, and afterwards Acheson admitted that the president had been "helpful." With the assistance of Hickerson and Achilles, and with the support of the French and the Dutch, Wrong even secured the re-inclusion of article 2, which Acheson, in deference to Senator Connally's wishes and the general sentiment of the Senate, proposed to exclude.[37]

The Canadian government had pressed strongly for the inclusion of article 2. In arguing for the article, Pearson and St Laurent told the Americans that political pressure at home made its inclusion politically vital. It was an argument that politicians could understand, and as a matter of courtesy and prudence politicians tend to defer to each other when it comes to reading the political temperature of their home country. No one called Acheson inept when he presented his gloss on the opinion of the US Senate, even though, as Truman showed, effective political management could dissipate much of that presumed sentiment. The Americans, similarly, did not question that if St Laurent and Pearson said that article 2 was an item dear to the hearts of many Canadians, it must be so. But was it?

In March 1948, squirming to escape from a free trade pact with the United States, Mackenzie King clutched at the idea of including trade in the security negotiations just beginning in Washington. It was a dodge, and his civil servants recognized it as such. Yet there was a point to including trade, economic policy, and other matters in the negotiation. Communism appealed because it presumed to satisfy mass needs, blending science and equality in a prosperous future. Pearson, Reid, and many others believed that the Western democracies must do the same, not using the same abhorrent methods, but rather proving that democratic ones would work too.[38]

Using a North Atlantic treaty to coordinate economic policy made sense. Mitigating nationalistic or exclusionary economic policies – and the list of potential signatories included some expert practitioners of "beggar-my-neighbour" economics – would reinforce, not weaken, the alliance. Or so Pearson thought. Acheson thought the contrary, that if the treaty tried to do too much and interfered in jealously guarded domestic jurisdictions, it would collapse. As Hume Wrong, echoing Acheson, pointed out to Escott Reid, "We are creating not a federation but an alliance."[39]

The details of trade policy and the manufacture of international institutions and commitments seldom engage public opinion for long. It is in the field of public opinion that the Canadian arguments for article 2 have tended to mislead. The Canadians used the political argument because, among politicians, it was powerful, not because it had any particular foundation in public perception or demand. Where Canadian public opinion did matter was in its near universal support for the North Atlantic Treaty and the widespread opposition to communism, the Soviet Union, and Stalin. The government had no option but to sign the treaty, endorsed as it was by Canada's two senior partners, the United States and the United Kingdom. Fortunately it did not have to choose: it got the treaty, and it got article 2.

The treaty had crossed its final hurdle. On 4 April 1949 it was signed in Washington (it is called by some the Treaty of Washington, though there are many other contenders for this title), bringing NATO into existence. Pearson attended and noted that the US Marine Band, on hand for the occasion, played the Gershwin tunes "I've Got Plenty of Nothin'" and "It Ain't Necessarily So."

❧

THE YEARS FROM 1945 TO 1947 SAW THE WORLD DIVIDED between East and West. The years from 1947 to 1949 formalized the division and established institutions that were to manage it for the next forty years.

Canadian needs in foreign policy were largely satisfied between 1947 and 1949. In the Gray Lecture Louis St Laurent outlined a view of the world with which most Canadians would have agreed. Canada was part of a community that included Western Europe and extended across the Atlantic to encompass both Canada and the United States. Before 1939 the British, whom Canadians had followed into the Second World War, led this community. Adrift because of the decline of British power and the consequent absence of British leadership, Canada worked to encourage the United States to take on the role of leader of the West. Canadians generally were gratified when the Americans did so.

The Canadians expanded their transatlantic connection by helping to establish a "broad" vision of the North Atlantic alliance. They did not do so merely because they favoured a particular form of alliance, but because a transatlantic community helped mitigate or even pre-empt a strictly European political vision. In Canadian minds, the survival of the West was of course at stake; but so was the survival of Canada.

The alternative superpower, the Soviet Union, did its best to stimulate Western fears, through the communization of east-central Europe and particularly the Czech coup in 1948. The Berlin Blockade reinforced those fears and probably guaranteed that the United States would join an alliance of some kind.

No one imagined in 1949 that the North Atlantic alliance would outlast the Cold War and still play a significant role at the beginning of the twenty-first century. NATO proved to have significance beyond the military and gave the reassurance of association and community that Pearson and the other Canadian diplomats of 1948-1949 were seeking. It did not do all they hoped, nor did it avoid conflicts among its members. Nevertheless it signified resistance to Communism and Communist expansion, and as such it was continuously popular, in Canada perhaps more than in some other countries.

CONFRONTING
A CHANGING ASIA,
1945-1950

Early in the morning of Sunday, 25 June 1950, North Korean troops swept across the thirty-eighth parallel, which divided Communist North from anti-Communist South Korea. Achieving tactical surprise, and outgunning and outclassing their opponents, they achieved a virtually complete victory. Within a few days the South Korean capital, Seoul, would fall; the rest of the South was surely not far behind.

The Korean War was the first armed test of the rivalry between East and West in the Cold War. It was the first test of American leadership of the Western alliance and at the same time the first test of alliance relations between Canada and the United States. It also signalled a change in the direction of Canadian domestic policy: rearmament and the maintenance of a large peacetime military became the order of the day. Although the war was fought in Asia, it had a profound impact on both Canada and Europe.

TURMOIL IN POSTWAR ASIA
Asia existed in the background for most Canadians, remote, fascinating, but also formidable and dangerous. The Orient featured in Western culture – in Canada as elsewhere – as a land of mysterious riches, tantalizing but forbidding. In the nineteenth century traders and missionaries sailed westward for East Asia, bearing otter pelts and the Christian gospel, and Chinese and Japanese immigrants sailed east, to North America's Pacific shores. Canadians, even missionaries, were sojourners in the Orient; their reputation at home was high and their influence considerable through their church supporters. Those Chinese or Japanese coming to Canada got a mixed reception; their

work was welcome, but their actual presence was not. From the beginning, such immigrants were harassed by racist policy and attitudes; by the early twentieth century, exclusionary policies virtually closed the doors of Canada and the United States to immigrants from Japan, China, and elsewhere in Asia.[1] As a result, the 1951 census revealed that only half of 1 percent of the Canadian population was of Asian origin. Moreover, the Second World War had severed Canadian contacts with East Asia as missionaries were expelled or interned, and commerce dried up. In 1941 Canadian troops took part in the unsuccessful defence of the British colony of Hong Kong, and spent four years in brutal Japanese captivity, but otherwise even hostile contacts with Asia during the war were few. China, at war with Japan since 1937, became a Canadian ally in 1941, and in 1942 Canada established diplomatic relations with the Chinese government.

There were, as it turned out, experienced personnel available to stock Canada's first mission to China. Officers of the Department of External Affairs included several children of missionaries, like Arthur Menzies and Chester Ronning out of the China missions, or Herbert Norman out of Japan. Some Canadian aid flowed to China during the war, $26 million worth, though it was dwarfed by the money and supplies directed to Great Britain and the rest of Europe, and there was some doubt as to how much of it served its purpose. In the aftermath of the war the racist Chinese Immigration Act – "a standing insult to a friendly people" – was repealed.[2]

Canadians who studied such matters were uncomfortably aware that the Japanese had been very successful in toppling the European colonial empires in Asia – British, French, and Dutch – that had been based on the same sense of racial superiority and exclusion that had characterized Canada's immigration policy. These empires were restored in 1945, but their political foundations were very shaky. Thoughtful observers concluded that the future even of the British Empire in Asia might be brief and dim. They watched attentively as the British struggled to keep their Indian Empire in order against a wave of nationalist and anti-colonial sentiment.

After the end of the war Canada had an embassy in the Chinese capital, Nanking, and a mission in occupied Japan. Events in Asia in the immediate postwar period were viewed through the prism of trade, and some time and effort were spent in the futile pursuit of Chinese trade. But whether Canada wanted it or not, it was politics not economics that dominated events in Asia – most significantly for Canada the departure of the British from India and its periphery in 1947-1948, producing four successor states: India and Pakistan in 1947, and Ceylon (now Sri Lanka) and Burma (now Myanmar) in 1948. The British had little choice but to abandon their empire: local nationalism made India all but ungovernable, and the British had bought a few years' peace only by promising to depart as soon as they could. The peace collapsed as they were leaving: the partition of India into Muslim Pakistan and secular (but majority

Hindu) India was accompanied by intercommunal riots and massacres, and a border war over Kashmir.

Canadians were less culturally and politically interested in the fate of the non-British empires in Asia. The alternative to the British policy of dignified abandonment of India could be seen in French Indochina and the Dutch East Indies, where France and the Netherlands attempted to re-establish colonial rule. War and civil war raged in those parts of Southeast Asia, and in Malaya, where a Communist insurgency attempted to drive out the British. Overshadowing Southeast Asia was civil war in China, between the Nationalist government of Chiang Kai-Shek and Communist rebels led by Mao Zedong. The Nationalist government was a byword for incompetence, brutality, and corruption, and reports from the Canadian embassy in Nanking did little but confirm its image. In 1948-1949 the Communists gained the upper hand and in the spring of 1949 took Nanking and Shanghai, driving Chiang Kai-Shek and the remnants of his armies to seek refuge in the offshore province of Taiwan. In October 1949 Mao proclaimed the Chinese People's Republic, which henceforth dominated all of mainland China. The Canadian embassy viewed the advent of the Communist government, on the whole, with relief.[3]

The "fall" of China made a tremendous impression in the United States, which more than Canada had strong political, economic, and religious links to East Asia. American opinion on the subject was divided. To Secretary of State Dean Acheson, the collapse of the Nationalist government was something that no amount of aid from the United States could prevent. That view appealed to the Canadian government, whose minister of external affairs, Lester Pearson, received the news of Communist victory in China dispassionately. But as Acheson hesitated over what to do next, Pearson also decided to wait and see.[4] Thus, while the United Kingdom and India extended diplomatic recognition to the Communists and moved their embassies to the new Communist capital in Peking (Beijing), Canada and the United States did not.[5] The Canadian and American embassies stayed in Nanking while their governments debated what to do. The Communist authorities in Beijing did what they could to help. Their propaganda mocked and denounced the United States at every point, while in December 1949 Mao travelled to Moscow to conclude a Treaty of Friendship and Alliance with Stalin and the Soviet Union (January 1950).

The United States had already been made nervous by the end – the untimely end, as the Americans saw it – of its atomic monopoly. In August 1949 the Soviet Union detonated a nuclear device. While the Soviets did not yet have a practical bomb, it was plain that they could soon build one and that at some point they would find a means to deliver it to North America. Until 1949 Canada and the United States had enjoyed strategic immunity from any plausible attack. Soon, perhaps very soon, they would not.

The China question, and the larger question of Asia, thus linked back to the Cold War. In the space of a year, the world's most populous country had joined the enemy camp. It did not take an overly active imagination to conclude that the odds against the West had suddenly increased. Asia, always so comfortably remote, suddenly seemed to acquire a new importance.

THE CHALLENGE OF INDIAN INDEPENDENCE

When India and Pakistan became independent on 15 August 1947, Canada promptly extended recognition and sent high commissioners to New Delhi and Karachi. India, Pakistan, and a year later Ceylon all chose to remain in the British Commonwealth of Nations. (Burma, also independent in 1948, did not and exited the Commonwealth along with Ireland.) Membership in the Commonwealth did not guarantee stability. Millions may have died in the partition of India and Pakistan, and organized fighting broke out in the state of Kashmir, which Pakistan and India both claimed.

India, with an estimated population of more than 350 million, was the giant among the newly independent countries of the Commonwealth. Its elite and much of its middle class spoke English – indeed, India probably had more English speakers than did Canada. Its government was democratic – a parliamentary democracy and, for a short time, a monarchy, also like Canada. The Indian government, proud and nationalistic and determined to rid itself of colonial remnants, did not intend to remain a monarchy for long, and as soon as it could – in January 1950 – it converted itself into a republic.

Canadians, if they thought about India at all, hoped that it would become a stable, parliamentary democracy like Canada. That India had a British heritage, like Canada, was advantageous in encouraging Canadian sympathy.[6] It was this British inheritance in an Asian country that attracted Canadians. Canadians did not have the imperial baggage of the British (or so they thought) and thus could from the start deal with the Indians on a basis of equality, without painful imperial hangovers – or so they thought. In fact, Canadian perceptions of India were self-contradictory, rather like the British inheritance. Bilateral relations could only go so far. Immigration remained a sensitive subject, which the government of the day was unwilling to tackle. For half a century Canadian policy had sought to keep Indian immigrants out of Canada. As a result, few Canadians in 1950 were of Indian descent. Nor was there any great disposition to be generous in terms of trade. The old imperial preferences remained, and there would be no further concessions.[7]

India's independence also raised the question of the country's historical strategic importance. India had not been a negligible factor in either the First or Second World War. Its troops had been a mainstay of the British army in the Middle East and the Mediterranean as well as the Far East. It was hard for the British to imagine that India was suddenly gone as a strategic prop for Western influence in Asia. The Canadians were even slower to grasp the point. As Hector Mackenzie has demonstrated, the Canadian government initially saw India, and the Indian question, in traditional Commonwealth terms.[8] Of course there had been changes but, Canadian politicians and diplomats hoped, not too many to be absorbed and managed. These included the question of whether India could remain in the Commonwealth as a republic – the minimum that Indian politicians and public opinion would accept. The British, hoping that the Commonwealth would remain a strategic unit, treated the question as a matter of the gravest importance, and consulted the Canadians, Australians, and New Zealanders on the matter. Eventually a solution was reached that accommodated the new Indian republic – and any future republic – provided it sought, and got, the agreement of the rest of the Commonwealth to its new status. In a Commonwealth meeting in 1949, such agreement was secured.

As a spate of former colonies, like India, declared their independence, the international community became increasingly concerned that the disparity in wealth between the newly independent countries of Asia and the older countries of Europe and North America would induce the Asians to distance themselves from the West. To this was added the Cold War and the fear that the West might be outnumbered and surrounded by a Communist alliance with the former colonial world. In the year of Communist victory in China, this did not seem an exaggerated fear. At any rate, events elsewhere in Asia sharpened the desire to hang on to the connections that remained between India and the West. When the Canadian Cabinet came to discuss India's republican aspirations in early 1949, the ministers were concerned with more than constitutional niceties. "There is obvious value," the Cabinet minutes stated, "in India's continued membership in the Commonwealth, from a political and strategic point of view ... This is of importance not only in terms of the Soviet menace but also as providing an important link between the peoples of Asia and the Western countries."[9] Pearson did not exaggerate his feelings when, in the House of Commons, he referred to India as "a bridge between the east and the west."[10] Pearson over the next few years would put a lot of traffic on that bridge, relying on liberal and democratic sentiments that he assumed Indian leaders shared with himself and other Western leaders.

It was more than an assumption. The first generation of Indian leaders, including the prime minister, Jawaharlal Nehru, and the defence minister, Krishna Menon, were largely British educated and several had lived for some time in Great Britain. Their world was, at least in part, the world of the British left, anti-colonial abroad and socialist at home. It was a world tinged with anti-American sentiment, resenting American power and exaggerating American defects, including American anti-communism. This anti-Americanism was accompanied by an assumption that the Soviet Union could not be as bad as depicted and that the Soviet menace was overstated. Such sentiments were intelligible to a generation of Canadian diplomats – including Pearson – who were British educated and inclined to sympathize with the British Labour Party.

Some Canadian diplomats, meeting the sophisticated entourage of Indian prime minister Nehru, were charmed. "Whenever he spoke, the elegance of his mind was as apparent as the elegance of his person," wrote Douglas LePan, a senior member of the Department of External Affairs. In discussions, Nehru demonstrated "at least as wide a knowledge of the range of western civilization as any of his Western colleagues," as well as a "wise and realistic" grasp of the political problems of Asia.[11]

Accord with the Indians was not complete. The Indians were determined to be neutral in the East-West conflict. Even Canadians, while leaning to the left in the late 1940s, grasped that in a contest with the Soviet Union the United States was definitely the lesser evil.[12] It followed that Canada's four major parties – Liberals, Progressive Conservatives, the Co-operative Commonwealth Federation (CCF), and Social Credit – all accepted NATO and favoured Western collective security. To Indian observers, it seemed that Canadians were excessively pro-American, and they were not impressed by Canadian attempts to explain the moral gulf between the West and the Communist bloc.[13]

Pearson himself was less than comfortable with Nehru, India, and Asia. Perhaps Pearson's sense of political reality seasoned his approach: not only Nehru but the left-liberal view of the world would have seemed strange to his voters in central Ontario. Fundamentally, however, Pearson faced towards Europe, not towards Asia. Asia might be of use in solving the problems of Europe, and Europe might help solve its own problems by getting out of Asia, yet Pearson also felt that Asia was impervious to his understanding. "Subtle yet difficult," was Pearson's assessment of Nehru. "An extraordinary combination of a Hindu god, and an Eton-Oxbridge type of Englishman." Pearson, an Oxbridge man himself, could understand the latter, but never the former.[14]

The principal medium for consultation and cooperation among Commonwealth nations was the Commonwealth conference, held always in London. Of Commonwealth nations, five – the United Kingdom, Canada, Australia, New Zealand, and South Africa – could be said to be "Western" in orientation, although only Canada and the UK were members of NATO, the formal Western alliance. The three Asian members, India, Pakistan, and Ceylon, were less certain. Pakistan's main external concern was India, and the Pakistani government was not averse to harvesting support from Western countries by opposing communism. Ceylon also pursued, in this period, an erratically pro-Western course.

In the aftermath of the first Soviet atomic explosion and the proclamation of the Chinese People's Republic, Pearson set out to explore Asia for himself. The occasion was a conference in January 1950 of Commonwealth foreign ministers in Colombo, the capital of Ceylon. Pearson saw it as an occasion for bridge building – for exchange, mutual understanding, and, he hoped, sympathy for the West among Commonwealth members. The Colombo conference achieved all three, but it was remembered for something else entirely.

The problem was that political sympathy for the West, for Western liberal societies, was thought by the centre and the left to be difficult to manage on a diet of poverty and underdevelopment. If the West could offer the underdeveloped countries a hope of improvement, a rise in their standard of living and an increase in their wealth, that might prove a firmer foundation for friendship, and perhaps alliance, than transitory political convenience. As an additional spur for the West, there was the spectre of communism in China, promising to end poverty and deliver justice. "We knew," wrote Douglas LePan, who attended the conference as an economic adviser, "that extreme poverty was endemic throughout the Indian sub-continent and in many other countries of South and South-East Asia." Independence had raised expectations without creating the means of satisfying those desires. The West, "on humanitarian grounds and in [its] own self-interest," must "try to reduce the disparity between rich and poor among the nations of the world."[15]

Until 1950 aid from rich to poor nations consisted mainly of disaster relief, succour from fire, flood, famine, or disease. Charity of this kind, however useful, could do little to reduce deep disparities or combat chronic poverty. Acting at the instigation of the Australian external affairs minister, Percy Spender, and the Ceylonese finance minister, J.R. Jayewardene, the Commonwealth delegates resolved to try something new – capital investment. The conference agreed to recommend to the members of the Commonwealth a program of investment and technical assistance in South and Southeast Asia, using the World Bank or the United Nations if possible, or bilateral aid if not.

Pearson received the proposal cautiously. The Canadian government took a dim view of vague but expansive spending, and the external affairs minister knew that in any case his ability to commit Canada to new expenditures was limited. On the other hand, given the sentiment of the conference and his own desire to promote closer and better relations, he was in no position to resist. Fortunately the practicalities were beyond the time and capacities of those attending the Colombo meeting: the details were to be sketched out at conferences in Sydney, Australia, in May 1950 and London in September. A Canadian contribution to aid was announced at the end of June, $400,000 to the Commonwealth and $750,000 to the United Nations. The fruit of the three conferences was the authorization of a plan for technical assistance for South and Southeast Asia (including but not limited to Commonwealth members), and the establishment of a supervisory bureau in Colombo. The Colombo Plan, as it became known, took on a life and an ideology of its own. Its roots, however, were firmly planted in the soil of the Cold War.[16]

After the Colombo conference, Pearson toured India. He had no success in reconciling India and Pakistan over Kashmir, and that issue was left to fester for the rest of the century. Canada did, however, work through the United Nations to bring an end to the open combat; UN observers, including eight Canadians – Canada's first peacekeeping force – supervised the subsequent ceasefire.[17]

TROUBLE IN KOREA

On leaving Colombo, Pearson travelled to Japan and stopped over in Tokyo. There he interviewed the American proconsul and allied supreme commander, General Douglas MacArthur. On internal Japanese affairs Pearson found MacArthur "out of touch," but he was less sceptical when MacArthur reviewed foreign policy. Communism, according to the general, was no great threat; in particular, the disturbed peninsula of Korea, divided between a Communist North and an anti-Communist South, presented no difficulty. It was in any case not "vital" to the interests of the United States.[18]

When Pearson got back to Ottawa, he found that his friend Dean Acheson had said much the same thing. Speaking to the Press Club in Washington, Acheson outlined American security interests in the Pacific. The line of defence started in Alaska and continued through Japan to the Philippines. Beyond that line, Acheson said, "no person can guarantee ... against military attack." There was, however, the Charter of the United Nations, to which victims of aggression could appeal.[19]

The origins of American policy in Korea were as much financial as political or military. The United States found itself occupying South Korea after the Japanese surrender in 1945. The occupation was expensive and politically troublesome. It seemed impossible to organize a stable government in the South, and equally impossible to come to an agreement with a Soviet-sponsored Communist regime in the North. Anxious to wind up the costly occupation, the United States turned to the United Nations to oversee elections – in both parts of Korea if possible and in the South alone if necessary.

To investigate the situation in Korea and to manage elections if they proved feasible, the United Nations established a Temporary Commission on Korea (UNTCOK). Seeking a friendly face on the commission, the American delegation to the United Nations asked the head of the Canadian delegation, J.L. Ilsley, to agree to Canadian participation. Ilsley, who was minister of justice and a senior member of the Mackenzie King government, saw no harm in the request, and agreed. So did Louis St Laurent, the external affairs minister.

According to the colourful account of the defence minister, Brooke Claxton, St Laurent then casually told a Cabinet meeting in December 1947 that "a man named Patterson" would be Canada's representative in UNTCOK. Claxton added, "Mr. St

Laurent's manner made it obvious that he regarded this as of so little consequence that it was hardly worth mentioning. But Mr. King blew a gasket! It is hard for anyone who was not there to picture the scene of this old man turning on the person who, within a matter of months, was almost certain to succeed him as prime minister, and then proceed to give him a going-over as if he was a naughty little school-boy who had committed a sin against the Holy Ghost." The members of the Cabinet sat paralyzed as the prime minister rumbled on.

"There is no more important element in public affairs," King lectured his colleagues, "than the foreign relations of a country, particularly if these relate to war and peace as this most certainly does!"[20] The United Nations was "a useless organization that had merely served as a forum for Soviet propaganda, and, in any event, Canada was not in a position to save the world like some latter-day Sir Galahad." The members of Cabinet, who thought they were appointing someone to an obscure UN commission, remained mute. King insisted the appointment be cancelled. St Laurent refused. A further meeting of the Cabinet on 22 December failed to resolve the issue.

Without knowing it, Mackenzie King had stumbled into a Cabinet crisis. If he persisted, St Laurent and Ilsley would have no option but to resign. Pearson, still St Laurent's deputy minister, would go too. Minister of National Defence Claxton decided that, if that were the case, he would also quit. In Claxton's version of events, he saw King and outlined the sequence of possible resignations. "Despite appearances to the contrary," Claxton wrote, "his mind still functioned better than most people's and it did not take him more than a second or two to appreciate the implications of what I had said." A way out of the crisis soon appeared. King now sought clarification from St Laurent about what the commission could do, and more important, what it could not do. He concluded that the commission would not work because of Soviet-American disagreement and that it would not proceed if it had to contemplate elections only in the South. Given this limitation on its activities, there was little risk of the commission causing new divisions or serving as the focus for a new quarrel between East and West. St Laurent reassured King that the peace of the world would not be endangered. As for King, the incident showed he was at the end of his tether; more and more his colleagues focused on a future without their ancient leader. As Claxton put it, "These were the last bellows of the leader of the herd before he cashed in his cheques."[21]

As it happened, the peace of the world was not endangered, but UNTCOK did prove to be a source of discord and division, just as King had predicted. The Soviets in North Korea refused to recognize the commission's mandate and obstructed its activities. The Canadian delegate, Dr James Patterson, consequently argued that if elections in both parts of Korea were not possible, UNTCOK should simply report the fact back to the UN and terminate its work. The Americans did not agree: they wanted elections, a South Korean government, and, in the not distant future, the chance to withdraw their troops from Korea. Over Canadian objections, the commission decided to proceed with elections in the South alone. With South Korea organized as a state, the Americans then pulled their troops out in 1949.

Neither the convolutions of a United Nations commission nor the ambitions of the great powers directly led to the eventual outbreak of war in Korea. The Americans asked for nothing more than to wind down their commitment to Korea, while the Soviet Union was looking elsewhere. True, the occupying powers had promoted their own systems, and the two successor states mimicked the system that defined and justified their existence. The governments of both Koreas were highly nationalistic as well as ideological, each desirous of overthrowing the other and unifying the Korean peninsula. North Korea took the initiative.

For many years there was doubt over who started the Korean War. This is a different question from who *wanted* to start the war, for both sides wished to do that. It is now clear, however, as was amply recorded by note takers at the time, that North Korean dictator Kim Il-Sung decided the time was ripe to overthrow the South Korean government of Syngman Rhee and unify the whole of Korea by force. Kim first approached Stalin for the necessary equipment and support. Stalin, discouraged by events in Europe but heartened by the Communist victory in China, was inclined to listen. The Americans, in the view of both Kim and Stalin, would do nothing. As we have seen, Acheson's remarks on the subject indicated as much, and Lester Pearson drew the same conclusion from his conversations with MacArthur. On 30 January 1950 Stalin instructed the Soviet ambassador in North Korea to "tell [Kim] that I am ready to help him in this matter." Mao Zedong, although more hesitantly, also decided that this was a risk worth taking, indeed hardly a risk at all. The Soviets and North Koreans then fabricated evidence of a South Korean attack in order to claim that the invasion of the South was really a counterattack. "It was a fake," according to the later testimony of a North Korean general, "disinformation to cover ourselves."[22] Supplied by the Soviet Union, encouraged by China, and protected by a body of lies that marched alongside his troops, Kim Il-Sung attacked.[23]

NORTH KOREA CROSSES THE LINE

No one anticipated that 25 June – a Sunday – would be anything other than a peaceful day in Canada. Prime Minister Louis St Laurent was at his country house in St Patrick, Quebec, and his minister for external affairs, Lester Pearson, had taken refuge at his cottage in the Gatineau Hills north of Ottawa. As prime minister, St Laurent had a phone installed, but Pearson had seen no such need. The minister was surprised late in the afternoon to see his secretary arrive. His news was startling: the North Koreans, it appeared, had invaded South Korea.

The senior officers of External Affairs were already meeting in Ottawa, with the undersecretary, Arnold Heeney, in charge. Heeney's "forte was organization, decisiveness, despatch," one of those attending later wrote.[24] Heeney assigned responsibility for the crisis to the United Nations Division rather than the Far Eastern Division, whose head was on vacation. The UN seemed the appropriate arm to deal with a war that everyone anticipated would be short, bloody only in Asia, and wordy in North America. Indeed, the Security Council was already debating the invasion.[25]

If in 1947 Mackenzie King had described the UN as a useless organization and a forum for Soviet propaganda, up until June 1950 it amply merited his description. That spring the Soviet Union thought it safe to boycott the Security Council to signal its displeasure that Communist China had not yet replaced the Nationalists as tenants of the China seat at the UN. The Security Council was the UN's most crucial organ, armed with the power to rebuke and repel breaches of the peace – provided, of course, that none of the five permanent members of the council vetoed such action. The Soviet Union could be relied on to use its veto on any serious occasion, and so the council languished, effectively paralyzed. Even with the Russians absent, the feeling of impotence lingered. As the senior Canadian delegate at the UN, John Holmes, watched the Security Council debate the issue of Korea on 25 June, he had little expectation that anything would come of it.

Action depended on the United States and, more particularly, on the American president, Harry Truman. Truman thought the invasion necessitated a strong response. If North Korea's aggression went unanswered and unpunished, it would set the world on a downward path to war, just as in the 1930s. The president immediately discarded MacArthur's and Acheson's carefully drawn perimeters. What mattered was setting a good example. Rather to the surprise of his advisers, and to the amazement of foreign observers, including the Canadians, he asked the United Nations to take action to repel the aggression. With the Soviet Union deliberately absent and thus unwilling to vote or veto, the UN rose to the occasion.[26] On 25 June the Security Council passed a resolution demanding the North Koreans withdraw. Two days later another resolution urged that the members of the United Nations "furnish such assistance to the Republic of Korea as may be necessary to repel the armed attack and to restore international peace and security to the area." In the meantime Truman made a statement announcing American armed support for the South Koreans. Thus the UN vote legitimized an action the United States was already taking. The vote had one other effect: it precluded the president's having to go to Congress because Truman's armed support for South Korea was ostensibly part of a UN action, not a declaration of war per se, and therefore did not have to be referred to Congress. Congress in this case did not object strenuously: nothing Truman did transferred any serious decision making from Washington to UN headquarters in New York. For the duration, US decisions would also be those of the UN, rather than vice versa.

Because Canada was not a member of the Security Council, it did not take part directly in the UN debates. The government, though surprised by the vigorous American response, approved Truman's action. The prime minister said so in the House of Commons on 28 June, telling MPs he hoped they would "applaud and support this act of high courage and firm statesmanship on the part of the government of the United States."[27] On 30 June he went further, sending Canadian naval units to the western Pacific. The House then recessed for its summer vacation, with the promise that if further Canadian aid proved necessary, Parliament would be recalled.

On 7 July the Security Council debated and passed a further resolution, drafted by the Americans but sponsored by the United Kingdom and France. This resolution clarified relations between the United Nations and the United States on Korea and defined the UN's mission. The purpose of the UN intervention was to help Korea "to repel the armed attack" of North Korea, and restore "international peace and security in the area." The resolution made no mention of any particular territory outside Korea, and the Canadians believed that it referred only to that country. It established a "Unified Command" and asked the United States to name its commander. In return, the United States would report to the UN on the operations of the Unified Command. This did little to alter the basic situation: the UN authorized, the United States disposed.

The Canadian government was happy to be using the UN as an instrument of collective defence in the Korean crisis. Practically, there was no alternative. NATO barely existed in June 1950, outside a few ministerial and official committees. The "United Nations" had after all begun as an alliance during the Second World War, with a collective purpose defined as defeating a common enemy. The fragmenting of that collective purpose caused some Canadians in the late 1940s to lose faith in the UN organization, only to have it revive in June and July 1950. There was again a common enemy even if, paradoxically, that enemy sat in the United Nations, was entitled to take part in its deliberations, and was only temporarily absent from its governing body.

The choice of enemy was important. Ottawa accepted the need for the war because it also accepted that international communism posed a threat to the Canadian way of life. This analysis was not far from the Americans'; indeed, it guaranteed that differences between Canada and the United States during the Korean War would be tactical, not strategic. Differences there would be, but as far as Canada was concerned they would never bring into question the existence of an alliance with the United States, or its basic purpose. While the Americans sometimes became exasperated by the Canadians, they too believed that Canadian contradictions were at worst misguided, and at best a useful caution. Nor should it be forgotten that during the Korean War there were several, sometimes many, American points of view, some of them identical to what the Canadian government was saying.

Although the authorization for armed response to North Korea's action came from the United Nations, this did not mean that conducting the war would be different from directing the Second World War. In the earlier war, basic decisions were taken by the great powers that contributed the vast bulk of troops and munitions. The same was true of the Korean War, except that in Korea the great powers numbered only one. MacArthur became UN commander, but he reported to the UN only through the American chain of command. Nor did the UN have any control over his conduct of the war. The UN was a debating and a talking body, and differences among its members automatically were magnified through speeches and publicity. Canadian-American relations became more than bilateral because of the UN factor, but the UN also magnified differences between the two countries. Because Canada and Pearson were well respected at the UN (and possibly because the US representative, Warren Austin, was not), the politics of the UN became another way for Canada to put pressure on the United States. But the UN was also another way for the United States to put pressure on Canada. The Americans needed not only support, but public support.

The war in Korea did not go well in July and August. Even the arrival of MacArthur seemed to make little difference to the fortunes of war. The North Koreans continued their advance, rolling up South Korean and American forces as they progressed. By August the Americans were confined to a small area around the port of Pusan, on the country's southwest coast, and the North Koreans were preparing for a final triumphant offensive.

The UN and the United States needed all the help they could get, and the American government pressed its allies for practical support. Pearson had already told the US ambassador that Canada would not "let the US down." Canadian naval aid was confirmed by the Cabinet on 14 July – three destroyers, to be placed under MacArthur's command. It was welcome but could do little to help on the ground. In the opinion of the US Chiefs of Staff, ground troops were required – from the UK, Canada, Pakistan, Australia, and New Zealand, in that order.[28]

Pearson was strongly in favour of doing more to assist the United States, but that was an issue that required the support of the prime minister and the Cabinet. St Laurent was irritated because the UN secretary general had announced an appeal for troops to the press before consulting Canada. This manoeuvre evoked the memory of Berlin in 1948 and Britain's imperious assumptions about Canadian aid. Now it was the turn of the United States, under the aegis of the UN, to occupy the imperial seat.

In Cabinet on 19 July Pearson told his colleagues that the Americans wanted support "mainly for psychological reasons," which did not mean those reasons were unimportant. A display of Western solidarity was essential for the impression it would make on the Communist world, as well as on the United States. As historian Robert Prince commented, "Like the US, Canada was looking at collective security through the lens of the international communist menace."[29] Sending troops was another matter. There was not enough money; there were not enough troops. The commitment of troops, once begun, might prove unlimited. The Cabinet decided to send an air transport squadron to help in the airlift of troops – American troops – from the United States to the Far East. After the meeting, St Laurent told waiting reporters, "Well, gentlemen, I hope to be out fishing again the day after tomorrow."[30] Told that the Americans wanted more, a Canadian official protested that the three destroyers already sent were no mere token. "Okay," an American diplomat responded, "let's call it three tokens."[31]

There was an interesting tangent in the Cabinet discussion on 19 July. In discussing the possibilities for intervention, Pearson mentioned the idea of an "international brigade," individuals recruited to serve not under a national flag, but under the UN's. "What our Minister has in mind," Arnold Heeney wrote, "is the possibility of a force (perhaps of divisional strength) which would be recruited in various countries, would be paid for by the United Nations and which would be trained and equipped by the United States." Such an idea inspired a flutter of interest in New York and Washington, but not where it counted. Dean Acheson thought little of the idea. The United States needed trained troops immediately, he told Pearson, although he added that, later on, "Canadian volunteers might be able to join with other forces in a special United Nations division."[32]

American criticism of Canada's meagre contribution annoyed Canadian officials. The Canadian military cupboard was bare; the Canadians had already sent what they could. To do more required a change of policy that would have far-reaching effects on the budget and the priorities of the Canadian government. It was also ironic because the Americans themselves had faced the same dilemma and, in the summer of 1950, had not entirely resolved it.[33] The Canadians had an additional reservation: wars in 1899, 1914, and 1939 had divided English- and French-Canadian opinion. Surely war in 1950 would do the same, especially if, as seemed likely, Canadian troops served in a Commonwealth unit, under British command. At least the UN alternative had some utility in fending off anti-British and anti-war sentiment in Quebec.[34]

The Canadian Cabinet was also distracted by a domestic event of no slight importance. Mackenzie King, age seventy-five, died at his country estate outside Ottawa on 22 July. King had, as we now know, a fascination with the world beyond and, more practically, with funerals. His former colleagues (most members of the St Laurent government had served in King's Cabinet) staged an elaborate state funeral in Ottawa, with bands and troops, and then accompanied the body on an official train to its resting place in Toronto. King, as the ministers knew, had strongly opposed involvement in military adventures overseas and in particular had conceived of Korea as the cockpit of a future war. Some members of the Cabinet still sympathized with King's point of view, but pressures were mounting. Other countries were contributing troops. Great Britain in particular decided in late July to send an infantry brigade, and Australia and New Zealand hastily followed suit.[35]

The British example weighed heavily on some Canadian ministers: Britain's wars were Canada's wars, in the view of many – perhaps most – English Canadians. If Canada did not decide to send a substantial military force, it would be isolated among English-speaking countries. Of course, the government had to consider the opinions of more than just English-speaking Canadians: public opinion in Quebec was another factor. St Laurent was prepared to disregard the potential divide. If Cabinet made the right decision, whatever that might be, Quebec would follow along. While travelling to and from Toronto the Cabinet reviewed the options; by the time the members got back to Ottawa, they were ready to take a decision.

The decision was a compromise. Canada would raise a special force of 4,000 to 5,000 troops. The prime minister and the minister of national defence addressed the nation over the radio on 7 August and called for volunteers. The response was immediate and enthusiastic, and the 25th Canadian Infantry Brigade Group was duly created. Hasty recruiting meant a fair number of the recruits were unsuitable.[36] Training would require up to six months, even though many of those who had signed up were veterans from the Second World War. Because military facilities in Canada were limited, the brigade was sent to the United States for training. The first units landed in Korea on 18 December 1950 and first saw action on 20 February 1951.

The Canadian "special service" brigade was raised as a Canadian, not a UN, unit. Nevertheless, Pearson had not given up on the idea of a UN force. On 4 September he told the House of Commons, "We have started something very important, the importance of which is very much broader than Korea. We think that by this precedent we have begun the establishment of United Nations forces, not only for Korea but elsewhere."[37]

The decision to send troops improved Ottawa's relations with the American government and, according to Robert Prince, none too soon. Some American officials had interpreted the month-long hesitation over sending troops as indicating that "Canada's commitment to troop support was lukewarm at best."[38] (Pearson and other Canadian officials noted the American complaints, and resented them.) There was always a risk in offending the Americans; denied on one issue, they might remember it when something else came up. Indications from the fall of 1950, however, suggest that relations were still close.[39]

❦

As FAR AS CANADA WAS CONCERNED, up to September 1950 all the battles of the Korean War were verbal. Yet the consequences for Canada and Canadian policy were, potentially, very serious. On one level, Canada met the crisis in a traditional manner, harmonizing its policy with that of its principal allies, the United States and the United Kingdom. The precedent of the Second World War was very recent and strongly influenced both public opinion and government practice. That precedent was both good and bad. English Canadians thought it was good; French Canadians were ambivalent. The Cabinet had to decide whether, for the fourth time in the twentieth century, Canada would send an expeditionary force overseas, to serve in an English-speaking army and in what was, basically, a cause led by English-speaking countries. The fact that the principal ally was now the United States rather than Great Britain or the British Empire did not necessarily console Canadian politicians and diplomats.

The decision to send a force was not made primarily because of Canada's United Nations obligations. Yet these were formidable on paper. Articles 42, 43, and 47 of the UN Charter laid down principles and procedures by which the UN might respond militarily to an international crisis. If the UN called, should not Canada respond? In principle the answer was an enthusiastic affirmative, but even Pearson and his colleagues found the principle a little daunting. Were Canada's interests best served by sending a brigade to Korea rather than Europe? Europe was not a UN theatre, Korea was, and so the answer should have been logically obvious. Of course, it was not. As John Holmes put it, in the spring of 1951, when the implications of the Korean War had become more obvious, "there is little advantage in being led by a glow of idealism into crusades which might better be avoided."[40] Korea, in Holmes's judgment, was an avoidable crusade.

Holmes wrote at a low point in Western fortunes, at a time when Korea seemed to be an endless quagmire, and the risk of a Soviet attack in the main theatre, Europe, appeared all too real. Yet it was hard to see how Asia could have been hived off in a separate compartment of the Cold War. Western tools for resisting communism in Asia were few, and for resisting aggression even fewer. The UN stamp on the US-led armies in Korea was convenient, but it was the US participation that was essential. Both these elements were to recur many years later; but for the time being the Cold War would make the Korean expedition under UN auspices a one-of-a-kind affair. Instead of prolonging the exercise, or extrapolating from the experience, it was time to put an end to the war, a process that would take much longer than actually preparing for and launching it.

6   FROM KOREA TO THE RHINE

The Korean War lasted far longer than anyone expected or wanted, yet no one seemed able to devise a way out of it. For a time it seemed to imperil the peace of the world, but for most of its duration – it lasted until July 1953 – it seemed like a morass where nothing of any importance could be won, and yet where it was supremely important not to lose.

For Canada, the years between 1950 and 1953 continued the transformation of external policy. The Cold War was in place and unquestioned. Korea was not precisely popular, but, because Canada's contribution was limited and Canadian casualties were few, it was not unpopular either. The war affected Canada politically and economically, but not because the government was pouring troops and treasure into the Korean peninsula. Rather, the government and the country were preparing for war somewhere else – in Europe. Rearmament was the key word between 1950 and 1953 – rearmament in preparation for mobilization.

In the conduct of foreign relations, Korea confirmed a pattern. The war necessitated close collaboration with the United States, politically, economically, and militarily. The Canadian contribution to the war was large enough to be noticed, though not enough to weigh decisively in the balance when important American interests were at stake. Self-respect was nevertheless served, and there was always the promise of more, should more ever be needed. Canada, its diplomats claimed, was showing that it was a true "middle power," able and willing if required to put its resources on the line.

The show of strength was a convincing backdrop to a foreign policy that attempted to preserve Western solidarity while smoothing the edges of the confrontation between East and West. Canada's policy would be close to but not the same as that of the United States. It would be the policy of an ally, not a satellite.

THE PROGRESS OF THE WAR IN KOREA

In mid-September 1950 the UN (and US) commander, General MacArthur, having received reinforcements, won a decisive victory over the North Koreans in a risky but successful amphibious landing behind their lines. Seoul was recaptured, and by the beginning of October the North Korean army had dissolved. MacArthur proposed to pursue the beaten enemy. "In war there is no substitute for victory," he later said, and most military commanders would have agreed with him. If North Korea were occupied and reunited with the South, there would be no further danger from that quarter, or so MacArthur thought. The North should be punished; merely repulsing its troops was hardly sufficient. In hot pursuit, MacArthur's troops, American and Korean, began to cross the thirty-eighth parallel into the North. Public opinion and political leaders in the United States overwhelmingly approved. The Canadian government had little choice but to follow the American lead, though with misgivings and hesitation. Publicly, at least, the Canadian government welcomed American success and hoped it would last.

As the military situation improved, the UN allies fell to quarrelling among themselves. In an ideal world, most of them would have been perfectly happy to see aggression punished and a clear victory recorded for international law. Unfortunately, North Korea was located next to the two most powerful Communist states, China and the Soviet Union. How would they respond to a policy of punishing North Korean aggression? The allies did not know, but some of them could guess – and few of the scenarios were positive.

MacArthur believed China and the Soviet Union would do nothing, and he was mostly right as far as the Soviet Union was concerned. Stalin refused to send in Soviet troops: that would be a prelude to a Third World War, which he preferred to avoid. Instead, he sent word to Kim Il-Sung that he should be ready to leave Korea. In Beijing Mao Zedong and his comrades had trouble making up their minds what to do. They feared the American intervention. Their regime was new and insecure, and the presence of a large American army on the frontier might encourage anti-communist resistance. On the other hand, China had been through thirteen years of war and civil war; the economy was disrupted, and it would be difficult to sustain another large-scale military campaign. Mao's government therefore made intervention in Korea conditional on Soviet material assistance, and only when they had that, on 13 October, did they decide to move.[1]

Mao claimed to see no great difficulty in winning a war against the Americans, saying "We'll see who is going to wipe out whom." Chinese threats of intervention were even made in the presence of foreigners. One witness, the Indian ambassador, duly passed the word on to Washington, where it was disbelieved or dismissed as propaganda.[2] Even in Canada, where as Denis Stairs notes "there was a genuine disposition to sympathize with New Delhi's position and an anxiety to ensure that the Indians were not antagonized by western ventures in Asia," the Indian reports were not considered to be "hard evidence."[3] Instead, the Americans and their allies sponsored and passed through the General Assembly on 7 October a resolution that provided a mechanism for the unification of Korea and authorized "all appropriate steps" for the stabilization of the country. Once a stable Korea was in place, the resolution promised, the UN troops would withdraw.

UN resolutions had no effect on the progress of the war. Both the Americans and the Chinese were anxious to bring the war to an end, though with opposite objectives. The Chinese began to move large numbers of troops secretly into Korea while an oblivious MacArthur prepared for total victory. Even when the presence of Chinese troops was detected, MacArthur did not comprehend the danger that faced his forces. As a result, at the end of November American and South Korean troops were heavily defeated and forced to retreat south. Seoul was lost again, though the Americans did manage to dig in a short distance to the south.

The defeat sent the US government into near panic, not so much because of the situation in Korea itself, but because of fears that Korea might be the first stage of a general Communist offensive in Europe as well as Asia. Canadian ministers and diplomats were sympathetic to, if sometimes sceptical of, American worries. "It seems to me," wrote C.D. Howe, the minister of trade and commerce, "that our friends in the United States are suffering from hysteria in a very advanced stage."[4] That observation was not really accurate when it came to President Truman, but it fitted General MacArthur's state of mind. Defeated though not routed, MacArthur saw salvation in widening the war by attacking the Communist Chinese homeland, using the Nationalist Chinese army as allies. To get his way, MacArthur was playing a political game, enlisting the opposition Republicans against his own president and ostensible commander-in-chief. Over the winter of 1950-1951 he did so frequently, much to the dismay of the Canadians and other American allies. Why not widen the war? MacArthur asked, rhetorically, for to his mind the answer could only be affirmative.

It was a challenging situation. On the one hand, Canada firmly supported the United States in Korea. On the other, it did not want to have to support the United States in China or Siberia or wherever MacArthur's imagination might direct his armies. MacArthur was much more than an insubordinate general; he had plenty of allies in US politics in 1950-1951. Truman might not agree with his mighty general, but the president for the moment was keeping his head down in the face of venomous criticism that he and his advisers were incompetent or worse. Though Canadian diplomats understood administration views, they were not part of Truman's inner circle; their reports offered little hope that things would change soon or for the better in American public life.

Truman had many admirable qualities, among them courage and common sense. He was outspoken, which was also admirable, but he was prone to gaffes. On 30 November, as news of defeat in Korea was rolling in, Truman told a press conference that the use of the atomic bomb had been considered and that the decision whether to use it or not rested with the theatre commander – MacArthur. It was the allies' turn to be hysterical. What Truman had said was not true. Using the bomb was never an option considered by his administration, and MacArthur did not have the right to order its use: only the president could do that.[5] But Truman's unguarded comment resulted in a few weeks of remedial diplomacy and an "emergency" visit from British prime minister Clement Attlee. By the time Attlee arrived, Truman appreciated his mistake and was prepared to offer clarifications, among them the fact that MacArthur did not have his finger on the atomic trigger.

Pearson was wary of offering "a homily" to the Americans on the subject of atomic weaponry. The bomb, he knew, was a deterrent to Soviet adventurism. Whether it would ever be used, he did not know, but, if it were, he wanted some kind of consultation in advance. This the Americans could not precisely offer, but they did promise to consult if time and other circumstances allowed.[6] With the atomic issues shoved to the side, Attlee delivered what was probably his real message. According to Secretary of State Dean Acheson, "He wished us to end our conflict with the Chinese in order to resume active participation in security for Europe." Perhaps withdrawal from Korea and handing over the Chinese seat in the United Nations to the Communist government in Beijing would not be too great a price to pay.[7]

On this subject Canada and the United Kingdom acted very much in concert, tactically and strategically. Attlee visited Ottawa immediately after his trip to Washington. The British, both in Washington and Ottawa, told the Canadians that in private Truman had offered as much reassurance as could be desired, including consultation with the Americans' former atomic partners from the Second World War, Britain and Canada. Acheson, however, had refused to let him say so in public.[8] On the other subject, what to do about Korea, there was more harmony between the British and the Canadians than between the British and the Americans. London and Ottawa agreed on the need to negotiate with the Chinese, placing on the table the Chinese seat in the UN and the possession of the island of Taiwan, occupied by the Nationalist Chinese.

The Americans were unimpressed by Attlee's and, by extension, Pearson's preferred solution. Truman was determined to press ahead in Korea, to achieve a better military balance before negotiating. Nor did it seem time to reward an enemy that had stealthily joined the war and caused large numbers of American casualties. Where Chinese intentions was concerned, the allies had little tangible to go on; Mao no longer divulged his thoughts on Korea to foreign diplomats.

ASIA AND THE DEFENCE OF EUROPE

The Western allies had to consider whether Korea could be considered in isolation or whether they faced the prospect of Communist attacks elsewhere. Beginning in mid-November 1950, Canadian Cabinet members began urgently to review the state of the country's defences, and the defences of its allies. In a paper sent to ministers by the chiefs of staff, the military argued that while the Soviet Union might prefer to build up its own defences and defence industry, it might also choose to strike at the West before NATO planning and reorganization improved collective defence. In response to ministers' questions, the chiefs estimated on 14 December that an attack in the coming summer was more likely than during the winter that had already begun.[9]

On 18-19 December 1950 ministers from the NATO nations gathered in Brussels to review the state of Western defence. The main business was the appointment of a supreme allied commander for Europe. They duly recommended General Dwight D. Eisenhower, the supreme commander during the Second World War, for the job. That done, Acheson sketched the state of the world as the American administration saw it. The Canadians present, External Affairs Minister Lester Pearson and Defence Minister Brooke Claxton, outlined how Canada saw the world – "that the Communists were prepared to risk a world war and that Europe must have first place in [the West's] global strategy." On his return to Ottawa, Pearson told the Cabinet that "responsible US officials stated frankly the opinion that Canada was not aware of the seriousness of the situation [in general] and was not taking adequate steps to meet it." Some Americans – though not "the more sober" members of the Truman administration – had come to accept "the inevitability" of war and this turn of thought must surely be making the Chinese and Soviets nervous. All this meant that "the next six months would be very dangerous."[10]

Pearson and Claxton presented their colleagues with an assessment of the probability of all-out war between the West and the Communist powers. They stressed that while Canada and the United States might disagree on details, they agreed completely on their fundamental analysis of the international situation – that is:

1 peace is now in jeopardy
2 the expansion of Soviet imperialism must be opposed
3 the principle of collective resistance to aggression must be maintained; and
4 the main front which must be defended is Western Europe.[11]

The Cabinet defence committee, which included all the senior ministers, decided that action on a large scale was both necessary and inevitable. The Americans must not think that they were bearing the burden of Western defence alone. Canada would contribute troops to Europe, plan for buying and producing armaments, and review radar warning systems on Canadian soil.

When Parliament met in January 1951, the government announced that it was prudently preparing for an uncertain future. Just as in the Second World War, there would be a munitions department – the Department of Defence Production – headed by C.D. Howe. Not surprisingly, the department closely resembled its wartime model. The government proposed to spend $5 billion on rearmament, a very large sum that represented 23 percent of gross domestic product. Defence spending, which bottomed out at $196 million in 1947, reached $385 million in 1949 and, with the war on, $787 million in 1950. In 1951 it would be $1.45 billion, rising to $1.95 billion in 1952. Defence became the largest single item in the federal budget, remaining so until 1964.[12] Such allocations reflected a revolution in the business of government and a startling change in priorities. Defence and foreign policy, at least as measured by the amount of money spent, moved to the top of the government's agenda, from 16 percent in 1950 to 45 percent in 1953. Total federal expenditure moved from $2.45 billion in 1949 to $2.9 billion in 1950, $3.76 billion in 1951, and $4.65 billion in 1952. The Cabinet endorsed all this on 24 January, with minimal dissent.

The St Laurent government had hoped to avoid this reversal of federal fiscal policy. Since 1945 taxes had fallen along with expenditures, while the government shed regulations as fast as it could. But the economy was booming; it swallowed the new spending burden with barely a hiccup. Gross national product rose almost every year after the Second World War, from just over $5 billion in 1945 to $10.5 billion in 1950, $11.77 billion in 1951, and $12.7 billion in 1952.[13] So although taxes rose in 1950, they went up only modestly. The increase in 1951 was much higher and hit personal income taxes in particular, but the purpose of the tax was as much to contain inflation by reducing spending power as it was to pay for defence. The federal government ran a large surplus before the Korean war, in 1949, and much larger ones during the conflict – almost $1 billion in 1951. The government was determined not to let the war disrupt the economy, and although there was inflation (there would have been more without the taxes), it was kept in manageable bounds.

Ottawa was not the only Canadian government affected by fiscal changes. A rise in Ottawa's spending and taxes meant a fall in provincial expectations of revenue and expenditure. St Laurent demonstrated the connection directly when he brought Pearson into a federal-provincial conference in November 1950 to discuss the international situation.[14] The provinces conceded Ottawa's primacy, some gracefully and some not. Yet all were by 1951 so used to federal predominance that a prolongation of its leading role did not seem inappropriate or unwelcome. The provinces thus became part of the consensus that underlay Canada's foreign policy in the 1950s.

The most visible sign of the new federal expenditure was a rise in the numbers of the Canadian armed forces. The force had been as low as 35,000 in 1947; it reached 47,000 in 1950, 68,000 in 1951, and 104,000 in 1953, when rearmament and mobilization were more or less complete.

The war sent thousands of Canadian soldiers, sailors, and airmen to Korea. Almost 22,000 soldiers went between 1950 and 1953, although they went on rotation, with peak strength in the Canadian brigade at 8,000 in 1952. The air force and navy played their parts as well. The Canadian brigade served as part of a British Commonwealth division, just as Canadian soldiers had served with the British army in the First and Second World Wars.[15] The brigade also used British-style equipment; as David Bercuson notes, because many of the soldiers were veterans of the Second World War, they were simply returning to equipment they already knew.[16]

The Korean War was not especially bloody as far as Canada was concerned. The Canadian army had 1,543 casualties in Korea, of whom 309 died in action.[17] By the time the main Canadian force arrived, the conflict had settled down to positional warfare; the Canadians incurred casualties at a far lower rate than in the First or Second World War. There were, inevitably, national comparisons. The Canadians did not operate as independent units, and their most senior officer was a brigadier, so the quality of autonomous Canadian generalship cannot be ascertained. There have been attempts, in history and memory, to assess the quality of the troops. In stories told after the war, the all-volunteer Canadians compared themselves favourably to the conscripted Americans. Certainly some Canadian units – for example, the Princess Patricia's Canadian Light Infantry, better known as the Princess Pats – performed outstandingly.[18]

The Korean experience might seem to have reaffirmed Canada's Commonwealth and especially British ties. Brigadier John Rockingham, the officer commanding the Canadian brigade, later observed that he preferred the British system of command to the American. On the other hand, he noted the regrettable disposition on the part of some British officers "to treat my staff as mere colonials."[19] British recollections of the war make it clear that Rockingham was not being overly sensitive. "The Canadians," according to a British junior officer and later historian, "did not quite fit in with the rest of the [Commonwealth] division." At least some Canadian units did not maintain "high standards" in "personal cleanliness, waste disposal and sanitation." "To many," including the officer-historian, "they seemed very American, steeped in a culture which owed less to Anglo-Saxon roots than to the great republic whose neighbours they were and whose culture they had now absorbed, far more perhaps than they themselves realized."[20]

Despite such assessments of the Americanization of Canadian troops, relations with the Americans were no better than those with the British. The Canadian government found itself repeating, with the Americans, the old pattern of non-subordinate alliance that had been so often played out in relations with the British in the First and Second World Wars. Ottawa highly valued the integrity of the Canadian brigade. On one occasion, when rebellion broke out among North Korean and Chinese prisoners of war, the American command hastily dispatched a Canadian unit to the rebellious camp. Immediately objections flowed into Washington, although in historian David Bercuson's view, Canadian objections were mainly political, not military. The prisoners' rebellion was messy and possibly controversial, and the Canadians wanted no part of it. Brooke Claxton, who was highly attuned to any incident that might affect the reputation of the Canadian army or portray the Canadian government as subservient to the United States, took the incident as another sign that the war was not being run satisfactorily.

Visiting Korea in January 1952, Claxton was unimpressed by the American commanders who were MacArthur's successors. He described one corps commander as all "bluff and bluster," which he used to conceal "his incompetence." The army commander, General James Van Fleet, Claxton described as not knowing "what it was all about. His principal staff officers were far too old for their jobs. They had all got into the habit of receiving and lying to Congressmen and they put on a similar show for us. Their estimates of military possibilities, ammunition expenditures, casualties etc. were fantastic."[21]

By 1952 Korea was a lingering sideshow. Claxton's main duties lay elsewhere. Considering that the main danger to the West lay in Europe and not in Asia, the Canadian Cabinet decided in April 1951 to send an army brigade to Europe. While the Canadian chiefs of staff hesitated, thinking the numbers too great while Canada was still involved in Korea, the Americans made it clear that they considered a brigade in Korea and a brigade in Europe barely adequate: the State Department urged pressure on Canada for more commitments.[22]

As in Korea, the Canadian brigade in Europe – at the time 5,500 soldiers[23] – formed part of a British command, the British being still the occupying power in northern Germany, where the brigade was stationed. British forces in Germany bore the rather grand title British Army of the Rhine (BAOR), and for the next twenty years that army was where, organizationally, the Canadians belonged. With similar traditions, a common military history, and identical uniforms, it seemed a natural fit.[24] Nonetheless, there were some initial misunderstandings. The British claimed the Canadian brigade as part of their occupying force – West Germany was still an occupied country and not a sovereign state – while the Canadian government saw it as a NATO contribution.[25]

In addition to the army brigade, the government agreed to send an air division to Europe – 6,500 airmen manning twelve squadrons of fighters that, when fully deployed, would be 20 percent of NATO's fighter strength. There would be a transcontinental radar screen across Canada, the Pinetree Line, thirty-two sites along the forty-ninth parallel, with about two-thirds of the cost to be paid by Canada. The object was to warn against attacks from Soviet bombers, a sign of the increasing vulnerability of North America to nuclear or other forms of aerial attack.

These commitments would not have been enough had the Soviets ever launched an attack in Europe. Each intelligence estimate of Soviet capacities seemed worse, from the Western point of view, than the one before. The Soviet Union, in the opinion of the Canadian government's military advisers, could easily conquer continental Europe. It had, according to US intelligence, sixty divisions in Germany and Czechoslovakia and twenty in Austria with which to strike west. Then, according to an estimate by American intelligence, the Soviets could move to attack the United Kingdom, sixty days after the arrival of Communist troops on the English Channel coast, or ninety days after the beginning of a war.[26]

The Soviet leadership, the Western powers acknowledged, had to this point preferred to act by proxy, using domestic Communist parties in the West to sow disruption and discord, or employing proxies like North Korea to test Western resolve. Nevertheless, the Soviet Union had a "marked predominance" over the Western powers in its armed forces and conventional weapons. The fact that Western countries were beginning to rearm might tempt the Soviets to move against NATO forces in Europe before they were able to repel such an attack. On the other hand, Communist dogma held that Western disintegration and Communist victory were certain: that by itself might stay Stalin's hand from a costly war that could at best only somewhat advance the date of inevitable triumph.[27]

To counter any Soviet attack, the Western allies – NATO – had very little. There were perhaps twelve divisions on the ground in Europe in the winter of 1951-1952, varying widely in readiness and equipment. To bridge "the Gap" between Western and Soviet strength, military planners under the allied (SHAPE) commander, General Eisenhower, proposed to raise Western forces to fifty divisions plus four thousand aircraft by the end of 1952. The NATO Council, meeting in Lisbon in February 1952, solemnly agreed.[28]

The interallied discussions of "force goals" produced a split between the Canadian government and its military, or at least the Royal Canadian Air Force (RCAF). Allied airmen meeting in Paris in the fall of 1951 produced a plan for a super allied air force, including almost a thousand aircraft from Canada (incorporating existing commitments). Brooke Claxton, horrified at the news, forced the RCAF to go back to the NATO planners and tell them that Canada would not be sending any more airplanes to NATO.[29] But at Lisbon the politicians merely nodded at the military's plans. Later they blamed the military for agreeing to things that couldn't be achieved. According to A.D.P. Heeney, by then Canadian ambassador to NATO, "the military ... were operating in a watertight compartment, insulated from the Council and making plans which, by any realistic assessment, they were quite incapable of achieving." The military, in their turn, blamed the politicians for their shortsightedness.[30]

The Canadians were not alone in regretting their hasty commitment to Lisbon force goals. The European allies also had second thoughts. Only the perception of an imminent Soviet invasion might have spurred action, and by 1952 there was neither the threat nor the perception of a threat. The Korean War had not expanded and there were no signs of imminent Soviet aggression. NATO did not achieve its force goals and, by failing to do so, closed the door on the idea of a conventional defence in Europe. The democratic governments of the Western alliance could not bring themselves to mobilize short of war; the rearmament already achieved would have to do. The French, the European ally with the largest army, were distracted and drained by a worsening colonial war in Indochina, while the British had economic problems that prevented their taking a dominant role in NATO's European army. NATO had admitted two new members, Greece and Turkey, in 1951, but they represented as much a drain as an asset in terms of expenditures.

That left two choices for NATO troops. There was the United States, which would do what it had to. And there was West Germany, still occupied, not yet a fully sovereign state, but with a government that was anxious to trade independence and the end of the occupation for German membership in and contribution to NATO. The United States, with little hope of getting troops any other way, actively promoted the idea of German membership in NATO. The Americans had still to overcome the hesitations and reservations of the allies, especially the French, to German remobilization. That, as Pearson told the Canadian Cabinet, would take time.[31] Germany would be very much in NATO's future but, as of 1952, not in its present.

Germany's fate was not in Canada's hands, and Canada had done very little to develop any sensitivity to Germany's political and economic development. Canadian troops were, however, stationed on German soil, near Hanover. To equip these new troops, and the others it was raising, Ottawa was tendering contracts through the Department of Defence Production at a rate of $10 million a week. At the end of the Second World War the government had kept a skeletal aircraft industry, with plants in Montreal (Canadair) and Toronto (A.V. Roe). Canadair produced, under licence, an advanced version of the American F-86 fighter, while A.V. Roe worked on a Canadian alternative, the CF-100. The CF-100s entered service in 1954, first for the air force in Canada and then for the squadrons in Europe.

Canada retained an atomic capacity but did not attempt to build or own atomic weapons. The West's atomic arsenal, as far as Canada was concerned, was the business of the United States, but Canada did contribute to the strength of the arsenal. Timely discoveries of uranium in northern Saskatchewan and central Ontario produced a bonanza for the government's uranium company, Eldorado Mining and Refining Limited. With uranium in short supply, the US government bought all it could to fuel the rapid expansion of its bomb stockpile. Towns like Uranium City, Saskatchewan, and Elliot Lake, Ontario, were created by the Cold War. Uranium production eventually rose to a value of $331 million in 1959; most of it went to the United States and was paid for in American dollars.

In the scientific area, Canada maintained its own atomic reactor at Chalk River, Ontario, and in the early 1950s began building a new one. To help finance the project, Canada proposed to make plutonium at Chalk River and sell the product to the United States. The Americans, as it happened, had enough plutonium, and so Canada did not become a major source, but in this and other ways the Canadian government made plain its support of the Western atomic deterrent.[32]

Atomic weapons were, of course, only one component of Western armaments. Strength, both economic and military, was computed in industrial – especially steel – capacity, and steel required raw materials. Such raw materials were a point of concern for the US government, where informed opinion was coming to the conclusion that the United States was running short of such commodities.[33] The Canadian government was happy to promote Canadian resources and industry as a cheap and reliable substitute for dwindling American supplies.

To feed the American steel industry, a consortium of Midwest steel companies established a Canadian subsidiary, the Iron Ore Company and developed iron mines along the Quebec-Labrador border. They also built a railway to haul ore. The arrival of twentieth-century technology and conveniences was deeply impressive for the inhabitants of Quebec's North Shore, hitherto a forgotten backwater. The need to accommodate ore freighters helped the US Congress agree to a St Lawrence Seaway, a deepening of the canals that led from Montreal to the head of the Great Lakes.

Everywhere one looked, there was investment and activity. Not all of it was defence related, but with the memory of the Second World War still fresh and the prospect of a Third World War just ahead, it was hard not to conceive of it in a strategic context. Its other context, one that was increasingly obvious, was the strengthening of Canadian-American economic ties. For the time being, the Cold War trumped Canadian nationalism in the minds of the public. It would not always be so.

PEARSON, ACHESON, AND THE COLD WAR

On 10 April 1951 Lester Pearson addressed a lunch-time gathering of the Empire and Canadian Clubs in Toronto, the city's leading forum for businessmen. Most of his speech – entitled "Canadian Foreign Policy in a Two-Power World" – was devoted to a survey of the principles that underlay Canada's participation in the Cold War, in Korea and within the Commonwealth. But what was "very much in my mind," Pearson told his audience, was Canadian-American relations. The destinies of the two countries, Pearson stated, were "inseparable in the Western Hemisphere," while "Canada's hope for peace depends largely on the acceptance by the United States of responsibility for world leadership and on how that responsibility is discharged."

Yet, Pearson acknowledged, there were problems in Canadian-American relations. There had been criticism in the United States of Canada's contributions to NATO and Korea, and resentment of Canadian policy differences with the United States. Canada had contributed vastly more than its share to the British loan in 1946, and the United States vastly less, but the Canadians had not seen the disparity as an occasion for vocal complaints. The relationship with the United States, in Pearson's view, needed more balance, certainly on the American side, and more regard for an ally. The Americans should not take Canada for granted (a familiar phrase that Pearson, probably deliberately, did not use). Summing up, Pearson told his audience that "the days of relatively easy and automatic political relations with our neighbour are, I think, over." On the positive side, that was because the US commitment to lead the Western alliance was firm, and the Americans no longer had to be coaxed or coddled. But they had to accept that Canada was "more important" – continentally and internationally – than it had once been.[34]

Pearson's motives for delivering the speech, and delivering it when he did, were complicated.[35] The main reason was Canadian diplomats' disillusionment, bordering on resentment, with American leadership of what had become the Western alliance.[36] The abrupt decision to change policy and go into Korea in June 1950, the apparent independence of General MacArthur to make pronouncements on foreign policy, Truman's careless remarks about the use of nuclear weapons, all suggested a government that might slip casually into a major international crisis and then expect its allies to help pick up the pieces.

MacArthur was particularly vocal in the weeks before Pearson spoke in Toronto. He wanted, it seemed, an expanded war. Pearson took MacArthur's pronouncements so seriously that he told the American ambassador that if the war expanded Canada would pull its troops from Korea. The ambassador reported this threat to Washington, where, in the press of events, it was ignored. But President Truman had finally had enough of MacArthur and his insubordination, and mobilized his administration to dismiss his country's most famous living soldier. It was not an easy decision, and it had its political costs. MacArthur was lionized by the opposition Republicans, delivered an address to Congress, and briefly was considered to be a real political factor, even as a potential president. Truman was correspondingly vilified, and with him prominent members of his administration such as Secretary of State Dean Acheson.

Pearson, meanwhile, found his remarks in Toronto had got him into hot water; it became his "first exposure to public outrage," as he put it.[37] His senior colleague C.D.

Howe privately expressed incomprehension at Pearson's remarks, and Pearson himself acknowledged that he had pushed as far as he prudently could have. (Howe probably considered Pearson's public statement ill advised, since on other occasions he had no hesitation in deploring American policy in private.) In the opinion of the Canadian ambassador in Washington, the minister had gone further than was advisable. Hume Wrong freely told his American contacts that the speech was, in his view, out of line. Pearson did not know how far he had irritated his friend and representative, but he could certainly sense the disapproval. "Having said my piece," he wrote to Wrong, "I will now lapse into my traditional Canadian-American speech pattern."[38] That pattern, he did not need to say, was muted if not banal.

In the aftermath of the MacArthur dismissal, Acheson tried to mend fences with Pearson, pointing out the problems the administration had with the right wing in American politics. Pearson sympathized with Acheson's problems, which were considerable, and with him viewed with deep apprehension the ill-considered policies of the Republican right wing, which amounted to a witch hunt at home and unilateral action abroad. Acheson had to shape his foreign policy both in response to the currents of international affairs and to the demands of American politics, which in 1951-1952 took a lurch to the right, towards nationalism and possibly isolation.

Pearson and Acheson shared similar backgrounds, although the political realities of their respective nations ensured that their policy perspectives differed. Both men were the children of Canadian parsonages, Pearson Methodist, Acheson Anglican. Opportunity took Acheson's family to the United States, where his father eventually became bishop of Connecticut. The senior Acheson never forgot that he came from British stock, and that he was a sometime soldier of the Queen, a veteran of the Riel Rebellion: on the queen's birthday the Acheson house proudly flew the Union Jack. Dean Acheson absorbed some of the imperialism of the period, without necessarily attaching the sentiment to Great Britain. He knew Great Britain and visited Canada, and had friends in both.[39] Working in the State Department, he could see clearly that British power was waning. Talking to Mackenzie King in 1945, he argued that the United States had replaced Britain as the leader of the West; Canadians, he implied, should adjust to this new reality. The reality included an acceptance of the inevitable complications of the American political system. American presidents and Cabinet ministers did not have their words and actions ratified by compliant parliaments. Some of them envied the Canadian system – for example Acheson's colleague, Defense Secretary Forrestal. Acheson did not worship Congress. In his memoirs, he recalled an occasion when a political hurricane struck, "a large mass of cumulonimbus cloud, often called [Senator] Arthur Vandenberg, producing heavy word fall."[40] It was not that Acheson (or Pearson) did not believe in the power of words, but Acheson, a skilled advocate, expected his arguments to persuade if not compel agreement. In any case, he expected his audience to accept that he represented a sometimes self-contradictory political system and that dealing with the United States sometimes meant that you had to take what you could get. An American patriot, Acheson believed that usually was no bad thing.

Acheson sometimes saw heavy rhetorical clouds advancing from the north, carrying the thunder of Canadian moralism if not showers of disappointment and disapproval. That moralism was reflected in article 2 of the North Atlantic Treaty, conveying the notion that NATO was different from what it was – a military alliance.[41] The disagreement re-emerged as the Korean War dragged on and the search for a settlement began. Discussions between the opposing sides began in mid-1951 and would drag on until the middle of 1953. The fighting continued, but after 1951 there was no great change in the battle lines. Pearson during these years exerted himself to bridge the differences between the two sides. Because he was president of the UN General Assembly for a year (1952-1953), and because his diplomatic skills were already becoming known and respected, he had some influence.

The basic terms of any settlement had already been decided on the battlefield. The two Koreas would continue to exist. The boundary would run more or less where the fighting had left it. The main question remaining was what to do with the prisoners of war held on both sides. Ordinarily at the end of a war prisoners are simply exchanged, but in this conflict not all the prisoners wanted to go home. Many North Koreans, and many Chinese, wanted to stay where fortune had landed them, and on this issue the talks stalled.

The Communists knew that their subjects' reluctance to return reflected on the character of what was supposedly the most progressive and socially harmonious system in the world, and naturally they tried every means to get their compatriots to return – voluntarily or by force. Pearson, and with him India, took the position that the POW question was a minor detail that must not stand in the way of an end to the war. The Americans – and South Koreans – saw the matter differently. Acheson viewed with great disfavour Pearson's attempts to finesse the issues outstanding between the UN forces and the Communists. "He was a pretty strong-minded person," Pearson recalled. "If you disagreed with him he didn't hesitate to let you know that you were wrong and sometimes you were crazy."[42]

For Pearson to preach the morality of peace while ignoring the immorality of handing unwilling prisoners back to an unpleasant fate under the Communists struck Acheson as hypocritical. He took his disagreement with Pearson to Ottawa in November 1952. Invited to meet the Cabinet, he repeated his arguments for a change in Canadian attitudes and policy. Pearson did not need to be present (he was at the UN in New York); the prime minister supported his colleague, as did the other ministers.

Acheson got deference and appreciation, but not satisfaction. Reflecting on the relationship between Pearson and Acheson many years later, the Canadian journalist Bruce Hutchison (a friend of both men), described "the strange relationship of affection and antagonism existing between two great men who, I think, could never understand each other." Acheson, he concluded, was "a stoic realist in the struggle for world power, Pearson a frustrated idealist in the struggle for world understanding."[43]

Behind these personal differences there were issues of policy, though in retrospect they were not as deep or important as they seemed at the time. On the American side, policy had to take into account the Pacific as well as the Atlantic, Asia as well as Europe, and keep domestic isolationists at bay. For Canada, Asia remained a distant distraction, sometimes annoying but seldom crucial. Asia was best left to the Asians – to the Indians, for example – for the lesson of Western imperialism and consequent meddling was that they left resentment in their wake. Western interests would be better served by a combination of economic aid and political distance. The real interest of the West, and of the United States, lay in Europe.

The problem was not Acheson but what lay behind him, and what might come after the Truman administration. "There is a feeling here in some official quarters," a British diplomat wrote from Ottawa, "that the US will not commit itself to Europe indefinitely. They feel that as soon as the military danger which NATO is attempting to meet becomes less intense the US will be inclined to turn her back on Europe or at least to regard Europe as no more important than the Pacific. This is another reason why Canada, which regards Europe as pre-eminent, is anxious to develop direct links, other than purely military ones, between the US and Europe, so that Canada would not be left as the only North American power in close association with Europe."[44]

FROM 1950 TO 1952 CANADA LOOKED BACKWARDS AND FORWARDS. The Canadian government worried that the United States might somehow back off from its commitment to lead the Western alliance. In Ottawa's opinion, the American political commitment to an active foreign policy remained fragile, and the federal government worried persistently that domestic political pressures might lead the US government into foolish or harmful actions. As a theoretical argument, this Canadian attitude has something to be said for it. There were elements in US politics and even in the US military who would have or could have led their country in dangerous directions, if they had been granted the opportunity. The actual US government was not so inclined, though it had its troubles with a rhetorically reckless opposition. The dismissal of MacArthur made plain where the Truman administration stood, and despite Canadian fears its commitment to Europe did not waver.

For Canada, Korea was a surrogate for Europe. Security concerns, shared with the Americans and with the other allies, drove Ottawa to send troops to Korea. The United Nations finally proved to have some raison d'être as a rallying point for those opposed to aggression. That this was because of a particularly egregious error in Stalin's diplomacy did not escape the Canadian government, but it suggested what might happen in happier times.

The UN allowed Canada to deploy to advantage some of the skills its politicians had developed in the parliamentary forum. Used to debate, and working in a debating shop, Pearson and other Canadian ministers did not find the UN especially strange. Using the political culture they shared with the British and the Indians, they did well in debate and shone in the politicking of the corridors. When, much later, Pearson tried to define the differences between himself and Acheson, he suggested that one was the experience of pragmatic electoral politics and the endurance that parliamentary debate promotes. Acheson preferred to lead from the front, Pearson from the flank or rear, guarding his flock, rounding up strays, making sure they were all in the paddock at voting time.

The outbreak of the Korean War catalyzed attitudes that until then had been merely latent. None of the signatories of the NATO treaty really knew how it was going to work out in practice, or what the Cold War would mean for their countries. For Canada, the Cold War diverted the government towards rearmament and channelled investment into uranium, the St Lawrence Seaway, and the iron ore mines of Ungava. Perhaps such investments would have been made anyway, but there is no doubt that the Cold War shaped just how and when they actually occurred. The Cold War also affected the balance of revenue and power between the federal government and the provinces.

All this occurred without undue strain on Canadian society. Canada could bear the burden because, by the early 1950s, it was much richer than it had been five or ten years earlier. Taxes went up slightly but prosperity rolled on. There was no choice between guns and butter: instead, Canada got some guns and lots of butter. The butter went to producing a society that continued to closely resemble that of the United States, which in the early 1950s was a byword for economic success. Only a few Canadians grumbled to the contrary.

7 THE ERA OF GOOD FEELING,
1953-1957

The 1950s were a period of almost uninterrupted economic growth. With a slight
time lag, Canada followed the styles and fashions of the United States, and Canadians measured themselves and their society against a standard established to the south.
From the outside, everything seemed to be working as it should. NATO was well established, and Canada played a respectable role in it. Defence cooperation with the Americans was working too, and working cordially. Public opinion was anti-communist
and pro-American, but Canada's other associations were not neglected. The British
Commonwealth was enjoying a renaissance. There was a glamorous new queen, Elizabeth II, and a famous old prime minister, Winston Churchill, was back at Downing
Street. Great Britain would be young again, and great again. The Commonwealth prime
ministers met regularly in London, trading opinions and ideas. Cordiality replaced
colonialism, or so it seemed.

The Cold War did not seem quite as bleak as it had. Stalin died in March 1953, and
his successors appeared not to be as sinister. With the war in Korea over, the only open
conflicts remaining were colonial hangovers, embarrassing to be sure, but no great
threat to the peace of the world. The French were at war in Indochina, the British in
Kenya, and soon there would be a war in Algeria too. The imperial powers reacted as
imperial powers did, trying to keep what they had as they were used to having it. Canadian opinion kept its distance, unengaged, while Canadian diplomats preached what
was at bottom an anti-imperial line.

They had room to preach. The United Nations could have been invented to display Canadian talents to advantage, particularly those of Canada's external affairs minister, Lester (Mike) Pearson. With their combination of friendliness and candour, based on a foundation of common sense, Pearson's virtues seemed (to Canadians) to mirror those of his country.

And Canadians were appreciated. George Vest, then a junior officer at the US embassy in Canada, remembered it as a gratifying, exciting post. "It doesn't matter what area you were in, for those who worked with them, this was one of the great periods of Canada. I mean, the prime minister was Louis St Laurent, the foreign minister, the external affairs minister, was Mike Pearson, the man in charge of the economy was a great old man named C.D. Howe. These people were tremendous leaders, very important, and they knew everybody in Washington and in New York and in Chicago. It was a very interesting time." The appreciation went beyond personal admiration for the men in charge. Vest continued: "The [US] military were impressed with what the Canadians were doing in the far north and what they were co-operating with our military on. The agricultural attaché thought Canada was one of the greatest things in the world and was going to be one of the breadbaskets of the future."[1]

There was excitement, but also stability. The St Laurent government had a secure majority – the largest in Canadian history up to that point – elected in June 1949. From 1949 to 1953, it carried on with the same finance minister, the same external affairs minister, the same trade and commerce minister, and the same minister of agriculture. Just under that level, there was a variation in offices but not in personnel: the senior civil servants traded jobs, as they had for the previous ten years. Why not? They were young enough – in their late forties or early fifties, with many productive years ahead.

THE POLITICS OF PROSPERITY

Canadians went to the polls on 10 August 1953. It was a dull election. The country was prosperous, the standard of living was rising, and employment was high. Issues were few: some minor scandals, provincial autonomy, promises of less government and lower taxes from the opposition Conservatives, and pledges of more government and better planning from the tiny Co-operative Commonwealth Federation (CCF). Prime Minister St Laurent treated the opposition's platforms with genial contempt. In a speech in Calgary, he called the promise of tax reductions "hot air," the kind of unprincipled tactic just tried in the United States. Canadians were above such flimflam.

Canadians evidently agreed. With 49 percent of the vote, the Liberals were in for another four years, holding 171 out of 265 seats in the House of Commons. Their closest rivals, the Progressive Conservatives, got a mere 51 seats, while the two minor parties, the CCF and Social Credit, had 23 and 15, respectively.[2] The Liberals had been in power for so long that some commentators treated them as a permanent government. Why should an election make any difference?

The year 1953 was the fourteenth consecutive one of high and stable employment. Politically, that issue cut two ways, both favourable to the governing party. Younger voters could remember little but economic growth. Naturally, they were inclined to vote Liberal. But there were also plenty of electors who remembered the 1930s and the Great Depression – the last time the Conservatives had been in power. "Tory times are hard times," the Liberals reminded Canadians.

Foreign policy barely surfaced in the election. There was no need. Canada was newly at peace, with an armistice in Korea two weeks before polling day. Canadian troops stood beside their allies in Korea and Europe, guarding the West's frontiers against communism. The Soviet Union was a formidable foe, but the death of Stalin lessened fears of another Communist attack like that in Korea. Communism, Canadians were tempted to conclude, had been successfully deterred by the West's show of resistance in Korea, and by constant vigilance elsewhere. And there was still the atomic bomb – something the West had more of than did the Soviets.

Canadians were content, even smug. When the world's economies were compared, Canadians were delighted that they were second in standard of living, behind the Americans but far ahead of anybody else – including the British, the Swiss, and the Swedes. As for the Soviet Union, even Communist censorship could not conceal that Russians lived in poverty if not misery. Russia was parodied in a popular comic strip as "Slobbovia," whose wretched inhabitants were mostly starving amid the snowdrifts.

Canada had no such worries. Its image abroad was benign – a land of space and opportunity. Canada, the US magazine *Fortune* told its readers, was "a businessman's country," Canadian business to be sure, but also beckoning to American investors. In a world of uncertainty, Canada was a solid prospect. Direct American investment accordingly rose sharply: $84 million in 1949, $200 million in 1950.[3] Total foreign investment naturally rose also: $4 billion in 1950, $6 billion in 1953, and over $10 billion by 1957. Of the foreign direct investment, 76 percent came from the United States in 1950 and 76 percent in 1957. This fact bothered some Canadians. Some could remember when – as recently as 1920 – most investment came from Britain. The investment balance in the 1950s was just another sign of Canadian dependence on its southern neighbour. And it implied a diminution in Canada's sovereignty: decisions that might have been made inside Canada, affecting Canadian jobs and Canadian industry, would be taken outside the country, in some anonymous office tower in New York or Cleveland or Pittsburgh. Such concerns were in the minority in the 1950s, though they were voiced frequently enough, and vocally enough, to come to Americans' notice.

The US embassy in Ottawa, normally a sleepy backwater, took to including a section entitled "Canadian nationalism" in its regular reports to the State Department in Washington. The American government's institutional memory told it that back in 1911 such nationalism had derailed a reciprocal trade agreement between Canada and the United States. Clearly Canadian nationalism could disrupt what the Americans hoped would be pleasant and harmonious relations with their northern neighbour: it would have to be watched.

Most of the time, relations were pleasant, if not entirely harmonious. American governments of whatever stripe preferred it that way. When in January 1953 the Truman Democrats gave way to the Eisenhower Republicans, there was no basic change in Washington's relations with Canada. The incoming secretary of state, John Foster Dulles, who was in his private life a cottage owner and taxpayer in Ontario, indiscreetly let a US Congressional committee in on his view of Canada. Canada was important, he told his audience in private session. It was important because of its real estate, strategically located on the flight path between the Soviet Union and the United States. Accordingly, Canada must be "humoured" from time to time, kept sweet and cooperative. American bombers needed to fly patrols over Canada, and practise their bombing runs, in case the day ever came when war broke out between East and West, between the Communist bloc and the Free World. In effect, Dulles was arguing that American strategic interests demanded certain concessions to American allies. In Canada's case, that might mean that the United States should refrain from particular kinds of behaviour – excessive protection of American domestic interests, for example. Canada was not a costly ally, requiring American foreign aid or gifts of military hardware. American policy should aim to keep it that way.

Canadian policy was a mirror image of American policy. Ottawa was wary of the sleeping dogs of Canadian nationalism. This did not mean that the government neglected Canadian interests. On issues such as American military overflights – practice runs for nuclear-armed American bombers towards Soviet airspace – the St Laurent government was determined to remind Washington that Canada was a sovereign country, an ally and not just another American state. And, perhaps because they were so frequently reminded of the fact, the Americans accepted that argument.

The best example of the cautious management of Canadian-American relations in the mid-1950s lies in trade. Trade between the two countries was large and growing. Both governments approved: more trade was better trade. On the whole, Canadian and American interests and policies were compatible and sometimes they were enthusiastically complementary. Both countries cooperated in the General Agreement on Tariffs and Trade (GATT), which the Canadian government viewed as "the best institutional safeguard yet devised to control and limit discriminatory trading practices and to encourage countries to ... move towards a free multilateral trading system."[4]

Under GATT the procedure was for principal suppliers of a commodity to manage negotiations concerning that item; thus, on a wide variety of trading items Canada dealt mainly with the United States in the GATT negotiations of the period: Torquay (1949), Annecy (1950-1951), and Geneva (1956).

Agreement on trade matters with the United States was extremely important for Canada, but at the back of their minds the Canadians had other, larger, economic interests in view. In the mid-1950s Canada and the United States were among the few countries without formal and very restrictive currency controls. The Canadians looked to a future in which the Europeans, having abolished such restrictions, would trade freely with Canada. If and when that happened, Canadian commentators tended to believe, sales to Europe would finally balance purchases from the United States, and Canada's trade imbalance – its massive deficit in trade with the United States – would be corrected.

The Canadian trade deficit reinforced another strong tendency in Canadian trade policy. Trade with the Americans seemed to mean an outflow of Canadian dollars to the United States in perpetuity. Canadian trade negotiators and, even more, politicians were therefore wary of anything that would direct more trade along the north-south axis. When the Americans raised the possibility of a special, reciprocal trade deal – which under the GATT rules would have to mean some form of free trade – Ottawa drew back.[5] Although some of President Eisenhower's officials continued to dream of a free trade regime in North America that would be a model to the world, American professional diplomats as well as their Canadian counterparts poured cold water on the idea. It would be too controversial; the Canadians might not like it; things were well enough just as they were. There were enough bilateral problems already.

Sometimes the parallels between the United States and Canada were too close for comfort. With similar landscapes and climates, the two countries were often competitors for foreign and domestic markets. American base metals producers fought – successfully – against imports of Canadian lead and zinc. American farmers persuaded their government to exclude Canadian oats from the US market. American farm subsidies produced bumper crops of surplus grain, which a generous American government then dumped abroad, supposedly to countries that could not afford to pay for it but, as time went on, increasingly to purchasers who once could have afforded to buy. Despite spasmodic attempts at managing the international trade in grain and other commodities, the United States pursued its own interest, leaving disrupted markets behind.

Eisenhower and St Laurent agreed that subsidies were a bad thing, and agreed too on their deplorable consequences. But what, Eisenhower asked, could be done? In the United States, trade policy was shared – more than shared – with Congress. Congress made laws in this field but also acted as a kind of alternate executive. Members of the House of Representatives and the Senate usually outlasted the two-term executives elected to the White House. The best Eisenhower and Dulles could do was to mitigate the problem, curbing Congress's worst excesses and trusting in luck and alliance solidarity to make up the difference with America's allies.

That strategy did not always work, as the example of wheat exports illustrates. Canada needed to export its wheat, and Canada's farmers needed the money from its sale. The Canadian government, poorer than the American, could not afford agricultural subsidies on the same lavish scale. When a market for Canadian wheat was swallowed up by subsidized grain from the United States, Ottawa was not able to step in with compensatory payments. Canadian wheat farmers, concentrated in the West, were furious. They barraged Ottawa with complaints, and elected opposition MPs to make their point more forcefully. St Laurent and his trade minister, C.D. Howe, did their best in meetings with representatives of the American government. Some were sympathetic; others, including Eisenhower's agriculture secretary, were not. It was "iniquitous," Howe fumed. Ezra Benson, the secretary of agriculture and a God-fearing man, was shocked that anyone could so characterize his conduct. But, rhetoric apart, there was and could be no move to reduce the iniquity.

American sympathy was more in evidence in oil, where the Eisenhower administration did its best to accommodate Canadian exports despite vigorous lobbying from American domestic producers and complaints from other oil exporters, such as Venezuela. The fact that Canadian oil was given privileged access to the American market greatly annoyed the Venezuelans and played a part in encouraging them to make common cause with other oil producers by forming a producers' association – the Organization of Petroleum Exporting Countries (OPEC). For the time being, OPEC languished in obscurity in a market dominated by the great American oil companies and propped up by ever-increasing American oil production. Not only were American oil companies dominant in the business (along with Shell, an Anglo-Dutch company), but the United States acted as the West's ultimate petroleum reserve.

When it came to defence and defence production, relations were also imperfect, though Canada had a large military commitment to the common defence. Canada's armed services stood at 118,000 people in 1955. All military personnel were volunteers, and they were backed up by a sizeable militia system of the kind that had sustained the war effort during the Second World War. For a country of Canada's size – 15.7 million in 1955 – this was a respectable effort, all the more so because it was backed up by the promise of an even larger force should war ever break out. Defence and defence production cost Canadians $1.9 billion in 1952, at the height of the Korean War, and not much less, $1.8 billion, in 1955. That year, defence made up 40 percent of a federal budget of $4.6 billion, or 23 percent of *all* expenditures by *all* Canadian governments, federal, provincial, and municipal. Defence was thus a major factor in Canada's federal balance, pumping up federal expenditures relative to those of provincial governments and helping to keep Ottawa fiscally predominant in the Canadian federal system.[6]

Yet even in multilateral defence there were whispers of nationalism. Most Canadian weaponry was either made abroad or based on foreign designs. The Royal Canadian Navy's aircraft carrier HMCS *Magnificent* was originally a British ship, as was its successor, the *Bonaventure*. Rifles were a Belgian design; tanks were British; helmets were British and then American. Aircraft were something different and something special. During the Second World War Canada created a domestic aircraft industry, using British designs and American production techniques. Canada, as we have seen, produced military planes, notably the F-86 fighter (an American design) in Montreal, and the unique CF-100 at A.V. Roe, a British-owned firm, in Toronto. The production of the CF-100 was fraught with problems, but because the plane, once in the air, was generally considered more than satisfactory, Howe, still the responsible minister, authorized A.V. Roe to build the next generation of fighter plane, a supersonic all-weather jet, the CF-105, nicknamed the Arrow. Meanwhile, the CF-100 had become a symbol of Canadian pride. Defence production became entangled with feelings of nationalism and self-sufficiency. These feelings were lively political considerations, and they made Howe hesitate when, in 1956-1957, he came to understand that the Arrow was simply too expensive for Canada alone to buy, and that neither the Americans nor the British wanted it.[7] The trouble was that aircraft were a high-tech symbol in other countries too, and governments were under severe political pressure to spend their defence appropriations at home, on locally designed and made aircraft. As it turned out, Howe left the problem of the Arrow for another government to deal with.

The same considerations applied to atomic energy, which like aircraft was an outgrowth of defence production during the Second World War. In addition to its uranium mine and refinery, Canada was also entering the reactor business. Atomic reactors produced abundant energy that scientists hoped could be used to heat boilers in power plants. Using cheap and abundant uranium fuel, atomic energy could be the answer to world poverty, revolutionizing the economies of the impoverished southern half of the globe. Canada's largest electrical utility, Ontario Hydro, was an early enthusiast for atomic power, while the Canadian government was delighted to substitute cheap Canadian uranium for expensive American coal. As Canada's atomic industry laboured to produce an economic power reactor design, the government indulged in some publicity abroad. India wanted to establish its own atomic research centre and was considering a British design for its first reactor. The director of Canada's modest international aid program suggested instead a Canadian reactor, based on NRX, a reactor designed in Chalk River with the cooperation of the British in the immediate postwar years, and after a friendly exchange between Prime Minister St Laurent and Prime Minister Nehru, a deal was struck.

As part of Canada's Colombo Plan aid, India got a research reactor (called CIRUS). Only afterward did the Canadians realize that they had not asked that the research be peaceful in nature. In response to a Canadian request for a supplementary agreement, the Indians noted that the Canadians had no hesitation in sharing atomic secrets with the warlike (but allied) Americans and British, and they treated Canadian misgivings as postcolonial hypocrisy. It was certainly true that Canada continued to be involved in the American defence program, and was using its Chalk River reactor to test some of the components for the first American atomic submarine.[8] Under the circumstances, the Canadians muted their objections, while vowing never to be so enthusiastically imprudent again where international atomic safeguards were concerned.

Both Canada and India got most of what they wanted from the research reactor deal. The Indians got an efficient and reliable research reactor, which they used to start up an atomic program. In the 1960s Canada designed and built its first atomic power reactors, the CANDU model, and India was a ready customer. The Americans were pleased too, because acceptance of a Canadian design was a further link between India and the West.

Canadians liked to pretend that their aid program was apolitical, offered without strings. But, as the Indian experience showed, that was not so. Indeed, Canadian aid always had a political dimension, internal and external. The Colombo Plan, as we have seen, was rooted in the Cold War as well as philanthropy. In a world where Canadians sometimes felt overwhelmed by American wealth and power, the Colombo Plan was a useful sign of a separate identity. In its first decade, Canada gave $331 million in Colombo Plan aid.

If the external politics of aid were mildly deceptive, there was no doubt of the internal politics that supported Canada's aid structure. Aid was a continuation of the old missionary impulse that before the Second World War sent hundreds of Canadian clergy abroad to dispense goodness and religion in Asia and Africa. That altruistic impulse continued after the war, often mixing with anti-communism (the Communists followed another god) and informed by the belief that the economic problems of the underdeveloped world were so great that they could be met only by aid on a governmental scale. Newly independent governments in Asia and later Africa liked it that way – the uncontrollable activities of volunteer missionaries impeded the development of local notions of sovereignty, which often included various forms of totalitarian control.

Aid cost much more than the earlier missionary endeavours. That by itself made aid a political issue in Canada. As Canadians saw it, aid was help for Canada's friends in war or allies in peace. Aid was something that allowed the British or continental Europeans to buy Canadian goods in the postwar period. It was natural to extend the principle – Canadian aid would allow underdeveloped countries to buy something from Canada, and not from somewhere else. Canadians gave raw materials, commodities, and foodstuffs, such as industrial metals, asbestos, fertilizer, wheat, flour, and butter, not to mention industrial equipment and educational tools. Canadian farmers, manufacturers, technicians, and other experts benefited through the supplies and services that aid generated.

What, besides reinforcing anti-communism, did Canadians of the 1950s think they were doing with aid? There is little doubt that the Canadian government believed that it was exporting a proven model of achievement – and that it hoped it was exporting Western values in a broad sense and not merely the tools for local economic success. Leaders in recipient nations may have believed this themselves; certainly they did little to discourage the notion. Hopes, especially for former British possessions, were high during the 1950s; it would take another decade, and a great deal more aid, to level expectations and to replace optimism with scepticism. For the time being, hopes were trumps.

NATO, NORTH AMERICA, AND EUROPE

Aid, no matter how meritorious, was a sideshow in Canadian foreign relations in the 1950s. The main event, the principal action, was in Europe. That was where Canada kept an army brigade and an air division, while Canada's navy trained for the arduous task of keeping the sea lanes to Europe open if and when the next war came. To do all that, Canada was a member of NATO.

What was NATO supposed to do? It was a military alliance, whose members stood ready to defend each other in case of Soviet attack. There was a chain of command that led from the Supreme Allied Commander, Europe (SACEUR in military jargon), first General Eisenhower, and then a succession of senior American generals, sitting in headquarters outside Paris, right down to forward Canadian units guarding the frontier between East and West Germany, with nothing but a minefield and some barbed wire between them and the Red Army. The only problem was that the Red Army was much bigger, a fact that Western intelligence faithfully reported and predictably exaggerated.[9] In fact, the Red Army in East Germany was bigger than all NATO units in West Germany combined, and behind the forward Soviet troops there was a line of supply and reinforcement that stretched all the way back to Moscow. In case of war, the Canadians were to conduct a fighting retreat, to the Rhine if possible, and then to the English Channel. As an early military plan assessed the situation, "even if it was possible to hold the UK, many years would elapse before we would be in a position ... to liberate Europe. By that time, Russian occupation would have put an end to Western civilization."[10]

NATO thus had a task and a purpose. The task was to replace military weakness with something more plausible, to make it possible to stop the Russians somewhere short of total land victory in Europe. The best way to do that was to avoid war altogether. The purpose was to shore up the political structure of Western Europe, which the alliance was supposed to be protecting. NATO, in other words, was about security, not victory. But for the Western Europeans it had another purpose. The two principal Western European military powers, France and Great Britain, were having problems in their colonial empires. NATO, with its American-based strength, relieved them of part of the burden of defending their homelands and permitted them to deploy part of what were still very large armies in their colonies, France in Indochina and then North Africa, Britain in Malaya, Kenya, and Cyprus.[11]

NATO had to be just plausible enough to persuade the Russians that an attack across the East German boundary was inadvisable. The alliance needed troops and weapons to do the job, and, because in the early 1950s there were not enough troops, the weapons had to be convincing. Lacking conventional force, NATO had no choice but to rely on atomic weaponry and on the United States. The two were symbiotically related. The United States, far and away NATO's largest and richest member, had until 1952 a monopoly on atomic weaponry in the alliance. The unwillingness or inability of the European allies to furnish NATO with conventional armies meant that it had to rely even more on the United States. The ultimate weapon was the American atomic bomb, which by then was coming to be called "the deterrent."[12] To shape the bomb to the needs of the battlefield, the United States experimented with smaller nuclear weapons of the kind that might be deployed by NATO commanders in a future European war. (SACEUR was of course an American, and no decision to use nuclear weapons would ever be left to local European initiative; only the American president had that option. It is however true that the president might be able to delegate the decision to SACEUR.)

The Eisenhower administration, headed by a former general with real knowledge of warfare, was prudent in its military plans. Although the country had military conscription (universally called "the draft"), the American government used this resource sparingly. A very large military implied very large costs, and Eisenhower believed that the economic burden of defence could defeat the United States. Nuclear weapons were relatively cheap and could take the place of many expensive army divisions.

The increasing availability of nuclear weapons gave rise to a new dilemma. Previously NATO's mission was unrealistic because it could not hope to perform its military task successfully. With nuclear armaments, however, NATO could defend Western Europe, but at the price of cutting a radioactive swath through the middle of Germany. As long as Germany was defeated and occupied, a pawn and not a principal in international affairs, that was politically feasible. But by the 1950s the allies had rid themselves of most of the costly burden of occupying Germany and were thinking fondly of the Germans' well-known military qualities, as well as their resurgent economy. German soldiers and German money would make NATO more plausible, and in the early 1950s the West German government was more than ready to make the necessary diplomatic and economic trade-offs to re-establish itself as a responsible world citizen. As Eisenhower built up the American nuclear arsenal – with incidental profit to Canada via uranium sales – he and the British government did what they could to bring West Germany into the alliance. The French, invaded twice by the Germans in the previous forty years, hesitated, but eventually the convenience of German troops proved too great to resist. After experimenting with several half-measures, including an integrated European army (called the European Defence Community), the French gave way and agreed to German independence within an expanded NATO. In 1955 West Germany (officially the Federal Republic of Germany) took its seat at the NATO table as a full, paying ally.

The cementing of West Germany into NATO relieved for the time being any anxiety that the country would drift eastwards, into unity and neutrality or some kind of compromise with the Soviet Union. The Soviet Union was, admittedly, becoming less repulsive after the death of Stalin and the ascendancy of Nikita Khrushchev, who was the predominant figure in Soviet politics after 1953. Pearson investigated in 1955 with a visit to the Soviet Union – the first Western foreign minister to do so since 1947. The visit produced a trade agreement, signed in Ottawa in February 1956. Pearson was lavishly received, a clear sign of the importance his hosts attached to the occasion. They hoped for an opening to the West, while Pearson and his staff hoped they were experiencing and demonstrating a "new look" in Soviet diplomacy.[13]

The Canadian government had its hesitations, but in the end it remained a convinced and loyal ally, accepting that American leadership, for all its occasional faults, was best. More, it was swept along in the American nuclear enthusiasm, and in 1954 agreed in principle to a revised NATO strategy that would place smaller ("tactical") nuclear weapons in the hands of the NATO armies in Germany. At first such weapons were few, but by 1957 they were readily available, and a decision was required over whether Canadian soldiers would have access – with permission and in time of war – to American nuclear warheads for ground-to-ground and air-to-ground missiles.[14] The weapons systems acquired or contemplated by the Canadian military assumed a nuclear role, but it should be remembered that these weapons were not intended to be used. Nevertheless, for them to have the necessary psychological deterrent effect, they had to be seen to be ready for use.

In truth, there was no real agreement on how, or whether, a nuclear war would take place. The three nuclear powers of the 1950s – the United States, Great Britain, and the

Soviet Union – all tested nuclear weapons of increasing size. Some tests were televised, in Canada as well as in the United States, to demonstrate to the public their government's (or their government's friend's) capacity for defence. The display was impressive, but there were long-term consequences to consider. Nuclear contamination was borne by the wind, and in some cases observers or even innocent bystanders were afflicted by radiation sickness. The growing nuclear stockpile did perform its primary function of persuading the other side that any war would be a very serious business; but increasingly nuclear weapons and the prospect of nuclear war demoralized civilian populations in North America and Western Europe. They had reason to be afraid. Asked in 1954 how big a nuclear weapon could be, the chairman of the US Atomic Energy Commission offhandedly replied, "As large as you wish: large enough to take out a city."[15]

By 1954 such cities could be in North America. In both the First and Second World Wars, North America was virtually immune to attack. Neither the Germans nor the Japanese had aircraft capable of reaching North America, and the possibility of seaborne invasion was remote. By the mid-1950s, however, the Soviet Union had bombers capable of reaching the United States and Canada from Siberian bases across the North Pole. For the first time, North Americans had to consider what they must do to defend against air attack.

The first requirement was detection. A radar fence was the best bet, affording the earliest possible detection of an incoming Soviet bomber force. Should the bombers get through, the Western alliance's economic heartland could be devastated. Worse still, the American nuclear deterrent, embodied in the American main bomber force, the Strategic Air Command, might be wiped out, leaving the West little option but surrender in the face of Soviet attack. "It is quite likely," the minister of national defence told the House of Commons in 1951, "that in a general war, Russia would launch bombing attacks against North America with either atomic or conventional weapons."[16] In such an attack it hardly mattered whether the Soviet bombers were targeting the United States or Canada.

There was no question that there had to be some joint defence against Soviet attack. But what kind, and how much? Canada by itself could not afford a full-scale detection and interception effort. Yet inviting the richer, larger neighbour to take over the job might endanger Canadian sovereignty. Counsel was divided in Ottawa. The military, particularly the Royal Canadian Air Force, urged maximum cooperation; in an expanded air defence program one probable result would be a larger and more modern RCAF. Diplomats and other civilian civil servants urged caution, much to the Americans' disgust. That position, according to one American appraisal, showed "a tendency to play down the effects of Canada's bilateral ties with the United States, to insist on the inviolateness [*sic*] of Canadian territory and to become easily irritated over what they consider our lack of appreciation of Canadian interests and views."[17] Those views reflected what the Canadians understood to be the fragility of Canada's sovereignty, which they took to be in danger of being forgotten rather than overridden. The Americans too had nationalistic sensitivities, as Canadians had good reason to know. By way of response to American obliviousness, one senior Canadian civil servant jokingly suggested asking for a Canadian base in New Mexico. Nothing less, he thought, would bring home to the Americans what it was they were asking for.

But the Americans were not seeking new bases in Canada. (They already had some in Newfoundland and Labrador, in arrangements dating back before Newfoundland's entry into Canada in 1949.) They were seeking radar lines, and they were willing to pay for them. The Canadians paid as much as they thought they could afford, and the Americans paid the rest. Three radar fences were eventually built: the cost of the Pinetree Line, just north of the US border, was shared; Canada paid for the Mid-Canada Line, along the fifty-fifth parallel; and the Americans paid for the Distant Early Warning Line (DEW Line) along the seventieth parallel, above the Arctic Circle. Given its location, the DEW Line was by far the most expensive; ironically, it may not have been needed: the Mid-Canada Line was able to do most of the job.[18]

The creation of the radar lines resulted in a construction boomlet in the Canadian North, benefiting suppliers, shippers, and labourers. Canada profited from an injection of technology, as Canadian high-tech firms found a domestic market for their wares. Not everything moved smoothly. Canadian officials had their access to northern radar stations restricted, more or less as the pessimists among them had expected. Under the mania of secrecy and security that characterized defence plans and projects in the 1950s, Canadian officials found they needed American permission to visit parts of their own territory.

There were larger issues at stake than concerns about Canadian sovereignty in the North. The credibility of the Western deterrent was strengthened. The existence of a series of radar fences extended the warning time for a surprise attack and gave the Americans precious hours to decide what to do under those circumstances. Neither side in these dealings felt it necessary to belabour the obvious: if the Canadians had not shared in the project, the Americans might well have done it on their own. Averting infringement of Canada's sovereignty on an issue judged crucial to the United States involved, ironically, giving the Americans largely what they wanted. Nor, on an issue involving such an important matter as defence against sudden attack, would the Canadian public necessarily have supported a more assertive or obstructionist attitude on the part of their government.[19]

Under the circumstances both sides tried to mitigate the possibility of divergence between Canadian and American defence plans. There was the Permanent Joint Board on Defence, but its duties were largely housekeeping. The International Joint Commission, whose powers were theoretically vast, confined itself to issues involving boundary waters. Large questions had to be considered on a higher plane, yet without a specific incident or question it was hard to persuade Americans on the political level to pay attention. St Laurent and Eisenhower therefore agreed to establish two Cabinet-level committees, one on economics and one on defence. There was no permanent secretariat, and on the American side preparations for committee meetings were a hasty affair. But the meetings were held, and there was an exchange of views – sometimes quite frank. The meetings were, as a result, important: importance is not always measured in terms of the stated purpose of a given committee or organization, nor is it always calculated in terms of agreements made.

On occasion the meetings were so uncongenial that they gave rise to extremely negative impressions. After a Cabinet-level meeting in 1955, for example, External Affairs Minister Lester Pearson decided that something, anything, must be done to shore up the defences of the Canadian economy to relieve its exposure to American indifference. He promptly sponsored a review of "Canada's economic prospects" under the direction of his long-time friend (and well-known economic nationalist) Walter Gordon. Gordon was known to believe that Canada's economy was too much influenced by the United States and that the amount of American ownership of Canadian companies was excessive.

Trade and Commerce Minister C.D. Howe did not take kindly to Gordon's ideas or, especially, his mandate, which implied that Canada's economy should have evolved differently. Howe was sensitive to Gordon's argument that importing American investment and American branch plants meant exporting decision-making jobs and, with them, some of the Canadians who should be running the nation's business. In several speeches in 1956 Howe warned American businessmen to respect the autonomy of their Canadian subsidiaries and the Canadians designated to run them. He hoped that such a warning would be enough; he may have feared it would not suffice.

Howe's policies were a mixture of free enterprise and his own brand of economic nationalism. Himself an immigrant from the United States, he did not believe that Canadians should trust the goodwill of the American government to look after their best interests. Most of the time, self-interest would do the trick – the self-interest involved in relations with a free-standing, bill-paying, autonomous neighbour. Experience with planners and committees made Howe distrustful of excessive government intervention in the economy, but a different kind of experience – procuring supplies for the Canadian economy during the Second World War – disposed him to believe in overall government direction of the economy.

On the subject of energy supplies, for example, Howe was a definite believer in a policy conceived and managed in Ottawa. American coal for Ontario factories and

American petroleum to heat Canadians' houses or power their cars were all very well and good, but they were a drain on the balance of payments. And who could say what the Americans would do in a crisis? At the very least, Canada must not be an abject dependant, begging for energy crumbs at the American table. When Imperial Oil (an American subsidiary) discovered large quantities of oil in Alberta in 1947, Howe was extremely pleased. More, he started to scheme to build an oil pipeline from Western to Eastern Canada, the country's first long-distance flow-through fuel line. Completed to Sarnia, Ontario, in 1953, it ran partly through the United States, avoiding northern Ontario's swamps and rocks, much to the disgust of Howe's own Northern Ontario constituents. Fuel and nationalism were clearly linked, both in the conception of an east-west Canadian pipeline and in the spending of valuable dollars in previously neglected regions.

The next pipeline, Howe decided, would be an all-Canadian project – at least in location. Unfortunately, there did not seem to be enough Canadian money or expertise available to build it. A pipeline was no place to experiment with investors' money, and the people who knew how to build them were mostly American. Such a pipeline would surely make money and pay for itself in short order. By Howe's measure, that meant there was no case for government ownership, which should be involved only where nobody else could or would do the job. Howe came up with a compromise. A trans-Canada natural gas pipeline would be built entirely in Canada. A private company would build it. That company would seek its funds in New York, where investors expected and demanded that it be under experienced management. Such management was available – from Texas, then the centre of the American oil industry. As a further complication, the Trans-Canada Pipeline firm was unable to finance the Northern Ontario link between the populated prairie natural gas market and the bonanza of Southern Ontario and Quebec. Thus, the government would have to pay for that. To this demand, Howe agreed.

All this had to be passed through Parliament in time for the construction season of 1956. The Liberal government determined to get the pipeline through and, in one of the great parliamentary battles of Canadian history, it succeeded. The Parliamentary debate was notable for the anti-American utterances of two of the three opposition parties, the Progressive Conservatives and the CCF. (The third opposition party, Alberta-based Social Credit, very much wanted the pipeline to go through.) The Liberals had the majority in Parliament and used it to pass the bill on time, using the parliamentary rule of closure to limit debate. The Liberals harvested reams of hostile publicity from the Canadian media, where the government was accused of being anti-democratic and dictatorial, and such feeling lasted long enough to be a factor in the general election of 1957. The Americans too got a rough ride in the press – not specific but generic

Americans, too brash, too domineering, and (especially in university common rooms) too vulgar. Canada was in danger of being taken over, the media claimed, of becoming a satellite of the United States.

These sentiments must be weighed against the equally definite admiration of American life and culture that was daily expressed by Canadians who tuned their televisions (as their parents had tuned their radios) to American wavelengths. Canadians bought models of American cars and stoves and refrigerators, made in Canada on short production runs and thus more limited and more expensive than their American cousins. Oceans of ink and forests of trees were expended on the question of the crucial difference between Canadians and Americans, a topic that was never resolved nor, as far as Canadians were concerned, exhausted. One Canadian ambassador, reflecting on his service in the United States, proposed a test. Ask any mixed Canadian-American group how many believed there was no difference between the two nationalities, and all or almost all the Americans would stand up. Subliminally, the joke suggests, and its audiences would presumably accept, that there is no other easy way to separate sheep and goats.

A sociologist, Seymour Martin Lipset, who in the 1950s was delving into the mysteries of Canadian prairie socialism, later quantified the difference. In terms of opinions and attitudes, he claimed, Canadians and Americans resembled each other more than either resembled anyone else. On issue after issue, the difference between them was 5 to 10 percent, as measured by polls.[20]

Many of the criticisms directed at Americans by Canadians would have seemed familiar enough south of the border. The context might have been slightly different: when Canadian critics said (and meant) "*all* Americans," American critics might have murmured "*some* Americans." Both sets of critics might well have agreed on the undesirable features of North American consumer society, on the herds of salarymen pouring into and out of faceless buildings and returning to featureless suburbs in the evening. One notable critic actually straddled the border – the Canadian-born but Harvard-based economist John Kenneth Galbraith, whose book, *The Affluent Society*, summed up the misgivings of a liberally inclined cohort of Americans about their society's mistaken turnings and wrong directions. Galbraith's book was instantly adopted by Canadian liberals too – though not by Liberals of the C.D. Howe variety. Some, indeed many, of the seeds of the anti-Americanism of the 1960s were sown in the pro-American 1950s.

Many Canadians of the 1950s sought, and found, alternative models. A small and slowly dwindling minority found solace in the contemplation of the Soviet Union or the newer Communist giant, China. Some found hope in world government, in the common aspirations of humankind, and in the United Nations. Many more tried to blend hope with nostalgia, and placed their faith in the British Commonwealth of Nations, and its mother country, Great Britain.

THE BRITISH COMMONWEALTH AND THE UNITED NATIONS

For many Canadians, Britain was still a vital and important source of pride and identity, and still the alternative to the United States as a cultural and political pole. For the British, Canada's booming economy and rising standard of living represented hope: it suggested the British Commonwealth of nations could be dynamic and prosperous, as well as inclusive.[21] The dominions, one official later reflected, "were of value no longer as appendages, but in themselves."[22] If there was a "golden age" of Anglo-Canadian relations, it was the 1950s, when a diminished Britain needed a close and faithful friend, and thought it had found one, free of the old taint of colonial subordination, in Canada. Many Canadians reciprocated these feelings.

Pro-British sentiment had a recent boost. Half a million Canadians had passed through Great Britain during the Second World War, a generation that was in its prime by the mid-1950s. And now, with the Canadian standard of living indubitably higher than that in Britain and likely to remain so, many British subjects took ship or plane for Canada. The proportion of Canadians of British stock actually increased in the years immediately after 1945, though that trend would not be maintained. Between 1946 and 1961, Britain sent almost 600,000 immigrants to Canada (28.5 percent of British émigrés), raising the number of British-born Canadians to nearly a million (5.3 percent of the total population).

As the decade drew on, the sense of opportunity in Anglo-Canadian relations gradually leached away. But in the first half of the 1950s, the Commonwealth meant hope. In London, before 1956, East met West, and developed, white North met underdeveloped, non-white South. The peaceful exchanges in the Commonwealth were potent symbols for Canadian foreign policy in the 1950s, in which pride in the past met hope for the future. Canada opted for building bridges from an obsolescent colonial past to a future that, however uncertain its outline, had at least some potential.

Economically, strategically, and politically, Great Britain still counted in Canada; and from the British point of view the Commonwealth also had considerable weight. To use the most easily quantifiable measure, Great Britain ranked second throughout the 1950s as a Canadian trading partner; and, together with the rest of the Commonwealth, it accounted for just under a quarter of Canadian exports and roughly 15 percent of Canadian imports.[23] That was only natural: next to the United States, Britain had in the early 1950s the largest economy among the Western powers. The British standard of living, while lagging behind the North Americans', was still higher than that of any other Western European country. The British fleet still sailed most of the seven seas, the British army was still large, and the Royal Air Force carried a British nuclear deterrent. Canadian troops served with the British army in Germany, and Canadian officers and diplomats served beside their British counterparts in NATO. Canada's largest mission abroad was not in Washington but London, and the Canadians who served there often enjoyed a common background in British universities.

Good, or strong, ties had existed before, but in the 1930s Canada played almost no international role, and during the war the British were preoccupied with their essential ally, the Americans, and had no time to render more than courtesy to the British dominions. Fortunately, from the British point of view, the Canadians had asked no more, and after the war there was occasion enough to warm the relationship. It is arguable, even probable, that the foundations as well as the practices of Anglo-Canadian relations were better between 1945 and 1955 than ever before – or, as it has turned out, since.

The excellence of Anglo-Canadian contact after 1945, and the continuing significance of Canadian economic and cultural relations with Great Britain, cannot mask the obvious fact that the United States was more important to both Canada and Great Britain, and remained so. The British Commonwealth might take 25 percent of Canadian exports, but the Americans took 50 percent and more. For imports, the American figures were higher still, while in investment the Americans far surpassed the depleted British holdings in its former colony. Canadian-American contacts were good, often friendly and almost always cordial. But they were not as close: the common flat North American accent concealed the fact that, as often as not, the neighbours were speaking different diplomatic languages.

After 1945 British diplomacy was both congenial and influential as far as the Canadians were concerned. Great Britain opposed the Soviet Union and denounced communism; British diplomacy was crucial in the formation of NATO; the British sought to establish a close, "special," relationship with the United States. Canadians applauded all these things. Thus, Britain's policy placed it in solidarity and apparent identity with its North American relatives. NATO and the "special relationship" looked west, across the Atlantic; both these policies engaged Canadian interests and support.

So did the stabilized Commonwealth, the political bridge to the new world of independent ex-colonial states. Canadians hoped for much from Indian independence. The Canadian government acted quickly to firm up that country's Commonwealth allegiance by accommodating the Indian government's desire to become a republic, the Commonwealth's first. At Commonwealth conferences, Canadian representatives listened carefully to Indian views and sought to accommodate them; at the United Nations, the Canadians worked with the Indians as far as possible, even when, as on the Korean War, India's positions were far different from those of the United States or even the United Kingdom.

The Indian prime minister, Jawaharlal Nehru, visited Ottawa early on and found it both familiar and deferential. "The atmosphere in Ottawa at that time was markedly British," Escott Reid, a senior diplomat, wrote, "and Nehru in heart and mind was at least half British." Prime Minister St Laurent noted that India had twenty times Canada's population; that country might be relatively poor and geographically remote, but he believed that its population was a better gauge of its ultimate importance for Canada.[24]

As a token of that importance, St Laurent and Pearson dispatched Escott Reid, one of the most senior Canadian diplomats, to New Delhi in 1952.[25] Reid's job was first and foremost to shore up existing personal contacts between India and Canada, not forgetting that India's significance to Canada, and vice versa, was more than bilateral. For India, Canada might supplement or in some circumstances circumvent relations with the United States, which were poor. For Canada, India was a bridge to the Third World – but not only the Third World. Despite misgivings in Ottawa over what Reid described as Indian naïveté toward China, the Canadians as well as the Indians hoped for improvements in relations with that Communist giant.

In 1952-1953 India and Canada worked closely together at the United Nations during the last stages of the Korean War. The American government, outgoing Democrats or incoming Republicans, was not impressed by this collaboration, which only helped reinforce Indo-Canadian diplomatic solidarity. India's profession of neutrality, which some Americans regarded as abstention from a moral cause, did not greatly concern the Canadians. Ottawa feared that American intransigence towards India might do more harm than good, alienating future good will. St Laurent visited India in 1954, and both he and Nehru worked hard at making their "special relationship" work. Lester Pearson, as external affairs minister, visited from time to time, and expressed his admiration for Nehru's subtlety and brilliance. With India's approval, in 1954 both countries were appointed to a truce supervisory commission for Indochina. Yet, underneath the cordiality, and the sense that the relationship *ought* to work, there was uneasiness, which Pearson shared. Perhaps Nehru's values were not the same as his own; perhaps he sensed a different calculus of interests behind the smooth Oxbridge façade of the Indian prime minister.[26]

Canada and India found the United Nations their most useful public forum. The United Nations in the mid-1950s was not exactly what its founders had imagined. The central organ of the UN, the Security Council, was paralyzed by the conflict between East and West and by the great power veto. During the Korean War the Americans, with an overwhelming majority in the General Assembly, had bypassed the Security Council using the "Uniting for Peace" resolution, which simply appropriated some of the Security Council's functions and granted them to a body that operated by a simple majority, and without a veto.

The General Assembly continued to be the centre of UN activity after the war. Yet it no longer reflected as much of the political reality of the world as it had: the great powers had a stranglehold on admission of new member states, and as a result a large number of countries were not members. The Americans were of two minds. In theory, they favoured a universal United Nations, with as many members as possible. But they also liked the convenience of an automatic majority and were uncertain what shift in power might result from new admissions. They had to consider their allies, in this case Nationalist China, still occupying China's UN seat and still with a veto.

The American sense of timing and occasion differed considerably from the Canadian in the bargaining related to the admission of new member states. In a complicated and prolonged negotiation, it was the Canadians not the Americans who prevailed: the Americans, hamstrung by their position as alliance leader, moved with the slowest members of the Western herd. The Canadians, unfettered by such considerations, eventually brokered a number of compromises and broke the admissions logjam.[27] Secretary of State Dulles was not pleased, but the deed was done.[28]

The outcome of the new admissions was a change in the nature of the UN membership, making it more representative of the world as it had come to be and creating a precedent for the admission of a flood of former colonies in the early 1960s.

Suez

In the mid-1950s the European powers continued to cling to empire. The British, free of India and Palestine, hung on in Africa. The French held on to Algeria. The Belgian and Portuguese colonial empires continued. Empire was not quite what it had been, however. The British faced rebellions in Malaya, Kenya, and Cyprus. These rebellions ate up money and troops. Some troops were available after the British foreign secretary, Anthony Eden, negotiated an end to the biggest drain on British military resources, the 80,000-man garrison at the Suez Canal, in 1954. In exchange for promises of good behaviour from the Egyptian dictator, Nasser, and goodwill for the future, the last contingent sailed away to Cyprus in June 1956. British troops may have left, but the Suez Canal remained not the property of the Egyptian government but of an Anglo-French company.

The withdrawal was a promising development. It also provided needed relief to British forces in NATO, which the government in London, by 1956 headed by the same Anthony Eden, had just increased to four divisions. It eased pressure on pro-Western governments elsewhere in the region. It appeased the nationalist government of Egypt, whose affections the British and the Americans were attempting to secure. It might, just possibly, assist the search for a stable peace between Arabs and Israelis.

To the Canadian government the Middle East had a fourfold importance. First, it had a general strategic value in the defence of the West, as the hinge between Asia and Africa, and between the Indian Ocean and the Mediterranean. It was an oil reservoir on which the European allies increasingly depended. Second, it was a region where the British and the Americans had parallel but not identical interests, with a proven potential for a clash. Third, it was a political theatre in which declining colonialism confronted anti-colonial nationalism – new countries versus old empires. Lastly, it was an area in which a substantial number of Canadians – mainly Jewish – took an interest, because of the newly founded Jewish state of Israel, and its struggle to establish itself in the face of Arab hostility, which had manifested itself in the first Arab-Israeli war, in 1948.

The Egyptian dictator, the populist and nationalist Gamal Abdel Nasser, was a master of verbal theatrics. Yet his rhetorical exaggerations boxed in his policies. To show that Egypt could not be bought, and that substantial Egyptian grievances remained even after the departure of British troops from Suez, he bought arms from Communist Czechoslovakia, even as he negotiated a development loan from the Americans and the British to build a great dam at Aswan on the Nile.

Pearson, as a NATO foreign minister, was concerned about the deal with Czechoslovakia, and he raised the subject in a 1955 visit with Nasser. The Egyptian leader defended his arms purchases as a necessary response to Israeli aggressiveness, even though he appeared to accept Pearson's argument that it would force Israel to buy arms of its own. Pearson left Cairo "without optimism" about a political solution to the underlying conflict.[29] The next month, meeting the Israeli foreign minister in Ottawa, Pearson was struck by Israeli intransigence and became increasingly pessimistic about the prospects for peace between Israel and its neighbours.[30]

It did not take much for the several instabilities of the Middle East to erupt into crisis. Distrust of Nasser and a well-founded fear that a loan to "pro-Communist" Egypt could not clear Congress caused Dulles to cancel the Aswan loan. The British followed suit. Nasser, in a stunning response, nationalized the Suez Canal on 26 July 1956. This action triggered rage in the British Cabinet, and especially in Anthony Eden. The British prime minister, thinking back to the evacuation of the Canal Zone, decided that he had been deceived and betrayed by Nasser. Eden was from the beginning inclined to military action. What he would do with victory – if he got it – he did not know: the overthrow and humiliation of Nasser and the restoration of British prestige were enough. Dulles, sensing Eden's mood, scrambled to buy time by convening a "Suez Canal Users' Association" (SCUA). Dulles wanted postponement for postponement's sake, while Eden hoped to demonstrate that even a distinguished and well-meaning international forum like SCUA could do nothing with Nasser. SCUA did consume time, as Dulles hoped. But it did not accomplish its larger object of gradually lessening tension. Its lack of substance was transparent. Pearson, from a distance, told the Canadian Cabinet on 27 September 1956 that there was still a "very real danger" that the British and French would act against Egypt.[31] Eden concocted an Anglo-French invasion force: it slowly dribbled to British bases in Cyprus, the nearest British territory to Egypt.

Meanwhile, rumblings within the Soviet empire distracted the attention of the world from events in the Middle East. First Poland and then Hungary disputed Moscow's absolute authority; by mid-October discontent in Hungary was turning into revolution. While Moscow decided what to do, the world nervously waited. No one noticed when British, French, and Israeli ministers met in Sèvres, outside Paris, to devise a secret plan for the invasion of Egypt. Israel would go first, providing the British and French with an excuse to protect the Suez Canal. With the rest of the world continuing to gaze anxiously at Hungary, the Israelis crossed the Egyptian frontier on 29 October. The British and French, true to their word, issued an ultimatum to the Egyptians – and the Israelis. It professed alarm that the Suez Canal was endangered, asking them to stop fighting and withdraw ten miles from the canal, which then would be "temporarily" occupied by the helpful British and French. The Egyptians refused, so the British and French bombed airfields outside Cairo. "I have an uneasy feeling," Pearson wrote, "that there is something going on between the French and the Israeli governments which the French have not bothered to tell us."[32]

With the bombing already underway, Eden sent a telegram to St Laurent, hoping for his "continued support." Eden knew this was nonsense: he had deliberately kept his distance from the Canadians over the preceding months. St Laurent was usually considered a calming influence: grandfatherly and courtly, he was an ornament at Commonwealth conferences. But cooperation with Great Britain was always a conscious exercise for St Laurent, a learned rather than an instinctive reaction. Faced with evasiveness and insincerity in London, he was deeply offended. Controlling his temper, he drafted with Pearson a reply that attempted to recall Eden to sanity. He told the British that they had jeopardized three important interests: the United Nations, which had been ignored, and whose position was therefore undermined; the Commonwealth, where India objected violently to the British action; and Anglo-American friendship, so important to Canada, and to the Western alliance. The Canadians were right on all three counts and right too that the British and French did not have the strength to defy the world by appropriating a piece of Egyptian territory. Far from giving Eden the automatic support he wanted, Canada remained publicly uncommitted.

With St Laurent's approval and support, Pearson flew to New York on 1 November. He had three objectives in mind. The most important was to preserve the Western alliance. The second was to reinforce the authority of the United Nations by persuading it to intervene in the dispute. The third was to salvage, if possible, the Commonwealth and repair relations between the Western powers and the Third World. Over the preceding few years Pearson had established a close working relationship with Dag Hammarskjöld, the UN secretary-general. Both men were anxious to reinforce the standing of the United Nations. Pearson had the experience, the range of contacts, and the diplomatic skill. Hammarskjöld, who was himself not deficient in these qualities, had the key UN position and an activist temperament.

Fortuitously, Eden had given Pearson an opportunity. In a debate in the British House of Commons on the afternoon of 1 November, he justified his impending intervention in Egypt as a "police action" to separate the combatants. Once that action was accomplished, he claimed to have no objection if the UN took over "the physical task of maintaining peace." A senior British official underlined the remark for Norman Robertson, the Canadian High Commissioner in London, and Robertson reported it immediately to Pearson. Very early the next morning, in the course of a debate in the UN over the Israeli invasion of Egypt, Pearson made the proposal for a "United Nations force large enough to keep these borders at peace while a political settlement is worked out."

Pearson did not have very much time, but he had some encouragement. The Americans liked the idea of a UN force and urged the Canadians on. Like Pearson, Dulles feared the consequences if the British proceeded; unlike Pearson, he had powerful weapons at his disposal. The British and French economies were vulnerable, and their currencies lacked sufficient reserves to back them up in a panic. They needed American economic support. If they invaded Egypt, Dulles and Eisenhower decided, they would not get it. Pearson knew this and acted accordingly. Backing and filling, abstaining on an American resolution that demanded an immediate end to the fighting in Egypt, Pearson hoped to straddle the British and American positions. By 3 November he had the elements of a UN peacekeeping force in play, had moved a resolution – drafted by Henry Cabot Lodge, the American UN delegate – establishing a peacekeeping force, and had lined up support from the Asian and neutral bloc. Just then, time ran out.

That the United States would not assist its allies was something Eden could not grasp. Assuming, wrongly, that his wartime comrade Eisenhower would fall into line and back up his most important ally, he gave the signal to attack. Believing, again mistakenly, that British and French forces could masquerade as UN peacekeepers, he saw no reason to hold back. Finally, the Anglo-French invasion force sailed for Egypt.

The invasion of Egypt coincided with the invasion of Hungary by the Soviet Union. Excited newscasters had difficulty choosing which crisis was more important. In Canada, English-Canadian public opinion battled with itself. Great Britain was at war. In every previous war, Canadian support was forthcoming. This time, to judge by the statements coming out of Ottawa, it was not.[33] This reluctance inflamed the Conservative opposition in Ottawa. Its members, especially John Diefenbaker, MP for Prince Albert, Saskatchewan, and prospective Conservative party leader, demanded that Canada back Britain.

Undeterred, Pearson proceeded with his resolution in the UN General Assembly. It had become more difficult, because the British and French had flouted the organization's express wish for an end to hostilities and no invasion. But their unilateral action had resulted in a run on the British pound and French franc; oil markets, afflicted by an Arab oil boycott, were in chaos; and the reality of the Americans' refusal to support the action could no longer be denied. As the extent of American displeasure became obvious, the British position softened. Canada entered a bargain with India, securing the passage of Pearson's proposal in return for Canadian support for an Indian resolution that condemned the British and French. The fact that Canada voted for such a proposition again caused a stir at home.

Reluctantly, the British and French agreed to a ceasefire without achieving their military objective, control of the whole Suez Canal. (The canal was blocked by the Egyptians, and stayed blocked for months thereafter.) The Canadian resolution had passed: a UN force replaced the British and French and stood between Arabs and Israelis.

There had been other UN forces, small and large. The biggest one was the UN army in Korea, which was the comparison most commentators drew. That army had been free standing, and though it had the cooperation of the South Koreans, it did not absolutely depend on their consent. Pearson's proposed force was much smaller. It was not intended as a fighting force. As Pearson said, "we would have been in the soup if this force had been charged with the job of 'enforcing' anything."[34]

Pearson had no idea of creating a permanent police force in the Middle East: the UN would avert further fighting, re-establish calm, and promote a peace settlement. He hoped to set a useful precedent for managing future conflicts, one that would encourage disputants to bring their problems to the international forum. But he also wanted to go further. He wanted UN forces to be an assertion of a dominant international interest over mere national priorities. This international police force should be insulated from every local whim – responsible first to the UN and only a long way after to local sovereign authority. This, the Americans told Pearson, could not be. There was a fundamental right to sovereignty in which the Americans themselves believed. Egypt wanted ultimate control over the duration and composition of the UN force's deployment. Nasser made the point by objecting to participation by Canadian troops in the newly titled United Nations Emergency Force (UNEF). The Canadian public were told that this was because Canadian uniforms and unit designations resembled those of the British, but in fact it was because Nasser thought the Canadian position in the UN debate too close to that of the British. Secretary-General Hammarskjöld, after discussing the matter with Nasser, confirmed and accepted the Egyptian position, noting that "Egypt's consent to [the] continuance of [UN] forces in Egypt [is] required."[35]

Once Nasser was reassured, Canada sent support troops to UNEF and remained a regular contributor for the next eleven years. The Canadian public gradually accepted that Canadian soldiers were playing an important and appreciated role, one that justified the shock of breaking publicly for the first time with Great Britain on an important issue of foreign policy.

The government in Ottawa paid a political price for Suez – though scholars disagree about how heavy that price was. In a debate in Parliament in mid-November, just as Canada was trying to get its contribution to UNEF accepted by Egypt, Prime Minister St Laurent let slip the remark that "the supermen of Europe" had had their day, and that the outcome of the Suez Crisis ratified that fact.[36] He was right. The crisis had demonstrated that on issues of war and peace the British and French could no longer afford to be independent actors. But the prime minister had committed the primary political sin of uttering a home truth in a memorable verbal package. Not all Canadians agreed with him, or, more important still, wanted to agree with him.

Conservatives in Toronto ⌐ the citadel of the Conservative Party, traditional and extremely anglophile – were enraged. The newspaper columnist Judith Robinson wrote: "Thus in one bitter and revealing phrase, the prime minister of Canada had made clear the end he wanted Canada's U.N. votes on the Suez Crisis to serve; the 'pretty close end' of France and Great Britain as world powers." Pearson did some explaining of his own, in a two-hour speech to Parliament. It did him little good with the opposition, which alternately condemned the United States and praised the British and French. "It was perhaps natural that [Pearson] should write off traditions he once shared and discount loyalties he no longer felt," the very Conservative *Toronto Telegram* said of Pearson's speech. "But it was stupid of him to forget the historic distrusts which endure just under the surface of Canadian-US relations, and to overlook the fact that much has happened in the years since the last war to renew and enliven those distrusts among ordinary Canadians."[37]

In Canada, there are two contrasting perspectives to the Suez Crisis: the reality of what actually occurred in 1956-1957 and the memory of the crisis viewed through the prism of later events. The remembered version of Suez is long-term. In it, Canada made a crucial and effective intervention in the Suez Crisis, rescued the British and French from the hole that their own imbecility had dug, and on the side established peacekeeping as a vocation for the UN and for Canada. In recognition of this achievement, Pearson – and, through him, Canada – received the Nobel Prize for Peace in October 1957. This interpretation of events works as far as it goes. But what did Pearson, and Canada, actually do in November 1956 to merit the Nobel Prize? That question can be answered on two levels. Technically, Pearson created and then stage-managed the principal Western reaction to the Suez Crisis. He was able to do so because his experience and his reputation among other diplomats at the UN gave confidence that he, if anyone, could turn the trick. "People kept rushing up to me, . Secretariat people, all kinds of people," John Holmes, a senior Canadian diplomat, recalled, "and they would say, 'What has he got? We hear Mike's got a proposal. It's high time. Can he do it?'"[38]

Pearson's job was to build a coalition from initially disparate if not hostile elements. His first stroke of luck was that senior British officials were themselves very dubious of their own government's policy. To quote John Holmes: "The most enthusiastic were the British, who thought their own policy was just appalling ... [They] were saying to us that if Mike can make a proposal saying that the UN will take over what the British and the French were proposing to do, then we can persuade Eden to get up and say if the UN is taking over, then we don't need to do it [invade Suez]." This left Pearson open to the charge that he was "playing the British game," which was in a general sense true, for the British game was very differently defined by many British diplomats than it was by Eden. Pearson also knew that the British would accept from him what they would not – or not yet – accept from the Americans.

Pearson was also fortunate that the basic objective of the US government was the same as his own. It was, after all, a draft *American* resolution that he moved in order to get UNEF launched. Yet without Pearson's superb tactical sense of the UN, of what was possible and what was not, the American draft might not have worked. Timing, as Pearson understood, was almost everything; provenance was the rest. It was important to move now, and it was important that Canada, not the United States, do the moving. "I gave him the paper," Henry Cabot Lodge remembered. "And he just looked at the paper and he said, 'Yes,' just like that, adding, 'Yes, I'll take it.'"[39]

The point on which the Canadian and American governments agreed was that the Western alliance was in danger as long as the British and French insisted on pursuing a policy that was beyond their ability to implement and that required allied, especially American, complicity to work. Nor was complicity too strong a word, given the ramshackle conspiracy that the British, French, and Israelis had cobbled together to justify the invasion of Egypt and the seizure of the Suez Canal.

The Western alliance was not the same after 1956. The British and French drew different conclusions from the experience. The British, under their new prime minister, Harold Macmillan, cleaved closely to the American alliance. The French largely took the view that the United States – and by extension Canada – had let them down. The French were, in the phrase of one of their historians, the "bad pupils" of the NATO class. NATO was not an equal partnership but a forum for American dominance.[40]

It took years for the truth of the Suez conspiracy to surface. The American government certainly had its suspicions at the time, and it may have passed them on to the Canadians. As far as public opinion was concerned, impressions were formed in the absence of detailed knowledge. Public opinion polling on the issue was imperfect: the only sample taken revealed 43 percent of Canadians in favour of the Anglo-French action and 40 percent opposed. That sample was, however, based on a "quick spot check" and was drawn only from Toronto.[41]

Suez played prominently in Canadian politics over the winter of 1956-1957. The government was thinking of calling an election in the spring, and Suez was an issue that rallied Conservatives around the issue of Canada's British identity. Anti-Americanism was reinforced by an unpleasant incident in April 1957, when the Canadian ambassador in Egypt, Herbert Norman, jumped to his death from the top of an office building. Norman had been publicly accused in an American Senate committee of hiding his communist past. The implication was that the Canadian government and Pearson, the responsible minister, had been harbouring an agent of the Kremlin for many years. Pearson defended Norman, both before and after his death. The external affairs minister had to span the positions of expressing regret for American conduct over the Norman affair, thereby appeasing public indignation, and keeping Canadian-American relations going. Washington was not especially helpful, offering lukewarm regrets while serving to remind Canadians that the American legislature, in this as in so much else, was a law unto itself.

Canadians did not need to be reminded. American trade restrictions, on lead and zinc, and on oats and barley, not to mention market-destroying wheat giveaways, strongly indicated that the American government consulted its own narrow interests first. The perception was not quite right, but, as with Suez, the explanation was complicated and nuanced – not the best message to broadcast from the hustings.

The Liberals saw no reason to worry: public opinion polls cast a sunny glow over the future; indeed, every public opinion poll since 1943 had placed the party first in the public's affections. That was true in the 1957 election as well, right up to and including polling day. The only problem was that the Liberals did not stand first in terms of parliamentary seats the day after the June election.

Foreign policy did not greatly assist the government in the 1957 general election. That was true on two levels. There was the underlying resentment of the United States and its conduct. The Liberals were regarded as the pro-American party, while the Conservatives (and the Alberta-based Social Credit) wrapped themselves in the mantle of imperial history and British patriotism. More specifically, the residue from the oil pipeline debate, which figured strongly in the election of 1957, was in part an anti-American issue, along with a thousand and one other irritations. The government responded as best it could, but its explanations were swept away.

Interestingly, in the 1957 election only three elements in the Canadian electorate held firm for the Liberals. The first was the French-Canadian segment of the population, which in 1957 as before remained faithful to the Liberal Party and its French-Canadian Catholic leader. The second was the Ottawa area, with its strong civil service component. While there were many civil servants who voted Conservative or CCF, there was little doubt that the Liberals were the "Ottawa party." Finally there were the armed forces, at home and abroad – that part of the population most affected by foreign policy. The armed forces felt that the Liberals had treated them well. They had little or no objection to contacts with the Americans, and many if not most strongly identified with their counterparts in the US military. If there were a segment of the Canadian population immune to anti-Americanism, this was it.[42]

There is no strong evidence that Canadians saw the 1957 election as a foreign policy debate. Yet the debate was there, the issues were mentioned, and there was a current of nationalism, in English Canada at least, that did not improve the Liberals' chances. And so they lost, though, significantly for the future of the party, external affairs minister Pearson kept his seat.

☙

NOT SURPRISINGLY, THE PERIOD FROM 1945 OR 1948 TO 1957 has been labelled a "golden age" in Canadian diplomacy.[43] It was the period when Canada was listened to, when it had influence, when Canadians counted. Canadians liked to tell themselves that their country was a Great Power in everything but population. That was a big but. With 16 million people in the mid-1950s, Canada lagged far behind the 200 million in the United States, or the 225 million in the USSR, or even the 50 or so million in Great Britain or France. And while Canada was still, in 1957, second in per capita income in the world, the gap between Canada and the countries of Western Europe was closing fast. Canada's abounding prosperity and rising standard of living (and the Canadian habit of making comparisons only with the United States) masked the fact that, relative to the rest of the world, North America was no longer unique or as isolated as it had been in 1945.

Canadians, English and French, enjoyed strong national identifications – different, as befitted different backgrounds and cultural formations, but centred on the notion of a Canadian national state. Quebec had not yet become the "national" alternative to Canada, as it would in later decades. The English-Canadian variant drew much of its strength from the recent experience of depression and war; and although the proportion of veterans was less in French-speaking Quebec, the same phenomenon could be perceived – veterans, for whom service in the national Canadian armed services had been a most positive experience.

General agreement on the principles and practices of Canadian foreign policy also fed a belief that that policy "made sense." In a homogenizing decade, there was no basic difference among Canada's major political factions on the Cold War, or NATO, or the confrontation with Soviet Russia. Nor was there any serious disagreement that Europe and of course the United States were the proper focus of Canadian attention. Canadians were in overall agreement as to what constituted "their" world. Asia was a source of mystery and danger, but in the 1950s concerns on that continent counted only as a distraction. Perceptive Canadians understood that the Americans were concerned about Asia because they had to be; the less tolerant considered American worries over China and Southeast Asia to be aberrations and compared American policy unfavourably with their own self-satisfied removal from the issues.

Canada's educational system equipped the government with a cadre of university-trained people who were recruited to staff the hard-working foreign service. Pearson could make the splash he did at the UN because he was backed by a studious and literate staff, who in the 1950s, as before and after, had a reputation for reliable professionalism. Perhaps more than at any other period, there was a reciprocal appreciation between the civil servants and the politicians, and the feeling that Pearson and the foreign service were symbiotic.

Canada in the 1950s could afford a good foreign service, as it afforded a large and well-trained military. Circumstances allowed a bigger Canadian role than in the past, and the experience of the Second World War justified it. The absence of other countries from the negotiating table – of Germany and Japan from the UN, for example – created a vacuum that Canada, among others, was able to fill. Pearson, a survivor of a much more modest Canada, the depression-ridden, semi-colonial country of the 1930s, did not presume too much on the fact. For those whose experience began with the war, the unbalanced world of the 1950s may have seemed not only expansive, but permanent. The notion of an activist Canadian role would later be called "Pearsonian." Part of the secret of Canada's success was that Pearson himself was not a "Pearsonian."

Canada's influence can nevertheless be exaggerated. Pearson was respected, even admired, by other diplomats. Yet Canada's ability to function effectively depended in part on its larger allies. The solution to Suez was not simply a Canadian creation but an idea hatched simultaneously in the British foreign service, the American UN mission, and Pearson's own mind. Pearson's was the hand that put the ingredients together, but the influence and power that made them possible were not Canada's.

Pearson had the remarkable gift of making it all seem painless. Circumstances allowed him to work a field he knew well, and instinct kept him grounded in reality. Much the same thing could be said of the Liberal government of which he was such a prominent part. Much later a member of that government, by then out of office, contemplated its decline and fall. "St Laurent made it all seem so easy," he sighed. "The Canadian people thought anybody could do the job, and so they elected anybody."[44]

8

DIEFENBAKER AND THE
DWINDLING
BRITISH CONNECTION

John Diefenbaker became prime minister of Canada on 22 June 1957 and exited the office on 22 April 1963. He left an imprint on Canadians' politics and on their historical memory; but he left less of a legacy to his country than he could have wished, or, certainly, imagined. Such was the power of his personality that it was impossible, almost fifty years later, to think of his time as prime minister as anything other than "the Diefenbaker era." It was, however, an era that John Diefenbaker did not understand and that he consequently failed to master.

To begin with, there was the personality. Diefenbaker was born with a sense of personal destiny and the ambition to pursue it. Yet he spent most of his life, until the age of sixty-one, watching fortune pass him by. Prairie lawyer (he lived in Prince Albert, a small city north of Saskatoon), provincial politician, backbench MP, Diefenbaker spent his life accumulating frustrations and, with them, resentments. When he was almost too old for the job, his party, the Progressive Conservatives, elected him leader in December 1956, the latest Tory in a long succession to assail the unassailable, the entrenched Liberal government of Louis St Laurent.

On 10 June 1957, the Liberals narrowly lost. Diefenbaker became the prime minister at the head of a minority government, but he faced a demoralized and disorganized opposition. Imposing his personality on events, he persuaded Canadians that his was a government that would ride with destiny and lead the country in a different direction. He was rewarded with a second mandate – this time a majority – on 31 March 1958. For the next four years he led a government with the largest majority, until then, in Canadian history.

Canadians saw a "Diefenbaker government." True, it was a Conservative administration, and there were personalities other than Diefenbaker's. Yet his flair for publicity, his powerful oratory, and even his physical presence (he was well over six feet, erect and dignified, with piercing blue eyes) permitted the prime minister to dominate his surroundings. He was quick witted, fast on his feet and with repartee. His knowledge of a subject might not be deep – he was not a well-read student of public affairs – but he was able to conjure up information and manipulate it quickly. Diefenbaker had, in other words, an unusual and formidable array of gifts. It was his misfortune and the country's that he had no idea what to do with them.

It was not that Diefenbaker was bereft of ideas or attitudes. He was often described, accurately, as a "Prairie populist." He believed that political strength flowed from the people; he believed, too, that it flowed to him. He had a strong sense of the past, if not of history. Most of Canada's recent past, indeed his own past, was bound up with the Liberal Party. The trouble with the Liberals, in Diefenbaker's opinion and that of other Conservatives too, was that they had severed their ties with "the people." The Conservatives had campaigned in 1957 under the slogan "It's time for a change," and once he was in power Diefenbaker was determined to change things.

As his official staff soon learned, the new prime minister was impatient of convention and suspicious of advice, especially if it came from those associated too closely with the previous government. Yet Diefenbaker had no alternative advisers, and as it turned out he had very little in the way of new policies. His views on foreign policy were, in a word, orthodox. He believed in the British connection and firmly believed that Great Britain was still "great." He admired the United States and practically worshiped the American president, Dwight D. Eisenhower. Mistrusting the Soviet Union, he accepted that Canada's place in the Cold War was firmly in the Western alliance. These views were hardly unusual among Canadians.

So far, it would seem, so good. Diefenbaker's early contacts with the American and British leaders, President Eisenhower and Prime Minister Harold Macmillan, were deferential if not effusive.[1] Broadly speaking, he was working within a framework of relationships that in the hands of his predecessors had proven popular within Canada, and effective without. Yet by the time Diefenbaker left office, his conduct of foreign policy was reviled by an important and growing number of Canadians, while his relations with both the Americans and the British were disastrous. Canada's influence in the world was declining, so much so that Canadians were forced to take note. Overseas, in Canada's NATO garrisons, the prime minister's portrait was used as a dartboard in military messes.

Diefenbaker, who expected to take credit for his conduct of a people's foreign policy, instead ended up taking the blame for a flawed performance. Inevitably, much of the criticism was excessively partisan or unfair, but it cannot be denied that the prime minister was the author of many of his own misfortunes. He was, to begin with, a bad fit with routine, and therefore the conduct of foreign relations. As one of his diplomatic aides, Basil Robinson, may years later concluded, Diefenbaker "had very little inclination or talent for negotiation in the substance of foreign policy. He did not appreciate the environment in which others were operating, and was not willing to give in search of compromise ... [For] those who wanted a creative, resourceful role for Canada in the world, Diefenbaker was not the answer."[2]

MINISTERING TO FOREIGN POLICY

Diefenbaker was not a diplomatic asset. Nor did he better his odds, and his country's, by putting his ministers to good use. He had two ministers of external affairs: Sidney Smith, from September 1957 until his untimely death in March 1959, and Howard Green, from June 1959 until April 1963. Each man had his virtues. Smith was affable and amiable, and for many years he had deployed these talents as president of the University of Toronto, Canada's largest university. Transplanted to Ottawa, to the unfamiliar terrain of foreign affairs, Smith was becalmed. Diefenbaker was not respectful of his ministers; even if he had been, most prime ministers find the temptation of easy publicity and cheap credit in foreign policy irresistible. Diefenbaker was no exception, and in Smith's time in office the prime minister regularly overrode his hapless minister.

Howard Green, Smith's successor, was a very different commodity. Green was a political veteran, MP for Vancouver Quadra since 1935, and a one-time candidate for the Conservative leadership. Failing in that ambition, Green loyally served whatever leader fate placed at the head of the Conservative Party. As a result he had Diefenbaker's qualified trust – as much as the prime minister gave to anyone. As minister of public works from 1957 to 1959, Green gained respect even from the opposition, and good notices in the press. As minister of external affairs, he won the reluctant admiration of professional diplomats. "Tall, white-haired and bespectacled," Basil Robinson wrote, Green "was a man of dignified bearing, a ready smile, and an appealing tendency to puncture solemnity with a huge, conspiratorial wink."[3]

Green was also a man with firm views and with the political ability – at least at home – to put them into effect. His subordinates at the Department of External Affairs appreciated his support; as important, they admired his effectiveness as a minister. While he was not especially knowledgeable about foreign policy, he was open to advice; perhaps fortuitously and certainly fortunately, he found himself in close agreement with his deputy minister, the very experienced Norman Robertson. Green was even able to manage the distrust and disappointment that Robertson and Diefenbaker felt for each other.

Green was less successful abroad. The minister adapted more readily to certain Canadian diplomatic attitudes than to others. He valued Canada's links to India – as Pearson had – and sometimes spoke hopefully of a mediatory role between the United States and the Communist bloc. Listening to Green talk about Canada's position "between two nuclear giants" at a NATO meeting in May 1961, the American secretary of state, Dean Rusk, was unimpressed. As he wrote his president, John F. Kennedy, Green "seemed to join the long parade of those who have wished to provide a bridge, meaning continuous concessions on our part to an insatiable power determined to pursue its world revolution by every available means."[4]

Many Americans darkly suspected that Green was anti-American, a suspicion that some US diplomats extended to Diefenbaker as well. Certainly Green had a deserved reputation for being pro-British, which in the context of Canadian politics could mean anti-American. He believed that Americans overstated their case, especially on East-West concerns, and relied excessively on the unquestioning loyalty of their allies. (Though he might not have known it, he agreed on these points with his predecessor, Lester Pearson.) Green did not always come down on the anti-American side of an issue and at times worked to moderate that tendency in his leader. In the summer of 1960, for example, when a worried and pessimistic Diefenbaker let the Americans know that Canadian-American relations were in a state of crisis, Green worked hard to persuade them that his chief was exaggerating.[5]

In tranquil times, Diefenbaker's diplomatic flaws need not have had much effect. Unluckily, his time in office demanded just the kind of creative diplomacy that came so easily and naturally to Pearson but not to him. Unluckily too, his style of government meant that his foreign ministers could not compensate for him. Ironically, Diefenbaker's first foreign policy crisis – the first of many – involved what most Canadians expected would be one of his greatest strengths, Canadian relations with Great Britain.

THE COMMONWEALTH FIASCO

British policy looked outward – out from Great Britain, to be sure, but out from Europe, where the British insisted on a separate mission and a distinctive destiny, apart from those of the Continent. If Britain did not face east, across the English Channel, then logically and necessarily it must face west, across the Atlantic, and beyond the Atlantic to the "white dominions," Canada, Australia, and New Zealand. In this English-speaking, transatlantic world, the United States took up most of the psychic and economic space, but there was still room for Canada, among others.[6]

Unfortunately for the British, the Americans and – more reflectively and more reluctantly – the Canadians did not consider that North America was a true alternative
to Europe in Britain's future. Canadian trade with Great Britain remained significant,
but proportionately and even absolutely it was not what it had once been. In 1957
Canada exported $727 million worth of goods to Great Britain, but $2.9 billion to the
United States. That same year, Canada had imports of $509 million from Great Britain,
and $3.9 billion from the United States.[7]

There figures were subject to several interpretations, which could lead to different
conclusions. The St Laurent government, along with most economists, believed that the
British were not exporting to Canada because they could not. Several trade-promotion
programs in the 1950s, either incomplete successes or outright failures, were a mute
testament to that reality. Yet there were those who believed, as late as 1957, that trade
with Great Britain could still be revived to its late, glorious levels. John Diefenbaker,
instinctively if not intellectually, was among that number.

Returning from his first Commonwealth conference in June 1957, just after taking
office, Diefenbaker let slip to a reporter that he thought Canada should strengthen its
British ties. It should do so by transferring 15 percent of its trade from the United States
to Great Britain. The remark caused a minor sensation at the time, and presumably it
was a lesson to the new prime minister that even the most casual remarks could have
policy implications. In later years Diefenbaker either pretended that he had not said it
or that it was a mere slip of the tongue with no serious repercussions. That was not the
case. Diefenbaker's loose tongue played to an attentive British audience. The British
government in 1957 faced a crisis in its own trade policy, and more broadly in its strategic situation. The British sat on the edge of a newly integrating Europe. Should they
join six other Western European countries in creating a Common Market, or should
they remain outside, where Britain had traditionally been and where many, probably
most, Britons believed they should stay?

The question was partly about self-image. Possessing, as they had for 150 years, the
largest economy and highest standard of living in Europe, the British took comfort in
the fact that they were not like other Europeans. Their real economic and social problems were at home, in the maldistribution of wealth and privilege, or so British politicians believed. At the same time, Britain's real foreign policy interests lay in a larger,
"Atlantic," community. The defence of Western Europe depended not so much on any
aggregation of Europeans as it did on the Americans, and by extension the Canadians,
who had come to Britain's aid before and would again if the issue ever arose. That was
the lesson of the Second World War, and it would be the pattern for a Third, if that ever
occurred.[8]

Links to the Commonwealth were far from insignificant. Trade with Australia and
New Zealand alone was more valuable in the early 1950s than trade with France,

Germany, the Benelux countries, and Italy combined.[9] The British resisted appeals from continental European governments, backed by pressure from the United States, to throw their energies and influence into constructing a united Europe by submerging the economic and political barriers that had for so long divided the continent. The British reasoned that joining Europe would require abandoning or reducing their overseas ties. They remembered that these ties, which were still substantial, had stood them in good stead in the Second World War.

Despite the relative decline of Britain's economic power, Canada still had an important interest in existing trading patterns with Great Britain. Canada exported paper, apples, wheat, and cheese to Great Britain, all under Commonwealth (formerly Imperial) Preference. If Great Britain joined Europe, these exports would be at risk. As time would show, such fears were far from irrational, for European protectionism, especially in agricultural products, was a fearsome thing. Nevertheless, on balance, informed Canadians cautiously agreed with informed Americans in what generally constituted the official line: the stability of Europe, the strength of NATO, the interest of the West in general, suggested that the British should unite with the other European countries while it could. As the outgoing Canadian defence minister had bleakly told his Liberal colleagues in May 1957, "The impression which some [in Britain] would wish to convey was that the UK remained an independent world power but this was no longer economically or physically possible."[10]

The British government did not see any urgency in dealing with these problems, to the extent that it even recognized them to be problems. It abstained from early versions of European unification – for example, the European Coal and Steel Community, negotiated in 1950. Surely without British participation the scheme would fail, or lead to Franco-German disharmony. So the British civil service argued, and the Attlee government, then in its last stages, could not disagree.[11] The British also remained aloof from negotiations for a customs union, as permitted under the GATT, among six Western European countries – West Germany, France, Belgium, the Netherlands, Luxembourg, and Italy. British ambassadors plausibly reported that these countries could not hope to reach agreement, or, if they did, that their local parliaments would toss out any treaty. When in March 1957 the six signed the Treaty of Rome, establishing a Common Market among themselves with tariff reductions starting in January 1958, the British were surprised and then alarmed. The treaty established a customs union, but it did not stop there: it made possible a high degree of economic integration among the partners. That fact alone made the European Common Market obnoxious to the British, who valued their own autonomy so highly that placing it in any common jurisdiction was, at the time, practically unthinkable.

The British hoped to retrieve the situation by establishing an inclusive European Free Trade Area (EFTA), of which the future Common Market would be a member.[12]

This ploy – taking advantage of lower tariffs without assuming any of the costs – did not appeal to the Common Market Six. The British were shut out and as a consequence were forced to look for alternatives.

The final details of the Treaty of Rome also caught the Canadian government by surprise. Canadians, Escott Reid later wrote, had subscribed to "the notion that a Free Trade area would weaken protection." Only later did they discover that such an area could be "in itself protectionist and restrictionist."[13] The trade minister, C.D. Howe, told the St Laurent Cabinet in April 1957 that the news was not as good as he might have hoped. Although Canada favoured European unity for economic and political reasons, and therefore found its achievement encouraging, the protectionist thread in the Treaty of Rome was worrying: "A number of important provisions ... appeared more damaging to trade than had been expected."[14]

At this point the government changed, and Diefenbaker, knowing little of the context of British policy, made his statement on trade. He was understandably surprised when, in the fall, London responded that it would be happy to negotiate a bilateral free trade area with Canada. Such an agreement – free trade – was compatible with the GATT. For the British government, caught short in its European policy, the Diefenbaker proposal seemed to be an oasis in the middle of a parched desert. The British Cabinet welcomed "the initiative by the Government of Canada," estimated a gain in trade of $625 million, and dispatched emissaries to Ottawa.[15]

The issue was complicated by the Canadian government's desire to host a Commonwealth Economic Conference. The British reluctantly agreed, hoping to please the Canadians, although they thought its agenda thin and its likely results meagre. (They were right, except on the all-important publicity front, where Diefenbaker hoped to impress domestic Canadian opinion.) In early September British ministers travelled to Ottawa and formally presented a proposal for a free trade area. Diefenbaker, by now thoroughly alarmed at what he had stirred up, protested that it was too much too soon. The Cabinet, equally perturbed, pondered how it might reject the offer without seeming anti-British; meanwhile ministers and their closest advisers held the matter in deepest secrecy.

The Commonwealth Economic Conference was duly held at Mont Tremblant, Quebec, and was pronounced a brilliant success by its Canadian hosts. The only problem was that the British openly referred to the free trade proposition, causing some embarrassment to Diefenbaker. Free trade with Britain was a major policy change, which Diefenbaker's political plans did not include. Those plans centred on calling another election, and soon, to give his government a secure parliamentary majority. He did not wish to awaken the demons of protectionism in Canada, especially when the protectionists included his firmest supporters in the business community.[16] He quickly moved to quash the furtherance of this embarrassing and politically costly development. Free trade with Great Britain could not be contemplated – at least not prudently contemplated, his advisers told him. Yet to deal with the subject openly would lead to damaging criticism and might even indicate that the prime minister was not fully in command of his brief or, worse still, his tongue. In top-secret talks with the British chancellor of the Exchequer, the Canadian government rejected any possibility of free trade. Outwardly the government maintained that nothing had happened. Canadian officials at home or abroad who wanted information had to learn the facts from their British colleagues, or from the Americans.[17]

Appearance was all. Diefenbaker planned to hold another election as soon as the time was right. He wanted to show the electorate, as one of his ministers later recalled, that he was "a combination of God, Moses, de Gaulle, Churchill, Napoleon, and a few others." The witticism originated with Quebec premier Maurice Duplessis, a Diefenbaker supporter, who added, "This combination usually wins votes."[18] The impression made on the British was secondary.[19] Their concerns were not Diefenbaker's, or Canada's.

Diefenbaker called his election for 31 March 1958, and he got his majority. "Dief" was now "the Chief." The Liberals, under their new leader, Lester B. Pearson, were reduced to 48 seats in the House of Commons, compared to Diefenbaker's 208. It should have been a happy conclusion for Diefenbaker. Pearson had won the Nobel Prize, but Diefenbaker was prime minister. But it was not enough. Pearson's prize gnawed at the Chief's spirit, reminding him that, electoral landslide or no, the Liberals remained a viable alternative to his government.

The British swallowed their disappointment with Canada, at least in public. The pageant of Commonwealth tours and conferences carried on, punctuated by royal visits in 1957, 1959, and 1961. Prime Minister Macmillan was faithful to the rituals established by previous British heads of government, touching down in Ottawa before or after his trips to Washington. Ottawa continued to be a major diplomatic post for the British, as London was for the Canadians.[20]

There were other disappointments in the relationship between the two countries. One involved the versatile Canadian supersonic fighter, the Avro Arrow, the CF-105. Avro, properly the A.V. Roe Company, was a subsidiary of a British conglomerate, Hawker Siddeley. The Liberal government had fostered Avro to help maintain an independent Canadian aircraft industry, with its own design and research capabilities. Ottawa hoped its British connection would furnish not merely a technological payoff but a line to British sales. Unfortunately the British had their own high-tech garden to cultivate and no money to spend on non-British production. Commonwealth or not, Canada could not jump the queue for scarce British defence funding. Diefenbaker turned to the United States to find orders for the Arrow, and there too he was refused. The Arrow proved to be more than Canada could afford, and had to be cancelled in February 1959. Unlike free trade, the demise of the Arrow was a public affair, accompanied by the loss of 14,000 jobs, and Diefenbaker reaped massive adverse publicity.

The Arrow decision was good public policy, badly managed. Its effect on Diefenbaker was to reinforce his tendencies, already pronounced, towards secrecy and concealment. Even worse, he veered into obfuscation and postponement whenever he scented the possibility of controversy. And at a minimum, the Arrow did nothing to help Anglo-Canadian industrial or economic connections.

The same was true of atomic energy, where in the mid-1950s the government's nuclear arm, Atomic Energy of Canada Limited, attempted to join forces with its British counterpart to formulate a common reactor design. Failing that, the Canadians hoped to persuade Britain's electrical production monopoly, a government organ, to buy Canada's own heavy water reactor, then in the prototype stage. That could not be, the British government decided. A British Crown company must show faith in local design, which was paid for by the British taxpayer. Although the head of the British electrical utility preferred the Canadian type of reactor, he did what he was told.

The final negotiation on Canadian reactor sales occurred in 1961-1962. It was not a good year for Anglo-Canadian relations. Two issues bedevilled the Macmillan and Diefenbaker governments that year: South Africa, and Great Britain's application to join the European Common Market. Neither government covered itself with glory in these two areas, and, where the Common Market was concerned, each suffered political damage as the result of the actions of the other. Yet of the two problems it was probably South Africa that did most to antagonize the British with the Canadian government. Unlike Suez in 1956, the damage was lasting.

Canada maintained distant but vaguely friendly relations with South Africa. Within the Commonwealth before the Second World War, the two countries often found themselves on the same side, in opposition to Great Britain's remaining imperial pretensions. During the two world wars, South Africa fought alongside the Commonwealth and the allies, and during the Second World War Canada established diplomatic relations with its distant partner.

South African domestic politics were the politics of race. There were white, black, and coloured – that is, neither black nor European – and there were two varieties of white, English speaking and Afrikaans speaking.[21] English speakers and Afrikaners broadly agreed on the politics of white supremacy, and their two major political parties supported a segregationist social system. The party in power after 1948, the Nationalists, was especially rigorous in its commitment to "apartheid" – literally, "apartness" for the races. Until 1960 South Africa was buffered by the existence of large colonial empires to the north, British, French, Belgian, and Portuguese. But in the space of four years, 1959-1962, the British, French, and Belgians packed up, and suddenly most of Africa was governed by black majority rule. Harold Macmillan came to Cape Town to tell the (white) South African parliament that "the winds of change" were blowing through the continent. Eventually they would blow clear down to South Africa.

The South African government prepared to meet the winds of change by implementing a traditional Afrikaner obsession: South Africa would rid itself of the British monarchy and become a republic, to take effect on 31 May 1961. This was narrowly approved in a plebiscite among the white population. At the same time South Africa wished to remain within the Commonwealth and to maintain a defence connection with Great Britain. To remain within the Commonwealth required the approval of the other members, because of South Africa's changed governmental system.

The government of India made it plain that it would not approve South Africa's application for readmission. Other Commonwealth countries in Africa and Asia took a similar line. The British government, mindful of large British investments and trading interests, and wanting to preserve its defence connection with South Africa, favoured that country's readmission. Australia and New Zealand had no trouble following the British lead. The issue would be decided at a meeting of Commonwealth prime ministers in London in March 1961. Where would Canada stand?

John Diefenbaker was initially ambivalent. He abhorred apartheid, but he hoped that the South African government could be induced to make concessions, however nominal, that would point in the right direction. When the South African government hardened its position, Diefenbaker hardened his. Warned that Diefenbaker was slipping into opposition, British Prime Minister Macmillan sent a lengthy telegram and then phoned, but failed to move him. Macmillan privately characterized Diefenbaker's position as "holier than thou," suggesting a preference for moralism over common sense. Because it was Britain that had large interests at stake, it should be the British who called the tune over South Africa, or so Macmillan believed.

But it was the British prime minister who refused to recognize the consequences of his actions. If South Africa remained in the Commonwealth, with British support, it could lead to the departure of some, possibly all, African and Asian members. Under such circumstances, the Commonwealth would either become a whites-only club, impossible to sustain, or fall apart. So Diefenbaker was advised by his most senior civil servant, the clerk of the Privy Council, Robert Bryce. Still, Diefenbaker was torn: the professional diplomats in External Affairs advised caution, and this time he weighed their advice carefully. Only during the conference, after much hesitation and a survey of Canadian editorial opinion, did Diefenbaker take a stronger line. In discussions with the other prime ministers, he held out for a condemnation of apartheid, while appealing for concessions from the South African prime minister. The latter, however, was uncooperative, and on the third day of the conference he withdrew South Africa's application for Commonwealth membership.

Diefenbaker was the only one of the white prime ministers to take an unequivocal stand against apartheid and to speak for a Commonwealth that refused to tolerate racial discrimination. His position was not pivotal, but it was important in preventing a split in the prime ministers' meeting between old and newer Commonwealth members, and between whites and non-whites. The Commonwealth might not immediately have perished immediately had South Africa not been expelled, but it would not have lingered long.

The British were used to fractious Commonwealth meetings and, in the past, had forgiven their ambiguous and sometimes disappointing results. The Commonwealth's preservation strengthened rather than detracted from Great Britain's larger interests. But the South African dispute, coupled with another, simultaneous quarrel, marked the beginning of a new phase in Great Britain's relations with its former empire, one that would eventually empty the Commonwealth of most of its significance.

The other quarrel of 1961 involved Prime Minister Macmillan's belated and reluctant decision to apply for British membership in the Common Market. He began planning the event in mid-1960, moving pro-European ministers into key posts, including the position of Commonwealth secretary.[22] After a trip to Washington and Ottawa in April 1961, Macmillan told his Cabinet that his "discussions had strengthened his view that far-reaching decisions would have to be taken soon about the United Kingdom's relations with Europe." These decisions would almost inevitably damage the "economic interests" of various Commonwealth countries, notably Canada.[23] To calm the waters, the Commonwealth secretary, Duncan Sandys, went on a tour of Commonwealth capitals. In July 1961 he arrived in Ottawa, preceded by dire warnings from the Australians about the hypocrisy, if not outright untruthfulness, of British reassurances.

As with the South African question, Canada's official position was at first hesitant. True, Canadian trade with Great Britain was at risk, and that was no small matter. On the other hand, it was politically unsafe to seem to block a necessary and possibly inevitable British policy simply out of economic self-interest. To put it another way, Canadian trade with Great Britain, though large, was not large enough to justify bringing on a crisis, and in any case many informed Canadians believed a united Europe to be desirable. Progressive Conservatives were frequently pro-British: to oppose the British government on a matter close to its heart might offend many of Diefenbaker's supporters.

Sandys did not convince his Canadian counterparts that they should joyfully accept the British overture to the Common Market. He pointed out that it was only an approach, a prelude to a negotiation, designed to see whether the European terms were good enough. These terms would have to include consideration for the Commonwealth and its trading privileges, or Macmillan could hardly consider proceeding. He concluded by asking the Canadians "not to be too hard on us if we do what you think we should not do."

His Canadian listeners took all this with many grains of salt. The external affairs minister, Howard Green, told the Cabinet that British admission to the Common

Market would be "simply disastrous for Canada." The trade minister, George Hees, who seems to have had only a nodding acquaintance with recent history, suggested that perhaps Canada should abort the application by offering "an alternative trade deal."[24] The best the Cabinet could manage was to resolve to wait and see, and hope that European terms would be so repugnant that the British would recoil from the negotiations.

The Diefenbaker government did not feel that it occupied a strong position over trade – or anything else, for that matter. Public opinion polls had turned sour: the government fell behind the opposition Liberals in 1960 and never again pulled ahead. Despite its massive parliamentary majority, the Diefenbaker government gave every sign of insecurity, and insecurity led to hesitation, a frantic testing of popular waters before any serious decision could be taken. Although the Diefenbaker Cabinet was essentially opposed to the British application, it never felt it had the strength to push its opposition. In September 1961, just before leaving for a Commonwealth economic conference in Accra, Ghana, George Hees worried to his colleagues that the public was "concerned about the government's apparently negative attitude."[25] Safely out of Canada, Hees and his colleague Finance Minister Donald Fleming indulged in some plain speaking at Accra. The British application, they argued, would damage the Commonwealth politically and sap the economic interests of its members. While Canada and other Commonwealth nations could not prevent the British government from going ahead, Hees and Fleming argued, the consequences would be dire and that fact should be made clear.

The Canadian position was unwelcome to the British delegates to Accra. They lost no time in briefing the press on how unhelpful and obstructive the Canadians were being. Directly through Canadian correspondents, and indirectly through British press reports, Canadian newspaper readers were told that Canada was being unhelpful to its senior Commonwealth partner. The effect may be gauged by a Cabinet discussion on 14 September, when Justice Minister Davie Fulton told his colleagues that the public saw Canada's position as "negative and defeatist." With Diefenbaker (as well as Hees and Fleming) absent, the Cabinet consensus was that Canada should accept British entry into the Common Market "as gracefully as possible," despite its previous, strongly expressed opposition.[26]

By this point opinion at home had congealed against Diefenbaker's position on British entry. Government ministers reflected ruefully that opinion was so pro-British that many Canadians believed that anything Britain did – including joining the Common Market – must be right. With an election in 1962 drawing closer, official Canadian statements became more temperate. Meanwhile, British negotiators at the Common Market headquarters in Brussels abandoned position after position, first on manufactured goods and then on agricultural products. British attempts to negotiate exceptions and long transitions for Commonwealth preferences were contemptuously rejected. (Concessions were made for kangaroo meat and frozen rabbits.) It became clear that the French in particular were attempting to raise as many barriers to British admission as possible; the British response was to meet each new obstacle with a new concession. When Macmillan again visited Ottawa in the spring of 1962, he got a cool reception. It was all the worse that in Washington the British prime minister had harvested good opinions of his course of action; by this point in the life of the Diefenbaker government, that was no recommendation.[27]

Diefenbaker complained about the course of the negotiations at a Commonwealth conference in London in September 1962. He played to residual British sentiment for the Commonwealth, and fears of Europe, and he undoubtedly caused some embarrassment for British ministers as they strove to pretend that Commonwealth economic interests and the Commonwealth as a political institution were not being damaged. Tight-lipped in public, members of the Macmillan government privately portrayed Diefenbaker as a loose-tongued "mountebank," seriously "muddled" and – by extension – unbalanced.[28] As Canadian reporters repeated their private comments without attribution, it is possible that the British contributed in a serious and effective way to the decline of Diefenbaker's reputation in Canada, at a time when he was already floundering politically.

Ottawa was aware of the French objections to British membership, which in a roundabout way were the same as Canada's. The French feared British entry and believed that the British, once admitted, would undermine French predominance in the Common Market; the Canadians feared British entry would mean a turning away from the Commonwealth and North America. Both governments were quite possibly right in their conclusions, but unlike Diefenbaker French president Charles de Gaulle could do something. On 29 January 1963 he announced that France would veto British admission to the Common Market.

Through the French action, the Commonwealth as an economic association got a reprieve. The British had to wait until after de Gaulle's death to be admitted to the European Common Market, in January 1973. Commonwealth preferences remained in place, though, with the diminishing importance of British trade, they were of steadily less significance to Canada. Despite the rebuff they had received from the Common Market, successive British governments never again took the Commonwealth as a serious alternative to Europe.

The Diefenbaker government sustained serious political damage at home because of its policy on British membership in the Common Market. It managed to offend two contradictory streams of Canadian sentiment: those that for reasons of tradition or other sentiment were strongly pro-British and those that maintained that for Britain, and for Canada, the realistic choice was to accept the economic and political inevitability of a declining Britain becoming part of a rising Europe. Those who valued the Commonwealth highly and those who valued it not at all were united against the Diefenbaker government's policy.

If Diefenbaker was once again politically unfortunate, does it follow that his government was mistaken to object to British policy? On the contrary: Canadian fears of the consequences of British membership – the devaluation of the Commonwealth and damage to Canadian economic interests – were well founded. Nor were the Canadians the only ones to object: in Commonwealth meetings the Canadians were far from alone. If Canadian policy was in some respects lacking, was British policy any better? Macmillan too confronted pro-Commonwealth sentiment in Britain (60 percent of the electorate according to some polls), and he faced it with evasion and duplicity – the same tools he deployed with his Commonwealth partners. The hollowness of his protestations that he would not proceed unless Commonwealth interests – British interests too – were safeguarded was an unfailing source of political weakness at home. Diefenbaker played to that weakness. When British ministers whispered that Diefenbaker was "muddled," they ignored the futility and contradictions of their own policy.

Diefenbaker became a political casualty in no small measure because of public disapproval of his policy on Britain and the Common Market. In retrospect historians have concentrated on his more dramatic disputes with the Americans as a prime cause of his unpopularity and political collapse in the spring of 1963, but the British factor should not be ignored. Arguably the British were more effective, more persistent, than the Americans in stimulating domestic dissatisfaction with Canada's prime minister.[29]

Diefenbaker was not the only political casualty of 1963. Worn out and discredited, Harold Macmillan resigned in October. His government, afflicted by scandals and confounded by its failure to achieve success in the Brussels negotiations – despite its ready sacrifice of its own principles and others' interests – could no longer pretend to have any answers to the question of Britain's future. Macmillan remained for many years on the fringes of politics, yesterday's man stoking yesterday's issues with his lengthy memoirs. In this he provided a model for Diefenbaker.

IT IS TEMPTING TO SUGGEST THAT ANGLO-CANADIAN RELATIONS never recovered from John Diefenbaker. It would be truer to say that they never recovered from the period 1957-1963. The issues placed before the politicians of the day overwhelmed the institutions – the Commonwealth being a prime example – that once could have dealt with them.

The Commonwealth enjoyed a renaissance in Canadian and British opinion in the 1950s. It did so for a number of reasons. First and probably most important, Great Britain was still regarded, and regarded itself, as a major power. Second and related to the first point, Great Britain was still the leading European power. Germany had not recovered sufficiently, while France, until de Gaulle came to power in 1958, accepted an automatic junior partnership with the British, as it had since the 1920s. Great Britain's economy was larger and its standard of living higher than those of other European countries.

The Commonwealth, trading on the recent memories of the war, and relying on the still significant economic links that bound its members together, mistook its real significance. It had been designed as a way station on the road from colonial status to independence. It preserved what were once real and binding associations within a looser framework. It replaced reality with symbolism. Diefenbaker accepted the symbols, but he, like many other Canadians of his generation, refused to believe that they represented a comforting past rather than an indefinite future. With the British application to join the Common Market in 1961, the economic aspects of the Commonwealth automatically became a residual question, a remnant of the past awaiting closure rather than a figment of the future.

In his approach to the South African question, Diefenbaker unwittingly furnished a clear road map of the Commonwealth's future direction. The South African issue, as he saw it, was pre-eminently symbolic. The retention of an apartheid South Africa in the Commonwealth roused memories of the less desirable aspects of colonialism, which the organization had been designed to bury. It threatened to undermine the Commonwealth's pretensions to universal values and universal scope. It might have alienated the Commonwealth's "South" – the underdeveloped former colonies – by drawing a line around the white or white-dominated "dominions."

Yet the departure of South Africa from the Commonwealth did not end the South African issue at Commonwealth meetings. Supplemented by the problems of another African ex-colony, Rhodesia (now Zimbabwe), it dominated Commonwealth meetings from the 1960s to the 1990s. In such meetings Canada usually took the "moral" position, arguing in the name of Commonwealth unity for the condemnation of racial discrimination. As a consequence, the British government repeatedly found itself in an uncomfortable minority. As the British saw it, they had real interests, economic and military, where the Commonwealth majority had only sentiments. Increasingly, they felt trapped in an institution they had once dominated, unable to reign and unable to master a desperately irritating situation. Later British prime ministers, Labour and Conservative, for the most part found the Commonwealth an irritation, and by the 1980s there were suggestions that British interests and membership in the Commonwealth were incompatible. Nigel Lawson, British chancellor of the Exchequer in the 1980s, referred in his memoirs to "the unpleasant and acrimonious spirit that had become customary at Commonwealth gatherings," a sentiment that many of his colleagues from the 1960s on seem to have shared. Yet even the combative British Conservative government in which he served proved unwilling and unable to sever the link that bound Great Britain to the decaying postcolonial symbol.[30]

Canada did not cause the conflicts between Great Britain and its former colonies. Nor was moralism in international politics a peculiarly Canadian tool. British governments, like other democratic administrations, found the use of morality or sentiment directed against them a difficult problem because it so easily resonated with their own population. When Diefenbaker turned the issue of British adhesion to Europe into the assertion that Britain was repudiating its traditions, he expressed the views of a very large number of Britons – perhaps even the majority – as Macmillan was uncomfortably aware. When he questioned whether a morally unworthy government such as South Africa's should be permitted to remain in a Commonwealth that boasted of its racial tolerance, he appealed to many of Macmillan's own subjects and undermined the British prime minister where it hurt – at home. And Macmillan returned the compliment. Yet the difficulties in Anglo-Canadian relations were more than merely personal. The British were, in the early 1960s, finally facing up to the dwindling of their power. Canada meant a lot to a country trying to shore up its international position by drawing on the sentiments and the interests of its traditional friends. Canada meant less to a country concentrating its resources and its interests on shoring up its position in Europe.

The shape of the transatlantic world was changing. It had been changing since the failure of the Anglo-French Suez expedition in 1956. That event had caused the French to think seriously about their connections with the English-speaking world, encouraging them in the path of European economic and political integration. The British became less important to the French, and the Germans more important. British economic weakness did the rest.

The Americans remained central. It was American policy to encourage European economic union and political rapprochement. Through the Treaty of Rome and the European Common Market, they got what they wanted. There was a price to pay, even for the United States, for the Common Market that emerged was highly protectionist, especially on agricultural products. There were growing problems with the American balance of payments, caused by a trade deficit and an outflow of American investment to Canada and Europe, problems that were not alleviated when in 1958 most European currencies were made convertible.[31] But the United States in the early 1960s was boundlessly prosperous, and very little of that prosperity flowed from international trade.

Canada was more affected, and less fortunate. In the climate of the 1960s, Canadians too would have to consider how their international connections were being reshaped. The decline of Great Britain removed a prop from Canada's sense of psychological security, as the American ambassador, Livingston Merchant, perceptively noted in 1962. "A significant fraction of the current Canadian malaise can be attributed to the decline in the power position of Great Britain, both in the world at large and vis-à-vis the United States. This phenomenon is more felt or sensed by Canadians than intellec-tually understood. It has the effect, however, of increasing the uneasy Canadian feeling that it is almost irretrievably exposed to the friendly embrace of the United States with no powerful mother country nearby to act as protector and refuge."[32] The effect, in Merchant's opinion, would not be to make Canadians more pro-American.

It would be a new and in many respects less happy world. Its first direct effect, as Merchant foresaw, occurred between Canada and the United States.

9   NUCLEAR NIGHTMARES,
1957-1963

The election of John Diefenbaker and his Conservatives was thought to herald a new turn in relations with the United States, one where the government would cultivate respect for Canada's British heritage and thus distance itself from the Americans. Things did not quite turn out that way. On some issues Diefenbaker was closer to the Americans than the Liberals had been, while on others his government simply carried on where the Liberals had left off. After all, the basic context of foreign relations remained the same. The Cold War did not end, nor did the spectre of nuclear destruction. If anything, the Cold War and the nuclear menace intensified during Diefenbaker's term of office. These were developments for which he was poorly prepared and for which, it soon became apparent, he had no answers.

OUR AMERICAN COUSINS

Canada had no constitutional connection to the United States, as it had with Great Britain. But it had a shared history, a common accent, and close if not entirely compatible political traditions. Migration between Canada and the United States was a southward flow, carrying Canadians to Massachusetts or California or Kansas. In return, the Americans shared their books, magazines, music, movies, radio, and television, with Canadians – or at any rate with the English-speaking variety.[1] (Francophones were not indifferent, especially to the music, but even there they were differently affected.) New York styles were, after a lag, Toronto styles. American fashions – intellectual, social, or political – were, or soon became, Canadian fashions. The year Diefenbaker became prime minister, 1957, was one when many Canadians, willingly or not, listened to Elvis Presley and Pat Boone, drove very large American cars from American-style suburbs to their American-style jobs in large and often American-owned corporations. There was even an American term – popularized by a best-selling novel that was also made into a movie – to describe it: "The Man in the Gray Flannel Suit." The "Organization Man" wore the suit, and wandered around in a "Lonely Crowd."[2]

Many Americans were acquainted with Canada but few studied it. Every year tourists thronged across the border in search of the spartan tourism provided by Canadian woods and water. American airmen and sailors were stationed in Newfoundland and Labrador. Businessmen crossed and recrossed the frontier. What they found was familiar. But if Canada was familiar, it was largely invisible. There were infrequent references in the American press, usually friendly. American policy towards its northern neighbour was sometimes set by accident, as it had been under the farm surplus act that had devastated Canada's overseas wheat markets in the interest of subsidizing American farmers. Sometimes it was set deliberately, as when American officials considered the election of John Diefenbaker in 1957.

Given Diefenbaker's nationalist rhetoric and the Conservatives' traditional identification with Canada's business class, the US embassy predicted a drift away from both the GATT and liberalized trade. Ottawa would probably reject the country's dependence on the United States and attempt to cultivate Great Britain. On the other hand, there were friendly enough references to the United States in the Conservative platform, and recognition of its role as the leader of the Free World. Meeting the American ambassador, Livingston Merchant, on the day he was sworn in as prime minister, Diefenbaker gave only a hint of trouble, and that over the perennial question of wheat exports. But on such an auspicious day, all it took was a congratulatory message from President Eisenhower to raise the prime minister's spirits.[3]

Although the 1958 election campaign had "subtle anti-American overtones" when it touched on trade and investment, there was little the Americans could complain of in those areas, apart from Diefenbaker's foray into trade diversion to Britain in 1957-1958.[4] In an early meeting of the Canadian-American ministerial committee on economics and trade, the American secretary of state, John Foster Dulles, sarcastically referred to the trade-diversion scheme, remarking that the Canadians would soon learn who could afford to pay for their exports. Dulles was undiplomatic but he was right, as Diefenbaker's ministers already knew. When it came to investment and trade, the Diefenbaker government parked its rhetoric and did nothing to deviate from the general policy laid down by its Liberal predecessor.

In some cases Diefenbaker and his ministers were significantly less nationalistic than the Liberals had been. In the months before the 1957 election, the Liberals had resisted the final conclusion of an air defence agreement with the United States. The government's military advisers differed from its civilian advisers – the Department of External Affairs – on the necessary safeguards for Canadian autonomy in an inevitably lopsided defence arrangement. The military wanted as much defence as they could get, as soon as possible.[5] After Diefenbaker's first electoral victory, they immediately approached the new minister of national defence, General George Pearkes. In a long and distinguished career, Pearkes had never been known for subtlety or hesitation, and he enthusiastically pressed the case for an immediate agreement. Diefenbaker took his minister's advice and, since the prime minister was temporarily also minister of external affairs, that was that. Only later were the diplomats informed.

Without this defence agreement, Blair Fraser, a journalist close to the previous Liberal government, commented, "consultation was compulsory. With it, as Diefenbaker learned to his great resentment in the Cuba crisis of 1962, consultation became more or less optional."[6] There is no doubt that neither Diefenbaker nor Pearkes fully understood what he was doing, a fact that even Canada's chief of defence staff, General Charles Foulkes, later called "unfortunate." To Foulkes's surprise, the new arrangement was not even discussed in the Cabinet defence committee. There was no exchange of notes with the United States, nor did the Canadian Cabinet pass an order-in-council formalizing what had been agreed. Instead, there was a press release on 1 August 1957, stating that a new joint air defence command for North America was being established. Perhaps unwittingly, the statement set the grounds for future confusion by adding that the new organization "extend[ed] the mutual security objectives of the North Atlantic Treaty Organization to the air defense of the Canada-US region." That was, very strictly speaking, true. "Objectives" was a vague word, promising much and saying little. But the North American Air Defence Command (it acquired the name shortly after being created, and thereafter was known by the acronym NORAD) was not a part of NATO, and NATO was not consulted about its establishment. Although NATO theoretically covered the defence of North America, the United States did not want Europe to have a say in the defence of American soil. This was fine with the Europeans, who saw NATO as an arrangement for the defence of Europe only and did not want to pay for the defence of the rich North Americans. It is clear that Diefenbaker and possibly Pearkes did not understand the separation the Americans had drawn between NORAD and NATO. Consequently the purported "link" between the two would be trotted out by Diefenbaker time and again over the next six years.

The agreement was an easy target for the Liberals during the fall 1957 session of Parliament. In response Diefenbaker chose to emphasize NORAD's NATO connection. In the spring of 1958 the defence command was regularized by an exchange of notes with the United States. The notes stipulated that there would be "the fullest possible consultation" between the two governments, "such consultation [being] regularly and consistently undertaken."[7] The notes also coincided with the news that the US Strategic Air Command was putting its bombers on a fifteen-minute alert.

The Diefenbaker government took few other initiatives with regard to Canadian-American relations. Tariffs were raised slightly in 1959-1960 but not enough to break the liberalizing tariff pattern set by the Liberals since 1947. Defence problems were regulated to the Americans' satisfaction, even if the Canadian performance on the details left something to be desired. The Conservative government, once in office, toned down its rhetoric about American domination of the economy. Even the problem with wheat was dealt with, although not quite as the Americans had anticipated.

Failing effective action by the US government to curb surplus-wheat disposal, Canada had to find markets elsewhere. As so often, the solution came not from any large government initiative but from an enterprising commercial representative, in this case the Canadian trade commissioner in Hong Kong. Chinese agriculture was in chaos thanks to the policies of Mao Zedong's Communist government. In one of the most dreadful famines in modern history, scarcity and starvation stalked the land. The catastrophe was kept secret, though occasional reports of food shortages surfaced. No one knows how many died of hunger in China between 1959 and 1961: estimates range from fifteen million to thirty million, or between 2 and 4 percent of the total population. As British historian David Reynolds commented thirty-five years later, "the most chilling aspect of what was probably the worst famine of the twentieth century is how little we still know about it."[8]

To mitigate the situation – solving it was beyond their ability – the Chinese Communist government was ready to spend, and roughly half of its hard currency spending between 1961 and 1964 was on grain. The Diefenbaker government did not know how drastic the situation was, and most of what Canadians have written on the subject, then and since, has dwelt on the commercial and political acumen of the Canadian politicians and wheat salesmen who negotiated sales to China.[9] The sales were useful from the Canadian point of view, granted, but they were necessary from the Chinese side. Canada created neither the demand nor what were uniquely favourable conditions for supply: the United States refused to sell its wheat to the Communist Chinese. Canada had stepped into what was, for a time, a seller's market.

The sales were not without controversy. China was a Communist power, and a formidable one. Arguably, the Canadian sales were strengthening the Communist regime – although this was at a time when the extent of the awfulness of that regime's conduct towards its own citizens was unknown in the West. Some members of the Canadian Cabinet had their doubts about trading with Beijing, and Diefenbaker had to intervene on the side of sales. The Americans were mildly obstructive: a particular variety of American grain-handling equipment was necessary to handle the shipments, but the US government took this to be "trading with the enemy." Diefenbaker appealed to

President Kennedy, who in the interest of good Canadian-American relations released the equipment.

The sales were impressive. The Canadian Wheat Board announced in 1961 that by December 1963 it would sell 3 million tons of wheat and 600,000 tons of barley to the Chinese – a total of almost 128 million bushels of grain. Sales in fact totalled 425 million bushels, worth $425 million. It was raining money in the parched desert of western Canadian agriculture. Nor did Canada sell only to China. The Soviet Union, though it lacked a famine of the same dimensions as China's, was also an eager customer. Sales (mostly of wheat) to the Soviet Union bulged up from $3 million in 1962 to $150 million in 1963, and to $316 million in 1964. The price of wheat also rose from $1.60 to $2.19 a bushel. Purring with satisfaction, prairie wheat farmers voted Conservative for a generation.[10]

There is no doubt that Diefenbaker and his minister of agriculture, Alvin Hamilton, acted promptly and effectively when opportunity was presented to them. The opportunity was a human tragedy on a vast scale, however, little understood at the time: the collapse of Chinese (and later Soviet) agriculture. Communism as applied to the soil was one of the twentieth century's great political, economic, and social failures. It sapped the economies of the two principal Communist powers and required them to divert scarce foreign currency reserves for the purchase of foodstuffs. As far as Canada was concerned, this was an economic miracle as the Soviet Union and China became regular and reliable customers for Canadian grain.

Economic linkages to the Soviet bloc (the "Second World" as it came to be called) remained important for Canada after 1960. Ottawa's view of the Communists was dualistic: they remained the enemy, politically and militarily, but they were also good customers. They were not allowed to buy everything; military and other strategic goods were banned from export under COCOM, an agreement among the Western allies to avoid strengthening the Soviets and Chinese militarily.[11] The Diefenbaker government drew no broad conclusions from the experience, but there was a feeling that trade with the Soviet Union and China might in some way help in breaking down the Communist monolith.

Washington maintained a posture of steadfast indecision in the face of these developments. The Eisenhower administration disapproved of large-scale economic contacts with the Communists, believing that they would ultimately sap Western resolve. It was not against all sales to Communist countries; some such states, such as Poland, ought to be encouraged to diversify their contacts with the West, including through subsidized American wheat.[12] American firms were prohibited from sales of most items to Communist countries, a prohibition that applied also to American firms located abroad. In other words, domestic law in the United States had extraterritorial application. American companies resident in Canada (corporate citizens of Canada) could, on some points, be called on to answer to their home government. In that case, US investment in Canada did make a difference to Ottawa's jurisdiction.

The US government saw the dangers in this situation and usually acted to finesse the problem. The importance of American investment abroad was greater than minor exports from American subsidiaries in Canada to Communist countries. And so generally, but not invariably, Washington winked at the sale of trucks to China from Ford of Canada or the sale of grain "vacuators" (American-made but sold through a Canadian agent) to those same Chinese. Nevertheless the issue of extraterritorial jurisdiction emerged at times between Eisenhower and his successor Kennedy, on one side, and Diefenbaker on the other.

Canadian-American relations were further complicated by the emergence of a Communist state in the Americas. On 1 January 1959, after a rebellion lasting two and a half years, revolutionaries swept into the Cuban capital, Havana. The outgoing dictatorship had few friends, even in the Eisenhower administration, but the existing Cuban political and economic system was closely identified with American interests. The revolutionary leader, Fidel Castro, was a romantic figure, young and vigorous. At first the North American media took him to be a kind of latter-day Robin Hood, and he was given star treatment on a tour of the United States and Canada in April 1959. Diefenbaker at the last minute refused to see Castro, perhaps because the Cuban had already stimulated misgivings in Washington. (Castro was not technically the head of government in Cuba, so there was an unofficial quality to his tour, a loophole seized on by Diefenbaker.)[13]

Castro was soon launched on a collision course with the United States. It was easy for him to portray the Americans as complicit in the age-old corruption of Cuban society, and easy too to link cleansing that society with the reduction or expulsion of American interests. Castro's actions against American investment ranged from restriction and harassment to outright confiscation, while at the same time he increasingly favoured the Communist Party and persecuted its opponents. The American government, gazing across the Florida Straits, concluded that if Castro walked like a duck and quacked like a duck, he must be a duck. It was a style of reasoning that had been discredited by the excesses of McCarthyism some years earlier, but in this case it proved correct. Castro was by 1960 committed to a Communist path and seeking friends not in Washington but in Moscow. But the evil reputation of McCarthyism – accusing the innocent without adequate proof – acted to deflect, in some circles in the United States and also in Canada, the alarm that might once have been felt about Castro.[14]

The US government, in no doubt as to Castro's hostility, reacted by freezing Cuban assets and restricting and eventually banning trade with the new regime. The Eisenhower government sought support from its allies, only to discover that Canada had its own views on the matter. Canadians also had investments in Cuba but found they were not as much of a target as the American ones were. Equally, there was business to be done supplying parts and equipment that the Cubans could no longer buy from the United States.

The American government found it had a tough job selling the notion to its Canadian counterpart that Castro was a Communist menace.[15] Canadians disliked the idea of coercing the Cubans. There was even, in theory if not practice, a certain fellow feeling about American investment and the question of the rights of small nations. The US treasury secretary told the National Security Council, a Cabinet-level body, in July 1960 about his recent discussions with the Canadians. "The Canadians were unwilling to accept any view of Cuban developments except the view that it was simply an internal revolution," he said. "They felt that the US was preoccupied with communism. They stated they could not imperil the free right of their banking institutions and businesses to take up any slack that might be created by US economic sanctions. Altogether it was a very disturbing conversation."[16] Worse, the Canadians had "the presumption" to tell the Americans that action against Castro would create ill feeling in Latin America against the United States.[17]

Although it irritated important American officials, division on Cuba was not a major item in Canadian-American exchanges. The Americans placed the issue where it probably belonged, in the unfathomable basket of "Canadian nationalism," which was used in the period to explain any and all actions that Washington considered irrational or inexplicable. At the same time, the Eisenhower administration was aware that there might indeed be grounds for Canadian feelings of resentment or inferiority. These showed up most often in economic policy.

FOOD AND FUEL

Grain was not an item that figured much in north-south trade. The Americans had plenty of grain and were reasonably successful at excluding the Canadian product. The Eisenhower administration was especially adept at catering to the farm vote and even, in 1955, secured the exemption of its agricultural subsidy programs from the GATT. The Canadians protested and grumbled: at that point the Canadian government would have preferred some form of free trade in agriculture, although eventually the Canadians themselves devised and implemented far-reaching forms of agricultural protectionism. An opportunity was perhaps lost in 1955 to secure a freer flow of agricultural products, but with the Americans leading the way the trend was firmly set towards protectionism.[18] The pursuit of individual advantage and the separation of agricultural interests from general trade policy contributed to a failure to act where the two countries' agricultural interests in fact converged. Between 1958 and 1963 the European Common Market (increasingly known by its formal title, the European Economic Community) erected a system of agricultural subsidies and tariffs that walled off continental markets from most North American agricultural exports. The result, known as the Common Agricultural Policy (CAP), was sometimes bizarre and certainly excessive. European farmers generated what later became known as the Butter Mountain and the Wine Lake; the CAP might also have been titled the Money Pit, for the billions of francs and deutschmarks that were poured into it. But the compromises that had helped to create a stable political system in the countries of Western Europe rested or perhaps squatted atop millions of contented farmers. This was something that North American politicians could understand even if, in their better moments, they did not like it.[19]

Effectively, the European past, full of quarrels and wars and centred on a restless Germany, was traded for the European present, a self-seeking but peaceful and slow-moving European political economy of which Germany was an integrated and satisfied part, moving in tandem with France as the effective engine of the European Community. This was certainly preferable to the unbridled nationalism that had brought on the World Wars, as Canadians as well as Americans saw it. The realities of the Cold War, plus the memory of the World Wars, were constant factors in shaping Canada's trade policy to accept the concessions necessary to keep the European balance steady.

The Cold War raised its head again in petroleum policy. For the Canadians, two distinct energy supplies were in question. There was oil, which travelled in liquid form through pipelines and could be carried across oceans in tankers. And there was natural gas, which, not being liquid or solid, could not be carried in large quantities but could be piped east and west or north and south within continental North America. Petroleum exports were a relatively recent problem for Canada, which until major discoveries in Alberta in the late 1940s had always been short of this form of energy. The St Laurent government promoted energy security for Canada, through pipelines to central Canada and Vancouver and through the development of power-producing nuclear reactors. It simultaneously favoured sales to the United States, which would help to pay the costs of the pipelines. Such sales would also assist the balance of payments, which throughout the 1950s was in deficit on American trade. At a time when, every year, geologists brought news of new oil and gas fields, the supply of petroleum seemed infinite, as did the prospects for profit.

The international petroleum trade, as well as the domestic oil business in the United States, was dominated by the "Seven Sisters," large multinational oil companies, mostly headquartered in the United States. These companies had been notably successful in discovering oil abroad, especially in the Middle East – so much oil and so cheaply that the international "offshore" oil price was half what it was in the United States. Cheap oil might have been considered to be a bonanza to an industrial economy like the Americans', but to the domestic US oil industry and its political supporters it was a threat. It was a threat that demanded a creative and imaginative response, which they were happy to provide. Their reasoning began with the undoubted fact that the United States' abundant supply of petroleum was a fundamental asset, not just for that country but for the Western alliance as a whole. In 1946-1947 and again in 1956-1957, the United States with its abundant oil had come to the rescue of an energy-starved Europe.[20] It might be thought that this was because the Americans had greater oil reserves than anybody else, but that was not the case – Saudi Arabia alone had many times the United States' reserves. The Americans did have lots of oil, but just as important they had an industry primed to pump it out of the ground. That industry would be forced to close down if cheap foreign oil were allowed to trickle into American gas tanks. The security of the United States and the entire West would suffer without a steady flow between pump and profit. Thus national security demanded that more and more high-priced American oil should surge into American cars, homes, and industry. In any case, foreign suppliers were overseas, and enemy naval action could mean that what they sent might never arrive.

In the 1950s there seemed to be lots of undiscovered oil, or so the geologists said. In 1960, however, there was a change: that year, for the first time, more oil was pumped than was discovered. American oil reserves went down, even as national security demanded that more and more American oil be expended. Because Congress was dominated by politicians from the main oil-producing states – Texas, Oklahoma, and Louisiana – and their allies, American petroleum policy rolled along just as it always had. Some members of the administration knew that depletion of American reserves actually added to American insecurity, but for the most part they prudently kept their mouths shut.

Where did Canada fit in this picture? Mitchell Sharp, who dealt with the question first as deputy minister of trade and commerce, until 1958, and later as a senior minister in the Liberal governments of the 1960s, once supplied a synopsis in a radio interview: "On petroleum, there was a very curious sequence of events. The Americans had a policy of limiting the imports of petroleum into the United States, in order to protect the domestic industry. However," Sharp added, "because of the very special relationship that existed between Canada and the United States there was an overland exemption applying to Canada, an exemption from these controls, these direct controls ... [There] was an understanding that we would restrain our exports of petroleum so as not to cause problems in the United States, because of the exemption granted to Canada."

Was this exemption typical of a "special relationship" between Canada and the United States? The answer appears, unhelpfully, to be both "yes" and "no." In a general sense, the answer was "yes." "Canadian-United States relations were the same as those you enjoy with the fellow next door," in the view of the economics counsellor at the US embassy in Ottawa. "For the most part you get along great, except that maybe you differ over whether he or you ought to mow that strip of weeds between your two properties."[21]

The United States had interests in Canada, and these were best safeguarded by accommodating the Canadians, if that could be done without too much political cost. President Eisenhower, with an eye to stabilizing and improving Canadian-American relations, exempted Canada from American petroleum import quotas. (Canada's perennial trade deficit with the United States was a factor in American decision making, then and later.) Eisenhower's action vastly irritated another major oil supplier, Venezuela, whose oil minister shortly began negotiations that led to the formation of an oil producers' group, the Organization of Petroleum Exporting Countries, better known as OPEC.[22] Despite promises to contain Canadian oil imports to the United States, they surged under the American exemption, further enraging the Venezuelans, who were only partly mollified by the explanation – proffered by Eisenhower's successor, Kennedy – that the Americans were really shoring up Venezuelan exports to *Canada*. That was because, as the historian Tammy Nemeth has shown, Eisenhower traded off Canadian access to American markets for a promise not to build an oil pipeline as far as Montreal, thus preserving eastern Canada as a market for overseas suppliers.[23]

Nuclear Dilemmas: The Berlin Crisis and the Nuclear Arms Race

Two spectacular foreign policy issues dominated the news at the end of the 1950s: Berlin, and with it Germany and the balance of force in Europe; and Cuba, the first Latin American country to stray out of the orbit of the United States and into that of the Soviet Union. In both cases the Soviet Union boldly tested the status quo, to the potential disadvantage of the West. As the Soviet leadership discovered, boldness was not precisely its own reward.

The danger of the situation in Berlin and Cuba lay in the development of nuclear weapons in the 1950s and the expansion of their means of delivery. The three atomic powers of the 1950s, the United States, the Soviet Union, and Great Britain, competed in the size and fearsomeness of their weaponry, believing that they were thereby adding to their military strength and international standing. NATO took the lead, deploying the growing American nuclear arsenal as soon as it became available.[24] But nuclear weapons turned out to be a double-edged sword, and it would become apparent that their growing size and number were not necessarily a military advantage.

At the time Diefenbaker took office, the Western allies still depended on the number and ingenuity of their nuclear weapons (mostly American but some British) to make up the difference between the size of their armies and those of the Soviet Union. The 1950s saw the development of the hydrogen bomb, which was much more destructive than the atomic bombs that had been dropped in Japan, but because both sides had the weapon it could hardly constitute a decisive advance.

Nuclear weapons had been made smaller as well as larger, ready for tactical use on the battlefield, under the control of local commanders – once the signal to use them had been given by the proper authorities in Washington. It seemed neat and logical – "small" nuclear weapons on a limited battlefield need not lead to larger weapons that would devastate whole countries and continents. The peoples of the West relied on the wisdom and sophistication of their strategists to know just when and how to apply these "limited" weapons in such a way as to lead to the defeat of the armies of the Warsaw Pact, the Soviets' military alliance with their East European satellites. Some strategists apparently believed a war fought with nuclear weapons feasible; others, evidently including Eisenhower and after him Kennedy, did not. Increasingly, it seemed, the public took the latter view. In the year Diefenbaker was elected prime minister, an Anglo-Australian novelist, Nevil Shute, published *On the Beach*, about the last stages of a nuclear war, in which a radioactive cloud slowly but inexorably extinguished all remaining life on earth. In book form or later as a popular movie, *On the Beach* told audiences in the West – there was no question of its being shown in the Communist bloc – that nuclear weapons were likely to destroy the societies they were designed to protect.[25] Other films, plays, and books argued the same point.

The spread of opposition to the use of nuclear arms occasionally distressed the officials guarding the nuclear secret, who understood that the deterrent factor of nuclear weapons depended on the belief that they could reasonably be used. If public faith in nuclear bombs were undermined, the defence of the West might crumble. In 1962 the Canadian Broadcasting Corporation televised British author Marghanita Laski's play *The Offshore Island*, in which the surviving but irradiated inhabitants of the British Isles are compulsorily sterilized by a humane but inflexible American officer to prevent genetic defects in what is left of humanity after a nuclear war.[26] Perturbed, the American ambassador moved to protest the play and its motivation – which only confirmed the play's message in the eyes of many of its viewers. That audience was not large – the CBC's serious drama did not appeal to most Canadians – but it was well educated and, likely, influential. Up to this point the Cold War had largely smothered the attractions of pacifism in Canada; nuclear fear helped revive them.[27] This fear was further fanned by the BOMARC missile fiasco.

The Soviet Union had, in 1957, tested an intercontinental ballistic missile (ICBM), and the Soviet leader, Nikita Khrushchev, had alarmed Western media and public opinion with his boasts about the power of his country's missiles. For the present, however, conventional bombers carrying nuclear bombs were still the real threat to North America. To combat this threat, Ottawa ordered an American defensive missile system, the BOMARC.[28] Equipped with nuclear tips, BOMARC missiles were designed to intercept and "cook" incoming Soviet bombers and their nuclear cargo. If fired from the northern United States, the BOMARC stood a good chance of exploding over Canada's populated areas. It therefore made sense for the Canadian government to suggest that the BOMARC move north. The Americans agreed.[29] With the BOMARC, the nuclear issue came home, to a public already seriously disquieted by the government's cancellation of the Avro Arrow.[30]

Canadian officials, including the clerk of the privy council, R.B. Bryce, and the undersecretary for external affairs, Norman Robertson, recommended the BOMARC, fully understanding that it would not work without nuclear warheads. (Bryce was so unperturbed by the prospect, he actually recommended two bases in the Ottawa area.) Ministers and their advisers believed that economic rather than political considerations were most important. The heavy burden of the cost of modern armaments clashed with Canada's desire to play a prominent role in the air defence of the continent.[31] The BOMARCs and other forms of nuclear weapons were cheaper than the conventional alternative. Canadians were not generally aware that their country was already an active participant in the preparation and deployment of nuclear weapons, although this was no secret. As we have seen, Canada supplied uranium for bombs, and in NATO agreed to the American doctrine of "massive retaliation," albeit with many misgivings.[32] Diefenbaker agreed to a "strike-reconnaissance" role for Canada's air division in Europe, which involved interdicting enemy lines of communication with tactical nuclear devices. And the Canadian NATO brigade would also be equipped with "Honest John" ground-to-ground missiles, nuclear-tipped, which might or might not blow the advancing Soviet tank armies into radioactive smithereens. (Opinions also differed on whether the Honest John was a reliable weapon.)[33]

Canada did not actually make nuclear weapons, and any warheads assigned to Canadian rockets or planes remained in the custody of the United States. Only when released by presidential order did the warheads become operational.[34] This detail did not appease the growing number of critics of nuclear weapons, who by 1959-1960 were multiplying in Canada as elsewhere in the Western world. Diefenbaker was sufficiently concerned by the public mood that he restricted Canadian participation in a simulated nuclear crisis, in which the Canadian and American governments were to demonstrate their determination and preparedness by fleeing to secret safe locations from which government could be carried on. (Canada's, in tribute to the prime minister, was popularly called the "Diefenbunker.") The American government was seriously annoyed, but Diefenbaker had a real point: drawing public attention to the effects of nuclear attack damaged morale and reinforced the government's critics. To put it another way, Eisenhower was staging the wrong play at the wrong time and as a result losing his audience.[35] Diefenbaker, perhaps the most theatrical of Canadian prime ministers, was obsessively determined not to alienate what remained of his own audience.

Public support was a real consideration: the government was well aware that its popularity was declining by the winter of 1959-1960. In the summer of 1960 the opposition Liberals passed the Conservatives in the public opinion polls and remained ahead thereafter. Diefenbaker faced an uphill fight, and, not surprisingly, he adopted a defensive political strategy. He decided to take no chances, and, as a consequence, he avoided decisions that might prove unpopular. He was assisted in this posture by the fact that his Cabinet and his senior civil service advisers were deeply divided over nuclear weapons. Some had, in fact, arrived at the view that the employment of nuclear weapons would amount to "global suicide," in the words of Norman Robertson. Even American officials were arriving at the same conclusion, as their staffs computed the millions or hundreds of millions of casualties that would occur in a nuclear exchange.

The potential destructiveness of such an exchange seemed to increase with each passing year. The panic that swept the Western world after the Soviet Union launched Sputnik, the world's first satellite in 1957, may have been a factor in determining the American presidential election of 1960. In any case, the new American president, John F. Kennedy, immediately ordered the biggest peacetime defence build-up in American history, vastly expanding the power of the United States to deliver a crushing blow to its Communist enemy. Such measures were directed against a phantom enemy because the fabled missile gap with the Soviet Union and its store of bombs and missiles was just that: a black hole of bravado, rumour, and fear mongering. American spy planes regularly returned from the Soviet Union to report that they had seen little or nothing of Soviet missile sites. Later, spy satellites brought the same news. The Soviets were playing an elaborate game of bluff, trying to impress the West with an illusion of weaponry when, in fact, they had little or none.

Khrushchev had an objective. He wanted to shore up the Communist regimes of Central Europe, especially East Germany. The East German regime was understandably unpopular at home; it carried the burden of Soviet occupation as well as of an inefficient economy. Although divided from West Germany by barbed wire and landmines, East Germany was not physically separated from West Berlin, occupied by the United States, Great Britain, and France under agreements made in 1945. The Western allies could maintain their position, and the population of Berlin, because those agreements guaranteed land, water, and air access to the city. West Berlin was a liberal, democratic, capitalist beacon for East Germans, and by their hundreds of thousands they moved there, simply walking across an imaginary line. By 1961 the Soviets estimated that 1.2 million East Germans had taken advantage of this large political loophole to improve their lot, materially and spiritually.

The Soviets knew that the Western powers in the mid- to late 1950s were divided on the best approach to the problem of the division of Europe and Germany, with the Americans and Germans taking a distinctly harder line than the rest of the alliance. The Soviets believed that West Germany aimed to acquire nuclear weapons, which filled them with dread. The British in particular were uncertain how to cope with

Soviet fears, in part because they fundamentally agreed with them. If the British were soft on the Berlin issue, the Canadians, among others, were also uncertain.[36] Beginning in 1958, Khrushchev turned his most effective weapon – his rhetoric – on to the status of Berlin. The West must withdraw, he proclaimed, or the Soviet Union would turn over to East Germany control of the vital access routes. Because the Western powers did not recognize the East German regime and on Berlin issues dealt only with the Soviet Union, this would place them in an impossible political dilemma. Khrushchev then imposed the first of a long series of deadlines, and waited.

The West was thrown into confusion. Nobody wanted to abandon Berlin, and yet maintaining their foothold in the city might mean war. Recognizing East Germany was unpalatable. The only realistic defence for the outnumbered allies in Berlin, and NATO forces elsewhere in Germany, was nuclear. "What happens if we don't?" American officers in Germany asked, referring to the use of nuclear weapons. There was no answer.[37]

Khrushchev's deadline proved adjustable and the Berlin crisis rose and fell according to the tides of Soviet-American relations. "Berlin is the testicles of the West," Khrushchev told his colleagues. "Every time I want to make the West scream, I squeeze on Berlin."[38] As predicted, the Canadian Cabinet screamed, or at least squeaked. Canada opposed threatening force over Berlin, believing that hostilities in Europe would lead to nuclear war. Such a decision indicated a real distrust of NATO's nuclear strategy among senior officials in Ottawa.

There were also objections of a more traditional kind. The Berlin crisis necessarily involved the whole of NATO, but it was being managed only by the three Western occupying powers, the United States, Great Britain, and France. The Canadian government would have preferred to bring the matter before the NATO Council, where all members could discuss it. This suggestion got short shrift from the Americans, British, and French, who wanted to preserve their privileged position.[39] In fact the Canadians had no concrete plans to put forward – merely the hope that the Western powers would be flexible. Diefenbaker did from time to time muse, in public and in private, about turning the city over to the United Nations. (It was a point that had been suggested by Harold Macmillan, and in 1959 Diefenbaker took British suggestions very seriously.) Some Canadian diplomats favoured renegotiating Western rights in Berlin, putting them on an apparently firmer and less provocative foundation. (This was originally another British idea.) Canadian hesitations over Berlin and Germany, some of which were leaked to the press, probably harmed Canada's position in Europe, where, as a Canadian diplomat, Henry Davis, reported, Canadians "were already suspected of being the 'avant garde' of the revisionists."[40]

The Canadian attitude was not sympathetic to the West German government, which saw an allied commitment to the eventual reunification of Germany as fundamental.

"Eventual" was the operative word, but the "commitment" seemed to be enough to keep West German politics on track. Many if not most officials in the Department of External Affairs took a different view, believing that the permanent division of Germany was an acceptable price for stability between East and West in Europe, and certainly desirable if the alternative were nuclear war. As Harold Macmillan put it, how could Britain go to war "for two million of the people we twice fought wars against and who almost destroyed us?"[41] It was a view that would have commanded much sympathy in Ottawa.[42]

This stage of the Berlin crisis eventually petered out in the summer of 1959. Khrushchev was invited to visit the United States, and for a time all seemed sunny in Soviet-American relations. Berlin took a back seat to rapprochement. Yet the issue had not been resolved as much as postponed, as the question of what to do about Germany was also postponed. The West had certainly not found a solution to maintaining a garrison in the heart of a Communist state. Canada had not been much help during the crisis. Canadian behaviour throughout was hesitant, contradictory, and, above all, ineffective. Neither Diefenbaker nor his external affairs minister, Sidney Smith, had any clear conception of what to do, while their officials bickered among themselves. Such policy directions as there were came from the British.

The possibility of confrontation arose again in the summer of 1961, when Khrushchev decided that he might be able to bully the new Kennedy administration into concessions. All he provoked was a further rise in American nuclear capabilities. Even before that became evident, the Soviets, responding to the increasingly desperate pleas of their East German satellite, which was losing population at the rate of 40,000 a month, solved their Berlin problem unilaterally. On 13 August 1961, East German police and troops sealed off West Berlin from East Germany. In doing so, they did not touch Western access routes. Over the next couple of months a concrete wall was built, circling West Berlin. It was destined to stand for the next twenty-eight years, providing the West with a magnificent symbolic justification for the Cold War, one that publicly admitted the failure of communism as an economic or political system.

Western statesmen waxed indignant at the Berlin Wall. Diefenbaker maintained solidarity with his allies and approved additional troops for Canada's armed forces. But the prime minister and his advisers were secretly relieved at the wall and the decompression of the crisis. The East Germans were worse off, with nowhere to go and no alternative but to remain in their grey, drab fragment of a country; but what was that compared to the danger of a nuclear war? No longer pressed by the East German government, the Soviets forgot about the status of West Berlin, accepting that it would remain part of the West. They accepted the status quo not only in Berlin but across the continent of Europe. Henceforth Soviet diplomacy in Europe was directed at preserving what they had, rather than expanding their zone of control.

THE CUBAN MISSILE CRISIS

The construction of the Berlin Wall in 1961 did not end the Cold War. Rather, it signalled a change of venue from Europe to the Third World or, as it was then called, the underdeveloped world. There had already been clashes between East and West, between Communists and anti-Communists, during the 1950s in Central America, Malaya, and Indochina. "Wars of national liberation," Khrushchev stated, were entirely permissible and indeed inevitable as the old colonial regimes gave way to the forces of freedom and progress.

Khrushchev was the last Soviet leader with a sincere and romantic attachment to communism. Marxist ideologues proclaimed that the Third World was ripe for the plucking. There, communism embodied the struggle for justice and liberation, however bankrupt it might seem in the developed world. Sensing that communism was checkmated in Europe, the Soviet Union was pleased to discover that faith in a happy Marxist future burned bright on a Caribbean island.[43] As an extra incentive, Cuba offered a chance to improve the strategic balance, which, thanks to Khrushchev's boastful diplomacy and the consequent American rearmament, was tilting strongly in the direction of the United States. The Americans had even placed missiles just across the Black Sea, in Turkey, something Khrushchev vividly resented but did not take any responsibility for. Instead, he decided to respond in kind.

Cuba's future was in some doubt. The Eisenhower administration broke relations and imposed an economic blockade. The Kennedy administration was even more hostile, and in April 1961 launched an ill-prepared invasion of the island from a brackish beach on the Bay of Pigs by an army of Cuban exiles. The enterprise failed, and American prestige was considerably damaged. So was the reputation of the new president: Diefenbaker, for one, concluded that Kennedy had shown he was rash and foolish. Nor did a visit by the Kennedy to Ottawa in May 1961 – his first outside the United States – help matters, for Diefenbaker emerged with a fixed dislike of the American president.

Castro, the Cuban dictator, needed protection, and the Soviet Union looked like a desirable champion. If there had been any doubt, the botched invasion showed that the American threat was real, and Castro hardly needed encouragement to look eastward for help. Gazing towards Moscow, he saw what he wanted to see – great military power coupled with a willingness to use that power in defence of socialism. He believed that a Soviet offer of "several hundred intercontinental missiles" would do the trick, as he later admitted.[44] It seemed natural for Castro to agree to a request from such a powerful ally to place some short- or medium-range missiles in Cuba. This despite the fact that by 1962 it was public knowledge everywhere – apparently everywhere but Havana – that the Americans enjoyed massive superiority in numbers of missiles and warheads.

In July 1962, the Soviet Union began to send to Cuba missiles with nuclear warheads and troops to guard them. This took months; by October or November, the missiles and their warheads would be operational. Outside Cuba, time passed uneventfully. Canada maintained diplomatic relations with the island, as did most Western European countries and Mexico. The Americans did not mind: "Canadian reporting from Habana is of great value to us," an American official wrote, though Canadian trade caused some concern.[45]

Cuba was not on the Canadian political horizon in the summer of 1962. Canada had a federal election in June 1962, in which Diefenbaker lost his parliamentary majority. The Americans prepared for their mid-term elections, to be held in November 1962, and, as the autumn drew on, seemed to concentrate on nothing else. But in October the American government, using aerial surveillance, discovered and confirmed the existence of the missiles and decided that it must do something to counter the threat. President Kennedy, in a televised address (televised in Canada too) at 7 p.m. eastern time on 22 October 1962, announced that he was setting up a naval blockade of Cuba.

Diefenbaker watched the speech without surprise. He knew from well-informed Canadian sources that a crisis was impending and that it involved Soviet missiles in Cuba. He already knew what Kennedy would say, having been specially briefed, along with the leaders of Great Britain, France, West Germany, and Italy, a few hours before. He did not need to be told that this was a risky business. If the Soviets chose to proceed, either by completing the missile sites in Cuba or by sending their ships to break the blockade, nuclear war would most probably result. In a nuclear exchange, much of Canada would probably be incinerated. No one, in Washington or Ottawa or even Moscow, could safely predict how Khrushchev would respond to Kennedy's policy of confrontation. If there was a response, it was quite probable that it would extend beyond the United States; in any case, given the nature of North American geography, Canada was bound to be sucked in. Yet the Americans intended to initiate their course of action without bothering to ask Diefenbaker's opinion.

Lack of consultation was not the only problem, though it was big enough. Diefenbaker was by October 1962 persuaded that Kennedy had joined the multiplying ranks of his antagonists, in a year when the prime minister's political future hung very much in the balance. Diefenbaker was right, although he ignored just how much his own behaviour had contributed to the situation. (For example, he had acquired a scrap of Kennedy's notes during the president's visit to Ottawa in May 1961 and, believing that they revealed an American plan to bully Canada into submission to US policy, threatened to make the document public.)[46] The characteristic folly of Diefenbaker's tactic – personalizing differences between himself and his opponents, real and imaginary – has obscured the fact that there were real differences of policy and even strategy between his government and the Americans. These Kennedy was trying to sweep away, in the name of alliance solidarity.

It was not surprising that Diefenbaker reacted tensely as Kennedy's envoy, the former ambassador to Canada, Livingston Merchant, explained what American spy planes had uncovered and what he claimed to be the American government's necessary response. Diefenbaker listened calmly, raising no substantive objections. Merchant was not among the prime minister's greatest admirers, but he thought that the briefing had gone well enough and that the prime minister accepted the American case for action against the Soviet Union's missile deployment. It followed, Merchant believed, that Washington should expect a statement of support from Canada, probably on 23 October. Instead, Diefenbaker spoke in the House of Commons only a few hours after seeing Merchant – though after Kennedy's speech. He had in the meantime received advice from the Department of External Affairs that there might be an analogy between the Suez crisis of 1956 and Cuba in 1962. Perhaps United Nations action was indicated, either through mediation or along the lines of Pearson's 1956 emergency force. And Pearson had won the Nobel Prize, a fact Diefenbaker had always resented and envied. Diefenbaker moved rapidly from thought to speech, vaguely proposing a United Nations investigation of the situation in Cuba, and seeming to cast doubt on the American position.[47]

The Cabinet met the next day, the 23rd, and the next, the 24th. Diefenbaker had before him a recommendation from the minister of national defence, Douglas Harkness, that Canadian forces in NORAD and in the North Atlantic be placed in the same state of readiness for attack as their American counterparts – a level that in the jargon of the military was called Defence Condition, or Defcon, 3. Diefenbaker – distracted by the notion of UN intervention, influenced by worries emanating from British prime minister Harold Macmillan, and prone to consider Kennedy a rash young man – temporized. At Harkness's insistence and after the Americans had moved to Defcon 2 (enemy attack imminent), Diefenbaker grudgingly gave permission for Canadian forces to go on the alert. Thanks to Harkness, they had already done so, without the prime minister's knowledge.

The Cuban crisis lasted for about a week. Finally, after some desperate diplomatic exchanges, the Americans and Russians agreed to a compromise. The Soviet Union withdrew its missiles and nuclear warheads in Cuba. The Americans privately agreed in return to withdraw *their* nuclear-tipped missiles in Turkey, a small concession because those rockets were considered obsolete even before they had been activated – ironically, on 22 October.

It was a humiliation for the Soviet Union, which had surrendered to the logic of force: American force in the Caribbean and the Atlantic, and in deliverable atomic warheads, far outweighed the Soviet Union's mostly phantom armoury. It was a disaster for Nikita Khrushchev, whose colleagues in the Soviet Politburo did not forgive their "hare-brained" leader's escapade. Khrushchev lasted not quite two more years in office and was then deposed, although not before signing a nuclear test-ban treaty in Moscow in August 1963. His successors were determined never again to allow themselves to be overborne by the Americans, and they accelerated the missile race with the United States. The Americans had meanwhile persuaded themselves that they already had enough weaponry to vaporize the world, and that their participation in a further nuclear weapons race was futile.

Diefenbaker's hesitation over Cuba did not go over well with the Canadian public. Contrary to the prime minister's expectations, Canadians expected him to act as a loyal ally, to do as his predecessors had done in the World Wars, and in Korea. Indeed, Diefenbaker's prevarications, circumlocutions, and qualifications aroused the same kind of uneasiness as Pearson's careful passage through the Suez crisis had done, and in many of the same people – those who expected that Canada in foreign affairs should show basic solidarity with its allies. That meant Great Britain in 1956 and the United States in 1962. People who thought this way were prone to vote Conservative, believing that this was a characteristically "conservative" position. The Cuban crisis undermined Diefenbaker's position within his own party and left him vulnerable in his final conflict with Kennedy.

DIEFENBAKER VERSUS KENNEDY

The June 1962 general election left Diefenbaker a minority prime minister with a majority temperament. Unaccustomed to compromise, rigid and proud, Diefenbaker proved to be as inept at political tactics as he was at diplomatic strategy. His weakness at diplomacy put him into an impossible political position, from which compromise and concessions were the only means of escape.

The issue was nuclear weapons, which in the summer and fall of 1962 moved rapidly up the scale of political priorities. Canada's commitment to acquire nuclear weapons for its troops in NATO was by then five years old, while the commitment for North American air defence, though less clear-cut, could be traced back to 1959. Kennedy had raised the topic time and again with Diefenbaker, and each time had been put off – in both senses of the term. Now the Americans returned to the charge, with a Diefenbaker who was even less psychologically able to deal with the issue.

The Cuban missile crisis highlighted the dangers of further drift. Diefenbaker himself seems to have scented the problem, hinting that he would finally decide the issue, this time in favour of nuclear weapons. His resolution quickly flagged, however, under pressure from Howard Green, still staunchly anti-nuclear. Diefenbaker did not pass over into the anti-nuclear camp: instead, he sat determinedly in the middle, refusing to choose. "What drove us nuts was his wishy-washy indecision," an American diplomat commented. "If he had said no from the beginning," a White House official added, "we could have dealt with it. But he said neither."[48] Instead, Diefenbaker proposed that warheads for Canadian BOMARCs be held at American bases adjacent to Canada, and rushed north for attachment in time of need. (A similar procedure would have been implemented in Germany.) This idea, or variations on it, was raised during negotiations in November and December. Not surprisingly, it went nowhere. There was not time, in case of a Soviet attack, to rush atomic munitions northward.

Christmas brought a farcical interlude. Canada was not directly involved, at first. The Americans faced the embarrassing necessity, as they saw it, of cancelling a joint rocket development program with the British. The British, who based their hopes for the modernization of their nuclear weaponry on this program, begged for an alternative. Kennedy and Macmillan scheduled a meeting in Nassau in the Bahamas, then a British colony, shortly before Christmas, to thrash out the problem.

The meeting was successful, certainly from the British point of view, as they acquired the American nuclear submarine type, Polaris. Incorporated in the Royal Navy, Polaris submarines would carry a battery of nuclear missiles. They would then cruise the seas bearing British bombs. From the American point of view, British dependence on the United States was again underlined. From the British point of view, a close relationship with the United States had once again paid off – a point that did not go unnoticed in Paris, where President de Gaulle kept a wary and jealous eye on such developments.

In Ottawa the substance of the Macmillan-Kennedy meeting was of less concern than its form. The two senior English-speaking leaders – neither of whom could stand Diefenbaker – were meeting on the North American side of the Atlantic without going through the then-standard ritual of consulting or informing the Canadians. Diefenbaker decided that if Macmillan were not going to come to Ottawa, he would go to the Bahamas. That it was December and that Nassau was hot may also have weighed in his decision. The freshly arriving cuckoo was met at the airport by the police band and all due ceremony and then conducted to Macmillan's nest. There Kennedy, who hoped to escape before Diefenbaker arrived, was persuaded to linger for lunch, which, by all accounts except Diefenbaker's, was a stilted and uncomfortable affair. In Kennedy's words, "There we sat like three whores at a christening," out of place and out of sorts.[49] Lunch over, Kennedy fled, Diefenbaker and Macmillan exchanged some formal thoughts on the state of the world and Anglo-Canadian relations, and Diefenbaker settled down to enjoy a week and a half of sun-baked vacation at a private villa put at his disposal. He seems to have had a jolly time, enlivened by self-serving press interviews that naturally emphasized the importance of the Nassau conference and Diefenbaker's role in it.

The sun may have shone on Diefenbaker's enterprise, but fortune did not smile upon it. His boastful interviews annoyed the Americans and infuriated the British. When, in late January 1963, Charles de Gaulle announced his inflexible decision to bar

British entry into the Common Market, there was natural, if unfounded, speculation that Diefenbaker's Caribbean posturing had something to do with it. The level of criticism left the Diefenbaker government with only a very narrow margin for manoeuvre. The prime minister faced the return of the minority parliament on 21 January 1963, and he confronted serious discontent within his Cabinet – discontent that he was unable to manage.

The focus of Diefenbaker's problems was the defence minister, Douglas Harkness. Harkness knew what his department wanted, and he agreed with it. Its Honest John missile battery in Europe was useless without nuclear tips, while the F-104s had nothing to do but train for a war the RCAF knew it could not fight. The BOMARC squadrons at North Bay, Ontario, and La Macaza, Quebec, had been ready – expensively ready – for months, and could do nothing. Loyalty to his leader and his party made Harkness bargain for months with the Americans for out-of-country nuclear storage, even though he knew that in the two or three hours that might elapse between the first warning of air incursions and the arrival of Soviet planes over their targets there would be no room for the time-consuming niceties of consultation, decision, and installation.

The failure to reach an agreement tried American patience sorely. Lunching in early December with Basil Robinson, minister at the Canadian embassy in Washington, Livingston Merchant was uncharacteristically blunt. He observed that "he didn't think Canada had earned, by its actions and by certain non-actions, the right to the extreme intimacy of relations which had existed in years past."[50] Merchant, twice American ambassador and an admirer of Canada, was polite. His successor as ambassador was not. W.W. Butterworth ("Walt" to his friends) was, like Merchant, a veteran of the US foreign service. A classmate of George Kennan's at Princeton, he had served in Canada during the 1930s, where he first met Pearson. Subsequently he occupied a variety of senior posts in the department and it was presumably as a compliment that Secretary of State Dean Rusk, another old acquaintance, appointed him to Canada in the fall of 1962. Butterworth knew that Canadian-American relations were rocky and that Diefenbaker was partly to blame. He came to Canada expecting trouble, and he found it.

Meeting Diefenbaker on 17 December, Butterworth reported to Washington that the prime minister was not in the best of health. "Although vigorous in speech and gesture, he struck me as being unwell and exhibited evident signs of palsy or perhaps Parkinson's disease." The subject of nuclear weapons was not raised; Butterworth dismissed Diefenbaker's views on other issues as uninformed.[51] In any case, when it came to nuclear weapons, the ambassador agreed, not with the prime minister, but with Defence Minister Harkness. In Harkness's view, the Canadian government was not living up to its pledged word.[52] The political situation also counted. Opposition leader Pearson knew that the Liberals continued to outpace the Conservatives in public opinion polls, and that on the question of whether Canadian forces should accept nuclear weapons, 54 percent of Canadians said yes. In Ontario, party polls put the figure at 70 percent, and in Quebec, 58 percent.

Christmas barely afforded a respite. Parliament adjourned, but the controversy did not. This became publicly evident when, on 3 January 1963, the retiring NATO supreme commander (SACEUR), General Lauris Norstad, made a farewell call to Ottawa. Asked by a reporter about the state of Canada's commitments in Europe, Norstad publicly confirmed that they had not been fulfilled. The associate minister of national defence, who was standing beside Norstad at the news conference, could only grin and bear it despite the damage the general was inflicting on the Diefenbaker government's carefully constructed system of obfuscation.

Norstad's remarks created a storm in Canada. It was not the storm that Diefenbaker expected, or wanted. Some Conservative partisans and anti-nuclear activists condemned the general's words, but among the public generally there was an uneasy feeling that he was right. Canadian soldiers and airmen silently applauded, a fact that was already known to the Liberal opposition. The Liberal defence critic, Paul Hellyer (briefly associate minister of national defence under St Laurent in 1957) had spent time in Europe in the fall of 1962, at NATO headquarters in Paris and among Canadian troops. He reported back to his leader, Lester Pearson, that there was a very serious morale problem in Canada's NATO units and that Canada's standing in the alliance was being undermined.

It was Pearson's turn to confront the issue. The Liberal leader was no enthusiast for nuclear weapons or the apocalypse they promised to provide. He had famously remarked to an interviewer that if push came to shove, he would "rather be red than dead" (an inversion of a catchphrase of the time). This was not the tough, muscular response required of true Cold Warriors, but as Pearson pointed out, it was coupled with the hope that communism, evil as it was, would not last forever and that he and people like him could work to overthrow it.

A nuclear holocaust was hypothetical – a terrible thing, but still the stuff of science fiction as far as a majority of Canadians were concerned. Politicians must live in the here and now, and what Canada confronted was an actual problem with its allies and alliances. NATO was a cornerstone of Canada's foreign policy and an asset in its foreign relations. Relations with the Americans should not be jeopardized, especially if the Canadian government had actually asked for the weapons – BOMARCs and F-101s – it now proposed not to use. Pearson, faced with a choice, made a decision: he would take nuclear weapons, as promised, and then, through negotiation and agreement, try to get rid of them. In reaching a conclusion, Pearson knew that nuclear weapons had the potential to be the winning issue if there were another election; some years later he told an interviewer that the nuclear controversy was "when I really became a politician."

But Pearson was the only witness to his final decision, and its motives.[53] He announced his nuclear policy in a speech in Scarborough, Ontario, on 12 January 1963. Canada under a Liberal government would honour its existing commitments and accept nuclear weapons for its NATO and NORAD forces. This would not mean an independent Canadian nuclear capacity, nor would it mean that Canadian soil would simply be a conduit for American strategy: "a US finger would be on the trigger," Pearson told his listeners, "but a Canadian finger would be on the safety catch."[54]

To Harkness, Pearson's speech meant that the government could now adopt nuclear weapons without fear of criticism. Diefenbaker, schooled in an older version of partisanship and demonstrating a classic opposition mentality, instead argued that the Conservatives' way was now clear: to oppose the Liberals, who in the meantime could be conveniently tarred with the charge of pro-Americanism. It was another, fatal blunder by Diefenbaker. He did nothing to heal the split in his Cabinet. Rather, in place of a serious discussion on policy, he summoned ancient demons from the Canadian past: the ghosts of 1911 and 1891, the anti-American elections that had produced Conservative triumphs in the face of Liberal "sell-outs" to the Yankees.

When Parliament reconvened, the defence issue was front and centre. The Cabinet was in almost continuous session as Harkness tried to find a way – a nuclear way – out of the impasse. Howard Green, his steadfast opponent, merely had to sit tight and do nothing. On 25 January Diefenbaker made a speech in the House of Commons that took both sides of the issue, and promised nothing. In orating, however, Diefenbaker characteristically went overboard in his description of negotiations with the Americans. The prime minister allowed that things were going well on that front – under the circumstances, a most incautious remark. The Americans were deeply irritated by two years of pointless chat; worse still, they were offended by Diefenbaker's loose-lipped performance in Nassau. The embassy in Ottawa urged Washington to do something "to sweep away the confusion which Diefenbaker's statement can cause in Canadian minds."[55]

In Washington, Undersecretary of State George Ball determined to take Diefenbaker to task. He found an ally in Kennedy's national security adviser, McGeorge Bundy, and willing hands in the State Department staff who had endured, once too often, what they judged to be Diefenbaker's erratic buffoonery. A statement rapidly took shape. On 30 January, Canadian diplomats were shown the text, while Canadian reporters were summoned to the State Department for an unusual briefing. The version of the history of the nuclear negotiations presented by Diefenbaker on 25 January was wrong and misleading, the Americans stated. Negotiations were not going well, and there was no mutually acceptable solution in sight. In effect, the State Department was calling Diefenbaker a liar.

"We've got our issue now," Diefenbaker gloated to his finance minister, Donald Fleming. His path was clear: he should call an election, make Canadian sovereignty the issue, and whip the Grits, just as his hero, Sir John A. Macdonald, had done in 1891. Once again, Diefenbaker's instincts failed him. Not only was the Canadian public unpersuaded of the iniquity of American interference, but many Canadians actually believed that the State Department was right on the facts, and right again on Diefenbaker. The pro-nuclear faction in Cabinet, perhaps half the ministers, also felt in their bones that the Americans were right, and that "our issue" was a bomb that would blow up in the hands of the Conservatives. Much against his will, Diefenbaker was backed into temporizing. There would be no election, but there would be plenty of rhetoric. The Cabinet continued what might be called its deliberations into the weekend of 2-4 February. After a bizarre exchange of insults and a display of histrionics by the prime minister, the defence minister resigned.[56]

Now it was the turn of the Liberals, who introduced a motion of non-confidence on the government's defence policy. If it could attract the support of the two minor parties, the thirty-member Social Credit and the eighteen-member New Democrats, the government would fall. This was more difficult than it seemed. On the substance of the issue, the acquisition of nuclear weapons, the NDP and at least half the Social Credit probably supported Diefenbaker in rejecting nuclear weapons. The division and dissension in the Conservative Cabinet, and its inability to enunciate a clear position, transferred the debate to a question of process: the inability of the government to manage defence policy, or any other policy for that matter. Despite this tack, it was possible up to the last moment for Diefenbaker to compromise with either or both of the minor parties. This he refused to do. Consequently, on 6 February the government was defeated in the House of Commons, 142 to 111. Subsequently, two more ministers resigned from the Cabinet, and a number of other Conservative politicians declined to run in the election that parliamentary defeat had made inevitable.

Diefenbaker proved to be more comfortable on the hustings than in the Cabinet. Shrugging off the resignations, he presented his case to the Canadian people in an election on 8 April. The wickedness of American interference was a principal theme, but one that was never developed to its full potential. Kennedy followed the election closely; sensibly, he curbed his instinct to publicly support the Liberals.

Nuclear weapons and what they represented – bad relations with the United States, indecision in the Diefenbaker government – were probably a winning issue for the Liberals in English Canada. In French Canada, however, that was probably not the case. A poll taken in March, as the campaign approached its climax, indicated that 57 percent of English Canadians thought that Canada should take nuclear weapons, while the largest group among French Canadians, 37 percent, thought it should not. So much for earlier polls that detected no great difference between Quebec and English Canada, even though there were plenty of public signs that opinions in French Quebec differed from views elsewhere in the country.[57] Pierre Trudeau spoke for many when he described Lester Pearson as "the defrocked pope of peace" and backed his local NDP candidate, the McGill philosopher Charles Taylor.

The Liberals won the election. Most American observers were pleased by the result; so too were the British. It was too late for Harold Macmillan, whose Cabinet was, like Diefenbaker's, in an advanced state of decay. But Macmillan rejoiced nevertheless, as did Mike Pearson's many British acquaintances. Some commentators, at the time and since, have translated the unquestionable rejoicing abroad, and especially in the United States, to mean that the American government took a direct hand in Diefenbaker's political death throes. Did he fall or was he pushed, one historian pointedly asked. Was the wish father to the deed?

To these questions, sensible and inevitable as they are, the answer is: He fell. Diefenbaker had many enemies, laboriously if sometimes unconsciously cultivated. But he had little need of them. His own efforts were usually, and in the nuclear weapons crisis amply, sufficient. As a political leader, Diefenbaker was incomplete. He trusted to luck and therefore to fortune. This made him an opportunist, a tactician of the moment. He appears to have had little ability to plan ahead and possibly little confidence in his own judgment. His hesitation paralyzed his Cabinet, neutralizing even the loyalty that perhaps half its members felt towards the man who had, after all, given the Conservatives their most decisive greatest political victory, in 1958.

Diefenbaker was unable to match politics with government. Trained and highly skilled as an impresario in the shadow world of politics, Diefenbaker was inclined to mistake the political impact of an issue for its substance – a natural conclusion for one who spent most of his political life in opposition. He liked delay but failed to understand that delay was a means to an end, not an end in itself. The fact that government is about choices and, therefore, decisions, and that his performance would be judged on his ability not merely to make correct and advantageous choices, but to make choices at all, eventually undermined his leadership and his government. Not all, indeed not even most, of his blunders fell into the field of foreign relations.[58] Yet foreign relations was the field most easily noticed, and the field least subject to domestic control or political management.

Diefenbaker's rigid personality and limited view of politics combined with another defect, a dated if not ignorant view of the world. He would have been perfectly happy – as most Canadians had been happy – with the world of 1950 or 1955. It was a Cold War world, to be sure, but it was also the continuation of the way things had been during the Second World War, a time in which Canada was active and important. In that earlier time as well, its two principal allies, Great Britain and the United States, were in a stable balance. British decline upset that balance, calling up new policies and producing uncertainty. Diefenbaker's political skills rose to the challenge of Britain's change of position, but his governmental skills (or lack thereof) did not allow him to ask what the eventual outcome of his confrontations with Harold Macmillan would be.

Similarly, Diefenbaker misconceived as much as he mismanaged relations with the United States. There was, as it happened, nothing wrong with his choice of issues: nuclear weapons, Berlin, Cuba. There was good reason to be concerned about American foreign policy. The strategy of nuclear deterrence, adopted and implemented by the American government in the 1950s, was a strategic dead end. As Soviet nuclear capacities grew, and the Soviet Union acquired the ability to strike North America with atomic bombs, the American government struggled with a series of half-measures – tactical nuclear weapons, limited nuclear wars, more and better rockets to replace aircraft. The nerve-racking confrontations over Berlin and then Cuba were the inevitable result. It was practically impossible for America's allies, including Canada, to discuss such matters with Washington because their dependence on American power made them perennial beggars at the strategic feast. Diefenbaker, mesmerized by Eisenhower and antagonized by Kennedy, did not even try to engage in serious discussions with the American leadership, difficult as that may have been, before crisis struck. He was consequently ill prepared to say or do anything when Kennedy sounded his battle horn and prepared for his confrontation with Castro and Khrushchev in 1962.

Diefenbaker had even less to say about US assumptions regarding the internal dynamics of the Western world. Fixated on the British and their trade dilemmas, the prime minister did not seem to notice – or, if he noticed, care – about the American design to craft a united Europe out of its several squabbling components. American statesmen had dreamed of a harmonious Europe since the 1920s, and after 1945 they had both the means and the incentive to forward their design. It was a grand vision, and one that many influential Europeans shared. It was also an incomplete vision, from the American point of view, as long as Great Britain remained fascinated by its overseas connections and particularly by its empire and Commonwealth. This latter the Americans were inclined to see as a wasting asset, a useless and even dangerous diversion for the British, who would be better occupied stamping their outlook on a united Europe.

The Americans may have been right: the inability of the Commonwealth to offer an alternative, economic or political, to a uniting Europe eventually drove Harold Macmillan to his desperate decision to seek membership in the European Common Market at almost any price. Diefenbaker unwittingly played a part in this drama through his offhand response to British overtures for a transatlantic bilateral free trade area in 1957-1958. It was not a shining hour for Canadian diplomacy – or for the British. Worst of all, it left unanswered the question of Canada's search for a stable position inside the Western alliance.

Diefenbaker's spectacularly bad personal relations with Kennedy have overshadowed the fact that there were large, unresolved questions in Canadian-American relations. The American official view of Canada – mirroring its unofficial view – was friendly enough and favourable enough. It was perhaps best encapsulated some years later by the American defense secretary Robert McNamara, in a speech in Montreal in 1967. Struggling to define the essence of security, he cited the "fund of compatible beliefs" and "shared ideals" that constituted "the character" of Canadian-American relations.[59] It was the kind of comment that caused Canadian editorialists, and other professional opinion-shapers, to complain that Canada was once again being taken for granted. Yet, at least on a good day, McNamara was perfectly right, and many Canadians then and earlier (and later too) would have agreed. His assumptions, widely shared among those who thought about the matter in the United States, caused the American government to downplay not merely Diefenbaker, but Canadian nationalism in general, as a minor irritant, an abnormality that would, eventually, pass.

And so, in the crisis of 1963, the Americans did not push, and had no need to. Even the press release of 30 January 1963, which helped to accelerate Diefenbaker's fall, was crafted below the presidential level, by assistants who expected that their master would approve.[60] He did approve and no heads rolled, as they would have if he had had any qualms or regrets. During the 1963 election, however, Kennedy practised a salutary form of sympathetic non-interference and was ready, if fortune decreed it, for four more years of John Diefenbaker.

The tale was different on the Canadian side. Diefenbaker's assistants were dismayed at the prime minister's increasingly erratic behaviour on the nuclear weapons issue. The reaction of his political associates we have already seen. The reaction of his military and civil service subordinates was equally pronounced. Canadian officials sometimes cast themselves as mediators, trying to settle squabbles among politicians; and sometimes they let their American counterparts know that they too disapproved of the instructions they have to carry out. Military officers were sometimes not even that discreet. It was a divided government as well as a divided country that Diefenbaker led – if led was the word.

On 8 April Canadians learned that they had elected another minority government, this time Liberal. On 22 April Lester B. Pearson was sworn in as prime minister, with the expectation that the controversy and bitterness of the Diefenbaker years were, at last, over. As far as the nuclear issue was concerned, he was right. As for the rest, Pearson could only hope for the best and count on his good relations with Kennedy to guide Canadian-American relations into a new era of good feeling. As so often, hopes were dupes.

❦

THE FIRST YEARS OF THE DIEFENBAKER GOVERNMENT were not especially dominated by foreign relations, yet by 1960 or 1961 there were signs that foreign policy would be much more of a problem than the government imagined. Initially, Diefenbaker was not hesitant in taking decisions or making commitments. NORAD, nuclear weapons, and the Defence Production Sharing Agreement all date from 1957-1959. They regularized the defence of the continent, settled questions of weaponry, and, through the DPSA, provided some compensation for the heavy defence expenditures Canada was making. Yet none of these measures guaranteed Canada's ability, in a crisis, to control its own destiny or even have a say in how that destiny was shaped. The Diefenbaker government paid close and constant attention to the shifting currents of public opinion, hoping to find guidance. Not finding it, the prime minister preferred to postpone decisions in the hope that something would turn up. In 1961-1963, it did.

The erection of the Berlin Wall in 1961, the Cuban missile crisis in 1962, and the issue of whether Canada would fulfil its commitment to nuclear weapons in 1963 all led Diefenbaker to bungle relations with the United States and cripple his own prospects for re-election at home. The Canadian government vacillated over the Berlin crisis, appearing at best unhelpful. And Diefenbaker's vague suggestion of a UN investigation of the situation in Cuba was hardly the firm support that either the Americans or Canadians themselves expected. The Cuban crisis destabilized Diefenbaker's position within his own party and left him weakened in his jousts with Kennedy. Finally, the prime minister's temporizing over nuclear weapons misread the mood of the Canadian public and brought about his own political demise. It would fall to Lester Pearson to shepherd Canada further into the 1960s.

10

INNOCENCE AT HOME:
ECONOMIC DIPLOMACY
IN THE 1960s

The April 1963 election that deposed John Diefenbaker was not as satisfactory as his successor, Lester Pearson, would have wished. In the campaign's last days support for the Liberals fell away. Although they increased their popular vote by 3 percent over the previous year's election and won many more seats, they lacked a majority in the House of Commons, with 129 out of 265 members. Urban Canadians by and large voted for the Liberals, at least in cities over 150,000, Edmonton being the only exception. But rural Liberals were few and far between (even in Ontario and Quebec), and Saskatchewan elected no Liberals at all.

Fortunately for the Liberals, the opposition parties disliked each other at least as much as they disliked the government. The two minor parties, Social Credit (twenty-four seats) and the New Democrats (seventeen seats), were glad to see the last of Diefenbaker as prime minister and were reluctant to do anything that would bring him back, so they were inclined to support the Liberals over the Progressive Conservatives in the House. Diefenbaker, embittered by his election defeat but encouraged by the ninety-five seats he retained, remained a political force. His followers knew that they had kept their seats largely because of the Chief's magnetism. Most of his opponents in the parliamentary party had left, or had been defeated, and for the moment he could concentrate on seeking revenge for his defeat. Revenge was a Diefenbaker specialty.

MINISTERS AND MEASURES

The heart of the new government – of any government – was the prime minister. Lester B. Pearson, "Mike" to his friends and admirers, was, along with Diefenbaker, the best-known and most familiar Canadian of his time. In government in one form or another since 1927, in the public eye since the mid-1940s, pleasant looking with an infectious grin and a jaunty step, Pearson combined an extraordinary reputation with a familiar, almost folksy touch. Canadians remembered him at the United Nations in the 1940s and the 1950s. Nostalgia coloured the Liberal 1950s as a time of prosperity, minus the rising unemployment and searing controversies that disfigured Diefenbaker's time in office. The Liberals were believed to be competent internal managers, and Pearson's Nobel Prize showed what the world thought of him. Canada's standing among nations needed to be restored. Pearson could do that.

To assist him, Pearson assembled a Cabinet of talented men. The most senior, in point of service, was Paul Martin, secretary of state under King and minister of national health and welfare under St Laurent. Martin had run against Pearson for the leadership in 1958. Sixty years old when the new government took office, he hoped to run again when Pearson retired. Martin was talented and experienced, not just in domestic policy but in foreign affairs, which he had studied as a young man. In the 1940s and 1950s he was Pearson's alternate at the United Nations and could boast at least a nodding acquaintance with senior diplomats around the world. He was a natural choice for secretary of state for external affairs, and he welcomed the portfolio, not least because he hoped it would be a natural stepping stone to the Liberal leadership. Ambition meant that Martin, in office, would conduct himself with an eye not merely to the present, but also to a future that he expected to be both rosy and rewarding. Martin made no secret of his ambitions, but he was content to wait until, in good time, Pearson retired.

Pearson's other senior colleagues, J.W. (Jack) Pickersgill, Lionel Chevrier, and Paul Hellyer, all ministers under St Laurent, also got prominent jobs.[1] Pickersgill and Chevrier worked mainly on the domestic side, but Hellyer became minister of national defence, having briefly served as junior minister in 1957. Hellyer had a strong and sometimes prickly personality and thrived on confrontation. In 1962-1963 he had counselled Pearson to reverse the Liberals' policy on atomic weapons, and one of his first tasks as defence minister would be to secure nuclear weapons for Canada's armed forces. Being defence minister meant overseeing the largest chunk of the federal budget and a network of bases from coast to coast, as well as units in France and Germany, a very complicated task. Hellyer's colleagues, including the prime minister, by and large left him alone to manage his department. It was a sign that the main business of the government lay elsewhere.[2]

The Liberals' chief organizer in the 1962 and 1963 elections was a newcomer to the Cabinet, Walter L. Gordon, a chartered accountant and corporate executive from Toronto. Gordon had made his name in advising and sometimes rescuing Canadian companies, buying, managing, and selling them as occasion and profit demanded. Back in the 1930s he had met and befriended Lester Pearson. Unusually though not uniquely among the Toronto business elite, Gordon favoured comprehensive social reform and supported the Liberals as the best vehicle to get it. In the 1950s Gordon became known for his nationalist views, especially in the area of economics, though they surfaced on political issues as well. In 1955 the St Laurent government appointed him to chair the Royal Commission on Canada's Economic Prospects. To no one's surprise, he used the commission to focus national attention on foreign (meaning American) investment. He let it be known that he opposed more American investment and had his doubts about investment already in Canada; at the same time, he opposed any serious alteration in Canada's protective tariff.[3]

There was no chance that the St Laurent government would adopt Gordon's positions on investment; in any case it did not have the time, going down to electoral defeat in June 1957. The Diefenbaker government remained mute on the issue, the prime minister no doubt feeling that he had troubles enough without adding economic adventurousness to the list. It was left to the Liberals to do what they would, or could, with Gordon.

Though he did not have the ear of the Conservative government, Gordon was more than a mere private citizen. He had Canada's largest newspaper at his side, indeed at his service. Back in the 1940s the Conservative government of Ontario had plotted the forced sale of the Liberal *Toronto Star* to pay succession duties and had passed legislation to that effect. The legislation generally was seen for what it was, a crude political ploy. When the Conservatives signalled that they would back off, Gordon was instrumental in reorganizing the newspaper and selling it to reliable Liberals, including the *Star*'s editor, Beland Honderich. Thereafter the *Star* gave Gordon's every utterance top billing, on page one.[4]

Gordon applied his undoubted organizational talents to the Liberal Party, recruiting new candidates and restoring its finances. In return, he asked for assurances from Pearson, first that the leader shared his economic views, and second that Gordon would be minister of finance in a future Pearson government. Pearson agreed to both points, apparently enthusiastically, and Gordon continued his work. The Liberals committed themselves to a social welfare agenda, entailing major commitments in pensions, education, and health care. It was on this platform – along with their position on nuclear weapons – that they ran in 1963.

Pearson kept his promise to Gordon and made him minister of finance. But Gordon's was not the only economic philosophy represented in the Cabinet. An alternative

Liberal tradition, derived from C.D. Howe, was personified by Howe's former deputy minister, Mitchell Sharp, who had been elected to Parliament in 1963 from a Toronto constituency. Sharp considered Howe a great minister and a true economic nationalist. Howe's nationalism expressed itself through growth and investment – through a sense of confidence in Canadians rather than a sense of dread of the foreigner.[5] Sharp took on Howe's old portfolio, as minister of trade and commerce.

When Gordon prepared a budget that incorporated measures against foreign investment, Pearson approved. Nor did Pearson object when, distrusting the capacities and viewpoints of his civil service advisers, Gordon brought in a team from Toronto to help him write the budget. The rest of the Cabinet, as was customary, heard budget proposals only on the day Gordon presented them, when copies of the budget speech had been printed and delivered. The budget included a takeover tax of 30 percent that was to be applied to foreign purchases of Canadian-owned stock, as well as a series of general tax hikes. It was intended as a major blow in a crusade for Canadian ownership and against American influence over Canadian business.

Gordon expected applause. He did not get it. His takeover tax was at the centre of a storm, as Canadians across the country derided and condemned his budget. Tom Kent, Pearson's principal domestic adviser, later wrote, "The atmosphere was one in which there was a danger of a sharp break in stock-market prices and perhaps the kind of financial panic that would produce [a] run on the Canadian dollar." As important, the tax was administratively difficult, perhaps impossible to collect equitably.[6] Gordon mounted only a feeble defence of his measures and then collapsed. The takeover tax was aborted. With it, much of the steam went out of Gordon's crusade for economic nationalism. The minister's prestige was shattered. As for Pearson, though he may have been economically illiterate, he could recognize a political liability when he saw one.[7]

The American government watched these events from a distance. Diplomats with service in Canada knew about Canadian nationalism and what it might do, but they had expected a bit more professional competence from the Pearson Liberals. Pearson might accept nuclear weapons and chat with Kennedy about baseball, as he did in a meeting at Kennedy's estate at Hyannis Port, Massachusetts, in May 1963, but political harmony plainly did not carry over to economics. Because the takeover tax disappeared so quickly, it never became a direct bone of contention, but it would surface indirectly in the summer of 1963.

The Kennedy administration had economic problems of its own. Money was flowing out of the United States – too much money, in the view of the American administration and international experts. So Kennedy moved to reduce the flow, imposing an interest equalization tax on investment abroad, stocks or bonds. (The idea was to make the cost of borrowing in the United States – which was low – the same as borrowing elsewhere.) The effect would have been to add at least 1 percent to the interest on

Canadian bonds sold in the United States, which could be expected to reduce the flow of US investment to Canada.[8] Gordon, still minister of finance, might have been expected to welcome the American measure – after all it did what he had proposed to do. But the difference between nationalist theory and economic reality was too great: Gordon rushed to make representations to Washington against the tax. Canada, he pointed out, had a chronic trade deficit with the United States; the American measures would make matters worse, for where would Canadians get American dollars to buy American goods if not through investment?

Ottawa got what it wanted, but it also got a lesson in continental economics. Canadians needed American consideration, and, because Washington viewed Canada as important to American interests, the Canadian government secured an exemption from the new tax. It turned out that Canadian nationalism had its limits, and American policy adapted to that. Fortunately, the political impact of Gordon's actions south of the border was mild, though in other circumstances that might not have been so. As the American undersecretary of state, George Ball, pointed out to the governor of the Bank of Canada, Louis Rasminsky, "your last budget hasn't made it easier for us to agree to do what we've just done,"[9] namely a favour to Canada.

If there was confusion over how Ottawa managed its budgets there was also confusion over how it managed federal-provincial relations when those relations affected foreign affairs. The federal government maintained that it alone had jurisdiction over foreign relations. Yet domestically there were vast areas where, at least in peacetime, the federal government had no authority. The issue arose when, in January 1961, the Diefenbaker government signed a treaty regulating dams and hydroelectric power on the Columbia River, which crossed and recrossed the border between Canada and the United States. The United States wanted the dams more than it wanted all the power generated by them, so the Diefenbaker government reserved for Canada some of the electricity to be produced by the Columbia. It would be used by the British Columbia electrical utility. Unfortunately, communication between Ottawa and British Columbia on the subject was not good – the Diefenbaker Conservatives were deadly rivals of the province's Social Credit government – and the Socreds simply refused to implement the treaty. Under the Canadian constitution, that was effectively that. The federal government could not impose its will on British Columbia. Nothing further was done while Diefenbaker was in office.

It fell to Pearson and Paul Martin to remedy the situation. British Columbia wanted money, not electricity. It did not matter that the province's demands were at best eccentric and at worst foolish: provincial autonomy was politically and legally absolute where natural resources were concerned, and Ottawa had no feasible way of changing the situation. And so a revised Columbia Treaty was negotiated with the Americans, following the provincial agenda. It was a reminder that even in foreign affairs Ottawa had to watch its step where provincial interests were concerned. Diplomacy, Canadian-style, did not stop at the border.

The Columbia River Treaty was not the only hangover from Diefenbaker. There was a virtual labour war on the Great Lakes, a result of dissatisfaction on the part of Canadian sailors with the conduct of the US-based Seamen's International Union (SIU). At the height of the Cold War, the St Laurent government had effectively invited the American SIU into Canada to replace a Communist-dominated Canadian Seamen's Union. By and large the Canadian labour movement had approved; as the prominent labour lawyer and future NDP leader, David Lewis wrote in 1950, "it is extremely desirable, in the present international situation, to oust Communist control from Canadian trade unions." Lewis had his reservations about some of the methods used, both by the SIU and government, but he and other labour leaders were able to live with the result through the 1950s.

The SIU's reign on the Great Lakes was peaceful on the grand scale but violent on the small. Sailors learned not to incur the wrath of the union or its all-powerful Canadian director, Hal Banks. (An American immigrant, Banks was accepted into Canada despite a criminal record.) Eventually, in the early 1960s, Banks provoked a full-scale revolt among his members that led to an established Canadian union – the railway workers – signing on the disgruntled seamen. The international union and the Canadian union battled it out around the Great Lakes. The SIU had the support of the American labour movement, while the Canadian rebels had the support of the Canadian Labour Congress and, for what it was worth, Canadian public opinion and the Pearson government. It was an unequal contest. The SIU was a major contributor to the Democratic Party in the United States, and the Kennedy administration – and, after Kennedy, Johnson – winked at its misdeeds. When Ottawa placed the SIU's Canadian branch under trusteeship, the American labour secretary, Willard Wirtz, denounced the action. Banks, who had meanwhile been tried and convicted of conspiracy to assault, departed Canada and resumed residence in the United States, where he lingered for many years, a fugitive from justice protected by his union's influence over the American government. After a spell of trusteeship, the SIU resumed its place on the Great Lakes, under different management. Whether that was a just solution or not, it proved to be a stable one.[10]

The SIU affair was a case, frequent in transborder relations, where Canadian actions affected important American domestic interests, as defined by American politics. It was Pearson's (and before him Diefenbaker's) misfortune to tread on sensitive toes in a number of areas. In one case, a large American bank (owned by the Rockefeller interests) took over a small, Dutch-owned Canadian bank, the Mercantile. It was, in theory, merely a transfer from one foreign owner to another, but to the Canadian government it was not so simple. The Rockefellers would wish to do something with the

Mercantile, while the previous owners had let it slumber. Heretofore, the banking sector had been all Canadian, as a small and specialized institution responsive to the wishes of the Canadian government and often acting in partnership with it. It was hard not to think of Canadian banks as an arm of government, at least on some occasions. Now an American bank, a very large American bank, was entering the game.

As finance minister, Walter Gordon regulated banks, and, when approached by the Rockefellers about the Mercantile acquisition, he warned that he did not think it desirable. When it went ahead, Gordon in response revised the Bank Act, not to reverse the acquisition, but to prevent the Mercantile (and any other bank more than 25 percent foreign-owned) from growing. The Mercantile Bank forthwith became an item in Canadian-American relations. Eventually, the bank agreed that it would issue new shares to bring its American ownership down to 25 percent, and after a battle in Cabinet between Gordon and his successor as finance minister, Mitchell Sharp, that was where the matter was left. Eventually, the Mercantile reduced its US ownership, expanded a bit, and was absorbed by a larger Canadian bank.[11]

American ownership and American content were issues in cultural policy as well. The government of Canada maintained its own cultural agencies – the Canadian Broadcasting Corporation and the National Film Board – to convey the Canadian experience to Canadians and any foreigners who might care to listen or watch. Government ownership stopped short of print media, where an abundance of newspapers and magazines flourished, or wished to flourish. American magazines and newspapers circulated freely in Canada, as they had done since the early nineteenth century.

Following the logic of the tariff, two magazines set up shop in Canada: *Time* and *Reader's Digest*. Among the most popular periodicals in the United States, they had the same appeal in Canada. Their Canadian editions, which had some Canadian content, competed directly and successfully with their domestic counterparts in circulation and advertising – too successfully in the latter's view. Complaints reached Diefenbaker and, later, Pearson. The question was pondered and restudied. The US government, prodded by *Time*, viewed the potential interference from Ottawa with alarm. Eventually the government, in Gordon's 1965 budget, disallowed tax deductions for advertising in all foreign media – or rather, all but *Time* and *Reader's Digest*. That, in the opinion of the *Globe and Mail*, was equivalent to locking in "the two biggest wolves with the sheep," but, given the vigour of American protests, it was as far as Ottawa dared to press. It was Gordon who took the brunt of Canadian nationalists' wrath.

New Life in the GATT

Although Canada considered itself a trading nation, the main source of prosperity and the rising standard of living in the country was investment – another reason why Walter Gordon's tinkering with the inflow of American dollars received such a sharp reception in 1963. The ratio of exports to the gross national product had reached a historic low in 1958 and 1959 – 14 percent.[12] Trade flows grew steadily, and Canada accounted for 5 percent or more of world trade at the time – but in effect in Canada, prosperity grew faster than trade. Nonetheless, Ottawa continued to look for ways to expand trade and penetrate new markets.

In 1960 a new body, the Organisation for Economic Co-operation and Development (OECD), headquartered in Paris, superseded the old Organisation for European Economic Co-operation (OEEC), an economic watchdog that had grown out of the Marshall Plan in the early postwar years. The OEEC had been a purely European organization, with Canada and the United States relegated to observer status. While its members had pursued liberalized trade among themselves, they had refused concessions to others. For Canada, then, the OEEC had been a disappointment.[13] In contrast to the OEEC, the OECD was a clearinghouse for information and discussion and had no executive functions. The Europeans had no objections to admitting Canada and the United States to membership, and over time it expanded to most of the developed world. In terms of influencing thought, discussing ideas, and exchanging information, the OECD was useful; in terms of actual trade policy it played "a relatively muted part," in the words of a Canadian trade negotiator.[14]

A less muted role was assigned to the General Agreement on Tariffs and Trade (GATT). From the Canadian point of view, the GATT was potentially invaluable, a multilateral brake on relations with the rich and powerful United States. But the success or failure of the GATT depended not on Canada, but on the United States. American policy on trade was really two policies – one for the administration, meaning freer trade, and one for Congress, which prevented the United States taking a strong lead at the GATT or anywhere else. Without American leadership, the GATT had foundered somewhat in the late 1950s.

The Diefenbaker government was not displeased at the slow progress of the GATT. The Conservatives were predisposed to protectionism, as their Liberal predecessors were to freer trade, but given the international political climate at the time, there had not been not much difference in results. Under President Kennedy, American policy began to shift, although that challenge was confronted by Pearson's government, not Diefenbaker's. There was a danger that the United States and the European Economic Community (EEC) would drift into opposite protectionist directions, something Kennedy was determined to prevent. Preventing it involved taking a broader approach to trade negotiations, setting to one side the item-by-item format that had characterized American trade policy since the Reciprocal Trade Agreement Act in 1934.

In what was a major legislative achievement, Kennedy persuaded Congress to pass the Trade Expansion Act in 1962, setting the stage for a new round of GATT negotiations, appropriately called the Kennedy Round. The Americans for the first time could

– and did – propose an across-the-board cut in all tariffs. This had been a gleam in the eye of Canadian trade negotiators since the Second World War. Ironically, now that it was offered, Canada was reluctant. The hesitation, if not outright opposition, was in the Pearson Cabinet. Mitchell Sharp, minister of trade and commerce, was a free trader by conviction, but Walter Gordon, minister of finance, was an instinctive protectionist. Other members of the Cabinet consulted the interests of the industries located in their constituencies and came down against substantial changes to the tariff. Canada was running a balance of payments deficit with the United States, and lowering tariff barriers would open still more industries to US competition. Yet Canada could hardly turn down a major American trade initiative, especially after Kennedy won the reluctant agreement of the Europeans to proceed.[15]

Unable to avoid the GATT negotiation, Ottawa asked for special consideration for the vulnerable state of the Canadian economy, signified by Canada's trade deficit. The Americans were helpful, though worried by what they called the "narrow and short-run self-interest that characterized the Canadian position." The Europeans were less sympathetic but finally agreed that the Canadians could negotiate on the basis of something other than an across-the-board cut.

Canada did offer large reductions in tariffs, though not across the board, and in return asked for "50 percent cuts in all items of actual or potential export interest to Canada." The Canadian delegation hoped for cuts in agricultural barriers, but was disappointed. Though Canada was an important player in the Kennedy Round, the main action was elsewhere, between the United States and the Europeans. Where Canadian and American interests coincided, there was some hope of progress; where they did not, there was none. Agreement was finally reached in June 1967, and the results were significant: Canada obtained tariff concessions affecting $3 billion in exports and in turn lowered tariffs on $2.5 billion in imports. But the main gain for Canada was with the Americans. As Michael Hart, a historian of Canadian trade policy, observed: "The much vaunted desire to diversify Canada's trading patterns had been throttled again by the reality that only the Americans had sufficient interest in the Canadian market to make concessions that were helpful to Canadian exporters."[16] The effect of Canada's determined participation in this multilateral trade forum was to reinforce trading links with the United States.

Those links were already being reinforced, and in a manner quite unexpected.

THE AUTO PACT

The Kennedy administration had great hopes for Canada when Pearson took office in April 1963. By the time of the American president's assassination in November, those hopes had, by and large, faded. The Gordon budget was the first blow. The subsequent Canadian appeal to sentiment and self-interest over the interest equalization tax had succeeded, but in a way that suggested that relations between the United States and its smaller neighbour were something of a one-way street. Then in November 1963 the Canadian government implemented an export subsidy program for automobiles. (It worked by remitting import duties on automotive components in return for improved export performance.) It was an attempt to strengthen Canada's small and costly automobile industry, which produced a limited number of models of American cars behind a high Canadian protective tariff, and at the same time to improve Canada's nagging balance of payments problem. As a result, Canadians paid up to 50 percent more for their cars than Americans did.[17] One American company, Studebaker, tempted by the subsidy, promptly shut down its US plant, and opened one in Canada.

When Washington got wind of the scheme, it protested. American law (and Canadian, for that matter) prescribed that subsidized imports be met with a "countervailing" duty that would remove whatever advantage the subsidy conferred. After repeated warnings, in April 1964 a countervailing action was launched. Walter Gordon was furious: his shouts over the phone entertained a group of American officials in Washington who knew that the Canadians had no adequate response.[18] The Americans, however, did. Instead of going to war over automobiles, they suggested, the Canadians should consider harmonizing automobile production into one free-trading, continental market. Conditions in the United States could hardly be more favourable, politically. The "Big Three" American automobile producers, General Motors, Ford, and Chrysler, also owned and operated Canada's car industry. Workers on both sides of the border belonged to the same union, the United Auto Workers (UAW). The Canadian industry was so small, relative to its American cousin, that it posed no great threat to the booming factories of Michigan and Ohio. The North American car market was simple – imports from outside the continent were few (8 percent of the market in 1966), and non-resident ownership negligible. This was a deal between North Americans alone, with no overseas complications. The US economy was riding high, and unemployment was low. All that was required was for Walter Gordon and his friends to suppress their Canadian nationalist reflexes.

That was not as hard as anticipated, but soothing nationalist fears required some tangible reassurance. Canadian and American negotiators produced an agreement abolishing tariffs on automotive products, but they added substantial safeguards designed to preserve the weak Canadian automobile industry. The Big Three could import automobiles and parts duty-free, as long as they maintained a certain level of production in Canada. In a separate exchange of letters, the Big Three also agreed to keep boosting their Canadian production proportionate to the growth in their sales in Canada. Only the Big Three were involved, for no other large companies produced automobiles in Canada. Under the circumstances, Gordon concluded that the Canadian industry was adequately protected and did not oppose the deal.[19]

The negotiations later provoked some reflections by an American participant, Julius Katz. "The thing about negotiating with the Canadians," he told an interviewer, "is that, at least in those days, you have two parties that are speaking the same language, I mean literally and figuratively. There are some minor cultural differences, but for the most part the negotiations are between people who think pretty much alike." The Canadians had their sensitivities, Katz added, "about absorption – being the 51st state ... The idea of free trade, complete free trade, would not have washed at that time."[20]

Lester Pearson and President Lyndon B. Johnson signed the Auto Pact, as it became known, at Johnson's Texas ranch in January 1965. Johnson steered it through the Senate with the support of the UAW and its influential president, Walter Reuther. (The Canadian arm of the UAW did not favour the agreement, nor did most local car executives.)[21]

The Auto Pact reshaped the economy of central Canada (mainly Ontario, although there was a General Motors plant in Quebec). Because most of the automobiles built in Canada were exported to the United States, it vastly increased the dependence of Ontario on the American market and made trade with the rest of Canada less important. Provincial officials were neither present nor consulted in the negotiation of the Auto Pact: it was purely an exercise of federal trade power, with far greater consequences than the simultaneous Columbia River dispute with British Columbia.

The Auto Pact was not much discussed at the time, except in the automobile industry and among economists. It played little part in the federal election of November 1965. Gradually, however, its effects became clear. Canadian costs were lower, and locating cheaper factories in Canada attracted American investment. Auto production in Canada rose. As a consequence, Canada's customary trade deficit with the United States shrank. In 1970 and 1971 Canada had a surplus in the automobile trade with the United States, much to the surprise of some American politicians. In 1972 matters returned to "normal," with an American surplus, which remained in place until the early 1980s.[22] Ultimately, the Canadian branch of the UAW became the pact's strongest supporter, continuing to support it even after the union seceded from its parent and formed the Canadian Automobile Workers (CAW) in 1984. Price differences in automobiles between Canada and the United States dwindled, and consumers pocketed the result. The Ontario economy prospered as car exports headed south – indeed by 2001 Ontario passed Michigan in auto production. Automotive products were consistently Canada's largest export – 23 percent of total exports in 1997, compared to 8.2 percent for agriculture (1.7 percent for wheat), 1.9 percent for minerals, and 11.6 percent for forest products in the same year. The Canadian economy, and more particularly the Ontario economy, had been reshaped: secondary industry grew as primary industry diminished in importance.

On the American side, things were not so rosy. The industrial heartland that had sustained the US economy in the 1950s and 1960s fell on hard times. The industrial states south of Ontario were derisively termed "the rust belt" as factories closed and production halted or shifted to the glamorous "sun belt" in the Southwest. Not surprisingly, American unions took a different view of the Auto Pact in the 1980s than they had in the 1960s. Business, however, continued enthusiastic on both sides of the border. Though it was doubtful that the Auto Pact could have been passed in the 1970s or 1980s, there was never quite enough political pressure to remove or abrogate it. It became the stuff of dreams for those who benefited from it, and nightmares for those who wondered what would happen if the Americans ever saw fit to abolish it.

The Auto Pact was remarkable for another reason. The GATT made no provision for sectoral free trade – that is, the abolition of duties on one set of products only. In order to secure the Auto Pact, Canada and the United States had to get an exemption from the GATT, at the time the Kennedy Round was being negotiated. Of course, the American creators of the Auto Pact saw the measure as merely the first stage in a rationalization (and integration) of the American and Canadian economies – a point that especially appealed to the very influential George Ball, undersecretary of state and Washington's chief economic diplomat. The GATT exemption was not attained without struggle, but ultimately the Europeans reluctantly granted it.

The Auto Pact increased the amount of foreign (mostly American) investment in Canada. In its first two years, more than $500 million was invested in the automotive industry in Canada, creating eighty-seven new plants (not to mention additions to existing factories) and 20,000 jobs.[23] Canadian-American interaction increased, to the point where it would have been difficult to sort out the auto industry into separate Canadian and American packages.

This continental integration of a very large industry was, however, curiously disconnected from the trend of public opinion in Canada, both as stated by polling companies and as interpreted by politicians and the media. The public reaction to the American economic phenomenon thus bears some examination.

Opinion and Politics

During Diefenbaker's term of office, polls showed Canadians felt more dependent on, somewhat resentful of, and at the same time friendly towards the United States. Opinion remained strongly anti-communist and, in terms of political foreign policy, generally pro-American. Annexation to the United States was favoured by perhaps 10 percent of Canadians, with opinion favouring that option strongest in Quebec, where 14 percent supported it in 1960 – meaning that elsewhere in the country 7 or 8 percent favoured it.[24] On economic policy, there was a drift away from unqualified approval of US investment, indicating that the nationalist concerns of Walter Gordon's 1958 royal commission report were having some effect. In a poll in December 1961, 38 percent took the view that the United States had "too much influence in Canada" – up sharply from 21 percent in 1957. Among those taking an unfavourable view, 30 percent cited the notion that "American capital controls our industry." By 1963, pollsters excitedly reported that the proportion of Canadians who considered US investment "not a good thing" had risen – to 29 percent from 17 percent in 1956. On the other hand, well over half of Canadians polled thought US investment a good thing.[25] The safest conclusion is that on the issue of American investment a growing minority – but still a *minority* – of Canadians thought as Gordon did; and perhaps, like Gordon, they had no practical idea what to do about it.

Gordon's economic measures managed to convey the impression that there would always be a tinge of anti-Americanism in Canadian life. But Gordon himself did not immediately or directly attract followers to his cause, and as finance minister he could not overtly campaign for new measures to limit American investment – Cabinet solidarity prevented that. Moreover, the kind of Canadian who supported and voted for the Liberal Party in the 1963 election was more, not less, likely to be pro-American. The Liberals enjoyed, more than the Conservatives, the favour of the affluent, the university-educated, and the urban electorate, and these people were on the whole inclined to view the United States benignly. They had not, and would not, read Walter Gordon's various books expounding his nationalist doctrines; those who tried found them tedious, and their remedies unexciting.

The fact that better-educated and better-paid Canadians supported the Liberal Party did not escape the notice of a professor of theology at McMaster University, George Grant. Grant came from Canada's academic elite, the son of the headmaster at Upper Canada College in Toronto and grandson of the principal of Queen's University. In Grant's family anglophilia was second nature, as it was among most upper-class or upper-middle-class English Canadians. Grant travelled to England to further his education and was caught there by the Second World War. In London during the war he knew Pearson, and one of his sisters was married to a prominent Canadian diplomat, George Ignatieff. Though he came from privilege, Grant did not come from money, and he regretted Canadians' postwar pursuit of affluence and materialism. And he did not like Pearson. Grant penned a long essay interpreting Canada's recent history, which in September 1965 was published under the title *Lament for a Nation*. Coincidentally the book appeared just as Pearson – on Gordon's advice – called a general election. It did not take long for reviewers and readers to discover that Grant had made Diefenbaker the hero of his *Lament*, and the Liberals into smooth, continentalizing, modernizing villains.

"Canada cannot survive as a sovereign nation," Grant wrote. It was too small, too weak, too subject to the overwhelming cultural and economic influence of the United

States. The natural supporters of an independent Canada, the moneyed elite, had abandoned the country by repudiating Diefenbaker and his Conservatives. (Grant had read his polling data.) The election of 1963 was proof of that. Canada would henceforth develop as a junior American nation, in the image of its richer, smarter, elder brother. Grant's book sold 7,000 copies immediately, and over the next three decades, 50,000. As Stephen Azzi notes, "Canadian writers are usually too cautious to use the word 'masterpiece,' particularly in reference to a Canadian book, but to many *Lament for a Nation* deserved this description."[26] "Masterpiece" or not, Grant's book gave anti-Americanism in Canada a voice, and made it a voice of dissent. Grant was especially popular among the young, who found his romantic view of Canada's past appealing, and his denunciation of the present convincing. Grant's past became "authentic" to his many readers and his many more admirers. Liberal society by contrast seemed inhumane, an unworthy pursuit.[27]

The general election of 1965 provided ironic justification of Grant's view of Pearson and his party. The only reason for the election was the pursuit of a parliamentary majority. The 1963 Parliament was working, after its fashion, and the Liberals were in no danger of defeat. But having called an election and put the country through a two-month political campaign, Pearson ended up where he had started, short of a majority.

The main consequence of the election was the formal resignation of Walter Gordon as finance minister. Gordon had given mistaken advice to the prime minister, and he owed it to him to resign. Gordon expected Pearson to dismiss the very idea and confirm his position. Instead the prime minister accepted the resignation, and an embittered Gordon departed the Cabinet. The US embassy rejoiced: "In my view," the ambassador wrote, "we will be far better off in over-all terms with a minority Liberal government without Gordon than we would have been with a majority Government with Gordon."[28] It was a poor prediction. Gordon soon discovered he could say much more outside the government than in it.

In his place, Pearson appointed the minister of trade and commerce, Mitchell Sharp, as minister of finance. Under Sharp, policy would take a very different direction than the one Gordon had tried to pursue. At a Liberal Party conference in 1966, Gordon proposed a series of resolutions that reflected his nationalistic beliefs, urging the government to "reduce foreign ownership and control of Canadian industry and resources to not more than one-third in the next twenty-five years." Sharp disagreed. In a speech to the conference he deplored "narrowly nationalistic policies" and opposed "penalizing enterprise just because it is foreign." Canadian ownership by all means, Sharp argued, but not in a negative and inward-looking spirit. In the subsequent vote, Gordon lost, and lost heavily, 650 to 100.[29]

Pearson sought to avoid a complete break with Gordon. He persuaded him to return briefly to the Cabinet in 1967 in a nominal post, where he remained for just over a year. Gordon's principal activity was to sponsor an economic study of foreign investment, conducted by academics recruited for the purpose. The result, called the Watkins report after its principal author, Mel Watkins, was published in the winter of 1968. Not surprisingly, it was close to Gordon's views and was greeted, especially by those who had not read it, as a manifesto of the new Canadian nationalism. The *Toronto Star* gave the report eight full pages, all favourable. In fact Watkins's analysis was mild and his prescriptions muted. It significance was more in its existence than in its careful suggestions for increasing Canadian participation in the ownership of foreign subsidiaries without resorting to wholesale nationalization or discrimination against foreign-owned businesses.

It was not the end for Gordon's brand of economic nationalism, but that nationalism now moved to the fringe of the Liberal Party, and beyond – to the left-wing New Democratic Party (NDP), and within the NDP to that party's left wing. Economic nationalism was not the only issue before the country, or even before younger Canadians, in the later 1960s. It would be the combination of economic nationalism with other issues that flavoured Canadian public opinion, and influenced Canadian foreign policy.

WHEN PEARSON DECIDED IN SEPTEMBER 1965 to call Canada's third general election in just over three years, he acted out of a sense of weakness. The Liberal government seemed always to be teetering on the edge of disaster, facing constant battles in the House of Commons against a Conservative opposition inspired and animated by the vengeful Diefenbaker. Pearson failed to inspire his followers to a strong response; instead, he appeared fumbling and inconsistent.

Nonetheless, real policy choices had been proposed and made. Economic nationalism scented the air, but did not penetrate into policy, after the abortive episode of Gordon's 1963 budget. Instead, Canadian trade policy took its cue from Sharp, a very different kind of nationalist from Gordon. Gordon's main foray into trade had precisely the opposite result to the one he had intended. Concern for an inefficient Canadian automotive industry and worry over Canada's balance of payments and trade deficit pushed the government into an ill-advised export-subsidy scheme. The American government recognized the financial and industrial problem and proposed a solution that eventually became the Auto Pact.

The most lasting and probably most important legacy of the Pearson government's economic policy was thus "born in the USA." It was manifested in scores of factories across Ontario and in the exponential growth of the Canadian automotive sector. It showed up, too, in the startling improvement in the Canadian balance of payments as cars, trucks, and auto parts became among the country's major exports, dwarfing the primary products that had once been Canada's staples. Under Lester Pearson, Canada was on the road to becoming a different country. It was just not quite the country that Pearson and Walter Gordon had intended.

11

INNOCENCE ABROAD: FUMBLING FOR PEACE IN INDOCHINA

In Canada the Vietnam War is remembered as an episode in domestic politics – riots, protests, dissent – or as a particularly unfortunate period in Canadian-American relations. The symbolism is not forgotten: a small Asian country confronting and ultimately fighting off an imperial superpower – an image that fits solidly into a century of anti-imperialist thought in Western countries. Diplomats recall the period with a shudder, remembering when diplomacy came up against public opinion and lost. "Quiet diplomacy," as far as Canadian-American relations were concerned, was a lost cause, as politicians desperately tried to appease irritable voters. There was no choice except expediency, and no alternative but surrender to what aroused Canadians loudly demanded. It was in some respects the well-intentioned diplomat's worst nightmare.

These images are true enough, as far as they go, but they apply mostly to the second half of Canada's involvement with Vietnam, from 1965 until the fall of Saigon to the Communists in 1975. They do not describe the first half of the Canadian experience in Southeast Asia, from 1954 to 1965, although the story of that early experience is an unhappy one as well. Canada in 1954 undertook to help clean up the aftermath of a colonial war that pitted East against West, South against North, communism against democracy, and the emergent nationalism of the Third World against the colonial hangovers of European imperialism. The Canadian government of the day, Liberal in politics and liberal in temperament, was a firm member of the Western alliance. Yet the government also saw itself as untainted by European – even British – colonialism, and as unmoved by the sometimes hysterical and always strident anti-communism that in the 1950s disfigured American public life. These qualities were considered moral assets, and in 1954 they were deployed in formerly French Indochina.

ORIGINS OF THE CONFLICT

Indochina was the jewel of the French colonial system. Before the Second World War, it was exotic, isolated, and remote, ruled by the French with an iron hand. French proconsuls governed its three components, Vietnam, Cambodia, and Laos, either directly or indirectly through puppet kings. During the war the Japanese disrupted French colonial rule, which was only uneasily restored in the face of a nationalist uprising in Vietnam, led by the Communist Ho Chi Minh. War resulted between the French and their local allies and Ho's Viet Minh movement. It was from the first a civil war as well as a colonial war, and in 1950, when Communist China extended recognition and aid to the Viet Minh, it also became a factor in the Cold War. The Americans responded by sending money, supplies, and advice to the French. They tried to procure help from their allies, including Canada, as well, but the Canadian government, its eyes fixed on Europe, refused.

The Viet Minh extended the war into all parts of Vietnam, and Cambodia and Laos as well. Finally, in May 1954, the Viet Minh forced the surrender of a significant French force at Dien Bien Phu. Faced with the prospect of total defeat within a few months, the French either had to receive additional help from the Americans or come to an arrangement with Ho Chi Minh. The Americans hesitated. If they intervened, it might well have to be with nuclear weapons and without allied support. An international conference was already meeting in Geneva to deal with the aftermath of the Korean War: it seemed advisable to wait and see what it could do.

As a participant in the Korean War, Canada was at Geneva, but as discussion moved on to Indochina, the Canadians, led by Pearson, left for home. "I would repeat," he wrote to St Laurent, "that it has been made clear to all concerned that we have not, and do not expect to have, any special obligation in respect to Indochina or any special claim or desire to be included in the formal Indochinese Conference."[1] The discussions among the powers remaining in Geneva lurched towards an agreement. The Soviet Union and Communist China had had enough of war in Korea and did not want another in Indochina, especially if there were danger of American intervention. The result was a ceasefire, or rather three ceasefires, one for each of the countries of Indochina. Ho Chi Minh and his followers received as a result of their victory the northern part of Vietnam, north of the seventeenth parallel, and agreed to withdraw their forces from Laos, Cambodia, and the southern part of Vietnam. Refugees might move to either zone. Refugee and military movements were to be supervised by an international commission comprising representatives from three powers – a number chosen to avoid deadlocks. The commission – or, rather, commissions, as there would be separate ones for Vietnam, Cambodia, and Laos – would prevent the importation of arms into the region, and the various states of Indochina were to refrain from external military alliances. Western and Communist countries (but not the United States or the existing government of Vietnam) at the conference then drafted a final declaration, which mandated free elections for all of Vietnam to be arranged not later than July 1956, two years in the future. To complicate matters, the United States and the government of Vietnam refused to sign the ceasefire agreement, although the United States publicly declared that it would not obstruct it.[2]

All sides had to cooperate, so it made sense to place representatives of the two sides, Communist and anti-Communist, on the three-nation International Commissions for Security and Control – universally abbreviated to International Control Commissions (ICC). The Communists settled on Poland as their representative. The large and important neutral country of India became the second member and chair of the commissions. But who would represent the West? The United States preferred Belgium, but the Indians and with them the Chinese thought Canada would be more suitable because Belgium, like France, was a colonial power. The Indians had other reasons. Prime Minister St Laurent had publicly discussed the end of French rule and the postcolonial future of Indochina during a visit to New Delhi in January. Canada made a point of listening to and cooperating with India. Canada had sponsored a nuclear reactor for India, CIRUS at Trombay.[3] Canadians, especially Pearson, were well regarded in New Delhi. Pearson, in one Indian's view, "had a fine sense of humour and always strove to find points of agreement between opposing sides and to put forward constructive solutions."[4]

The British prime minister, Anthony Eden, informed the Canadians of their selection for the ICC in terms that he knew they couldn't refuse. "Chou En-lai said to me this afternoon that it was time that agreement was reached on the question of the composition of the International Supervisory Commission. He accordingly proposed that this should consist of India, Canada and Poland. Molotov afterwards told me that he agreed."[5] The initial Canadian reaction to this unanticipated membership was incredulity, followed closely by resignation. Canada had not sought membership, and did not want it, but would agree to the seat in the larger interest of ending the war and avoiding another. The Canadian government, like Canadians generally, knew Indochina only as a blip on a map, and through the dramatic news reports of France's defeat.

The members of the ICC met in New Delhi in August 1954, and then moved on to Hanoi, still under French occupation but destined to be the capital of the Communist state of North Vietnam (properly the Democratic Republic of Vietnam). Pearson instructed the Canadian delegation carefully. They should show "objectivity, impartiality and fairness" in their conduct. They should be careful of contacts with the French and the Americans. They should especially try to get along with the Indians, who provided the commissions' chairmen (there were three – one for each commission) and most of the administrative staff. Canada's goal was "security and stability in Southeast Asia." The Indians, Pearson thought, would cooperate. "In ultimate objectives," he wrote, "Indian policy does not differ radically from our own, in the sense that we both wish to avoid a general war and to see formerly dependent peoples achieve independence and free, as opposed to Communist, self-government."[6]

There were many roads to security and stability and only a few of them passed by the commissions. The French and the North Vietnamese were the two main parties to the ceasefire agreement in Vietnam. The French disengaged speedily from North Vietnam and pulled out all their troops in the North by the spring of 1955, as required by the terms of the ceasefire. A million refugees, mainly Catholic, moved south in the wake of the French, to the vast irritation of the Communists in North Vietnam, who, with the help of the Poles on the ICC, did their best to limit the haemorrhage at the border. Communist troops moved north, or buried their arms and faded into the population in the south.

The attitudes and conduct of the Communists during the evacuation of the northern refugees alienated Canadians on the Vietnamese commission.[7] It was the beginning of a long process of disillusionment – a primer on Communist chicanery. The Poles invariably supported the North Vietnamese. The level of cordiality on the ICC gradually sank, though to watching Americans, it seemed the Canadians on the commission failed to act forcefully enough in combating Polish wiles.[8] The Poles actually thought the Canadians were doing their utmost to be fair. The Polish delegate, Mieczyslaw Maneli, later wrote: "In this period of my work with my Indian and Canadian colleagues, I was struck by their loyal cooperation. It was a period when most of the cases were against the Southern authorities; whenever there was justifiable suspicion that the Southern authorities were treating their citizens in an inhumane manner, the Canadian delegates never hesitated in condemning the crimes. I always considered this to be extremely significant."[9]

Once the evacuation of the North was completed, the Vietnamese commission transferred its main activity to Saigon, the southern capital, while maintaining an office in Hanoi. It also established "fixed teams" of military observers at strategic points around the countryside, to monitor flows of arms and signs of warlike activity. In the North, the commission was soon isolated. Staffers were carefully watched and their movements restricted. Only by accident could the northern teams see something worth reporting. Even if they had a chance to investigate, the Poles, usually with the support of the Indians, could be relied on to frustrate it.

The Vietnamese commission was not the only one facing significant challenges. In Cambodia, the government was run by a prince, Norodom Sihanouk, who attempted in his fashion to balance Communist and American influence in his country. The

Canadian commissioner, Arnold Smith, described Sihanouk and his policies in 1956: he was "a spoiled and highly emotional young man" but also "a brightly intuitive and shrewd politician." Sihanouk claimed in private that his anti-American statements were directed at getting the United States to offer unconditional aid while persuading the Communists that they should leave him alone. Perhaps in the short term this worked, but Smith's "feeling [was] that our Princeling [had] been too clever by rather more than half." The Communists would not be satisfied, in Smith's opinion; and in the long run neither would the Americans. Sihanouk nevertheless managed to hold on for the next sixteen years, before being overthrown in an American-approved coup.[10]

Laos was a sleepy place. Its tiny political elite, divided into pro-Western, neutral, and Communist factions, squabbled among itself. The pro-Communist forces, the Pathet Lao, occupied an area along the Chinese and North Vietnamese borders, and commission activity in the mid-1950s was devoted to finding a way to bring them into alignment with the rest of the country.

SQUABBLING OVER THE SPOILS

Cambodia was peculiar, Laos somnolent, and South Vietnam chaotic. There were still substantial French forces in the South, and France was responsible for maintaining the South's end of the ceasefire agreement concluded at Geneva. Against that prospect was the inescapable fact of military defeat, and the acceptance in Paris that further effort in Indochina was impossible. Worse, a rebellion broke out in Algeria in November 1954, which absorbed all available French military resources. Thus, Paris had to keep on at least minimally good terms with the United States, which was taking a larger interest in Vietnam.

If a continuing French role in Indochina existed mostly in the imagination of a few unreconstructed French officers and diplomats, American influence could also be exaggerated. In North Vietnam, American prestige was non-existent, and the US consulate in Hanoi soon closed. In Saigon the Americans dealt uneasily with the government of the State of Vietnam, nominally a monarchy under an emperor, Bao Dai, who preferred Cannes to Saigon. In the last stages of the Indochina war, the emperor appointed Ngo Dinh Diem, an administrator and politician, as premier of his semi-autonomous government. Diem had earlier chosen exile rather than collaborate with the French, but he was fervently anti-Communist, a nationalist, and a devout Catholic. He was also a man of singularly rigid views and character.

Diem has often been portrayed as a puppet of the Americans, but that conclusion does violence to his historical role. Diem had a clear agenda, and made little secret of it. He wanted, first, to get rid of the emperor and concentrate power in his own hands. Next, he wanted to get rid of the French and their local allies. Finally he wanted a united Vietnam, obviously under his own authority. To get what he wanted, he was prepared to use whatever means came to hand, and in the circumstances of 1954-1955 that could only mean the Americans. He understood that the first step in dealing with the Americans, as with other optimistic Westerners, was telling them what they wanted to hear. That meant he had to appear as a man of the twentieth century, an Asian democrat committed to some extent to the virtues of republican government. He also had to be effective, and in 1954-1955 Diem moved swiftly to show that he was the man of the hour.

The Canadian delegation to the ICC misunderstood the dynamics of Vietnamese politics and underestimated the man of the hour. This was to some extent a functional problem. Diem, after all, did not recognize the Geneva agreement the commission was supposed to enforce. He wanted nothing to do with the ICC, which symbolized the division of his country, if not worse. Instead, the commission dealt with the parties to the ceasefire, the French and the North Vietnamese. The French looked after the ICC in Saigon, furnished accommodation and other facilities, and served as interlocutor when the commissioners had to address someone.[11] The commissioners believed that it was possible, with French cooperation, for the ICC to supervise elections in 1956, as the Geneva final declaration promised, leading to the reunification of the country and the triumphant conclusion of the commission's mandate.

The commission dreamed its dreams. So did senior Canadian diplomats, especially the high commissioner in New Delhi, Escott Reid. Reid had long been seduced by the notion that Canada and India should act as a bridge between East (meaning the Orient rather than the Communist bloc) and West, and between the underdeveloped world and the advanced and prosperous countries of Europe and North America. Indochina seemed an ideal proving ground for his theories. Creating the Indochina commissions had actually brought East and West into intimate contact, not in the antiseptic climate of the United Nations or the controlled atmosphere of his small diplomatic staff, but in the day-to-day business of observation and negotiation. For most Canadians who served in Indochina, this was their first taste of the East; for the Indians, with colonial rule only seven years back, it was not their first experience with Westerners. Moreover, the decisions the Indians took would have repercussions in their own neighbourhood. The Canadians, when they finished, could go home across a wide ocean; but Indochina, some of the Indians reflected, was practically next door. If Canadians on the commissions conducted themselves within the confines of a general Canadian foreign policy, their Indian counterparts did the same with regard to Indian foreign policy. And Canadian and Indian policies were not the same.

There was one further complication, originally mechanical but with strong policy implications. The commissions consumed a great many Canadian resources: diplomatic from the Department of External Affairs; and military from the Department of

National Defence. In theory the ICC expenses were paid by the signatories at Geneva, channelled through the two co-chairs of the Geneva Conference, Great Britain and the Soviet Union. But payments took time, and not everything could be covered. So, in the short term there was inconvenience and in the longer term distortion of other Canadian priorities that would have to be pared back. As the undersecretary for external affairs, Jules Léger, wrote Pearson in 1954, the whole cost of Canada's participation on the ICC would not be less than $4 million a year, which might occasion "shock ... when the size and cost of the operation was realized."[12]

Indochina was not, by Canadian diplomatic standards, normal. Facilities were primitive, even by the standards of tropical posts, health was a problem, communications difficult, and recreation limited.[13] As a hardship posting, an Indochinese tour of duty was limited to a year, and families, if any, had to be left behind. Understandably the government tried to select single personnel, who in addition had to be young and healthy. The first shock to personnel was the blast of sultry tropical air. It was an age before general air conditioning in Southeast Asia, and the hotels judged suitable for Canadian diplomats and soldiers were not cooled. As a consequence, noted a departmental inspection team in 1964, "virtually all members of the staff in Saigon spend a good deal of their free time in air-conditioned bars and cafés rather than in their hot, bleak hotel rooms. This inevitably gives rise to intimacy with the bar girls and more often than not ends up with one girl sharing the member's bed and board. Such arrangements seem to be accepted in the Catinat Hotel particularly as a matter of course."[14]

It took time for this situation to develop: more time than Pearson had imagined in 1954. Initially, he had hoped that there would be elections, but the problem with elections grew the more the Canadians looked at it. Pearson attempted to persuade American Secretary of State Foster Dulles that if they were held a majority might well support Diem, not Ho,[15] but it was clear that this could happen only if the commission or some other international supervisory body took control of the electoral process, North and South. It was very doubtful that the North Vietnamese would ever agree to such a condition, and even more unlikely that the ICC, with its Indian swing vote, would be able to manage the issue through "compromise," voting first for one side and then the other in an attempt at balance.[16] The Indians believed in compromise for its own sake, regardless of the issue at hand. This tactical approach satisfied neither of their ICC partners, and there was a strategic problem as well.

In 1954 Pearson had laid down that Canada's and India's "ultimate objectives" were the same. At the time the few Canadians knowledgeable about India were persuaded that this was so, and the high commissioner in New Delhi, Escott Reid, was an especially fervent believer in the notion. The ICC would be its first test before a larger audience. The numbers and rotations of Canadian personnel assigned to the ICC meant that as early as 1955 there were significant numbers of serving officers, mostly young, with Indochinese experience. Escott Reid learned this when he came to Ottawa on home leave in the summer of 1955 and "was asked to give a report on India at a meeting of the senior officers of the Department ... In my talk I spoke of the intent which I understood lay behind the acceptance by France and Britain of the Geneva settlement: that it was not possible to hold a line against Communist expansion in Vietnam, but that it was possible to hold a line at the border between Laos and Cambodia on one side and Vietnam on the other, and that France and Britain had implicitly acquiesced at Geneva in Ho Chi Minh taking over the whole of Vietnam as the result of elections. This, I said, was the Indian point of view and I agreed with it." It quickly became clear that the officers of the department did not. "The roof fell in on me," Reid wrote. "Officer after officer at the meeting attacked me for my callous, immoral proposal which would betray millions of anti-communist people in South Vietnam into the clutches of the communists of North Vietnam."[17] The prospect of a speedy wind-up of the commission was draining away. The senior officers were right, but in a larger sense, so was Reid. There had to be a political settlement that the North would accept, and the Indian model was closer to it than the one Reid's colleagues might have had in mind.

By then it was already unclear who could enforce the "Indian alternative," as presented by Reid. Diem in 1955 eliminated rival political factions in Saigon (including a criminal gang, the Binh Xuyen, in cahoots with the French), staged a referendum that eliminated the emperor, and, at the beginning of 1956, told the remaining French forces to pack up and go. They did. To let the commission and especially the Indians know what he thought of them, he staged a riot that plundered their possessions.[18] As Diem consolidated his power, the ICC soldiered on. The Canadians, still assuming that elections would be held, hired a political scientist specializing in elections to assist them. Diem allowed the ICC to stay in Saigon and its various "fixed team" posts around South Vietnam and even gave it minimal logistical support. At the insistence of the Americans, he apologized for his riot, but he was determined that elections would not be held.

American policy towards Vietnam, and Diem, was by no means clear. The American emissary, General J. Lawton Collins, had studied Diem and did not like what he saw. He recommended the United States extricate itself from South Vietnam as quickly as possible. Secretary of State Dulles took the opposite position. President Eisenhower eventually had to decide, and chose Diem.[19] Diem would now receive the support he needed. As another American official put it, a bit later, it was "Sink or Swim with Ngo Dinh Diem." Dulles said as much to Pearson in what was described as an unhappy interview early in 1956. The ICC – and Pearson – accepted the situation; even the Indians decided that it was more important to carry on with the commission than to exit on a statement of principle. Pearson did toy with the idea of pulling out altogether but eventually settled for "a policy of stalling," continuing with the commission as "the best chance of keeping the peace and holding the line in Asia."[20]

North Vietnam was dismayed that there would be no elections and hence no unification, though the Communist leadership knew that Ngo Dinh Diem was unlikely to agree to reunification on Hanoi's terms.[21] There is not much doubt that the Indians were right when they told Reid the North Vietnamese assumed that the South Vietnam government would collapse, using the fig leaf of elections in 1956. When the fatal date rolled around, the North Vietnamese found that their senior Communist partners, the Soviet Union and China, were not willing to back them in demanding that elections take place in both North and South. Diem, and with him the Americans, gambled that the North would accept the situation. For a time it looked as if they might have won. North and South Korea existed, and East and West Germany: Why not North and South Vietnam?

HOPING FOR THE BEST

From 1956 to 1960 Canada's Vietnam policy was to go with the flow. Ngo Dinh Diem was a political fact of life. The United States fed its – and his – appetite for security by sending in clandestine weapons, while the Communists did much the same in the North. Life on the ICC drifted into a routine of trips North, trips South, trips out, reports and debate. The Canadians pressed for Commission action on myriad complaints from both sides, which the Poles obstructed, while the Indians dithered. The Laos commission, with little to occupy itself, was wound up. Paul Martin, the minister of health and welfare, visited Saigon in 1956 and met Diem, a fellow Catholic, and all seemed to be well. Doubtless Martin was hoping for favourable optics at home among Catholic voters. In Ottawa, St Laurent gave way to Diefenbaker, but where Vietnam was concerned there was no thought of a change of policy. The fact that Diem seemed to be maintaining, if not improving, his position had its own logic, even for the Indians and Poles.

As we have seen, Vietnam was far from the only flashpoint in Cold War politics in the late 1950s. The Soviet Union meddled with the West, first in Berlin, then in Cuba. As it did so, its eastern door came unhinged: Soviet relations with Communist China plunged into crisis. From 1958 or 1959 on, the two Communist powers viewed the world through different lenses and drew different conclusions. Smaller Communist powers were called on to take sides. Predictably, the Communist countries in Europe (except for tiny, remote Albania) sided with Moscow. North Vietnam attempted to straddle the chasm, but by the time the Sino-Soviet split became official and public, in 1960, the North Vietnamese leadership had taken the country's destiny in its own hands. In 1959 it decided to renew the war in the South, authorizing local Communists to take armed action against Diem, with the assurance of support from the North. That year, guerrillas began to assassinate local agents of the Diem regime.[22]

Events in Vietnam were for some time overshadowed by those in neighbouring Laos. Ill-advisedly, the Eisenhower administration decided that Laos was the frontier of freedom. For four years, between 1959 and 1962, American leaders contemplated events in the tiny kingdom, solemnly debating which Laotian faction chief better exemplified the values of freedom and democracy. The US ambassador in Laos fought a rearguard action for a sense of proportion, but in a debate of this kind local expertise can only count for so much. The Canadians were drawn into conferences in Geneva where the balance of power in Laos was discussed. Their role was to be ready to cooperate in case the Laotian ICC was reactivated, as it inevitably was. Canada reluctantly returned to the Laotian capital, Vientiane.

When Eisenhower handed over the American presidency to John F. Kennedy in January 1961, he spent most of the time briefing his young successor over Laos, which he appears to have thought would be the birthplace of a third world war. These thoughts were concealed from the Canadians, as from the other allies, though the Canadians suspected that behind the frantic Laotian negotiations there might lurk the threat of atomic weapons as the ultimate equalizer. These fears were not entirely misplaced, but fortunately they were never realized.[23]

The situation in Laos alarmed the Saigon government, as it should have. Geographically, the country offered a route from North to South Vietnam, avoiding the heavily patrolled frontier between the two Vietnams – where, incidentally, the ICC maintained one of its "fixed teams." Diem also took fright at the many schemes for "neutralizing" Laos, a formula that, applied to Vietnam, would have meant sharing power with the emerging guerrilla forces. He therefore urged the Americans to stand firm in Laos.

The ICC was an unhappy witness to a steady rise in violence in South Vietnam. Assassinations ate away at the foundations of Diem's government. Large areas became "unsafe" and travel possible only in military convoys. The South Vietnamese, the Americans, and the Canadians on the ICC, blamed external forces, namely the North Vietnamese. The North Vietnamese, and the Poles on the ICC, blamed misgovernment and justified the violence as a people's insurrection. Both sides were, of course, right. To counter what was seen as a form of invasion, the Americans sent "advisers" to bolster the military in the South, and then helicopters and pilots to fly them. A US Military Assistance Advisory Group (MAAG) duly appeared to coordinate the American program. The United States justified its aid to Diem by pointing to evidence that North Vietnam was clearly supplying the rebellion in the south with men and with arms. Briefly, in 1961-1962, the Indians and Canadians on the ICC cooperated to produce a majority special report condemning the North for "inciting, encouraging and supporting hostile activities" in the South, in contravention of the ceasefire agreement. The report also condemned the large-scale American aid as clearly prohibited by the same agreement.[24]

The special report, the Canadians hoped, would give the ICC some badly needed credibility in South Vietnam. If that were so, it might give the commission a new lease on life and make it a genuinely moderating force. Certainly the South Vietnamese and the Americans were pleased. The report was in many ways a propaganda victory for the South, and the North took it very much in that way. The North rejected the report and its conclusions, and argued that the very idea of ICC condemnation of subversion – an internal matter – was forbidden by the terms of the Geneva ceasefire.

The Canadian delegation to the ICC hoped that the special report had marked the emergence of an Indo-Canadian majority on the commission, able to investigate and report impartially on violations of the ceasefire. The fact that the report even-handedly condemned the South and the Americans as well as the North would demonstrate the "objectivity, impartiality and fairness" that Pearson had once hoped would govern the conduct of the ICC. But that was not to be. As reported by the British ambassador in Saigon, the commission enjoyed a brief period of "unprecedented popularity" in the South following the publication of the special report, but thereafter it "lapsed into inactivity, increasingly conscious of its fundamental impotence and bedevilled by financial worries."[25] The Indian chairman retreated into formalism, refusing to publish a legal report that his delegation had helped draft, thereby disappointing the Canadian delegation.[26]

In 1963 Canada's disappointment turned into frustration. The Pearson government had not placed Indochina very high on its list of priorities, but as the year wore on it was obvious that the situation in South Vietnam was becoming dangerous. The Communist guerrillas, called Viet Cong by their enemies, were able to defeat whole battalions of government troops and found means to defend themselves against American helicopter attacks. Junior American officers in Vietnam talked freely to reporters about the incompetence of the South Vietnamese army and the cowardice of Diem's government, and Vietnam became a front-page embarrassment for the Kennedy administration. Senior American officers in Saigon and the American ambassador stoutly clung to Diem as the only hope of success in Indochina, but they had to argue their case in the face of his manifest lack of success in defeating Communist guerrillas. Kennedy resisted demands from his military advisers for stronger action in Indochina, but he had nothing else to put in place of the already failed policy of aid and more aid for the South Vietnamese. Kennedy and Pearson discussed Vietnam at Kennedy's seaside home in Hyannis Port in May 1963, and the president seems to have told the prime minister of his desire to get out of Vietnam; unfortunately he had no idea how to do so. Democrats were mesmerized by the "loss" of China to communism and the subsequent criticism that had crippled the Truman administration. If Kennedy "lost" Vietnam in the same way, it might unleash a new wave of McCarthyism in America. So, curiously, the pursuit of "success" in South Vietnam was a defence against a more militant anti-communism in American politics.

Events in Vietnam accelerated, and, to the distress of a new, youngish, and activist Canadian commissioner, Gordon Cox, the ICC stood by, unable to act with any resolve. Cox certainly brought enthusiasm to his task, but some observers questioned whether he brought judgment. The British ambassador later rather loftily criticized Cox's performance, but his remarks have the ring of truth. "He [Cox] came to Saigon, his first Head of Mission post, with the evident intention of making his mark. At a time when experienced observers had lost confidence in President Diem's ability to bring the war to a successful conclusion, he elected to commit himself strongly to an optimistic view. This meant that during the first half of 1963 he was very much closer in his views to the American Embassy than to ourselves. With their encouragement, he applied himself assiduously to attempts to make use of the ICC machinery to secure condemnation of North Viet Nam, while turning a blind eye to American breaches of the Geneva Agreement."[27]

Kennedy replaced his ambassador in Saigon in the summer of 1963, sending a prominent Republican politician, Henry Cabot Lodge. Lodge had no doubts about what should be done, which was to get rid of Diem, a point Kennedy could not bring himself to face. His administration was divided, but finally the Americans in Saigon were authorized to nod when senior Vietnamese officers suggested a coup. The coup duly occurred on 1 November 1963; in the course of it, Diem and two of his brothers were murdered.

Cox was embittered by the assassination and by his failure to turn the ICC into anything more than a debating society where sterility alternated with passivity. "I would be less than honest if I were to confess to anything other than a sense of futility and discouragement," he wrote in February 1964.[28] He made no secret of his view that the murder of Diem was a grave mistake (or worse), attracting the ire of Ambassador Lodge, who was implicated in the event. Lodge painted Cox in his dispatches home as eccentric if not disloyal, and welcomed his abrupt departure in June 1964. When Cox paid a formal farewell call, Lodge could barely contain himself. Cox spoke of North Vietnamese preparations for war, and saw no sign that Hanoi would ever accommodate US desires. "He [Cox] hoped the US would not lay NVN waste, as had been hinted," Lodge wrote. "I assured him we would not. All of the above must be taken with a large grain of salt having in mind Cox's several sets of prejudices."[29]

Cox's superiors saw him as both pro-American and a Cold Warrior – as indeed did some of his American colleagues. He had made the mistake of alienating a powerful American politician whose own competence at his post was doubtful.

THE CANADIAN-INDIAN CRISIS, 1964-1965

The ICC had become a problem of the first importance for the Canadian government.

Over time Ottawa had poured soldiers and diplomats into the enterprise, with no useful result. The only positive thing to be said for the ICC was that nobody wanted to disband it. North Vietnamese, South Vietnamese, British, Soviets, and Americans all argued that its disappearance would be a blow to peace, a final admission that the Geneva Agreement of 1954 was inoperable and that consequently peace had finally broken down. That argument had admittedly become rather thin by 1964-1965, with full-scale war just around the corner, and so a variant appeared: the ICC might prove useful in winding up the war that was coming. However the ICC was viewed, Ottawa had determined that the drain on Canadian diplomatic resources should not be allowed to continue.

Under these circumstances, the Canadian government decided to try one more time to turn the ICC into something more than a waiting room for unspecified future events. In doing so Canadian diplomats drew on a decade of frustration and irritation directed not so much at the Poles – as Communists they would behave like Communists – as at the Indians. The crisis began with a further increase in the hostilities in Vietnam. In August 1964 American ships fired on North Vietnamese patrol boats in international waters in the Gulf of Tonkin. As we shall see in the next chapter, that move caused a great stir in the United States and proved to be a harbinger of what was to follow in Vietnam. For the moment, however, it was an issue for the ICC, to which the North Vietnamese complained. It became clear that the Indians and Poles on the commission would likely issue a condemnation of the American action, and that this would not be balanced by any reproaches directed towards the North for infiltration and subversion.

To their existing complaints of inefficiency and inaction, the Canadians now added unfairness. In trying to address these issues, the Canadians had their eyes on more than just the ICC. Securing a condemnation of the North or even a balanced report might make the Americans happier with Canada and even put off the day when they would choose to send troops to Vietnam. The issue was fought between the latest Canadian commissioner, Blair Seaborn, and the Indians in Saigon, but it also became a matter between Ottawa and New Delhi. The undersecretary for external affairs, Marcel Cadieux, raised the subject with the Indian high commissioner in Ottawa and with the Indian Ministry of External Affairs via the Canadian high commissioner in New Delhi, Roland Michener. As Louis Rogers, the senior officer dealing with Asian affairs in Ottawa put it to a British diplomat, "the Indians seemed to think that, as in the past, they would be able to 'take the Canadians up and down the garden path' but that this time they would find that the Canadians were in earnest ... Throughout our conversation Rogers manifested the most extreme frustration towards the Indians."[30] The campaign lasted for the best part of a year, from the summer of 1964 to the summer of 1965. When it was over, nothing had changed for the better, and relations between Canadians and Indians on the commission had been strained to the breaking point.

Why did the Canadian campaign to secure a more effective commission fail? It is not enough to say that it was one-sided, though it might be argued that its perspective was narrow. The objective was a balance, not a simple whitewash of American or South Vietnamese misdeeds or a blanket condemnation of the North. Nor is it sufficient to argue that Indian policy was also narrowly self-interested, concocted with an eye to Soviet support for India over China, or against Pakistan in the eternal rivalry of the subcontinent. It is clear that Canada's attempt to appeal to common values – which is really what the quest for an impartial and balanced commission was about – did not weigh sufficiently in the balance. Indians in Saigon, and in New Delhi too, judged the commission to be a frail instrument. Attempting to turn it into an effective instrument for investigation and judgment was akin to putting an engine in an oxcart. And where would it go? The cause of the Saigon government was surely lost: What practical or useful purpose would be served by propping up Saigon? Unfairness and imbalance, exercised on behalf of the winning side, had their advantages.

The key point in the failure of Canadian diplomacy, and the only one under Canadian control, was that the Canadians were, contrary to Louis Rogers, not "in earnest." If Ottawa thought the commission futile and frustrating, it could withdraw, and, under the circumstances of 1964 or 1965, that would probably have been enough to terminate the ICC. The decision whether to stay or go belonged to the political level, to Pearson and Martin. Martin went a considerable distance in protesting and complaining to New Delhi about Indian conduct on the ICC, but he never took it to the point of winding the commission up; even if he had, it is an open question whether Pearson would have agreed with him.

When the Indian prime minister, Lal Bahadur Shastri, visited Ottawa in June 1965, he and Pearson had a discussion on Vietnam that was described as more lengthy than fruitful. In essence the Indians thought that the United States ought to be more accommodating – like the more realistic Canadians. Nevertheless, "the bitter frustrations which the Canadians have been experiencing over Indian tactics in the Commission over the past year were not allowed to protrude above the smooth surface of this ministerial visit."[31]

A few weeks later, Martin finally had to make up his mind over what to do about the ICC. His subordinates pressed for withdrawal, but the minister hesitated. "I had an opportunity of discussing the future of the Commission with the Minister yesterday," an official wrote, continuing,

> From my discussion, I would take it that the Minister does not favour Canadian withdrawal from the Commission at this time for the following reasons among others:
>
> 1 Unilateral Canadian withdrawal in present circumstances could be held to add a further complicating element to the situation in Vietnam;

2 Membership in the Commission does give us a *locus standi* in international discussions of the Vietnam problem;

3 Membership in the Commission also enables us to resist pressure for direct Canadian involvement in the Vietnam situation;

4 The possibility of the Commission being able to play some part in moving toward a solution of the Vietnam problem cannot be altogether excluded, however remote the prospects may appear at the moment.[32]

A functional commission having failed, and withdrawal being excluded, there was only one alternative left: Canada could downgrade the ICC, stop its crusading attempt to make the commission functional, and leave the diplomacy of Vietnam to higher authority. The ICC was, as Douglas Ross noted, "effectively dead" after 1965, though its ghost lingered until 1973 and another phantom peace superseded it.[33]

CANADA, THE UNITED STATES, AND THE ICC

Canadian delegations in Indochina were necessarily in frequent contact with their American counterparts. It was not working contact – that was with the Poles and the Indians, and with the commissions' Laotian, Cambodian, and North and South Vietnamese hosts. But the Americans were nearby, they spoke the same language, and they were usually friendly.

In the commissions' early days, American representatives in Indochina took an urgent interest in what they were doing – in redeploying troops and in managing the outflow of refugees from North Vietnam. When North Vietnam closed up and the American consulate in Hanoi closed down, the ICC became a source of whatever information there was about the mysterious North. Canadian, civilian but especially military, travellers were regularly debriefed on what they saw in the North, which was almost always what the North Vietnamese permitted them to see.[34] Canadians, it should be noted, were not the only source of information. Indian diplomats and especially the Indian military from time to time told the Americans what they could about the North.

The news from Hanoi was not always what the Americans wanted to hear – though it depended on which American was doing the listening. It also mattered which Canadian was doing the reporting. A May 1965 report from a Canadian, David Jackson, in Hanoi, faithfully transcribed in the US embassy, began: "Settling of sultry summer over Hanoi and long day of new working routine has failed to discourage local authorities from maintaining tempo of seemingly endless civil defense preparations."[35]

Contacts between Canadians and Americans in Saigon were not usually at a very high level. The military talked to the military, but not at any exalted rank, and, as the American embassy grew, the American ambassador became an increasingly grand and remote figure, never more so than when the imperious Henry Cabot Lodge held the post in 1963-1964. (A Canadian diplomat did, however, date one of his family members.) The British embassy in Saigon represented British interests, which were important because Great Britain was one of the two co-chairs of the Geneva Conference and thus, along with the Soviet Union, the official paymaster and reporting centre for the ICC.

Initially, during the mid-1950s especially, Canadian reports and British analyses were freely interchanged, usually in London, where the Foreign Office's expertise in the area was greatly prized by the Canadians. There were local differences, never more so than when Gordon Cox was Canadian commissioner. When the pro-American Cox offended the US embassy, he found little sympathy for his position in the British embassy, which found him entirely too "American" for its taste.

All in all, where the Americans were concerned, the Canadian presence on the ICC was useful but remote, friendly but, except on a very few issues, not especially important. Washington marched to its own drummer – and of course, down to 1963, to Diem's. But not to Ottawa's, a conclusion that was reciprocated both in reports from Saigon and in discussions in Ottawa. In Vietnam, Canada and the United States were allies of a kind, but of a distant kind.

❦

THE SAD STORY OF THE INTERNATIONAL CONTROL COMMISSIONS is instructive. Canada, wealthy, Western, and willing, undertook to facilitate peace in Indochina, an area where it had no expertise but, as important, no axe to grind, in 1954. Canada had experience of international commissions, mostly along the border with the United States, and knew, or thought it knew, how they worked.

In India, the commission chair, Canada had an ideal partner – English-speaking and imbued with British traditions of fair play, but also motivated, like Canada, to prevent war, a war that had already harmed a Canadian ally, France, and threatened to drag in the United States. The Indians, it should be stressed, were the most important power on the ICC. Because they handled the administration of the commissions, they also had the largest delegation by far, and the day-to-day conduct of business depended on the capacities of the Indian chairmen and their staff.

Not for the first time, a common language was no bar to misunderstanding and misconstruction. Culturally, the Canadian staff on the commission found the Indians a foreign puzzle. Most of them had little previous experience with India, or any other part of Asia, and they found Indian ways of doing business strange and slow at best. The Canadians had little use for enforced leisure; that, coupled with their living conditions in the steam bath of Saigon, turned them into a parody of a colonial garrison or occupation army, complete with black market and prostitutes.

The year-by-year grind of life in Saigon and Hanoi gradually wore down the mortar from the Canadian-Indian relationship. As Marcel Cadieux put it in a report on a frosty interview with the Indian high commissioner, "a whole generation of Cdn officials had served in Commissions and ... their experience had affected Cdn-Indian relations. Their views on Indian policy had become much more concrete and detailed and this process had had a very sobering effect. Quality of relationship between Indian and Cdn officials had changed as result of experience in Indochina."[36]

Canada and India did not always disagree, but by themselves they could do little about the return to war in Vietnam. The decision in 1955-1956 to forget about elections and hope for the best was mutual, even if arrived at separately and for somewhat different reasons. It was a gamble that, under the circumstances of 1956, may have been justified because North Vietnam had little support outside its own resources, and thus nothing with which to resume the war. A few years later that was no longer so, and in 1959 the North Vietnamese decided to proceed with reunifying their country by force of arms.

They might not have succeeded had the Ngo Dinh Diem regime in South Vietnam managed to construct a viable political base, but it did not. Nevertheless, Diem's political skill and courage should not be underestimated. When effectively deployed, as they were in 1954-1955, Diem's qualities were more than sufficient to outmanoeuvre the French and ensnare the Americans. Diem too gambled for high stakes, for by bringing in the United States and its wealth and power he raised expectations among his patrons that he ultimately failed to satisfy. The consequence, in his case, was his overthrow and death.

The Americans gambled on Diem and then on his successors. The stakes were high and luck was against them. The failure of their luck helped bring on a military effort that was intended to contain and end the war but instead encouraged it to spiral out of control. To this spectacle the Canadians in Saigon were helpless witnesses. But then, so were Canadians in Ottawa, as the next chapter will show.

VIETNAM
AND CANADIAN-AMERICAN
RELATIONS

12

Crossing the border from the United States into Canada was less than momentous for young Americans coming to Canada in the 1960s: "Then it occurred to me that at some point we must've passed into Canadian waters, across that dotted line between two different worlds," wrote American novelist and Vietnam veteran Tim O'Brien.[1] The farther shore of the Rainy River looked just the same, but to O'Brien's protagonist it was "a different world." There was indeed a difference. O'Brien's world was beset by a distant and apparently pointless war, its young men, like O'Brien himself, destined for the military, for the United States had conscription, the draft. The other world, on the surface exactly the same, just across the Rainy River, or the forty-ninth parallel, or the Niagara, on the way to Winnipeg or Vancouver or Montreal, had no war, and no draft.

O'Brien's character chose not to land on the Canadian shore. He did not become a "draft dodger," but rather returned home to family, country, and war. Canada remained an imaginary refuge to him and to most of the two million American military personnel who went to Vietnam. Others chose not to go. "I felt okay about not having gone to Vietnam," Larry Martin recalled in Vancouver in the mid-1980s. "The rite of passage in our case was coming to Canada, a strange country." At the time, it seemed that the consequences of this right of passage might be permanent: the prospect of an American amnesty for draft evaders was unthinkable. "When you came to Canada, you never expected to go home."[2] A very large number of young Americans – probably around 50,000 – did the same.[3] They found a country remarkably similar to their own and sympathetic support in Canada's cities, especially among people their own age. As one summed it up, "If this is jail, it sure is a big, beautiful one."[4] Later, the war over, many returned to the United States, but many stayed.

The arrival of draft dodgers posed a problem for the Canadian government. It was not, strictly speaking, a legal problem. The dodgers could not be extradited to the United States, because an extraditable offence must be a crime in both countries. There being no draft in Canada, evading the draft was no crime. The problem was complicated by the nature of the Canadian immigration service, which like many other government departments offered preferential and secure employment to Canadian war veterans. Most immigration officers, those who greeted and sifted through inbound travellers to Canada, fell into this category. They were prone to regard draft dodgers and, worse, deserters from the US military as highly undesirable immigrants; in this they did no more than reflect the conservative side of Canadian opinion.[5]

The government in Ottawa was, however, Liberal, and on this issue tended to be liberal as well. As a minority government it was especially sensitive to the currents of Canadian opinion. Vietnam could affect the Liberal Party's voting base, over the longer term; in the short run, it was a litmus test for the left-leaning New Democratic Party, on whom the government ordinarily relied for support in securing a majority in the House of Commons. Mitchell Sharp, a senior minister under both Pearson and Trudeau, explained that "the general feeling in the circles in which I moved in the civil service and in the public service was that the Americans had made a mistake" in going into Vietnam. If the war was a mistake, then it followed that "when we thought about de-serters: [we asked] from what?"[6]

Less visible and less discussed was the movement of young Canadians in the other direction. Roughly 20,000 to 30,000 Canadians served in the American armed forces during the Vietnam War, and 111, according to official figures, died. Their names are carved in the Vietnam War memorial, a giant black wall, in Washington.[7]

There were differences over the war in the United States. But there were also differences in Canada, among Canadians, between those who sympathized with the war and supported the official American war effort, and those who disagreed and supported the unofficial American war resistance. As a result, the history of Canadian relations with the United States during the Vietnam War is both official and unofficial, less the history of divergence than of similarities, as two governments struggled with a newly intractable public opinion.

An Unhappy Public and Uneasy Policy

The political problems of Canadian-American relations in the 1960s began much earlier than that unhappy decade. In some senses they had always been present, because Canadians had from the beginning sought to find and define differences between themselves and Americans. Naturally the effort implied such differences should, if possible, cast a favourable light on Canadians. In discovering American defects, Canadians often relied on American sources and opinions, and on American self-dissections, and with a generally free press in the United States these were plentiful.

The resemblance between Canadian and American opinion on political issues – on any issue – was marked.[8] Differences there were: down to the 1960s, polls suggested that Canadians were more conservative and less adventurous than Americans. On the great issues of foreign policy, however, North Americans had similar views, opposing communism, fearing war, supporting NATO, and blaming the Soviets. As we shall see, general public opinion surveys during the 1960s show more similarities than differences between Canadians and Americans on questions of foreign policy, including Vietnam.

But how to interpret public opinion? Did all opinions count equally, and did they equally influence the makers of policy? Polls conducted in 1962 suggested that there was a substantial divergence between the views of political leaders and those of the general population. As a survey for the Canadian Peace Research Institute put it, "Most Canadians regard Communism as a danger to the West, but are by no means unanimous on how this danger should be handled." Asked whether they agreed that "the West should take all steps to defeat Communism, even if it means risking nuclear war," 42 percent of a national sample agreed, while 47 percent disagreed. But among a sample of business people, presumably better educated and better informed than the general population, the proportion disagreeing rose to 86 percent; among political leaders, it was 81 percent.[9] The difference between the political elite and the general population crossed party lines. Labour leaders and the leaders of the left-leaning Co-operative Commonwealth Federation (CCF) and its successor, the New Democratic Party (NDP), were more likely to agree – but these were labour and political leaders, not the rank and file. Nor were the differences transitory. A subsequent survey in 1964 led a prominent journalist, Blair Fraser, to the conclusion that "a majority of Canadians differ sharply from the majority of politicians, regardless of party." Perhaps the most striking figure reported in the survey was that 41 percent of Canadians generally favoured "a hard line against [the] Communist bloc" but that only 4 percent of politicians did.[10]

Conducting Canadian-American relations always ran the danger of awakening the restless dragon of Canadian nationalism. Nationalism took many forms, and many of those forms were anti-American. Yet that sentiment coexisted with an acceptance of American influence, or American money, or American culture – or all three. Experienced politicians like John Diefenbaker oscillated between pro- and anti-American poles almost by instinct. The more self-conscious Pearson was aware of the contradictions imposed on him by the divisions and overlaps in Canadian opinion. They were present in his own Liberal Party, and between the Liberal Party and the general population.

Pearson, like other thoughtful Liberals, worried about his party's place in the political spectrum. Many Canadians in the 1950s had seen the St Laurent government as too complacent, alienating important parts of the electorate. In 1960 labour leaders and survivors of the old CCF decided to form a "new party" that would appeal to progressives generally, including left-wing Liberals. In 1961 this "new party" became the New Democratic Party. To counter the possibility of a drift to the NDP, Pearson encouraged the Liberal Party to move to the left – though no further left than American Democrats at the same time. The result was a broadly reformist platform that the Pearson government after 1963 was committed to enacting. The reformism was allied to, but not the same as, Walter Gordon's nationalism. It was more closely linked to a craving for a new approach to foreign policy. For this Pearson, with his Nobel Peace Prize, seemed well equipped.

"Peace" suggested that Pearson should exploit the sense among Canadians that, after the Cuban Missile crisis, the Cold War had thawed. War with the Soviet Union no longer seemed likely, though China lurked as a peril in the public mind. If the Cold War was less dangerous, there was less need to follow American leadership, and less need, too, for high defence spending.

To this we should add the perennial problem of Canadian sentiments about the United States, so apparently favourable in the early 1960s. As an American diplomat who later made a specialty of Canada and Canadians noted in 1961, "American officials who follow United States-Canadian relations closely will be aware of the often contradictory elements of Canadian attitudes toward the United States, which frequently are amalgams of intimate knowledge, ignorance, affection, resentment, self-satisfaction, and feelings of inferiority."[11]

Most critics focused, not on what Canadian-American relations usually were, but on what might be or should be – at least in the critics' view. For Canadians, relations between the two countries were not a means of expressing similarities but of defining and even amplifying differences. The American ambassador during the Pearson government, W.W. Butterworth, contemptuously explained to the State Department that the root of English-Canadian nationalism was "a desire to prove they are not what they suspect, a second-class American."[12]

Pearson also had to take into account French-Canadian views. These were not, in the 1960s, entirely favourable to the United States. According to a Gallup Poll taken in August 1964, "Ontario is most satisfied with Canada-US relations, with 75% saying they are excellent or good. Quebec is least satisfied. Sixty-one percent say excellent or good; 33% say fair or poor."[13] Yet Quebec too was subject to the American lure. Though members of the Quebec elite often looked to France (and even occasionally to Great Britain) for style and opinions, more looked to the United States, like their English-speaking compatriots. As an "advertising guru," Jacques Bouchard, put it in 1978,

"Québécois assume their Americanness and clearly prefer 'the American way of life' to the European way. Their daily behaviour proves it beyond a doubt."[14] The stage was set for the same bifurcation of opinion as in English Canada.

In the first poll to sound out Canadian opinion over American intervention in Vietnam, in July 1965, 44 percent of Canadians approved and 33 percent disapproved. Among the university-educated, however, approval rose to 51 percent and disapproval sank to 25 percent. (The number of university-educated in the survey was admittedly not great.)[15] The university-educated were, in the 1960s, the strongest supporters of the Liberal Party (49 percent in 1965, 60 percent in 1968).[16] By this measure, Vietnam should not have been a major problem for Pearson. But university-educated could mean many things. It included different age groups. Generation probably counted for as much as education, and for the generation that had gone through the Second World War, and had benefited thereafter from a free education for veterans, the Americans seemed to be doing the right thing, responding to aggression before it got out of hand.[17] A university education probably signified greater affluence, for there was a clear correlation between level of education and income. The university-educated were still a small minority in the Canadian population, because the baby boom had by this point only barely arrived at the gates of academe. Initially, the Canadian polls paralleled American ones in showing that more Canadians approved of the war than disapproved. The balance tipped, as it did in the United States, only in early 1968, when the news media concluded that there was no light at the end of the Vietnamese tunnel. Yet for the Pearson government, the balance had tipped three years earlier, and with it tipped the political fortunes of Canada's external affairs minister, Paul Martin.

Lester Pearson was not quite the indispensable man for the Liberal Party. He might be an international celebrity, but he was politically unskilled. His conduct of the dismal 1958 election campaign ever after served as a benchmark for political naïveté in Canada. He recovered, rebuilding the party, but in the 1962 campaign the Liberals' standing in the polls dropped with every passing week. In 1963 the party barely missed the glittering prize of a parliamentary majority.

Pearson's Liberal colleagues drew conclusions. "He's here because we're here," more than one minister decided (the actual phrase is Mitchell Sharp's). As prime minister, Pearson could insist on his prerogatives to direct government business, reward the deserving, and steer the government's political direction. Yet behind his back his ministers were not entirely content. Leaks to the press proved the Liberal ship was not watertight, while its crew was often at odds with itself.

Foreign policy was Pearson's specialty, but there was no question of the prime minister taking on the heavy duties of running the Department of External Affairs. The job was a political prize, and it went to the Liberals' most senior MP, Paul Martin. Martin had been member of Parliament for Essex East, in the Ontario city of Windsor, since

1935.[18] A graduate of the University of Toronto, Martin actually took classes from Professor Lester Pearson, and had known him for almost forty years. Martin chose to earn his living as a lawyer, though on the side he pursued an interest in international affairs, training, reading, and speaking on the subject.

After being elected to Parliament, Martin spent almost ten years on the backbenches. His colleagues knew he wanted to be a minister, and Mackenzie King occasionally toyed with "that lugubrious fellow Martin" before finally appointing him to the Cabinet in 1945. He stood aside – according to his own account – when King and St Laurent appointed Pearson secretary of state for external affairs in 1948, and seconded Pearson's efforts as foreign minister. Martin on occasion substituted for Pearson as head of the Canadian delegation at the United Nations and in that capacity helped broker a deal that brought new members into the organization in 1955, preserving its founding principle of universality. Martin became known as a valuable "political" minister, never at a loss for words, reliable and ready when the party called. He also had a less useful reputation as intensely ambitious, determined to succeed to the Liberal leadership. When the occasion offered, in January 1958, Martin lost to Pearson – knowing that almost all his former Cabinet colleagues were supporting his rival.

Martin soldiered on, proving a valuable support to Pearson in opposition. He could speak on any issue, and at length, qualities valuable in opposition. Under the circumstances, he could not be denied the prize of External Affairs – and it appears that Pearson never thought of denying him. Senior, experienced, and knowledgeable, Martin finally had the field he wanted on which to prove his talents. His department and the Prime Minister's Office shared the venerable East Block of the Parliament Buildings, and the two men slipped into an easy habit of consultation over foreign policy questions. Cabinet colleagues did not contest the way foreign affairs were handled. They would have agreed that after Diefenbaker, the subject needed care and feeding, and Martin's talents, even his long-windedness, seemed made to order. His ability to deploy these talents made Martin amiable and useful, but it did not necessarily make him impressive. Some thought he had difficulty distinguishing small points from large issues. Some were uneasy at his ability to reinterpret the record in his own favour. Many of them would have agreed with the American official Bill Bundy, who when asked to summarize his impression of Martin said that he was "pas sérieux," someone not to be taken seriously.[19]

Yet foreign officials and diplomats had to take him seriously, although that task was complicated by another factor: Martin tended to overestimate Canada's weight in the international system. Perhaps fond memory overcame grim reality: in the 1950s, under Pearson and before Europe and Japan had recovered economically and politically from the war, Canada had indeed had more weight in international discussions. While Martin was certainly not Pearson, it was probably Canada's reduced comparative importance and not his personality that counted for more – or rather less – in international discussions.

Martin was in many respects an orthodox Cold Warrior. He had visited Vietnam in 1956, met Ngo Dinh Diem, and approved of him. He saw the International Control Commissions (ICC) as an instrument for countering Communist propaganda, and he supported his officials when they attempted in 1964-1965 to make it more impartial and more useful. He was mindful that the distance to all-out war in Vietnam was getting steadily smaller, and the ICC's potential as a roadblock must not be ignored. He might have reflected that Canadians expected no less, and on the surface, well into 1964, he would have been right.

Canadian views about communism were not entirely consistent or straightforward. Dislike of communism among university faculty and the moderate left had been tempered by the American McCarthyite experience of the 1950s and the Ban-the-Bomb movement of the early 1960s. The view was increasingly common that American anti-communism was hysterical and exaggerated, and that a close eye must be kept on Americans' regrettable propensity to go overboard when they spotted, or thought they spotted, a communist.

There was also a trend in opinion, small but discernible, that divided "youth," however defined, from its elders. Not for the first time in Western history, youth in a time of affluence rejected what it took to be the values and practices of its elders. Society had achieved plenty, but at a price – rigid systems, conformity, and impersonality were the inner cost of a thoughtless if affluent "consumer society." That society's latest innovation, the giant computers used by big business, big science, and big government, were fed a regular diet of punched cardboard cards that had to be kept pristine, unfolded, and untorn. "Do not fold, spindle or mutilate," was the instruction printed on computerized bills sent out to consumers; "do not fold, spindle or mutilate" was the youth culture's warning to its elders.

Youth culture was, of course, not uniform. Much of it was inward-looking, concentrating on cultural fads, and passive in relation to politics. As the 1960s wore on, "alienated youth" seemed to grow in number and, with them, a "countercultural" lifestyle. But other segments of the youth culture, especially in the early 1960s, were active, and actively engaged in political causes. It is tempting to speculate that in any society there is always an "anti-establishment" minority prone to the promotion of good causes and to protest against bad ones. In Canada, this minority seems to have been absorbed in the Ban-the-Bomb movement of the early 1960s and, when that failed, to have moved on to the cause of civil rights in the United States. Given the efforts of the Kennedy and Johnson administrations to combat discrimination, it was difficult to cast the United States government as deep-dyed or whole-hearted villains over that issue. Vietnam would prove to be another matter. (Mention should be made of a third "youth" group, those who were neither anti-establishment nor countercultural. This group, possibly a majority, did not act as a distinct entity, but mirrored the views of its elders. But by that token they did not require special analysis, or merit propitiation.)

Paul Martin, at sixty-one, was not especially attuned to the youth culture. His whole background of hard work, application and ambition was antithetical to the counter-cultural and anti-establishment wings of the youth culture. He and his colleagues were more plugged into the views of "opinion leaders" – professors, church officials, and journalists, for example – what in another country and culture would be called the intelligentsia. These groups, by the nature of their work or lives, were more likely to be in contact with younger people, and the linkage between them and youthful dissent could be (and was) significant, especially because they could act both as an influence on and a conduit for the views of alienated youth. Because of their position, they had a strong influence on the educated bureaucracy, on educated politicians, and on the two parties that competed for their favour, the Liberals and New Democrats.

Despite the nuclear issue, left-leaning academics were inclined, in 1963-1964, to take an optimistic view of international affairs. The signing of a nuclear test-ban treaty in Moscow in August 1963 took some of the heat off the nuclear issue. (The defeat of the right-wing Republican presidential candidate by Democratic incumbent Lyndon Johnson the next year was taken as another good sign.) Stability along the East-West frontier in Europe let some of the tension out of the Cold War. Decolonization in Africa, where the British and French were bailing out of their colonies, was another favourable sign. There was trouble in Southeast Asia, between Indonesia and its neigh-bour Malaysia, and the British, Australians, and New Zealanders had found it neces-sary to station 50,000 troops there. The Americans had a smaller number of soldiers in Vietnam, which appeared to be in perpetual turmoil. But Vietnam, at the beginning of 1964, did not seem a serious issue. Not yet.

LOGICAL DEDUCTIONS, 1964

The coup that overthrew Ngo Dinh Diem brought neither stability nor victory to South Vietnam. In Saigon, the military staged an apparently endless series of coups against a background of rioting Buddhists and student demonstrations. American generals and Cabinet officers flew back and forth between Washington and Vietnam. In the White House, President Johnson tried to focus on the issue of the day, or rather year, because 1964 was an election year and he did not want Vietnam to become an issue in the campaign. As leader of the most powerful Western country, Johnson had an alliance to balance, and he did not want Vietnam to become an issue between the United States and its allies.

Yet the lack of success of Johnson's policies made Vietnam an issue that would not go away. The South Vietnamese army could not defeat the Viet Cong guerrillas in the countryside, nor could the successive military governments in Saigon offer an alternative to the revolutionaries. The only hope of avoiding defeat lay in cutting off supplies from North Vietnam to the insurgents, and, without American troops, the only way of doing that lay in persuading the North Vietnamese to stop sending them. That possibility became the subject of an anxious conference at the US embassy in Saigon on 19 April 1964 between Secretary of State Dean Rusk and the American ambassador to Vietnam, Henry Cabot Lodge. Lodge had a bold proposal. As the notes of Bill Bundy, assistant secretary of state for the Far East, indicate, Lodge urged "that we make fullest use of a diplomatic intermediary to Hanoi, as we begin an ascending scale of actions, and that such an intermediary be used to tell (not to negotiate with) the DRV [North Vietnam] at the highest possible level that the US would be forced to take military actions, but ... if Hanoi desisted from its effort" it could instead receive "food supplies" and a partial American withdrawal of its military advisers from South Vietnam.[20] In suggesting an intermediary, Lodge had Canada in mind, and in particular Geoffrey Murray, whom he had known at the United Nations in the 1950s.

Canada was about to become involved in a very sensitive diplomatic mission – that is, if Ottawa agreed. Rusk and the Johnson administration certainly had no misgivings about the choice of Canada or a Canadian to take a message to Hanoi. Johnson's relations with Pearson were placid, if not deep. The president was polite, though not especially interested in what the Canadian prime minister had to say, as an early meeting in December 1963 made plain. In this case, however, all Pearson had to say was "yes."

Rusk came to Ottawa to meet Pearson and Martin on 29 April. Before his arrival, the Department of External Affairs had decided on the person to succeed Gordon Cox as ICC commissioner. The appointment of J. Blair Seaborn, who had previously served in the embassy in Moscow, had passed the Cabinet in mid-April.[21] When Rusk brought up the possibility of a change in personnel in Saigon with Pearson and Martin, they had a name. Rusk described Seaborn to Lodge as "an expert in communist affairs." Seaborn, Rusk, Pearson, and Martin agreed, was to take up his duties on the ICC as soon as possible, and Cox was to leave ahead of schedule.[22]

Seaborn's task was carefully defined. He was to carry an American message to Ho Chi Minh. "We," Rusk wrote, "want to know whether [Ho] considers himself overextended and exposed, or whether he feels confident that his Chinese allies will back him to the hilt." That was only the first point. The second was to tell the North Vietnamese "the full measure of US determination to see this thing through," including a determination "if it becomes necessary to enlarge the military action." Third, Seaborn was to assure the North Vietnamese that the Americans had no ambitions in the area and did not even want to place permanent bases in South Vietnam or Laos. Finally, he was to offer the inducement of trade and food if only "peaceful conditions were to prevail." Commenting from Saigon on Rusk's report of his Ottawa visit, Lodge suggested strengthening Rusk's language and sharpening Seaborn's objectives.[23]

Two senior American officials travelled to Ottawa to brief Seaborn as to what he was to say to the North Vietnamese. One of them, Chester Cooper, gave a succinct description. "The American bargaining position," he wrote in 1970, "was just about nil; the South Vietnamese forces were being mauled; there were not enough American advisers in Saigon to influence the tide of events, but there were more than enough to give us the onus of running the country; opposition to the war was already evident and growing in the United States. Although Seaborn pressed for something nourishing to put before the North Vietnamese, he gracefully accepted the thin gruel he received."[24] During the meeting. Paul Martin gave the Americans his view – namely, that an international conference was his preferred outcome. That was, in the Americans' view, not likely, because of its weak bargaining position in the spring of 1964.

On 28 May, the same day as the meeting in Ottawa with Seaborn and Martin, Johnson and Pearson met in New York City, where they reviewed Seaborn's mission and what he might say. Johnson reiterated the negative and positive inducements Seaborn was to carry, and claimed that he was a man of peace. Pearson for his part warned about the dangers of a wider war, one that might escalate to include the use of nuclear weapons. Johnson was reassuring, but allowed that the United States might have to take "carefully limited" action against the North. He did not say what that might entail.[25] Pearson and Johnson having reached agreement, Seaborn packed his bags for a mission the department code-named "Bacon."

Cox, who knew nothing of what was in store, carried on with his regular duties and at the end of May travelled on the ICC plane to Hanoi. The mission in Saigon suddenly received a telegram from Ottawa: Cox was to return to Saigon immediately and prepare for departure. He packed his bags, made his farewell calls, and left. En route he met Seaborn in Hong Kong for a hasty greeting and briefing.

Seaborn had an unenviable task ahead of him. He met North Vietnamese prime minister Pham Van Dong in Hanoi on 18 June and delivered the message from Washington. Johnson was a man of peace, Seaborn informed the North Vietnamese, but he was firm. He wanted North Vietnam to cease interfering in South Vietnam and to accept the 1954 division of the country. Johnson would not withdraw American troops, and, if forced "to choose between withdrawal and escalation, he would choose escalation." Pham was unimpressed. The rebellion in the South was the people's will, and that drove the resistance to the Saigon regime. North Vietnam's help to the insurgents was "limited," he said, and his government would not tempt the United States to retaliate against it by imprudent actions. But if it came to war, North Vietnam was prepared and would withstand whatever the United States threw at it. If the United States accepted the situation and withdrew, there could be some kind of neutralist solution for South Vietnam, a coalition of Communist and non-Communist forces. This might be accomplished through international negotiations of the kind French president Charles de Gaulle had already suggested.

Seaborn came away from meeting Pham with an "impression of quiet sincerity, of realization of the seriousness of what we are discussing and of lack of truculence or belligerency." He found confidence, not despondency, in Hanoi. In the view of the North Vietnamese leadership, the US threats of military action were futile. The Americans could do their worst: they would still lose.[26]

Seaborn was not the only visitor to Hanoi that summer. Chinese premier Zhou Enlai spent four days there at the beginning of July. He amplified an earlier commitment by Mao Zedong that China would support North Vietnam no matter what the United States did or tried to do. If the United States sent troops, so would China.[27]

Failing to secure a positive response to their carrot-and-stick message delivered through Seaborn, the United States supported South Vietnamese raids on the North Vietnamese coast. A clash resulted, when North Vietnamese patrol boats attacked an American destroyer. The Americans retaliated; more important, Johnson used the incident, which took place in international waters in the Gulf of Tonkin, to obtain a Congressional resolution of support for his policy in Vietnam. The Gulf of Tonkin resolution gave Johnson the power he wanted, to pursue either war or peace in Indochina. Its effect was that of a conditional declaration of war. According to Senator J.W. Fulbright, the resolution "would authorize whatever the Commander in Chief [Johnson] feels is necessary."[28]

The Gulf of Tonkin incidents (there were two, one imaginary on the Americans' part) and the Congressional resolution formed the background to Seaborn's next visit to Hanoi, in mid-August. As instructed, he informed his hosts that American opinion was solidly behind Johnson, as reflected in the nearly unanimous support for the Gulf of Tonkin resolution in the American Senate. Pham, more angrily than before, repeated that American actions were unjustified and doomed to failure.

Seaborn's instructions for this meeting had passed through Ottawa; reading them, the Department of External Affairs instructed the Canadian commissioner not to repeat the Americans' more threatening talking points, which were little more than assertions of American power. Repeating those, Seaborn was told, would make the Canadians seem "unthinking mouthpieces."[29] That decision underlined a difference in Canadian and American objectives: Ottawa wanted to find a way into negotiations, while Washington did not want to negotiate, except on how much it might take to buy the North Vietnamese out of the war. The fact that the Seaborn missions produced no outcome was of no great concern to the American administration. The point was that a "peaceful" alternative had been proffered and not accepted. Now planning for sterner measures could go ahead. With Johnson's triumphant re-election in November 1964 – ironically, as the peace candidate against a much more extreme opponent – the way was clear. By early December 1964 the American government was ready for war. All that was lacking was a suitable occasion.[30]

BAD POLITICS MAKES FOR BAD DIPLOMACY

The Auto Pact, not Vietnam, dominated Canadian-American relations during the first months of 1965. In January Pearson and Martin flew to Texas to visit Johnson at his ranch and sign the agreement. The informality, which Pearson did not like, was interpreted to the Cabinet as a sign of favour. But the Auto Pact was not the only item under discussion. The president raised in pressing form the question of Vietnam. The United States wanted and needed help there: What could Canada provide? Not much, Pearson replied. "Canada could not consider participating in any military or para-military fashion, nor in any way which would conflict with her responsibilities as a member of the International Control Commission," the prime minister told the Cabinet. At the same time, Canada would not protest help from other nations to South Vietnam.[31]

Two weeks later, on 9 February, the Cabinet discussed the prospects for South Vietnam. The United States had just conducted a retaliatory air raid on North Vietnam in response to a Viet Cong attack on a US helicopter base. Plainly the war was heating up. There was no reason for optimism, Martin told his colleagues. Citing Seaborn's reports, he said that "the United States was now embarked on a hopeless course since the [South] Vietnamese people had no will to fight and there were no prospects for strong civilian leadership." The best that could be hoped was an international conference that would wrap up the situation as it had done in 1954, but the situation in South Vietnam was so bad that the United States had virtually no bargaining position. The American government therefore wished to await events, although, according to Martin, there was a division of opinion in Washington as to what to do next. In effect, the Cabinet was told that there were no prospects for a strong civilian government in the South but that the United States wished to hold on until one emerged.[32]

Pearson was already aware that American counsel was divided. En route to Ottawa from Texas in January, he stopped in Washington to meet Vice-President Hubert Humphrey. In his previous incarnation as a senator, Humphrey had told Pearson that he opposed further American involvement and favoured withdrawal; as vice-president he continued to think withdrawal was the best policy. A few weeks later Humphrey sent Johnson a memorandum to this effect; as the historian David Kaiser has observed, "Humphrey [then] found himself excluded from the highest councils of the administration for months."[33]

Pearson evidently mulled over the state of American opinion and the balance of policy in Washington for several months. He and Martin listened carefully to Canadian views about the state of Vietnam, as expressed by the press,[34] by other politicians, and by the intelligentsia. They did not like what they heard. Negative reports came from friends in the United States, including the journalist Marquis Childs and "persons highly placed in the United States government who were loyal to Johnson but disagreed with his Vietnam strategy and hoped to moderate it" – presumably a reference to Humphrey. Pearson also discussed Vietnam with his family, including his son Geoffrey, a foreign service officer who had served in New Delhi.[35] Significantly, in early March Pearson told the Cabinet that "Canada was in danger of being overwhelmed by United States influence in a variety of ways." Vietnam might be one of these ways.[36]

Opportunities for Canada to prevent further escalation were diminishing. On 2 March the United States began "regular, gradually intensifying air attacks against North Vietnam." This was Operation Rolling Thunder, which aimed to discover at what point the North Vietnamese would rationally conclude that enough was enough, and cease their intervention in the South. (The American air force believed that, despite its name, Rolling Thunder was little more than a distant squeak. Its carefully calibrated pressure was in fact foolish: only a massive attack would produce the desired political results.)[37] In March the United States landed marine units to protect bases at Pleiku and Da Nang. These forces were the forerunners of a much larger ground army, to which Johnson was already secretly committed. Yet knowing that this American war – for so it was – was not popular, the president preferred to proceed by small steps, announcing one commitment at a time while concealing what was in store. This stealthiness became standard procedure for Johnson, and it would lead, inescapably, to trouble.[38]

There was also the pressure implicit in what became by early 1965 daily press and television coverage of Vietnam. In early 1965 it was still largely a tale of hopelessness and folly, but not directly threatening because the Vietnamese appeared to be the principal actors. By March, with the Americans taking over the war, it went further. In that month the CBC broadcast the sensational news that the United States was supplying the South Vietnamese army with poison gas. The CBC compared it to the use of chlorine gas by the Germans on Canadian troops in the First World War. Other commentators called the use of gas in Vietnam a racist act, comparing it to the dropping of the atomic bomb on Hiroshima and Nagasaki. By the time the truth caught up with the rumour – the Americans had supplied tear gas to the Vietnamese – the issue had been raised in Parliament, and the Canadian government found itself in the uncomfortable position of justifying or explaining away an alleged American atrocity.[39]

As American troops began to engage the enemy in the summer of 1965, stories multiplied. Morley Safer, a Canadian journalist working for CBS News, reported in

August on US Marines burning down a Vietnamese village believed to be harbouring Viet Cong guerrillas. The report was accompanied by vivid film footage of marines casually using lighters to set fire to thatched roofs. The report, repeated in Canada, caused a sensation in the United States. The Pentagon demanded that CBS recall Safer. "Canadian military friends of mine," wrote the assistant secretary for public affairs in the US Defense Department, "who know Mr. Safer personally, tell me he has long been known ... as a man with a strong anti-military bias."[40]

The impact of sceptical and unfriendly reporting was felt in Canada. Early in March 1965, Undersecretary for External Affairs Marcel Cadieux sent a briefing note to his minister, Paul Martin, in preparation for a meeting with the foreign affairs group of the Liberal caucus. "Continued implicit support for the American position is difficult in the face of Canadian public opinion, the articulate section of which seems uniformly against the United States," the minister was told. It was important to distinguish Canadian attitudes from American, and not to seem to be just a mouthpiece for the United States.[41]

Pearson thus had reason to focus on Vietnam: time was apparently running out, a serious Canadian-American division seemed to be in the making because of Canadian unhappiness with the war, and the key to that crisis was in the United States. President Johnson was not seeking advice from American allies, so there was little hope of making an impression that way; besides, Canada was not willing to pay the political price of sending official aid to the South Vietnamese. Pearson decided to use the occasion of a speech at Temple University in Philadelphia to try to slow the tempo of American mobilization for war. He would propose a pause in Rolling Thunder.

The draft speech was circulated to the Department of External Affairs and to its minister. Both immediately pointed out that if the speech were intended to positively influence Johnson it would not achieve its object. Martin threatened to resign, but that failed to deter Pearson. (Pearson, too, thought Martin "pas sérieux.") The speech, as delivered, was hardly a revolutionary document. It did not question Johnson's motivation or the larger themes of American policy. It went out of its way to applaud American sacrifice and leadership. Canadians, Pearson said, supported American "peace-keeping and peace-making policies in Vietnam." Then, as Pearson's biographer notes, he "significantly" added: "We wish to be able to continue that support." The best way to shore up public opinion would be to test Hanoi's willingness to talk peace, through "a suspension of air strikes against North Vietnam *at the right time*" – the "right time" being, in Pearson's view, right now. Two months of bombing, Pearson thought, should have given the North Vietnamese a "loud and clear" message. If the North did not respond, or proved obstreperous, then "increased military strength [might] be used against the armed and attacking Communists."[42]

Mild and conciliatory as he was, Pearson was telling Johnson his policy was mistaken and was offering him an alternative, withdrawal, and a tactic, negotiations, he did not want. Pearson had refused to give the White House an advance copy of his speech. Johnson got the message, in terms of both policy and politics. He called Pearson with an invitation the latter could hardly refuse: lunch the next day at the presidential retreat of Camp David. There, in a classic confrontation, Johnson ranted and raved at the astonished Pearson. "You pissed on my rug," he told the prime minister, meaning that commonly accepted diplomatic practice did not allow foreign visitors to interfere in their host's domestic politics. That had in fact been Pearson's objective, but, as Johnson's response indicated, it had not worked or worked sufficiently to derail or deflect presidential wrath. The prime minister had to reflect that Canada had a great many interests still at stake, not least the recently signed Auto Pact, still awaiting passage, with presidential support, through Congress.

Shaken, Pearson on returning to Ottawa wrote a lengthy explanation to Johnson. In content, the letter repeated the idea of a useful bombing pause as a means of isolating and pressuring the North Vietnamese, but in tone Pearson was contrite. But sugarcoated or not, the message found no reception in Johnson. Pearson thereafter occupied the "No. 1 kennel" in Washington.

The Canadian ambassador in Washington, Charles Ritchie, had advised against Pearson's speech at Temple. He worried that Canadian comments on the war were not only damaging the country's basic interests, they were essentially mistaken, for Ritchie did not oppose the war. Nonetheless, the ambassador was the Canadian on the spot in Washington, and he took the brunt of Johnson's resentment:

> The last time I saw the President, Johnson, was on my departure from Washington, where he gave a small farewell luncheon for myself and the departing German Ambassador. He started up by saying Germans [are] good friends of the United States. We turn to them and we rely on them. He said, Ambassador I want you to convey that so that was that. And he paused and he said, The Canadians are very clever, very clever ... Yes, they're clever. They come down here and tell us how to run the war in Vietnam and then they screw us over the Auto Pact. Oh yes they're very clever.[43]

Johnson had the opportunity to take out his feelings on Pearson in a more concrete way, because the Auto Pact was still unpassed. But he did not. He did not start a cycle of retaliation against Canada, even if, after 1965, he did not go out of his way to help Pearson politically. The Auto Pact moved through Congress and was duly implemented. It was a sign that Johnson's approach to many aspects of foreign policy was less personal and more rational than many commentators have allowed.[44] American interests in Canada were important, and so was American trade. Politics was politics, and trade was trade. Canada's "special relationship" with the United States was economic, and under Johnson it barely suffered a hiccup.

Johnson may have concluded from his interview and correspondence with Pearson that he could safely ignore Canadian views on Vietnam. That was no change: in 1964, when Seaborn was employed as intermediary, Johnson had used Canadians but had not consulted them. Now Pearson had had his say and retired from the field. It is not quite accurate for the American historian and former diplomat Paul Kattenburg to say that "the Canadians offered no serious objections to the US course during most of the war,"[45] but it is true that Canadian official objections were, after April 1965, muted.

Not all of the fallout from the speech was negative. In Cabinet, Pearson received thanks and appreciation from his most anti-American minister, Walter Gordon, who "expressed warm agreement with the speech by the Prime Minister ... He felt there had been general agreement with it in Canada."[46] Pearson tried to befog even the British by prevaricating about Camp David in an interview with the British High Commissioner, claiming that the session had been basically friendly and constructive.[47]

The impetus to maintain normal or non-confrontational relations between Canada and the United States was strong on both sides of the border. It should not be forgotten that most Canadians, in the spring of 1965, still broadly approved of Johnson, as they did of his war. Most Americans approved of their northern neighbour: Canada was probably the last country they expected to quarrel with. There would have been a political cost for both Pearson and Johnson had they stepped outside the established routines and expectations of Canadian-American relations.

There were also broadly economic considerations in keeping relations on track. These were not unimportant, but neither should they be exaggerated. A Defence Production Sharing Agreement had been in effect with the United States since 1959 and was renewed in 1963. The idea was to balance Canadian defence purchases in the United States with American purchases in Canada, and the agreement had met that objective. With the build-up in Vietnam, American purchases in Canada rapidly reached $260 million in 1965 and $300 million in 1966. The Canadian government did not ask where or how the Americans intended to use what they bought, though it was obvious that some commodities, such as napalm and other chemicals, were destined for Southeast Asia.[48]

Military exports to the United States fitted into an economic and conspiratorial analysis of the "true" motives for Canadian policies on Vietnam. Marxists argued, and some non-Marxists accepted, that Pearson and Martin were in it for the money – not personally, of course, but on behalf of large Canadian and American corporations. Some even argued that Canadian companies had an interest in Vietnam, and that the point of the war was to keep South Vietnam an exploited vassal state in the American economic empire. The latter was nonsense: Canadian investment and trade with South Vietnam and all of Indochina were and remained insignificant.[49] Where the Defence Production Sharing Agreement was concerned, the Canadian government was firm: it was a reciprocal obligation to an ally, conceived and justified under NATO. As a consequence, the government absorbed a great deal of indignation from the same intelligentsia that had helped stimulate Pearson's ill-fated intervention at Temple University. Pearson had not managed to appease his domestic critics for long.

Would Canada's position have improved had it taken Johnson's hints and sent actual military help for the American cause in Vietnam? The answer is probably not. Australia and New Zealand both sent soldiers to Vietnam. Yet neither ally was regularly or adequately consulted about the course of the war: their role was to support the United States and suffer the consequences. Those consequences, in Australia especially, were significant in terms of domestic opposition; by the end of the war it was difficult for Australian soldiers to wear their uniforms in public for fear of provoking an incident. South Korea and the Chinese Nationalist regime on Taiwan also sent troops to Vietnam, while various Southeast Asian countries like Singapore vociferously supported American efforts. Singapore is perhaps the exception among the allies. It did not seek to influence the war nor did it send troops, but its leader, Lee Kwan Yew, advanced his country's interests by "unstinting declarations of support for the US war effort in Indochina." In return he received "favors ... in ample measure." Although, the war over, Lee speedily established relations with the Communist regime in the united Vietnam,[50] his effusive support for American policy should not be completely discounted.

The situation in Southeast Asia was fluid in 1964-1965. Not only Vietnam but Indonesia threatened to slide into the Communist camp, and Indonesia was a much larger, richer, and strategically more important country than Vietnam. It seemed that the erratic policies of Indonesia's president Sukarno, who leaned heavily on Communist support, could have no other end. If Indonesia had gone Communist, Malaysia and Singapore would have been imperilled, while Australia would have had to live with a Communist neighbour. Abruptly, in September 1965 the Indonesian military staged a coup d'état. Unlike the various Vietnamese coups, this one had overwhelming force. The Communist Party was savagely suppressed (the party had its own record of savagery). The next year Sukarno was out, and a right-wing military government took his place.

With hindsight, we can see that the balance of power in Southeast Asia shifted as a result of the Indonesian coup, and shifted permanently. Though the United States obviously approved of the coup, it had not been closely involved in planning it; the Indonesians on their own, and in their own country, had accomplished what billions of dollars and thousands of American troops could not do in Vietnam. The coup had little effect on the American prosecution of the war. Troops continued to arrive in Vietnam, the bombing campaign against the North went on, and opposition at home grew. The Johnson administration held to the position that Seaborn had conveyed in 1964: it wanted an end to infiltration of the South by the North.

The Merchant-Heeney Report and the 1965 Election

The politicians anticipated as much as they reflected the trend of public opinion. The most striking example was the fate of the so-called Merchant-Heeney report. Livingston Merchant was the distinguished former American ambassador to Canada, and Arnold Heeney his equally distinguished Canadian counterpart. Johnson and Pearson in January 1964 asked the two men to examine the conduct of Canadian-American relations and make recommendations for improving them. Merchant and Heeney produced a generally sensible and good-humoured document that argued that the two countries could and should compose their differences through a process of regular consultation and "quiet diplomacy." The words were almost a tautology. Most diplomacy is by its nature quiet and, given the unspectacular nature of most Canadian-American interaction, it was hard to see how the Canadians and Americans could differ from this standard practice even if they wanted to.[51]

The Merchant-Heeney report was intended to improve relations between Canada and the United States. Using recent cases from Canadian-American relations, it urged principles for automatic and rational consultation between the two countries. It also recommended resolving differences between Canada and the United States "in private" as far as possible. In "normal" times, if the period before 1965 is taken as normal, the report's advice would have been unexceptionable. But so rapidly had Canadian public opinion moved – or rather the mood of the vociferous part of the public – that the report instead provoked irritation if not rage from some critics. Charles Lynch of the *Ottawa Citizen* complained that Merchant and Heeney had confirmed "our lackey status." A former member of the Diefenbaker Cabinet argued that the report made Canada "a lap dog" of the United States.[52]

In September 1965 Lester Pearson, in an attempt to win a majority in the House of Commons, called an election for 8 November. It was a frustrating and ultimately futile campaign: it improved Liberal standing in the House by only two seats, still short of a majority.

Foreign policy was not much of an issue in the election, but Vietnam had already made inroads in Canadian public opinion. Ministers were obliged to face the unfiltered public, and the result was disturbing. Martin found it expedient to claim in rural Ontario – no hotbed of urban radicalism – that Canada was trying to mediate in Vietnam. Vancouver was notorious for its rowdy audiences, and Martin found it best to be prepared when he held an election rally there. "I asked the organizers of the meeting ... to bring in the most powerful loudspeakers they could find. True to form, the anti-Vietnam war protesters tried to take over my meeting, but the loudspeakers enabled me to prevail."[53]

The trend only got worse. By mid-1966, only 35 percent of Canadians approved the war, while 34 percent disapproved. In the same period the proportion approving continuation of the war sank from 66 percent to 45 percent, while the number favouring American withdrawal rose from 20 percent to 35 percent. Quebec was the region most strongly against American policy and most strongly in favour of US withdrawal.[54]

There are no polls showing the impact of Vietnam specifically on the Canadian political elite, but there are some shedding light on the attitude of Liberals and Conservatives in 1967-1968 on a number of foreign policy issues. Asked whether Canada should bring its foreign policy more closely into line with that of the United States, only 13 percent of Liberals and 19 percent of Conservatives agreed. Asked whether Soviet Communism was still a threat to Canada, 47 percent of Liberals and 42 percent of Conservatives said yes. This ambiguous result was on a core issue, perhaps the central question, of the Cold War.[55] It suggested that many Canadians were ready for a change in direction, in policy, and in leadership. The Vietnam war was the occasion for this sentiment but there were other, deeper causes: the arms race, nuclear fear, and a growing sense that the USSR did not, after all, pose an immediate mortal peril.

THE RONNING MISSION

The war was nonetheless first in people's minds. The arrival of US troops in Vietnam did not immediately turn the tide of the war, as many Americans – even sceptics – had expected. It did lend some evenness to the battlefront, and it coincided with the installation of a slightly more stable government in Saigon under General Nguyen Van Thieu, who would remain in power almost to the end of the war. Militarily, the United States was now better able to fight the war.

In terms of public opinion and diplomacy, however, the new situation made little difference. Elite opinion in Canada and around the Western world – outside government – was almost entirely convinced that the Thieu government was a corrupt, repressive tyranny. By contrast, North Vietnam was usually portrayed as a genuine people's state led by the elderly and possibly saintly Ho Chi Minh. Ho's sins, if any, paled by comparison with Thieu's, or Saigon's generally.[56] Thus from the beginning the United States was condemned to fight on behalf of a regime or a cause whose legitimacy was seriously questioned at home and in the West in general.

A contemporary indication of the relative standing of Thieu and Ho may be found in the memoirs of a Canadian diplomat, Chester Ronning, a missionary child who had a long diplomatic career and who played a major role in Canadian relations with China. Ronning had played a useful role at the Geneva conference in 1954 and in subsequent negotiations over Laos. He knew the Vietnamese leaders, and, just as useful, he knew senior Chinese leaders, such as China's perennial premier, Zhou Enlai. They understood his views were sympathetic to their own, as Ronning freely admitted.

Meeting Thieu in Saigon, Ronning heard the general complain that he dared not stir from his palace for fear of assassination. "I chose not to mention," Ronning wrote, "how many people of Vietnam, both North and South, had told me about their respect and support for Uncle Ho, whom they considered to be the father of their country. If Thieu had been loved by the Vietnamese, perhaps he too could have walked home without an armed guard." Ronning might have reflected that the rigidly controlled people of North Vietnam dared not act in any way out of turn, while Thieu's own organs of repression were not functioning nearly as efficiently as those of the beloved Ho.[57]

The arrival of American troops was accompanied by an aerial campaign, bombing the North and its supply routes to the South. Neither troops nor aircraft seemed to make much impression on Hanoi's determination to prosecute the war. The North Vietnamese merely announced that no negotiations for peace could take place until the United States stopped the bombing, removed its troops, and recognized the rebels as the true government of South Vietnam. Then and only then would the North consider a "neutral" regime in the South. Not surprisingly, these were difficult terms for Johnson to accept, especially as American casualties began to mount. In response, Washington ratcheted up the number of troops, with no apparent effect except to increase the number of US protesters against the war.

As the war heated up, the Johnson administration began to probe the question of whether the North was ready to talk peace. Averell Harriman, a senior politician and diplomat, was commissioned to find out what he could and to use what avenues he could command. News from the North was, as always, scarce. Scenting a possibility and reasoning that Chinese influence might be brought to bear, as in 1954, Paul Martin decided to play the Canadian card one more time. Chester Ronning made no secret of his admiration for "people's revolutions." He resolutely approached Mao's China with a blind eye and a deaf ear, qualities the Chinese leadership appreciated. Martin reasoned, probably correctly, that if anyone could talk to the Chinese, Ronning could. He believed, also correctly, that Chinese views counted heavily with the North Vietnamese leadership.

China was no bystander in the war. Politically, it guaranteed North Vietnam that if the United States directly invaded the North with ground troops, the Chinese would also become directly involved. Though the Americans did not precisely know this, they usually assumed that an invasion of the North would precipitate a wider war.

The Chinese helpfully hinted as much, and the Americans listened. Militarily, by 1965 the Chinese already had substantial numbers of troops in the North, manning anti-aircraft and missile batteries, building factories, bridges, and roads, and keeping the North Vietnamese infrastructure in repair. At their peak, in 1967, 170,000 Chinese troops served in Vietnam. Manpower released by Chinese specialists could be sent south, to the war. Economically, the Chinese sent supplies of all kinds, from shoes to sugar to artillery shells.[58]

The Chinese nevertheless were not especially eager to go to war. For one thing, Mao Zedong had decided to implement a "Cultural Revolution," which turned society upside down and inside out for several years as mobs of Red Guards roamed the streets attacking Mao's enemies, real or fancied. The Cultural Revolution was about to start just as Paul Martin decided that Chester Ronning, friend of the Chinese people and their leaders, would be an ideal go-between. He was not to carry American messages, as Seaborn had done. His task was merely to discover whether the two sides would talk to one another, and he was to explore Chinese views of the matter. At a time other than the Cultural Revolution, such a plan might have made sense. As it was, the Chinese proved unreceptive, even to well-meaning diplomatic probes.[59] Accordingly, things did not work out quite as planned. The Chinese refused to admit Ronning, who had by then reached Hong Kong. They did not "consider the time ripe as yet" for discussions about Vietnam.[60] So he proceeded to Saigon, where he met with Thieu and Henry Cabot Lodge, who had returned for a second round as American ambassador. Next stop was Hanoi, where in the company of the Canadian ICC Commissioner, Victor Moore, he arrived on the ICC plane.

The North Vietnamese received Ronning well, even lavishly. He met the premier, Pham Van Dong, and round after round of officials. From Pham he gleaned that discussions with the Americans could begin if the bombing stopped. Opinions differ as to how significant or genuine this offer was, and even as to whether Ronning interpreted Pham's words correctly. Yet there could be little doubt that the North Vietnamese had taken the approach seriously, and that they thought something would come of it. Because the contact was kept strictly secret, propaganda did not seem to be in question.

The Americans were sceptical of what Ronning brought back, but not so sceptical that they refused to countenance another mission. Air raids on North Vietnam were postponed while Ronning was in Hanoi for his second visit, and when it was over Bill Bundy came up to Ottawa from Washington to listen to Ronning's report. Martin summarized the results for the Cabinet on 21 June. The North Vietnamese, he told his colleagues, "were not ... prepared to accept the position which Mr. Ronning had put forward on the basis of discussions with the US administration, to the effect that the Americans would cease bombing if 'reciprocal action' were taken by the North Viet Namese." The North wanted the bombing to stop, and in return promised little or nothing.[61] Bundy was unimpressed. In a dinner meeting with Martin and senior officials from External Affairs, Bundy found more support than did the minister.[62]

But Martin was not quite through. He entertained notions of using the ICC collectively rather than Canada singly as a forum for negotiations, or as the nucleus of a future international conference. He followed as closely as he could Polish attempts later that year to establish contact between the United States and the North Vietnamese. The parallel between Canadian and Polish efforts to bring the war to an end is striking, but in both cases the result was the same: neither belligerent wanted to end the war badly enough. For both the military solution remained an option.

Pearson was not especially impressed by what Martin was trying to do or had done. Pearson had known the minister for forty years, beginning as his teacher in university, and may have suspected his minister's motives were self-aggrandizing. "Mike was angry and distressed," at the failure of the Ronning mission and the continuing war, as Pearson's biographer wrote. "His relationship with Martin suffered accordingly."[63]

UNSUCCESSFUL DIVERSIONS

Canadians as a whole did not have to focus on Vietnam in 1966-1967. The year 1967 was the centennial of Confederation: there was a World's Fair in Montreal, Expo 67, and Canadians were prepared to celebrate. Expo proved a runaway success, thanks largely to the hundreds of thousands of Americans who attended. But Vietnam kept intruding. The Canadian government invited President Johnson to visit Expo, but by then a major consideration in the president's trips was whether he would face hostile demonstrations. The issue was raised between the State Department and Ambassador Ritchie. The latter "was at some pains to assure [the department] that ample security precautions would be taken in connection with any visit to Canada by President Johnson. He said his government could give as absolute assurance as it was humanly possible to do. He mentioned in particular that recent legislation empowered Quebec and Expo 67 authorities to deal firmly and expeditiously with political demonstrators."[64]

That Canadian authorities had to offer such assurances to protect the US president from public disapproval indicated that for many Canadians there must be something wrong with the United States itself. That was not news to many Canadians, like George Grant or Walter Gordon, but it gave new life to their views. They could read and cite what Americans themselves were saying about the war and the government that was prosecuting it.[65] Those who supported the American cause had to tread carefully in the face of public scorn. Nor was there any avoiding the issue, as the war dominated the media.

But the war was not the only source of unrest south of the border. The mid-1960s witnessed great social disruption in the United States – assassinations, riots, rising crime, and racial tension. A beleaguered and bewildered Ambassador Butterworth, overwhelmed by the bad news, criticized the Canadian coverage. "Pearson govt," he telexed home in 1967, "is fanning, whether purposely or not, anti-Americanism in country. Best known and most visible evidence of this development is in govt crown corporation CBC's TV public affairs program Sunday Night (formerly This Hour has Seven Days, now The Way it is) continues to carry slanted and venomous attacks on US policy and US society. Recent shocker was half-hour US-made documentary film of race riots in US cities this past summer which was psychedelic presentation attempting to show American society as welter of fear, hate, depravity, rot, and disintegration."[66]

It was not easy to be an American diplomat abroad in 1967, and Butterworth was cracking under the strain. Only in his dreams did Pearson have control over the CBC; a prime ministerial attempt to intervene with the network would certainly have become public, and where Vietnam or the United States generally was concerned Pearson and other ministers knew better than to try. Butterworth should have emphasized, more than he did, that much of the material he disliked was "US made." Anti-Americanism, as much as official propaganda, was "made in the USA." By 1967 attacks on the nature of American society and calls for the dismantling of American capitalism were commonplace on US campuses. In American universities, liberals suddenly found themselves perched uncomfortably on the right, as revolutionary enthusiasm spread towards the centre. Canadian university presidents nervously glanced southward and saw riots sweeping Columbia, Berkeley, Harvard, and Cornell. Several professors from Cornell packed their bags and moved to Canada to escape gun-toting students who had decided that the next American Revolution should start in the Finger Lakes.

The link between Vietnam and anti-Americanism was made early and firmly in Canada. What is interesting is that this was not strictly a Canadian phenomenon, and not restricted to the subject of Vietnam, but a process that moved in tandem with events and opinion in the United States.

⁂

THE VIETNAM WAR MAY BE TREATED ON A NUMBER OF LEVELS. It was an alliance question, involving US leadership of the Western alliance. Paradoxically, the US government thought it had demonstrated leadership by proving its reliability and its willingness to shoulder burdens and sacrifice in the interests of the Western alliance as a whole. It proved the "moral" case for the West by resisting the "immoral" transfer of tens of millions of Indochinese to Communist rule. Yet it did so against the inclination of most of its allies and apparently against the will of most of the South Vietnamese it came to Southeast Asia to save.

Diplomatically, Canada's position was also a paradox. Canadians, including most of the diplomatic part of the Canadian government, accepted that submission to communism was undesirable, both for the people of Vietnam and for the West in general. The ICC itself was an illustration that cooperation with the Communists was at best difficult; it was an organization that could survive only by doing essentially nothing, accepting stalemate as a way of life.

Life with Uncle Sam in Saigon was never close or easy for Canadian diplomats, though easier and closer for the Canadian military. The United States was the dominant foreign power in the South, so far ahead in its sacrifices for the alliance and the South Vietnamese that its position was both self-contained and self-referential. The servants of the US government, in other words, acted as if they did not need allies – certainly not the kind of allies with whom they needed to consult. Leadership of an alliance, it turned out, could not really be shared with the allies.

This was not news for the Canadians. Vietnam presented, in exaggerated form, some of the problems of alliance with which they were already familiar in Europe. That could be borne in Europe, in the 1960s as in the 1950s. What was uniquely difficult about Vietnam was that it became linked to the domestic situation in Canada.

The 1960s were a time of dissatisfaction and restlessness. The postwar era was coming to an end, and the generation that had provided leadership for Canada – the men (and a few women) who remembered the First World War and the interwar period – was giving way to younger people. Half the country was under the age of twenty-five in 1965, and the postwar baby boom gave a lively tone to life and therefore politics. The Canadian political system was resilient and flexible and for the most part it absorbed youthful energy and ferment, but some of that energy remained outside established politics. It found form, strength, and purpose in the issue of the Vietnam War.

In numbers, conviction, and the ability to make trouble, the anti-Vietnam War movement pressed hard on Canadian politics, as it also did in the United States, Great Britain, and France. Vietnam was fought out among the Canadian elite, the well educated and the affluent, rather than among Canadians in general. In this, it closely resembled the anti-Vietnam event in the United States. On the Canadian left, the NDP, which prided itself on representing the voice of progressive people, had to scramble to deal with the shouts of even "moderate" students. The Liberals, who defined themselves in the 1960s as a more moderate, realistic, and reasonable form of the NDP, shifted in the direction of anti-Vietnam demonstrators, probably in about the same way and at the same speed as the Democrats in the United States. Even the Progressive Conservative party drifted uneasily between support for the United States and passivity in the face of public uproar in Canada.

In the end, Canadian politics did contain and moderate the anti-Vietnam movement, preventing it from fulfilling the romantic revolutionary dreams of its leaders. Circumstances helped: a spectacular change in personalities and also in political generations in Canada in 1968-1971 symbolized openness to change and to the agenda of the newly enfranchised baby boomers. The revolutionaries, as usual, went too far and went on too long. Mass demonstrations had a shelf life as spectacle and event, but eventually their pointlessness became apparent. The war gradually drew down in the early 1970s and was resolved by an American acceptance of defeat and withdrawal in 1973. Virtually overnight the Vietnam issue disappeared. With nothing left to hold it together, the revolutionary movement dispersed, in Canada and in the United States.

The Vietnam War did less damage to Canadian-American relations than might be supposed. This was because domestic disapproval in the United States developed at about the same rate as disapproval elsewhere in the Western world. When Canadian politicians reacted to pressure from domestic forces, American politicians and diplomats knew what they were talking about. Their own children were also in the streets. Johnson, Rusk, and McNamara were political ghosts long before they gave up power. As a member of the Johnson administration reflected about the year 1968, the Canadians did not have to pay attention to what Johnson said any longer. They merely had to await whatever the American electorate produced in that year's elections, confident that whatever that was, it would not be Johnson.

The year 1967 was thus the culmination of the older and the beginning of the newer Canada. The centennial looked back with pride and forward with confidence. With the spring of 1968, there was a new prime minister, an election, and a new set of issues. One of those issues also involved foreign relations, but this time it was relations with France, and between English and French Canada. As the Americans struggled to extricate themselves from the Vietnam swamp, Canadians turned to the question of satisfying Quebec and fending off France.

13 NATIONAL UNITY AND FOREIGN POLICY

Louis St Laurent had, in 1947, laid down both an external and an internal function for Canada's foreign policy: abroad, it should express Canadian values; at home, it should serve the cause of national unity. As every Canadian politician knew, "national unity" meant the cultivation of harmony between English and French Canadians. Three times in St Laurent's lifetime, English and French Canadians had confronted each other over questions of foreign policy, each time over Canada's participation in a war abroad. National unity survived, but the exercise was a dangerous one.

As minister for external affairs and later prime minister, St Laurent kept an eye on the diplomatic service and secured the appointment of a French-speaking diplomat, Jules Léger, as undersecretary or permanent head of the department. The department did, in fact, recruit with an eye to French speakers, who made up 21.7 percent of its serving officers between 1945 and 1965. (The figure may not seem impressive compared to the 30 percent or so of French Canadians in the general population; but it was better than any other Ottawa department.) At the "senior level," however, there were only 21 French-Canadians, compared to 102 of their English-speaking counterparts.[1]

Coming to Ottawa was a wrench for some French Canadians: the national capital was predominantly English speaking, and in the civil service the language of work was English. Language apart, the federal civil service offered more scope and more freedom for those Quebeckers who did not like the clerical and conservative climate of opinion in *la belle province* during the 1950s. Though Pearson and his staff were working in English, they were doing exciting things, and Quebec definitely was not. The Union

Nationale government of the province was a limited government, frugal and cautious. Although Premier Duplessis explored the possibility of opening a Quebec office in Paris, he balked at the cost, and when he died in September 1959, nothing had been done.

A New Politics in Quebec

The conservative Duplessis style of government did not long survive the old premier. The provincial Liberal Party won the June 1960 election, and Jean Lesage became premier. Lesage had an ambitious program to reform and modernize the province, but he proved to be less the master of events than their creature. The reforms he set in motion (the "Quiet Revolution") depended heavily on using the powers of the provincial government to carve out cultural, economic, and then political space for Quebec's French majority. In the process, without entirely intending to, he came into conflict not merely with the existing regime in Ottawa, but with the Canadian balance of powers.

At first the clash could be viewed as an ordinary partisan disagreement. The government in Ottawa was Conservative, and Lesage was Liberal, and a former federal Cabinet minister at that. Yet it was not the federal Liberals or their leader, Lester Pearson, who benefited from the ferment in Quebec. Pearson failed to win even half the province's seats in the elections of 1962 and 1963, despite a roster of star candidates, some closely connected to Lesage. Worse still, not all Quebec's politics were electoral politics. In May 1963 bombs exploded in mailboxes in the affluent English districts of Montreal. Over the next five years explosions became a familiar routine – not merely in mailboxes, but in armouries and even in the Montreal stock exchange. The Front de Libération du Québec (FLQ) was announcing itself.

The name of the FLQ was modelled on those of revolutionary movements in various colonies, most notably Algeria where the Front de Libération Nationale (FLN) had just won its struggle against its colonial power, France.[2] During the Algerian war (1954-1962) Canada had been unsympathetic to France, as it was to other European colonial powers – that is, Canada was as unfriendly as an ally might be. The notion of Algeria's anti-colonial struggle attracted more than the government's lukewarm interest. Intellectuals, particularly in Quebec, were fascinated by the significance, and perhaps the inevitability, of what was happening in Africa and Asia. Quebec too, some of them reasoned, was occupied by a foreign colonial power. "Unlike our traditional nationalists," Gérard Pelletier wrote, "the neo-nationalists of the 1960s enthused – at a distance – over the National Liberation Front. They actually identified with the Algerian rebels. They were beginning to promote the thesis that was shortly to become the basis of their movement: Quebec was also oppressed by 'Anglo-Canadian colonialism.'"[3]

Most Quebec opinion found the idea preposterous. But since this was not electoral politics, the fact that only a tiny minority supported a given proposition hardly mattered. The minority was almost entirely composed of intellectuals who as a matter of course assumed that they spoke for the larger society or, at the very least, the society's best interests. Certainly, as elsewhere, the intellectuals had access to the media and helped shape the information that reached their fellow citizens. Nor were they or their views as isolated as believers in the raw data of elections or public opinion polls liked to think. When it came to resenting English Canadians or English-Canadian behaviour, the nationalist minority suddenly became much larger. Even moderates believed that English Canadians had from time to time abused their majority position in Canada. For moderates, the solution was to persuade English Canadians to behave better and act as true partners; for radicals, it was better to get rid of them altogether by separating Quebec from Canada.[4]

Between radicals and moderates there were a hundred shades of opinion. That was nothing new – disagreement over French Canadians' political options was as old as Quebec politics. But until the 1960s nobody but Canadians and the rare foreign specialist displayed much concern for the subject. The French-speaking motherland took little interest in its transatlantic connections; much more pressing matters weighed on French voters and their governments – wars, invasions, occupation, and coups d'état. Only in 1962, with the end of the colonial war in Algeria, did France appear to stabilize. Canadians and their governments took this as a sign of hope. What they did not suspect was that for the first time in two hundred years France could take an interest in what was happening on the banks of the St Lawrence.

CANADA AND FRANCE

Canada and France had never ceased entirely to communicate after the British conquest of 1760. Books, travellers, and ideas passed back and forth, demonstrating as often as not how far apart republican and anti-clerical France and its former North American colony, deeply Catholic in religion and ideology, were becoming. There had been relations of a formal and consular kind between France and British North America since the mid-nineteenth century. French Canadians had an ambiguous relation with the country of their ancestors. It was undoubtedly the cultural metropolis, but it was distant, a country of tourism, or study, or occasionally exile. Family links were few, and not supplemented, because almost all French-Canadian families had come to Canada before 1760. There was almost no reinforcing flow of immigrants from France. There were, in 1961, 36,103 French-born inhabitants of Canada, compared with 969,715 born in the British Isles – and the number of the French had almost tripled since 1941. In 1965, 3,396 persons of French birth came to Canada, compared to 36,000 from the British Isles, 28,000 from Italy, 7,000 from Germany, 6,000 from Greece, and 6,500 from Portugal – to take only European examples.

It was true that hundreds of thousands of Canadians had spent time in France – the soldiers of the First and Second World Wars and in the 1940s and 1950s were probably the most important connection between the two countries. Canadians occupied an honoured place among France's allies and in the memories of the historically minded. In 1961 there were still Canadian troops in France, in air force units under NATO command. From all appearances Canada and France were and would remain cordial allies.

Economic links between the two countries were modest. Canada lent a significant amount of money ($200,000,000) to France after the Second World War as a contribution to economic reconstruction.[5] There was some French investment in Canada – enough to be noted, but ranking after American, British, Dutch, and Belgian in value. Canada imported $96 million worth of goods from France in 1965, and sent $87 million worth in the other direction.

During the war French scientists had served in Canada as part of the atomic bomb project, and General Charles de Gaulle, leader of Free France, visited the country in 1944 as a welcome ally in the war against Germany.[6] Some of the general's followers knew that Free France was less popular in Quebec than the collaborationist and traditionalist Vichy regime in German-occupied France, but the general made no public allusion to the fact, and he glossed it over in his memoirs. After the war, French president Vincent Auriol visited Canada, to a mixed reception, especially in Montreal, where in ultra-Catholic circles the French republic was still viewed with deep suspicion. Louis St Laurent made a formal visit to France in 1951 and passed through Paris as part of a world tour in 1954, but the visits seem to have made little impression on him. When he was external affairs minister, Lester Pearson was a frequent visitor to the French capital, but more because Paris was the headquarters of NATO than for bilateral reasons. At the time, Canadian-French relations were sometimes disturbed by Canada's anti-colonial attitudes at the United Nations and Ottawa's reluctance to subscribe to the French cause in Indochina or Algeria. Maurice Duplessis did not visit France at all during his long premiership: he preferred baseball games in New York, though he did once travel to Scotland, where he had some ancestors, and attended a "highland games" event while there.[7]

During the 1950s France was convulsed by colonial wars. The war in Algeria toppled the French Fourth Republic and brought back to power General de Gaulle in 1958. De Gaulle had his hands full over the next few years, facing down two attempted coups d'état before he was finally able to bring the war to an end in 1962. Recognizing that colonial empires of the old kind were doomed, he granted independence to most of France's remaining colonies, replacing imperial rule with indirect influence and military support, as required. French Africa became French-speaking Africa; with the exception of Algeria, where recent memories prevented too close an attachment, the region remained part of France's sphere of influence. The key difference was that France paid far less, in money and blood, for influence than it had for colonial rule. Yet the former colonies where France wielded influence were neither big nor especially wealthy. For de Gaulle, the apparent shrinkage of French prestige and influence posed a challenge, one he was not disposed to avoid.[8]

QUEBEC AND INTERNATIONAL AFFAIRS

The use of French was shrinking in a world where English had become the lingua franca of international communication. In France, English was fashionable as well as useful – from signs to slang, there was clear evidence of the advance of English. In Quebec, purists deplored the incorporation of English phrases or English slang in common speech. In most of the stores of downtown Montreal, in corporate offices, in management generally, English was the essential language. French speakers were sometimes told to speak English, or more often met with blank incomprehension. French seemed to be relegated to merely a local dialect. Immigration continually reinforced the English community. The sense that French was threatened was a theme underlying the Quiet Revolution. Historically, a high birth rate had sustained the French population in Quebec, but in the 1960s its birth rate was falling.[9]

Under the circumstances, it was not surprising that the Lesage government, as part of its modernization program, reached out to France. Early in 1961 the premier announced the establishment of a *délégation générale* in Paris, and in October he travelled to the French capital to open it. He was received with all the honours appropriate to the head of a sovereign government, rather than as the premier of a non-sovereign province. He had lunch with President de Gaulle, laid a wreath at a ceremony at the Arc de Triomphe, and with his accompanying ministers met with the French foreign minister, Maurice Couve de Murville.

Lesage was careful not to go too far. Quebec, he emphasized, was part of the Canadian federation, and his *délégation générale* would act in cooperation with the Canadian embassy in Paris. The federal government spoke for Canada as far as international treaties were concerned. But, he added, Canadian provinces were practically autonomous in "industry, commerce, education and culture." That was not quite the case, as Lesage knew. The federal government had exclusive responsibility for "trade and commerce," including trade treaties, and it played an active role in developing and shaping Canadian industrial policy. Even in the area of culture, the federal government represented Canada in international bodies such as UNESCO. But the limits of provincial jurisdiction were certainly broad, and up to that point they had never been tested as far as foreign affairs were concerned.[10]

There was no novelty in Canadian provinces maintaining offices abroad, for the promotion of trade, tourism, and even immigration. Some of these offices dated back to the nineteenth century; sometimes useful, sometimes not, they were at worst a convenient way of rewarding faithful friends or disposing of embarrassing nuisances. There was always the implication that on local matters a provincial government could represent its interests better than Ottawa could, a manifestation of the rich vein of federal-provincial conflict that has always bedevilled Canadian politics. With Quebec, there was the added issue of language. The Canadian embassy in Paris, to take one example, had a staff that was predominantly English Canadian. Personnel at the Department of External Affairs worked in English.[11] But between Quebec City and Paris, matters would be dealt with in French, and only in French. Even for French-speaking Canadian diplomats who were fluent in English, it was tempting to represent Quebec only, and forego the fatigue of bilingualism.

As the Quiet Revolution went on, Lesage's initiative gathered momentum. The premier at first argued for the full exploitation of Quebec's constitutional powers in order to build a "provincial state," planned and, up to a point, directed from Quebec City – and run in French. This was the approved French model of state building, and the province's intellectuals, politicians, and bureaucrats increasingly looked to France for precedents and advice in economics, as in culture. (The distinction between intellectuals and bureaucrats was blurred, for Lesage recruited heavily in Quebec universities.) Increasingly, Quebec civil servants hankered for a public, formal link that would ratify and solidify the province's special relationship with France.

If Quebec were truly autonomous, such a link would be no problem. But Canadian practice suggested that the components of the federation should run their significant external contacts past Ottawa. What Quebec was seeking was no transboundary agreement on parking tickets or licence plates but something with symbolic implications. Should Quebec go ahead? Should Ottawa consent? What did Quebec want?

The Lesage government was divided on the answer. The more traditional wing of the province's Liberals, which probably included Lesage himself and the party's English-speaking component, believed that Quebec should stop at economic modernization and political reforms. Broadly speaking, this was also the agenda of the national Liberal Party and its provincial affiliates elsewhere in the country, and it might have been the basis for a political accord. Lesage valued his links to the federal Liberals. The first part of his career had been in Ottawa, and it was always possible he might return there as national Liberal leader and prime minister after Pearson. Pearson himself thought as much: Lesage was his logical successor, reaffirming Quebec's place in Canada and French Canadians' stake in the governing of the whole country.

Lesage was torn. He was tempted by federal ambitions but also sensitive to events inside his province. Appeals to French Canadians' sense of ethnic nationalism strengthened the Liberal Party in a provincial election in 1962, called over the issue of nationalizing Quebec Hydro. In other provinces, nationalization of electricity providers was an issue easily interpreted as good government and modernization; in Quebec, it carried the added meaning of bringing under French-Canadian and French-language control an industry hitherto dominated by Montreal's English-language business community.

For the first time, there were misgivings among those studying Lesage's political course. A Montreal editor and law professor, Pierre Trudeau, raised doubts about what Lesage was doing. He was, it seemed, going beyond what a provincial premier ordinarily did, or should do. Speeches by Lesage's energy minister, René Lévesque, seemed to suggest that Trudeau was right. Lévesque "started making speeches in support of a steel industry in Quebec," one of Trudeau's associates, Marc Lalonde, recalled, "on the theory that somehow we had to have it."[12] Quebec's economic destiny was being interpreted as different, indeed separate, from that of the rest of Canada. And if that were true in economics, why not in other fields – education or culture? The logic of such questions pushed Lesage away from Pearson and Ottawa.

In culture, the lead was taken by Georges-Emile Lapalme, like Lesage a former Liberal MP, but a man even less likely to be positively influenced by that fact. As minister of culture, Lapalme entertained his French counterpart, André Malraux, during the latter's visit to the province in October 1963; the two dreamt up cooperative enterprises. The main significance of the visit seems to have been to persuade Malraux that events were moving in Quebec.[13] Admittedly Malraux's main currency was words and ideas. Lesage would have preferred French investment, but for the time being it was thoughts, not deeds, that counted. France would influence Quebec by example and would observe rather than intervene actively in events.

That trend changed with the creation of the Quebec Department of Education in 1964. Every other province had such a department, but in Quebec education had been at one remove, run by confessional authorities, Catholic or Protestant, with state subsidies. The establishment of a formal department was an assertion that it was the state, not the church, that would have the primary role in the new Quebec. To underline the fact, Lesage appointed Paul Gérin-Lajoie as minister. Gérin-Lajoie was a lawyer and constitutional expert as well as a standard bearer of the cause of liberal reform – and he was a nationalist. To him, effective education meant strengthening the French language, and reinforcing French meant further, extensive contacts with France. The minister saw no reason why contacts with France in this field should be run past or through English-dominated Ottawa, and he brought his constitutional law training to bear on the problem. The definition of foreign affairs, he noted, had greatly expanded to include areas never contemplated in the nineteenth century. What did this mean in the context of the Canadian constitution?

On 12 April 1965 Gérin-Lajoie addressed the consular corps of Montreal. He had news for them: Canada had not one sovereign jurisdiction in foreign affairs, but two – federal and provincial. The federal government had authority over only those subjects assigned it by the constitution – trade, defence, and perhaps "political" foreign policy generally. The provinces, following seventy years of judicial rulings, controlled the rest. That meant that only the provinces could speak with authority on subjects such as natural resources or education; while the federal government could speak, it could do so only with their permission or, at best, their cooperation. This "defective" system should be replaced by direct contacts between the provinces and foreign governments. As a start, the consuls should be aware that their diplomatic privileges depended not on Ottawa, but on Quebec City.[14]

How would the federal government respond? Pearson and Lesage, accompanied by some of their senior officials, met to discuss the point at the Queen Elizabeth Hotel in Montreal. Lesage wished to put the Gérin-Lajoie initiative before his Cabinet, but he wanted to let Pearson know what he proposed. "The Quebec premier used such a technique on several occasions," Tom Kent, Pearson's policy adviser, later wrote. "Nationalist sentiment, even within his Cabinet (then including René Lévesque), was strong enough for him to feel that, as he put it, his political life was 'a struggle to control a bear.' The technique helped him to propound a position strong enough to please the nationalists internally while keeping the temperature of federal-provincial relations as low as possible."[15] Next, with Allan Gotlieb, a senior member of External Affairs' legal bureau, and with the agreement of the minister, Paul Martin, and the deputy minister, Marcel Cadieux, drew up a response to Gérin-Lajoie's pretensions.

Only the federal government had an "international personality," Martin (and Cadieux) proclaimed. Thus, only the federal government had the power to enter agreements or treaties with other sovereign states. No other federal state allowed its component parts to make agreements abroad without clearing them with the federal authorities. Only Ottawa had "exclusive responsibility for the conduct of external affairs as a matter of national policy affecting all Canadians." This did not mean that Ottawa would unreasonably obstruct constructive provincial contacts with other countries, but the principle that foreign relations must be conducted under Ottawa's general authority was clear.[16]

Lesage drew back. He did not question Ottawa's treaty power, he said on 24 April. He meant only that Quebec should "negotiate and finalize agreements within provincial jurisdiction." Practically, this agreed with Gérin-Lajoie, but Lesage offered a theoretical fig leaf to the federal government to cover its inability to implement treaties that fell within the provincial sphere. Ottawa and Quebec sought to span the gulf between their positions with a bridge of ambiguity. Both Canada and Quebec were engaged in discussions with France. Canada sought a Franco-Canadian umbrella agreement designed to cover provincial contacts, while Quebec sought a purely bilateral accord with France. In what seemed like a race between the federal and provincial governments, it was the federal government that emerged, in 1964, with an "accord-cadre" or umbrella agreement that legitimized Quebec's contacts with France as occurring with federal permission.

This outcome was not especially satisfactory for Quebec nationalists, whether separatists or merely autonomists. It was more pleasing to Ottawa, where some politicians and diplomats suspected that the whole point of Quebec's quest for an agreement with France had been to assert its independent authority to conclude an international agreement – an attribute of state sovereignty. At about this time Jean Chrétien, then a young Liberal MP, had an illuminating conversation with Claude Morin, Quebec's deputy minister for federal-provincial affairs and, it was widely believed, the mastermind of the provincial government's quest for autonomy. "I remember being told by Claude Morin," Chrétien later said, "we'll separate from Canada the same way that Canada separated from England: we'll cut the links one at a time, a concession here and a concession there, and eventually there'll be nothing left."[17]

Achieving Canadian independence from Great Britain had taken fifty years or more, and Morin did not have anything that long in mind. One way of accelerating the process was through the cooperation of a foreign state, which could only mean France. If France treated Quebec as effectively independent, this would set a precedent that other states would eventually follow. For Canada to react negatively to honours lavished on Quebec visitors to France, or to contacts between two French-speaking governments, would risk provoking a negative reaction and making conversions to the cause of sovereignty among Quebec voters.

APPEASING FRANCE

Ottawa was not without tools in the struggle against Quebec independence. France had interests in Canada, investments and trade connections. France and Canada were allies, formally through NATO and informally in the aftermath of two world wars. Canada was not unpopular in France, and ordinary French citizens certainly did not see Quebec as an urgent cause justifying the diversion of their country's foreign policy into a new and unfamiliar channel. The French government had other interests and priorities besides Canada, some conceivably more important than interfering in North America. But did de Gaulle see it that way?

The French president had begun to take an interest in Quebec around the time of an official visit to Canada in 1960.[18] The Quebec *délégation générale* intrigued him, and he took an increasingly close interest in events in the province. In 1961 he considered that contacts with Quebec had to be pursued even if they were disagreeable to the government in Ottawa. By September 1963 there is evidence de Gaulle had formed the conclusion that Quebec would ultimately become an independent state.[19]

Pearson hastened to visit Paris in January 1964.[20] The visit was superficially cordial and, to the Canadians, apparently satisfactory. Pearson was keen to convince the French, de Gaulle in particular, that there could be a special connection between Canada and

France and that France occupied a place in Canadian hearts and policies similar to that occupied by the United States and Great Britain. He succeeded in convincing them of almost the opposite. On concrete issues, Pearson had nothing to offer regarding the purchase of French aircraft for the government airline, Air Canada; nor would he sell uranium to France so it could build up its military stockpile. Canada freely sold uranium to the Americans and the British, and cheerfully bought US aircraft for its airline. De Gaulle made it clear, publicly and privately, that he had problems with the style and substance of American leadership of the Western alliance, but there too Pearson had little to offer. The prime minister was at pains to emphasize Canada's good relations with the United States, and the centrality of American influence in Canadian life.

Pearson was unimpressed by de Gaulle's arguments. A few weeks later he told George Ball, the American undersecretary of state, that de Gaulle was fifty years behind the times, rigid and unbending in his attitudes. The French president was equally unimpressed by Pearson and did not exert himself to be pleasing to his guest. A French historian describes Pearson's reception as "cold," and that seems to be correct.[21]

Practically, Pearson could do little to appease de Gaulle. The Canadian government depended on close relations with the United States, and the 1963 election showed that Canadians expected as much. Canada accepted the American nuclear deterrent, and the government broadly approved of American policy in NATO. Relations with Great Britain were less close or cordial than they had once been, but there was no great cause for dispute or controversy there. France was important to Canada for one reason and one reason only – French favour or, at worst, French neutrality would help maintain the internal political balance at home.

The obvious anxiety that Pearson betrayed during his trip to France struck de Gaulle as proof of personal weakness and, worse, of the weakness of the Canadian state. Canada, de Gaulle concluded, was ultimately doomed, whatever well-intentioned but naïve people – like Pearson, but also like some of his own officials – might say. From early 1964, he moved to recognize and encourage differences between Quebec and Canada, with decreasing concern for Ottawa's reaction. Canada and France remained, officially, allies, but there was little serious communication between them at the policy level. De Gaulle would go his own way, and he would travel without Canadian baggage.

Essentially, de Gaulle envisioned a distancing between North America – meaning the United States – and Europe. The Americans had their interests, and would pursue them, but they were different from Europe's interests. Canada didn't exist in this equation; to insist on a Canadian position, or to argue that European and North American interests ought to remain the same and in an American-led alliance, was antithetical to the vision of the French president. Within that perspective, Canadian views must either be disregarded, or, if they had some support, opposed. For the next few years, no day was complete without a pronouncement from Paris – on the Third World, on the

Soviet Union, on international monetary policy, on the unity of Europe "from the Atlantic to the Urals," or on Vietnam. On all points, de Gaulle differed from the United States and on most of them, though he did not point it out, from Canada.

The Canadians did their best. If de Gaulle was unhappy with the existing structure of NATO, Pearson allowed that he had his doubts. He speculated in public in February 1965 that it might be time for Europe to assume responsibility – within NATO – for its own defence, leaving the North American members to look after their own side of the Atlantic.[22] On another issue, the American-sponsored Multilateral Nuclear Force (MLF), Canada echoed French objections.[23] Given that de Gaulle opposed the project, its failure was certain; Canada's position was, accordingly, a realistic acceptance of the inevitable. Yet the alternative to the MLF was an independent French nuclear capacity, the *force de frappe*, and the addition of another member to the nuclear club.[24]

Early in 1966 de Gaulle announced that France would pull out of NATO's military organization, though it would remain a formal member of the North Atlantic alliance. As a consequence, NATO headquarters had to leave Paris, and allied NATO troops had to evacuate their bases in France. The expulsion included Canadian troops, and Canadian officials in Paris and Ottawa were duly notified that they had a year, until March 1967, to close Canadian air bases at Marville and Gros-Tenquin.

Pearson was furious. He remained, in his heart and by conviction, an alliance man. The lessons of the thirties bit deeply: only consultation and solidarity among the democracies, based on their shared ideological and other interests, could work. Initially, the prime minister sarcastically asked the French ambassador if the evacuation order included Canadian war graves, a comment he repeated to Lyndon Johnson. Pearson's strident initial comments worried the Americans; Johnson told his staff that he did not intend to let Pearson lecture him on American relations with France.

But what could Pearson do? Foreign policy was a difficult issue in the mid-1960s, especially where the American alliance was involved. The shadow of Vietnam reached into Europe, and for much of Canadian public opinion, especially on the left, de Gaulle's withdrawal from an American-led military alliance was a very good thing. NATO was no longer a major priority with Canadians and especially, as Pearson knew, with politically active opinion. This was another point where the prime minister's subtle interpretation of Canadian interests differed from that of public opinion, though on a much less sensitive or dangerous issue than Vietnam. Finally, France was France, potentially a factor in Canadian domestic politics, and Quebec was Quebec, sensitive to "Anglo-Saxon" slights. Opinion in Quebec might well oppose a strong line on France, and Canadian policy must take that possibility into account.

Damage control was indicated, and Paul Martin did his best. French officials, he argued, were far less disposed than de Gaulle to question US policy or confront NATO.[25] Admittedly, NATO had to pull its military bases and headquarters out of France, but did it follow that the alliance should remove its political headquarters? So, at least, Martin told the allies, as they debated what to do. The Americans were impatient with Canadian stalling on the move from Paris, but as usual they attributed Martin's interventions to his domestic problems. His hesitation could be irritating. "Paul Martin," Secretary of State Dean Rusk reported to President Johnson, "looking over his shoulder at Quebec, was our most difficult problem." But Martin agreed to the relocation of the military headquarters to Belgium and, finally, to the transfer of the North Atlantic Council to Brussels. As over Vietnam, some of his diplomats were unhappy at the minister's management of the issue; and as with Vietnam, the Americans knew it.[26]

Marcel Cadieux echoed the department's misgivings. By 1966 Cadieux and Martin coexisted uneasily; there had been a bitter personal quarrel between the two men, and it removed ordinary constraints of respect and loyalty as far as the undersecretary was concerned. Martin knew it, as did the prime minister, but for the time being there was nothing that could be done. Martin could not replace or repudiate Cadieux, as this would dishearten French-Canadian federalists. And so the undersecretary carried on. "Encore une perle pour la collection," Cadieux would write, as he recorded another *bêtise* from his minister. "Ambitious, ignorant, shallow or dishonest," was Cadieux's condensed view of Martin. He exaggerated, but there was a kernel of truth in his observations. As over Vietnam, it was the minister's ambition that dominated and inevitably created difficulties and outright failures.[27]

Cadieux had early concluded that France was up to no good in Canada, and he made no secret of his belief. Over lunch, he told the American ambassador that the French were using Quebec as part of a general anti-American strategy. There could be no doubt that France was trying to break up Canada. De Gaulle was taking every opportunity to encourage pretensions towards "separatism" on the part of Quebec leaders of all shades of opinion, and Cadieux "cited the manner in which members of the Quebec Cabinet were invited to the Elysée [de Gaulle's presidential palace] without the Canadian Ambassador."[28]

What especially worried the Canadian government was the possibility that the French president and his entourage were coordinating their actions with the government of Quebec. There were plenty of avenues for contact, through the *délégation générale* in Paris and the French consulates general in Montreal and Quebec City – and of course the embassy in Ottawa. Cadieux warned all foreign missions in Canada that they should deal only with the federal government, but that edict proved difficult to enforce. In any case, "unofficial" visitors from France kept the cauldron bubbling.[29]

In private and public, the Canadian government kept as silent as it dared on the issue of NATO. It kept silent as it became evident that the Canadian ambassador to France, Jules Léger, was being cold-shouldered by de Gaulle and his officials, and that Quebec politicians travelling to France were receiving increasingly grand receptions from the French government. (Ironically, Léger was a strong advocate of the French position on NATO, a view that placed him at odds with Cadieux and the department in Ottawa.) Canadian ministers received the minimum ceremonies compatible with diplomatic life. When Paul Martin raised these difficulties with his French opposite number, Maurice Couve de Murville, the reply was always the same: these were minor matters best ignored. Franco-Canadian communiqués consequently remained relentlessly cheerful.

On the next issue to arise in Franco-Canadian relations, Ottawa took even greater care to keep silent. The governor general, Georges Vanier, wished to visit France, where he had once served as ambassador. Vanier had also been Canada's representative to the Free French, and thus to de Gaulle, during the war. There was, apparently, a strong personal connection, which mirrored Ottawa's view of what Franco-Canadian relations should be. A visit from his old acquaintance would serve to remind de Gaulle of what France had once received from Canada, and what it might hope for in the future. It would also be a visit from one French-speaking head of state to another, a public display for Canadians, especially French Canadians, of the success of Canada's bilingual experiment.

De Gaulle found the proposed visit embarrassing. He could hardly resist receiving a comrade in arms from the war in which his own reputation was founded. Yet he did not wish to provide a demonstration of Franco-Canadian harmony, and even less of English-French harmony in Canada; on that subject, his opinion was evidently increasingly entrenched. He therefore took refuge in a technicality. Canada was a monarchy, and Elizabeth II was its head of state. Vanier was only her viceroy, in effect her deputy. Though he did not say so, de Gaulle implied that Vanier's position was closer to that of a colonial governor, while Canada's position as a sovereign state was under this interpretation dubious, to say the least.

So Vanier might be received, but only as an old friend and important personage, and definitely not as head of the (or a) Canadian state. De Gaulle distinguished between personal sentiment and the interests of France, which did not include recognizing Canada through its governor general. Under the circumstances, the visit was impossible. Deeply offended, Vanier cancelled his project. The Vanier incident was, however, much more than a personal affront – it was an indication that de Gaulle had cast his lot with Quebec's separate destiny.[30]

Centennial Blues

Vanier and de Gaulle might still have found occasion to trade reminiscences. Canada was going to celebrate its centennial in 1967 with a lavish celebration centred on a world's fair in Montreal – Expo 67. Representatives of virtually all countries were invited to Canada; the invitations would, of course, include de Gaulle. The program for heads of state had a standard form – a stop in Ottawa, followed by a visit to Montreal and its exhibition. Vanier would take care of the greetings and local entertainment in Ottawa, and the commissioner general of Expo and his staff in Montreal would do the rest.

Although de Gaulle had been invited in September 1966 to attend the centennial and visit Expo, his response did not come until the spring of 1967, by which time the centennial celebrations were already well launched. Nor did de Gaulle accept the federal invitation, but that of Quebec. Governor General Vanier did not have to cope with this latest incivility; he died in January and was hastily replaced by Roland Michener, a distinguished former politician and Canadian high commissioner to New Delhi.

There was another change in personnel. The Lesage government went to the polls in June 1966, expecting to be handily re-elected. To his surprise and considerable humiliation, Lesage was narrowly defeated, winning fifty-one seats to the Union Nationale's fifty-five. True, the Liberals won a substantial plurality of the popular vote – 47 percent to the Union Nationale's 41. But as Daniel Johnson, the Union Nationale leader and new premier of Quebec, put it, "If you take away the English-speaking vote in Montreal, if you take away the votes that are English, Jewish, I am sure that the Union Nationale had a very strong majority of the francophone vote."[31]

Johnson was a different character from Lesage, and he held very different views about the future of Quebec and Canada. Lesage was, at bottom, a convinced Canadian federalist in what was becoming the Quebec Liberal style, using nationalism as a vehicle to shore up the Liberal vote. Lesage had experience in Ottawa and strong federal connections. Johnson, on the other hand, was a purely provincial figure, a former Cabinet minister under Duplessis, a man generally considered a lightweight – by Lesage, among others. Johnson was in reality a smooth and very supple politician; many thought he was willing to ride whatever wave would carry him to power, and keep him there. Between 1962 and 1965, Johnson had reoriented himself away from orthodox federalism and towards a group of nationalists in his own party, and there is no doubt that he encouraged talk of separatism and independence among his followers. Johnson himself talked on both sides of the issue – fiercely while in Quebec, and more moderately outside the province.[32]

In the 1966 campaign, Johnson spoke for the many Quebeckers, especially in rural areas, who thought the province was changing too much and too quickly. But once in power, he did almost nothing to reverse Lesage's policies, while he maintained most of the Liberal government's official advisers. On the constitutional front, and in foreign affairs, it was difficult to predict what the new premier meant to do. In 1965 he had produced a book titled *Egalité ou indépendance*, arguing that Quebec should achieve "equality" within Canada or seek independence. For the conservative-minded, and the traditionalists in his own party, Johnson seemed to prefer "equality" and staying within Canada. For the nationalists, he presented the arguments for independence.

Most Canadians outside Quebec, and many inside the province, were unable to fathom what Johnson meant by "equality or independence." His position was clearer than federalists believed. Quebec should be "equal" in Canada. There would be two Canadas, English and French, with equal standing and equal power. No longer could the English-speaking majority impose its views on the French minority. Instead, the English would have to treat the French with the respect that had so often not been accorded in the past. If they did not wish to do so, there was always independence. Strategically bold and far-reaching in his policy, Johnson was also extremely cautious tactically, and it seems fair to conclude that he wanted to use independence in pursuit of equality.[33]

Johnson quickly perceived that de Gaulle and France could be of use to him, and de Gaulle came to the same conclusion. The French president could serve to illustrate the possibilities of "independence" while conferring prestige on his local allies, Johnson and his followers. For de Gaulle, Johnson was a shrewd, provincial politician of a kind not unknown in France. He saw in him what he wanted to see, a Quebec nationalist steering towards independence but needing encouragement and direction.[34] De Gaulle was, of course, just the man to offer both, and he took Johnson's election as a sign that he should do so.

When invited to visit Expo 67, de Gaulle was coy. Only in February 1967, pressed by Johnson, did he make up his mind: he announced that he would come to Quebec City and then to Montreal.[35] The visit was scheduled for late July. Long before then, it became clear that there would be difficulties. De Gaulle wanted to visit Quebec City first, then Montreal and Expo, and, finally (or perhaps), Ottawa. He would not only be visiting Quebec first, but primarily, treating the federal government as marginal at best. His arrangements were therefore made first with the government of Quebec and confirmed by a visit to Paris in May 1967 by Premier Johnson.[36] Johnson hoped to encourage de Gaulle. "Mon général," he is reported to have said, "Quebec needs you." Then Johnson added, "It's now or never." De Gaulle naturally agreed. He had something in mind, and it was clear to him that there would never be a better occasion – indeed, given his age, there might never be another occasion at all.[37]

The federal government reluctantly went along with what they knew of de Gaulle's plans. The Department of External Affairs studied what was likely to happen and reached a guardedly optimistic conclusion. Problems there were, and de Gaulle's actions were not entirely predictable, but on balance there was reason for hope.[38] Perhaps the department was misled by its contacts with the French embassy, which like most of the rest of the French foreign ministry did not wish to see relations with Canada disturbed.[39]

External Affairs, through its minister, advised Pearson that "best results will probably be secured through a judicious mixture of alertness, firmness and friendliness, which has served us well to date."[40] Canadian policy towards France was definitely, even desperately, friendly, but it had not been firm, and if this advice was any indication it was not especially alert. As for serving Canada well, the de Gaulle visit was about to plunge Canada, and Franco-Canadian relations, into a prolonged and profound crisis.

The shape of the crisis was determined well in advance. The Canadian government was divided: Martin and Léger hoped for the best, Cadieux feared the worst, and Pearson drifted uncomfortably in between.[41] Mitchell Sharp, the finance minister, inclined to optimism. "France," he told an American diplomat in June, was "attempting to gain influence in Quebec by playing up French-English Canadian difficulties. The Federal Government, however, was on to France's game and was interposing itself between France and Quebec in a manner which both undercut France and gave the appearance of increased Franco-Canadian ties. In any event, he opined, Quebeckers were not enamoured of France. They considered themselves French North Americans."[42]

The federal Cabinet was nevertheless uneasy. They discussed the visit at length: some ministers argued that the federal government should stand firm on setting the agenda for de Gaulle's visit. On balance, however, the ministers agreed that there was more to be feared from a cancellation than from going ahead. Paul Martin, passing through Paris, bore his colleagues' reservations in mind when he saw de Gaulle on 16 June; faced with the general's charm, and with an apparently conciliatory attitude, he decided not to spoil the occasion by bringing up Canadian complaints about the behaviour of French and Quebec officials. As Dale Thomson commented in his study of the de Gaulle visit, "Almost desperately anxious to have the visit go smoothly, he appears to have been taken in." De Gaulle, for his part, seems to have decided that nothing should now stand in the way of his visit to Quebec and consciously applied a little hypocrisy to the task.[43]

The federal opposition parties, Conservatives, New Democrats, and Créditistes, resembled the Liberals in their contradictions and hesitations. The Conservatives in particular were consumed by factional disputes in the spring and summer of 1967 (Diefenbaker would be deposed at a convention in September), but they also worried at length about the balance of forces in Quebec, and where their political advantage and the national advantage lay. Johnson and his government varied in their hopes and fears, some towards the federalist side, some towards separatism and independence, while the opposition Liberals in Quebec City mirrored the divisions of the government. No major party had as yet broken with the Canadian federal system: in the 1966 provincial election, the supporters of independence had harvested only 8 percent of the vote and in the minds of mainstream politicians represented a shrill, radical minority.[44]

De Gaulle intended to change all that. "I am going to strike a strong blow," he told his son-in-law, General Alain Boissieu. "Things are going to get hot. But it is necessary."[45] According to his education minister, Alain Peyrefitte, the French president had long ago made up his mind on the desirability of achieving Quebec independence, and by the spring of 1967 had decided to use his official visit to Canada as a pulpit for preaching the separation of the province.[46] De Gaulle and the Johnson government took the next step. They insisted on controlling the general's itinerary: Quebec City first, of course, nodding to a minimal and barely tolerated federal presence, a motorcade along the shores of the St Lawrence, and a triumphant arrival in Montreal on 24 July. The visit to Expo would follow, and finally de Gaulle would go to Ottawa to meet with federal government representatives. Whether the general ever intended to complete the final part of his journey is open to serious question: his main object was Quebec, and the federal government represented, to him, little more than a phantom or, at most, an obstacle to be overcome. Cooperation did not appear on the general's agenda.

De Gaulle landed in Quebec from a French naval cruiser, the *Colbert*, on 23 July. (The cruiser was named after one of Louis XIV's ministers, who had helped develop the colony of New France.) There was official entertainment in Quebec City, where the federal presence was distinctly secondary. Louis St Laurent, in retirement in the city and indisputably a distinguished son of the province, had to be invited to the provincial government's banquet, but in compensation he was seated as inconspicuously as possible, far away from de Gaulle, Johnson, and the other dignitaries of the moment. Perhaps it was just as well: he would not have enjoyed what the general had to say.

De Gaulle made it clear that he was in Quebec to celebrate "the advent of a people." Soon, he hoped, the French of North America would "become their own masters," and then work out their destiny – including "their independence" – with the English Canadians. There was still the possibility of ambiguity: de Gaulle might have been referring to *Canadian* independence vis-à-vis the United States ("their colossal neighbour.") But there was no doubt that the general regarded Quebec's past as well as its present as something to be overcome, and discarded, in favour of a new identity and a new relationship with the rest of Canada. That could be *égalité* on the Johnson model; it could also be (and in de Gaulle's opinion ought to be) *indépendance*.[47]

As long as de Gaulle stayed in the realm of ambiguity, the Canadian government would – however unhappily – accept his behaviour. Nervously, Pearson awaited the next day. July 24 was reserved for a triumphant motorcade along the north shore of the St Lawrence, on an old highway renamed for the occasion the *Chemin du Roy*. A public holiday was proclaimed. Union Nationale organizers were instructed to get out the crowds: they arrived by the school bus load, waving French and Quebec flags provided by the provincial government. There was no question of Canadian flags. As de Gaulle's procession advanced, the general was treated to enthusiastic demonstrations by separatist militants, waving signs: *Vive la France*; *Vive de Gaulle*; and, of course, their main slogan, *Vive le Québec libre.*

De Gaulle responded to the crowds. As he moved towards Montreal, his language and his attitude grew increasingly excited. For the first time, Johnson became nervous. "If he continues like that," he said after listening to de Gaulle's lunchtime oration, "by the time we get to Montreal we will have separated." As they drove on during the afternoon, Johnson pointedly told de Gaulle of his hopes for a federal-provincial conference scheduled for November. That would not do, the president replied. It would only snuff out the cause. "A deficient regime, he remarked, could not be reformed from within."[48]

Awaiting de Gaulle in Montreal was a municipal reception followed by a banquet, hosted by Mayor Jean Drapeau. Drapeau and his guests had a long wait, because de Gaulle and Johnson were making slow progress from one crowded town to another, but finally they arrived, just as twilight was drawing on. Drapeau had his own perspective on what was taking place. The mayor had started out as a nationalist politician, but his career in municipal politics had refined his view of the world. Montreal was, and had been since the 1760s, a bilingual city. It flourished on the basis of mutual tolerance between French and English, but also for the city's immigrant communities.

In Montreal de Gaulle met the same fervent crowds he had seen throughout the day. He was grateful for the enthusiasm, he told Drapeau. Drapeau dryly responded that it was what "a great cosmopolitan city" would naturally do for a great man. "Cosmopolitan" was not precisely what de Gaulle wanted to hear, and characteristically he ignored the term. He was in Montreal only to speak to the "French of Quebec." And, of course, he wanted to speak. There was a balcony to hand, and a crowd outside. There was also a microphone, provided, some later said, by the local correspondent of the French broadcasting system, RTF.

Drapeau had foreseen the problem. Unfortunately, he told de Gaulle, the microphone was not functioning. The mayor knew that this was so: he had had the sound system disconnected. As luck would have it, and unbeknown to the mayor, there was a technician standing by and within earshot. There was no problem, he assured de Gaulle. He could quickly get the sound working. Assured that his words would carry, de Gaulle stepped on to the balcony.

It had been quite a day, the general told his audience. He had passed through scenes of joy that reminded him of only one thing. Lowering his voice in the manner of bedtime-story tellers, de Gaulle explained, "I am going to tell you a secret that you will not repeat. This evening, here and all along the route, I found the same kind of atmosphere as that of the Liberation." This was, of course, the Liberation of France in 1944 – from the Nazis. The president thanked his listeners for the "unforgettable memory of this evening in Montreal." If it was not unforgettable, de Gaulle was about to make it so. "Vive Montréal!" he shouted, his voice rising and continuing to rise. "Vive le Québec! Vive le Québec libre!"

The scene was recorded for most of Canada to watch on the 11 o'clock news, which led off with the item. As soon as it played, phones started ringing, and telegrams poured in to Ottawa. Pearson himself was on the phone, trying to locate Martin and Léger, while Martin played hide and seek with Couve de Murville, the French foreign minister. (Couve, by all indications, was appalled: he would later describe the general's actions as "une connerie."[49]) It was difficult, this time, for Martin to deny that the news was bad, but, typically, he argued that it could be worse: it would be worse if, for example, the federal government reacted negatively to de Gaulle's statement.

Pearson could not afford to agree with his foreign minister. The prime minister was personally offended by the implied comparison of English Canada to Nazi Germany. The reaction of most of his ministers, Liberal MPs, and the media made it plain that English Canadians were very upset indeed. If he failed to say anything, Pearson risked disrupting his party and his government. There was in any case no further possibility of appeasing de Gaulle; that strategy had just reached a spectacular and definitive dead end.

THE AFTERMATH

While Pearson met with his Cabinet in Ottawa, de Gaulle spent 25 July touring the Expo site in the company of its Canadian commissioner, Lionel Chevrier. According to witnesses, de Gaulle and his staff lost no opportunity to insult their Canadian escorts. Even de Gaulle's Quebec hosts were disconcerted by the president's choice of the separatist slogan in his speech the previous night. Something surely would now happen.[50] De Gaulle lingered over the French pavilion, but gave the Canadian one a bare ten minutes.[51] Everyone, including de Gaulle, was awaiting word from Ottawa.

It came in the form of a televised address by the prime minister. De Gaulle's remarks, Pearson bluntly stated, were "unacceptable." Mouthing the slogan of Quebec separatists was of course improper, as were the remarks about liberation. "The people of Canada are free," Pearson said. "Every province of Canada is free. Canadians do not need to be liberated." He would have further discussions with de Gaulle the next day when the general arrived in Ottawa; and he hoped for the best.

De Gaulle seized the moment. "We're leaving," he told his staff. A French aircraft picked him up at Montreal airport, and it was back to Paris, not on to Ottawa. In Ottawa, Pearson dropped in on his old friend, the governor general. Together they picked over the delicacies assembled for the never-to-be-held banquet for de Gaulle, and together they contemplated the mysteries of life.

A small cottage industry grew up to interpret what de Gaulle really meant when he shouted "Vive le Québec libre!" on the evening of 24 July 1967. First, there was Jean

Drapeau, who within days argued that de Gaulle had simply been carried away by emotion.[52] Then there were the pollsters. In a poll in August 1967 they offered Quebeckers a choice of meanings for de Gaulle's words. Over half chose the following: "The general meant that Quebec is actually free and that he is glad that this is so." Only 17 percent maintained that he meant to urge Quebec to separate from Canada. Since he had meant nothing by his remarks, it followed, in the minds of a majority of Quebeckers, that Pearson had been "too hard." Forty percent nevertheless believed that de Gaulle, presumably in the spirit of charity, should have gone to see Pearson anyway, in Ottawa.[53]

Apologists for de Gaulle have taken their cue from this early poll. Some argued that he had been carried away by the moment and had said what he said without really intending to. Some argued that there was a different meaning to de Gaulle's speech. Many of these writers argued that Pearson, and English Canadians generally, overreacted to the oration. The fact that de Gaulle was bitterly denounced from Newfoundland to Nanaimo only confirmed that Canada was a divided country and provoked a French-Canadian counterreaction. Yet the unconcealed joy with which many French Canadians received de Gaulle's words was not in the first instance a response to English Canada; rather, he had caught their sentiments well enough and, alone among serious centennial speakers, had given them tangible and (to them) respectable form.

Canada certainly appeared to be divided in the summer of 1967. But the division, as de Gaulle would certainly have pointed out, was already there. He exploited Quebec nationalism and separatism, but he did not cause them. Quebec had always been divided among optimists who sought reconciliation with the rest of Canada and pessimists who argued that French Quebeckers must rely on themselves alone and abandon the false formulas of Canadian federalism.

The centennial and Expo were intended to remind Canadians of what, together, they had accomplished in the hundred years of federation. The celebrations evoked a prideful sense of nationalism, everywhere but among Quebec nationalists. And Quebec nationalists and *indépendantistes* were on the upswing in 1967, as they had been for some years.

In the immediate aftermath of de Gaulle's eruption, almost all Quebeckers took a position. Jean Lesage was against, and said so. François Aquin, a Liberal MLA, promptly resigned from the party to sit as an "independent" (and supporter of independence) until a party more to his liking came along. That happened in the fall, when the Quebec Liberal Party split. The majority backed Lesage and federalism; the minority marched out of the hall behind René Lévesque. (Lévesque himself was none too pleased at de Gaulle's intervention, which he considered a distraction.[54]) The next year Lévesque and his followers constituted the Parti Québécois, whose mission was to promote Quebec sovereignty.

De Gaulle counted on Daniel Johnson to shape the consequences for Quebec of the Montreal speech. Had not Johnson appealed for help for Quebec as recently as their interview in Paris in May, and had not de Gaulle responded successfully? He had succeeded in one thing – he made Johnson uncomfortable. Instead of endorsing the general's message, Johnson retreated into ambiguity. It has been said that he threatened Pearson with secession if Ottawa broke diplomatic relations with France, but there has been no corroboration for this assertion. The premier's health was tricky, and he needed rest far from his duties. He went to Hawaii, in the company of some of his more federalist friends. There he learned that Quebec businessmen, especially French-speaking businessmen, thought matters had gone far enough, and that the province would suffer serious economic damage if Johnson took another step towards independence.

Vacation over, Johnson returned to Quebec. He had to conduct the province's business, and the rhythms of Canadian politics reasserted themselves. There was a conference of the provinces in Toronto in November, and Johnson had to be there. As he habitually did with English Canadians, Johnson played the moderate: there was hope for Canada; the crisis would be resolved; all would yet be well.

That left de Gaulle in Paris, dancing the separatist minuet without a partner. The general did his best. He knew that reaction in France to his pronouncements in Canada was sceptical if not hostile. He whipped his Cabinet into silence. Public opinion polls showed that 45 percent of French men and women disapproved of de Gaulle's foreign policy after the Quebec escapade, while only 18 percent approved. It was a turning point in de Gaulle's popularity, at least where foreign policy was concerned, and he never fully recovered.[55]

Naturally, the general was undeterred. In August he ordered that French aid for Quebec increase.[56] That was government aid: hopes for investment from the private sector were dashed on the shoals of French financial prudence. He rejected suggestions from the French embassy in Ottawa that now was the time for reconciliation with Pearson. In November, coinciding with Johnson's visit to Toronto, de Gaulle held a press conference to denounce plurilingual countries as a delusion, bound to fail. Canada was naturally his prime example, but the general threw in Nigeria (then in a state of civil war) and Cyprus for good measure. "Save us from our friends," one of Johnson's aides murmured.[57] But, for de Gaulle, Johnson was a friend no longer. To his consul general in Quebec, whom he had authorized to run his mission independently of the embassy in Ottawa, tainted by federal connections, the president stated that Johnson was after all "a politician and not a statesman." But de Gaulle had demonstrated that he did not have the means to keep Johnson's friendship. If economic risks were a measure of the viability of independence – and they were not the only one – then France did little to improve the odds. De Gaulle complained loudly inside the confines of his

Elysée palace about the unpatriotic attitude of French businesses, unwilling to put their money into Quebec, but he could do little to alter the situation.[58]

After 1967 Johnson inclined – "chose" is too strong a word – to continue inside Canada. As a result, de Gaulle's immediate policy for Quebec and, by extension, Canada was frustrated. He had taken a chance in creating an international incident in Canada. He managed to stir up some trouble in Quebec, but not enough, from his point of view. Nor was his policy well received in France. Newspapers and politicians – all but those directly beholden to de Gaulle and his party – criticized his actions. How much damage was done to de Gaulle's domestic prestige is debatable, but it was surely a factor in the decline of his presidency in the year that followed. Domestic disruption and an economic crisis in 1968 kept French mischief making in Canada to a minimum; in May de Gaulle even had to make sure of the reliability of the French army in Germany in case he had to use military force to put down a potential rebellion in Paris.[59] The next year, following a reverse in a referendum, de Gaulle quit as French president; two years later he was dead. As far as the independence of Quebec was concerned, de Gaulle had lost his race with time.

CANADA SURVIVED DE GAULLE, though not without damage. He may have accelerated the separatist timetable in Quebec, and he obviously contributed to ill feeling between French and English Canadians. The centennial was more of a mixed memory than it should have been, and the image of Montreal and Expo was slightly tarnished. As time passed, de Gaulle was remembered in English Canada more for his exploits as leader of Free France than as the architect of Quebec separation; in that role he was more sorcerer's apprentice than sorcerer.

The year 1967 was more than a hundredth anniversary; it marked the end of political generations in France and in Canada. Pearson and de Gaulle were both veterans of the First World War as well as senior players in the Second. Neither man was at his best in 1967. De Gaulle sought to compensate for France's decline by raising its oldest colony from the dead, and, because he felt the pressure of age and time, he tried to do it in a hurry. Pearson, knowing that the bright and brassy façade of the centennial and Expo masked serious weaknesses in Canada's basic political structure, overestimated the damage de Gaulle could do. Instead of refuting French pretensions, the Canadian government sought to avert or appease them. In the process Ottawa confirmed in French eyes that it was negotiating from weakness; the result was more, not less, bullying and interference.

The French poltergeist was not completely exorcised. Subsequent French governments, for diverse reasons, continued to interfere in Canada, and Quebec nationalist politicians, for their own reasons, continued to invoke the spectre of French support. They remembered only the loud noise de Gaulle made in 1967; they forgot that it was Johnson who had invited him to Canada, and Johnson who discovered that after de Gaulle flew off, Quebec was still in Canada, and that very little had changed.

14

CHANGING THE MEANING
OF DEFENCE

In celebrating its centennial, Canada set its best before the world and presented a vision of the future, symbolized by Expo 67. In the same year, the host city of Expo, Montreal, opened its subway, the Metro, and inaugurated its big-league baseball team, the Expos, Canada's first. In vision, design, and sports, Canada through Montreal was showing that it had come of age. Across the country, prideful citizens erected auditoriums, civic centres, and hockey rinks as a symbol, but also as a gift, from their generation to their children and grandchildren.

The centennial also commemorated the achievements of the past. Speeches, books, and documentaries recalled what Canadians had done. *Canada's First Century* was one such product, the work of Donald Creighton, the dean of Canadian historians. Creighton also helped edit the Canadian Centennial Series, a collection of histories that tried to sum up what Canadians of the present knew about their compatriots of the past. Not to be outdone, the government sponsored a military tattoo, with marching bands, which tried to illustrate three centuries of Canadian military achievement. Bands played "Marching to Pretoria," commemorating the Boer War of 1899-1902, "Tipperary," for the First World War, and "The White Cliffs of Dover" for the Second. The culmination was contemporary soldiers, in the blue berets of United Nations peacekeeping, marching under celebratory fireworks.[1]

Most Canadian soldiers were not serving with, or under, the United Nations. Though UN service was popular with politicians, and with the left-leaning section of Canada's political class, the main commitment of Canada's armed forces – land, sea, and air – was to NATO. It was an expensive undertaking, but NATO was an unquestioned part of Canada's foreign policy, as it had been since the foundation of the alliance in 1949.

The two most prominent instances of Canada's peacekeeping in the 1960s were as much the product of NATO as they were of the United Nations. The United Nations Emergency Force in the Sinai was very much the result of Canadian fears of a rift between Great Britain and the United States. The emergency had by 1967 lasted over ten years; no one could honestly say when it would end. The more recent Canadian force in Cyprus reflected Canadian fears of war between two other NATO allies, Greece and Turkey; sending troops also obliged the senior NATO partner, the United States, as well as Great Britain. Domestically, the Cyprus mission reflected the eagerness of the external affairs minister, Paul Martin, to put "his" stamp on a peacekeeping force. If it had worked for Pearson, Martin may have reasoned, why not for him?[2]

Canada's defence policy, in its older NATO and newer UN aspects, seemed to be one of indefinite commitments, overseas garrisons that once in place could not be withdrawn. The commitments were heavy, but until the mid-1960s they were firmly supported by public opinion. NATO was, however, an American-led organization, and American leadership, because of the Vietnam War and simultaneous unrest in the United States, was coming under fire. In a public opinion poll in Canada in 1968, 37 percent of Canadians agreed that the United States was "a sick society," though 45 percent disagreed. In Quebec, 41 percent agreed and only 30 percent disagreed, the most radical sample in Canada.[3] Such anti-American sentiments were a major factor affecting support for NATO. A study conducted for the Department of External Affairs, which found that a majority of Canada's largest and most influential newspapers were either "consistently anti-NATO," or "generally and increasingly anti-NATO."[4]

Accepting the leadership of a "sick" country certainly did not attract some Canadians, and the argument that it was inescapable, inevitable, or traditional did not appeal to others. The freshly appointed minister of justice, Pierre Elliott Trudeau, was one of these. Talking to a British television interviewer, Trudeau claimed that since 1949, "Canada's foreign policy was largely its policy in NATO, through NATO."[5] By implication, that would have to change, though in a Pearson government how it would change was not obvious. Under Pearson, defence had been and still was an issue, perhaps the weak point of Canadian foreign policy.

DEFENCE

Canada's defence forces in 1963 consisted of 123,000 personnel. That year marked the beginning of a decline from their postwar high of 126,000 the year before; by 1967 their number had reached 106,000. It was a sign that the Pearson government did not give defence or the armed forces the same high priority that they had received during the Berlin crisis. Along with declining numbers, there was a general lack of clarity about the role the government intended for the armed forces.

In the fiscal year 1963-1964, Ottawa spent $1.7 billion on defence, roughly 23 percent of its total budget, far more than on any other category in the federal cornucopia, including health or social welfare. So it had been since the onset of the Korean War in 1950: every year, in every budget, defence was first. Public opinion, and the politicians who expressed it, had few qualms about military spending. Some might quibble over details, but with the exception of a few pacifists and the fringes of the left, there was no quarrel over the principle.

The Pearson government, with great fanfare, released a White Paper on Defence in 1964. It nodded towards the presumed popularity of peacekeeping for the United Nations, as well as towards efficiency and savings through the elimination of duplication in military administration. It promised large sums ($1.5 billion) to replace aging equipment: the new ships, planes, and armoured personnel carriers would go towards reinforcing the forces' traditional roles. As Minister of National Defence Paul Hellyer later explained, the Liberals were not seeking to change or withdraw from Canada's existing commitments. "If that were the objective, why on earth would we have launched a 1.5 billion dollar, 5 year re-equipment program? ... For a UN role alone, an order of blue berets and billy sticks might suffice."[6]

Most of Canada's soldiers, sailors, and airmen served not with the United Nations but at home, or with NATO. The army in particular cherished its European brigade, resisting arguments that would have seen the military refocus on the defence of North America. Traditionalists liked the association with the British, with whom the brigade served – though there was little the British could or would do to buy Canadian equipment in return.[7] Things were no better when it came to planning the brigade's use in battle: as the historian Isabel Campbell concludes, "There was strong disagreement between the Canadians and British on the operational role of the brigade, at least insofar as the Canadians were informed about British plans." One military planner reported in November 1958 to the vice-chief of the defence staff that the brigade's tactical position "violates nearly all our tactical beliefs."[8] Cuts in British defence spending as early as the late 1950s degraded the quality of British troops in Germany, and by extension imperilled their Canadian allies.[9]

The government kept Canadian aircraft manufacturers alive with contracts to manufacture Canadian variants of American fighter planes for the Royal Canadian Air Force.[10] The traffic was not entirely one-way: the Americans liked the short take-off and landing (STOL) aircraft made by de Havilland of Canada in Malton, outside Toronto, and bought upwards of 1,200 de Havilland models under the Defence Production Sharing Agreement (DPSA).

As long as public opinion accepted the necessity of the defence burden, it was possible to continue paying for an entirely professional armed force, supplemented by an extensive militia system. In the 1950s the cost of the military seemed bearable. In 1963, however, when Pearson and the Liberals came to power, they promised to expand and complete Canada's social safety net, expanding pensions and adding a public health care system. The military budget had new competition in Ottawa, just at a point when Canadians were beginning to reconsider their role in the military balance of the Cold War. The result was a prolonged crisis over government priorities that lasted for almost ten years.

Defence minister Hellyer knew that the military budget had to fit in the overall federal budget and that non-military items in that budget were about to become very costly. Diefenbaker's cancellation of the Arrow and his hesitations over nuclear equipment had been costly, not merely in money but in time. Inside his department, pressures were mounting. The armed services needed or would soon need new planes, tanks, and ships, and the money to buy them. If the money were unavailable outside the defence establishment, perhaps it could be freed up internally: unification of the armed services beckoned, with its promise of efficiency and therefore savings, and Hellyer followed.

Hellyer was in for a fight, but its ferocity must have surprised him. The battle over unification consumed the minister's energies for the next four years. The greatest opposition came from the navy, but it was not lacking elsewhere. Pearson occasionally wobbled, as he did with other controversial ministers, but in the end gave the necessary support to see Hellyer's program through. The defence minister even merged the uniforms, decreeing the same dark green colour for army, navy, and air force. The uniform was not, at the time, a great success. It violated service identities and shook the military's sense of continuity. It may have adversely affected morale. Finally, in 1967, unification passed through Parliament. It was what one historian called a pyrrhic victory. Hellyer hoped that a streamlined military would be effective, efficient, and, most important, attractive to federal budget makers. Instead, he found that economy was the watchword in Ottawa's finance department where the armed forces were concerned.[11]

Soon afterwards Hellyer departed National Defence. He had made sweeping changes, but the military hardly had time to digest them. More changes were on the way.

PEACEKEEPING AND THE MIDDLE EAST CRISIS OF 1967
Peacekeeping was originally tried out on distant frontiers, an expedient designed to keep war at bay. It used small teams of military observers sent by the United Nations to enforce precarious ceasefires. These small missions were supposed to add the weight and prestige of the United Nations to a doubtful peace, and they made a modest contribution in that regard.

The UN force in the Sinai was larger and more important than the others, and derived from a more important international crisis. Eleven years after its formation in 1967, it was still there, standing along the armistice line between Israel and Egypt, on the Egyptian side of the border. The Israelis would not allow the United Nations Emergency Force (UNEF) on their territory; the Egyptians permitted it as long as their sovereignty was unaffected. A UN garrison occupied Sharm el-Sheikh at the southern tip of the Sinai Peninsula. It commanded the sea lanes to the Gulf of Aqaba, leading to the Israeli port of Eilat. As long as the UN stayed, Eilat flourished.

Canada had no direct interest in the Egyptian-Israeli dispute. During the 1940s and 1950s Canadian policy mimicked American and British policy, keeping a certain distance from entanglement in a difficult if not intractable problem. The 1948 war that established the state of Israel had routed the Arab forces, including Egypt's, and thereafter Israeli military power kept the surrounding Arab countries at bay. Some 700,000 Arab Palestinians, who had fled their homes during the 1948 fighting, squatted miserably around the periphery of Israel, a perpetual reminder of the outcome of the war and a constant provocation to Arab governments to return, eventually, to the fray.[12]

The 1956 war did nothing to lessen the tension between Arabs and Israelis. Indeed, it may have aggravated the situation, because it enhanced the prestige of the Egyptian leader, Gamal Abdel Nasser, who aspired to unify the disparate Arab nations under his direction. The existence of Israel, Nasser proclaimed, was ample evidence of the need for unity. Having grasped the issue, the Egyptian leader did not dare to let it go: he could not appear a moderate on the issue of Israel even if, from time to time, he seems to have wished he could. Extreme in rhetoric, Nasser most of the time was moderate in practice. His moderation was quite possibly related to his assessment that, militarily, Israel was more than a match for all the Arab countries put together.

Israel occasionally demonstrated its military power through raids on its eastern neighbours, Jordan and Syria. One such raid, in the winter of 1967, set off a chain of events. The Syrians, whose government was effectively a client of the Soviet Union, understood that by themselves they could not cope with the Israeli army. They therefore appealed to Nasser for help, while the Soviets, in an act of stunning irresponsibility, falsely informed the Egyptians that the Israeli army was concentrating in great force against Syria.

Nasser reached for his favourite weapon, the microphone, and issued a series of blood-curdling threats against Israel. He began moving army units into the Sinai, close to Israel. To maintain his credibility with his own people, and with other Arabs, he chose to go one step further. The UNEF stood between Egypt and Israel: if Nasser's threats were to be credible, Israel's UN shield must be removed. At first, the Egyptians tried to occupy only one UNEF position, at Sharm-el-Sheikh, controlling Israel's only access to the Red Sea, the Indian Ocean, and beyond. This had the advantage that the Egyptians would still be shielded by the rest of the UNEF, to the north along the Sinai frontier with Israel.[13] The UN secretary-general, U Thant, protested that Nasser and the Egyptians could ask only for the removal of the UNEF as a whole. Accordingly, on 18 May, Nasser ordered U Thant to withdraw the force from the Sinai. U Thant consulted diplomats from the countries supplying UNEF troops, and ascertained that the non-aligned countries supplying the bulk of the force would withdraw their troops as soon as Nasser requested them to do so. Canada, through its UN delegate, George Ignatieff, asked for delay and consultation, but on this matter the Canadians were in the minority.[14] Mindful that the UN force was stationed on Egyptian territory with Egyptian consent, U Thant believed he had no choice and promptly agreed to Nasser's request.

Too promptly, Pearson believed. Withdrawal was not a blow for peace and thus was contrary to the spirit, if not the letter, of the UN Charter. Pearson argued, as he had in 1956, that the United Nations interests were superior to the sovereignty of any single member – a difficult doctrine, because it theoretically undermined the basis on which most UN members had consented to join the international organization. It left Pearson open to the criticism from Third World representatives that he did not mean to assault the sovereignty of all states – merely countries like Egypt, non-Western and recently independent. Pearson certainly distrusted the use to which Egypt and possibly Israel would put their sovereignty. The preservation of peace was, in his opinion, an international interest superior to untrammelled sovereign authority. He had so argued in 1956 against Britain and France as well as Israel and Egypt, when the UNEF was established, and he argued the case again in 1967. During the 1956 crisis, then secretary-general of the UN Dag Hammarskjöld had tried to secure Egyptian consent to limitations on its ability to remove the UNEF as and when it wanted, but he had failed.[15] It was in that sense that U Thant's deputy, Sir Brian Urquhart, later commented, "Mike was right" about the nature of peacekeeping.[16]

U Thant ignored Pearson's pleas, believing them legally unfounded, as undoubtedly they were. Instead, the secretary-general visited Cairo to speak personally to Nasser and to beg for restraint. Instead, the Egyptian leader followed the logic of his occupation of Sharm-el-Sheikh and on 22 May formally announced that he was closing the entrance to the Gulf of Aqaba to Israeli shipping. "For Israel," as the historian Avi Shlaim has pointed out, "this constituted a casus belli. It cancelled the main achievement of the Sinai campaign [of 1956]."[17]

The United States and Great Britain anxiously conferred. The Egyptian blockade was a serious provocation to Israel. The Israelis wanted to know what the Western powers intended to do about it, with the implication that if they did nothing Israel would have to solve the problem for itself. Pearson, meeting Lyndon Johnson on 25 May after the American president's brief visit to Expo, argued strenuously for a UN role in any solution.[18]

Egyptian actions and inflammatory rhetoric alarmed Jewish citizens in Canada and the United States. Some 15,000 people attended a rally in Montreal, and another sizeable gathering was held in Toronto. Sam Bronfman, a Canadian multimillionaire, led a delegation to Ottawa to push Pearson, Martin, and the opposition leaders for support for Israel.[19] When Pearson and Johnson spoke, they were already under considerable domestic pressure to do something to avert the destruction of Israel and possibly another holocaust.

The hope for a UN-guided solution faded after U Thant visited Nasser. Anxious above all to show that only Arab interests would guide him, Nasser refused to do anything that might defuse the tension. As far as Egypt was concerned, Canadian support for U Thant's mission and, before that, the continuation of the UNEF (which the Egyptians had defined as "an army of occupation") was provocative and pro-Israeli. A Canadian-Danish resolution in the Security Council calling attention to the consequences of Nasser's blockade of Israeli shipping merely confirmed Egyptian suspicions.

Originally, the UN force expected to withdraw in an orderly fashion. Its 800-strong Canadian contingent, which handled logistics and communication, would stay until near the end, leaving at some point in the summer.[20] On 27 May, however, Nasser demanded that the Canadians leave within twenty-four hours, citing Canada's alleged "support for imperialism and Zionism." Ottawa complied: an airlift promptly removed the Canadians from the Sinai. The first evacuees reached Canada on 30 May, to be greeted by defence minister Hellyer.

Nasser's sudden outburst was interpreted as "a blow" to Canada's prestige, as it may have been. But it removed Canadian soldiers from what was about to become a battleground. The remaining UN troops had to endure the unpleasant fortunes of a war in which they were no more than hapless bystanders. The departure of the Canadians also removed the possibility that the Egyptians would attempt to hold them hostage in return for Ottawa's silence on or acquiescence to Nasser's actions.[21]

The key decisions were made in Washington and Israel. On 3 June the Israeli prime minister was told that the United States "would welcome an independent Israeli strike to shatter Nasser." The next day the Israeli Cabinet decided to go to war.[22] Hostilities broke out with a surprise Israeli attack on 5 June. Egypt, Syria, and Jordan were ranged against Israel, which was outnumbered and appeared to be outgunned. Yet within a day the Israelis had wiped out the Egyptian air force. Within five days they had occupied the Sinai up to the Suez Canal, and driven the Jordanians out of Jerusalem and the West Bank of the Jordan River. In a final offensive on the sixth day of the war (which became known as the Six Day War), the Israelis turned on Syria and occupied a strategic stretch of Syrian turf overlooking Israel, the Golan Heights.

As the magnitude of the Israeli victory became apparent, the Soviet Union busied itself to save its Arab friends and clients. Canadian television carried non-stop debates at the UN Security Council, resulting in highly favourable TV exposure for the Canadian delegate, George Ignatieff – and, coincidentally, in very unfavourable exposure for the Arabs, whose ambassadors, like Nasser himself, orated to audiences at home rather than to the council or, beyond it, viewers in North America and Europe. The Arab position thus came across as rigid and fanatical and, in the light of the crushing Israeli military victory, faintly absurd.[23]

The Arab failure was not only military but economic. The Arabs had oil but not the ability successfully to use it as a weapon. The United States had sufficient oil reserves to carry the Western powers through any Arab oil boycott, and consequently the West could ignore threats of retaliation.

When a ceasefire took effect in the Middle East on 10 June, Israel was indisputably the region's major military power. Moreover, during the brief war, the Israelis had more than doubled their territory and had added 800,000 unwilling Arabs (mostly Palestinians) to their population. The task now was to maintain control, or to use it to bargain for a stable settlement that would guarantee not merely the existence but the security of Israel. In that task Israel would be less successful than it had been militarily.

The impact on Canada of the Six Day War was considerable. Canadians, who took pride in their peacekeeping enterprises, were surprised and somewhat offended that others did not share their enthusiasm. In the 1967 crisis, Canadian diplomacy fluttered around the margins of great events. Paul Martin and, behind him, Pearson did their best to avert war, but without making much of an impact in Israel or Washington or, for that matter, in the Security Council, where Soviet obstructionism and Third World pride blocked Western attempts to master the crisis short of war.

Nor had Canada been especially successful in influencing American policy – an important point, because the United States was the only country that could have dissuaded the Israelis from attacking the Arabs. Johnson did spend time discussing the crisis with Pearson during his visit to Canada on 25 May, but there was little to build on in terms of trust or mutual confidence. Pearson and Martin's reluctance to commit Canadian support and resources to a proposed maritime force that would have kept the sea routes to Israel open did not impress Johnson, who was already impatient with what he took to be Canadian preachiness and prevarication over Vietnam. After the meeting, Johnson's staff allowed it to be understood that the visit to Pearson was not a real consultation or a meeting of minds, but a "pseudo-event – an outing to Expo which was endowed with trappings of diplomatic significance so that it would not appear as just an outing."[24]

On the other hand, Johnson did not single out Canada as a wobbly ally, not to be seriously involved when it came to making the final decision over what to do in the Middle East. Pearson was not alone in the White House kennel. Johnson was almost as impatient of Britain's prime minister, Harold Wilson. As for France, de Gaulle was, as far as he could be, on the other side, tacitly supporting the Arabs rather than Israel. When the United States government signalled Israel that it had no objections to an attack, it acted without telling – much less consulting – *any* of its allies.[25]

These nuances were not apparent to the Canadian public. There, the overwhelming reaction to the outcome of the Six Day War was relief, mixed with satisfaction that Nasser had apparently got his just desserts at the hands of the Israelis. Relief was mixed with regret, where Canadian foreign policy was concerned. The expulsion of Canadian troops from Egypt was clearly a reflection on Canada's acceptability as an international peacekeeper in the Middle East, although it did not necessarily preclude Canadian troops from being used in other regions with different quarrels.[26] Nor had Canada's diplomacy presented the Americans, Israelis, or anybody else with viable alternatives that might have delayed or prevented the onset of war.

Canadian views on the Middle East became less neutral in the aftermath of the war. Canadians became more receptive to pro-Israeli and pro-Zionist views. Peter Dobell, a perceptive observer, commented in 1972 that "since the expulsion of UNEF in 1967, there has been no strong argument for restraint, and the well organized Jewish lobby in Canada has pressed relentlessly for support of Israel." The Jewish community, in Dobell's opinion, owed its influence to its "wealth, ... financial support for the Liberal party, their superb organization and their concentration in the large cities which vote Liberal."[27] He added that at the time there was no Arab counterweight: Arab Canadians were few and scattered, and their influence politically negligible. Nor was pro-Israeli sentiment restricted to the Liberal Party, as time would show. Liberals and Conservatives harkened to the concentrations of Jewish voters, especially in Toronto, where on economic issues the Conservatives were competitive with the Liberals in affluent Jewish areas. All things being equal, Jewish voters were ready to vote Conservative, provided they were reassured that Canada's relations with Israel would not suffer thereby. Reassurance was not far off.

The collapse of one peacekeeping effort did not mean the collapse of all. Even along the Arab-Egyptian frontier one small UN team, the United Nations Truce Supervision Organization, or UNTSO, which predated the UNEF, survived and carried on. The UN Force in Cyprus (UNFICYP), which included a large contingent of Canadians, was also unaffected. There was no public demand to bring all the troops home, or to wind up cooperation with the United Nations. For the moderate left, the United Nations was practically immune to criticism. For the centre and moderate right, the UN did no particular harm and even some slight good. If support for UN actions enhanced the attractiveness of Canada's defence policy, then such support was positively desirable. For there was an uneasy sense that Canada's defence policy needed all the support it could get.

REVAMPING NATO: THE HARMEL REPORT

Canadian defence policy turned on the North Atlantic alliance. Canada maintained a brigade group and an air division in Europe, and contributed ships to anti-submarine activity in the North Atlantic. Because of Pearson's victory in the 1963 election, these forces were equipped with nuclear weapons, greatly to the satisfaction of Canada's various NATO contingents.

But there were problems. Not everyone in the Liberal Party was happy with the nuclear option. Pearson himself had said that he hoped Canada could negotiate its way out of its nuclear commitments. The military did not take the remark seriously at first. After all, what else could the CF-104s (known as Starfighters) or Honest Johns use except nuclear warheads? The government had no answer, but as time passed and the stock of Canadian Starfighters diminished, the military noticed that they were not being replaced. Out of an original 126 planes, 36 were gone by 1966. The government's response was to reduce the number of Starfighter squadrons rather than try to bring the existing ones back to full strength. The Starfighter commitment made by the Diefenbaker government, Hellyer stated, had been a mistake; presumably he was rectifying it by running down the Starfighter squadrons.[28]

Canada's air division in Europe, once twelve squadrons, was down to six by 1966. When the French government expelled Canadian and American forces from French bases in 1966-1967, the Canadian government pulled back two more, leaving only four, and with obsolescent planes. Essentially, the government had decided to terminate Canada's nuclear role in NATO, by ensuring that Canadian forces were incapable of performing it. Pearson and Martin managed to convince their Cabinet colleagues to approve a continuing, five-year commitment of Canadian forces to NATO, but only with difficulty.[29]

There was nobody to listen to complaints from the military. Two of the opposition parties, the New Democrats and the Quebec-based Créditistes, would have wished to go further, faster, to reduce Canada's armed forces. The Progressive Conservatives were convulsed by leadership problems and took an attitude to military affairs that was at best inconsistent if not downright opportunistic. In this atmosphere, the Liberals were the best of a bad lot.

An American diplomat summarized a confused defence debate in the Canadian Parliament in 1966, informing Washington that the discussion "illustrates the nature of the parliamentary hostility to which current defense policies are subjected in the House of Commons and to some extent explains why it is unlikely that the present Government would be able to take on a greater defense burden even if it were disposed to do so (which it is not)." Under the circumstances, Canadian defence policy could be summarized in one phrase – spend not, and hope for the best. The best idea around, according to cynics in Ottawa quoted by the same US diplomat, was "the hope that some way can be found to reduce Canada's defense commitments to the Western Alliance, and to enable it to devote more of its efforts to its peace-keeping capability."[30] Pearson complained, though in private, that one of the ideas behind NATO was that the Europeans would eventually take over the burden of their own defence, once they could afford to. By 1966 nobody could deny that Europe was fully recovered from the war and that the European Common Market was a notable success. But the only new and notable defence development was France's withdrawal from NATO's command structure and the expulsion of Canadian and American troops from French soil.

The Canadian government was accordingly predisposed to notions of détente between NATO and the Soviet Union. Nor was Canada alone. Other countries too were finding NATO a greater burden than they had bargained for. The British were an exception to Europe's abounding prosperity, at least in the sense that British economic growth lagged behind that of continental Europe. Yet Conservative British governments pursued a policy of military grandeur. British garrisons dotted the Indian Ocean and the Persian Gulf, and fully 68,000 British troops were engaged in a war in Southeast Asia – not in Vietnam, but in Malaysia. The British kept the pound high, so as to pay for their foreign commitments, only to find that it remained at a reasonable level only by constant infusions of American money. The money was willingly supplied by an American government that was itself stretched to the military limit by the Vietnam War.

The price was an endless series of financial crises, as the British and Americans bailed out the pound sterling. Finally, in 1967, the British Labour government under Prime Minister Harold Wilson had had enough. Wilson almost halved Britain's defence forces, down from 700,000 to 375,000; to accommodate the cuts, Britain would withdraw from "east of Suez," with the exception of the symbolic garrison of Hong Kong, by 1975. Later, under continued economic pressure, the date was advanced to 1971. The savings gleaned by abandoning Britain's overstretched commitments could be applied where it really mattered, on the central front in Europe, under NATO. But it would be a much reduced and far less ambitious British role, even in Europe.

Although Wilson hardly modelled his defence or foreign policy on Canada's, his measures effectively meant that the two countries' policies proceeded on parallel tracks. The result was growing pressure on NATO to be something more than a strictly military alliance. Much of the alliance's time in 1966 was occupied in coping with the effects of France's abrupt withdrawal from a military role, and with the relocation of NATO headquarters to Belgium. The disruption and displacement masked another development that, in the end, proved to be much more important, and possibly even crucial to the survival of the alliance.

In the aftermath of the Berlin crisis, the Cuban missile crisis, and the Test Ban Treaty of 1963, relations between the United States and the Soviet Union slowly improved. "Europe was quite secure militarily now," President Kennedy concluded in early 1963.[31] In the opinion of the historian Marc Trachtenberg, "the Cold War had become a different kind of conflict, more subdued, more modulated, more artificial, and, above all, less terrifying."[32] Conflict was certainly not over: the leadership of the Soviet Union was determined to rectify the nuclear balance by making its nuclear forces the equal of those of the United States, and the Cold War flashed and flared in Asia, Africa, and Latin America, instead of Europe. At the same time, the United States was becoming convinced that nuclear supremacy was a strategic dead end, and Washington was more and more determined to modify its strategy to ensure that its conventional forces – and those of its allies – provided a viable alternative to a rush into nuclear war.[33]

What should NATO do under these circumstances? The allies were uncertain. Nuclear defence might be immoral and politically uncomfortable, but it was relatively inexpensive. Conventional defence was uncertain, and expensive. The allies were not obliged to participate in the Vietnam War – though it was clear that help from almost any source would be welcome. NATO meetings became a forum for venting the allies' disapproval of Southeast Asian adventure. As far as Paul Martin and Pearson were concerned, this became a point in NATO's favour – a clear demonstration that membership in the Western alliance did not imply slavish conformity with the American anti-communist crusade. Martin, instructed by Pearson, made the point to Walter Gordon, who had publicly criticized Canadian membership in NATO and NORAD, by taking him along to a NATO meeting in Luxembourg in June 1967, so that he could listen to European criticism of the Vietnam War. Martin found Gordon's reaction satisfactory, though Gordon later seems to have had second thoughts.[34]

With NATO's mandate in question, the Belgian foreign minister, Pierre Harmel, proposed two study groups, one made up of the European allies, the other of Canada and the United States, to study NATO's future role. For Canada, Harmel's bifurcated concept was mischievous if not dangerous: it recalled the "dumbbell" idea of NATO – a North American group linked to a European group – proposed by George Kennan back in 1948. It contributed to Canadian worries that NATO had "forgotten" Canada – that the alliance was really about European-American relations, with no consideration given the other North American ally.[35] As the American ambassador to NATO, Harlan Cleveland, put it, "when Pierre Harmel first started talking about what came to be known as the 'Harmel Plan,' he was talking not about the transatlantic bargain but about the need to organize in 'caucus' the European bargainers. Some new European solidarity, he thought, should be the centerpiece of NATO's Study of Future Tasks."[36] Martin attached high priority to convincing Harmel to modify his proposition into a single study. Because the Americans wanted the same thing, Harmel conceded the point. The North Atlantic Council, meeting in December 1966, then resolved on the study.

It was the result, not the process, of the Harmel study that proved most important. There had been previous studies of NATO with much distinguished input, including Pearson's, but there had not previously been any great inclination to change. In 1967 there was. France's partial withdrawal, and the possibility that it would take advantage of the twentieth anniversary of the alliance in 1969 to announce its complete departure, concentrated the minds of the remaining NATO partners. The Americans, for their part, worried that a nuclear-tipped NATO would in a crisis be provocative and ineffective, leading to a general nuclear exchange between the United States and the Soviet Union, with catastrophic consequences. President Johnson and Secretary of State Rusk were open to alternatives in dealing with the Soviet Union. Détente in Europe might be possible; it was at the very least an option worth exploring. Finally, the Germans were hopeful that their ultimate goal, the reunification of their country, might be accomplished if there first were détente in Europe.[37]

After some hesitation and considerable negotiation, the North Atlantic Council adopted the Harmel report in December 1967. "Military security and a policy of détente are not contradictory but complementary," it declared. The alliance must do its best to shore up its defences, because "instability and insecurity" still characterized East-West relations in Europe. The emphasis on "collective defence" nevertheless had a positive and beneficial effect, for it was "a stabilizing factor" and "the necessary condition for effective policies directed towards a greater relaxation of tensions." The objective must be "the use of the Alliance constructively in the interest of détente." Finally, "the participation of the USSR and the USA will be necessary to achieve a settlement of the political problems in Europe."[38] In the words of the American ambassador, "The North Atlantic alliance was now in the peacemaking business."[39]

The benefits of the Harmel exercise were substantial for Canada. In terms of domestic politics, it helped mend NATO's image. A later Canadian study concluded that the report was "very much in accord with Canadian thinking," and "a development that would justify Canada's continued involvement" in NATO.[40] Internationally, the Harmel exercise and report defused the impact of France's partial withdrawal from NATO and may have helped keep that country in the alliance. Canada and the United States remained players in negotiations over European security, something that the French in other circumstances might have wished to avoid.[41]

A final result of the report was that NATO modified its internal structures to create a Nuclear Planning Group (NPG). The departure of France actually cleared the way to this innovation: the French government's views on nuclear control and strategy were so much at odds with those of the United States that no agreement had hitherto been possible. The NPG consisted of the United States, Great Britain, Germany, and Italy, as permanent members (with Canada left out).

It was unclear how NATO would negotiate with the Soviet Union. There had been false starts before, and the Harmel report could have been a signpost pointing to another dead end. It did not prove to be so, but for the time being hope and scepticism coexisted in Canadian attitudes towards European security. In any negotiations, Canada, through NATO, would have a seat at the table. However strained Canadian relations with NATO, the United States, or Europe might be, it was almost inconceivable to admit that Canadian interests were not bound up in the security of Europe. How bound up, and to what degree, remained open questions.

THE MID-1960S WITNESSED THE CONTINUATION of long-established trends. Canada maintained its preference for multilateral engagement, while shaping its policy according to the state of relations with its closest allies, especially the United States. There was no defining moment in which circumstances abruptly and radically changed, merely a steady progression of events following predictable patterns. Trade with the United States rose, absolutely and proportionately; trade with the rest of the world, except Japan, failed to rise as fast. American investment rose, as it had since the 1940s.

Europe recovered, as Canadians could see when they compared what their dollar could buy in 1960 with what it could buy in 1970. But not quite all of Europe. Canadians could buy fewer francs and marks to the dollar, but the rate of the British pound plunged – $2.70 in 1960 to $1.55 in the early 1970s. In the United Kingdom energies during the early 1960s were directed at defending the pound, and with it Britain's presumed international standing. Relations with the British grew more distant in the 1960s, not because of any conscious decision by the Canadian government, but because Great Britain's deteriorated financial position, reflected in continuous exchange crises, made that country unable to improve its position as a Canadian trading and investment partner. That for Britain was a very small part of a much greater problem. Much more important was the fact that, despite sacrifices, Britain was unable to maintain its position as a global power. But absent the sacrifices, absent also would be the "Great" part of "Great Britain."

Until the mid-1960s Great Britain kept a major presence "East of Suez," with a large army and naval establishment in Malaysia and Singapore, bases in the Indian Ocean and in the Mediterranean in Malta and Cyprus, and protectorates in the Persian Gulf. Despite major cuts to defence spending, the British exchange position failed to improve. By the early 1970s the British Empire had shrunk to the British Isles themselves, and an assortment of offshore islands, of which Hong Kong was the most significant. The British government sought refuge and solace in the embrace of Europe, applying for the second time in 1970 to join the European Common Market. Despite hesitations and misdirections, this second quest would ultimately prove successful, and on 1 January 1973 Great Britain became a formal member of what was by then called the European Economic Community.

There was nothing in any of this that took Canadians or their government by surprise. British decline seemed to be an immutable fact of life. The important consideration for Canada was that nothing was taking Britain's place. Trade with Europe grew, but not apace, and given the protectionist habits of European governments, led by France, it would never grow enough.

Nor were problems limited to economics. NATO papered over divergences among its members, but fissures over policy sometimes amounted to chasms. Dean Acheson, a founder of NATO, liked to remark that it was nothing more, and nothing less, than a military pact, and that it derived its strength from that fact. The departure of France from the military side of the alliance in 1966 indicated what French president Charles de Gaulle thought of the alliance's future, even if, for the time being, he accepted continued membership in NATO's political structure. Creative diplomacy during 1966 and 1967 averted what could have been the unravelling of NATO precisely by giving the organization a role in coordinating Western policy towards the Soviet bloc, and by admitting that détente in Europe might be a proper object for alliance diplomacy.

Canada's role in these events was on the whole marginal, even if the events themselves were important for the country. A self-centred Europe, preoccupied by its own formidable problems, would search for continental solutions first. Non-European interests, even those of allies, came afterwards. The Canadian contribution to European defence, Pearson suspected, bought Canada very little influence on the continent. The price of real influence remained incalculable, but even if it could have been formulated or estimated, it was not politically achievable.

Pearson in 1949 had understood that NATO could be achieved because a sense of common danger overcame national particularities. As the danger faded, so did the desire to sacrifice for the common defence. Pearson had wanted to use the opportunity – fleeting as he knew it to be – to add non-military responsibilities to the alliance, as represented in the North Atlantic treaty's Article 2. Acheson, on the other side, believed that adding culture and social policy to NATO's responsibilities might be too much sharing, even in the perilous circumstances of 1949. In the new circumstances of 1966, however, it was Acheson who advised that "we must seek to strengthen NATO by something new, so that we don't end up with 'the same old NATO slightly weaker.'"[42] The answer to this challenge was the Harmel report and the changes it would set in motion.

As on Vietnam, domestic opinion limited Pearson's room for manoeuvre regarding NATO. Canadian public opinion approved the treaty in principle, as far as anyone could tell, but it was an opinion difficult to mobilize unless there was a direct, Europe-related security threat. Opinion in Quebec, and elite opinion, was cooler than the sentiments of the "average" Canadian. Quebec, meaning French Canadians, liked military commitments – foreign obligations in general – less than other Canadians did. Meanwhile, polls showed that party activists, the kind of people who showed up at Liberal or Conservative Party functions, were increasingly sceptical about NATO and the United States. Under the circumstances, Pearson and Martin inclined to the view that a significant section of Liberal supporters might view with a jaundiced eye vigorous leadership and strong support for the Western alliance. There were votes to be found in medicare and regional economic development, but there were few or none to be had in exchange for up-to-date tanks and planes. The will to act was muted, if not paralyzed, by the lack of significant expressions of domestic support.

If NATO failed to attract domestic support, the United Nations remained throughout the decade a "good" cause. The trouble with the UN was not the lack of expressions of support – there were plenty of those – but the lack of any popular means of embodying that support. Enthusiasm for the UN bubbled along the surface of politics and in editorial columns, but the depth of pro-UN sentiment remained highly doubtful. Canadians were disappointed but hardly enraged by the course of events in the Middle East in 1967. If the UN was less strong than Pearson had once hoped, it was a matter of regret but only mild concern.

And so Canadian policy drifted, buffeted by contradictory currents in international affairs and domestic opinion. Some interpreted this situation as proof that Canadian foreign policy was frozen in time – the 1950s, to be precise – and that it was obviously time for a change. A better reading would have been that Canadian policy was paralyzed, by the lack of significant motivation for change and by lack of agreement on the direction of that change. Ferment there was, but it was not the churning of deep currents. It was, rather, mostly gas.

15 NATIONAL SECURITY AND SOCIAL SECURITY

Dissatisfaction with the United States and disillusionment with the United Nations were prominent themes in Canadian foreign policy in the winter of 1967-1968. Nor was the sense of an unsatisfactory present confined to foreign relations. Politics in Canada were at an impasse, and the political system itself came into question under pressure from Quebec nationalism. It was time for a change, to find someone or something that would cross the political and social crevasse that had opened up under Canada's national institutions.

The media narrowly interpreted the political deadlock strictly in terms of party politics. In fact, the Pearson government had been quite successful in passing its legislative program through Parliament. In particular, it had enacted an ambitious program of old age pensions and universal medical care. The question confronting the government, as the centennial summer of 1967 drew on, was how to pay for it all. The finance department began to scour the government's cupboard for possible savings, and it did not take long for defence to again come under scrutiny.

The debate was kept secret, inside the government. Pearson and his colleagues were well aware that certain decisions would have to be made, and soon. NORAD would be up for renewal, and though some of the ministers wished to drop the agreement, it was clear that the US government would not take that to be a friendly act. At a meeting of the Permanent Joint Board on Defence in June, the US delegation let it "be known that any [Canadian] wavering on [the] alliance as exemplified by NORAD [was] likely to affect [the] core of [the] US-Canadian defense relationship." The Canadian chairman, A.D.P. Heeney, was as reassuring as he could be, while conveying that some Canadian "Cabinet members, including the Prime Minister, had considerable misgivings about [the] continuation of [a] NORAD-type arrangement."[1]

Perhaps, while renewing the North American Air Defence Agreement, the government might find savings in Canada's contribution to continental air defence. Then there was NATO, where it might be possible to trim without affecting the core of the Canadian garrison in Germany. There was always peacekeeping. That was in bad odour because of the painful demise of the United Nations Emergency Force in the Sinai back in the spring. There were, it was argued, "very few places where a commitment of actual resources was required," either in peacekeeping or in defence generally. Truncating peacekeeping was definitely the military's preference. With that in mind, the government's military and diplomatic advisers presented a memorandum to Cabinet proposing modest cuts to troop strength – perhaps 4,000 to 6,000. Cabinet approved the proposal on 12 September.[2] It seemed to be a prudent reinforcement of Canada's existing position and commitments just as the country embarked on a season of political change.

THE OLD GUARD RETIRES

In September 1967 the Progressive Conservatives took the first step in changing the political landscape in Ottawa, replacing their dysfunctional leader, John Diefenbaker, with the younger, more cerebral, but certainly less charismatic premier of Nova Scotia, Robert Stanfield. In December, Pearson took the next step. He wanted to retire from politics, he told the press, and would do so just as soon as the Liberals could summon a convention to replace him. Replacing the man rather than the institutions he headed had its attractions. The balance of generations was shifting in the 1960s, as the baby boomers reached their teens and, ultimately, began voting. The first candidates in the field were tried and true members of the existing political system – Paul Martin, the external affairs minister, aged sixty-five, and Paul Hellyer and Robert Winters, veterans not only of Pearson's Cabinet but of Louis St Laurent's back in the 1950s. Mitchell Sharp, the finance minister, joined in – a mere fifty-six. Thirty-eight-year-old John Turner, the youngest candidate, was handsome and undeniably youthful.

But the times were not normal. "Youth" had greater numbers, more money, and wanted better opportunities than any previous generation in Canadian history. There were so many young people that a slogan like "Don't trust anybody over thirty" seemed to have some meaning, and some relevance, to those who wanted to harvest youthful energies and votes. The candidate that caught their imagination was not under thirty; indeed, at forty-eight, he was considerably older than Turner. But he gave every impression of youth and vitality – and unconventionality.

In February 1968 Pierre Elliott Trudeau, minister of justice since 1967, a member of Parliament and a professional politician only since 1965, declared he would run in the April Liberal leadership convention. Trudeau had been a professional intellectual, irreverent and anti-authoritarian, a rich man's son who could afford to shrug at Quebec's traditions and its parish-pump, tub-thumping nationalist politicians. He deplored nationalism as he had seen it in Quebec, and believed as strongly in federalism, Canadianstyle, which he saw as an opening to the world. In addition he believed it to be a sensible balancing of powers between local and larger national interests. Trudeau immediately attracted the support of younger Canadians.[3]

There was another aspect to Trudeau's relationship to the world, and to Canada's foreign policy. Trudeau was not exactly an enthusiast for Pearson's approach to government. Government in Canada was overextended at home and abroad. At home, Canada had undertaken a vast new pension scheme and was embarking on a national medicare program. The minister of finance could barely see how to pay for these things. At the same time, Canada had peacekeepers in Sinai and Cyprus, a garrison in Europe, and observers in Indochina. It boiled down to defending the West, supporting the United Nations, stretching its resources in the name of maintaining an international order that, as often as not, did not want to be maintained, and certainly did not thank Canada for it.

As minister of justice Trudeau had gathered around him a small group of advisers, including Allan Gotlieb, the legal adviser at the Department of External Affairs, Max Yalden, another External Affairs lawyer, and Ivan Head, a former foreign service officer then teaching law at the University of Alberta. Broadly speaking, Gotlieb and Yalden stood for what might be called a realistic approach to Canadian foreign relations, responding as they saw it to the "disillusionment" of Canadian public opinion, especially after the fiasco of the UNEF. Canada's foreign policy, Gotlieb told Trudeau, had become the handmaiden of a misguided devotion to international institutions. Along the way, Canada's national interest had been lost, or at least submerged, and Canada had earned itself the reputation of an international busybody. "No more helpful fixers," Trudeau said, or was believed to have said.

It was one of those decisive phrases that helped define Trudeau's moment in Canadian politics. It was clear and decisive, yet the clearer and more decisive it was, the less practical it might prove to be. Other currents were at work, contending for Trudeau's attention and time. There was the weight of experience, and existing habits of thought. Canada did not after all propose to abandon the United Nations. Pearson had sent him down as part of Canada's delegation to the General Assembly, and Trudeau had found the experience irritating. He considered it a place that specialized in windy insincerity, an artefact frozen in time, but in defending his approach to international affairs he did not fix his eye on or shape his policy around perceived UN deficiencies; he merely hoped to avoid the place as much as he could.

But what to substitute for existing policy, which Gotlieb dubbed "false internationalism"? Canada could, for one thing, stop making rhetorical pronouncements that had the effect only of annoying its allies – the United States, in particular. Canada could concentrate on bilateral relations rather than multilateral institutions, even in trade. Canada could de-emphasize the multilateral approach to disarmament, or to Law of the Sea, in favour of a more limited but more self-interested approach, one that would admittedly violate recent Canadian practice. Canada could explore the Third World – la Francophonie and Latin America, in search of advantage. All this, Gotlieb suggested, would help construct a more realistic and effective foreign policy.[4]

Of course, the race for the Liberal leadership did not focus primarily on foreign-policy issues, but there were implications for foreign relations nevertheless. Trudeau successfully positioned himself as the candidate of change. Elect Trudeau and renovation would follow. The phrase of the day was "participatory democracy," an exciting slogan unfortunately devoid of concrete meaning. Trudeau mobilized enough enthusiasm to squeak out a narrow victory in the convention in Ottawa early in April 1968, and on 21 April he became prime minister. His first action was to call an election for 25 June.

The Liberal convention had taken place against the background of the Vietnam War. Worse, riots swept the United States following the assassination of the civil rights leader Martin Luther King during the week of the convention. As the Liberals cheered and partied with their new leader in Ottawa, Canadian diplomats in Washington nervously watched from the roof of the embassy as rioters advanced. (The disorder stopped several blocks away.)

The rejoicing in one country and the rioting in the other seemed to underline the difference between Canada and the United States, and between Canadians and Americans. Canada had not had a serious riot, with loss of life, in living memory. (On the other hand, there had been terrorist acts in Quebec, with potentially more serious consequences for Canada than any of the American riots had for the United States; but in the euphoria of 1968 nobody drew attention to that fact.[5]) William Kilbourn, a prominent Trudeau supporter and a professor at Toronto's York University, bestowed the title "Peaceable Kingdom" on a new and highly positive collection of essays about Canada.

Trudeau's "New" Foreign Policy
What views, what attitudes, and what aptitudes did Pierre Trudeau bring to the direction of Canadian foreign relations? On the most general level, as Canadians were aware, Trudeau was the foe of convention and orthodoxy. He questioned axioms, disputed

doctrines, and poked sticks at sacred cows. He wore sandals and ascots to the House of Commons, contravening what must have seemed an unalterable dress code. He was, he once said, a "citizen of the world," a man with a preference for the greater over the lesser, for the broader over the narrow, unwilling to be fenced in by mere national boundaries.

Trudeau was widely travelled, and his travels had made some impression on him. He had seen the United States and Europe, including Germany, in the 1930s. In the 1940s he had studied at Harvard, the London School of Economics, and the Sorbonne. He had visited Communist Yugoslavia, toured the Middle East, and passed through wartorn China and Indochina in 1948-1949. He had seen more of the world than most Canadian diplomats, let alone most Canadians, and he was receptive to what he saw. Whereas an earlier generation of Canadians saw the non-European world with an eye to its improvement through the application of Christianity or capitalism, Trudeau saw the desire of very different peoples to improve their own lot, without obtrusive help or direction from Western countries, however friendly or well intentioned.

Nor was the prime minister a cold warrior of the older style. He was no friend of communism, but he disapproved of the exploitation of anti-communism by unscrupulous politicians in Canada and the United States during the 1950s. He visited Moscow for an economics conference in 1952 at a time when to do so was to invite the suspicion if not conviction that one was "soft on communism." For a short time, Trudeau went on the American government's list of suspected pro-communists and had difficulty getting into the United States as a result. Thereafter, he took a sceptical view of militant American anti-communism, especially when it was directed at revolutionary movements in Asia or Latin America.

The tensions of the 1940s and 1950s had created militarized alliances – another problem for Trudeau. The prime minister did not object to alliances, and accepted the need for a balance of power between the Soviet Union with its satellites in the Warsaw Pact and the United States with its allies in NATO. But he did not wish Canada to be too enthusiastic a participant. Trudeau worried about nuclear arms and what they might do. In the 1963 general election, he campaigned for the New Democratic Party and against the Liberals over the issue of nuclear arms, something that Liberal stalwarts never quite forgave him for.

Five years later, Trudeau had not entirely changed. He had come to accept the Liberal Party as a better political vehicle than the NDP, and he accepted party discipline. As a member of the Pearson government, he maintained Cabinet solidarity, but inside the Cabinet he was a notable critic of Canada's commitment to NATO and its closeness to the United States. Talking to a former military officer (and his campaign director) during the 1968 election, Trudeau asked, "Why would a guy as smart as you waste his time in the military?"[6] The military, in Trudeau's view, undeservedly dominated Canadian foreign policy.

Trudeau's pronouncements may have given the impression that he had a strong sense of where Canadian foreign policy ought to go. But this was not entirely the case. He believed that foreign policy should be ethically based and that, like other areas of life, it should be firmly based in reason, even in dialogue. As it turned out, however, Canada's policy in NATO and the position of its armed forces were less important to the prime minister than the means by which these policies were arrived at.[7] In the Pearson government, it was clear that foreign policy was reserved for Pearson as prime minister and Paul Martin as external affairs minister. Discussions of foreign policy in Cabinet were few and far between; even when there were questions, the answers remained the same. That, Trudeau decided, would change. The conclusions, he may have also believed, would change as well, but the answer was less important than asking and discussing the question.

Trudeau was in a strong position vis-à-vis his Cabinet. True, he was only recently a Liberal MP and Cabinet minister and his victory at the convention was narrow, but he immediately consolidated his position by calling a general election, which he won with a clear parliamentary majority and a strong plurality in the popular vote. "We're here because he's here," ministers said. Trudeau was not only prime minister: he was the party chieftain.

The new prime minister's intelligence was unquestioned. Nobody was quicker at a briefing, though sometimes getting him to open his briefing books was a chore. Trudeau did not take advantage of his position to impose preset views on his staff or colleagues. With the exception of Quebec, a subject where the prime minister and his intimates had firm views and where it could be reasonably argued the electorate had ratified them, Trudeau was open to forceful argument and new information.

The great issues of Canadian foreign policy – the Vietnam War, NATO, and relations with the United States, Europe, the Soviet Union, China, and the rest of the world – did not change after Trudeau arrived in power. There were established policies for all of these, most dating back to the 1940s. In addition, there were questions of money and equipment, for the aircraft and tanks used by the Canadian forces in Europe were growing old, and replacing them would be expensive. If Canada's commitments were to be met, that was what would have to be done.[8]

Surely, Trudeau thought, something more could be accomplished. But there were difficulties. The civil servants who implemented Canadian external policy argued that it reflected intractable facts. There was a Cold War between liberal democratic societies on one side and communist dictatorships on the other. Canada was naturally on one side of the conflict, and Canadian policies flowed from that fact. Marcel Cadieux, the undersecretary of state for external affairs, vigorously defended the morality and the appropriateness of Canada's existing commitments. The morality that Cadieux saw was not quite the same morality that preoccupied Trudeau, and the undersecretary confessed himself baffled by the new prime minister.

Cadieux was, in Trudeau's mind, an absolutist. He remembered him from the early 1950s, when he had briefly served in Ottawa, and knew that Cadieux passionately believed that communism of any variety represented an evil, and that most kinds of communism also represented a threat to Canadian security and values. Trudeau took a longer view. No society was absolutely right, he thought, and no society or country held a unique key to eternal truth. The Cold War was costly, dangerous, and, worst of all, unending. It had produced great evils, like McCarthyism in the United States, the hysterical repression of dissent by the supposed monopolists of virtue. The atmosphere of the Cold War had deafened the West to reason and blinded it to opportunities.

It was time to try something different. "How different?" was the question. Pearson himself, who had done more than anyone else to define and create Canada's Cold War policies, had sensed that some movement and some change might be desirable and possible. In late 1967 he and Paul Martin had commissioned Norman Robertson, a senior Canadian diplomat and an old friend of Pearson's, to study the main lines of Canadian external policy and to recommend whether change was necessary. Robertson recommended against radical change. NATO was not what its critics claimed it was, a Cold War artefact frozen in time. In 1967 the alliance had redefined itself during the crisis provoked by de Gaulle's semi-withdrawal. The Harmel report laid down that NATO should be both a defensive military alliance and an active player in European diplomacy. NATO's debates were sometimes time consuming, and occasionally messy, but, as Vojtech Mastny observes, "this expression of diverse interests was its abiding strength," the "soft power" of the West.[9]

The Harmel exercise had shored up NATO's sense of purpose at a moment when several allies, not just Canada, were restive about the alliance. Canada was well represented in NATO's existing structures. Robertson argued that NATO, valuable in itself, gave Canada "an extra margin of security" with the United States.[10] Nevertheless, Robertson conceded that foreign policy had become "reactive" rather than "creative." Perhaps there was an opportunity to reverse the emphasis; if so, further study would be necessary.[11] These observations were predictable; so was the reaction to them. His critics sneered that Robertson was defending policies he had designed himself. In effect, too much knowledge was a dangerous thing.

Robertson's report arrived just as the new government took office, in April 1968. The new minister of external affairs, Mitchell Sharp, was of much the same generation and background as Robertson and Pearson, though with an emphasis on the economic side – a former deputy minister of trade and commerce in the 1950s and minister of trade and then finance under Pearson. Intelligent, energetic, and persistent, endowed with all the bureaucratic virtues, Sharp naturally was imbued with a sense of hierarchy. As a civil servant he had presented his ministers with alternatives, advised them as to the right one, and then implemented their decisions. Now he had moved up, but it was the same system and he was comfortable in it. For Liberals, Sharp was a link to the business community, to the prosperity and growth of the 1950s, a symbol of moderation and common sense.

Sharp was politically adept. He thought the crisis with Quebec was crucial and accepted that Trudeau was the best man to deal with it. Trudeau's bravura performance at the 1968 Liberal convention and during the subsequent election confirmed Sharp's view that the new prime minister was the man for this season. Indeed, Sharp had helped make Trudeau's victory possible by abandoning his own floundering campaign for the Liberal leadership just before the convention met and announcing his support for Trudeau. At the convention Sharp sat conspicuously next to Trudeau in the hall, reassuring wobbling delegates who might otherwise have found the minister of justice unsettling.[12] It followed that Sharp could have his choice of portfolio in Trudeau's Cabinet, and he got it: External Affairs. He became a senior minister in a Cabinet that drew on new and younger blood, including several ministers who were known or thought to be opposed to Canada's membership in NATO, Donald Macdonald from Ontario and Gérard Pelletier from Quebec among them.

Sharp understood that addressing unease over Canada's foreign policy was his major priority. He had to have his colleagues behind him, especially Trudeau, and that meant addressing their concerns. Trudeau insisted (and placed in the Liberals' election platform) that foreign and defence policy be reviewed. Reviewed they would be. Because the most important concern was NATO, Sharp set up a task force to study the problem. For most of the rest of 1968, civil servants scurried about Ottawa trying to review, summarize and reconcile their point of view with Trudeau's. They did not succeed.

The civil servants, officers, and ministers supporting Canada's existing commitments to NATO – and it is fair to say that most did – focused on the importance of Western solidarity as a political factor in East-West relations. Trudeau and those who thought as he did reasoned differently. They concentrated on the instrumentalities of NATO – the means the alliance chose to defend itself. That meant nuclear weapons. It also involved the character of American politics and decision making, which the intellectual left and centre-left in Canada and the United States considered deeply flawed, from McCarthyism to Vietnam.[13]

Trudeau's passionate opposition to nuclear weapons should have come as no surprise. They were consistent with his earlier statements and with faltering public support in Canada: by 1966 more Canadians opposed nuclear weapons than favoured them.[14]

If nuclear weapons were an issue, Trudeau could count on substantial support. Alliances and Canada's membership in NATO were another matter.

The Soviet Union and communism did not seem as fearsome by the mid-1960s as they had ten or twenty years before. In the 1940s communism was a serious political force in France, Belgium, and Italy. By the 1960s the political threat had disappeared, while the military threat remained. Indeed, with nuclear weapons on both sides it had grown.

Soviet behaviour throughout the Cuban missile crisis in 1962 had reinforced the impression that the Russians would do or try practically anything to get their way. But in the mid-1960s Soviet repression at home and in its European satellites seemed to have diminished. In particular, Czechoslovakia in 1967-1968 came close to lifting repression altogether. "Socialism with a human face" was proclaimed. If the liberalized society of Czechoslovakia were the end result of twenty years of Communist rule, perhaps there was hope for real compromise and true rapprochement between East and West.

In August 1968 the Soviet government crushed these hopes. It decided that the Czech experiment had gone entirely too far. No liberal Czech government would wish to remain under Soviet tutelage, and, if that were so, the Soviet Empire might be rolled back, country by country. Leonid Brezhnev, the Soviet leader, could not imagine abandoning any part of the empire inherited from Stalin; it was not something that he or any Soviet leader could tolerate if he wished to survive politically. Summoning the aid of more obedient satellites, the Soviets invaded Czechoslovakia and overthrew its government, installing a compliant regime in its place.

Western governments expressed outrage at Soviet behaviour that was, in truth, outrageous. Canada proclaimed that it would accept Czech refugees who had escaped over the border to Austria and Germany, and 13,000 came in 1968-1969. In private, however, Canadian officials doubted that there was much to be feared – or much to be done. The American delegation at NATO told its government in the winter of 1969 that the Canadians lagged behind most of the other delegations in drawing conclusions from the Czech affair: "They have consistently put a lower estimate than most of the Soviet threat to Western Europe, even after Czechoslovakia, and while they have not conspicuously favored an early return to pre-August contacts with the Soviets, they have generally minimized the importance of defense efforts as part of a balanced approach to East-West relations."[15]

At home, the Department of External Affairs continued to argue the existence of the Soviet threat. To this it added the virtues of NATO solidarity and the benefits Canada derived from being a prominent member of the Atlantic alliance. Such, at least, were the conclusions of a lengthy exercise conducted by some of the department's most senior staff, mixed with representatives of other departments, and called in the fashionable jargon of the day STAFEUR.

STAFEUR ranged widely. It even considered whether Canada could enhance its social services with the money saved from reducing the military. In the end, however, the committee recommended keeping and even enhancing Canadian commitments to Europe. The prime minister did not like STAFEUR's report. "Trudeau made it perfectly plain that he hoped our recommendation would be for a downgrading of Europe in the Canadian perspective, and a complete withdrawal of Canadian troops in Europe," the co-chairman of STAFEUR later wrote.[16] Trudeau had promised a re-examination of Canadian policy, but the result was an affirmation of existing policy. He called for another, and it duly came, with the same message. Apparently convinced that there was support within Cabinet for a radical change in policy, convinced as well that there were grounds for believing that the Soviet danger was not what External Affairs portrayed, Trudeau demanded a third report. It said much the same thing. The official advice of the departments of External Affairs and National Defence was that Canada should stand by existing commitments.

The departments were not on as firm ground as they thought. True, there was no widespread concern about the bases of Canada's foreign relations.[17] Polls taken in the late 1960s and 1970s showed that a majority of Canadians had positive views of the United States and Americans. Fifty-eight percent told interviewers that the United States was Canada's "best friend." In what was described as "the foreign policy elite," fully 71 percent thought that the United States had "a benign impact on the world," and 53 percent thought that the United States treated Canada better than it did other countries.[18]

Not for the first time, public opinion polls did not help design Canadian foreign policy. As in the early stages of the Vietnam debate, the opinions that counted were the views – the certainties – of the educated and interested minority. In large numbers, academic commentators deplored nuclear weapons, asserted that there was hope for détente with the Soviet Union, and expressed their resentment of the United States and, to a lesser degree, Europe. Trudeau, coming from that particular group, even if he did not entirely represent its opinions, naturally listened when professorial voices spoke. (He later changed his mind and practice when the left-leaning academy deserted him over Quebec.)

The academy was not unanimous. Like the political world, it was changing generations. The older generation – those over forty-five – was inclined to go along with existing practices and policies, the "quiet diplomacy" of the Merchant-Heeney report. The younger generation, professors in their late twenties or thirties, were more likely to demand change. "An independent foreign policy for Canada?" asked University of Toronto political scientist Stephen Clarkson. By all means, he answered, in a book that used the question as its title. Canada's alliance policy was ten years out of date. Nor could the secretiveness or elitism of existing policy be defended in a "mass democracy."[19] The appearance of Clarkson's book alarmed External Affairs, which belatedly realized that, in the words of a senior official, an "unfortunate communications gap" had opened between itself and "the academics."[20]

There was little difference between the arguments of younger academics and those of Trudeau's entourage. Canada was spending large sums for European defence, but the Europeans were doing nothing for Canada. Canada had stepped forward to provide needed troops and money while Europe was recovering from the Second World War; by 1968 Europe was fully recovered, and rich. Yet Canada still sent troops and money. Why? As Trudeau put it to one of his ministers over lunch, "Well, my view is that the Germans are a lot richer right now, so I do not understand why we are spending hundreds of millions of dollars to keep troops over there, when the money is badly needed back here."[21]

Economically, the European Common Market excluded Canadian agricultural products and subsidized sales of European wheat in Canada's remaining markets. Canada spent much on NATO; NATO spent little in Canada. When asked exactly what advantages Canada derived from its participation in NATO's councils, ministers had no answer, at least as far as Trudeau was concerned. Failing to get the advice he wanted, Trudeau turned to Ivan Head, the foreign policy adviser in his own office.

Head was ready. Relatively young, at thirty-eight, he had been a foreign service officer (FSO) in Canada's high commission in Malaya. Leaving the foreign service – an act that at the time was unusual and earned him disapproval from the department's senior officers – he taught law and ended up in Trudeau's office when he was minister of justice. Head moved from being an adviser on law to an adviser and speechwriter on many things, and then the many things narrowed to foreign affairs.

Head was certainly more liberal than the average foreign service officer, though he maintained contacts in his old department and believed that many junior or middling FSOs thought as he did. The department, he thought, was frozen in time. The Soviet Union it depicted was more fearsome and dangerous than it really was, and the policies it defended, particularly NATO's nuclear response to war in Europe, were much more risky than politicians generally realized. Canada had put its eggs in the basket of Europe and the United States, ignoring the underdeveloped and decolonized countries of Asia, Africa, and Latin America. It was common gossip among younger diplomats that Canadian policies did not produce the results that senior staff thought they did. It was time for a change, or at least for a proper argument about change.

Head put together a team to draft an alternative for Cabinet. Trudeau approved, and the team, called "the non-group" to underline its clandestine status, worked secretly along lines indicated by Head and the prime minister. Trudeau tried out some of its ideas in a speech early in March 1969, and he carried others in his head when he went to Washington later that month to meet with President Richard Nixon.

Trudeau scheduled a Cabinet session on foreign and defence policy for 26 March 1969, a Saturday. To prepare for the meeting, External Affairs Minister Sharp and his colleague National Defence Minister Léo Cadieux met with their senior advisers in Sharp's office on the preceding Friday. Cadieux was an amiable and attractive ex-journalist from Quebec; he liked his department and did his best to forward its interests in Cabinet. The two men basically agreed on what Canada's policy should be: the national interest demanded that Canada continue to play an active and useful role in NATO's defence structure in Europe, which involved maintaining most if not all of Canada's European garrison.

Cabinet meetings were preceded by the arrival from the Privy Council Office of massive briefing books designed to inform ministers on subjects to be discussed. Sharp in his memoirs comments on "the sudden and enormous increase in documentation" that occurred under Trudeau.[22] Generally briefs came from the departments whose business was under consideration, and when Sharp and Cadieux opened their books in the presence of their senior staff they found their expected departmental contributions. But there was also a paper headed "A Study of Defence Policy." Its provenance was unclear, but the intention was obviously to have it discussed as an unorthodox alternative to the orthodox contributions from External Affairs and National Defence. This was the "non-group" paper. It argued for the reduction over ten years of Canada's armed forces from over 100,000 to 50,000, the withdrawal of some or all forces from Europe, and the curtailment though not complete elimination of commitments to NATO. Instead, Canada's armed forces would for the most part work at home, with excursions abroad for peacekeeping.

Astounded, Sharp and Cadieux asked the civil servants to leave. Cadieux picked up the phone, reached the prime minister, and spoke – loudly. Sharp then took the phone, to ask if the prime minister preferred the advice of some other individuals to that of his ministers. If so, the ministers, particularly Cadieux but also Sharp himself, would be justified in resigning.[23] Trudeau, momentarily outfaced, agreed to withdraw the paper, and not to refer to it in the next day's Cabinet meeting. But because every minister had received the paper and presumably read it, much of the damage from Sharp's point of view was already done. On the other hand, Cadieux's explosion made Trudeau realize that he might face one and possibly more resignations if he proceeded with the proposals advocated in the mysterious paper.

Discussion the next day began with an examination of why and whether Canada should be aligned in the Cold War and proceeded to consider whether NATO was the right instrument. There were known neutralists in the Cabinet, including two of the prime minister's closest friends, Jean Marchand, the manpower minister, and Gérard

Pelletier, the secretary of state, but Eric Kierans, the postmaster general, and Donald Macdonald, the president of the Privy Council, took the same line as Pelletier and Marchand.[24] Nonetheless, the neutralists were outnumbered: the Cabinet supported alignment and NATO, and the continuation of Canada's military role in Europe. That was as far as the pro-NATO forces could take it: the price of continuing in NATO would be a substantial reduction in the number of troops deployed to the alliance and, equally important, a redefinition of the tasks they were called on to perform. If part of Canada's air and land contingent stayed in Europe, it would be without nuclear weapons.

It is natural to ask whether the views of the allies counted for anything on an issue that dealt with Canadian alliance commitments. The answer is that they did, but only indirectly. In a meeting with American Cabinet members some months later, Sharp took the position that the cuts were, in his words, "not negotiable."[25] The Department of External Affairs was anxious and attentive where the allies were concerned, and represented their probable reactions to the rest of the government. It was clear enough that the other active partners in NATO would deplore any reduction in their collective military power. The Americans were known to be curious, and worried, about what Trudeau and his ministers would do, though president Nixon had told Trudeau in March 1969 that the possibility of reducing European commitments was interesting. Nixon faced some pressure in Congress to withdraw some or all American troops, so Trudeau's idea was familiar.

The Europeans naturally thought differently. The French premier, Couve de Murville, when asked by Trudeau in September 1969 about the withdrawal of Canadian troops, advised against it. The Germans had not been asked, though their foreign minister, Willy Brandt, was scheduled to visit Ottawa early in April. When he arrived, he found the decisions had already been taken and announced, though he argued as best he could against them. Returning to Bonn, he sent Canada a message described as "so forthright his ambassador delivered it with trepidation."[26] It did not matter; nothing Brandt or Germany might say would have deterred Trudeau at this stage.

What Trudeau finally announced was in part the decision taken by the Cabinet and in part a compromise worked out between himself and his ministers Sharp and Cadieux. Cadieux's departure would have weakened the government by showing that it was not a wholehearted participant in NATO. The Liberal Party would have divided on the issue, which might even have brought down the government. It was better to keep the peace at home and use Cadieux to keep the peace abroad. A NATO meeting was pending, and it would be better by far for Cadieux to defend the policy to the allies than to have a new and untried defence minister perform the task.

Cadieux and Sharp did what they could in meetings with the allies. Nobody liked what they had to say, but there were degrees of reaction. The British fulminated through their defence minister, Denis Healey, although it should be remembered that Great Britain was itself in the process of withdrawing most of its overseas garrisons and halving its armed forces.[27] The Germans were disappointed, as they should have been, as the affected Canadian forces were based in Germany.[28] Moreover, they considered that the process by which the policy was arrived at, with its lack of real consultation, was at the very least cavalier. The Americans disapproved but took the view that they could do little to alter the situation and that, if they pressed the Canadians too hard, they might actually make things worse. The Americans might have reflected that they had been stripping their army in Germany of its best troops to provide reinforcements for the war in Vietnam; by 1969 the Seventh Army in Germany was but a shadow of its former self. (They might also have considered that the Canadian contribution was not crucial – Canadian reductions were a political rather than a military issue.)

Cadieux's representations had their effect. There was sympathy, if not support, in some quarters in Washington. A senior American official urged Nixon's national security adviser, Henry Kissinger, to go easy and go slow. "If we escalate our language and force a confrontation *now* we will probably magnify the consequences of the Canadian decision out of all proportion," Helmut Sonnenfeldt wrote. "There is still room for negotiation, as hinted by Cadieux. We should not slam the door."[29] The American defence secretary, Melvin Laird, did not follow the advice, but he did nothing that would actually cause the Canadians to have serious second thoughts.

There were short-term considerations that restrained American reaction, but there were longer term ones too. Canada's reputation in the United States was good. Surveys through the 1970s demonstrated as much. "The majority of Americans combine a poverty of knowledge with great affection for the country [Canada] and its people," two analysts wrote in 1979. "Ninety-three percent of the masses and 98 percent of the elite have been found to express positive sentiments towards Canada, a greater degree of warmth than is expressed towards any other country," according to surveys in the early 1970s.[30]

In fact there was no room for real negotiation. Trudeau was not overly concerned with the opinions of Canada's allies. The Europeans were assumed to be self-interested and resistant to concessions that might have balanced or justified the continuing costs of Canadian deployment on the continent. The result reflected the differences of opinion within the Liberal Party, and in the country, between those who believed that NATO no longer responded to any credible threat to Canadian, American, or European security and those who argued that the Soviet Union still represented a military threat to Western Europe and therefore to Canadian interests. Within the party, the balance still weighed towards NATO, as was reflected by a series of foreign policy resolutions at the Liberals' annual meeting in 1970. Canada should remain in its military alliances, the delegates decided, and should not use money currently spent on the military for causes like increased foreign aid. Only 136 out of 773 voting delegates supported Canadian withdrawal from NATO or the NORAD pact with the United States.[31]

Sharp described the conclusion to reduce forces and stay in NATO as a compromise. Visiting Norway in June 1969, he stressed that the Canadian decision was "necessitated by anti-NATO sentiment of influential domestic intellectual groups" and that the "decision to remain in NATO was [a] happy compromise which should be recognized as such by Canada's allies." He explained that the Trudeau government wished to reorient Canada's defence effort towards North America, where Canada was at present unable to put up even a convincing display of force. He was, he said, "surprised by Europeans' reaction to Canada's troop reduction decision" and spoke of British Defence Minister Denis Healey in "bitter terms." In fact, Sharp told the Norwegians, he hoped "to emphasize European relationships." The Norwegians were astounded and "mystified" by how this last claim squared with Ottawa's decision to reduce its contingent of troops in Europe on account of security requirements in North America.[32]

Sharp might have answered that it didn't square, but that, over time, he would try to reconcile the irreconcilable. He had time and patience on his side. For the moment, Head was triumphant. A Gallup poll, Head wrote to a friend, showed a narrow majority of 51 percent of Canadians "in favour of what we had done." It was, he claimed, a triumph for reasoned argument and "carefully formulated" policies.[33] A generation later Head reflected in a conversation with the author that the battle over NATO was a contest between an expert and well-entrenched bureaucracy and the will of an elected government. In that battle, after considerable effort spread out over most of a year, the government had prevailed, as it had to. Had the issues been clearly laid before the public, there was a very real question as to which position – the pro-NATO arguments of the bureaucrats or the anti-nuclear and anti-NATO assumptions of some politicians – would have prevailed.

The idea that there was a battle of opposing views would have come as news to most Canadians. The bureaucracy kept its views to itself; only the well informed knew that there was disagreement between Trudeau and his supporters and the official foreign policy establishment. Public opposition to the government by the civil service was virtually unthinkable in the Ottawa of 1969. Even had the pro-NATO forces wished, it was clear that the two main opposition parties, the Progressive Conservatives and the NDP, would not have been much more welcoming than the Liberals. The NDP voted in 1969 to get out of NATO, while prominent Conservatives were numbered among NATO's stronger critics.[34] In that sense, Trudeau was fortunate in his opponents, who chose not to try more overtly political methods to have their way, even when they considered the government to be deeply mistaken.

AFTERMATH AND AFTERMYTH

The immediate consequence of the Trudeau Cabinet's decision was that, starting in 1970, more than half the Canadian forces stationed in Germany were withdrawn. Their nuclear weapons role was terminated at the same time. The remaining troops, reduced in size and status, no longer had a clear role to play in NATO defence. They migrated south, from Soest, their previous base, to Lahr, an enlarged air base near Stuttgart, and from direct cooperation with the British to a somewhat anomalous role in an American-defended area.

Remnants of both the air force and army stayed in Europe. As a result, Canada fielded three fighter squadrons and a tank force. The "non-group" planners had hoped to get rid of both, turning the Canadian forces into a lightly equipped and highly mobile formation, but they had failed. Perhaps the continuation of some old roles occurred because of the stubbornness and traditionalism of the armed forces, as some argued. Be that as it may, the Cabinet agreed on the overall composition of the armed forces and the final disposition of the European garrison. Cadieux made the announcement in September.

The resolution of the controversy over NATO was not the end of the re-examination of Canadian external policy, merely the conclusion of its most urgent phase. Trudeau was determined that every aspect of Canadian policy be examined, and to that end the Department of External Affairs created another internal task force on Latin America, and yet another on the United Nations and related questions, such as disarmament. George Ignatieff, who chaired the latter exercise, later wrote of "the mind-numbing futility of these so-called liaison meetings. Interminable hours were spent discussing competing or overlapping jurisdictions and responsibilities, and on the rare occasions when a decision was reached, it invariably represented the lowest common denominator among divergent points of view."[35] Marcel Cadieux said the same thing more sedately. The reviews, he wrote, "restrain our ability to be creative on current problems. The sooner the review phase was over, the more resources we will have for initiatives and operations."[36]

The slow grinding of the foreign policy task forces certainly met Trudeau's requirement for process. Process there was, but it was slow. The easiest way to agree was to have more of everything. There would be more engagement with Latin America and cooperation with the United Nations. Eventually, in November 1969, External Affairs presented the Cabinet with "a conceptual framework within which to consider the external policies and programmes of government." The main points deserve to be quoted:

1 Foreign policies are basically an extension of internal policies, conditions and interests;

2   To establish the right priorities, to identify divergent policies and to achieve some
     degree of coherence it is necessary to look at foreign policy in its totality;

3   In the seventies, Canada is likely to be as active in the foreign field as in the past
     but in different, perhaps more modest ways;

4   Continuous coordination will be necessary within the Government to ensure
     optimum effectiveness.[37]

Geoffrey Murray, the department's review coordinator, next tried to illustrate graphi-
cally how these considerations could work. The result was a hexagon, grouping foreign
policy issues under six heads: "Sovereignty and Independence," "Peace and Security,"
"Social Justice," "Quality of Life," "Harmonious Natural Environment," and "Economic
Growth."[38] The result looked like a ouija board or, as one minister put it, a stop sign. It
might be better, ministers decided, to leave the graphics out of the final, published
product. Trudeau himself read the draft review, and the hexagon went back in, though
it was removed again later. The drafters continued to work, adding papers on international development, the Pacific, and an updated study of relations with Europe. There
was no American study, so references to the United States were sprinkled through the
review. Not surprisingly, it took months of drafting and redrafting for the final product to reach the point where it could be tried out on the public.

The foreign policy review was published as a statement of government policy (a
White Paper) in June 1970, two years and two months after the Trudeau government
took office. The "conceptual framework" was still there, even if the hexagon was not.
The title – *Foreign Policy for Canadians* – was didactic, and the publication took the
form of six colour-coded pamphlets: on the United Nations, international development, the Pacific, Europe, Latin America, and a general overview. Every word was carefully weighed, every page the result of detailed scrutiny.[39]

There was no doubt that the review reflected the same approach to foreign relations that had appeared during the consideration of NATO in 1968-1969. Then, some
ministers asked where and how, precisely, NATO benefited Canada, rejecting answers
that from the questioner's point of view were imprecise or too general. "Canada, like
other states, must act according to how it perceives its aims and interests," the White
Paper proclaimed. Foreign policy was the outward projection of "national policies."
Diplomats would have to get busy, remember that they were Canadians first, and set
about peddling Canadian products in the pursuit of "economic growth."

This was an implied criticism of the way Canadian embassies did their business.
Some diplomats thought it a distortion. George Ignatieff, a veteran ambassador, protested that he had "sold pigs" in Belgrade and "appalling pickles" in London. Others
had done the same. Pearson, reading the pamphlets in retirement at his Ottawa home,
was so incensed he penned a furious essay denouncing the review and the attitudes

that had given rise to it. How could "peace and security" rank *third* in the government's priorities, behind "economic growth"? Why was peacekeeping placed after "light aircraft manufacture"? "National interest" as defined in the White Paper, Pearson wrote, is "a shaky and misleading formula for policy." He continued: "The promotion of national interest in the narrow, traditional sense merely evokes resistance from other nations, also in the name of national interest, and this inevitably leads to confrontation and conflict." A true understanding of national interest involved "co-operation with others ... leading to a world order which promotes freedom, well-being and security for all."[40] Canada's national interest, Pearson concluded, was not well served by the government's policy.

The former prime minister did not have to run his critique past layers of watchers and minders in the bureaucracy. It was the product of a single mind and pen, and as a result it read trenchantly and coherently. That was more than could be said for *Foreign Policy for Canadians*. So anodyne was its language and so broad its categories that, as one critic helpfully observed, it could be read as justifying either international crusading or self-absorbed economic diplomacy.[41]

Pearson was not the only reader to have his doubts. External Affairs Minister Mitchell Sharp later wrote that the White Paper "was full of generalities and was bound to raise controversy." He was comforted that "so quickly did the world change that it wasn't long ... before these papers became outdated and largely irrelevant." There was one aspect of the White Paper for which Sharp was prepared to take credit, or blame: the omission of a separate pamphlet on the United States. That was because relations with the United States were "so pervasive" that the general paper was really an analysis of relations with the giant neighbour.[42]

Over the long term the White Paper probably did little harm to Canadian policy. It offered little that would guide analysts of Canadian foreign relations. The hexagon was a curiosity, soon forgotten. The pamphlets retreated to library shelves, where they linger, unread if not unseen, to this day. Canadian diplomats had to confront new problems and new crises, and there was never time to consult the White Paper to see which principle, which side of the hexagon, should prevail under the circumstances. But the review was significant of a new trend: governments and other large organizations were becoming enamoured of endless self-study. "Strategic reviews" became fashionable, along with "mission statements" and other forms of self-direction and self-analysis. These are seldom adventurous and almost never far-sighted. Like *Foreign Policy for Canadians*, they give employment to graphic designers and copy editors. Like *Foreign Policy for Canadians* they subtract from an organization's ability to do its work.

It was a paradox that it was Pierre Trudeau who brought the mechanical side of bureaucracy into full flower in Ottawa. A romantic, dashing, committed figure, Trudeau became the autocrat of the Cabinet table, dictating not the conclusion of an issue but the process by which a conclusion was reached. The results of his activity were often not what he anticipated or bargained for. Intending to bring foreign policy back under political direction, he found that the political balance dictated a shapeless compromise that destroyed the effectiveness of Canada's NATO contingent in Europe – by halving the force and rendering its weaponry useless – yet maintained the remnant in Germany for a further twenty-four years, until 1992. A proponent of clarity, public information, and public participation, he was responsible for the production of a definition of foreign policy that nobody could understand, let alone agree with.

THE DECISIONS OF 1968-1969, and the policies that resulted, shaped Canadian policy towards the Cold War and beyond. Ottawa spent less on conventional defence and more on foreign aid; through the 1970s it would spend more, much more, on the domestic side of policy. These policies responded to the imperatives of internal politics. They conformed in a way to the prescription Trudeau's advisers laid down in 1968 and that was reflected in *Foreign Policy for Canadians* in 1970. And they shaped reactions abroad to, and opinions of, Canada.

One American secretary of state, Lawrence Eagleburger, tried to sum up the impression Canada had made on him (he had been a professional diplomat before he became a political appointee). In his time, at least in the 1970s and 1980s, Canada was simply not politically very significant: economically it was another matter.[43] It followed, though Eagleburger did not say so, that to make a political impression Canada would after 1969 have to punch far above its weight. Put another way, Canada's arguments in foreign policy forums would have to be especially convincing, because they could not be especially forceful.

16 THE 1970s BEGIN

The 1970s were a decade of reversals. The Vietnam War, the great issue of the late 1960s, dragged miserably to an end, leaving the United States politically becalmed. Scandal drove an American president, Richard Nixon, from office in 1974, enfeebling the moral authority of the US presidency and of governments generally. The economy slowed and sputtered under the impact of "stagflation" – stagnation and inflation – for which government appeared to have no cure. Simultaneously, a series of sharp rises in energy prices, starting in 1973, eroded the gas-guzzling, electricity-squandering freedom of the North American way of life. For the first time since the 1940s, shortages and line-ups at gas stations became a daily routine.

No country was prepared for these developments, though some governments welcomed them. Energy-producing countries stood to benefit. Saudi Arabia, Kuwait, Libya, Venezuela, Indonesia, Nigeria, and many other oil-producing states boomed as oil prices rose tenfold and untold quantities of wealth poured in. After years of Western arrogance, with the memory of colonies and protectorates still fresh, here was the great turnaround. In Moscow, hearts soared. The Soviet Union produced oil and gas in quantity. Both meant money and a reprieve economically, as the USSR rejoiced in finally finding a major commodity to export – one more lucrative than revolution or even the arms trade. Militarily, the Soviets had built up a pile of rockets and nuclear warheads that equalled and even surpassed the American pile. Parity had been reached; could superiority be far behind? The Soviet elite was already looking around with new confidence. They drew happy conclusions from Vietnam and the diminution of American self-assurance. They had always believed that socialism was inevitable; perhaps it was inevitable sooner rather than later.

Politically, this apparent reversal of fortunes manifested itself at the United Nations. Third World countries – the former colonies and their associates – had become the overwhelming majority of UN members, seventy-seven out of 127 in 1970, with an automatic majority that erased the old Western domination of the General Assembly. It was not the Soviet Union that had colonized and dominated Africa, Asia, or Latin America, but Western Europe and the United States. (Central Asia was for the time being ignored.) Despite American protests that the United States was itself an anti-colonial country (as it was, in terms of encouraging the disappearance of the old colonial empires), Third World states resented its power and wealth. In the 1970s, relatively few Third World countries maintained the democratic forms with which the colonial West had endowed them, and, even when they did, formal democracy sometimes masked an authoritarian reality. Authoritarian regimes, in turn, found it convenient to blame some of their deficiencies on colonial hangovers, and they were enthusiastically supported by groups of anti-colonial intellectuals in the West. The Western reaction to the postcolonial pretensions of Third World states therefore lacked intellectual support and, depending on local politics, political consistency. A long revenge now began in the minds of the anti-colonial delegations that thronged to New York.

Appearances were deceiving. The Third World that vaunted its numerical superiority at the UN was lacking unity outside the rarefied atmosphere of the delegates' lounge in New York. Latin American military dictatorships that faced Marxist rebels at home sat uncomfortably beside doctrinaire Marxists from Africa. Economically, the Third World was also incoherent, with national interests directly clashing. The "petro-states" extracted high oil prices from Tanzania and Botswana as well as the United States, sending the economies of their African neighbours into a tailspin. If the Third World was based on a sense that a shared colonial history made for common economic as well as political interests, the swelling of Saudi bank accounts suggested that the richest and the poorest parts of the Third World were drawing apart.

Even apart from the illusions (and occasional realities) caused by the oil bubble, there were changes afoot. Japan suddenly discovered economic strength, which by the end of the decade appeared to rival that of the United States. True, Japan was aligned with the West, and in the 1970s it became an advertisement for the virtues of capitalism and entrepreneurial skill. Old postcolonial "underdeveloped" countries, like Malaya (reconstituted as Malaysia), South Korea, and Singapore also began to flourish. Whatever the secret of their success (and opinions varied), it was certainly not Marxist socialism.

The Trudeau government in Ottawa was only partly prepared for these changes. That did not mean that it did not have views, but inevitably they were views based on the experience of the 1950s and 1960s. Perhaps Trudeau and his immediate colleagues could be forgiven, from the perspective of 1969 or 1970, for thinking that they had a novel and practical insight into the realities of the Third World. But as time passed, the insights grew dim and dated. Trudeau did have the advantage of a ready-made political basis for whatever he might propose. The Canadian Liberal Party was an alliance of many views and factions, an agglomeration of people, policies, and attitudes accumulated since the Great Depression and the Second World War. Most Liberals believed that there was a direction to events, and that the key to understanding them was Progress. Keynesian economics explained and prescribed domestic policy, justifying an interventionist state, particularly of the "mixed" (public-private) Canadian kind. The prosperity of the 1950s, channelled and redirected in the equally prosperous 1960s, justified the notion that Canada, under expert direction, had found a governmental goose with a supply of golden eggs that would pay simultaneously for the welfare state and "peaceable kingdom." So prosperous was Canada that the question of how to pay was not addressed.

Trudeau and his immediate entourage, particularly Ivan Head, believed that the disruption of the West and the rise of the Third World were no surprise. There was a turning of the tide in human affairs – it was decolonization, a shift of political power away from white-skinned Northern countries towards the Third World. Economic power must shift as well. Canadian foreign policy must be conducted on two planes, one short-term, looking to Canada's historic links to Europe and its economic dependence on the United States, the other gazing south into a future dominated by Asia, Africa, and Latin America.

Trudeau's aspirations to change the direction of Canada's external attachments gradually dribbled away. It did not take long for his ambitions to wither – though it is arguable that they never quite died. The first lesson that any Canadian prime minister must learn is that an autonomous foreign policy is not a luxury often enjoyed by smaller powers. Trudeau's short-term policy had to respond to crises as they happened, not as they might occur in some distant idealized future. The short-term expedients also proved to have a long life, longer than the new policy directions Trudeau so confidently anticipated.

CANADA AND THE THIRD WORLD

The Third World, Trudeau told a Calgary audience in May 1968, was crucial to Canada. A focus on Southern regions was not simply a matter of altruism, noted Trudeau: an impoverished world was an unstable world. In terms of stability and security, the Third

World was not far from Canada's door. Nor should foreign aid be seen as a one-way transaction: "We must never forget that in this process Canadians are beneficiaries as well as benefactors."[1]

Canada met the Third World in a variety of forums: formally at the United Nations, the British Commonwealth, and through bilateral diplomatic contacts, informally through travel, trade, immigration, and missionary activity. Since 1949 Canada had participated in aid programs for underdeveloped countries through the Colombo Plan, acting through its External Aid Office. Governments of the day justified the aid by referring to generally accepted nostrums. Poverty caused discontent, and discontent caused instability. Instability was the breeding ground of communism; aid, therefore, was an economic pre-emptive strike. Canadian officials took pride in Canada's approach to the Third World as less rigid and confrontational than that of the old colonial powers, preoccupied with self-justification and self-interest, or the United States, obsessed with anti-communist ideology. Canada was even prepared to overlook the frequently extreme rhetoric of Third World governments, in the interest of building bridges and shoring up relations.[2] One obvious bridge was in the area of foreign aid, and we will turn to that first.

There was never enough aid, and aid programs never seemed to do what was necessary.[3] Canada was not a major giver, a role reserved for richer and larger countries like the United States. Yet Canadian aid was not insignificant: the country transferred technology as well as goods and money, most notably nuclear reactors to India and Pakistan. The export of nuclear technology fitted well into a pre-existing scientific base in both recipient countries, which did not necessarily mean that the Canadian and Indian (or Pakistani) governments agreed on all the purposes of nuclear science. The Indian government pursued the development of nuclear weapons prototypes and resisted all Canadian attempts to rein in its strategic enthusiasms.

Difficulties between India and Pakistan would lead the two countries into war in 1971. The war greatly improved India's position, detaching East Pakistan and creating the independent (though still Muslim) country of Bangladesh. The United States tilted towards Pakistan, and India tilted towards the Soviet Union, a deplorable fact but not something that Canada could remedy. "India," the Department of External Affairs noted in 1973, "is in a position of pre-eminence in South Asia." Moreover, it "has made no secret of its interest in being regarded as a great power or at least a potential one, possibly on a par with China, but definitely on a par with Japan." Canada's interest in India was in the stability of the world's largest democracy and, more generally, in the stability and if possible the tranquillity of the subcontinent. Commonwealth contacts, important in the 1950s, declined in succeeding decades. In 1975 the Department of External Affairs reminded Trudeau that "the Indians have displayed little real interest in the Commonwealth as a political forum and appear to regard it as an aid/trade association." Bilateral relations turned largely around Canadian aid, which was significant; indeed, India absorbed 20 percent of Canada's foreign aid in the mid-1970s.[4]

A visit to Canada by the Indian prime minister, Indira Gandhi (the daughter of Jawaharlal Nehru, India's first prime minister), in June 1973 did little to improve overall relations. The next year India detonated what it called a "peaceful nuclear device," using plutonium manufactured in a research reactor supplied by Canada as part of its aid program. The explosion coincided with the Canadian general election campaign in 1974, which did not improve the government's temper in having to deal with the controversy over India's expanding nuclear program – and Canada's role in it.[5]

Over the years, Canada had tried to convince India not to use its nuclear program for weapons development. The test was proof of the failure of Canada's influence. Ottawa was indignant, but the Indian government remained deaf to its protests. As the Canadian high commission in Delhi reported, the test was, from the Indian perspective, "morally right because Indians say its purpose is peaceful ... and legally right because [the] letter of an agreement had not been violated." This was true enough. "Indians are extremely sensitive to criticism but they are also extremely insensitive to other people's sensitivities, and then fail utterly to understand we are reacting to violation of [the] spirit of [our] relationship."[6] To drive home Canadian anger, Trudeau froze nuclear aid.

Canadian aid spoke English until the 1970s. In the early 1960s, when independence swept through Africa, aid from Ottawa remained largely restricted to former British, rather than former French, colonies. This caused problems in Quebec: separatists cited it as proof positive of obtuse anglophone domination of Canadian policy, while federalists argued that Ottawa must change its anglophone biases before it was too late. Trudeau, strongly supported by his colleagues Jean Marchand and Gérard Pelletier, saw reform of the foreign aid system as a major priority for this reason.

First, the government reorganized. Foreign aid had a mixed past since its origins in Colombo Plan assistance in the early 1950s. Most of the time it had lived in the Department of Trade and Commerce: "Aid was trade and trade was aid," in the view of an aid veteran.[7] In 1960 an External Aid Office was created, reporting to the minister of external affairs. It oversaw a gradual and not entirely consistent increase in Canada's aid budget. Pearson and the Liberals took a favourable view of external aid, which was propelled by the fashionable economic theories of the day. These theories dictated heavy capital investment in items such as railways and heavy industry, items that more or less matched what Third World governments thought every self-respecting country required.[8]

In 1966 Pearson reached outside the bureaucracy for a new head of the External Aid Office: he appointed Maurice Strong, a youngish (thirty-seven) and very successful businessman. On Pearson's promise that he could reshape Canada's aid program, Strong took the job. He expanded the office's capacities, but it still fell short of what he wanted. Eventually, in 1968, the External Aid Office was sublimated into the Canadian International Development Agency (CIDA), a much grander and more expensive affair. Under Trudeau, Strong's mandate was if anything expanded. Foreign aid had acquired its own constituency among educated and well-intentioned Canadians; for good or ill, over the next forty years CIDA's non-governmental connections, fervent, opinionated, and often impractical, were both its greatest support and its greatest handicap. Strong sought publicity for his agency, and over time his and its activities became widely known and favourably viewed among political and intellectual elites in Canada. That did not necessarily translate into enduring popularity, as we shall see.

Having changed the organization, the government changed the policy. Strong wanted to eschew "direct aid" of a highly prescriptive and politically sensitive kind, and substitute support for developing nations' "self-help."[9] There was no difficulty getting the Cabinet to agree to more aid to French-speaking Africa.[10] If Canada did not give the francophone Africans aid, and plenty of it, Quebec and France, the still dominant ex-colonial power, might find a damaging purpose for the valuable sovereign attributes of the independent (but still French-dominated) African countries. France and the French government had something to lose if Paris officially treated Quebec as a sovereign entity; but if Gabon or some other African state did, there was little Canada could do to retaliate, and little or no domestic political fallout to fear. Sure enough, when, early in 1968, Gabon invited Quebec to a gathering of French-speaking countries, all Ottawa could do was fulminate and cancel its non-existent relations with Gabon. (De Gaulle actually relished the idea that Canada might as a result of the incident break relations with France; he would then, he told his intimates, establish relations with a sovereign Quebec.)[11]

Gabon might be explained away or ignored, but the effect of two or three more such incidents, inside Quebec and internationally, would be harmful. Canadian sovereignty would become controversial, the position of the provinces – especially Quebec – doubtful. And France's ability to interfere in Canadian affairs would be enhanced.

The French bureaucracy was divided on the issue of using Africa as a means of afflicting Canadian federalism. That might be the policy of the French president, who was the most important individual in the state, but many in his foreign office and military, not to say the French political system at large, disagreed with him. De Gaulle's crusade to patronize Quebec appeared to many French citizens to be quixotic, responding to no discernible French interest.[12] De Gaulle and his adherents had been able to run much of the country's foreign policy on the cheap, including the maintenance of an informal empire in Africa. French influence depended on the presence of French troops to bolster unstable regimes, but also on French aid. If Canada began to compete in aid, the governments of francophone Africa might decide to exercise their sovereignty apart from French advice.

There followed a complicated contest for influence in francophone Africa. The prize, from the Canadian point of view, was the neutralization of French efforts to use African governments to advance Quebec's international status. Paris would have preferred to see Quebec alone invited to francophone cultural and educational conferences, on the grounds that only Quebec could speak, in French, for the French inhabitants of Canada. Ottawa resisted, promoting invitations to other provinces housing substantial French-speaking minorities. Ottawa sent high-level delegations to compete with Quebec's and to undertake visible and audible propaganda on Canada's behalf. On one occasion, the Ottawa and Quebec delegations shifted each other's flags around, from prominence to obscurity and back, giving the whole episode the title of "la guerre des drapeaux" – the flag war.[13]

Federal efforts were greatly assisted by the fortuitous and precipitous departure of Charles de Gaulle from the French presidency in January 1969. During 1968, de Gaulle faced labour unrest and a student rebellion, and although he prevailed over his opponents, he had to seek assurances from the French army that they would stand by him if necessary, and if called upon. Compared to these intense domestic crises, Quebec must have seemed insignificant, even to de Gaulle.

De Gaulle's departure diminished but did not end official French antagonism to Canada. Nevertheless, de Gaulle, absent, was greatly to be preferred to de Gaulle, president. His successor, Georges Pompidou, put Quebec lower in his list of priorities, though he could not ignore it altogether. Pompidou drew his political strength from many of the same elements that had supported de Gaulle, and he stepped carefully around Gaullist minefields. His major priority was reversing the former president's stand against Great Britain joining the European Common Market; with that in hand, he may have been reluctant to spend political capital on minor issues like a rapprochement with Canada. On Quebec, the French government would tolerate a certain freedom of action for the Gaullists.

A few French functionaries, particularly Jean-Daniel Jurgensen, the associate political director at the French foreign ministry, and Bernard Dorin, Philippe Rossillon, and Xavier Deniau, civil servants and minor politicians, took an "ultra" view of Canada and did their best to encourage Quebec independence. In one notorious instance, Jurgensen offered René Lévesque's fledgling Parti Québécois $300,000 for expenses in the Quebec provincial election of April 1970. Lévesque prudently refused, rather to Jurgensen's surprise; doubtless this kind of activity was closer to the political norm in France.[14]

In April 1970 the quasi-federalist Liberal leader in Quebec, Robert Bourassa, defeated Jean-Jacques Bertrand, the indisputably federalist premier of the province.

Bertrand led a nationalist party, the Union Nationale, that was ambiguous on the subject of Canada. Bourassa's problem was the reverse. The new premier's credentials as a federalist were relatively weak, but he headed a federalist party, and federalism was the position of most Quebec voters. At thirty-six Bourassa was also very young for a Canadian political leader, and at first he was uncertain of what his policy ought to be. Trudeau overshadowed the premier and pre-empted the role of spokesman for the province's interests, and Bourassa was careful not to disturb the prime minister on any particular issue.

Displacement and moderation in both Paris and Quebec City opened the way, politically, to a resolution of the question of relations between the states that made up "la Francophonie." Canada promoted a vision of a francophone version of the Commonwealth; it would include French-speaking Belgium and, if possible, Switzerland, and as many other countries as cared to join. It would also include prosperous Canada, which was in a position to back its membership with money. The French were undecided. France was unused to the possibility of disrespectful treatment, and the prospect of a "French Commonwealth" gave severe heartburn to those officials who knew what the British model had turned out to be.

The French bureaucratic reaction was to reduce in size and capacity the prospective organization. Suitably shrunken, it was brought to birth at a conference hosted by Canada in October 1971. In deference to the varying sensibilities of the Canadian participants, the conference started in Ottawa and moved to Montreal for its conclusion.[15] The new organization, known as the Agence de Coopération Culturelle et Technique (ACCT), had its headquarters in Paris. Canada even supported a noted Quebec separatist, Jean-Marc Léger, for the post of secretary-general, securing his appointment in spite of a pronounced lack of enthusiasm from France. The French, in riposte, multiplied the number of secretaries-general and minimized the "perks" of the office. There would be an official limousine to tootle around Paris, but three secretaries-general would have to share it.

On the question of aid to Africa under Trudeau, it was not Africa's needs that were foremost, either to the Canadian government or to its French and Québécois antagonists. Just as in its dealing with the United Nations under Pearson, or with the Colombo Plan, aid to Africa fitted neatly into larger Canadian concerns, in this case national unity, and relations with France, as previous aid programs had fitted into the Cold War. French-speaking African states were able to reap collateral advantages from the priorities of Canadian politics, both in terms of direct aid and through the establishment of the ACCT.

The ACCT had become a side issue in Canada by the time it was founded. Quebec's relations with France were governed by the fact that the Bourassa government (which remained in office until 1976) wished to avoid confrontation with Ottawa and did not wish to indulge in a "flag war" or any other symbolic dispute with the rest of Canada. Speaking to an American diplomat, the French foreign ministry's desk officer for Quebec

> confirmed the Canadian Embassy's view that both Ottawa and Paris are anxious to avoid any problems. Madame Haulpetit-Fourichon said that the Ottawa-Paris-Quebec triangle seemed quiet for the moment and was likely to stay so for the foreseeable future. However, she concluded that while it was unlikely that French policy would ever return to the days of "Vive le Québec Libre," she personally believed it "impossible" to pre-judge France's reaction should Quebec be governed by a leader less willing than Bourassa to cooperate with Ottawa and more actively seeking closer ties with France.[16]

Aid for francophone Africa was of course only part of the foreign aid picture, though a most important part. Trudeau increased the amount of Canadian foreign aid; it rose as a proportion of Canada's gross national product, though never to the magic 0.7 percent level that enthusiasts considered appropriate.[17] CIDA was the dominant agency, but it ran athwart the fact that public opinion was beginning to take an increasingly sceptical view of aid programs. In the early 1970s, with prosperity still unbroken and unemployment relatively low, there was more money than CIDA could handle; later, in less favourable economic times, financial or political support shrank. Canada reached its peak in foreign aid in 1975, at 0.54 percent of GNP; by 1981, with Trudeau still in power, it had sunk to 0.37 percent.

There was always an enthusiastic minority that could be counted on to boost direct foreign aid, a minority that, under Trudeau, was close to the dominant views of the top level of the political class, and to the thinking of the Prime Minister's Office. Other politicians practised risk aversion by seeking to convert foreign aid largesse into local procurement, sometimes with bizarre results. "With regard to procurement restrictions," one expert commented in 1976, "the Canadian record is a poor one."[18]

Admittedly, the alternative of "self-help" did not always work. In Tanzania, which had an eloquent and attractive socialist president, Julius Nyerere, Canada helped finance projects the Tanzanians themselves identified – a waterworks, a large bakery, hydroelectricity, and railways. The idea was that Canada would contribute knowledge and equipment, and train local management and labour for enterprises that were already up and running and ready to be handed over. But the date of handing over the bakery, or the waterworks, continually receded. The bakery was simply uneconomical, producing bread that cost 60 percent more to make than it could be sold for. As for the waterworks, the only way it could be kept going was through continual infusions of Canadian aid. Not every aid project was a fiasco, even in Tanzania, but the ones that failed were the ones that received publicity.[19]

POSTCOLONIAL AFRICA AND THE COMMONWEALTH

Canadian policy towards Tanzania – a former British colony – had a strong political dimension. Through the Commonwealth, Canada was linked to an ever-expanding group of former British colonies. At first, Trudeau's perspective on the organization was highly qualified. The Commonwealth embodied British and imperial traditions, meeting in imperial splendour in London. When Trudeau attended his first Commonwealth conference, in London in January 1969, he staged an irreverent, but carefully choreographed, pirouette at a royal reception. It could be interpreted as high spirits, and was, by those friendly to Trudeau. Others took it as a juvenile gesture of disrespect and, in truth, it was probably both.

If Trudeau initially found the Commonwealth encumbered with too many imperial trappings, too much a place where the British enjoyed an undeserved (and unequal) dominance, he soon discovered attractions.[20] Trudeau was temperamentally averse to the carefully staged public pantomimes of the United Nations, where the deaf talked to the deaf, at length. It took considerable persuasion from his senior staff to get him to attend the 1969 Commonwealth meeting, but in the end he conceded the point. There would be interesting people there, such as Lee Kwan Yew, the prime minister of Singapore, whom Trudeau had already met.[21] The Commonwealth heads of government (not all Commonwealth countries had preserved the parliamentary system, and heads of government were often presidents) spoke at length, but in private. They had a common language and to some extent a common understanding. The Commonwealth, in short, held the possibility of being an "authentic" experience, which appealed to the romantic in Trudeau. And so he said in public – a good place for discussion and honourable disagreement.

But the organization was confronted with the problem of history. There were two perspectives on Commonwealth history. From the perspective of Canada and the other "old Commonwealth" countries, the Commonwealth was a useful achievement and its history reflected that fact. To the African and Asian members, the history of the British Empire embodied historical injustices, which would have to be repaired before the members could truly meet and discuss as equals. Trudeau saw a forum for discussion; the Africans saw a last chance for action – on Rhodesia and South Africa.[22]

The Commonwealth by the 1960s had evolved through several stages. At first, between the wars, it was an alliance of Great Britain and its self-governing former colonies. In peacetime, it was a difficult and fractious organization, but for the most part it held together. When war came in 1939, only Ireland stood aside. The end of the war forced Great Britain to come to terms with economic shrinkage, at a time when maintaining the empire required greater and greater resources. Forced to choose between economic logic and its empire, Great Britain began to abandon its empire, particularly in Asia. For a time it appeared that it could hang on to its African colonies, but by the late 1950s that too was beyond its capacities. Beginning with Ghana in 1957, every African colony under direct British control received independence.

The Commonwealth received its direction, such as it was, from periodic meetings of heads of government, usually prime ministers. While the memory of empire was fresh, and the first generation of postindependence political leaders remained in power, attendance at these meetings was good. Discussions could be acerbic, but there was relatively little to decide except agendas, procedures, and communiqués.

From 1960 on the Commonwealth's political focus was Africa. The decision to refuse membership to apartheid South Africa coincided with the appearance of new African members in the Commonwealth, and they and their issues began to dominate the agenda. As the historian J.D.B. Miller observed, "Africa represented dynamism, spectacle, conflict, and the expression of radical principle."[23] The impact of African issues was multiplied by the struggle for civil rights in the United States; it was easy for Canadians to link the fight against discrimination and inequality in Africa with the same struggle in the United States. Although Trudeau had not anticipated it, Canada was inescapably drawn into the African imbroglio, as a member of the Commonwealth and of the United Nations, where African votes had a clear political weight.

There were plenty of colonial or postcolonial issues to clear up. Great Britain had encouraged white settlement in East Africa, especially in Kenya and Southern Rhodesia. The settlers, though a tiny minority, received a form of self-government that excluded the African majority of the colonial populations. Under British pressure, the settlers gave up in Kenya, Northern Rhodesia, and its neighbour Nyasaland, but in Southern Rhodesia they were too well entrenched. Instead of acceding to British urgings, the Southern Rhodesian whites declared unilateral independence in 1965. The British did not move to restore their jurisdiction by force, relying instead on diplomatic pressure and economic sanctions.

The Southern Rhodesian problem was linked to the question of white domination in adjacent South Africa. The latter was a significant economic and military power and there was no disposition within Britain to challenge its government by force. Great Britain had significant economic interests as well as military links there. Because British public opinion was generally liberal, it would have been exceedingly difficult for Britain's political leaders to express anything resembling approval of or tolerance for white rule in Africa. Its diplomatic position was to be disapproving but inert, hoping that the leaders of South Africa and Southern Rhodesia would find the grace to transform themselves and their countries. It was hope without substance that characterized British policy, and most Western countries followed or imitated the British example.

That was not sufficient for most African countries. As the next Commonwealth conference approached, in Singapore in January 1971, the British knew that African issues must be addressed – meaning that Britain's African policies would come in for criticism.[24] The British argued that they needed to maintain cordial relations with the South African government in order to keep a naval base at Simonstown, to secure the sea lanes around the Cape of Good Hope and in the Indian Ocean. The British prime minister, Edward Heath, refused to compromise, while some African heads of government indicated that unless they received satisfaction they would pull out of the Commonwealth. Trudeau, speaking to Mitchell Sharp from Singapore, informed him that "the British had made up their minds and it seemed that they were not prepared to pay a very high price for the Commonwealth." The best that could be done, Trudeau continued, was to hope that nobody actually quit the organization.[25] The Canadian prime minister played a large role in reconciling the irreconcilable. In the event, the Singapore meeting pronounced firmly against racialism of all kinds but, at the same time, recognized the autonomy and ability of each member country to interpret its own security needs. Trudeau's role at Singapore was widely praised, both by the African countries and by the British.[26]

Foreign Policy for Canadians had identified social justice in southern Africa as a goal of Canadian policy. It was obviously a distant goal, since Canadian policy could do little directly to hasten the end of the racialist regime in South Africa. As for Rhodesia, Canada was even more distant, without a diplomatic or consular presence. The embassy in Pretoria urged moderation on the part of Ottawa, that it was better to exert some mild influence than none at all should either country be moved to sever ties.[27] Diplomatic relations were maintained, and until 1979 trade continued as normal. South Africa even continued to enjoy the old "British preference" it had been granted as a member of the British Empire back in 1932.[28]

In the meantime, the Rhodesian issue had found a solution of sorts. Unable to stand both economic sanctions from most of the world and a guerrilla war, the racialist regime in Rhodesia sued for peace. Canada had made noises from time to time that it would support or contribute to a Commonwealth force in Rhodesia, and there was some expectation that Canada would help finance a transition government as the country moved to Black majority rule.[29]

The domestic impact of the South African issue was as significant as its external ramifications. Since the late 1940s liberal opinion in Canada had regretted and then deplored that country's white supremacist government. The brutal use of police power and the suppression of civil liberties ate away at the liberal conscience. For most liberals, South Africa was nevertheless one issue among many; in terms of its effect on Canadian politics it ranked well behind nuclear weapons, the arms race, foreign ownership, and the Vietnam War. Nor should it be forgotten that "liberal" Canadians divided their political support between Trudeau's Liberal Party and the New Democratic Party, which on this issue offered much more rhetorical comfort to anti-apartheid groups in Canada.[30] For most Canadians, it must have seemed that South Africa and its problems were a permanent fixture on the international scene, rather like the Soviet Union and Communist China, similarly deplorable situations but strongly entrenched and virtually certain to endure.

At the beginning of Trudeau's mandate, an African country did briefly dominate Canadian newspaper headlines and television coverage. The issue was not South Africa, but a civil war in Nigeria, where the Ibo minority attempted to secede in 1968-1970, setting up their own country, known as Biafra. In order to suppress the Ibo rebellion, the Nigerian government imposed a blockade on the rebel regions. The Ibos claimed distress and even starvation caused by the government's policy, which amounted, so Ibo publicists claimed, to genocide.

Ottawa was not eager to take a position on Biafra. Nigeria, like Canada, was a multi-ethnic federation, and its troubles gave comfort to those who, like Charles de Gaulle, believed that such countries were unnatural and ought not to exist. Perhaps Trudeau was thinking of federal analogies when, in August 1968, he stopped to answer a reporter's question about Biafra. What did his government intend to do? Instead of obfuscating, Trudeau replied directly. "Where's Biafra?" he asked. It was a legalistic answer – Biafra did not exist as an internationally recognized country – to a humanitarian question, which a more experienced politician would either have ignored or answered vaguely. Trudeau's response was all the worse because it seemed to be playful – when Biafra was at the very least a grave issue. The rejoinder immediately infuriated Canada's moral minority. "Incredible," was the mildest comment; others believed the response was "callous" and betrayed "astonishing ignorance."[31] Up to this point, Trudeau had enjoyed a favourable rating from the press; Biafra proved to be the first occasion on which his reason did not appeal to their passion. (Passion is more telegenic, and much more quotable.) As Head and Trudeau remark, the Biafran war "took on a life of its own and quickly built up into a major bone of contention for the Canadian government, which steadfastly championed the principles of federalism and of negotiated settlements of grievances." All very rational: but for an excited press and Biafran enthusiasts it was not the answer they wanted to hear.[32]

The Biafran rebellion was finally crushed at the beginning of 1970. Harsh as the Nigerian government's measures may have been, they did not amount to genocide. After the war, Biafra was reintegrated into Nigeria, and the Ibo minority continued to play a part in that country's chaotic and frequently unsavoury politics. In terms of Canadian policy, Biafra illustrated how a Canadian domestic issue – federalism and secession – could be projected into foreign policy. As important, Biafra represented the first but not the last time that the Trudeau government differed from liberal-minded interest groups. As such, it probably had an impact on a whole range of issues, from South Africa to cruise missile testing.

CHINESE PUZZLES

One of the most domestically important and yet one of the most inconsequential of Trudeau's foreign policy initiatives was the recognition of Communist China. The question of whether to recognize had been debated ever since the proclamation of the People's Republic of China in October 1949, following Communist victory in the Chinese civil war. The victory was not absolute: the defeated Nationalists withdrew to the island of Taiwan to lick their wounds. Ordinarily, Canada would have recognized the Communist government on the mainland, as it recognized a whole variety of other unsavoury regimes from Poland to Argentina, but the Korean War intervened. Before the war broke out, India and Great Britain had recognized and exchanged diplomats with Beijing; Canada and the United States had not. During the war, with Chinese troops fighting the United Nations, there was no question of recognition. For the rest of the 1950s, and the 1960s, the United States set itself against recognition, and, like Canada, maintained relations with the Nationalists. (Canada did not keep an embassy in Taiwan, but Taiwan kept one in Canada.) As time passed, and the Communist government remained stable and apparently immovable, Canadian diplomats came to favour recognition, but American pressure was sufficient to keep the Canadian government in line. The outward sign of Western solidarity on the issue was the annual vote at the United Nations to keep the Nationalist government occupying the Chinese seat, which included the rights and privileges of a permanent member on the Security Council.

The erosion of Western dominance at the United Nations with the rise of the Third World made the annual Chinese vote a problem. Every year the issue came up, and every year the United States had a more difficult task in continuing to exclude Communist China. Even the Canadian government and Paul Martin, Pearson's external affairs minister, were beginning to chafe at American direction. In 1966 Martin went so far as to propose a compromise at the UN, which would have recognized both Chinas, while handing Beijing the Nationalist seat. The Canadian delegation found its proposal drew little attention and less support – a sign, as one of them later said, that Canada's prestige and influence at the UN were waning.

Under Mao's direction China increasingly went its own, radical way. Disputing Soviet policies of "peaceful coexistence" with the West, China built its own atomic bomb (first tested in 1964). In the mid-1960s, Mao launched the Cultural Revolution, which disrupted Chinese society for a decade, bringing misery to millions. Perhaps the most important effect of the Cultural Revolution and the other Mao-induced social convulsions of the 1949-1976 period was the retardation and even reversal of Chinese economic development; secondarily, the effect was to keep Mao securely atop the quaking pyramid of Chinese society.[33]

Some of the bad news from China penetrated Canada, as it did other Western countries, but compared to South Africa or even the Soviet Union, China was a hermetically closed country and Mao's worst atrocities were secret. Perhaps as a consequence, Communist China retained its admirers in Canada; even more important, it did not acquire a circle of hostile critics. Support for Nationalist China was limited to certain groups inside the Chinese community and a few right wingers and particular business interests.[34] That was nothing compared to the approbation the government would harvest. Non-recognition of Communist China was blamed on the United States (accurately enough). The United States was also blamed for the excesses of anti-communism, from McCarthy to Vietnam. Anti-Americans and anti-anti-communists (despite the name, a fairly common breed, especially among intellectuals) would therefore approve Canadian recognition of Communist China.[35] And opposition to the recognition of Communist China had been weakening in the United States itself. There were still vociferous anti-communists there, but there were increasingly large numbers who thought that rigid anti-communism was counterproductive and foolish. In March 1969 Democratic Senator Edward Kennedy called for the admission of Communist China to the UN, a straw in the wind noted by President Nixon.[36]

Getting to recognition proved to be a complicated and prolonged affair, with negotiations set in Stockholm. Canadian diplomats handled the discussions with considerable aplomb. The Chinese side responded carefully and firmly, but with a positive end in view. Finally, in October 1970, Canada and China reached agreement. Canada would not have to acknowledge specifically Beijing's claim to Taiwan, but instead announced through External Affairs Minister Mitchell Sharp that it would be inappropriate for Canada to question the Chinese government's claims to territory, or vice versa. Taiwan promptly withdrew its ambassador from Ottawa and sold its embassy. The new Chinese embassy settled down in a converted convent on the banks of the Rideau River. Canada naturally sent a senior diplomat, Ralph Collins, to Beijing; surprisingly, the Chinese sent a very senior political figure, Huang Hua, to Ottawa.

Throughout the negotiations with the Chinese, the Canadian government carefully kept the Americans informed. (By coincidence, news of the Canadian-Chinese negotiations leaked while Sharp was in Washington in April 1969, and he confirmed the news at a press conference there.) When recognition finally came, there was some predictable irritation expressed by the American government, but not much, and not for long.[37]

Richard Nixon had long since concluded that American policy towards China was damaging US interests, and almost as soon as he became president, he set about to change that policy.[38] Discussions with the Chinese began in Warsaw in January 1970; by July 1971 Nixon's national security adviser, Henry Kissinger, was in Beijing, laying the groundwork for a presidential visit the following February. Ironically, Nixon got to China even before Trudeau. Trudeau's visit occurred in October 1973. He got a warm reception, an interview with the ailing Mao, and considerable time with the Chinese premier, Zhou Enlai. There were warm toasts, optimistic agreements, and useful outcomes. Trade, already substantial, increased, although, after the Kissinger and Nixon visits, Canada had to compete with the United States in its previously cosily restricted wheat market.[39]

In an era when little was known about the nature of the Chinese government, Trudeau's thawing of relations with Beijing earned little but praise in Canada. From a practical point of view, it is difficult to disagree with the decision to open relations, and it probably produced favourable results in trade and other contacts. The context was set not by anything Canada did, but by the defrosting of American relations with China. Nixon's dramatic reversal of twenty years of American policy showed what experts already knew: the Communist world had split, and China was no longer counted an ally of the Soviet Union. Indeed, the Chinese kept an anxious eye out for signs of Western dissension and weakness, even urging the French to draw closer to the Americans, in the interest of a common defence against the Soviet Union.

THE TRUDEAU GOVERNMENT'S RELATIONS WITH THE THIRD WORLD should have been the most innovative sector of its foreign policy. Fixated as always on process, Trudeau and his disciples reorganized Canada's foreign aid machinery. Concerned to demonstrate that Canadian foreign policy should represent francophone interests, and spurred by competition with Quebec, Trudeau advanced Canadian aid into France's African sphere of influence. Unexpectedly, Trudeau began to appreciate the Commonwealth, for which until then French Canadians had shown very limited enthusiasm; but Trudeau liked the freer exchange of views at meetings of Commonwealth heads of government. More noticeably, and more important in terms of Canada's domestic politics, the Liberal government recognized the Communist government of China and exchanged ambassadors with Beijing.

Yet Third World relations was one area in which Trudeau's objectives, and therefore Canada's, were not met. Western aid did not transform the economies of the Third World, and the basket cases of the 1960s remained the basket cases of the 1980s. The proposed international aid standard, 0.7 percent of GNP, was not reached, at least not in Canada's case. And it is debatable whether it would have made much difference if Canada had achieved the magic digit.[40]

There may even have been a contradiction at the heart of Canada's Third World policy. Trudeau's aid machinery ground away in Ottawa, planning, granting, and auditing, and Canadian-funded projects sprouted accordingly. Yet there was little permanent change in Canadian relations with the Third World or its component countries as a result, and the benefits to the local populations were at best arguable. Nonetheless, there was occasionally a strong thread of realism in Trudeau's diplomacy. Canada's Third World policy did most good, or did least harm, where it was attuned to local realities. In the case of Biafra, intervention was beyond Canada's power, either diplomatically or militarily, and it is reasonable to conclude that Trudeau's aloof posture did least harm, which is not to say that harm was not done. In the case of China, recognizing the Communist regime in Beijing was simply to come to grips with the facts on the ground: China existed and must be dealt with.

In the long run, the realistic thread predominated, making for policy that was less moralistic and less interventionist than many of Trudeau's supporters would have liked.

17

PARALLEL LIVES:
NIXON MEETS TRUDEAU

The shape of Canada's relations with the United States was imposed by geography, history, and circumstance. The political geography of the eighteenth century ensured shared rivers, lakes, plains, and mountain ranges. The technology of the nineteenth bridged the rivers and polluted the wind currents, carrying American effluents to Canada, and vice versa. Railways, airways, and highways linked Canadian producers and American consumers, and carried American products, from machinery and citrus fruit to magazines and newspapers, north. Canadians followed those same routes south; almost 900,000 Canadian-born lived in the United States in 1970, adding family connections to the other north-south linkages.[1] Added to these were the Canadians who retired for the snowier part of the year to Florida, to live under the palms for the winter.[2] All this added to Canadian-American interconnections.

Canadian politicians liked to talk of Canadian-American relations as if they were shaped by Canada alone. The reverse was more often the truth, though the impact on Canada of American initiatives was as often as not unconscious. The most important example of an unconscious initiative was in immigration. In the mid-1960s Congress set out to amend long-standing injustices in the American immigration law. The result was a revised act that ended discrimination against whole regions and therefore whole races.[3] A side effect, largely unnoticed in Canada, was that unrestricted admission of Canadians (among other North and South Americans) to the United States came to an end. Free passage of emigrants, which had existed as long as Canada – indeed, much longer – suddenly vanished, and Canada was treated, where immigration was concerned, like any other country.

Trudeau Views the Americans

Trudeau had lived in the United States for a year when he was a student at Harvard University. Later, his roving included a visit to a conference held in Stalin's Moscow, and this caught the eye of American officials. The US government reacted by barring Trudeau from visiting the United States for a few years in the 1950s. Fervent anti-communists later maintained that Trudeau was little more than a fellow-traveller for the Soviet Union.[4] That was not the case, but what was true was that Trudeau was less influenced by the United States, its politics, or its values than any other twentieth-century Canadian prime minister. Attempts to get him to pay attention to most contemporary American phenomena failed. "The only American media he bothered following was American movies," his campaign manager once lamented.[5] The Cabinet, however, placed foreign investment (meaning American) on its list of priorities in 1971.[6]

Politically, Trudeau did not worry unduly about American influence over Canada or Canadian policy. The United States was a great power, and great powers had their interests, including the security of their neighbourhood. Canada was affected; that was a fact of life. He does not seem to have considered the United States to be especially malignant, a point that might have reassured Americans, except for the fact that he extended the same consideration to the Soviet Union – in the jargon of the time "equivalence." The Soviet Union was a great power like the United States, and like the United States had a sphere of influence that it believed guaranteed its own security. That fact explained, though it did not excuse, the Soviet invasion of Czechoslovakia in 1968. It also explained the West's almost purely symbolic response. Western reaction to the invasion was strictly limited, in effect recognizing that what the Soviets did behind the Iron Curtain was primarily their own affair. Other Western statesmen thought as Trudeau did, it appeared, sometimes without recognizing the fact. Not long after the Czech problem subsided, Trudeau scheduled a visit to the Soviet Union for October 1970. Domestic events intervened, and the visit had to be postponed, but it was a sign of détente and, as such, was highly valued by the Soviets.[7]

When Trudeau did visit the Soviet Union in the spring of 1971, there was little of substance to discuss. A few minor agreements were cobbled together for signature, primarily because there had to be *something* to sign. The Canadians appreciated the time spent with the Soviet premier, Alexei Kosygin, technically Trudeau's equivalent, and also met the actual political head of the Soviet Union, the Communist Party chief, Leonid Brezhnev. The visit gave Trudeau, and perhaps Westerners generally, reason for hope. One version of the trip "indicated that the Canadian Party had been encouraged by the 'sophisticated realism' of the Soviet leadership. [A Canadian diplomat] said that he personally had perhaps tended to underestimate the Soviet leadership and that the results of the trip had indicated that it was more competent and imaginative than he had thought."[8] The Soviet leadership might well be ready for realistic negotiations, on security in Europe, on arms control, on détente.

What was remembered about the visit to the Soviet Union was less the Canadian-Russian agenda than certain remarks made by Trudeau, when he publicly spoke about the "overwhelming presence" of the United States in Canadian life. American diplomats winced, and in the opinion of the Canadian ambassador to Moscow, Robert Ford, they had reason. According to Ford, Trudeau's statement and his choice of words were revealing: "I am ... certain that it was a psychological lapse, since it reflected a deep-seated distrust of the United States and a friendly feeling toward the Soviet Union on the part of the prime minister."[9]

THE AMERICANS VIEW TRUDEAU

Equally revealing was American reaction to Trudeau. It went beyond Trudeau's remarks in the Soviet Union, though of course the response varied according to the personality involved. Nixon disliked Trudeau, who was such a study in contrasts to himself. Nixon's national security adviser and foreign policy guru, Henry Kissinger, did nothing to contradict the president. In the view of the US ambassador, William Porter, Kissinger "imitated Nixon's attitude toward Canada" and neglected the northern neighbour, to the ambassador's distress.[10] Later, Kissinger appraised Canada and Trudeau more shrewdly. Canada, Kissinger believed, acted in counterpoint to the United States. "We are so powerful," he argued in 1974. "Whatever identity they have, they get in opposition to us." As for Trudeau, Kissinger considered him "intelligent, foppish and a momma's boy." It was not a bad analysis, though later Kissinger gilded it for his memoirs.[11]

The US embassy had a mixed impression. Trudeau, one American diplomat later argued, was "brilliant, and we recognized the man's brilliance, and his experience, but we were impatient with his advice at times, [his] sermonizing, and his needles." It was necessary to pay attention, but not too much attention, to what Canada said; the same diplomat observed "that Canada really is a minor Power, that it usually doesn't matter what policy positions Canada takes because it can do nothing about most of them." As far as Canada's relationship to the United States was concerned, the diplomat agreed with Kissinger, "Trudeau had to assert policy independence from us for [domestic] political reasons and ... this situation is a basic Canadian problem."[12]

Certainly *Foreign Policy for Canadians* offered the Americans no reliable guide to Canadian policy. A perceptive domestic critic observed that it could be read either as encouragement for international crusading or for the promotion of economic self-interest. Certainly there were no insights to stir the attention of Nixon or Kissinger. The United States had big problems, from Vietnam to the nuclear arms race, and on most of these issues Canada had little or nothing to contribute. Kissinger prided himself on his realistic approach to international politics; great powers had great interests, and frequently had them in common. Kissinger proposed to focus on these things, leaving other countries and lesser problems to the housekeeping staff at the State Department.

Yet Canada counted for something. Kissinger later cited its "somewhat aloof position combined with the high quality of its leadership," which gave it "an influence out of proportion to its military contribution."[13] It was a flattering appraisal, not entirely borne out by Kissinger's behaviour at the time.[14] Canada did not figure on Kissinger's list of countries or issues that merited automatic presidential consideration, and Washington had, at best, only slight interest in Canadian views on issues that *did* concern the American administration.

Nixon was a known political commodity. He had been Republican senator from California and then Eisenhower's vice president. He advanced through extreme and sometimes unscrupulous partisanship, positioning himself as a stalwart anti-communist when that position paid high political dividends. Defeated successively for president of the United States and governor of California, he temporarily left politics. (It was during this period that Nixon acquired some Canadian experience, acting as a lawyer for some American firms investing in Canada.)

Narrowly winning the presidential election of 1968, Nixon immediately hired Henry Kissinger to become his national security adviser. It was a position that afforded access and influence to its holder, even though in the hierarchy of American government it ranked below the secretaryship of state. The national security adviser wielded power as and if the president desired, and Nixon did so desire. Secretive and devious, highly intelligent and exceedingly unscrupulous, Nixon was determined to bring the most important foreign policy issues under his direct control. The others he left to his secretary of state, William (Bill) Rogers, a prominent New York lawyer, and his former senior law partner. Almost from the beginning, however, it was clear that Rogers had far less authority than Kissinger on such important subjects as negotiating peace in Vietnam, or relations with the Soviet Union. On the other hand, Rogers did manage relations with Canada.

Rogers led a Cabinet delegation to Canada in October 1970, just at the time of the FLQ crisis, and found his Canadian hosts somewhat distracted. These Cabinet-level meetings had begun in the 1950s in an attempt to bring Canadian questions forcibly to the attention of the higher levels of the US government. The 1970s meetings were the last. American diplomats found it too difficult to bring their Cabinet officers up to speed on Canada. They would open their briefing books only after getting on the plane to Ottawa. Their performance suffered accordingly, and they were consequently often at the mercy of the better-informed Canadians. The Canadians for their part found the process very unsatisfactory because there could be no real discussion or understanding of what were to Canada important subjects.[15] It did not matter to the Americans that Canada sent a senior diplomat, Marcel Cadieux, to Washington as ambassador. Cadieux was a man with interesting and well-informed (and notably anti-communist) views, which at home he frequently expressed. In Washington he had nobody important to talk to. Like other ambassadors, he talked only to the secretary of state; the Soviet envoy, by contrast, had an entrée to Kissinger and, through him, to the president.

Canada was handled by the State Department, or officers in other executive departments, like Treasury or Commerce. That did not mean it was badly treated. Dr Helmut Sonnenfeldt, on Kissinger's staff, dealt with Canadian issues that reached the National Security Council. He relied on a younger staffer, Denis Clift, to keep an eye on Canada.[16] Clift had been to Canada as a teenager, had distant Canadian relatives, watched Canadian tourists, and had "hazy, rosy, positive impressions." These, he later wrote, "would sharpen and be calibrated," but they were the basis for a longer regard for the country.[17]

Sonnenfeldt and Clift were sympathetic and helpful, but one thing they could not do was get Cadieux an appointment with their all-powerful boss, Kissinger. When Soviet premier Kosygin visited Canada, returning Trudeau's visit the previous year, Cadieux tried to brief Kissinger on his impressions. "Cadieux has been anxious to have an opportunity to see you for some time," Sonnenfeldt wrote to his superior, "and this occasion presents him with a peg. He is quite pro-US and has been deeply disturbed about adverse trends in US-Canadian relations and what he feels may be some misunderstanding here of Trudeau personally."[18] But no meeting was forthcoming: Kissinger had more important things to do.

The absence of direct, high-level communication of policy did not necessarily mean disharmony. Trudeau's encounters with Nixon were cool, formal, polite, and generally productive. "It cannot be said that Nixon and Trudeau were ideally suited for each other," Kissinger wrote. Nixon would have been tempted to identify the sophisticated and non-conformist Trudeau with his "enemies" in the eastern establishment. Trudeau was a Harvard graduate, and Harvard men had to work overtime, as Kissinger did, to curry Nixon's favour. Trudeau seems to have perceived Nixon's intelligence, and quickness of thought, and "treated Nixon without any hint of condescension when they were together," while Nixon "accorded Trudeau both respect and attention,"[19] in public at least. Trudeau did not expect that Nixon would pay much attention to detailed

Canadian views. It was enough for him to know whether Canada was in general sympathy or agreement with Nixon's policy. Much of the time, apart from Vietnam, it was.

THE CONTINUING IRRITANT OF VIETNAM

Vietnam remained the single most poisonous issue in Canadian-American relations. Canada's opposition to the war was shared by virtually all of the Western allies. It was worse in those countries, like Australia and New Zealand, that had actually sent troops to Indochina; their governments could not avoid taking an overtly pro-war stance, and they reaped vast unpopularity as a result. Because Canada was not overtly committed to the war, Ottawa had the luxury of drifting with the tide of public sentiment and allowing its anti-war inclination to be understood rather than explicitly stated. Because Trudeau had a parliamentary majority, and party discipline was strong, his government did not have to fear serious political consequences by remaining aloof.

Neither Trudeau nor Mitchell Sharp, his external affairs minister, had any personal agenda where Vietnam was concerned. They passed through the federal election campaign of May-June 1968 without any of the disturbances and confrontations on the issue that characterized the campaign of 1965.[20] Trudeau felt less engaged than his predecessor, Pearson, in the future of the Western alliance,[21] while Sharp realistically assessed the situation as one where Canada could do little good and might as well not try. The Cabinet, for its part, decided in January 1970 that participation in any future peacekeeping exercise should depend on the reasonable prospect of its success.[22] But Sharp also let his American counterpart, Bill Rogers, know that if the end of the war required Canada to play a role on an armistice or truce commission, it would be ready.[23]

In the meantime, the government could only watch what the war was doing to Canadian views of the United States. The signs were not good. Bookstore shelves were crowded with titles like *An Independent Foreign Policy for Canada?* (the answer was yes) or *Death Goes Better with Coca-Cola* (advising against the consumption of American mass culture) or *The New Romans* (featuring on its cover a potbellied unmistakably "American" type dressed up as a Roman centurion). Such titles meshed with public opinion polls, which showed a drift away from the pro-American sentiments of the 1950s and early 1960s. In 1956, 27 percent of Canadians polled agreed that "the Canadian way of life was being influenced too much by the US." Fully 63 percent disagreed with the statement. By 1966, 53 percent thought American influence in or on Canada was excessive; by 1974 the figure was up to 57 percent.[24] A poll in 1969 found that only 24 percent of Canadians thought Canadian-American relations had recently worsened, compared to 48 percent who thought the two countries were drawing closer together. Yet the people "who saw a deterioration in Canada-US relations pointed to 'Canada's independent foreign policy' and criticism of the Vietnam war as the basis for their opinion."[25] A surge of Canadian nationalism suddenly became manifest. In universities, anything Canadian – Canadian history, literature, political science – suddenly became popular. As the historian Doug Owram put it, not being American conferred "moral authority"; put another way, not being American meant being Canadian.[26]

Such anti-Americanism was not uniquely Canadian. Anti-Americanism has always been a peculiarly American product: throughout US history, dissenting groups have denounced the evils (often magnified) of their sinful land. One of Canada's founding groups, the United Empire Loyalists, was American, and the question of differentiation between loyal (British) and disloyal (pro-American) Canadians was central to English-Canadian politics in the nineteenth century. During the early stages of the First and Second World Wars, young Americans enlisted in Canada's armed forces while their own country was still officially neutral; of course, when the United States entered those wars these pro-Canadian or anti-German actions were officially authorized or ratified.

The Vietnam War was different. The young American men coming to Canada were trying to *avoid* the fight. There were other creative ways of avoiding a ticket to Vietnam. Deferments (effectively indefinite postponements) were freely available to college students, and the older you got, the less likely you were to be called up. Enlisting in the armed forces' reserves, if you chose the right unit or right kind of service, was also good for a postponement of rigorous duty overseas, as various prominent Americans (including future vice president Dan Quayle and president George W. Bush) discovered.

The Vietnam War made major demands on American manpower. The war required more young men than the existing system could comfortably supply, and so deferments shrank and draft calls rose. The war could not be disregarded as something distant or remote; it was as close as the next mail delivery bringing "greetings" from Uncle Sam. In the mid-1960s disturbances began on American campuses, reaching national and indeed international prominence in 1967-1968. In 1968 the Democratic national convention in Chicago was disrupted by riots, simultaneously broadcast in living colour in both the United States and Canada.

Draft dodgers continued to flow into Canada. The American government for its part did not press the issue. As one White House official, William Macomber, put it in a letter to an indignant Congressman in 1969, "Not much can be done to prevent movement of draft evaders to Canada, short of drastic measures which would have side effects adverse to our national interest." He added, "nevertheless we have on a number of occasions informally let the Canadian Government know of our concern."[27]

Nixon was determined to end the damaging internal effects of the war. His administration practised "Vietnamization" of the war, replacing American combatants with Vietnamese soldiers, while continuing an intense bombing campaign against North Vietnam. Negotiations with the North Vietnamese went forward in Paris, with the object of a triumphant conclusion before Nixon's campaign for re-election in 1972. It was a rocky road: the North Vietnamese had not given up hope of military victory, nor had the Americans. But at least Nixon's new policy meant that the greatest political pressure point, the draft, was beginning to subside.

It was not the war that brought on a crisis in Canadian-American affairs, or at any rate not directly. It was the much more traditional and mundane matter of trade and economic relations.

Economic Shocks from Washington

Canada traded more with the United States than with any other country; virtually every year after 1945 the proportion of exports going to, and imports coming from, the United States increased. This was not a matter of deliberate policy, at least not in the first instance. Every Canadian government after 1945 hoped to diversify the country's trade, and every Canadian government left office with the proportion of American trade increased.

The components of trade did not remain the same. At first, Canada sent mainly raw materials or semi-processed products to the United States. It was customary to use the expression "hewers of wood and drawers of water" to describe Canada's role in the American scheme of things, sending natural resources south and receiving in return US mass-produced goods, which were cheaper than those made in Canada. Canadian nationalists were deeply suspicious of the Auto Pact of 1965, believing that it was a harbinger of the deindustrialization of Canada. Canada had almost always had a trade deficit with the United States, and automobiles and automotive products were a large part of that deficit.[28] In economic negotiations with the Americans, Canadian diplomats usually secured exemptions or "special" treatment because of their country's imbalance of trade and payments with the United States. If the Americans had problems with trade or with trading partners, it was always with somebody else. Or so the Canadians thought.

By the late 1960s trade was a source of increasing anxiety in the United States. There were regular trade deficits. Money flowed abroad to service American investment. Governments tried to stem the outflow with a variety of ingenious devices, but the deficit continued to rise. American industry, and American industrial workers, began to worry about imports. Sometimes, in politically sensitive areas, Washington made concessions to domestic sentiment. American purchases of uranium, once a source of tremendous profit to Canadian exporters, were restricted after 1966 to Americans only, in defiance of US commitments under the General Agreement on Tariffs and Trade (GATT). For the most part, however, Democratic and Republican administrations stuck to freer trade as the best policy.

Nixon was no exception. The president believed in free trade and resisted early attempts by a Democratic Congress to dilute trade policy with a dose of protectionism.

Like other postwar presidents, Nixon saw a connection between political influence abroad and a policy of freer trade. But protectionism appealed to precisely those voters – industrial workers in declining industries beset with foreign competition – that Nixon needed for re-election. Within the administration, the balance began to shift towards protectionism, and towards Treasury Secretary John Connally, a former Democrat and former governor of Texas who, so it was thought, was crucial to Nixon's success in the approaching election. Connally projected toughness. It was a quality Nixon greatly admired – so much so that the president saw Connally as his natural successor.[29]

Nixon's principal foreign policy adviser, Henry Kissinger, took little interest in economics.[30] His gaze, in 1970 and 1971, was firmly fixed on Vietnam, the Soviet Union, and China, and he had little time for lesser issues, including, for the time being, relations with the allies. Connally was a more significant figure in the administration than Secretary of State Rogers, and it was Connally who took command of the problem of the American trade deficit.

"Command" was the operative word. Connally took a broad view of American power. The United States was the biggest and the most important country in the Western coalition. All its allies depended on American strength, and they should pay heed to American needs, which after all maintained that strength. Connally played on the resentful strain in Nixon's personality. In one of his television addresses, Nixon spoke scornfully of a United States afraid to use its power as "a pitiful, helpless giant." In 1971, as he informed his staff, "we have too long acted as Uncle Sugar and now we've got to be Uncle Sam."[31]

Vietnam apart, the single most serious problem confronting the Nixon administration was economic. The United States had for some time been running a balance of payments deficit, caused, as mentioned, by an outflow of dollars to fund American investment abroad. In 1971 came a shock: the United States was running its first trade deficit since the nineteenth century.[32] This was by definition an unnatural state of affairs, requiring swift remedy.

For months the Nixon administration debated what was required. Everything was up for discussion. If Washington was reconsidering its commitment to free trade, it also had to review the Bretton Woods system, under which the United States had taken a leading role in trying to ensure the equilibrium of the global economy. Could the United States afford to go on being the world's bank of last resort when foreign claims on that bank, in dollars and gold, outweighed what the US government had available to meet them? The US dollar was overvalued, and maintaining a gold exchange regime was no longer possible.

The United States needed a breather from such pressure. In early August 1971 new demands on US gold and dollar reserves gave Nixon an excuse to act.[33] In deep secrecy he assembled his economic advisers at the presidential retreat at Camp David, Maryland. Nixon had recently electrified the world with his dramatic reversal of twenty years of American policy on China: now his advisers urged him to do something equally impressive with respect to economic policy, something of "Peking proportions."[34] One group urged the president to close the "gold window," to end the convertibility of US dollars into gold. Another urged a series of urgent measures to protect American industry. Urgent and temporary measures were permissible under the GATT, and many countries, including Canada, had taken advantage of the provision. Connally took the lead. To protect American industry against the predatory policies of its allies, Connally settled on a series of demands. American trading partners must raise the value of their currencies and abandon restrictions on American trade. If the United States had a trade deficit with a given country, it was a sign of unfairness that must somehow be righted. To induce change, Connally prepared a range of import surcharges and export incentives. "My basic approach," the treasury secretary argued, "is that the foreigners are out to screw us. Our job is to screw them first."[35]

Connally's chosen method was what Henry Kissinger later called "brutal unilateralism," mitigated only by the thought, perhaps the conviction, that, left to themselves, the allies would do nothing to solve what the United States government perceived as a crucial problem.[36] His approach is revealed by a discussion among Nixon's advisers at Camp David on the merits of negotiating changes to interest rates with the allies, as opposed to a sudden and unilateral move. The protagonists are Connally; the undersecretary of the treasury, Paul Volcker; and the chairman of the president's Council of Economic Advisers, Arthur Burns:

> *Connally:* So the other countries don't like it. So what?
> *Volcker:* But don't let's close the window and sit – let's get other governments to
>   negotiate new rates.
> *Connally:* Why do we have to be reasonable? Canada wasn't.
> *Burns:* They can retaliate.
> *Connally:* Let 'em. What can they do?
> *Burns:* They're powerful. They're proud, just as we are ...[37]

Connally essentially wanted to devalue the US dollar in order to make American exports cheaper for foreigners to buy; alternatively, he wanted to force the allies to increase the value of their currencies. The object was to reduce or abolish the American imbalance of payments. Up until this point, the United States had made its currency the cornerstone of the Bretton Woods financial system, promising to exchange its dollar for gold at the rate, unchanged since the 1930s, of $35 an ounce. Connally was convinced that the United States could not maintain Bretton Woods and overcome a too high dollar, and so Bretton Woods had to go. But if the United States devalued its dollar, other countries could devalue their currencies too. Connally had to prevent other countries from lowering the value of their currency. He devised an import surcharge, a tariff on tariffs, so to speak, that could be announced, waved before other countries, and then rescinded if they promised to behave and not follow the United States in devaluation. The final part of the package was a program of domestic wage and price controls.[38]

Up to this point, Canadian officials might not have objected. Connally, however, went one step farther. Canada, he had decided, was part of the problem.[39] The key was the Auto Pact.[40] By 1971 it was clear that what had been intended as a mild alleviation of a chronic and heavy Canadian deficit in the automotive trade had turned out to be something completely different. In 1970, for the first time anyone could remember, Canada ran a surplus in trade with the United States in automobiles and automobile parts.[41] That was part of a global surplus in merchandise trade, and those were the figures Connally had to hand when he decided to revise American trade policy. In terms of the total number of automobiles produced in the two countries, Canada's share had risen from 7.1 percent in 1965 to 12.6 percent in 1970.[42] For the Canadians, therefore, Connally reserved a surprise: cancellation of the Auto Pact. That would certainly send a message to Canada: 32 percent of Canadian exports to the United States were automobiles or automotive products.

Connally secured Nixon's consent and, equally important, his support. The two men decided they must move quickly, with barely a day and a half between the basic decision and its announcement. One commentator later marvelled "how few of the key decisions had been thought through."[43] Nixon would personally announce Connally's economic package in a televised address on the evening of 15 August 1971. The machinery of the American government lumbered into gear. There would have to be copies of Nixon's speech and press releases dealing with every part of his economic ultimatum to be fed to a presumably ravenous press corps the evening of the speech. All these items had to be typed, mimeographed, stapled, and sorted. That took staff, more than Connally or even Nixon had available. Casting the net for available labour, White House officials pulled in State Department officials – the individuals who would have to handle the fallout.

One conscript was a vacationing diplomat posted to the US embassy in Ottawa. As Emerson Brown sorted through the press releases, he found the one announcing the cancellation of the Auto Pact. He did not relish returning to Ottawa to tell the Canadians that the United States had just unilaterally repudiated an important treaty. He took his views to Secretary Rogers, who mustered his credit with the president to pull the Auto Pact announcement at the last minute. The disappearance of part of the press package forced the renumbering of great piles of paper, to the intense annoyance of the White House press secretary.

Not knowing that they'd only narrowly avoided a huge economic blow, the Canadians were not pleased by what Nixon announced on 15 August. At first, the Canadian reaction was that there had been some kind of mistake, that Canada had been accidentally included in an all-embracing category of offending foreigners.[44] Inquiries in Washington produced the assurance that Canada was definitely part of the package. How prominent a part, nobody let on.

In Ottawa, Mitchell Sharp was acting prime minister while Trudeau was on holiday. As such, he was in charge of the official reaction. "I thought it was part of a dream," he said later.[45] Finance minister Edgar Benson was on a wine tour of Europe; he hastily packed his bags and trademark pipe and headed home. Prime Minister Trudeau was cruising the Adriatic; prudently, he decided that he should let Sharp handle the problem. The problem swiftly became a crisis once it became clear that Canada was included and as the media speculated as to what it might all mean.

Officials decided that a firm response was in order. "The point of the whole thing, Mr. Sharp, is confidence," the deputy minister of finance, Simon Reisman, said. Sharp did not think so, at least as far as he personally was concerned. He avoided going in person to Washington; instead, Benson would lead the Canadian delegation. He was expected, along with another eight or nine finance ministers from allied countries. They had a role to play, scripted by Connally. The Canadians were the United States' largest trading partner, accounting for 25 or 26 percent of US imports,[46] and Connally hoped to use negotiations with the Canadians and the Japanese as a means to prying concessions out of the Europeans.[47] Public concessions from the Canadians were therefore necessary. Theatrics were an essential part of Connally's approach. As Kissinger later waspishly commented, "For Connally, a victory was meaningless unless his victim knew he had been defeated."[48]

The secretary's impressive office in the Treasury Department was the stage. Washington's August heat provided atmosphere – the fires of a sweaty hell. Rumpled and perspiring, Benson and his delegation sat in front of Connally's elegant desk (it had belonged to Alexander Hamilton, the first secretary of the treasury) and listened to the secretary's indignant speech. It was for a moment a surreal experience, as Connally's words seemed to have no relation to Canada. Little wonder: he had picked up the wrong papers and was reading from his denunciation of Japan. The script was replaced, and the secretary started over, but the meeting had begun to unravel.

The Canadians were uncooperative. They protested their innocence; they invoked the laws and customs of international trade; they told the secretary that he was mistaken.

At one point Reisman shook his cigar indignantly and the ashes drifted down over the Hamilton desk. The meeting ended without agreement, and without repentance from the Canadians.

It was the first of many encounters, all fruitless. The two sides did not even agree on facts – the Canadians had one set of economic figures, the Americans another.[49] It is difficult to know if the Canadian meetings were unusually unpleasant or unfruitful, but as summer turned into fall it became clear that Canada was not the only ally to feel badly treated. Kissinger began to take notice. Connally's trade theatrics were interfering with progress on disarmament, on détente, on China.

Back in Canada, Trudeau was perturbed. Tried-and-true methods of dealing with the Americans, the arguments and personalities that had always been effective before, were not working. He turned to Ivan Head for advice, and Head turned to Kissinger, who was, in a sense, his American counterpart. Kissinger knew matters were not going well. His deputy, Helmut Sonnenfeldt, warned in October that "our relations with Canada have gone downhill unnecessarily, partly because of our bad manners."[50] Kissinger arranged for Trudeau and Nixon to meet in Washington in early December 1971. The two leaders chatted with Head and Kissinger, while their deputies tried again down the hall. Predictably, the subordinates replayed their existing lines and emerged, exhausted and ill-tempered, to be sunnily greeted by the two leaders, who proclaimed that they had reached a meeting of minds. As Head put it, they resolved "the impasse to the complete satisfaction of each." The surcharge on Canadian products was lifted, and "no further demands would be made with respect to the value of the Canadian dollar."[51]

It was, apparently, a happy ending. Perhaps Nixon had decided to let well enough alone. He had got most of what he wanted, a revaluation of the Japanese yen and European currencies, ratified in a meeting at the Smithsonian Institution in Washington that Canada also attended. It did not matter that the Canadian dollar stayed where it was (at the time above par with the American dollar). Nor did it matter that the surcharges were lifted: most Canadian exports to the United States entered duty free, and the surcharge was a percentage of an existing tariff. A percentage, any percentage, of zero remains zero. Nixon might also have been thinking of a forthcoming visit to Canada, scheduled for April 1972. That was an election year, and the signs of a successful presidency had to be plainly visible. If there was to be a visit to Canada, it must go well; and cancellation was not a good option, as the Canadians set great store by presidential visits. Nixon so far had made none, though he had been practically everywhere else. As far as Canada was concerned, a presidential visit was desirable; Trudeau, who also expected an election in 1972, needed evidence to set before the public that relations with the United States were in good hands.

Despite the apparent accord of the December meeting between Trudeau and Nixon, Connally did not give up. He wanted the Canadian dollar up, and safeguards in the

Auto Pact down. Nixon had removed the dollar from discussion. That only ensured that Connally would focus his fire on the Auto Pact.

Connally and his Canadian counterparts therefore continued to bicker and snarl into the spring of 1972. In February Sonnenfeldt warned that Treasury had "raised the possibility of suspending the US-Canadian Auto Agreement and the Defense Production Sharing Arrangement with Canada." He continued, underlining the sentence for emphasis: "*This memo is to alert you to the problem and to the urgent need to moderate Connally before an unnecessary foreign policy crisis with adverse domestic political implications erupts.*"[52]

The impasse was complete. Connally would settle for nothing less than the removal of all Auto Pact safeguards, and the Canadians would not agree to that.[53] Some of the American officials attending the talks were disturbed and embarrassed by Connally's hard line. Harold A. Scott, assistant secretary of commerce, was moved to write to Kissinger early in April:

> With the exception of the White House meeting on 6 December 1971, the mood throughout was conciliatory, courteous and characterized by the Canadians' desire to be helpful without abandoning their traditionally tough negotiating stance and their acute awareness of their domestic political climate.
>
> In my opinion, having been present at all of the meetings, had the United States ever made a firm proposal the Canadians would have gone further than the point where conversations had terminated. Not knowing, however, what were the United States objectives they were cautious on commenting on individual points until the dimensions of the entire package were clearly visible to them.[54]

Scott urged an end to the pointless confrontation with Canada, and his wish was fortuitously granted.

For several months Connally had been rubbing up against a White House staff that thought him a loose cannon. For his part, Connally thought that Nixon's entourage ignored his authority and interfered in his department.[55] The Canadian problem was one among many, but it occurred just as Connally decided that he and the White House staff were no longer compatible. On 18 April 1972 he met with H.R. Haldeman, Nixon's assistant, to tell him it was time to leave before an unseemly political quarrel inside the administration occurred. If he left now, he argued, he and the administration could remain friendly, and he could chair a front group, Democrats for Nixon, for the campaign.[56]

And so the impasse between Canada and the United States was solved. The Nixon visit to Ottawa was key: it had to be seen to succeed, and a quarrel over the Auto Pact would not do that. Second, Connally had to go. He went, not because of Canada, but

Canada was one beneficiary of the happy fallout from his departure. Replacing Connally was George Shultz, a businessman and former professor, and a notable contrast in style and substance to his predecessor.

THE END OF VIETNAM

Out of office, Connally was not necessarily out of power, but his career was hostage to Nixon's fortunes. When the president insisted on burglarizing the presumed secrets of his nearly impotent opposition, and lied about his actions, he eventually became the centre of what was probably the greatest political scandal in American history. Triumphantly re-elected in November 1972, he was driven from office in August 1974, and Connally went down with his political master.

Nixon managed to be re-elected without ending the Vietnam War. He had succeeded, by the summer of 1972, in withdrawing all ground combat troops, thereby ending the constant political drain of nightly televised casualty figures. But the United States was still engaged by air and sea, bombing selected North Vietnamese targets and giving air support to the South Vietnamese forces. Air raids produced air casualties and added to the sizeable number of American prisoners of war in North Vietnamese hands. The fate of the POWs became an item for the final settlement with North Vietnam.

Negotiations between the United States and North Vietnam continued in Paris. The North Vietnamese had concluded that Nixon would be re-elected, and that the Soviet Union and China did not wish the war to continue.[57] The shape of things to come was by the fall of 1972 fairly clear. There would be a truce, the United States would withdraw its forces, the South Vietnamese government would remain in place, existing forces would remain where they were, and there would be a pretence that the North and South Vietnamese sought a lasting peace. Kissinger hoped to reinforce it with promises of lavish aid to South Vietnam should war break out again. The talks were an electoral asset, and Nixon's officials allowed it to be known that "peace was at hand" – or, as a Canadian diplomat in Washington quipped, "at least at arm's length."

While the peace talks proceeded, the International Commission for Supervision and Control (ICC) lingered in Saigon in suspended animation. The commission had little to do, and nobody took its presence very seriously. Canada had reduced its contingent to a level consistent with somnolence. Protests at home against Canadian "collusion" with the Americans forced the government officially to limit contacts between the ICC and the American embassy and military.

It may seem surprising that the Canadian government was willing to repeat the experience of the ICC, letting it be known that if peace broke out Canada would be willing to facilitate it. External Affairs Minister Mitchell Sharp and his American counterpart, Bill Rogers, discussed the question of such participation periodically, but it was never urgent, and life, including political life, went on. Opposition to the Vietnam War was a fact of political life in the 1970s, ever present in newspapers and on television. The conclusion of a column in the *Toronto Star* in May 1972 gives the flavour: Vietnam, it said, "is a war in defence of the enthronement of technology, and Our Side is waging it in the only way we know: with money, and marvellous machines, and vast bureaucracies, and sophisticated poisons and automated warriors who never see the wounds inflicted by the buttons they push. That's how we are waging it, and we are losing. No wonder Richard Nixon is a desperate man."[58]

On 1 September 1972 Trudeau called a general election, set for 30 October. It was a contest he confidently expected to win, but he was quite wrong. Although the country was generally prosperous, Trudeau seemed to have done nothing in particular – nothing that firmed up support from those new voters he had attracted in 1968. The Liberals barely squeaked through, reduced from a strong majority in the House of Commons to a two-seat plurality over the Progressive Conservatives. Until Parliament reconvened in January 1973, Trudeau could not claim to have much more than a housekeeping mandate.

At this point, the United States called. The peace talks were in their final stages. There would be an international control commission to supervise the peace. The United States wanted Canada as a member: Would the Canadians serve? Marcel Cadieux delivered a qualified yes. According to American notes, the "response was ingeniously couched in language designed to preserve Canada's traditional attitude towards [the] nature of control machinery," but also reflect the "tenuous political situation prevailing in Ottawa."[59]

The war had one final spasm. With negotiations at a standstill, Nixon authorized the intensive bombing of the heavily defended North Vietnamese capital, Hanoi, and its port, Haiphong. The bombing, which took place between 17 and 29 December, apparently killed about 1,500 civilians along with an unknown number of military. Reaction around the world was highly unfavourable. With peace almost assured, these raids seemed pointless and cruel. They were also costly for the United States, which lost fifteen giant B-52 bombers in the brief campaign. Negotiations resumed in Paris on 8 January 1973, and a treaty was concluded on 23 January.

Reaction in Canada to the Christmas bombing was nearly hysterical – and virtually unanimous. With the minority Parliament about to meet, consideration of the public mood became a delicate and important consideration for the Trudeau government. Reading the newspapers and watching television, it was clear that the United States had few defenders. Moved by the public outrage, Ottawa sent no fewer than three notes to the United States complaining of the bombing.[60] Parliament met on 4 January. For the Liberals, the key consideration was securing the support of the New Democratic Party (NDP) to ensure a majority vote in the House of Commons. For the NDP and especially its supporters, the most important issue was the American bombing of North Vietnam, and the Liberals framed their policy accordingly. "Seizing the initiative from the NDP," Sharp later wrote, "I sponsored a resolution in the House of Commons on 5 January 1973." The resolution "deplored" the recent bombing, hoped it would not recur, and expressed "grave concern" over the continuation of hostilities. It was something no party dared vote against.[61] Voting for it, MPs were also giving the Trudeau government a new lease on political life. Had Trudeau been defeated in the first vote of the session, he would have had little option but to resign in favour of the opposition leader, Robert Stanfield.

The resolution generated varied reactions in Washington. State Department officials were by and large unconcerned and accepted the assurances of Canadian diplomats that the Trudeau government was simply playing a political game, with no real significance for Canadian-American relations. Nixon, however, was enraged. When Trudeau sent him a letter, the president refused to reply. When Trudeau's mother died, Nixon refused to send the customary letter of condolence.[62] The president further instructed that Canadian diplomats in Washington were to be shunned. Invitations to the embassy were to be refused, nor were Canadian diplomats to be received at the State Department. It was absurd, and as an absurdity it was ignored in spirit if not in form: it merely resulted in the transfer of Canadian-American business to Washington restaurants.

The prohibition was all the sillier because it occurred just as the Paris talks produced agreement. Canadian participation in a new commission was now needed and had to be negotiated. A hundred details needed to be settled – matters of cost, duration, and administration. The Canadian government had to deal not only with the American government, but with the Poles, Indonesians, and Hungarians, the likely partners on the new supervisory commission. The commission was broadly like the old ICC, as its name reflected – International Commission for Control and Supervision (ICCS), although it had an even, rather than an odd, number of participants. Majority votes were no longer possible, but, as the old ICC showed, majority votes made no difference anyway.

Experience suggested that the ICCS would work as long as the participants agreed on its immediate objectives. Getting the Americans out of Vietnam was possible and desirable, and that alone justified the Canadian commitment. The Cabinet weighed the arguments, and agreed. Canada would join the commission, but only for a sixty-day trial period. If the commission did not work, Canada would leave.[63]

As with the ICC, the Canadian delegation to the ICCS was a mix of civilians and military – 290 individuals, all told. Their chief was Michel Gauvin, an experienced foreign service officer and Canadian ambassador to Greece. Gauvin moved to Saigon on secondment from his Greek job – a sign that his role was expected to be strictly temporary. He arrived in Saigon on 29 January to greet his Polish, Indonesian, and Hungarian colleagues. They had much to do and in the glare of human-interest publicity, given the return of the American POWs. On the surface, all went well. Behind the scenes, the two Communist delegations dragged their heels, cooperating only if the Indonesians could devise an expedient compromise. The work took time and was not completed when Sharp's first sixty-day deadline approached.

Sharp understood that Vietnam was a pre-eminent example of public diplomacy. Activity was measured in sound bites and television exposure, and so, although he already knew what facts he would find, the minister set off on a well publicized fact-finding mission to Saigon and Hanoi. There, he heard the same old song, familiar from years on the old ICC. Peace was fragile, and the peacekeeping structure more fragile still. To help keep the peace, Canada must stay, no matter how discouraging the circumstances. Back in Ottawa, the minister reported to the Standing Committee on External Affairs and Defence of the House of Commons. Circumstances were difficult, to be sure, but he insisted that the ICCS was doing important work. Soon the Americans would be gone. Sharp announced a ninety-day extension.

The ninety days were difficult. An ICCS helicopter was shot down by North Vietnamese troops stationed in the South, killing, among others, a Canadian army captain. Evidence of truce violations piled up. When these involved the North Vietnamese, the Poles and Hungarians refused to do anything. Neither the North nor the South believed in the peace, and it was only a question of time until full-scale war broke out again. It was plain what the future would hold. "An atmosphere of futility began to pervade the ICCS headquarters in Saigon, which occupied the same bedraggled compound that had housed the old control commission," an American reporter wrote.[64] From Saigon, Gauvin conducted a running commentary. The technique was promptly dubbed "open-mouth diplomacy," and, like Sharp's well-publicized hesitations, it managed simultaneously to inform the public about what Canada was doing and prepare it for the removal of the Canadian presence.

In May Ottawa again considered what it should do. Gauvin advised departure: the internal contradictions of the mission were too great.[65] The United States pressured Canada to stay. Kissinger pointed to improvements in Canadian-American relations and hinted that these were owing to, and depended on, Canada's continuing membership in the ICCS. Sharp laid the alternatives before the Cabinet, recommending that Canada terminate its part in the "charade." The Cabinet agreed. When Sharp informed Kissinger that he would soon make the decision public, Kissinger begged for a postponement. That could not be, Sharp replied, but he would agree to let the Canadian troops associated with the commission stay an extra month, until the end of July 1973, if that would help. Kissinger accepted, and the matter was decided.[66]

To no one's surprise, the North Vietnamese gradually improved their military position in the South, and the government in Saigon was unable to muster the wit or the will to resist them effectively. In the winter of 1975 the North Vietnamese began an offensive that took them all the way to the Southern capital, which they reached on 30 April. The chargé of the Canadian diplomatic mission there had left some time earlier, after shipping out the embassy car.

The fall of Saigon was a nine-day wonder. It was marvellously photogenic: footage was broadcast around the world of Americans, other Westerners, and some Vietnamese scurrying for rescue helicopters from the roof of the US embassy. There followed a longer tragedy, less publicized, as Communist rule clamped down on South Vietnam. The outside world learned what was happening mostly through a flood of refugees – "the boat people" – who risked the South China Sea to escape their homeland. Many came to Canada. The influx was slow at first, 9,000 between 1975 and 1978, but during the brief Joe Clark government 34,000 came, 21,000 of whom were privately sponsored.[67]

The end of the war removed the most acute unhappiness in Canadian-American relations. It was not that the two governments had ever clashed over the issue. Except for atmospherics, Pearson and Trudeau were circumspect where the war was concerned. Trudeau in particular believed it was quite beyond Canada's power to influence, let alone solve. Rather, Vietnam poisoned public life, sapping the morale of friends of the United States, while enabling those who hated Americans, or imperialism, or capitalism, to have a field day.

The end of the war was a defeat for the United States but a reprieve for American society. The defeat was noticed and much commented on in Moscow. The US political system had not produced victory after all, despite American wealth and power and technology. That must mean that history, and time, were on the Communists' side, as Marx and Lenin had predicted. American reluctance in the mid-1970s to get involved in Communist-sponsored conflicts in Angola, Mozambique, or Ethiopia encouraged the belief that the United States was on the decline, and that Moscow-supported adventures abroad would find success.

Domestically and internationally, the end of the war calmed political passions. In Canada, the revolutionary left no longer had a cause to rally around. Even more moderate leftists lost focus. The first half of the 1970s was characterized by riot and protest, especially on Canadian campuses; the second half, by contrast, turned away from issues of war and peace to questions of economics and inflation. There were other problems in the 1970s, not susceptible to military solutions. They centred on the questions of energy, especially oil.

PIERRE TRUDEAU'S RELATIONS WITH RICHARD NIXON WERE NOT AS GOOD AS HE THOUGHT, but better than most Canadians believed, then and later. The years of Nixon's presidency, 1969 to 1974, were overshadowed by the Vietnam War, but like the Democratic Johnson administration before it, Nixon's Republicans refused to let the war stand in the way of maintaining good relations.

Good relations with Canada were important to the United States, but not because of politics or political issues like the war. Canada was by far the major American trading partner and a principal repository of American investment. That this was so was demonstrated by an uncharacteristic American lapse into cowboy diplomacy in 1971-1972 under the leadership of Treasury Secretary John Connally. Connally sought to bully US economic partners – including, and especially, Canada – into surrender, though on what terms no one could be sure. In the case of Canada, Connally stimulated eight months of tense economic negotiations, but despite threats from the American side nothing came of it. For Canada, it was a negative triumph that preserved intact the Auto Pact of 1965. Compared to the economic issues at stake, Canada's political relations with the United States passed like shadow play: fearsome images reflected on a screen, masking the strong economic ties that bound the two countries together.

18 THE PURSUIT OF PROMISES

When Trudeau first became prime minister and proclaimed a change in the way Canada would relate to the world, he chose an opportune moment. The Cold War in Europe, symbolized by the nuclear arms race, the endless crisis over Berlin, and the Cuban missile crisis of 1962, had reached an impasse. The Soviet Union learned not to challenge the United States and its allies directly, and instead quietly built up its military strength. The United States, having projected determination and inspired confidence over Cuba in 1962, sought to shore up its strength and reinforce its reputation through the Vietnam War. It did neither. The war undermined the political consensus inside the United States that was the real foundation of American foreign policy, while Western countries made it plain that the Cold War alliance had its limits. The problem for the United States was less the policies of allied governments than the growing anti-Americanism among their citizens. As in Canada, by the end of the 1960s a substantial proportion of European public opinion was convinced that the United States was a real menace to peace, while the Soviet Union was little more than a steady and reliable neighbour.

The creative diplomacy of Richard Nixon and Henry Kissinger sought to restore American power by limiting its application and lowering its costs, political and economic. They sought an accommodation based on shared interests with the Soviet Union and China, while exploiting the divergence between those rival Communist powers. The foundation for this "détente" was laid by a Test Ban Treaty in 1963, ending atmospheric nuclear tests among its signatories. The Soviets later claimed that the Vietnam

War had subverted the détente created by this treaty, and certainly during the mid-1960s Soviet-American relations were testy.

China rejoiced in the Vietnam War and cheerfully fuelled the North's war effort. The Soviet Union felt reluctantly compelled to follow where the Chinese led; the provision of supplies became an incident in Soviet rivalry with China. The war did not bring the two powers closer together. While it was going on, Soviet and Chinese troops clashed along their frontier, while the Soviet authorities considered a surprise nuclear strike on their erstwhile ally.

The West did not create Sino-Soviet antagonism, but Kissinger was more than willing to exploit it. The two antagonists were kept roughly in balance, each one linked to the United States and the West by separate arrangements. Head and Trudeau later wrote approvingly of Kissinger's reaching out to China and the Soviet Union. Besides acknowledging the inherent intelligence of this move, they took it as confirmation of the wisdom of Canada's slightly earlier initiatives, although, they later added, "one could not expect any acknowledgement to this effect from a superpower."[1] Sniff.

TAKING STOCK IN EUROPE

The depressurizing of East-West rivalries left the West free to seek an alternative to confrontation, as laid down in NATO's Harmel report, adopted in 1967. The adoption of Harmel's principles gave American allies some room for manoeuvre. The British wound up most of what remained of their overseas military commitments, further shrinking their empire. For most of the 1970s, Britain's domestic political and economic situation preoccupied its politics and governments. France, as always, aired its well-publicized differences with the United States, but French policy in the 1970s was more concerned with optics than with substance.

France was prosperous, compared to Britain, but both countries paled in comparison to West Germany, officially the Federal Republic of Germany. West Germany's economic recovery was complete by 1970. The West Germans enjoyed the largest population and the biggest economy in Western Europe. Without question, West Germany was the economic engine of the European Economic Community (EEC). It was also the European mainstay of NATO, home to most of the alliance's armies and weaponry, as well as the main zone of confrontation with the Soviet tank armies across the Iron Curtain. But Germany was still a country divided. Seventeen million Germans remaining under the Soviet occupation that operated through the local Communist tyranny in East Germany, officially the German Democratic Republic (GDR).

The fate of the GDR remained a lively though not usually dominant issue in West Germany. It was sufficiently important to factor in West German politics and to inform the approach of the Bonn government to East-West relations. The West Germans pursued an *Ostpolitik* – "Eastern Policy" – that aimed to reduce tensions and build links with the East, reassuring the Soviets while maintaining West Germany's ties to NATO and the EEC. *Ostpolitik* was first and foremost a German policy, adopted for German needs, but it had a fortuitous effect on what later became détente. *Ostpolitik* sought to stabilize Europe, a notion that meshed well with Kissinger's concept of détente. Moreover, by accommodating *Ostpolitik* within NATO, the alliance avoided unnecessary friction with West Germany, and kept moot the question of German neutrality. Not that everything went smoothly: the European allies were certainly keen not to be left out of Soviet-American talks. They were afraid that the United States would forget or compromise their interests to reach a superficial accord with the Soviet Union.[2] The Americans for their part did not want their own position compromised or undermined by European or Canadian desire to reach an agreement with the Soviet Union.[3] It was not an unreasonable concern: a true meeting of the minds with the allies was difficult to achieve, and in any case neither Nixon nor Kissinger was given to sharing responsibility in foreign policy. Without *Ostpolitik*, and the prospect of a stabilized Europe, it was hard to conceive of successful détente between the West and the USSR.[4]

For years the Soviet Union had worked to separate the two halves of NATO. Europe's destiny, the Soviets argued, pointed one way; North America's (meaning the United States') another. Although aimed at the United States, this policy was especially displeasing to Canada, whose policy had always attempted to maintain and expand Canada's European connections. When he visited Moscow in 1971, Trudeau therefore sought reassurance from Soviet premier Kosygin that if East-West negotiations were contemplated Canada would not be left out. It would have been equally to his benefit to have sought reassurance from the United States that the interests of the allies would be remembered in negotiations between Nixon and Brezhnev. Either way, Canada's interest in better Soviet-American relations was great. If it came to Soviet-American cooperation, Canada would not object.

Inevitably the Soviet Union and the West had different ideas when it came to defining a proper East-West relationship. The Soviets were fond of the words "peaceful coexistence," which had a particular meaning when it came to East-West relations. Canadian diplomats, and especially the experienced Canadian ambassador in Moscow, Robert Ford, believed that the Soviets were willing to abandon only direct confrontation, with its attendant political and military dangers. They did not renounce the goal of a world free from capitalism or the eventual triumph of socialism in general and the Soviet Union specifically.[5]

Ford was not especially worried about his own government's attitude to this intransigence, for it was not Canada that would make the difference in East-West negotiations. What was worrisome was that Nixon and Kissinger, in their lust for a public foreign policy coup in the US election year of 1972, would agree to something that essentially advantaged the Soviet Union.[6] In 1971 Trudeau avoided the pitfalls of Soviet-speak when he and Brezhnev signed a harmless "protocol" providing for Soviet-Canadian consultations – all couched in the future indefinite tense. Nixon, in contrast, unwittingly conceded what the Soviet leaders considered to be a real triumph through a concession of strategic arms parity.[7]

From the Soviet point of view, détente logically fell into three parts. The Soviet Union signed a strategic arms limitation treaty (SALT) with the United States. East-West discussions dealing with security in Europe proceeded, essentially defining security as the stabilization of the existing political division of the continent. But in Africa and Asia, and on the high seas, the Soviet Union proceeded with a policy of expansion and adventurism, sustaining client states in Angola, Mozambique, and Ethiopia and providing extensive support for Castro's dictatorship in Cuba.

Castro for his part propped up international socialism by sending expeditionary forces to Africa.[8] The United States and NATO became alarmed at the projection of communist power into Africa. As a result, strategic assessments in the later 1970s took on a pessimistic cast, to which the Soviet Union's own policies contributed mightily. Simultaneously Castro rebuffed American attempts to ease relations with his island nation.[9]

The Soviet armed forces grew steadily throughout the 1970s. Tanks stationed in the Soviet part of Europe increased by almost a third, armoured personnel carriers by 79 percent, and artillery by 38 percent.[10] Starting in 1977, the Soviets deployed new and powerful rockets in Europe, upsetting the strategic balance and making a mockery of détente. Finally, in 1979, the Soviet Union occupied by force the neighbouring country of Afghanistan, helping set in motion the events that would destroy the Communist system and the Soviet Union itself.

On the Western side of the détente ledger, there was talk. From the Canadian point of view, the greatest store was placed on Mutual Balanced Force Reduction talks (MBFR), a continuation of disarmament discussions dating back in various stages to the 1950s. These began in 1973, in Vienna; they would last until finally terminated in January 1989.[11] Less important, and less hopeful, the Canadians thought, were discussions on reducing tensions in Europe, to which the Americans and Canadians were invited. Détente made possible the Conference on Security and Cooperation in Europe (CSCE). Preliminary talks took place in Helsinki in 1972, followed by detailed negotiations in Geneva in 1973-1975. Trudeau followed these events only generally, while Mitchell Sharp, as external affairs minister, gave his ambassadors (successively Michael Shenstone and Thomas Delworth) their head.

Sharp attended the opening session of the CSCE, in Helsinki in 1973. For the minister, it seemed that the conference was "a rather forlorn hope." But it was important for the hundreds of thousands of Canadians who had been born behind the Iron Curtain, to whom it represented the prospect, however distant, of family communication and reunification, and perhaps even liberalization and freedom for the countries they had fled. It was an occasion for the Liberals to cement their links to most of the immigrant communities of Canada; but it might be more.[12]

The negotiations dealt with three areas, called in conference jargon "baskets." The first was security – essentially securing the boundaries and confirming the division of Europe. The second was economics and technology. Basket three, on human rights, was labelled "Cooperation in Humanitarian and Other Fields." The Canadian delegation took a strong interest in this basket, as did various voluntary humanitarian organizations – part of what in the 1990s and later would be called "civil society."

The treaty that resulted from the CSCE discussions was signed in Helsinki in August 1975. It gave the Soviet Union pretty much what it wanted in baskets one and two – indeed the Soviets were so eager to get an agreement that they lost the initiative in the overall negotiations. As Delworth later argued, "the Soviet Union was on the run throughout the talks."[13] In terms of basket three, the Soviets promised to respect human rights, foster family reunification, and allow a certain amount of external interest in how they conducted themselves domestically and with their allies. Some Soviet leaders found these provisions alarming, but spurred on by Foreign Minister Andrei Gromyko's sense of the advantages of baskets one and two, they swallowed it. Like the Soviet policy of Third World adventurism, this too would have unexpected consequences. Ironically, the hard-liners were right: the CSCE opened a window on the West, and thereby helped undermine Soviet order.

In hindsight, it may seem surprising that the Soviet Union could deal with the United States from a position of strength, essentially as an equal. Brezhnev himself admitted in a speech to the American Congress that the Soviet Union had its problems, though prudently he did not elaborate on them. He did have some arguments on his side. The Soviet Union did have a substantial pile of nuclear warheads, and rockets to deliver them, and that fact was naturally impressive. That they were growing was not a subject Kissinger wished to dwell upon. The Soviet armed forces were large and apparently formidable. There was, of course, a social and economic cost to such militarization, which Western academic analysts generally ignored.[14]

Beneath the burden of military power, the Soviet economy was palpably sputtering. Canadian diplomats in Moscow reported that the civilian economy was no longer delivering the goods, that during the 1970s the Soviet standard of living was falling, not rising.[15] That it could nevertheless sputter along was owing to the structure of the Soviet economy – low or no wages for large segments of the workforce – and favourable economic relations with its unlucky satellites in Europe.[16]

Petro-Politics

Not only the Soviet economy was sputtering in the 1970s. In the West, including Canada, unemployment slowly rose while government spending seemed to do little but encourage inflation. This phenomenon, dubbed "stagflation," undermined the public's belief that governments could reliably manage the economy or economic conditions.[17] This change in public perceptions would eventually fuel the conservative revival of the 1980s, with definite effects on foreign policy, economic and political. For the time being, in the 1970s, it merely led to a souring of the public mood and a diminution of tolerance for large and expensive public projects.

The government reacted to the economic downturn in a number of ways, which sometimes were not compatible. It lowered tariffs to battle inflation, and it raised them to protect jobs. It fiddled with domestic programs and unemployment entitlements. It fretted with the question of "control" of the Canadian economy, promoting studies and agencies to slay the dragon of "foreign" – meaning American – investment. No part of the economy was more subject to foreign control than the oil sector, where, from extraction to refining to retail sales, foreign oil companies predominated, as Canadians were reminded every time they filled up at Esso, or Sunoco, or Texaco.

The Liberals were uneasily aware that to their left the tides of nationalism and anti-capitalism were rising. With the Trudeau government dependent on the NDP for parliamentary survival, its ear was more closely attuned to voices that argued that Canada had too much foreign ownership, too much foreign direction, and too little Canadian management. That management could be private or, preferably for the NDP, public but it must be Canadian. To show the way, the government in 1973 pushed through Parliament legislation creating a national oil company, Petro-Canada, which soon found a major role in public policy.

The conception that private enterprise was at best irresponsible and at worst evil was enhanced by a political-intellectual development of the late 1960s. In 1962 an American scientist, Rachel Carson, published *Silent Spring*, a book denouncing the careless and dangerous practices of large industrial corporations. The economy, she argued, was slowly poisoning the environment. Carson's analysis had its roots in conservationism, the idea that nature should be preserved or conserved against human depredation. It was a problem that in the 1950s and early 1960s was presumed to have been solved. Industry and especially industrial science were held to be the secure foundation of a prosperous society, not merely harmless to the environment.

Western society in the 1950s and 1960s had revelled in increasing physical abundance, reflected in the extraction and conversion of minerals into everything from skyscrapers to clothing to fuel. Fuel was cheap and getting cheaper: oil hovered around US$3.00 a barrel for the first twenty-five years after 1945. Taking inflation into account, a barrel of oil cost 40 percent less in 1970 than in 1945. Cheap oil meant increased consumption. As long as that consumption was based on stable or increasing oil reserves in the West, it could be sustained. But what if Western wells ran dry? What if (eventually) everybody's oil wells gave out? What then? The question became increasingly pertinent, as American production had exceeded new petroleum discoveries since 1960. In Canada, production first exceeded new reserves in 1970. And oil was only one of many dwindling resources.

A group calling itself the Club of Rome achieved considerable success putting about the theory that human population was outstripping available resources. As a Canadian advocate of the club later put it, resource failure was not only inevitable but imminent. "In the view of many of us," Dr. J.R. Whitehead, then principal science adviser in the Privy Council Office, later wrote, "even in the 1960s, we were already passing the level of world population that could conceivably be sustained. Even if, by some miracle, all politicians in the world could be persuaded to work cooperatively and rationally towards the slowing of population growth, it was already very late. The process should have been started years before; now, in the 1960s, it was desperately urgent."[18] The club's founder and moving spirit, the Italian Aurelio Peccei, visited Ottawa and dined with Trudeau and some senior advisers (including Jean Chrétien). He found them a sympathetic audience, which translated into occasional financial support for the club's activities from the government of Canada.

The Club of Rome had a problem. Its analysis and its proposed solutions were unpopular, if not politically poisonous. No politician could appear before the electorate and advocate a massive change in lifestyle or a reduction in habits of consumption. Warnings of scarcity did no good as long as the scarcity was notional rather than actual. It required a touch of stringency, some real shortage, to cause the club's prescriptions (which Peccei embodied in a book, *The Limits to Growth*, in 1972) to be accepted.[19]

There were those who took the idea of scarcity of natural resources very much to heart and who were ready to oblige. Oil scarcity was a theory that petroleum producers found very interesting. Oil was absurdly cheap. If it was recognized to be scarce and getting scarcer, then its price should rise. A prudent oil producer could both raise the price and restrict supply; oil in the ground was money in the bank.

These developments put in peril Canada's domestic and foreign oil policies, which were based on surplus rather than scarcity and on a careful balance between cheaper foreign imports and more expensive domestic production. Since 1961, Canadians west of a line near the Ottawa valley purchased Alberta oil at $3.00 a barrel, while Canadians east of the line bought oil from Venezuela at $2.50 a barrel.[20] Atlantic Canadians liked their oil cheap, as did Quebeckers. Being part of Canada did not oblige Quebeckers to "buy Canadian." They could have their cake and eat it too, and, if not, there was always the possibility they would leave the country. Although other Canadians were not actively considering this option, regional delicacy – the balance of power and advantage among Canada's parts – inhibited Ottawa from integrating supply and prices in all parts of the country.

Externally, Canadian oil policy consisted of trying to sell as much Canadian oil to the United States as possible. Canadian oil was abundant and secure, Canadian envoys argued to sceptical Americans. The Americans had their own priorities, foremost among them American oil producers who for years had used the argument of "national security" to keep foreigners out and US prices high. The Canadians combined enthusiasm for a continental energy policy with a proposal to run a pipeline through Canada from new oil discoveries on Alaska's North Slope.

At the same time, Canada resisted American desires to establish a tanker route from northern Alaska across Canadian Arctic waters to ports in the eastern United States. The Americans sent a reinforced tanker, the *Manhattan,* through the Arctic in 1969 to test the waters. Canadians protested furiously. The Arctic waters were not international but Canadian; any spillage from a tanker would have a devastating impact on the fragile Arctic ecosystem. The Americans defended their right to traverse what they claimed to be international waters, even if the waters were mostly solid ice. The result was a standoff. The *Manhattan* got through, but the voyage was so time consuming and costly that it deterred further such attempts. The Americans made clear their position on Arctic waters, and the Canadians disagreed with it. But lacking a concrete issue, the question subsided.

The Nixon administration, under pressure as a result of dwindling US oil reserves, slowly concluded that a continental policy would be best. It wanted "a common oil policy, connecting current and future Canadian reserves to our market."[21] The Americans offered full access to the American market in return for common planning for energy shortages. (They were worried about the security of eastern Canada's oil supply.) It took the Americans some time to make the offer; by the time they did, Canadian ardour had cooled. Nixon's August 1971 economic "shokku," as the Japanese termed it, and the acrimonious trade discussions with Secretary Connally did not improve the atmosphere. The "climate does not seem an appropriate one," Canadian negotiators told their American counterparts in October, suspending the energy talks.[22]

The Americans raised energy during Trudeau's visit to Washington in December 1971 and again during Nixon's visit to Ottawa in April 1972.[23] In December the prime minister already knew that the Americans wanted much but were offering little.[24] The Americans needed oil, and the Canadians wanted a pipeline piggyback connection that could bring their own oil and gas down from the Beaufort Sea – a project that would be economically unfeasible without the American link. That Nixon could not grant. Alaska wanted a trans-Alaska pipeline – an entirely Alaskan route, from the

Arctic Ocean to Valdez on the Pacific, whence the oil would be shipped south by tanker. What Alaska wanted, it got. The Canadians protested – with considerable prescience, as it turned out – that the decision was environmentally unsound and that a tanker accident was virtually inevitable. The American decision left Canada to consult its own interests, and to wait on events.

Canadian production of oil and gas had reached the limit of capacity by early 1973. Although pipeline capacity had expanded, there was not much more fuel to ship to the American market unless shipments to Canadian customers were cut back. Anticipating that possibility, the Trudeau government introduced a licensing system for oil exports.

For years discontent had been building among international oil suppliers at the dominance of the oil market by the United States and the great international oil companies, all but one of them American-owned. Oil prices had dropped in real terms, while the American government played complicated domestic political games designed to placate the interests of American suppliers. In reaction, a small group of oil producers, led by Venezuela and Saudi Arabia, formed the Organization of Petroleum Exporting Countries (OPEC). By 1971 OPEC included most of the world's major non-Western oil producers. OPEC members began to change the terms on which they sold oil, at first modestly and tentatively, and then increasingly boldly. The oil companies complained to the US government, which paid little attention. In 1973 that government had little attention to spare, being convulsed by the tremendous domestic political scandal that was Watergate, but in October it had no choice but to turn its attention to a first-class international crisis.

On 6 October 1973 the armies of Egypt and Syria attacked the state of Israel. The Egyptians in particular were initially victorious, inflicting painful casualties on the Israelis, but eventually the Israeli armed forces turned the tide. A historian of Arab-Israeli relations calls the result "something of a draw," and in terms of its eventual effects that may have been so.[25] For a few weeks in October, however, it seemed as though the very existence of Israel was threatened. To preserve that country, the United States intervened with massive shipments of arms. That intervention was decisive. Israel was preserved, the war ended without either side gaining a decisive advantage, and finally, in 1978, Egypt, the most important Arab state, made peace with Israel.

The possibility of an eventual peace between Israel and its Arab neighbours was certainly an important consequence of the war. Equally important, however, was the weapon the Arabs chose to retaliate against the United States and the other Western nations that sympathized with Israel. In the last stages of the war, on 19 October, the Arab oil-producing states announced an embargo on shipments of oil to the United States and to other countries sympathetic to Israel. They then raised the price of oil from $3.00 to $5.00 a barrel, effective immediately, and announced progressive reductions in oil production until Israel withdrew from the territories it had occupied in 1967. These moves shattered Western solidarity. As the historian Ethan Kapstein put it, "The Europeans got the message loud and clear." Only Portugal allowed US planes bound for Israel to land and refuel, while the British and French cheerfully sold arms to various Arab states – but not to Israel.[26]

There was no politically effective pro-Israel lobby in Great Britain or France, but there was in Canada. Mitchell Sharp, who represented a largely Jewish riding in north Toronto, knew that Israel was important to his constituents "as the symbol of the survival of the Jews" after the Holocaust, as one rabbi put it. Canadian bilateral relations with the countries of the Middle East were mostly economic: political issues were dealt with, gingerly and hesitantly, at the United Nations. As Peter Dobell suggests in his study of Canadian foreign relations in this period, "Canada failed to anticipate events in the Middle East and to look out for its long-term interests."[27] It might be as true to say that the Canadian government hesitated to define what those interests might be.

Ottawa balanced between a commitment to the survival of Israel and an uneasy awareness that an Arab-Israeli compromise must be achieved if there was to be any hope of a lasting peace. The balance was symbolically demonstrated during a visit by External Affairs Minister Sharp to the Middle East in 1969. He visited Israel, and so he had to visit Egypt. Canadian officials told their American counterparts that "the meetings with Israeli and Egyptian officials proved to be a dramatic learning experience for Minister Sharp who had never visited the Middle East before. He came away deeply disturbed at what appears to be the absolute opposite positions taken by the two sides."[28] David Taras, in a study of Canadian-Israeli relations, attributes the "even-handedness" of the Canadian position to a balance between economic pressures resulting from the Arab oil embargo and the political representations of the Canadian Jewish community and its supporters.[29]

The economic pressures were very real. An anticipated shortage of Canadian supply – the transcontinental pipelines had reached capacity and demand kept rising – caused Canada to impose export quotas in the fall of 1973. Protests would be futile, the Americans were told.[30] The beginning of the rise in oil prices that September caused Ottawa to freeze the price of domestic oil. Imported oil would be subsidized so as to bring it down to the domestic level. The subsidy would be paid for by a tax on Canadian oil exports, bringing their price up to world levels. But what if there were not enough imported oil? The Atlantic provinces and Quebec depended on imports, and the Arab oil boycott, if extended to Canada, would cause misery there – not enough oil to heat homes, not enough gasoline to keep cars or trucks on the road.

No one knew whether Canada was a target of the Arab oil boycott or not. "The Canadians were ... concerned that they, too, might be subjected to a total boycott by the Arabs. Their foreign policy has been similar to that of the United States, and they are expecting the worst," American officials quoted Energy Minister Donald Macdonald as saying in October 1973.[31] Ottawa ordered its agencies to buy as much oil as they could, wherever they could, at whatever price. As Kapstein observes, "this was perfectly rational crisis behavior."[32].

The oil export tax fell mainly on shipments to the United States. That country had many problems to confront in October 1973. First, there was the problem of the Middle East, and the distinct lack of allied solidarity with regard to the region. On this score, the Americans were not unhappy with the Canadian government: "Canadian statements and actions in the Near East crisis," an American official wrote, "give us no apparent cause for offense." Nevertheless, a discussion with Donald Macdonald became "quite heated" when the energy tax was raised.[33] Under the pressure of shortages, Washington briefly considered retaliation.

Running down a list of possible retaliatory actions, ranging from cancelling the Defence Production Sharing Agreement of 1959 and ending intelligence cooperation to recalling the ambassador, the Canadian desk at the State Department advised that American interests would suffer considerable harm. Even unilaterally constructing a North Dakota engineering project called the Garrison Diversion, for which there was considerable local political support (and which the Canadians opposed because it would affect the water quality of Canadian streams) was not a good idea. In a revealing explanation, George Springsteen, an American official, demonstrated just how close American and Canadian interests – or the perception of their interests – were. "Many in the US, including top level officials concerned with environmental matters, share Canada's view," Springsteen wrote. "We would also probably be contravening the existing US-Canada Boundary Waters Treaty. Continuation with the project as now planned could be illegal, as well as contrary to our own environmental, agricultural and budgetary interests."[34] The division in the American government extended to Nixon's energy czar, William Simon, who reversed a position devised by the State Department, judging it unfair and excessively self-serving.[35]

Fortunately Canadian officials were keeping the Americans informed of what they were planning with regard to energy policy, promising that Canadian supplies to exposed Americans in the northern states would not be jeopardized. Canadians were selling to the United States at world prices, but the availability of Canadian oil probably acted as a modest brake on world prices.[36]

The crisis passed in the spring of 1974, when the Arab petro-states declared the boycott at an end. Production cutbacks were ended, but prices were not rolled back. The result was substantial inflation, which characterized western economies, including Canada's, for the rest of the 1970s.

Canadian-American oil discussions made little difference to the policies the Canadian government was following with regard to domestic oil supply and prices. The

Trudeau government, it should not be forgotten, was under extreme political pressure, its survival depending on a fragile balance of parties in the House of Commons. Following a Canada-first oil price policy, ensuring supplies to the Atlantic region and Quebec, and creating a Canadian oil company as a counterweight to the foreign oil giants were all politically popular policies. Trudeau was rewarded when, in the spring of 1974, he called a general election. The government's policies were popular, as a triumphant Liberal campaign showed. Canadians re-elected the Liberals, this time with a majority. Trudeau had received a second lease on political life, along with a valuable political lesson.

The mid-1970s were a time of relative stability in oil prices. The United States tried to shore up its position in the Middle East by strengthening its relations with Saudi Arabia and non-Arab Iran, using politics to reinforce economics. But an era had ended. Along with the defeat in Vietnam, the oil boycott and energy shortages spawned a sense that events were out of control or, at any rate, out of American and Western control.

For Canada the period was taken up by discussions with the Americans about pipelines from the Alaska oilfields to the midwestern and eastern United States. These would have to travel across Canada, a prospect that encouraged dreams of construction jobs and lucrative contracts. There was also the possibility of linking an American pipeline to Canadian oil and gas fields, particularly in the Beaufort Sea, east of Alaska, but the most practical route, along the Mackenzie River, proved to have too much local (mostly Native) opposition and political baggage attached to it. The two countries actually reached an agreement in 1977 to build a pipeline along the route of the Alaska Highway, but nothing came of it.[37]

THIRD OPTIONS AND DEAD ENDS

The experience of John Connally and the "shokku" of 1971 caused considerable reflection in Ottawa. Mitchell Sharp, the external affairs minister, had thirty years' experience at managing relations with the United States. Suddenly, in August 1971, the old rules seemed no longer to apply. The acutely frustrating negotiations that followed made Sharp worry that depending on the United States as an economic anchor might be unwise.

Trudeau and Nixon had asserted in 1971-1972 that Canada and the United States had distinct interests. Nixon even stated in a speech to the Canadian Parliament that "we have very separate identities" and that the two countries had "different interests." Yet in private discussions Nixon also stated that "altogether, Canada's position is one of 'paramount importance to us.' The US sees the relationship in terms of long-term goals and short-run problems."[38]

In retrospect, it is not unreasonable to conclude that the "special relationship," though shaken by Connally, was not dead. For reasons ranging from strategy to sentiment, the

United States treated Canada as a country whose interests were important, and complementary to American interests. Even in defence, where Trudeau was making cuts, Secretary of Defense Melvin Laird recalled that "Canada has tremendous strategic value in terms of surveillance and defense against Soviet bombers or submarines approaching the United States." While it was true that the Defence Production Sharing Agreement of 1959, governing joint defence procurement, resulted in a Canadian surplus, it would be unwise to abrogate it or alter it in a way that would apply "Buy American" provisions. That, Laird wrote, "would be seriously prejudicial to our complex defense interests in Canada."[39] It was clear that around Washington there was a strong disposition – everywhere but in Connally's office – to keep relations with Canada as they were. Canadian officials and politicians, however, drew a different conclusion.

Had the United States actually done what Connally seemed to threaten, choking off crucial Canadian exports and redrawing trade relations to suit itself, the economic and social consequences in Canada would have been grave. Canada had followed the call of geography and it had led to prosperity, but that prosperity entailed a high degree of dependence. Not for the first time, in 1971-1972 Canadians contemplated the consequences of that dependence with an eye to improving trade with partners other than the United States.

Canadian-European trade relations were managed through the General Agreement on Tariffs and Trade (GATT), and especially through the Kennedy Round, which had concluded in 1967 and had produced major cuts in tariffs on manufactures but little on agricultural products. Not surprisingly, the best results for Canada in the Kennedy Round came in reducing barriers to Canadian-American trade. Negotiations with the European Economic Community, on the other hand, were acrimonious. From the Canadian point of view, Europe conceded virtually nothing to Canada except through the "most favoured nation" feature of the GATT. From the European perspective, it was just the reverse.[40] There was no desire for a new GATT round, because Europe and the United States could not agree what a new round should do. Multilateral trading mechanisms were marking time in the early 1970s. If a Canadian initiative were to take root, it would have to be somewhere else, and in a different form.

There was no particular sentimental or political bond between Canada and Europe. When Europe thought of North America, it thought of the United States. Canada was not part of the European consciousness as it had been of the British. Moreover, given Ottawa's recent unilateral reduction of its NATO contingent, the time was not propitious for discussions with Europe of closer trade relations.

If Britain was fading in Canadian statistics and Canadian consciousness, the reverse was also true. The Commonwealth had occupied a large place in British affections and priorities in 1961-1962, when the British government first tried to enter the European Common Market. That was no longer the case by 1970. Edward Heath, who became Conservative prime minister that year and chief British negotiator with the European Economic Community (EEC) in 1961-1962, no longer cared much about the Commonwealth, nor was he especially enamoured of the transatlantic bond to the United States. He persuaded Georges Pompidou, the French president, that the Great Britain of 1971 was no longer an outward-looking imperial nation. On that reduced basis, Pompidou was ready to grant Britain admission to the EEC, and on Europe's terms.[41]

The Canadian government took an interest in the British negotiations with Europe. Canada still had preferential tariffs from the British, which would be lost when Great Britain joined the EEC. Europe's Common Agricultural Policy discriminated against non-European agricultural products and subsidized the produce of European farmers. Thus, Britain's admission to the EEC would mean Canada's bidding farewell to exports of wheat and apples and cheese to Great Britain, which would have to supply itself with expensive European equivalents. The Canadians demanded compensation from Britain and the EEC for lost advantage and lost markets, and Canadian negotiators proved tough bargainers on the issue. Nevertheless, the Canadians did not forget that it was the continent, not the United Kingdom, which offered the best prospects for trade.[42] Canada's position weakened accordingly, and its hope for concessions came to naught.

Great Britain, along with Denmark and Ireland, officially joined the EEC on 1 January 1973. The Six that had formed the original European Common Market were now the Nine, and soon they would be the Twelve, as Greece, Spain, and Portugal joined. Europe was a powerful trading bloc, and with the British inside it accounted for 12 percent of Canadian trade in 1973. That was enough for the Canadian government to give trade with Europe some consideration.

Europe was not the only major Canadian trading partner outside the United States. Japan had been rising steadily in importance, and Canadian economic relations with that country were good. The Japanese were interested in Canadian raw materials and agricultural products, to be shipped through Pacific ports. In 1973 trade with Japan was 7 percent of Canada's total; better still, trade was about two-to-one in Canada's favour. In the view of Michael Hart, an historian of Canadian trade, "Japan seemed to offer great potential as a trading partner with a future."[43]

The notion of expanded ties with Europe was present in *Foreign Policy for Canadians*, the government's 1970 policy statement. In the fall and winter of 1971-1972 the Department of External Affairs considered how best to justify and then develop an approach to Europe, and by April 1972 it had worked out a rationale. Devised by Klaus Goldschlag, a senior official, it laid down three alternatives or "options" for Canadian policy. These were, broadly, the status quo, "closer integration with the United States," and the pursuit of "a comprehensive long-term strategy to develop and strengthen the

Canadian economy and other aspects of its national life and ... reduce the present Canadian vulnerability."[44] Put that way, it was clear what the best choice should be. The foreign economic policy preferred by External Affairs became known as the "Third Option."

In April 1972 the department explained what it wanted: "Option 3 ... if it is to make sense and to be feasible, must be conceived as seeking important but limited changes in some dimensions of our relationship with the United States, which continues to involve extensive interdependence. The main burdens of the strategy initially are likely to be carried by domestic economic measures combined with vigorous efforts to diversify our economic relations, notably with Europe and Japan, and support for international efforts to restore or reconstruct international trading and monetary rules and mechanisms."[45]

The Cabinet wrangled over the Third Option: ministers from Western Canada consented on the understanding that Japan figure equally with Europe in the policy. On that basis Sharp announced the new policy in the dying stages of the 1972 election campaign. (The timing was coincidental: trade policy, especially a relatively sophisticated and theoretical trade policy, was not a vote grabber.) Canada would now seek a special relationship with Europe and Japan.

The Europeans were puzzled and not especially receptive. The French, who exercised disproportionate influence in the EEC, were especially sceptical. The French government, still Gaullist, could not bring itself to treat Canada as a serious country. The French finance minister, Valéry Giscard d'Estaing, took the view that Canada, English Canada at least, was doomed to be absorbed by the United States – a natural process, in his view. Nevertheless, if Canada made a formal approach, there must be a European response; courtesy demanded no less.

First, the Canadians and Europeans had to determine what Canada wanted. Canadian diplomats and ministers made clear that Ottawa was not offering preferential access to Canadian raw materials such as uranium.[46] It was therefore easy for the Europeans to agree that Canada could not establish a preferential relationship with Europe to replace the vanished British economic connection. GATT rules precluded anything short of a free trade area, an impossibility for the Europeans. An exclusive connection between Europe and Canada would complicate relations with the Americans, creating needless resentment and perhaps pressure to open the door wider – a lot wider – to include the United States. The idea of an enclosed European community would be lost.

External Affairs spent most of 1973 and 1974 formulating a proposal that could serve as the basis of negotiation. Forced into a practical framework, the Third Option began to shrink. Canada sought a "contractual link," one that would supplement, not contradict, the GATT. The Europeans were unimpressed. At a meeting in New York in September 1974, Canadian and European diplomats agreed they would undertake discussions in the hope that "the very act of negotiating" would lead to a definition of common interests and hence some kind of common link. The "very act of negotiating" involved discussions not only with the EEC's supervisory commission but with the various member governments. These governments needed to be reassured that the Canadian proposal would not lead to aggrandizing the powers of the commission, something the British and French in particular did not want.

Eventually, early in 1976, serious negotiations began and swiftly achieved completion if not success. In July a formal agreement was signed in Ottawa. The agreement did nothing to alter existing trade relationships. Canada and Europe gave each other most favoured nation status, but that was already granted under the GATT. There would be friendly consultations. There would be a Joint Cooperation Committee. There would be good feelings and good wishes.[47]

Canada went through a similar process with Japan, although in this case there was only one negotiating partner rather than nine sovereign interests to satisfy. The same constraints were imposed by the GATT. There was an exchange of visits, the Japanese prime minister coming to Canada and Trudeau returning the favour. In October 1976, during Trudeau's Japanese visit, a Framework Agreement for Economic Cooperation was signed. A Joint Economic Committee on a ministerial level was created. (This joint ministerial device is a favourite when no substantive agreement can be achieved. First tried with the Americans in the 1950s, it has seldom produced useful long-term results.)

A great deal of Canada's diplomatic expertise, time, and personnel were invested in the pursuit of the Third Option. It would be pleasant to report that the results were commensurate with the investment. But in both the short and the long term, this was certainly not the case. Economic relations with Europe and Japan and, most importantly, with the United States continued much as before. No special advantage was conferred on Canadian exporters or investors as a result of the agreements with Europe or Japan. There was an exchange of ambassadors with the EEC, but that exchange owed little to the Third Option.

One result of the Third Option was a gulf between the officially stated policy of the government and the practices and objectives of Canadian business. Business people were not enamoured with the policy. Except for those firms already engaged in Europe, the United States was the preferred market. The Japanese continued to seek Canadian raw materials exports but considered Canadian manufactures to be a doubtful commodity. As for investment, Canada was a small market, with a labour force prone to strikes. It was not an encouraging prospect from the Japanese standpoint. Canadian exporters, in turn, continued to regard Japan as a closed economic system.[48]

Ottawa was not unanimously committed to the Third Option. The Cabinet itself was divided, with only Trudeau and Mitchell Sharp genuinely interested.[49] Economic bureaucrats tended to view the Third Option exercise as an annoying and costly diversion of resources. Bureaucrats were not united on the subject, especially as the policy continually failed to bear fruit. As one diplomat remarked to a sceptical academic audience, "We are born into the Church of the Third Option, christened in it, married and buried in it. But in between ..." In between there were other things to do, and no time to waste.

The Third Option exercise was not especially innovative but was Canada's historical preference. Perched politically between the United States and Europe, Canadians relied on a tension between the attractions of Europe and America. Until the 1970s, Canada enjoyed a special relationship of sorts with one European country, Great Britain, through politics, culture, and economics. As Great Britain became less and less interested in and less capable of sustaining a relationship with Canada, there was a temptation to substitute the rest of Western Europe, and Japan, in the hope that they might together balance the attractions of the United States. The problem was that Europe and Japan had no interest in doing so.

The distance between Canada and Western Europe was widening in the 1970s, not contracting; at the same time, Canada's relationship with the United States was expanding and deepening, whether Canada liked it or not. That fact may account for the mild American reaction to the Third Option. "Well, there go the Canadians again," Ford's national security adviser remembered thinking. The Third Option was to be expected, but not taken seriously.[50] The Americans had no difficulty in assisting Canada in another foreign policy priority in 1975-1976, as what would become the G7 took form.

The economic sabre rattling of 1971 – the "shokku" – plus divergence on energy concerns suggested to the leaders of France and Germany that it would be a good idea to coordinate the economic policies of the major Western powers. The largest Western economies were those of the United States, Germany, Japan, France, and Great Britain, and the leaders of those five countries initially met in France in 1975 at the invitation of Valéry Giscard d'Estaing, the president of France.

Giscard's interest in a summit of heads of government coincided with an American realization that there was no effective mechanism for coordinating the economic policies of the Western democracies. The oil crisis and the Middle East impasse had driven a wedge between the United States and its European allies. Henry Kissinger, secretary of state under Gerald Ford, Nixon's successor, believed the United States had to act quickly to repair, or in some areas (such as energy) create, allied relationships. The notion was discussed among the French, Americans, British, and Germans in the summer of 1975. They agreed to expand the discussions from their original, narrowly monetary, focus to "encompass a much wider and more fundamental range of politico/economic issues, but with the emphasis on informal, and very private discussions."[51] With Japan's economy rapidly growing, it was impossible to ignore the Japanese, and so they would be invited. As the venue, Giscard chose Rambouillet, one of the French government's inexhaustible store of elegant chateaux. Giscard as host had control of the invitations. They went to the obvious "big five." But Italy, the European economy next in rank below that of France, Germany, and Great Britain, had protested its exclusion. Italy was a neighbour and a European, and France extended it an invitation. Up to this point, there was a logic to the invitations. The five original summiteers represented the largest economies of the world. The size of the Italian economy, however, was surpassed by that of Canada. The designers of the summit, George Shultz of the United States, Giscard, and Helmut Schmidt, had noted the importance of Canada in a conversation in Paris in September and had agreed at that time to include Canada if Italy were invited.[52]

The Canadians pricked up their ears. If Italy was to be invited, then obviously Canada should be as well. Giscard now had second thoughts. He would offend some of his supporters by giving credence to the idea that Canada had international importance. It would add another non-European participant to the conclave, one, moreover, that was close to the United States. The British and Americans protested on Canada's behalf. President Ford actually considered refusing Giscard's invitation if Canada were not invited. Giscard, in Ford's opinion, "was abusing the technical advantage of being the host." Rather than cause an international incident, the US president decided to get even. The United States would host the next economic summit, in Puerto Rico, and they would simply invite Trudeau to attend.[53]

External Affairs Minister Allan MacEachen fulminated in public, denouncing the French, but Canadian diplomats were quick to comment, in private, that the minister could not have meant what he said. It would be counterproductive to pick a quarrel with France after years of "laborious and lengthy efforts to bring Canadian-French relations back to ... normalcy."[54] Canadian protests were met with genial and unyielding indifference from the French.[55] Giscard did attempt an explanation in a letter to Trudeau, arguing in effect that he acted according to immutable laws of protocol, if not the configuration of the constellations that were, presumably, unintelligible to non-Frenchmen.[56] But thanks to Ford and Kissinger, in 1976 Canada joined the economic summits, then called the Group of Seven, or G7.

In the 1970s Trudeau's contribution to the G7 was modest. He liked Ford, and Ford's Democratic successor, Jimmy Carter, and Ford and Carter returned the compliment. Carter preferred Trudeau's conciseness and sharp intelligence to the windy sermonizing of German chancellor Helmut Schmidt. Some Canadians sympathized with Carter; observing Schmidt at close quarters as he toured Canada, they noted what they considered to be his contempt for the country, and for Trudeau. According to Trudeau's external affairs minister, Mark MacGuigan,[57] however, Schmidt and Trudeau often thought along the same lines, to the point where Trudeau sometimes voiced what Schmidt was thinking, though in his own manner and style.[58] It helped relations that the external affairs minister, Mark MacGuigan, found the German foreign minister, Hans-Dietrich Genscher, both congenial and impressive.[59]

Trudeau performed ably at the summits, though not enough to overcome Giscard's indifference. He got along well with the successive British prime ministers Harold Wilson and James Callaghan.[60] By the late 1970s the summits were becoming well established and were starting to develop their own bureaucracy, including the institution of "sherpas," senior officials who were to escort and guide their respective leaders to the summit.

The early summits coincided with a shift in economic thought. In France and Germany especially, there was a reaction to the inflationary trend in American public finance, and towards a restriction of government spending.[61] Keynesian pump-priming was out, and high interest rates were in. Most of the participants at the early summits were liberally inclined, and their discussions do not seem to have been especially disputatious.

Trudeau later wrote that he enjoyed the informality of the summits. Apart from the British, he probably had the most experience in attending such gatherings, because of the Commonwealth heads-of-government meetings. Trudeau had tried to alter the Commonwealth meetings in the direction of informal exchanges, to end the rigid posturing of formal speeches, and he had had some, though not complete, success. When he hosted a Commonwealth meeting in Ottawa in the summer of 1973, he shaped its agenda and its meetings to allow for a maximum of informal discussion.[62] (Behind the scenes there was a great deal of careful preparation, personally supervised by Ivan Head, who visited each Commonwealth capital and recorded what interested each leader.)[63] Certainly, Canadian observers believed that Trudeau's procedural reforms helped preserve the Commonwealth meetings. At the G7, each leader brought two ministers into the room (finance and external affairs, in Canada's case); it was, however, usually the leaders who spoke. The result, according to Trudeau, was a thorough discussion and greater understanding, if not always agreement.[64]

NEW WORLD ORDERS

The oil price shock was the first occasion when a group of countries usually considered to be underdeveloped or less developed had managed to reverse the terms of their trade with the developed world, and to extract large sums of cash in return for their raw material, oil. The impact on the petro-states was dramatic. Jeddah in Saudi Arabia became one of the most expensive places to live in the world. Thanks to the country's oil revenues, the sparse Saudi population paid no income tax and imported workers from abroad. Kuwait selected from among the world's best architects to design its new public buildings, including a parliament and central bank.[65]

The effect elsewhere in the Third World was different. The economies of most African states – those without oil – regressed as they siphoned off money to pay exorbitant fuel costs. Aid programs could not make up the difference. In Canada's case, as rising costs consumed the federal budget, the government felt it could afford less, not more, in aid. Aid expenditures began to sink.

The oil price rise was not universally seen as a bad thing, even among those most negatively affected. It furnished a model for breaking the tie of dependency that linked the underdeveloped world to the developed, in which poor countries traded on rich countries' terms, to the advantage of the latter. What had been done with oil might be done with some other commodity, or many commodities, turning what had been a buyer's world into a seller's market.

The notion of development was a progressive idea. Countries became more developed, acquired education for their people, and developed cities, manufacturing, and services. There was nothing new in this. The Soviet Union, so it was thought, had willed an entire economic infrastructure into existence, at vast cost but also in adverse circumstances.[66] The Chinese government believed it was doing the same. They were, of course, creating late-nineteenth-century economies that were between fifty and a hundred years out of date. Even Quebec's modernizing separatists believed that their province could never be a proper country without its own steel industry, and they proceeded at great public cost to create one.

Underdeveloped countries added the argument that they were underdeveloped because of the nature of the old colonial system;[67] but their model of development was often taken from their former metropolitan power. In the old colonial system, it was the imperial powers that set prices and shaped markets; it was time for their former colonies to turn the tables. Conceding developing countries the power to fix prices for their products helped alleviate an intellectual conundrum for aid givers, many of whom felt uneasy over the nature of aid and its objectives.[68] Thus, while Canada continued to dispense traditional forms of aid, the Trudeau government also took an interest in Third World efforts in the United Nations to develop a New International Economic Order. In 1964 the UN had established a Conference on Trade and Development, which had met sporadically thereafter. A special session of the United Nations General Assembly in May 1974 passed a declaration that demanded a just price for raw materials. Nations should exercise absolute authority to run their economies as they saw fit. Developed countries should grant trade preferences as well as aid. It did not mention the recent precedent of oil; it did not need to.[69] The following December the General Assembly adopted the program laid down by the special session.

Canada was a country that produced raw materials, and some of Trudeau's entourage, especially Ivan Head, believed it had much in common with Third World producers of raw materials. Head argued as much in *Le Monde* in 1974, and he had plenty of company at home, especially in universities, and around the world.[70] In March 1975, over the fierce opposition of the Department of External Affairs, Head persuaded Trudeau to deliver a speech in London in praise of what he called "the global ethic," one "that abhors the imbalance in the basic human condition."[71] That was all very well, but what if it meant standing aside from Canada's allies in the developed world, or, worse still, offending voters at home?

Trudeau and Head understood that there would be a cost to an effective program of development assistance. It was a cost that, in their view, a rich country like Canada ought to be able to meet, but they recognized that a willingness to meet it could only be the product, as they saw it, of a "sophisticated and widespread" understanding of the importance of the problem.[72] At this point some of the Cabinet drew back. Preferential trade agreements with former colonies were fine in theory, but they must not damage the interests of Canadian industry or Canadian workers. It was unlikely that the political system could easily swallow economic concessions to Third World countries that directly affected Canadians. As prosperity faded during the 1970s, more and more Canadians concluded that charity began at home.

THE 1970S WERE THE CULMINATION OF A GENERATION of rational planners, competent organizers, and visionaries. Trudeau's government, although it did not entirely realize it, was the result of thirty years of anticipation, planning, intervention, and invention. In that sense, Trudeau and his principal foreign policy adviser, Ivan Head, were less innovative than they thought.

Circumstances were not always kind. Initially, Trudeau was lucky. When he took office, the great postwar economic boom had a few years yet to run. Canada was a country of constantly rising living standards, and its people were correspondingly optimistic. The twin monsters of the oil price rise and stagflation ended all that. Thereafter, Trudeau had a shorter lead for his innovations and less impact on the direction of Canadian policy. The 1972 election was a harbinger of things to come. By 1978 there was a craving for safety and predictability and consequently less tolerance for a policy that planned for long-term benefit over short-term advantage. As a politician, Trudeau learned to prefer short-term electoral success over almost any alternative. It made for good politics, certainly; but it made for sporadic and often inconsistent policy.

Trudeau had his share of good fortune too. The United States might have been a major complicating factor in Canadian foreign relations. Under Nixon, Ford, and Carter it was not. The end of the Vietnam War, and the manner of its ending – an American defeat – blunted the desire in Washington to take major initiatives in foreign policy. Many Americans judged that the allies who had hung back and refused to send troops to Vietnam had been right all along. The notion that there might be advantageous alternatives to militant and universal anti-communism prepared the way for Henry Kissinger's policy of détente. Greater American suppleness towards the Communist world permitted others, including Canada, to be similarly flexible.

Trudeau's flexibility satisfied some of his domestic constituency. Canada's political and intellectual elites preferred policies that not only avoided war but aimed at stability, if not permanence, in international arrangements. Because that was also the basic attitude of the American government in the same period, Trudeau could both appear to be a cooperative ally and indulge the preferences of Canada's articulate political class. In this respect, he was no more than a man of his times.

The times, however, were about to change.

19

CANADA FIRST,
1976-1984

The years from 1976 to 1984 are a study in contrasts in Canadian foreign policy. Any general history of the period would see those eight years as the climax of the Cold War, when the tension between the Soviet Union and the United States reached a new height, and, having peaked, began to decompress. The world was as dangerously divided in the late 1970s and early 1980s as at any point since 1945. Canadian politics and policy concentrated on domestic events, in an ironic reprise of Trudeau's 1970 White Paper and an unconscious parody of St Laurent's forgotten dictum that Canadian foreign policy must reflect Canada's own basic values and interests. Politically, those values at the end of the 1970s were contradictory and conflicted; Canadian foreign policy took on a provisional character. "Foreign countries," Arthur Andrew observed, "had the impression that Canada was in narcissistic disarray."[1]

The dominant issue was, of course, Quebec. The province passed from an uneasy federalism to a provisional separatism, and back, between 1976 and 1984. The eternal constitutional question with Quebec was supplemented in the late 1970s by a dispute with the western provinces that centred on oil, oil revenues, and the effect of an oil bonanza in the Canadian West on the national economy. Since the subject was oil, the object was Alberta. These parallel disputes consumed Canadian politics for Trudeau's last eight years in office. If during that period Canadian foreign policy was sometimes wobbly and inconsistent, the reason was clear: the problem of Quebec threatened the survival of the country, and consequently whether Canada would have any foreign relations at all, while the quarrel with Alberta looked to modify what kind of country foreigners would perceive.

QUEBEC SEPARATISM, CANADA, AND THE WORLD

Quebec was never absent from the Trudeau government's agenda. It was obvious that many French-speaking Quebeckers were unhappy with their place in Canada and believed that the six million French speakers in the valley of the St Lawrence ought to form not merely a nation but an independent nation. National liberation was something of a global fashion in the 1960s, which Quebec mimicked even if it were not yet able to implement it. French Quebeckers might be dissatisfied, might nurture a sense of grievance, but the legends of injustice, oppression, and suppression were not as vivid in Quebec as elsewhere. But the 1960s were an era of disturbance, and the whiff of revolution was in the air, mixed with incense and pot. The turmoil reached a climax in 1970, with the kidnapping of the British trade commissioner in Montreal, James Cross, and the kidnapping and murder of the provincial minister of labour, Pierre Laporte.

After Laporte's death, Quebec society drew back from the brink. The cause of independence, disparaged as separatism among English-speakers, was channelled into party politics, and a political party, the Parti Québécois (PQ), was formed to promote it. The party had a credible politician, René Lévesque, at its head. Lévesque, an attractive and magnetic if not precisely charismatic personality, drew supporters from among the province's intellectual community and, especially, from French-speaking youth.

The PQ was strategically placed. "Softer" nationalists, those who did not espouse formal independence as a goal or solution to Quebec's problems, gravitated to the Liberals, who stretched out to accommodate them, and who then became a quasi-federalist party, dissatisfied with Canada as it was, but never enough to go over to independence. Robert Bourassa, the young Liberal leader, and premier of the province from 1970 to 1976, proclaimed that he was a devotee of "fédéralisme rentable" – "profitable federalism." Consciously or not, Bourassa – an economist by training – put a price on Quebec's allegiance. That left "pure" federalism to the federal Liberals, and Trudeau, who was not reluctant to take up the cause.

From the federal government's point of view, international circumstances were more benign in the 1970s than in the 1960s where Quebec was concerned. The main difference was an evolution in the politics of France and developments in Quebec's relations with that country. Paradoxically, on the level of public opinion, the French were probably more disposed to the idea of Quebec independence in the 1970s and 1980s than they were in the 1960s; what was lacking was a French politician willing to put the idea into effect, or to forward it on the French political agenda.

France was prosperous in the 1970s, and more or less content. There was a balance of interests in French politics; swings from right to left to right were getting smaller, as government passed from centre right to centre left, and back again. France was increasingly integrated in Europe, and European interests and priorities had repercussions in that country. A united Europe might originally have been designed to place Germany under a kind of permanent surveillance, but it had its effects on all the European partners, turning them inward and replacing or at least modifying older traditions of nationalist politics with a new conception of the common interest. Where de Gaulle cherished dreams of France across the seas, his successors believed that the transatlantic region was primarily the interest and business of the United States. They had difficulty seeing Canada, but they had difficulty seeing Quebec too. France's interventions in Quebec still had the capacity to make mischief, but if independence were ever to come about it would be because of internal events, not external inducements.[2]

Quebec's "transatlantic" status was evolving, in fact, changing. In the 1950s Quebec was, according to public opinion polls, the most anti-American part of Canada. In the 1960s radical separatists saw the United States and capitalism as major obstacles on the road to the independence of the socialist republic of Quebec. The United States was the citadel of capitalist imperialism, which kept the whole world in chains, Quebec included. "Le Vietnam aux Vietnamiens," demonstrators chanted. "Le Québec aux Québécois."[3]

In the 1970s radical separatism was denatured, often by the same people who had been radical militants in the 1960s. They and their successors sometimes saw the United States as neutral; as often, they liked the United States and admired Americans. The PQ leader René Lévesque had served as a war·correspondent with the American army during the Second World War and all his life maintained an affection for Americans, whom he saw as distinctly preferable to English Canadians. Lévesque, no Francophile, believed that too close attention from France to Quebec might backfire with the Quebec electorate.[4]

It logically followed that the United States, not France, would be the key to Quebec's independence. Americans vacationed in Quebec, and sometimes came to live there. Quebeckers voyaged south, in search of the ocean (which they found in Maine, at Old Orchard and other beaches) or heat (which they found in Florida).[5] Except for a few eighteenth-century relics, Quebec cities looked like their American counterparts. For two centuries the Roman Catholic Church had tried to keep secular, English-speaking, and Protestant influences – American as well as English-Canadian – at bay, but those defences collapsed in the great secularizing wave of the 1960s. Nor did Quebec entirely escape the homogenizing wave of the American media, though more than English Canada it preserved its own distinctive television soap operas even while its children listened to American popular music and strove to imitate it.

On 15 November 1976 the PQ under Lévesque narrowly defeated Bourassa's Liberals. Bourassa's term of office had been beset by strikes, disruption, and discontent. There were rumours of scandal, faithfully repeated by the media. The premier's dismal record allowed the PQ to run as the party of good government, promising to hold a referendum that would give Lévesque only a mandate to negotiate a political divorce coupled with an economic union with the rest of Canada – a proposition called "sovereignty-association."

Lévesque's victory had been widely predicted, but when it happened the shock was profound. Never before had there been the serious possibility that a Canadian province would secede. In Ottawa, the Trudeau government went into crisis mode, mobilizing the government's resources against the danger of separatism. The real fight, Trudeau correctly decided, would be over Lévesque's promised referendum. Until that was held, there would be a constant struggle for the hearts and minds of French Quebeckers.

Trudeau and his entourage immediately identified the attitude of the United States as a crucial factor. Relations with the Americans would help determine whether independence would be seen as a risky business by the Quebec electorate. If the Americans showed uncertainty or hostility to the project of Quebec independence, many Quebeckers would draw back. Independence was all very well, but independence plus uncertainty, if not actual economic loss, was not a useful gamble.

American diplomats were familiar with Canada's political troubles, especially separatism. Even in the 1950s Americans observed the cultural and economic divide separating English and French Canadians. In the 1960s, the US embassy commented on the inability of the Pearson government to lay the issue to rest, while in 1970 the regularly scheduled meeting of Canadian and American Cabinet officers coincided with the height of the terrorist crisis. Secretary of State William Rogers, leading the US delegation, commented: "The most striking single aspect of our visit to Ottawa was the preoccupying, almost obsessive, concern of the Canadians for the survival of the Confederation. Canadian ministers and officials spoke freely in private conversations about the possibility of a break-up of the country, even speculating about what choices might then be made by the different regions and provinces. In the formal discussions, the dominating Canadian theme was the search for national unity. And as is to be expected, attitudes toward the United States are colored by this constant concern for holding Canada together."[6] Surprised and disturbed by the apparent fragility of the Canadian political system, Rogers and his entourage did their best publicly to shore up the Trudeau government.

Until 1976 discussion anywhere about Quebec's separation from Canada was theoretical and remote. Devising an actual policy was quite a different matter. Knowing that the US embassy would be speaking to Washington on the matter, a parade of anxious visitors, official and unofficial, called on the American ambassador, Thomas Enders. The ambassador commented that his visitors were "genuinely uncertain what Washington's reaction to the PQ victory would be."[7]

At that point, there was a change of administrations in Washington. The Democrat Jimmy Carter defeated the Republican incumbent, Gerald Ford, in the November elections but would not take office until January 1977. Enders immediately briefed Carter on the situation in Quebec and Canada. There were two questions to consider. First, should the US government view the separation of Quebec and the possible destruction of Canada with judicious neutrality? Second, what should Washington do if (or when) the government of Quebec attempted to establish a relationship with the United States? Canada was too close a neighbour, and too similar a country, for the United States to be indifferent. A democratic, transcontinental federation, Canada paralleled its southern neighbour in more than geography. There were tremendous economic, strategic, and political interests at stake. As for what to say to or about Quebec, Enders recommended "that we comport ourselves in such a way as to leave no doubt of any possible support to Quebec." Enders later recalled that nobody in his government disagreed with that proposition.[8]

The governments of Canada and Quebec had competing pitches to put to American audiences. Lévesque spoke first, to the Economics Club of New York, in January 1977. His speech drew comparisons between Quebec's struggle for independence and the American Revolution two centuries earlier. The argument was strained and historically fanciful, and, as far as the audience was concerned, Lévesque "laid an egg."[9] Trudeau's response was already in train. In November 1976, shortly after the Quebec election, he had been invited to address a joint session of Congress, the first time a Canadian prime minister had been so honoured. Trudeau rose to the occasion in a speech delivered on 22 February 1977. The medium, in this case, was the message. Trudeau and Canada had the prestige to command such a pulpit, and the ability, in Trudeau's case, to reaffirm his faith in federalism. This time, the parallel between Canada and the United States was obvious and acceptable to his audience.[10]

Subtly but unmistakably, the US government made it clear that a united Canada was preferable to any alternative on offer. The Americans also rebuffed Quebec's attempts to establish a formal relationship. Lévesque himself did not want to go too far too fast. As Allan Gotlieb, then undersecretary of state for external affairs, later put it, "on the whole Mr. Levesque's approach to foreign affairs was more incremental than revolutionary."[11]

The American attitude helped the atmospherics of the Canadian-American relationship. Trudeau and Carter thought similarly on world problems. In the first part of his administration, Carter tried hard to reach an accommodation with the Soviet Union, while in other parts of the world, like Central America and Africa, he refrained from deploying American power. Difficult problems were handed to Vice President Walter Mondale, a former senator from Minnesota, assisted by an experienced staffer from the National Security Council, Denis Clift. Mondale met the Canadian ambassador, Peter Towe, regularly, which the Canadian embassy rated as "probably unique on the Washington diplomatic scene." Other Cabinet-level officers were equally cordial, and the overall effect was from the Canadian point of view extremely positive. "Our dealings with the Carter Administration [are] the smoothest in recent history," Allan Gotlieb, the undersecretary, purred in 1978.[12] Ambassador Towe described the atmosphere as the best since the 1950s, when Hume Wrong was an intimate friend of Dean Acheson.[13]

Carter's cooperation did not go unrequited. Trudeau was happy to provide extra Canadian oil shipments to cope with a harsh winter in the northern tier – a useful gesture for Carter. There was cooperation from the Carter administration on a number of other items as well, though with less happy results. Ottawa and Washington sought to negotiate their way out of competing claims on the North Atlantic fishery – a problem since 1776. The two countries clashed over the maritime boundary in the Gulf of Maine, which had important implications for the harvesting of scallops by one or the other partner. On one occasion, the Canadian navy moved a boundary marker, almost provoking a response (and a possible confrontation) from the US navy; but the American navy was told to stand down, and the incident passed.[14] The Canadians assigned Marcel Cadieux to the maritime boundary question: he proved a tough and very successful negotiator. He was in fact too successful, for the treaty, duly presented to the US Senate, was obnoxious to powerful senators and languished there for several years until withdrawn by Carter's successor, Ronald Reagan. There was also frustration in Ottawa over Carter's inability to resolve the gas pipeline issue, and there were difficulties over the Law of the Sea.[15]

Trudeau approved other items in Carter's foreign policy, especially his treaty with Panama, providing for an eventual American withdrawal from the Canal Zone, a postcolonial remnant.[16] The treaty was controversial in the United States and probably damaged Carter's domestic political standing; Trudeau pointedly showed his support by attending the signing ceremony in Washington.[17]

Trudeau's successful foreign linkages, especially with Carter, meant that French support for separatism, and even covert promises that France would be the first to recognize an independent Quebec, had far less importance inside Quebec than they might have a decade earlier. With Carter's policy fixed, even promises by the separatists that they would maintain Quebec membership in NATO and NORAD had no effect. As a result, foreign relations played very little part in the first Quebec referendum, held in May 1980. Trudeau and federalism won by a sizeable margin (60 to 40 percent). For the balance of his time in office, Quebec separatism was dormant, though not yet dead.

THE END OF DÉTENTE

At the end of the 1970s a series of events signalled a change in the diplomatic climate. Beginning in 1977, the Soviet Union deployed medium-range ballistic missiles, called SS-20s, in Eastern Europe. In 1978, Cuban troops arrived in Ethiopia to shore up that country's Marxist regime. In 1979, Soviet troops intervened in neighbouring Afghanistan, already a Soviet satellite, and ignited a ten-year struggle between Soviet power and Muslim guerrillas. These events had their roots in Soviet politics, although they were also probably inspired by a Soviet conviction that the United States, weakened by the Vietnam War, distracted by the energy crisis, and bogged down in a hostage crisis in Iran (where the staff of the US embassy had been kidnapped by Iranian fanatics) was in no shape to respond.

It was a serious misjudgment.[18] Jimmy Carter's national security adviser, Zbigniew Brzezinski, told the president that it was unclear whether there was a grand design or whether the Soviets were merely being opportunistic.[19] Brzezinski urged a firm response; in contrast, Secretary of State Cyrus Vance counselled calm, arguing that the Soviets were overreaching and would inevitably fail. Either way, Carter faced a serious dilemma. Polls showed that Americans considered their government adrift, weak, and uncertain. Carter dared not risk further erosion in his standing with a presidential election looming in 1980. The Europeans were also a problem. The Germans and the French saw the Soviet missile deployment as a direct threat; unless NATO and particularly the United States responded, Western Europe would be hostage to Soviet nuclear blackmail.

It was Afghanistan that occupied the headlines and dominated public debate in the United States. Carter announced a halt to American sales of wheat to the Soviet Union and proclaimed a boycott of the next Olympic Games, to be held in Moscow.[20]

In Canada, news of Afghanistan had to compete with domestic events, which included a federal election campaign in the spring of 1979. Foreign policy had played a marginal role in the election, mostly on issues that revolved around Israel. Trudeau's government was cautious on the question of Israel. Generally, Canada supported UN resolutions that asked Israel to withdraw from its 1967 conquests and return to its prewar boundaries; on the other hand, Canada did not ask that Israel do so before its security was guaranteed.[21] The Israeli government, then headed by the right-wing politician Menachem Begin, had been pressing Canada to recognize its capital as Jerusalem – thereby accepting the legitimacy of at least part of Israel's conquest of the Arab West Bank in the 1967 Six Day War. This Canada, like other Western countries, had not done, basing the policy on UN resolutions that looked to the restoration of the pre-1967 borders. In 1976 the Democratic presidential candidate Jimmy Carter had promised such recognition. Once elected president, Carter conveniently forgot the promise when it became clear that Arab opinion would be profoundly offended.

Menachem Begin, on a visit to Canada in 1978, urged Trudeau to grant recognition. When Trudeau demurred, Begin told him he would make Canada's non-recognition an issue with Jewish voters in the soon-to-be-held Canadian election. Trudeau replied that Begin's tactic would not "be very courteous – or very effective."[22] But Begin did it anyway, setting the scene for Trudeau's Conservative opponent, Joe Clark, to capitalize on what he perceived to be a Liberal political faux pas. Clark promised to do what Trudeau would not, as part of a series of dramatic election promises. The object was to detach traditionally Liberal Jewish voters from Trudeau. To a limited extent it was successful, helping Clark improve his standing in Toronto in a closely fought election where every seat counted. Trudeau lost the election, and Clark formed a minority government in June 1979. Trudeau never forgot the incident; it certainly did not improve his opinion of Begin, or of Israel.[23]

Clark now had the job of implementing his promise. There was a political premium on doing so, as his standing with the electorate was at best uncertain. Many expected that Clark would be unable to master the Ottawa bureaucracy – a sore point with Conservatives since Diefenbaker's experience in the 1960s.[24] Thus, it did not help that officials strongly advised the new prime minister not to recognize Jerusalem, and that even his newly appointed clerk of the Privy Council counselled delay. But Clark needed to look decisive and masterful more than he needed to look reflective or deliberative. He made the announcement of his Jerusalem policy one of his first official acts as prime minister. The promise was received with satisfaction by some spokespeople for the official Jewish community, but it did not command universal support among Canadian Jews.[25]

The reaction to Clark's initiative was not exactly what he might have desired. As predicted, Arab governments were wrathful. There would be economic consequences for Canada, and Canadians would not like them. There were suggestions of an oil boycott directed at Canada, which would have affected 10 to 15 percent of the country's oil imports. Canadian business, with exports to and contracts in Arab countries, panicked. Canadian media gave the story unrelenting attention, most of it unfavourable. Clark learned that all but one of his Cabinet opposed the move.[26] Finally, on 23 June, Clark had had enough. The promise was withdrawn but not repudiated. Instead, the Jerusalem issue was handed to a special fact-finder, former Conservative leader Robert Stanfield, who was to study Canada's Middle East relations and recommend ways of improving the country's standing in the region. Six weeks later, Stanfield was back, stating that moving the Canadian embassy would complicate the prospects for a lasting peace. The embassy move should, therefore, be shelved. It was an inglorious beginning to the Clark era, an era that proved remarkably short-lived.

Clark promised to govern as if he had a majority. Relying on the precedent of 1957, he believed that if the Liberals forced another election by defeating him in Parliament he would win overwhelmingly. Trudeau resigned as Liberal leader, just as the Clark government readied itself to present a contentious budget to Parliament. To Clark's considerable surprise, the budget was defeated on 13 December 1979. Parliament was dissolved and a new election called for February 1980, which, partly because of the Conservatives' doubtful record and partly because of the unpopularity of the budget, Clark lost. Trudeau returned to lead his headless party, becoming prime minister for the second time, in March 1980.

Reporters noted that several Conservative MPs, including the minister for external affairs, Flora MacDonald, were absent from the crucial vote to approve the budget. It was reported that MacDonald was in Brussels for a NATO meeting and had been unable to get back across the Atlantic in time. In the excitement nobody asked what NATO was doing, or why MacDonald's presence in Europe might have been important. She had been attending a NATO ministerial meeting whose principal purpose was to lay down the alliance's response to the Soviet SS-20 deployment. NATO, the ministers decided, would pursue a "two-track" strategy. First, the allies would balance the Soviet missiles with missiles of their own. Then, from a position of strength NATO would bargain with the Soviets over arms control.[27] The position of strength involved siting 108 Pershing II missiles and over 350 cruise missiles in Western Europe.[28] Canada, through MacDonald and other ministers, accepted the "two-track" decision; it remains unclear just how active the Canadians were in the discussion. Canadian troops in NATO had reverted to a non-nuclear role, and Canada was not expected to take any of the burden of the deployment.[29]

None of the Western responses to Soviet aggression had quite the desired effect. The Soviet invasion of Afghanistan continued, devastating that country, wasting Soviet resources, and demoralizing the Soviet armed forces, for whom victory was never within reach. Carter's most effective riposte to the Soviets was to supply arms and supplies to Afghan resistance forces through Pakistan.

The effectiveness of the US wheat boycott depended on the Soviets not having other sources for grain. Canada was a potential supplier, and there were anxious discussions with the Americans as to whether Canada would refuse to sell extra grain to the Soviets.[30] In the middle of the anxiety over turmoil in Iran, the Olympic boycott, and the wheat embargo, the Canadian government changed again, from Clark back to Trudeau. Clark had been sympathetic to the American position, as far as a prairie, wheat-growing power base would allow him to be. He terminated flights to Canada by the Soviet airline, an easy decision. Canada would not join the embargo, Clark had decided, but it would not sell any more wheat than normal to the Soviet Union.[31]

On the Olympic issue, Trudeau later explained in his foreign policy memoirs that the experience of the 1976 Olympics and the Commonwealth Games in 1978 persuaded many Canadians – himself included – that boycotts were a futile form of protest. Trudeau may well have had little patience for showy but ineffective forms of diplomacy, which led to self-defeating if highly public pseudo-actions. Instead, he punted the decision to the Canadian Olympic Committee, which duly endorsed Carter's boycott. The prime minister's lack of enthusiasm for the boycott was obvious throughout the episode.[32]

ADVENTURES IN NATIONALISM

Trudeau had many challenges to confront after his return to office, and many of these had a foreign policy element. In addition to Soviet aggression in Europe and Afghanistan, there was revolution in Iran, followed by a war between Iran and Iraq that resulted in a new round of oil price increases. The American economy sputtered in the dying days of the Carter administration, and Ottawa was soon facing a new, Republican administration in Washington. Domestic policies, such as a national energy policy and repatriation of the constitution, also had a clear foreign policy components.

Unexpectedly, Trudeau had appointed Mark MacGuigan as his new minister of external affairs. MacGuigan, a law professor and long-time member of Parliament, represented Windsor, on the border with Detroit. Partly for that reason he was sensitive to American concerns. At any rate, he was much more inclined than Trudeau to cast a friendly eye on the United States. Trudeau cited both these factors in appointing MacGuigan, adding that he also appreciated his colleague's coolness and rationality in dealing with public issues.[33]

In its final months in office, the Carter administration made the reluctant decision to put an end to the stagnation that had characterized the US (and Canadian) economy in the 1970s. The Federal Reserve Board reduced the US money supply. Inflation, at 12 percent in 1981, stopped as interest rates rose into the teens (as high as 21 percent in Canada that same year). Unfortunately, the economy stopped too, and both Canada and the United States tumbled into recession. Perhaps more than any other single event, the recession of 1981-1982 harmed the Trudeau government, as it blighted the prospects of the ordinary voter – the kind who until then had been the backbone of the Liberal Party.[34]

One repeated theme in Canadian foreign policy has been the tensions between the federal and provincial government in areas of overlapping jurisdiction, such as trade and energy. The federal trade power was weak, while provincial control over sectors such as energy was strong, as Diefenbaker had discovered over the Columbia River Treaty in 1960-1961. As Alberta's oil revenues rose in value, the Alberta government began to wonder whether it should directly represent its interests with the principal customers for its oil and gas, the United States. In 1972 the newly installed provincial Conservative government of Peter Lougheed speculated that it should begin "enlarging associations with the US Government and business representatives, and speaking on behalf of the Alberta Government on economic issues, primarily in the energy field."

It considered establishing a "listening post" in Washington, one that would not be attached to or absorbed in the existing Canadian embassy, where Alberta would "would lose its identity."[35]

As a result of the earlier phase of the oil crisis, the price increases of 1973-1974, the Canadian government had worked out a set of policies that included an export tax on oil and gas and a two-price system, with a lower price domestically. Relations between Ottawa and the government of Alberta were not good, as the two contended for control of oil and gas pricing. Essentially, Alberta's case was that the province had historically received world prices for its wheat and other agricultural products, while paying high prices for domestic manufactures sheltered behind Canada's tariff wall. That was not quite true, because Alberta had received an artificially high protected domestic price throughout the 1960s for its petroleum from the unwilling or possibly unwitting consumers of Ontario, but it was true that Quebec and the Atlantic provinces imported even cheaper overseas oil.

Trying to adjust oil-pricing policy, the short-lived government of Joe Clark ran squarely into differences between the Conservative government of Bill Davis in Ontario and that of Peter Lougheed in Alberta. Thus, the task of adjusting oil policy was squarely in the hands of Pierre Trudeau and the Liberals when they returned to power in March 1980. Their return coincided with the Iran-Iraq war and a sharp rise in energy prices. Oil prices moved from about $14 a barrel in 1978 to $35 a barrel in 1981, rises that most Canadians blamed not on the war but on the international oil companies. The stage was set for a heavy dose of nationalism, a made-in-Canada energy policy aimed not so much at the Middle East or OPEC, but at Esso, Shell, and other corporate malefactors.

Trudeau had concluded that one of the problems with his governments in the 1970s was that policy had been studied to death. As a result, much had been said and little had happened, except that, year by year, the federal deficit and the national debt grew. In secret, his finance minister, Allan MacEachen, and his energy minister, Marc Lalonde, and their top officials prepared a new policy that aimed to capture as much of the actual and anticipated rise in oil prices for Canada as possible. The Trudeau government saw oil as a goose that would lay endless golden eggs – enough, perhaps, to finance the deficit and pay for new social programs, or perhaps to buy back control of strategic sectors of the Canadian economy from foreign (read, American) investors.

Trudeau had already experimented in a mild way with limiting foreign investment. In 1974, during his minority government, Trudeau bowed to the nationalist New Democratic Party by introducing the Foreign Investment Review Agency (FIRA). FIRA scrutinized foreign takeovers of Canadian firms, rejecting those not deemed to be in the national interest. Its nationalist bark was definitely worse than its regulatory bite, and over time only a small proportion of proposed takeovers were actually rejected. The

FIRA process took time, and time was money, and the lawyers and accountants who guided applications to and through FIRA cost money too. Foreigners complained, and not just Americans; over time, complaints from Europe were probably just as audible as those from south of the border.

Now MacEachen and Lalonde returned to the charge. Guided by an official who had produced a PhD thesis on the development of socialism in Tanzania, they drafted a series of measures that were incorporated in MacEachen's first budget, presented to Parliament at the end of October 1980. Because it was part of a budget, and therefore subject to great secrecy, MacEachen's oil and gas policy, labelled the National Energy Program (NEP), was not subject to the usual discussion in Cabinet or among officials.

The NEP prescribed a heavy dose of nationalism. It embodied a series of measures designed to encourage Canadian ownership and to discourage if not penalize foreign investment. Tax concessions and subsidies were available to Canadian-owned firms but not to foreign ones. In federal territories, the government simply appropriated a proportion of oil and gas reserves already owned by private companies.[36] All this was contrary to the custom that foreign investment, once established, should be treated according to the same rules as domestic investment – a practice embodied in, among other things, the GATT.

The US embassy was furious, but it could do little. The presidential election was a week away, and President Jimmy Carter looked likely to lose – as he did, by a very large margin. Until the new American administration took office on 20 January 1981, it was unlikely that Washington would do much, and it did not. It is hard to know which government was the more enraged by the NEP – the United States, or Alberta. In the case of the United States, the incoming Republican administration of Ronald Reagan proved much tougher, and much more nationalistic, than Jimmy Carter's mild liberalism. The Reagan administration therefore applied unrelenting pressure until it got some concessions from Trudeau and company – a rollback of the appropriation of oil reserves by the federal government, for example. While the dispute raged on, oil prices, which the NEP assumed would top $60 a barrel, began to fall steeply. As the oil boom unravelled, so did the rationale for the NEP, which by the fall of 1983 had become a nightmare for Ottawa, as the federal government strove to prop up the Canadian firms it had encouraged to become big players in the oil and gas market. Washington sat back and waited for what it correctly assumed would be the inevitable denouement.[37]

Alberta furiously reacted to what its government saw as a transparent attempt to move the centre of gravity in the Canadian oil business from Calgary (and Edmonton) to Ottawa. Eventually, in 1981, the provincial government (still Conservative and still headed by Peter Lougheed) reached a compromise with its federal counterpart based on the assumption that with oil prices soaring there would be enough money to provide a bonanza for all. It was an assumption that proved sorely mistaken, but even while the going was good, and while oil prices were still rising, it left a sour taste in the Lougheed government's mouth.

REPATRIATING THE CANADIAN CONSTITUTION

After Quebec and a Canadianized oil patch, there was one more major item on Trudeau's agenda: the constitution. This was not ordinarily a problem in Canadian international affairs, although in the 1960s the Quebec and French governments had made it so. There were, it was true, overlaps between federal and provincial powers, and sometimes these gave rise to ferocious battles. But, apart from the French, no foreign power actively meddled in Canada's constitutional affairs, or tried to adjust the federal-provincial balance of powers.

One foreign power was passively involved in the Canadian constitution. Canada had been part of the British Empire and, throughout the twentieth century, continued to recognize the British monarch as its own sovereign. In the late 1920s the British government had moved to divest itself of its residual control over the self-governing parts of the empire, including the Dominion of Canada. In 1931 it passed the Statute of Westminster, which abolished the power of the British Parliament to legislate for or otherwise interfere with Australia, New Zealand, and South Africa. Canada was the great exception, because its provincial and federal governments were unable to agree on how to amend the British North America Act, Canada's constitutional statute, as regards the division of federal and provincial powers. Thus, any amendments that affected the division of powers in Canada continued to be passed by the Parliament in Westminster rather than by any Canadian authority or combination of authorities. Several amendments were passed in this way, always at the behest of the Canadian Parliament, acting through the federal government in conveying its wishes to its British counterpart. The British were obliging and refused to "look behind" the Canadian requests for amendments.

Over the years Ottawa convened federal-provincial conferences with the idea of solving the constitutional conundrum. The conferences of 1950, 1964, and 1971 failed. Provincial jealousies proved too much to overcome, and Quebec, especially in 1964 and 1971, was an immovable obstacle. The Bourassa Liberal government was a special problem: Bourassa had an advanced constitutional agenda that involved squeezing extra powers out of Ottawa, either for Quebec alone or for all the provinces. The Quebec premier was well aware of the role of the British government and Parliament in Canadian constitutional issues, and when he hosted a dinner for the visiting British prime minister, James Callaghan, he asked that Britain not act on any constitutional amendment if Trudeau alone asked for it. Callaghan refused, and the conversation languished.[38]

Trudeau's return to power in the 1980 general election, with seventy-four out of seventy-five House of Commons seats from Quebec, and the defeat of Lévesque and the separatist option in Quebec's referendum that same year decisively altered Canada's political circumstances. It was Trudeau, not Lévesque, who could thereafter claim to speak for Quebec. After the 1980 referendum, as another premier irreverently put it, Lévesque was a political eunuch.

Trudeau did not to let this opportunity go to waste. In September 1980, after the predictable failure of another federal-provincial conference to agree on amending the constitution, the prime minister announced that he would go it alone. As it happened, Ontario and New Brunswick supported him, but the other eight provinces were opposed. Regardless of provincial support, Trudeau was determined not only to secure a formula for amending the Canadian constitution inside Canada but also to get a Charter of Rights and Freedoms included in the package. This was a major reform indeed. Even more radically, Trudeau announced that once his amendments passed the federal Parliament, they would be sent to London for passage, with or without provincial support.

With some difficulty, Trudeau forced his constitutional amendments through Parliament. He had the majority necessary to do so. He had a legal basis as well. He defeated in the courts provincial attempts to scupper his chosen method of constitutional amendment: the Canadian Supreme Court conceded that he had the power to do what he was doing, even though exercising that right was neither "customary" nor conventional.[39]

Once Trudeau's constitutional package cleared the Canadian Parliament, it would have to go before the British Parliament. This took time, which gave the Canadian government the opportunity to prepare the way in Britain. It seemed likely that at some point in 1981 the Canadian government would transmit the Canadian parliamentary resolution to the British government. Accordingly, in June 1980 Trudeau spoke to the British prime minister, Margaret Thatcher, advising her of what was to come.[40] He did not, however, go into detail. Thatcher responded that "if you ask us to act, we will have to do so."[41]

In October 1980 Trudeau announced that he would seek both an amending formula and a Charter of Rights, both to be passed by the Canadian Parliament and then the British Parliament. He then sent two missions to London. The first consisted of Mark MacGuigan, external affairs minister, and John Roberts, the minister of science, technology and the environment. The two ministers briefed the queen, who proved interested and sympathetic. Thatcher was another matter. She objected to the Charter as a complication that might embroil her in trouble with her own backbenchers, since such a document was contrary to the declared policy of her government. Nevertheless, Thatcher did not protest too much, and MacGuigan and Roberts left satisfied.[42]

The second mission was more political, consisting of Yvon Pinard, president of the Privy Council, who went to London to discuss timetables with Thatcher's House leader, St John Stevas. Stevas was actively discouraging. There was no telling when a Canadian constitutional bill could pass the House of Commons; worse, a "Bill of Rights" would be difficult for the British Parliament to swallow. Pinard took the warning badly, but Stevas had a point.[43] The Thatcher government was new and untried; the prime minister did not yet have unquestioned dominance over her party; the British House of Commons, on non-essential matters, could be unruly and fractious.[44] Trudeau wanted the British government to designate the Canadian constitution as a matter of premier importance and insist that its MPs vote for it. Meanwhile, interested parties in Canada were trying to influence the British Parliament to reject what they perceived as Trudeau's hijacking of the Constitutional amendment process.[45]

The British government was divided on the issue. Stevas was against the Canadian package. The Foreign Office favoured the Canadian case, as, apparently, did Lord Carrington, the foreign secretary. Thatcher was described as firm and unyielding in public on the Canadian question but uncertain and unwilling in private.[46] She sent her defence minister, Francis Pym, to Canada to explain to his Canadian counterpart the difficulties she foresaw. The British High Commission in Ottawa uttered discreet warnings, and in at least one case, a not-so-discreet warning. Speaking to an NDP member of Parliament, Sir John Ford stated that the constitutional package had not the slightest chance of being passed by the British Parliament. As a result, at Canadian insistence, the British high commissioner departed his post, though without being declared persona non grata.[47] The year 1981 was not the happiest in Anglo-Canadian relations.

Canadian diplomats and other visitors to London reported that the battle over provincial rights and other questions (Indian rights were a particular sore point) was going badly. The Foreign Affairs Committee of the British House of Commons took up the Canadian case and grilled witnesses on the subject of the Canadian constitution. Some of those witnesses were known not only to be favourable to the Quebec government but actually employed by it. Ottawa, on the other hand, took the illogical position that it was a sovereign government and that it would be improper and offensive to Canadian dignity to appear before another nation's sovereign tribunal – even on an issue where the whole point was that Canada's sovereignty was incomplete. When the British committee reported unfavourably on Trudeau's constitutional amendments, no one was very surprised.

The publisher of the Toronto *Globe and Mail,* Roy Megarry, at home a strong opponent of Trudeau and all his works, made a frantic speech in London begging the British to do the right thing and defeat the Canadian constitution. When Thatcher saw Trudeau at a Commonwealth Conference in Melbourne in September, she told him that all she could promise to do was to bring the Canadian package forward. What MPs would do with it she could not say. Perhaps the eight dissenting premiers would descend en masse on London to oppose the Trudeau scheme in person. By the fall of 1981, even support from Ontario and New Brunswick was crumbling, a very bad sign for the constitutional package.

At the last minute, Trudeau and his justice minister, Jean Chrétien, plucked victory from the jaws of defeat, cobbling together an agreement between Ottawa and (finally) nine of the ten provinces. It involved some modifications to Trudeau's proposals; more followed at the insistence of pressure groups in the weeks that followed. The equation had shifted to Ottawa and nine provinces on one side and the separatist government of Quebec on the other.

Thatcher now scheduled the "Canada Bill" for debate and managed to give it first reading before Parliament rose for Christmas. There were some last-ditch legal manoeuvres by Native groups demanding the British refrain from passing the bill, but the British courts rejected their appeals. The bill passed the British House of Commons on 8 March 1982 and received royal assent on 29 March. The queen signed the new constitution in a public ceremony on Parliament Hill in Ottawa on 17 April, with Trudeau standing proudly by.

Trudeau's constitutional reform may rank as his major legislative achievement. It bore the unmistakable stamp of his personality, both in content (the Charter of Rights) and style (the determination to go it alone if necessary). While it impinged on the conduct of Canadian foreign policy, if only because it absorbed so much energy and attention, it had little to do with day-to-day relations between Canada and Britain. It did not help relations between Pierre Trudeau and Margaret Thatcher; it complicated her political life at a difficult time for a cause (the Charter) in which she did not believe. The constitution was soon forgotten by the British. It had the great advantage, from the British point of view, that once passed it would never return.

CRITICAL TIMES CALL FORTH STRONG MEASURES. Canada between 1976 and 1980 faced a crisis of national unity that threatened the country's existence. There had never been so serious a crisis before, threatening to divide Quebec from the rest of Canada. To meet the emergency, the Trudeau government subordinated all other considerations to winning a referendum that would reaffirm Quebec's place in Canada. Foreign policy played a role in the eventual federalist victory in the Quebec referendum of May 1980. American national interest dictated a supportive attitude from the US government, from the liberal Carter to the liberal Trudeau.

French influence, compared with the 1960s, took a distant second place – an indication, perhaps, that France would not derive any strong advantage even if the separatists won. Winning both an election and a referendum within the space of three months was a heady tonic for Trudeau and the Liberals. In the fall of 1980 they embarked on two controversial initiatives – the repatriation of the constitution and the National Energy Program – one successful, one not. Characteristically, the government's political judgment proved superior to its economic understanding. The requirement that Canada's constitution be amended in Great Britain was a ludicrous anachronism and, more importantly, the cause for endless dispute between the federal government and the provinces. The patriation of the constitution was a political triumph for Trudeau and, despite moments of deep unhappiness between Canada and Great Britain, Canada's unwilling and unwitting partner in the exercise, it caused no lasting damage to relations between the two countries.

The sharp rise in oil prices after 1978 gave Ottawa occasion to expand its role in Canada's oil markets. Managing oil and oil prices was apparently supported by Canadian public opinion, which blamed secret corporate forces for the sharp rise in oil prices and profits. Securing a place for Canada at the table of the giant international oil companies thus became a desideratum for the Canadian government. In 1980, through his National Energy Program, Trudeau did just that.

The sequel showed that daring was no substitute for thought. In the belief that once international oil prices had risen they would stay high, the Trudeau government set down a national strategy, financing the government's and the country's future out of high-priced gas bubbles. The market did not respond appropriately. Sagging oil prices popped the bubbles, and the NEP became a burden, not an asset.

Trudeau gambled a great deal on the NEP, and ultimately lost. He provoked domestic conflict between Ottawa and Alberta and a lasting sense of grievance in western Canada, not to mention damage to the Liberal Party's standing as a national political force. Abroad, the NEP offended the American government, just as it was passing from the mild policies of Jimmy Carter to the assertive nationalism of a new Republican administration. The United States, like Great Britain, was turning to the right at the beginning of the 1980s. There was a bite in the wind as far as Trudeau was concerned. Perhaps the winds of change, political but ultimately ideological, were blowing in another direction.

20 RETURNING TO THE CENTRE

The sixteen years that Pierre Trudeau was in office were, for many public servants, the worst of times. This may seem paradoxical. Trudeau by background and training resembled the members of the senior bureaucracy. He had friends in the public service, and he had been a civil servant himself. The essence of bureaucracy is predictability, the application of routine to problems. Routine is the product of systems. The systems governing the Canadian public service had, by the time Trudeau came to office, been in place for about fifty years – not a long time compared to older bureaucracies in other countries. That meant that the first, innovative, phase of bureaucracy, the design and implementation of systems and procedures, was not long in the past; and some of the first generation – Pearson, for example – were still around or just recently departed.

Trudeau found the results entirely too predictable for his tastes. He did not question that the system worked, but considered that it did not produce the best conclusions. Some of the senior mandarins in Ottawa were aware of the prime minister's critical eye and consequently found Trudeau's gaze on them and their departments deeply unsettling. The department that got the most attention, to its lasting regret, was External Affairs.

"The arrival of Pierre Trudeau in the Prime Minister's Office was a much greater shock to the Department's system than the arrival of John Diefenbaker had been,"[1] one senior diplomat later wrote. Like Diefenbaker, Trudeau was no great respecter of diplomats. But Diefenbaker had only resented the diplomats' politics; Trudeau seemed to disapprove of them root and branch. Early in his term as prime minister he flippantly remarked that he could get as much information from the *New York Times* as from his foreign service. While, like so many of Trudeau's comments, it was not meant to be taken entirely seriously, it revealed something of his attitude. Trudeau seems to have retained and refined bad memories of his encounters with the Canadian Foreign Service when he toured the world in the late 1940s. As one of the diplomats concerned later showed, these resentful memories were greatly exaggerated.[2] Nevertheless Trudeau believed what he believed, and his views, unfounded or not, counted, although in this case they could be blunted by his first minister of external affairs, Mitchell Sharp.[3]

Trudeau was not alone in his criticism of Canada's style of diplomacy: External Affairs' performance was under attack from many directions, by politicians, academics, and the concerned public, ranging from those who disliked the "quiet diplomacy" of the recent past to those who simply disapproved of particular foreign policy issues, like Vietnam.[4] Liking neither content nor process, Trudeau struck out in a new direction. Soon after taking office, rejecting External Affairs' existing processes, he set up his own: his own foreign policy adviser, ensconced in the Prime Minister's Office, who doubled as his speechwriter for foreign affairs.

What Trudeau did take seriously, apart from ideas, was process. He wanted things done right, rationally, and not instinctively or axiomatically. The Canadian civil service was in need of overhaul: hidebound, encrusted with traditions, promoting by longevity, it was no instrument for a government that thought of itself as activist and innovative. The contest of strength between the departments and the government in March 1969 around Canada's role in NATO was only a preliminary skirmish. Centring on policy, the issue was really fought on External Affairs' turf and on its terms, though it did not seem like it at the time. On that occasion, the diplomats and their political allies fought Trudeau to a draw, on a subject of his choosing. But having won the battle, the diplomats lost the war.

THE STRUCTURE AND PERSONNEL OF THE "DEAR DEPARTMENT"

The instrument to Trudeau's hand was the reform of the civil service. At its higher levels, the Department of External Affairs took itself too seriously. The "dear department," as some ironically called it, recruited from the Canadian elite; alone among Ottawa ministries it had a substantial bilingual capacity.[5] The proliferation of the best and the brightest was part of the problem. Even great powers had problem finding enough interesting jobs for their talented diplomats to practise on. International agencies like the United Nations in New York and Geneva, UNESCO in Paris, and the General Agreement on Tariffs and Trade, also in Geneva, helped a bit, as did the sudden multiplication of countries suitable for missions. Independence brought embassies, and embassies required ambassadors. Many of the new posts were pleasant but dull; some were distinctly unpleasant – and dull. The number of good jobs remained about the same, in Ottawa and abroad.

External Affairs worked according to the principles of merit and seniority. It was the prewar and wartime generations who got the plum positions, for the most part, for the "founders" of the department were only just reaching retirement age in the 1960s. Younger people could wait, or could try to bring themselves to the attention of the minister or deputy minister. "Young" was a relative term. The veterans' intake after the Second World War brought plenty of youngish and talented people into the foreign service, and well into the 1970s this was the dominant group in the department.[6] Those who had joined in the 1950s and 1960s would have to wait. Given the small numbers of Canadians born in the 1930s, this generational structure made some sense; but after 1965, with the baby boomers arriving on the job market, that no longer applied. The civil service swelled at the bottom, with the "invasion" of recent university graduates.[7] As a social system, External Affairs had arteriosclerosis.

The embodiments of the clash over External Affairs were the undersecretary, Marcel Cadieux, and the machinery of the Privy Council Office (PCO) incarnated in Michael Pitfield. Cadieux considered the foreign service to be a kind of missionary order whose members owed their department an exclusive and intense loyalty.[8] Pitfield was a bright Anglo-Montrealer who had served in Ottawa in a variety of venues, from the office of the minister of justice to Government House, fetching up as an assistant Cabinet secretary and heir presumptive to Gordon Robertson, clerk of the Privy Council. In 1974 Trudeau elevated Pitfield, still in his thirties, to be clerk and thus senior civil servant in the Canadian government. It was the outward sign of an unusually close political-bureaucratic relationship between the two men.[9]

Trudeau admired and respected Pitfield; he signed on to Pitfield's prescription for the civil service and, by extension, the foreign service. In Pitfield's view, the senior management (and perhaps the senior officers as a group) of External Affairs did not see that their present position was untenable. The department was not well managed, even in the opinion of many of its officers. There was resentment of the presumably lavish diplomatic lifestyle, and a sense that this was the main reason that some officers joined and remained in the department.[10] Unless there was reform, the bad and the good would both eventually be swept away. In his own mind at least, Pitfield intended to preserve the best of what existed. Such change would have to be forced on the existing establishment. "The collectivity which was External failed to meet the challenge of 'reborning' itself," so somebody else would have to do it.[11]

The first fact to be faced was that there was a pool of talent in External Affairs that was underemployed. Intelligence and competence were the crucial qualities, it seemed to Pitfield and Trudeau; if an individual had those, the rest could be learned on the job. They would siphon talent from External Affairs and use it elsewhere in the bureaucracy. The government drew off several of the department's brightest stars, including Basil Robinson and Allan Gotlieb, and sent them as deputy ministers to other ministries. Though both would later return, as successive undersecretaries, their departures broke the mould. Because Robinson had been a crucial manager in External Affairs, his departure made a considerable difference in how the department ran itself.[12]

The next stage followed. Efficiency was the name of the game, and one road to efficiency was the elimination of duplication and the consolidation of compatible if not identical functions. This notion, irresistible because simple and saleable to voters, was attractive to politicians. It had produced the integration of the armed forces in the 1960s. In the 1970s and '80s it was the turn of Canada's foreign services. There were three of these. External Affairs and its foreign service officers (FSOs) generated policy and ruled over political affairs. The trade commissioner service of the Department of Industry, Trade and Commerce (formerly just Trade and Commerce) provided information and other forms of assistance to Canadian business. The trade commissioner service had a long history – longer than the foreign service itself – but it drew on different talents and operated in a very different way. Yet with homogenization and the portability of talent as the government's watchwords, bringing the trade commissioners and the FSOs together made sense. Finally, there was the immigration service, part of the Department of Citizenship and Immigration, whose job it was to encourage the right kind of immigration, as defined by government, and prevent the wrong kind. Immigration was politically highly volatile, an area where it was impossible to satisfy an electorate profoundly split on the questions of how much and which kind of immigration to permit.

A task force made recommendations on integration. The departments resisted for what now seem to be good reasons – the different tasks and talents required for "political" foreign policy as opposed to trade and immigration – and the government proved less committed to implementing than imagining the integration of the foreign services. Instead, the government tried an Interdepartmental Committee on External Relations (ICER), which flourished briefly in the early 1970s and then declined into talkative immobility.

Meanwhile, something more immediately painful was occurring. In 1969-1970 the government suffered a fit of economy and ordered retrenchment in all directions. The Department of External Affairs' budget was cut by $7.5 million. Because most of the department's cost was personnel rather than programs, it was on personnel that the blow fell. Seven foreign posts were closed, and 60 FSOs lost their jobs, along with 110 support staff.[13] The resulting bitterness was immense. Morale, as might be expected, suffered. Although there were many subsequent disagreements between the foreign service, or some of its members, and the Trudeau government, this was the item that produced the most serious grievance. "I think the events of the late 1960s were badly handled," one of Trudeau's senior associates later admitted. "[They] were traumatic, but were in a sense inevitable."[14]

Events reflected a clash of bureaucratic philosophies. Modern bureaucracies have been built on specialization and routine – professionalism, in short. A recruit joins a department or agency, either already equipped with specialized training, as in science, law, or languages, or able to learn on the job – usually both. There are advantages to predictable relationships, rewards, and outcomes, and benefits from camaraderie – the sense of being together with the same objective in the same enterprise. On the other hand, there were many examples where "generalization" worked. Politicians were an obvious example, moving from job to job and place to place. In the American system, the political level of government was expanding the trend away from professionalization, which bit deeper with every passing generation. Some American diplomats were amused to see (and envious of) the privileges – allowances and offices – of their Canadian counterparts.[15] Some Canadian observers were less amused, though equally envious.

Pitfield represented one kind of challenge to the foreign service. Ivan Head represented another. Head talked to the prime minister about policy, however much he tried to be careful not to step over the line, and tried not to be "a vest-pocket Kissinger," a miniature of his powerful counterpart in Washington. In some ways, having someone like Head, who could deal with his analogue, Kissinger, was an advantage. The Canadian ambassador in Washington did not like it, certainly, but it was not an issue on which his minister, Mitchell Sharp, was prepared to go to the mat with the prime minister.

Sharp and his senior staff tried to adapt to the times. The department established a Policy Analysis Group (PAG) in 1969, to respond to the government's obsession with planning. It was somewhere between a think-tank and a prophetic social science institute. After an initial bout of enthusiasm it languished, despite changing its name to Policy Planning Secretariat. "Methodology sometimes seemed more important than substance," one traditionally oriented diplomat lamented, "the medium driving the message."[16] On one occasion, the department even sponsored a survey of its employees' opinions on Canadian-American relations; the exercise was appropriately named Operation Delphi, after the ancient Greek prediction factory. The views expressed were refreshingly conventional, even though all levels of the department were plumbed in Delphi's questionnaire.[17]

Sharp shied away from conflict with Trudeau. He had little enough to dispute with the prime minister, and he accepted that prime ministers needed publicity more than mere ministers. There was no point in objecting to the publicity of summits, for example. Within his department, Sharp was respected. He was, after all, a professional, he knew what he was talking about, and he took a commonsense approach to international issues, like the International Commission for Control and Supervision mission to Vietnam in 1973. He had the gift of making idealism practical, of seizing the essence of a situation while discarding, as and when necessary, its superfluous aspects. Cool and logical, Sharp often took his opponents by surprise; and they were never more surprised than when he prevailed. His talents could not preserve everything External Affairs wanted, but his ability and prestige limited the damage of what could not be helped.

After the 1974 election, Trudeau replaced Sharp with Allan MacEachen, a senior Liberal from Nova Scotia. MacEachen was qualified by education, experience, and intelligence, and, like Sharp, by political seniority. Liberals considered MacEachen a more overtly political animal than Sharp, and he was renowned (and greatly appreciated) for his parliamentary skills, which in matters of detail far surpassed Trudeau's.[18] The government's survival in the minority Parliament of 1972-1974 was largely MacEachen's handiwork, as was the successful campaign in 1974. MacEachen liked External Affairs, plainly. It was his choice in 1974, and he only reluctantly responded to Trudeau's plea that his talents were needed elsewhere in 1976. When, later, MacEachen wanted out of the difficult and politically unrewarding Finance portfolio in 1982, Trudeau did not hesitate to move him back, and he remained in External Affairs until the expiry of the Trudeau government in 1984.

MacEachen was aloof and often inaccessible. Some of his officials found his work habits a mystery; some wondered whether their minister was simply "lazy."[19] When occasion demanded, however, he did what was necessary. Nor did he lack for opinions on foreign policy. Like Sharp, he did not want to upset Canada's traditional relationships. Like Trudeau, he took a lively interest in the Third World. Unlike Sharp, he was not prepared to tolerate the continuation of Ivan Head as Trudeau's foreign policy adviser. Head must go, and he did, leaving for the position of president of the newly created International Development Research Centre (IDRC), a few blocks from Parliament Hill. A change in job title and geography need not have made a difference, but they did. Trudeau called on Head from time to time, and the two remained friends, but from then on the Department of External Affairs regained some ground in formulating foreign policy.

MacEachen's successor, Don Jamieson, was probably MacEachen's political equal, but until Trudeau made him minister of industry, trade, and commerce in 1975 and then minister for external affairs in 1976, he was essentially a regional figure, dominant if not invulnerable in his home province of Newfoundland, but little known outside. His civil servants knew that there was only one topic guaranteed to attract Jamieson's undivided attention – fish. Like MacEachen, Jamieson brought an attitude to his work.

He was notably pro-American in a government thought to be lukewarm on the subject. Since Jamieson's appointment coincided with the Parti Québécois victory in Quebec and the need for Canada to seek friends in the United States, his attitudes suited the government's needs.[20]

Finally, there was Mark MacGuigan, minister from 1980 to 1982, when he made way for Allan MacEachen. MacGuigan was not politically senior. In his own region, southwestern Ontario, he was known as a client of Paul Martin, whose Windsor seat he inherited. MacGuigan was more intellectual, certainly, than Jamieson, but like Jamieson he soon acquired a reputation for being pro-American. That did Jamieson no harm, but for MacGuigan it was political poison, as he later recognized.

MacGuigan was not close to Trudeau, and the prime minister often seemed to respect neither his political position nor his policy. MacGuigan swallowed hard. "I felt Trudeau was irrationally aggressive, suspicious, towards the Americans," he said in an interview in 1988. Sometimes MacGuigan prevailed in Cabinet when Trudeau was opposed, as in cutting off aid to Cuba, or in taking a harder line than Trudeau wanted over Poland. The two were not well teamed when it came to dealing with the Americans. Still, after Jimmy Carter was voted out of office, MacGuigan was useful in helping Trudeau deal with a new and altogether less sympathetic American administration, under Ronald Reagan. (MacGuigan later characterized the Reagan era in the United States as "psychologically unbalanced."[21]) He was unusual in liking Reagan's first secretary of state, General Alexander Haig, whom he considered an Atlanticist and at least aware of Canadian concerns; but in the view of many critics, the two men were too cozy. Being known as "Al's pal" did MacGuigan's political standing at home no good.[22]

The deputy ministers, or undersecretaries, advised on policy but on large issues did not have the deciding voice. The first clash between Trudeau and the Department of External Affairs over NATO made that perfectly clear. Although External Affairs managed to salvage much of its existing position, that was because the Cabinet was divided and because Mitchell Sharp and Léo Cadieux, the defence minister, were prepared to make it an issue. Marcel Cadieux, the undersecretary at External Affairs, seems to have done little but irritate the prime minister.

Marcel Cadieux was entirely committed to his task of preserving the status of the department, and brought his "fulminating personality" (a description by a fellow diplomat) to bear. Cadieux and Trudeau did not get along, though they shared many of the same attitudes and enjoyed many of the same enemies. Where Charles de Gaulle was concerned, Cadieux was especially passionate: he was to de Gaulle, a friend remarked, as Captain Ahab to the great white whale in *Moby Dick*. On that subject at least, Trudeau was more dispassionate than Cadieux. At best, the undersecretary approached Trudeau with wary respect, but no affection.

Cadieux had mixed success as undersecretary. He did his best to maintain high standards in the department and to encourage an intellectual approach to the problems of foreign policy. Many of his colleagues listened admiringly to his expositions: "I always wanted to hear what Marcel had to say," Reeves Haggan, one of the minister's assistants, recalled.[23]

Cadieux switched positions with A.E. (Ed) Ritchie, the ambassador to Washington from 1966 to 1970. Ritchie was a dominant personality, but like his minister, Sharp, he cooperated in Trudeau's and Pitfield's reshaping of the civil service machinery. Ritchie did not spare himself, and the pressures of his job brought on a stroke in September 1974 that effectively disabled him. His replacement was Basil Robinson, who held the job for two years. An able assistant, indispensable in earlier posts in Ottawa and Washington, Robinson found the top job not to his liking, and left early. He had returned to External Affairs from service as deputy minister in another department. So did his successor, Allan Gotlieb, who had once been the legal adviser in External Affairs. Gotlieb was unquestionably a heavyweight, once close to Trudeau and still, in 1977, close enough. Like his minister, MacEachen, he rejoiced in Head's departure.

Gotlieb was an active undersecretary. He adopted and promoted the idea that Canada was "a principal power" based on the importance of its natural resources and its intellectual and technological capacities. It was a powerful idea, a refreshing contrast to the pessimistic views that had characterized Canada as irretrievably a dependent of the United States. But the notion could be taken to extremes, as in descriptions of Canada as possessing "assets priceless to the industrialized world."[24]

There was a wary respect between Gotlieb and the prime minister, best illustrated by an occasion when Trudeau was about to depart for one of the G7 summits. The department had sent Trudeau a briefing book, and Gotlieb and some of his senior assistants arrived at Trudeau's office to discuss it. Trudeau announced that he had not read his material. Unperturbed, Gotlieb told the prime minister that it was advisable for him to read the notes, and that he and his officers would wait until that was done. Trudeau promptly resumed his task, read his brief, and returned as requested to discuss it.[25]

Gotlieb was aware that External Affairs was threatened by the homogenization of the civil service into one great interchangeable (the dreadful term "fungible" was just creeping into use) mass. He sought to restore his department's prestige and enhance its function by making it a "central agency," a term carefully reserved for the most important departments. With Pitfield's cooperation, he won Cabinet approval for External Affairs' new role. When another efficiency exercise occurred under the short-lived Clark government, Gotlieb and his department survived it handily, emerging with enhanced operational authority. In 1981 Gotlieb departed to become ambassador in Washington, in time to escape another turn of the wheel in Pitfield's mind.

The clerk of the Privy Council had become convinced that External Affairs could best be reinforced by integrating the trade commissioner service with the foreign service. This was a notion that deputy ministers, until this point, had resisted, both in External Affairs and Industry, Trade and Commerce, the latest incarnation of the old Department of Trade and Commerce, where the trade commissioners resided. It was a bad idea that, like most bad ideas, had a superficial plausibility. External Affairs was said to be weak in economics, and indubitably the trade commissioners performed an economic function. So External Affairs and Industry, Trade and Commerce were to be integrated. For good measure CIDA and the immigration service were thrown in. Trudeau and Pitfield appointed a new undersecretary, Gordon Osbaldeston, to carry out the merger. Osbaldeston was himself a trade commissioner, no recommendation to the foreign service.

The result was a physical and bureaucratic monstrosity. The name said it all: External Affairs and International Trade Canada (EAITC). Large numbers of bureaucrats had to be shoehorned into External Affairs' Pearson Building, and large numbers had to be exported somewhere else. The diplomats sniffed suspiciously at the arrival of the trade commissioners, whose virtues they generally failed to appreciate. They especially did not appreciate losing their private offices, which only the most senior retained. There were now three ministers who had to be accommodated in the department – External Affairs, Trade, and Immigration – not to mention deputy ministers. The undersecretary was the lightning rod for discontent. Osbaldeston also reaped the resentment of the trade commissioners, who found their own identity and functions frequently subordinated to those of the main department. External Affairs had been augmented and diluted, but it had not really been "integrated": the primacy of the political remained.

Osbaldeston did not stay. After his patron Pitfield was appointed to the Senate, Osbaldeston replaced him as clerk of the Privy Council. In his place, Trudeau appointed Marcel Massé, who had been clerk of the Privy Council briefly under the Joe Clark government but had not suffered permanent career damage. (Despite being a Tory appointee under Clark, Massé eventually emerged as a Liberal, elected to Parliament and appointed a minister under Jean Chrétien in the 1990s.)

Massé completed the reorganization of the department. He created five geographic branches, each of which included economic and political components. The branch heads would report to one minister on trade and to another on politics and to another on immigration. It was a conception only a theorist would love; it did not add to the efficiency or coherence of the resulting policy: the responsible officers were stretched too thin because of the variety of their responsibilities.

Massé was the last undersecretary to practise in External Affairs under Trudeau. The prime minister's time had run out, and on 29 February – 1984 was a leap year – he announced that he had taken a walk in the snow, had reflected, and would resign. That took another four months, until the end of June, when a Liberal Party convention selected John Turner, the former justice and finance minister, to be Liberal Party leader and prime minister.

Turner appointed Jean Chrétien to be external affairs minister, but it was a short posting. The Liberals promptly called an election, and Chrétien spent most of his time as minister on the hustings. In September the Liberals suffered the worst election defeat in their history, Turner resigned, and a new Progressive Conservative government took office.

New Times and Old Ideas

By 1980 the memory of Trudeau as young and fresh and daring had faded. He had outlasted almost all of the leaders in office in 1968: of that group, only Leonid Brezhnev remained in Moscow. Trudeau represented a generation that accepted the political and social compromises that had emerged from the Second World War. He had no qualms about a large role for the state, and he usually responded sympathetically to considerations of social welfare and the agenda of the moderate left. Canadian politics was like that – a blending rather than a confrontation of ideas: it was hard to find, in the late 1970s, any politician who did not see the nature as well as the function of politics as compromise.

Thus, Trudeau was not entirely prepared for the political revolution that followed the emergence of Margaret Thatcher as British prime minister in 1979. Thatcher was, in the conventional terms of 1970s politics, on the right. Yet she did not represent the British establishment nor did she come from an especially privileged background. She undoubtedly viewed Trudeau as a child of privilege, effete if clever; there were many like him in British politics and government, and it was a group or a class to which she was temperamentally allergic. Thatcher ignored Trudeau when she could, but when they met they were destined to clash.[26]

The real differences between Trudeau and Thatcher lay in the realm of ideology, in the assessment of Western relations with the Soviet Union, and in the relations of the rich and industrialized North with the underdeveloped and impoverished South. There was ample room for disagreement, and given the two personalities, room was required.

There was a clash of generations as well. Trudeau was the personification of the liberalism of the 1960s; Thatcher evoked an earlier, harder era, one that had been left behind by the welfare state. It comforted her opponents to class her as a throwback to an earlier, benighted, and selfish capitalism, as "the Great Hen squawking self-congratulations over the City," as one of them put it.[27] Unfortunately, that categorization failed to explain her appeal, which stretched far beyond the shores of the United Kingdom, and even extended into Canada.[28]

In fact, the generations were reversed. Thatcher was not a throwback but a harbinger. Unlike Trudeau, she was responding to the very real problems of the 1970s, and, although only six years younger, she was speaking for a different generation for whom the axioms of the 1960s either did not apply or no longer worked.[29] She had come to power in 1979 after a decade of stagflation, strikes, power shortages, and domestic conflict. She and her acolytes promised to end "the insufferable, smug, sanctimonious, naïve, guilt-ridden, wet, pink orthodoxy" that in their view had signally failed to produce what it promised.[30] After decades of labour disruption, deteriorating public services, and a winter in which the dead remained unburied – because of another labour dispute – the British electorate had had enough. Thatcher's qualities included, in MacGuigan's phrase, "vigour and rigour," which appealed to a desperate electorate. But, MacGuigan had added, "she entirely lacked a social conscience."[31] That was to become apparent as Thatcher confronted the "soft" issues of international affairs, like foreign aid and human rights.

Trudeau of course did not figure on Thatcher's agenda, nor did Canada. For the time being she had enemies closer to home, the "wets" in her own Cabinet, not to mention the powerful British trade union movement. Much of her time was spent bringing her party to order and imposing her brand of renovated capitalism on Great Britain.

Thatcher did have opinions on the Commonwealth.[32] She had a sentimental regard for Britain's imperial past, and she felt a cultural affinity for English speakers abroad, but she did not relish what the Commonwealth had become. She dreaded Commonwealth conferences where the members – she claimed – spent all their time talking about South Africa and sports. It took some persuasion, mixed with the sheer inertia of the institution, to convince her to attend. Commonwealth conferences took an immense amount of high-level time, and time for Thatcher was in short supply. She was saved, politically, by the Argentinian military government that in 1982 decided to solve its problems at home by adventuring abroad, invading and briefly occupying an offshore British possession, the Falkland Islands.

Thatcher sent a small armada to reconquer the islands, succeeding in a short, sharp campaign. Canada had economic interests in Argentina (the Argentines had bought a CANDU reactor), but that did not prevent Trudeau from stating that Canada was "100 percent behind the British."[33] Presumably Thatcher appreciated Canada's support; but she knew that it was not very covert American support that secured the British victory, underscoring for her the importance of close ties to the United States, and in particular to Ronald Reagan.[34]

In the aftermath of the Falklands War, Thatcher handily won re-election and, with it, dominance over her party and country. Secure at home, she preached abroad, where she won the deserved nickname of "Iron Lady" from the Soviets. Her renewed lease on power allowed her to implement a close alliance with Ronald Reagan, whose views on communism and the Cold War were similar to her own, if less extensively articulated.[35] Together they made a formidable combination, one that as far as Trudeau was concerned was unbeatable.[36]

Reagan, as president of the United States, was inescapable for Trudeau: they must meet, they must transact business, or establish an atmosphere where their subordinates could do the work. Doing business with Reagan was something Trudeau found hard to do, and he did not try very hard. If Trudeau found Thatcher frustrating, he thought Reagan infuriating. There was no meeting of minds between the two men; at times Trudeau seems to have thought there was no mind to meet. "Grade 2," he snarled, pacing in a garden in Bonn during a G7 summit. That at least was in private. In public, according to Mark MacGuigan, Trudeau's external affairs minister from 1980 to 1982, the prime minister was "wilfully nasty to Reagan." When the president spoke to the press, Trudeau would follow shortly afterwards, contradicting what Reagan had to say.[37]

Reagan deflected argument and, with it, unpleasantness. He knew (as did his aides) that he could not hope to match someone like Trudeau in mastery of facts and details, and so he simply ignored them, speaking from cue cards and relying on a disarming charm to keep his opponents at a distance.

Early in the Reagan administration, relations between Canada and the United States plummeted in a dispute over Trudeau's National Energy Program. At one point, the administration considered whether it should take stronger measures against Canada – for example, by excluding it from the G7 summit meetings, something that would certainly have attracted Trudeau's attention. In the end, as always on such occasions, the Americans decided that there were too many interests at stake. They tolerated Trudeau, but they did not like him.

When Allan Gotlieb was sent to Washington in 1981 as ambassador, he discovered that Trudeau's credit did not run as far as it had under Jimmy Carter. In his recollection, "there [were] a lot of people in the extreme right wing circles in the United States who were saying that Mr. Trudeau was not reliable." Trudeau, members of the administration believed, thought the Soviet Union and the United States "morally equivalent."[38] They were not wrong: in MacGuigan's opinion, Trudeau "was equally persuaded of the evils of American militaristic capitalism" as of Soviet defects.[39]

Trudeau for his part believed that Reagan's distaste for the Soviet Union – the "evil empire" as he once called it – was hysterical. It was more important to shore up relations with the Third World, as he tried to do through a North-South dialogue, than to waste money in confronting the Soviet Union. Within the limits of Canada's resources, the prime minister believed, he had done what was necessary to keep Canada's armed forces, including its NATO garrison, credible. He gave the Department of National

Defence a budget increase and, in a time of high inflation, guaranteed it against inflation for five years.

The government bought CF-18 fighters for the air force and German Leopard tanks for the army, the latter purchase strongly urged by the German chancellor, Helmut Schmidt.[40] The CF-18s reassured the Americans, who were increasingly and justifiably sceptical of Canada's ability to contribute to the defence of North America. "With the arrival of the CF-18," one of Trudeau's military planners remembered, "we had another, 130-odd first line fighters that could be thrown into air defence if necessary."[41] In addition, Canada offered its territory as a testing ground for American cruise missiles, with Trudeau deflecting considerable domestic criticism as a result.

Cruise missiles were a particular target of the peace movement of the late 1970s and early 1980s. The movement was an international phenomenon that arose around the time Reagan was elected president. Much of its composition was predictable: veterans of the anti-Vietnam and anti-nuclear movements, and left-wing activists generally.[42] One Canadian peace activist later ruefully wrote, "In 1977, I discovered to my dismay that although advocacy groups tend to attract more than their share of truly wonderful human beings, they also attract more than their share of full-blooded loonies."[43] There was in fact a direct and quite logical connection between the anti-nuclear power movement and the anti-nuclear bomb movement, as there had been earlier between the ban-the-bomb movement and the anti-Vietnam activism of the early and mid-1970s.

The movement also appealed to people who were too young to have been engaged in earlier foreign policy disputes. Their interest may have been piqued by a number of strongly anti-war movies at the time. *Threads,* a British movie made for the BBC, depicted both the outbreak and aftermath of a nuclear war. *War Games* showed a teenage computer hacker almost starting the Third World War by breaking into a military computer and thoughtlessly playing around. *By Dawn's Early Light* replayed one of the themes of the 1964 classic *Dr Strangelove.* Nuclear war was also a theme in song and in fiction.[44] Studies have shown a surge in "nuclear war fiction" starting around 1980, peaking around 1986 or 1987.[45] Anti-war themes may not have been dominant in something as large and diverse as mass pop culture, but it would be surprising if there were not a link between anti-war culture and politics.

In one case there was a direct link. Ronald Reagan watched an American made-for-TV movie, called *The Day After* (1983), set in and around Kansas City during and after a nuclear attack. It left him, according to a diary entry, "greatly depressed," as presumably were the millions of Americans and Canadians who watched it.[46] Nuclear weapons were a risky business, and Reagan seemed to be taking risks.

In May 1983 Reagan and Trudeau clashed at the G7 summit held in the restored colonial town of Williamsburg, Virginia. By then the summits were heavily scripted, following preliminary meetings of high-ranking officials. When the summits dealt primarily with economic matters, Trudeau had tended to listen; economics was not a subject he instinctively cared for. He was, however, deeply interested in questions of international security and the promotion of peace. Canadian diplomats urged the inclusion of a declaration of international security on their foreign colleagues at a preliminary meeting in Paris, and the subject of international security made it on to the agenda. Reagan and Thatcher had a specific idea in mind: they wanted an endorsement of the imminent deployment of Pershings and cruise missiles in Europe. They had brought a draft communiqué to that effect.

In the first day's meeting there was no great dissension, but in the second Trudeau and François Mitterrand of France made it clear they wanted no such endorsement. A fierce debate followed, lasting seven hours. "Trudeau was clearly afraid of provoking the Kremlin," Reagan's biographer wrote. At the time it was not Reagan who responded to Trudeau, but Margaret Thatcher. Trudeau, according to Thatcher, was "a solace to the Soviets."[47] Reagan was appreciative. "I thought at one point Margaret was going to order Pierre to go stand in a corner," he wrote in his diary.

Curiously, Trudeau did not mind. "Isn't she magnificent?" he murmured to his external affairs minister during one of Thatcher's summit diatribes.[48] The balance in the summits tilted: Thatcher, who was outnumbered and probably outgunned in the summits of 1979 and 1980, when Carter was the American representative, easily created a "special relationship" with Ronald Reagan that lasted for the duration of his presidency. The addition of the conservative German chancellor Helmut Kohl in 1982 effectively made the G7 a conservative forum. Yet Mitterrand and Trudeau were not entirely without effect: the summit's final communiqué was milder than it might otherwise have been, and there were some conciliatory words for the Soviets.[49] (There was a useful complement to the attraction between Trudeau and Mitterrand: the French president visited Canada – all of Canada – in a gesture that went some distance to repairing the rift between the two countries.)[50]

Trudeau was already disposed to regard Reagan as dangerous and, according to some of his close advisers, as a fool.[51] The president might not have noticed, but his entourage, alert to any possibility of bad publicity or atmospherics, did. Reagan embarked on the largest peacetime rearmament program in American history. Much of the money went towards new technology for which the Soviets had no match. When Reagan announced that the United States would pursue a missile defence shield, or Strategic Defense Initiative (SDI) – which his critics rudely labelled "Star Wars," after the phenomenally successful science fiction movie series – Soviet nervousness seems to have verged on panic.

In the fall of 1983, Trudeau decided to use the prestige and protocol of his office to promote better feelings among the nuclear superpowers. He would, he told his staff, personally undertake a "peace mission," visiting leaders east, west, and in between. Trudeau did see most of the world leaders he wanted to see. In India, he saw the belligerent Indira Gandhi, and in China, Deng Xiao Ping, the leader there. In Washington he saw Ronald Reagan and did his best to convince the president that he, Trudeau, saw him as a well-meaning man of peace. Reagan was polite, even cordial, but the real American view of Trudeau's missions was conveyed by Lawrence Eagleburger, a senior State Department official, who incautiously remarked that he wondered what the Canadians had been smoking.[52] For six months, Trudeau traversed the globe on a mission that many at home considered quixotic, or cynical.

Cynical it was not. The immediate occasion was the destruction by the Soviet air force on 1 September 1983 of a Korean airliner (flight KAL 007) that had strayed deep into Soviet airspace.[53] Two hundred and sixty-nine passengers and crew went down with the plane, including ten Canadians. It was a brutal and foolish act, for which the Soviets initially refused to accept any blame whatsoever.[54] To many in the West, it was typical of the Soviet Union, a sign the Communist bloc was dangerous.

Fortunately the Western public did not know the half of the problem. The Soviet leadership was decaying, aged men clinging to office without anything new or hopeful to offer their people. They were deeply divided between those who wanted to pursue détente with the West and those who believed, evidently sincerely, that under Reagan the United States was getting ready to attack the Soviet Union. In November 1983 Western leaders came to realize just how volatile the situation was. A NATO military exercise, "Able Archer," had to be cancelled when Western intelligence discovered that the Soviets were putting their nuclear forces on alert against an imminent NATO attack.[55]

Moreover, in October 1983, six weeks after the Korean airliner incident, Reagan sent troops into the Caribbean island of Grenada, a member of the Commonwealth, where they overthrew the local Marxist regime.[56] Trudeau protested the American action, without effect. The prime minister had no alternatives to offer, and local Commonwealth governments enthusiastically supported what the Americans had done.[57]

The peace movement in the West failed to prevent the deployment of the Pershing and cruise missiles in Western Europe, in response to the earlier emplacement of the Soviet SS-20s. The balance of politics in the West was definitely not what the Soviets hoped for, and the advantage went to Reagan, Thatcher, and Kohl.[58]

The Soviets were a problem. The aged Leonid Brezhnev had finally expired in November 1982, to be replaced by the chief of the secret police, Yuri Andropov. Andropov had no time for foreign leaders: he was seriously ill, and in January 1984 he followed Brezhnev into the tomb. The Andropov funeral gave Trudeau an opportunity to travel to Moscow. He discovered that the new Soviet leader, Konstantin Chernenko, was barely functional and that there really was no capacity in Moscow to listen to what he had to say. He sought consolation by visiting some of the Soviet satellites in Eastern Europe.

Standing on the tarmac in Prague as Trudeau disembarked from his plane, a Czech official observed to a Canadian diplomat that the visit was a great honour. "But," he added, "why is he here?"

As history would later reveal, a much more significant exchange between Canada and the USSR had already occurred. Its roots lay in 1974, when the Soviet Union assigned a senior Politburo adviser, Aleksandr Yakovlev, to be ambassador to Canada. The appointment was primarily to get him out of the way, for Yakovlev's views were unpopular with Brezhnev and his friends in Moscow.[59] Ivan Head, Trudeau's adviser, discovered that Yakovlev was an interesting and accomplished man. Head recommended him to the prime minister, and Trudeau and the ambassador hit it off; Trudeau saw more of Yakovlev over the next ten years than any other foreign diplomat.

The Soviet leaders would not have known what to do with this special relationship with Trudeau even had they wanted to take advantage of it. But Yakovlev had some friends back in Moscow, and in 1978 one of them, Mikhail Gorbachev, became minister of agriculture. Through Trudeau, Yakovlev got the Canadian minister of agriculture to invite Gorbachev to visit Canada in 1983.

The trip was less important for the bilateral discussions that took place, or for any impression Gorbachev might have made on Canadians, than for the impression that Canada – and by extension Western liberal capitalist society – made on Gorbachev. Coming from a society where plenty was a function of privilege, and scarcity a way of life, the Soviet minister was astonished by Canadian farms, homes, and supermarkets. He allowed himself to be grilled by a Canadian House of Commons committee, another and very different experience from what he knew at home.[60]

At the time, of course, Trudeau and his ministers could not know that Gorbachev would prove infinitely more important in Soviet history than the doddering Chernenko. Yet Trudeau seems to have made a good impression on Gorbachev. Two years later, out of office and visiting the Soviet Union, Trudeau was called to Moscow to talk to Gorbachev in his new role as Chernenko's successor and Soviet leader. Gorbachev sought the former prime minister's impressions of Reagan. No doubt their conversation was franker and more sincere than any exchange Trudeau ever had with Reagan himself.

PIERRE TRUDEAU SPENT ALMOST SIXTEEN YEARS as prime minister of Canada, from 1968 to 1984 with a short interregnum in 1979-1980. By the time he left office, he was the senior head of government in the Western world. He was the best-known Canadian of his generation, and he left his stamp on his country. The crisis of Quebec brought Trudeau into politics and propelled him into office. It was primarily owing to his efforts that Quebec separatism was frustrated for a generation and that Canada remained a united country into the twenty-first century.

To his contemporaries, Trudeau brought a sense of style and intelligence, a hard-edged brilliance that many, even most, Canadians admired for years after he left politics. There was a sense that Trudeau represented Canada notably around the world, that he left an impression wherever he went. Although he appeared to like foreign travel, representation abroad was only part of the prime ministerial job; much of the time, it was the prime minister's role to appear like a *deus ex machina* in an eighteenth-century opera, sing a diplomatic aria or two, shake hands, and depart – on to the next appearance, or home.

It mattered, up to a point, that Trudeau made a favourable impression on other heads of government, but the continuity of any foreign relationship depended either on the weight of a bilateral relationship – the amount of trade and investment, for example, or sentimental connections, or security concerns – or on the quality of Canada's routine representation, on those who remained behind after Trudeau left the scene. (And in terms of the quality of the foreign service, it is questionable whether Trudeau left Canada's diplomatic establishment in as good shape when he left as when he arrived.) It is unclear that Trudeau enjoyed a "special relationship" with any particular foreign leader, even those most likely to agree with him, or to cooperate with Canada.

It is certainly true that Trudeau got on better with liberals than conservatives abroad, as at home. His relations with Jimmy Carter, Helmut Schmidt, James Callaghan, and François Mitterrand were cordial and apparently useful, but it would be too much to describe any of them as soulmates. In the case of the United States, the prime minister usually behaved as his script demanded. It was a subject he did not especially understand or care to understand, but he knew that reasonable relations with the United States were a sine qua non for any serious Canadian leader. Relations with the United States were too large to be ignored or dismissed; fortunately, the American government also saw the weight of the American relationship with Canada, and judged it too important to be needlessly jeopardized.

Nevertheless, Trudeau could be difficult. His relations with the United States in the early 1980s were complicated by the prime minister's mistrust, if not outright contempt, for the ceremonial charade of Ronald Reagan's White House. The foreign minister of the day, Mark MacGuigan, later summed up his impression of Trudeau: "He had a mind of astounding brilliance in the service of very unworthy passions."[61] The Americans were not oblivious: "We put up with Trudeau for so long," one of Reagan's staff moaned, not long after Trudeau left office.

In his time as prime minister, there were only three large issues where Trudeau took command. The most important was the earliest, the foreign policy review of the late 1960s; but it resulted, at most, in a readjustment rather than a reformulation of Canada's foreign policy. The second was the issue of Quebec, and its cousin, the constitution, an internal problem in which Trudeau took a vivid interest. There, circumstances abroad favoured Trudeau. No foreign power except the United States took a close interest in the question, and the United States for its own reasons took Trudeau's side. Finally, there was the "peace mission" of 1983-1984, an expression of genuine concern, but on a question about which Trudeau in the end could do little.

During Trudeau's time on the world stage, he moved from representing hope, or dynamism, or the shape of things to come, to being the symbol of an earlier era. He embodied the hopes and the enthusiasm of the baby boom generation, though he himself was no baby boomer. He was out of place with the generation of the 1980s, and out of sorts with the world that time had created. It remained, as always, to be seen whether his successors would be more in tune with the spirit of a new decade.

CONCLUSION:
MULTILATERAL BY PROFESSION,
MUDDLED BY NATURE

Between 1945 and 1984 Canada pursued a policy of alliance and engagement in and with the world. It was not a world that the Canadians of 1945 would have wished on themselves, but they adapted quickly and readily to a situation over which they had little control.

Forty years is a long time, and in Canada as elsewhere one generation gave way to another. Veterans of the First World War – Lester Pearson and John Diefenbaker – dominated the period to 1968. The next prime minister, Pierre Elliott Trudeau, had not even been born when that war ended; his brief successor in 1979-1980, Joe Clark, was born only a few months before the Second World War broke out.[1]

The Cold War also had two diplomatic phases. In the first, down to the mid-1960s, the Western powers – and by extension Canada – were frightened by the image of a powerful, expansionist, ruthless Soviet Union and its handmaiden, international communism. This phase culminated in the Cuban missile crisis of 1962, which was as traumatic in Canada as elsewhere. Afterwards, in the second phase, there was the long decompression of détente. Yet détente ended in another crisis, in 1983-1984, when for the second time the world seemed to teeter on the verge of war.

Survival, international, national, and personal was, as we now know, in question throughout the Cold War. The question of survival became urgent very soon after the Second World War. The end of that terrible war was achieved by the use of a terrible weapon, the atomic bombs dropped on Japan in August 1945. Canada's ally, the United States, made and used the bomb, but Canada participated in its construction and supplied the raw materials and some of the technology for much of the American atomic arsenal, then and later. The newly founded United Nations – Canada was a founding member – could do little to control atomic weapons. The United States had atomic weapons, so the Soviet Union must have them too: the balance of power was supplemented by the balance of terror between the United States and the Soviet Union – the ability of each side to annihilate the other.

War was followed by Cold War, and the Cold War dominated Canadian foreign policy from 1945 through the 1980s. Winning, losing, or simply fighting the Cold War had drastic implications, but, in an imperfect world, there was security in numbers and in alliances. Canadians had little difficulty in choosing sides in the Cold War. History, values, and strategic necessity dictated Canada's participation in the Western alliance in the late 1940s. A liberal democracy, Canada sought the company of other similar nations. Closely linked to the United States and Great Britain, Canada followed its interests. The Soviet Communist model held no charms for all but the tiniest minority of Canadians: solidarity with its allies and opposition to the spread of communism were and remained fundamental policies for all Canadian governments. Canada, having helped found the UN, helped design NATO. Canada sent troops to Europe, and to Korea, and at home prepared to mobilize for what seemed at times to be an inevitable war.

These policies abroad depended on a firm foundation at home. To maintain defence, the Canadian government devoted most of its budget to the military for the first two decades after 1950. Public opinion supported the choice.

The fact that the United States was Canada's principal ally in the Cold War and its major trading partner occasioned some uneasiness. Canada was roughly one-tenth the size of the United States in population and had a lower standard of living. These facts weighed on many Canadians, evoking fears for Canada's identity, independence, and sovereignty.

Canadians – some of them, at any rate – found or hoped to find an identity through foreign policy. Canada was small but rich, technologically advanced, and domestically tranquil through the 1950s. Its gross national product placed it among the richest six or seven nations from the 1940s through the 1970s, and that fact, as much as any other, helps to explain the country's ability and willingness to be engaged abroad. Canada could afford an expensive military, professional and well equipped. It could field a diplomatic corps that in training and experience compared well with its British and American partners. Canada could provide aid, which by the 1970s was dispensed in substantial sums. Through the United Nations, NATO, and the Commonwealth, and specialized agencies like the International Monetary Fund and World Bank, Canada could search for partners, actual and potential. The partners were available, because Canada had what they wanted – sometimes money and supplies, sometimes military assistance, and sometimes simply diplomatic expertise. The various partnerships helped balance the relationship with the United States. As a "middle power," it was argued, then and since, Canada mattered – to Canadians, certainly. But to others? It is entirely possible that Canadians confused multilateralism, a small power's logical policy, with a higher status. Canada was multilateral by inclination even if, much of the time, the fruits of multilateralism too were difficult to imagine, let alone seize.

The 1940s and 1950s are sometimes called the "Golden Age" of Canadian diplomacy, and they are associated with the name of Lester B. Pearson, external affairs minister from 1948 to 1957. (Pearson's influence, however, derived in large part from the firm support given him by the prime minister, Louis St Laurent.) Pearson projected an image that matched the Canadian self-image. He stood – and, just as important, seemed to stand – for good conduct in international affairs, reliability, and firmness. He was rewarded with the presidency of the UN General Assembly and the Nobel Peace Prize. Canadians took pride in his achievements, either at the time or, in the case of his political opponents, some years later. In taking pride, there was among Canadians a certain amount of self-regard. They forgot that the Peace Prize was awarded to Pearson, not to Canada.

Pearson had some very un-Canadian characteristics. Sceptical and open-minded, he had a quicksilver quality. It was hard, always, to grasp where he was heading, but in his sense of timing and opportunity he had few equals. Yet Pearson had his limits. He hewed closely to the Western alliance and understood that, without American leadership and American contributions, the Western cause would be lost. He may have overestimated the Soviet challenge, and certainly he had through his later career a very healthy dread of nuclear warfare.

Pearson dealt easily with Americans in international, multilateral forums. He was less comfortable, and less skilled, in bilateral relations. In some respects that did not matter. Canadian-American relations were mainly economic, and self-sustaining; when they required management, they were managed by others. Though Pearson presided as prime minister over the conclusion of the Canadian-American Auto Pact in 1964-1965, it was not "his" project but the product of his professional advisers.

Pearson's prominence in Canadian diplomacy in the 1950s and 1960s gives rise to the question of whether there was any particular opposition at home to his policies, or whether there was a partisan political difference over foreign policy. Certainly there were atmospherics, political noises off intended to convey to the electorate that there were deep and abiding issues of principle between Pearson's Liberals and the opposition Progressive Conservatives, which could or should have produced a difference in policy. Yet the Conservative interlude of John Diefenbaker did not break the sequence of Canada's international policy. Such a thing was inconceivable and to Diefenbaker, a Cold Warrior, pro-British, and, in essentials, pro-American, impossible. When

Diefenbaker nevertheless managed to blunder into a confrontation with the popular American president John F. Kennedy, he found his followers swiftly abandoned him to return to the safe harbour of Pearson and alliance solidarity, in the federal election of 1963.

Ironically for Pearson, his time as prime minister was consumed largely by domestic issues, and when foreign policy was involved, as over the Vietnam War, he found domestic public opinion divided, difficult, and intractable. The most spectacular foreign policy crisis of the 1960s had all these characteristics, but it was not Vietnam. It was, rather, the irruption into Canada of the French president Charles de Gaulle, which gave an international dimension to Canada's domestic unity crisis. De Gaulle's attempt to encourage Quebec separatism soon collapsed into implausibility and irrelevance; but he was not wrong in discerning a possibly fatal weakness in Canada's political structure.

Quebec dominated Canadian politics for the next generation, which was not Pearson's, but his successor's. Pierre Elliott Trudeau had opinions on foreign affairs, certainly. He came from the left, and at times had been publicly doubtful about the wisdom of the Cold War consensus that supported Canada's alliance policy. In office, however, Trudeau was cautious, steering carefully among the competing views of his Cabinet and party colleagues.

In the end, circumstances demanded less of the Trudeau government in foreign policy than of its predecessors. The Vietnam War ended, the Cold War decompressed into détente, and Canada turned to economics and the Quebec issue. Trudeau developed a taste for world travel, which was gratified not so much by Canada's political standing, as by its economic clout and by the United States' need for company in what became the Group of Seven summits. In a modest way, Canada's economic diplomacy expanded under Trudeau. As Lawrence Eagleburger, then a senior American diplomat, later remembered, Canada counted economically – though not otherwise.[2]

In the end, Trudeau's foreign policies (apart from those dealing with Quebec) probably owed more to international trends and domestic budgets than to fixed convictions about the United States, the Soviet Union, and the balance between them. Pearson implemented a welfare state, enacting medicare and a more complete pension system; the effects were soon reflected in Canadian budgets. In 1964 Canada spent 4 percent of GNP on defence. By the end of Trudeau's term in office, 1984, the figure had fallen to 2.1 percent.[3] There is no doubt that Canada's military was weakened as a result, down in numbers and often deprived of new equipment.

Cuts to defence budgets are sometimes attributed to Trudeau's lack of affection for the military, and that may be part of the story – but not all. When discussing foreign and defence policy, Canadians have a tendency to look inward, but on issues like defence spending Canada was not alone. In the United States, defence remained the major part of the budget until about 1970. As Trudeau was reducing the military's call on government funds, so were his counterparts, presidents Nixon, Ford, and Carter. By the end of the Cold War – albeit after a major rearmament under Reagan – the United States was spending double on social programs what it was spending on defence.[4] Canada was not alone in its reaction to the international oil crisis, to the stagflation of the 1970s, or in its gradual turning away from the liberal solutions and statist policies that grew out of the war and dominated its public policy down to the 1980s.

The year 1984, like 1968 or 1945, thus marked a generational transition but also an ideological change. Domestically, it was symbolized by the defeat of the Liberal Party in the elections of September 1984, and the arrival of Brian Mulroney and the Conservatives in power in Ottawa. In foreign policy it was signalled by a new emphasis on bilateral relations with the United States, as against the multilateral policies of Pearson and Trudeau. After 1984, Canadian governments faced out, but very largely in one direction, south, and had a different agenda from those that went before. The generation of 1984 needs another book.

NOTES

INTRODUCTION

1 John Bartlett Brebner, *The North Atlantic Triangle: The Interplay of Canada, the United States, and Great Britain* (Toronto: Ryerson Press; New Haven, CT: Yale University Press, 1945).

2 Canada's colonial ambiguities could easily be mistaken for isolationism, and some imperceptive observers in the 1930s did just that. But while there were Canadian isolationists before 1939, they were mostly in French Canada. Even the anglophobic O.D. Skelton, the undersecretary of state for external affairs from 1924 to 1941, was never in doubt that the majority of English Canadians would want to be at Britain's side should war come. I differ on this point with David G. Haglund, who in his otherwise excellent *The North Atlantic Triangle Revisited: Canadian Grand Strategy at Century's End* (Toronto: Irwin, 1998), 23-5, gives Canadian interwar "isolationism" more currency and a more definite shape than it actually had.

3 The line is from *My Fur Lady*, a McGill University review that unexpectedly drew audiences from coast to coast in 1957.

4 Haglund, *North Atlantic Triangle Revisited*, 32, 46-9.

5 A point made by former secretary of state Lawrence Eagleburger when I interviewed him in Washington in April 2002.

6 Norman Hillmer, "Are Canadians anti-American?" *Policy Options* (July-August 2006): 63-5.

7 Haglund, *North Atlantic Triangle Revisited*, 46.

CHAPTER 1: CONSTRUCTION AND RECONSTRUCTION

1 I am greatly indebted to my friend Roger Sarty for supplying these figures, which he points out are quite rough.

2 On liberal politics see Robert Latham, *The Liberal Moment: Modernity, Security and the Making of the Postwar International Order* (New York: Columbia University Press, 1997), ch. 1.

3 See Leigh Sarty, "A Middle Power in Moscow: Canada and the Soviet Union from Khrushchev to Gorbachev," *Queen's Quarterly* 98, 3 (1991): 556-7.

4 On salaries, see John Hilliker, *Canada's Department of External Affairs*, vol. 1, *The Early Years, 1909-1946* (Montreal and Kingston: McGill-Queen's University Press, 1990), 192, 245-6, 280-1. Hilliker notes that the salary level during the war was low, but that in universities was lower still: see Robert Bothwell, *Laying the Foundation: A Century of History at the University of Toronto* (Toronto: University of Toronto Department of History, 1991), 86-8, 100, 109, 110-11.

5 John Holmes, *The Shaping of Peace: Canada and the Search for World Order, 1943-1957*, vol. 1 (Toronto: University of Toronto Press, 1979), 233-4, refers to Robertson's "high intelligence" and "unique authority."

6 Adam Chapnick, *The Middle Power Project: Canada and the Founding of the United Nations* (Vancouver: UBC Press, 2005), 151, points out that the dominant accounts of Canadian diplomacy in this period derive from civil servants' memoirs, which naturally stress professionalism as a key value.

7 Born in Romania, Mitrany practised political science at the London School of Economics for most of his career.

8 Hilliker, *External Affairs*, 1:255-6; Holmes, *Shaping of Peace*, 1:72-3. Hume Wrong was the official responsible for translating Mitrany's theories into King's statements.

9 Quoted in Costas Melakopides, *Pragmatic Idealism: Canadian Foreign Policy, 1945-1995* (Montreal and Kingston: McGill-Queen's University Press, 1998), 6.

10 King had protested against a "British" security sphere at a conference of Commonwealth prime ministers in London in May 1944.

11 Quoted in Holmes, *Shaping of Peace*, 1:235.

12 Memorandum of 2 November 1939, and King diary, 25 October 1944, quoted in James Eayrs, *In Defence of Canada*, vol. 3, *Peacemaking and Deterrence* (Toronto: University of Toronto Press, 1972), 139-40.

13 The electoral period was longer in 1945 than it would be in the 1980s and after.

14 Holmes, *Shaping of Peace*, 1:240-1.

15 Ibid., 256-7. In a meeting on 14 May King used the example of provincial jurisdiction over education as an area where there should be "no intervention" from the UN.

16 Ibid., 259-60. Canadian "smugness" seemed to find a particular focus at the UN, to the irritation and despair of British officials: UK National Archives, DO 181/87, Sir Patrick Dean to Lord Amory (British High Commissioner in Ottawa), 24 November 1961 and other missives.

17 Latham, *Liberal Moment*, 96-8, identifies collective security as a component of "the liberal tradition."

18 On this point see Akira Iriye, *Global Community: The Role of International Organizations in the Making of the Contemporary World* (Berkeley and Los Angeles: University of California Press, 2002).

19 Arthur Silver, *The French-Canadian Idea of Confederation, 1864-1900* (Toronto: University of Toronto Press, 1982), makes the point that the Catholic Church and international Catholicism provided a plausible substitute for British imperialism in the hearts and minds of French Canadians during the nineteenth century.

20 On the League of Nations Society, see Donald Page, "The Institute's 'Popular Arm': The League of Nations Society in Canada," *International Journal* 33 (Winter 1977-1978): 28-65.

21 Iriye, *Global Community*, 18.

CHAPTER 2: REAL PROSPERITY AND ILLUSORY DIPLOMACY

1 Interestingly, as the economist Pierre Fortin later concluded, military wages strongly benefited those areas with high enlistment rates: thus, Quebec lagged economically in terms of its standard of living. "The Canadian Standard of Living: Is There a Way Up?" C.D. Howe Institute Benefactors Lecture, 1999, www.cdhowe.org/pdf/fortin.pdf.

2 Roosevelt was delivering his annual State of the Union speech to Congress on 6 January 1941. The speech is still worth quoting: "In the future days which we seek to make secure, we look forward to a world founded upon four essential human freedoms. The first is freedom of speech and expression – everywhere in the world. The second is freedom of every person to worship God in his own way – everywhere in the world. The third is freedom from want, which, translated into world terms, means economic understandings which will secure to every nation a healthy peacetime life for its inhabitants – everywhere in the world. The fourth is freedom from fear, which, translated into world terms, means a world-wide reduction of armaments to such a point and in such a thorough fashion that no nation will be in a position to commit an act of physical aggression against any neighbor – anywhere in the world. That is no vision of a distant millennium. It is a definite basis for a kind of world attainable in our own time and generation."

3 See the argument in Robert Bothwell and William Kilbourn, *C.D. Howe: A Biography* (Toronto: University of Toronto Press, 1979), 201-2; but see the conflicting reasoning in Reginald Whitaker, *The Government Party* (Toronto: University of Toronto Press, 1977), 156-8.

4 The RTA was an act, not a constitutional amendment; what Congress had given to the executive it could take away, if it wished.

5 The failure to achieve progress on international commercial policy is examined in Kathleen Rasmussen, "Canada and the Reconstruction of the International Economy, 1941-1947" (PhD diss., University of Toronto, 2001), ch. 5.

6 The agreement, to be perfectly clear, did not anticipate and in fact forbade the piling up of a Canadian surplus; but this occurred anyway.

7 Rasminsky in January 1945, quoted in Bruce Muirhead, *The Development of Post-War Canadian Trade Policy: The Failure of the Anglo-European Option* (Montreal and Kingston: McGill-Queen's University Press, 1992), 16.

8 See Douglas LePan, *Bright Glass of Memory* (Toronto: University of Toronto Press, 1979), 53-110.

9 Rasmussen, "Canada and the Reconstruction of the International Economy," 317.

10 "His feelings for Britain were ... a fluid mixture of resentment, rivalry, and regard." John Lamberton Harper, *American Visions of Europe: Franklin D. Roosevelt, George F. Kennan, and Dean G. Acheson* (Cambridge: Cambridge University Press, 1996), 36.

11 See Robert Bothwell and John English, "Canadian Trade Policy in an Age of American Dominance and British Decline, 1943-1947," *Canadian Review of American Studies* 8, 1 (1978): 54-65.

12 On this point see Rasmussen, "Canada and the Reconstruction of the International Economy," 351-2, and Thomas Zeiler, *Free Trade, Free World: The Advent of GATT* (Chapel Hill: University of North Carolina Press, 1999), 48-9.

13 William Roger Louis, "The Dissolution of the British Empire," in *The Oxford History of the British Empire,* vol. 4, *The Twentieth Century,* ed. Judith Brown and William Roger Louis (Oxford: Oxford University Press, 1999), 331-2, notes the vast overseas costs the British were still carrying in 1946-1947; in doing so he misstates the amount of the US loan and fails to mention GATT as a way station on the road to dissolution of the British Empire.

14 Bruce Hutchison, a well-connected Ottawa reporter, commented that Gardiner was "the archpriest of protectionism in practice. For the old doctrine of low tariffs he had substituted the principle of farm prices guaranteed by the state." Bruce Hutchison, *The Incredible Canadian* (Toronto: University of Toronto Press, 1953), 414.

15 Charles Wilson, *A Century of Canadian Grain* (Saskatoon: Western Producer Prairie Books, 1978), 878-9. The relevant clause was 2(b).

16 Plus $30 million to the Dutch East Indies, not yet independent as Indonesia.

17 One such Canadian, Brigadier Charles M. Drury, was in charge of UNRRA programs for Poland and in that capacity had a ringside seat for observing the communization of that unhappy country.

18 F.H. Leacy, ed., *Historical Statistics of Canada,* 2nd ed. (Ottawa: Statistics Canada, 1983) (*HSC*), tables H148-160.

19 US National Archives, State Department Records, 842.20 Defense/4-2745, W.L. Batt to Edward Browning and Robert Turner, 27 April 1945.

20 *Canada Year Book, 1947* (Ottawa: King's Printer, 1947) (*CYB*), 879; in 1939 the United States supplied 65.9 percent of Canada's imports, the United Kingdom 15.2 percent. That same year, the UK took 35.6 percent of Canada's exports, and the United States 41.2 percent. The last year that the UK took more Canadian exports than the United States was 1941: 39.7 percent compared to 38.2 percent: *HSC,* G389-400.

21 *CYB, 1947,* 879.

22 Clifford Clark memorandum, "Outline of Discussions during Trip to Washington and New York, September 16-20, 1947," n.d., *Documents on Canadian External Relations (DCER),* vol. 13, *1947* (Ottawa: Department of External Affairs, 1993), 1423.

23 Ibid., 1423-4. Clark did in fact plan for a drastic situation (Plan A) and a less drastic one (Plan B).

24 The Canadian diplomat John Holmes attributed the US cooperation to "those friends in the State Department who recognized how we had kept Britain going [through the Canadian loan] before

they could act." Holmes, *Life with Uncle: The Canadian-American Relationship* (Toronto: University of Toronto Press, 1981), 24.

25 Atherton to Secretary of State, 29 October 1947, *Foreign Relations of the United States*, vol. 3, *1947* (Washington: Government Printing Office, 1972), 127-8.

26 Woodbury Willoughby, Memorandum of conversation, 29 October 1947, ibid., 129.

27 Quoted in Norman Hillmer and J.L. Granatstein, *Empire to Umpire: Canada and the World to the 1990s* (Toronto: Copp Clark Longman, 1994), 196.

28 The notion of a union of democracies around the Atlantic was very much in the air at the time, represented by a best-selling book, *Union Now*, by Clarence Streit.

29 *Life* was the creature of its right-wing publisher, Henry Luce, a strong believer in American manifest destiny. Luce saw Canada as culturally similar to the United States, and as politically reliable. Canada did not, in 1948, enjoy the reputation of being a semi-communist state drowning in socialist experimentation, as right-wing Canadians and Americans would later depict it.

CHAPTER 3: REALIGNING CANADIAN FOREIGN POLICY, 1945-1947

1 Interestingly, Franklin D. Roosevelt saw as early as 1920 that the erosion of British power would mean that the United States would replace Great Britain as the centre of attraction for the British dominions, including of course Canada. See John Lamberton Harper, *American Visions of Europe* (Cambridge: Cambridge University Press, 1996), 37.

2 William Roger Louis, "The Dissolution of the British Empire," in *The Oxford History of the British Empire*, vol. 4, *The Twentieth Century*, ed. Judith M. Brown and William Roger Louis (Oxford: Oxford University Press, 1999), 332-9, observes that the British dreaded above all becoming mired in an endless and unwinnable series of civil wars in their empire.

3 Quoted in ibid., 329.

4 The story of the Canadian contribution to the atomic bomb is in Robert Bothwell, *Nucleus* (Toronto: University of Toronto Press, 1988), 3-82.

5 Canada had a small uranium deposit at Great Bear Lake in the Northwest Territories. More important, it had a uranium refinery – the only one in allied hands. Attracted by the uranium, by the proximity to the United States, and by the fact that Canada was not merely allied but British, the British government located a laboratory in Montreal at the beginning of 1943. They found to their distress that the Americans had already tied up the uranium and the refinery. The Montreal laboratory thereafter occupied a relatively subordinate place in the atomic project. It developed a different kind of atomic reactor from the one the Americans were pursuing: a test model started up in September 1945 but the full-scale version began to function only in 1947.

6 On this point see Spencer Weart, *Nuclear Fear: A History of Images* (Cambridge: Cambridge University Press 1988), 3-74.

7 The first quotation is from an interview I conducted in 1985 with Sir Michael Perrin. The King diary reference for 11 October 1945 is quoted in Robert Bothwell, *Eldorado* (Toronto: University of Toronto Press, 1984), 159.

8 David Holloway, *Stalin and the Bomb: The Soviet Union and Atomic Energy, 1939-1956* (New Haven, CT: Yale University Press, 1994), 96, 132-3. See also Simon Sebag Montefiore, *Stalin: The Court of the Red Tsar* (London: Weidenfeld and Nicolson, 2003), 440-3.

9 Acheson experienced Mackenzie King's way of politics when, in the fall of 1939, he tried to get Jewish relatives of his friend Felix Frankfurter into Canada and out of Nazi Europe. He failed.

10 Library and Archives Canada (LAC), Pearson Papers, MG 26, vol. 3, Lester Pearson to Hume Wrong, 1 October 1945.

11 King's wishful thinking is concisely summarized in Jamie Glazov, *Canadian Policy toward Khrushchev's Soviet Union* (Montreal and Kingston: McGill-Queen's University Press, 2002), 8-10.

12 Quoted in Vladimir O. Pechatnov, *The Big Three after World War II: New Documents on Soviet Thinking about Post-War Relations with the United States and Great Britain* (Washington, DC: Woodrow Wilson International Center for Scholars, Working Paper No. 13, July 1995), 9 , 12. The first quotation is from Ivan Maisky, the former ambassador to London.

13 On the officials' attitudes, see Glazov, *Canadian Policy*, 7-8.

14 LAC, External Affairs Records, RG 25, file 2AE-1(S), Dana Wilgress to L.B. Pearson, undersecretary, 25 May 1948.

15 Reginald Whitaker and Gary Marcuse, *Cold War Canada: The Making of a National Insecurity State, 1945-1957* (Toronto: University of Toronto Press, 1994), 12. What made the difference between Canadian and American opinion was French Canadians, solidly anti-communist and therefore anti-Soviet even during the war.

16 See the accounts in Albert Legault and Michel Fortmann, *A Diplomacy of Hope: Canada and Disarmament, 1945-1988* (Montreal and Kingston: McGill-Queen's University Press, 1992), 57-65, and Margaret Gowing, *Independence and Deterrence* (London: Macmillan, 1974), 1:87-92. The Canadians were not charmed by the American proposal, which the leader of the Canadian delegation described as "insincerity from start to finish," but it must be admitted that the official American plan had no better press among American diplomats.

17 LAC, Mackenzie King Papers, J4, vol. 344, C237724, Hume Wrong to Mackenzie King, 18 December 1945, enclosing three dispatches.

18 The best account of the speech and its context is Fraser J. Harbutt, *The Iron Curtain* (New York: Oxford University Press, 1986).

19 King's reaction on the day of the speech contrasts with Pearson's professional caution, saying that Churchill was using "pretty strong language ... but ... our end was protected, and ... he of course was speaking for himself." J.W. Pickersgill and Donald F. Forster, *The Mackenzie King Record*, vol. 3 (Toronto: University of Toronto Press, 1970), 182, 183-4.

20 Ibid., 185-6.

21 The royal commission published its report later in 1946. Prosecutions of alleged spies followed, although the most important spy, Dr Allan Nunn May, had moved back to Great Britain and was arrested and prosecuted there. Mostly idealist or ideological concerns motivated the Canadians involved, a fact that greatly alarmed security authorities in Canada, the United States, and Great Britain. Ironically, later spies in Canada were motivated mostly by money, which Canadian and other Western spy-hunters had downgraded as a motivation based on the Gouzenko experience.

22 On the Anglo-Canadian project see Bothwell, *Nucleus*, 63-82, 112-6; Gowing, *Independence and Deterrence*, 1, 323-4.

23 Bothwell, *Eldorado*, 160-3, 169.

24 The Canadian occupation force was based on the 3rd Canadian Division of about 20,000 men, which remained in Germany through the winter of 1945-1946. The decision to withdraw was heavily criticized in Canada, even by normally Liberal supporters. On the other hand, public opinion was evenly divided outside Quebec; in Quebec it was strongly supportive of the government. See F.H. Soward, *Canada in World Affairs: From Normandy to Paris, 1944-1946* (Toronto: Oxford University Press, 1950), 27-8; Angelika Sauer, "The Respectable Course: Canada's Department of External Affairs, the Great Powers, and 'the German Problem,'" (PhD diss., University of Waterloo, 1994), 263-4.

25 The King diary chronicled the prime minister's low spirits and feelings of inadequacy during the conference: *Mackenzie King Record*, 3: ch. 9.

26 Glazov, *Canadian Policy*, 11-15, provides an able summary of the period.

27 United Kingdom, National Archives, FO 371/62420/XC026705, E. Bevin, "Effect of Economic Situation on Foreign Policy," 12 February 1947. I am indebted to Francine McKenzie for this reference.

28 Ibid.

29 Coal shortages helped drive British and American (and eventually French) policy in occupied Germany towards a resumption of normal coal production and hence to a less rigid and less unforgiving economic and political regime: Ethan Kapstein, *The Insecure Alliance: Energy Crisis and Western Politics since 1944* (New York: Oxford University Press, 1990), ch. 2.

30 Quoted in David Reynolds, *Britannia Overruled: British Policy and World Power in the Twentieth Century* (London: Longman, 1991), 167-9.

31 Anne Deighton, *The Impossible Peace: Britain, the Division of Germany, and the Origins of the Cold War* (Oxford: Oxford University Press, 1990), 120ff.

32 Truman Library, Truman Papers PSF, file Canada – William Lyon Mackenzie King, Acheson to Truman, 22 April 1947.

33 Louis St Laurent, *The Foundations of Canadian Policy in World Affairs* (Toronto: University of Toronto Press, 1947).

34 Grant Dexter memorandum, 3 June 1947, quoted in R.D. Cuff and J.L. Granatstein, *American Dollars, Canadian Prosperity* (Toronto: Samuel Stevens, 1978), 23.

35 Wrong to Pearson, 31 May 1947, *Documents on Canadian External Relations* (DCER), vol. 13, *1947* (Ottawa: Department of External Affairs, 1993), 1407-12.

36 Wrong to Pearson, 5 June 1947, *DCER*, vol. 13, *1947*, 1415.

37 Richard C. Gardner, *Sterling-Dollar Diplomacy: The Origins and Prospects of our International Economic Order*, 2nd ed. (New York: McGraw-Hill, 1969), 312-15.

Chapter 4: Dividing the World, 1947-1949

1 Lippmann quoted in Don Cook, *Forging the Alliance* (New York: Arbor House/William Morrow), 103-4.

2 In particular, General Maurice Pope; in early discussions with the Americans the idea was suggested that Canada might find itself at war before the Americans did, as in 1914 and 1939: American representatives found this view highly improbable: John Holmes private papers, F.H. Soward, "A Survey of Canadian External Policy," mimeo, ch. 3, 68-9, courtesy of the late John Holmes.

3 Library and Archives Canada (LAC), Brooke Claxton Papers, vol. 221, Claxton draft memoirs, iv, 958.

4 L.B. Pearson, undersecretary for external affairs, to Mackenzie King, 23 November 1946, and Mackenzie King statement, Canada, House of Commons *Debates*, 12 February 1947, quoted in J.T. Jockel, *No Boundaries Upstairs: Canada, the United States, and the Origins of North American Air Defence, 1945-1958* (Vancouver: UBC Press, 1987), 28-9. The "Maginot Line" refers to the fantastically expensive but also futile French defence system constructed along the border with Germany in the 1930s.

5 *Documents on Canadian External Relations* (DCER), vol. 14, *1948* (Ottawa: Department of Foreign Affairs and International Trade, 1994), 793ff, especially Claxton to St Laurent, 30 June 1948, and Pearson to Claxton, 14 July 1948; see the overview by James Eayrs, *In Defence of Canada*, vol. 4, *Growing up Allied* (Toronto: University of Toronto Press, 1980), 38-51. On the blockade, see Thomas Parrish, *Berlin in the Balance* (Reading, MA: Perseus, 1998).

6 See, for example, Reid's memorandum of February 1946, "An Approach to Some of the Basic Problems of Foreign Policy," reproduced in his *On Duty: A Canadian at the Making of the United Nations, 1945-1946* (Toronto: McClelland and Stewart, 1983), 152-9.

7 As had others: see Joint Intelligence Committee, "Strategic Appreciation," Appendix A, March 1947, *DCER*, vol. 13, *1947*, 353: "All we need assume is that the governing class of the Soviet Union is anxious to maintain the existing system in the area now under Soviet political control and that this involves a desire to expand the defence area of that system."

8 Escott Reid, *Radical Mandarin* (Toronto: University of Toronto Press, 1989), 224-5.

9 Escott Reid, "The United States and the Soviet Union: A Study of the Possibility of War and Some of the Implications for Canadian Policy," 30 August 1947, *DCER*, vol. 13, *1947*, 367-82.

10 Such penetration had occurred before, in 1814, when the tsar's armies reached Paris; afterwards, Parisian opinions reached into the Russian governing class, subverting the Russian political system. Stalin was well aware of the events of 1814, both as a high-water mark of Russian power and for the impact of Western political ideas on Russia.

11 R.M. Macdonnell to Pearson, 25 September 1947, *DCER*, vol. 13, *1947*, 387-9.

12 Ford to Pearson, 10 October 1947, ibid., 395-6.

13 Ritchie to DEA, 6 November 1947, ibid., especially 415.

14 MacKay to Pearson, 22 November 1947, ibid., 425-6.

15 Wrong, "Comment on Draft Memorandum," 5 December 1947, ibid., 438-42.

16 Wrong, "Influences Shaping the Policy of the United States towards the Soviet Union," 4 December 1947, ibid., 442-9.

17 LAC, St Laurent Papers, box 167, file "Notes on Commonwealth and International Affairs, 1947," no author, "General Canadian Policy at the United Nations," 20 October 1947. On the other hand, the United Nations was not completely discordant between 1945 and 1949: in disputes over Palestine, Kashmir, and Indonesia the UN produced agreement (and subsequent UN action) between the United States and the Soviet Union.

18 Escott Reid, *Time of Fear and Hope: The Making of the North Atlantic Treaty* (Toronto: McClelland and Stewart, 1977), 30-1. The speech had been cleared by the undersecretary, Pearson, with the consent of the minister, St Laurent.

19 J.W. Pickersgill and Donald F. Forster, *The Mackenzie King Record,* vol. 4 (Toronto: University of Toronto Press, 1970), 107ff, diary entry for 24 November 1947.

21 Ibid., 127-8.

20 Ibid., 119, diary entry for 4 December 1947.

22 Cook, *Forging the Alliance,* 109. Cook was a reporter in London for the *New York Herald Tribune* in 1947-1948.

23 King Record, 4:165, diary entry for 10 March 1948.

24 Ibid., 167, diary entry for 11 March 1948.

25 Pearson, "Proposed Pact of Mutual Assistance," quoted in James Eayrs, *In Defence of Canada,* vol. 4, *Growing up Allied* (Toronto: University of Toronto Press, 1980), 69.

26 Ian Q.R. Thomas, *The Promise of Alliance: NATO and the Political Imagination* (Lanham, MD: Rowman and Littlefield, 1997), 33.

27 As early as November 1946 Pearson wrote, "the USSR is ultimately bound to come into open conflict with western democracy." In response, the Western powers would combine and cooperate. Paper of 12 November 1946, preceding a Cabinet discussion of 14 November, *Documents on Canadian External Relations,* vol. 12, *1946* (Ottawa: Information Canada, 1977).

28 The thirteen were the United Kingdom, Canada, France, Belgium, Luxembourg, the Netherlands, Norway, Sweden, Denmark, Iceland, Eire, Portugal, and Italy. The door was left open for Germany and Spain to join when they acquired permanent or acceptable governments.

29 The text of the final position paper of the Pentagon meetings is in *Foreign Relations of the United States (FRUS), 1948,* vol. 3 (Washington: Government Printing Office, 1972), 72-5.

30 Wrong to Pearson, 19 May 1948, quoted in Eayrs, *In Defence of Canada,* 4:80-1; John Milloy, *The North Atlantic Treaty Organization, 1948-1957: Community or Alliance?* (Montreal and Kingston: McGill-Queen's University Press, 2006), 22-3, documents British opposition to melding an Atlantic alliance with European union and, more broadly, to economic and social cooperation.

31 LAC, King Papers, J4, file 2315, Pearson to King, 22 July 1948.

32 The historian Vojtech Mastny observes that the blockade "was very much Stalin's personal undertaking, managed more casually than it deserved." Mastny, *The Cold War and Soviet Insecurity: The Stalin Years* (New York: Oxford University Press, 1996), 47ff.

33 Memorandum by the participants in the Washington Security Talks, 9 September 1948, *FRUS, 1948*, 3:237-48, especially 245.

34 Milloy, *North Atlantic Treaty Organization*, 24.

35 Cook, *Forging the Alliance*, 203.

36 As Escott Reid observed, "Italy became an original member of the North Atlantic alliance even though the President of the United States didn't want it, the leading members of the Senate Foreign Relations Committee didn't want it and Britain, the Benelux countries, Canada and Norway were strongly opposed" (*Time of Fear and Hope*, 200).

37 Wrong's support was reluctant. Like Acheson, he saw little point to article 2, and he disapproved of Pearson's and Escott Reid's enthusiasm for the item: ibid., 173-6.

38 Given the poverty and chaos into which the socialist "system" collapsed, this argument will seem bizarre to readers of the twenty-first century, but from the perspective of the time it was very powerful. On this point see Mark Mazower, *Dark Continent: Europe's Twentieth Century* (New York: Knopf, 1999), 267-9.

39 Wrong is quoted in John Holmes, *The Shaping of Peace* (Toronto: University of Toronto Press, 1982), 2:113.

CHAPTER 5: CONFRONTING A CHANGING ASIA, 1945-1950

1 Prior to 1923, Chinese immigrants to Canada had to pay a very high "head tax." Between 1923 and 1947, they were virtually excluded from entering Canada as permanent immigrants. The Japanese were limited by a quota agreed to with the Japanese government. Japan was not much more enthusiastic about Japanese emigration than Canada was about receiving Japanese immigrants.

2 Henry F. Angus, *Canada and the Far East, 1940-1953* (Toronto: University of Toronto Press, 1953), 29.

3 A contemporary Canadian reaction may be found in the diary and letters of Chester Ronning, a Canadian embassy official in Nanking, published as Ronning, *A Memoir of China in War and Revolution from the Boxer Rebellion to the People's Republic* (New York: Pantheon, 1974). Ronning greeted the new Communist regime as "at long last, ... people ... who wanted to help the common people of China" (139).

4 Steven Hugh Lee, *Outposts of Empire* (Montreal and Kingston: Montreal-Queen's University Press, 1995), 25-6.

5 It is instructive to note that the UK embassy in Peking lived a shadowy existence for years, under the care of a chargé d'affaires. British recognition, in short, did the British little good. The Indian embassy, however, swiftly became a principal point of contact between the Beijing government and the outside world.

6 For a very pro-British point of view, which in tone is probably close to that of conservative Canadians in the 1950s, see Nirad Chaudhuri, *Thy Hand Great Anarch!* (New York: Addison-Wesley, 1988).

7 On this point see *Documents on Canadian External Relations* (*DCER*), vol. 16, *1950* (Ottawa: Canada Communication Group, 1996), 1292-7.

8 Hector Mackenzie, "An Old Dominion and the New Commonwealth: Canadian Policy on the Question of India's Membership, 1947-9," *Journal of Imperial and Commonwealth History* 27, 3 (1999): 88-9: "The principal focus for Canadian policy-makers had been on the constitutional options and consequences for the Commonwealth, with less attention to the political, strategic, or economic value of India to the organization itself or to the western alliance ... That demonstrated the considerable difference in interest and perceptions between the Canadian and British governments."

9 Cabinet conclusions, 17 March 1949, quoted in Mackenzie, "An Old Dominion," 82-112.

10 Quoted in James Eayrs, *In Defence of Canada*, vol. 3, *Peacemaking and Deterrence* (Toronto: University of Toronto Press, 1972), 257.

11 Douglas LePan, *Bright Glass of Memory* (Toronto: McGraw-Hill Ryerson, 1979), 172; John English, *The Worldly Years: The Life of Lester Pearson, 1949-1972* (Toronto: Knopf, 1992), 36-7.

12 This generalization excludes the minuscule Canadian Communist Party, which paid close attention to Soviet interests and to the paycheque it received from Moscow.

13 See on this point Greg Donaghy and Stéphane Roussel, "A Liberal Idealist in a Hard-Power World" in *Escott Reid: Diplomat and Scholar*, ed. Greg Donaghy and Stéphane Roussel (Montreal and Kingston: McGill-Queen's University Press, 2004), 3-9.

14 Ibid., 32, 37.

15 LePan, *Bright Glass*, 152.

16 On the origins and history of the Colombo Plan, see Ademola Adeleke, "Ties without Strings: The Colombo Plan and the Geopolitics of International Aid" (PhD diss., University of Toronto, 1996).

17 Robert A. Spencer, *Canada in World Affairs: From UN to NATO, 1946-1949* (Toronto: Oxford University Press, 1959), 118-20.

18 English, *Worldly Years*, 41-2.

19 Dean Acheson, *Present at the Creation: My Years in the State Department* (New York: Norton, 1969), 356-7; the account in James Chace, *Acheson: The Secretary of State Who Created the American World* (New York: Simon and Schuster, 1998), 268-9, argues that Congressional rejection of aid to Korea played a larger role than anything Acheson said.

20 Library and Archives Canada (LAC), Brooke Claxton, memoirs, vi, 1124ff, Claxton Papers, MG 32 B 5, vol. 221. The Cabinet minutes for 18 and 30 December 1947, when Korea was discussed, are regrettably laconic. See the "Cabinet conclusions" for those dates on LAC, www.collectionscanada.ca/archivianet.

21 This account follows the Claxton memoirs, ibid.; J.W. Pickersgill and Donald F. Forster, *The Mackenzie King Record*, vol. 4 (Toronto: University of Toronto Press, 1970), 133-53; Dale Thomson, *Louis St. Laurent: Canadian* (Toronto: Macmillan, 1967), 221-4; Denis Stairs, *The Diplomacy of Constraint: Canada, the Korean War and the United States* (Toronto: University of Toronto Press, 1974), 8-17; David Bercuson, *True Patriot: The Life of Brooke Claxton, 1898-1960* (Toronto: University of Toronto Press, 1993), 190-2.

22 See the analysis in John Lewis Gaddis, *We Now Know: Rethinking Cold War History* (New York: Clarendon Press, 1997), 70-5. Stalin's closest colleagues believed that the Soviet dictator had gone too far in encouraging the North Koreans: Simon Sebag Montefiore, *Stalin: Court of the Red Tsar* (London: Weidenfeld and Nicolson, 2003), 538-9.

23 The lies were not sufficient to deceive the governments of the Western powers in 1950 but they did convince those who wished to be convinced; for many years after, these "useful idiots," to use Lenin's phrase, proclaimed the innocence of North Korea and the guilt of the South Koreans and the Americans.

24 Stairs, *Diplomacy of Constraint*, 31-2; LePan, *Bright Glass*, 206.

25 Robert Prince, "The Limits of Constraint: Canadian-American Relations and the Korean War, 1950-51," *Journal of Canadian Studies* 27, 4 (1992-1993): 129-52.

26 The Americans bet that the Soviet delegation would be slow – too slow – to change its boycott policy, as every detail of Soviet behaviour abroad ultimately depended on Stalin's permission, and that proved to be so: Chace, *Acheson*, 285. On the UN resolutions and Pearson's statement, see Stairs, *Diplomacy of Constraint*, 34-51.

27 Stairs, *Diplomacy of Constraint*, 68-9.

28 Secretary of State to all diplomatic missions, 29 June 1950; Livingston Merchant to Dean Rusk, 19 July 1950, enclosing Chiefs of Staff list of proposed contributions, *Foreign Relations of the United States, 1950*, vol. 7 (Washington: Government Printing Office, 1976), 231-2, 432-5.

29 Prince, "Limits of Constraint," 137.

30 Bercuson, *True Patriot,* 209-10.

31 Prince, "Limits of Constraint," note 57.

32 LAC, DEA Records, vol. 4737, file 50069-A-40, pt. 27, Arnold Heeney to John Holmes, 21 July 1950; and Hume Wrong to Pearson, 22 July 1950, ibid., pt. 2.

33 The American defence debate centred on an April 1950 policy paper called "NSC (National Security Council) 68," a highly contentious analysis of Communist (especially Soviet) intentions and capabilities. NSC 68 argued not merely for American rearmament but for American mobilization, in the face of the budgetary cheese-paring of the Truman administration, which until then had concentrated on reducing taxes and consequently defence. See Ernest R. May, ed., *American Cold War Strategy: Interpreting NSC 68* (Boston: Bedford Books/St Martin's Press, 1993).

34 This Canadian preoccupation was well known elsewhere in the Commonwealth: Ian McGibbon, *New Zealand and the Korean War,* vol. 1, *Politics and Diplomacy* (Auckland: Oxford University Press, 1992), 111-12.

35 Technically the Australians and New Zealanders announced their contribution before the British did, but they knew of the British intention and were anxious to seem to be taking the initiative: William Stueck, *The Korean War: An International History* (Princeton, NJ: Princeton University Press, 1995), 72-3.

36 Of the 8,000 men recruited for the "special force" destined for Korea in its first two months, 1,500 deserted while 2,000 had to be discharged: Ted Barris, *Deadlock in Korea: Canadians at War, 1950-1953* (Toronto: Macmillan, 1999), 36-8.

37 Speech of 4 September 1950, House of Commons, *Debates,* 1950, 2nd session, 224.

38 Prince, "Limits of Constraint," 141.

39 See, for example, Heeney to Pearson, 4 October 1950, *DCER,* vol. 16, *1950,* 170-1, in which Acheson urged Canadian membership on a UN commission as the best way of heading off pressure for American membership. Obviously Acheson expected his critics would accept Canada as a kind of "virtual" United States.

40 Trinity College Archives, John Holmes Papers, memorandum, 12 May 1951.

Chapter 6: From Korea to the Rhine

1 John Lewis Gaddis, *We Now Know: Rethinking Cold War History* (New York: Clarendon Press, 1997), 79-81.

2 On 25 September the Indian ambassador in Peking was given a warning that China would intervene, and reported accordingly. Denis Stairs observes that this "and subsequent warnings ... were destined, like the prophecies of Cassandra, not to be believed" (Stairs, *The Diplomacy of Constraint: Canada, the Korean War and the United States* [Toronto: University of Toronto Press, 1974], 126). Cassandra's prophecies were, of course, accurate; but the evidence now suggests that for three weeks after 25 September the Chinese leadership had not made up its mind what to do.

3 Ibid., 127.

4 Howe was writing in December 1950; quoted in Robert Bothwell and William Kilbourn, *C.D. Howe: A Biography* (Toronto: McClelland and Stewart, 1979), 254. Howe was considered to be one of the most pro-American members of the government.

5 Connoisseurs of artful blather should read the defence of Truman's remarks by Dean Acheson in his book, *Present at the Creation* (New York: New York University Press, 1969), 478. Acheson does add that the press distorted Truman's remarks and that Attlee and others had got a wrong impression.

6 Pearson to Wrong, 4 December 1950, with enclosure, "Korea and the Atomic Bomb," 3 December 1950, and memorandum of conversation between George Ignatieff and R.G. Arneson, 6 December 1950, *Documents on Canadian External Relations (DCER),* vol. 16, *1950* (Ottawa: Canada Communication Group, 1996), 253-5, 265-8.

7 Acheson, *Present at the Creation*, 481; see also the memorandum dated 8 December 1950 by the chief of the US and Far Eastern Division in DEA, Herbert Norman, in which he argued for a negotiated settlement, failing which the UN forces would probably be driven out of Korea. At that point he also argued that the West should prefer "cutting one's losses" to any prolonged confrontation with China: *DCER*, vol. 16, *1950*, 275-8.

8 Hume Wrong, Memorandum of conversation with Sir Oliver Franks, 13 December 1950, *DCER*, vol. 16, *1950*, 298-9.

9 Library and Archives Canada (LAC), St Laurent Papers, box 277, file "External Affairs: Commonwealth Prime Ministers' Meeting," Paper no. 31(50), 21 November 1950, and "Supplementary Memorandum on the Imminence of War," 14 December 1950.

10 Cabinet conclusions (minutes), 21 December 1950, *DCER*, vol. 16, *1950*, 1154-6.

11 Pearson and Claxton, "The International Situation," 28 December 1950, ibid., 1159-62.

12 F.H. Leacy, ed., *Historical Statistics of Canada*, 2nd ed. (Ottawa: Statistics Canada, 1983) (*HSC*), 2, table H19. Economic analysis is from Robert Bothwell, Ian Drummond, and John English, *Canada since 1945: Power, Politics, and Provincialism*, rev. ed. (Toronto: University of Toronto, 1989), 134.

13 All these figures are in current dollars; if constant dollars are used, the economy grew by 33 percent between 1945 and 1952.

14 Dale Thomson, *Louis St. Laurent, Canadian* (Toronto: Macmillan, 1967), 301-3. Thomson, who was then St Laurent's secretary, noted that Ontario's premier "proved himself a model of conciliation and understanding," while even the premier of Quebec, Maurice Duplessis, also proved "surprisingly co-operative." It is hard not to see a connection between the positive mood and the grave international situation.

15 The Canadian government was initially reluctant to participate in a Commonwealth Division but in December 1950 gave in to British pressure and agreed to its formation: William Johnston, *A War of Patrols: Canadian Army Operations in Korea* (Vancouver: UBC Press, 2003), 138-9.

16 David Bercuson, *True Patriot: The Life of Brooke Claxton, 1898-1960* (Toronto: University of Toronto Press, 1993), 217.

17 Figures are from H. Fairlie Wood, *Strange Battleground: Official History of the Canadian Army in Korea* (Ottawa: Queen's Printer, 1966), 257-8.

18 Clay Blair, *The Forgotten War: America in Korea, 1950-1953* (New York: Doubleday, 1989), 837-9, describes a battle at Kapyong in April 1951 that resulted in presidential citations for the Princess Pats as well as Australian and American units.

19 Quoted in Johnston, *War of Patrols*, 140-1.

20 Michael Hickey, *The Korean War: The West Confronts Communism, 1950-1953* (London: John Murray, 1999), 282-3.

21 LAC, Claxton Papers, vol. 31, Claxton to George Ferguson, 27 May 1953.

22 Bercuson, *True Patriot*, 227; see also Queen's University Archives (QUA), Grant Dexter Papers, vol. 6, file 38, Bruce Hutchison memo, 24 October 1950, in which Pearson quotes the US army chief of staff, General Lawton Collins, as telling him that the United States did *not* want a Canadian brigade in Europe.

23 It actually rose by the mid-1960s to 7,000: Isabel Campbell, "Harmony and Dissonance: A Study of the Influence of Foreign Policy Goals on Military Decision-Making with respect to the Canadian NATO Brigade in Germany, 1951-1964," (PhD diss., Laval University, 2000), 5.

24 Campbell, ibid., 117-24, examines the nature of the fit. There were many examples of positive interaction with the British army on both an official and unofficial level. Nevertheless, British custom – for example, the highly privileged treatment of officers – was not always Canadian practice. There were also occasional clashes between Canadian and British soldiers in German streets and bars. On a higher level, the Canadians suspected the British of sharp practice on matters such as exchange rates.

25 Campbell, ibid., 96, notes that "the principle of equality of Germans was a key element in the Canadian plan to convert them into western allies." As Urs Obrist has demonstrated, "An Essential Endeavour: Canada and West Germany, 1946-1957" (PhD diss., University of Toronto, 2006), the German government used relations with Canada – not an occupying power – as a sign of its return to respectable international status.

26 Defence Liaison (2) to Pearson, "Probable Soviet Campaigns in the Event of Total War in 1951," 1 June 1951, enclosed in Pearson to St Laurent, 6 June 1951, LAC, St Laurent Papers, box 175, file "External Affairs, Defence, 1948-1951." See also Sean Maloney, *War without Battles: Canada's NATO Brigade in Germany, 1951-1993* (Toronto: McGraw-Hill Ryerson, 1997), 35, which estimates Soviet divisions in Germany at twenty-seven, with twelve Polish divisions presumably also available.

27 Note by the Secretaries to the North Atlantic Military Committee, "Estimate of the Relative Strength and Capabilities of NATO and Soviet Bloc Forces at Present and in the Immediate Future," 10 November 1951, Parallel History Project on NATO and the Warsaw Pact, Documentary Collections, http://www.isn.ethz.ch/php/documents. The document is classified "Cosmic – Top Secret."

28 The Lisbon goals were thought to be unfeasible even by the Soviets, who were unimpressed by this exercise in fantasy: Vojtech Mastny, "NATO in the Beholder's Eye: Soviet Perceptions and Policies, 1949-56," Cold War International History Project, Working Paper #35 (Washington: Woodrow Wilson Center, March 2002).

29 James Eayrs, *In Defence of Canada*, vol. 4, *Growing up Allied* (Toronto: Toronto University Press, 1980), 223.

30 Quoted in ibid., 223.

31 LAC, Privy Council Papers, Cabinet conclusions, 5 February 1952.

32 It is possible that the progenitors of the new Canadian reactor, called NRU, knew very well that its plutonium was unlikely to be needed in the United States, but that assigning it a role as a "war industry," so to speak, would be more likely to get it funded by the government.

33 Bothwell and Kilbourn, *Howe*, 250-1. On the other hand, US domestic rivalry was fierce, and American rivals often blocked Canadian supplies: ibid., 254-5.

34 "Canadian Foreign Policy in a Two-Power World," 14 April 1951, Department of External Affairs, *Statements and Speeches*, 51/14.

35 It was actually the second speech of its kind, following an address to the Canadian Bar Association on 31 March (*Statements and Speeches*, 51/13). In this speech Pearson argued that support of the Western cause "if it is to have any value, does not mean an automatic response of 'Ready, aye Ready' to everything that Washington proposes."

36 One diplomat, Lou Rogers, complained to Escott Reid on 2 April 1951 that the United States disregarded "any link between thought and action that did not mirror American policy." Rogers's letter is quoted in John Milloy, *The North Atlantic Treaty Organization: Community or Alliance?* (Montreal and Kingston: Montreal-Queen's University Press, 2006), 67.

37 Quoted in Geoffrey Pearson, *Seize the Day: Lester B. Pearson and Crisis Diplomacy* (Ottawa: Carleton University Press, 1993), 78.

38 LAC, Howe Papers, vol. 178, file 90-29, Howe to Howard C. Sykes, 16 April 1951; John English, *The Worldly Years: The Life of Lester Pearson, 1949-1972* (Toronto: Knopf, 1992), 2, 60-1; LAC, Pearson Papers, MG 26, Pearson to Wrong, April 1951. Astonishingly, the relevant volume (1951) of the *DCER* contains nothing on this issue. See English, *The Worldly Years*, 59-63.

39 There is a very perceptive and persuasive analysis of Acheson's character and views in John Lamberton Harper, *American Visions of Europe: Franklin D. Roosevelt, George F. Kennan, and Dean G. Acheson* (New York: Columbia University Press, 1994), 235-45.

40 Walter Millis, ed., *The Forrestal Diaries* (New York: Viking Press, 1951), diary entry for 17 August 1948; Acheson, *Present at the Creation*, 71.

41 Acheson was fond of reiterating this point. See, for example, his essay, "Canada: 'Stern Daughter of the Voice of God,'" in *Neighbors Taken for Granted: Canada and the United States*, ed. Livingston Merchant (New York: Praeger, 1966), 134-47.

42 Clair Balfour, "Pearson Recalls the Acheson Years," *Globe and Mail*, 15 October 1971.

43 Bruce Hutchison, *The Far Side of the Street* (Toronto: Macmillan, 1976), 282-6.

44 United Kingdom, National Archives, DO 127/117, J. Thomson to Bourke Cockram, Commonwealth Relations Office, 6 September 1951, enclosing his memorandum, "Canadians' Views on NATO, etc."

Chapter 7: The Era of Good Feeling, 1953-1957

1 Georgetown University Library, Foreign Affairs Oral History Program, Canada Country Collection, George Vest interview, 1989.

2 There were also five independent members of Parliament.

3 Investment can be either *direct* or portfolio. *Direct* is long-term investment in a firm by shareholders, usually in a firm controlled by those same shareholders; *portfolio* is investment in securities and does not imply control.

4 Department of External Affairs memorandum, 1954, quoted in Bruce Muirhead, *The Development of Postwar Canadian Trade Policy: The Failure of the Anglo-European Option* (Montreal and Kingston: McGill-Queen's University Press, 1992), 143.

5 In a meeting between President Eisenhower and Prime Minister St Laurent on 8 May 1953, Eisenhower and his advisers advanced the idea of a customs union and the Canadians retreated: *Foreign Relations of the United States* (*FRUS*), *1952-1954*, vol. 6 (Washington: Government Printing Office, 1987), 2090-1; *Documents on Canadian External Relations* (*DCER*), vol. 19, *1953* (Ottawa: Canada Communication Group, 1997), 1006-10; Donald Barry, "Eisenhower, St. Laurent and Free Trade, 1953," *International Perspectives* (1987): 8-10.

6 All figures from F.H. Leacy, ed. *Historical Statistics of Canada*, 2nd ed. (Ottawa: Supply and Services, 1983) (*HSC*), tables D125, H148, H160, and H161.

7 Howe understood that Canada could make the Arrow, and may even have thought it a superior aircraft. As one of his colleagues, Douglas Abbott, later explained to me, "Clarence [Howe] used to say we could grow bananas in Canada, if we wanted to pay for them."

8 The head of the US Navy's nuclear submarine project typically tried to conceal what they were testing at Chalk River. The Canadians, who were naturally and prudently curious about what they were putting into their reactor, took the American officials sent up to supervise the tests on a prolonged tour of Ottawa bars until their sealed packages could be examined and appraised. It was a reasonable safety measure, but the resulting information was also valuable for Canada's domestic power program.

9 Vojtech Mastny concludes that "In any case ... the putative Soviet action would have been well short of the dreaded assault by the 175 combat-ready divisions recurrent in NATO's annual 'Estimates of Soviet Strength and capabilities' from 1950 to 1955." See Vojtech Mastny, "Did NATO Win the Cold War? Looking Over the Wall," *Foreign Affairs* 78 (1999): 177.

10 See the 1950 planning document MC 14, quoted in Sean Maloney, *War without Battles: Canada's NATO Brigade in Germany, 1951-1993* (Toronto: McGraw-Hill Ryerson, 1997), 36.

11 On this point see David Calleo, *Rethinking Europe's Future* (Princeton, NJ: Princeton University Press, 2001), 100-1.

12 According to the *Random House Dictionary of the English Language* (New York: Random House, 1973), a deterrent was a "military strength or an ability to retaliate sufficiently to frighten an enemy from attacking."

13 Leigh Sarty, "A Middle Power in Moscow: Canada and the Soviet Union from Khrushchev to Gorbachev," *Queen's Quarterly* 98, 3 (1991): 557-61.

14 The Canadian brigade group in Germany was still assigned to the British Army of the Rhine, which was already equipped with tactical nuclear weapons.

15 Lewis Strauss, quoted in John Lewis Gaddis, *We Now Know: Rethinking Cold War History* (New York: Oxford University Press, 1997), 225.

16 Brooke Claxton, February 1951, quoted in Joseph Jockel, *No Boundaries Upstairs: Canada, the United States, and the Origins of North American Air Defence, 1945-1958* (Vancouver: UBC Press, 1987), 41.

17 See the 1951 survey, quoted in ibid., 48.

18 Such at least is Jockel's conclusion: ibid., 90.

19 There were criticisms nevertheless. Judith Robinson, political columnist in the Conservative *Toronto Telegram*, commented on Canadian-American relations in 1955 as follows: "So here we are among the banana republics, a satellite state proclaimed by Pearson. Purdahed behind the atomic curtain by the Canadian we hired to look after our international interests while we were still a sovereign nation, here we are." Judith Robinson, *This Is on the House* (Toronto: McClelland and Stewart, 1957), 61.

20 Seymour Martin Lipset, *Continental Divide: The Values and Institutions of the United States and Canada* (New York: Routledge, 1990), 212.

21 Take the interesting Hammond Innes novel (and later movie), *Campbell's Kingdom* (London: Collins, 1952) or the reference in Nevil Shute, *In the Wet* (London: Heinemann, 1953), 136-8, in which a French-Canadian prime minister, Auguste Delamain, provides a Canadian asylum for a refugee royal family.

22 Joe Garner, *The Commonwealth Office, 1925-68* (London: Heinemann, 1978), 279.

23 *Canada Year Book, 1961*, 970-1: Trade of Canada with Commonwealth and Other Countries, 1946-60.

24 Escott Reid, *Envoy to Nehru* (New Delhi: Oxford University Press, 1981), 4.

25 See Greg Donaghy and Stéphane Roussel, eds., *Escott Reid, Diplomat and Scholar* (Montreal and Kingston: McGill-Queen's University Press, 2004).

26 John English, *The Worldly Years: The Life of Lester Pearson, 1949-1972* (Toronto: Knopf, 1992), 36-7.

27 A discussion between Paul Martin, minister of national health and welfare and head of the Canadian UN delegation and his American counterpart, Henry Cabot Lodge, is instructive: "Lodge emphasized [to Martin] that [Nationalist] Chinese would not have to bear consequences, but it would be the US and Canadians ought to help US. Martin, however, merely said he would think about it." US Mission at the UN to the Department of State, 16 November 1955, *FRUS, 1955-1957*, vol. 11 (Washington: Government Printing Office, 1988), 369-70.

28 The deed involved an elaborate trade-off of Western and Communist candidates for membership. Sixteen countries were admitted in December 1955; Outer Mongolia and Japan were vetoed in a tit-for-tat exchange between the Soviet Union and Nationalist China.

29 Pearson memorandum, 11 November 1955, quoted in English, *Worldly Years*, 124.

30 English, *Worldly Years*, 124-5.

31 Quoted in ibid., 132.

32 Pearson to Jean Désy, 30 October 1956, quoted in ibid., 134. The Canadian high commissioner in London, Norman Robertson, was similarly uninformed.

33 Pearson ran his proposed course of action past the Canadian Cabinet on 7 August 1956 and found that several ministers expected that Canada would automatically endorse the British position. With St Laurent's support, Pearson received a free hand to do whatever he thought best to avert a war and the possible breakup of the Commonwealth: John Hilliker and Donald Barry, *Canada's Department of External Affairs*, vol. 2, *Coming of Age, 1946-1968* (Montreal and Kingston: McGill-Queen's University Press, 1995), 124.

34 Quoted in Norman Hillmer, "Peacekeeping: Canadian Invention, Canadian Myth," in *Welfare States in Trouble: Historical Perspectives on Canada and Sweden*, ed. J.L. Granatstein and Sune Akerman (North York, ON: Swedish-Canadian Academic Foundation, 1995), 164.

35 US Mission at the UN to Secretary of State, 19 November 1956, *FRUS, 1955-1957*, vol. 16, *Suez Crisis* (Washington: Government Printing Office, 1990), 1154-7.

36 The complete phrase was: "The era when the supermen of Europe could govern the whole world has and is coming to a pretty close end."

37 Robinson, *This Is on the House*, 82-3. James Eayrs, *Canada in World Affairs, 1955-1957* (Toronto: Oxford University Press, 1959), 187, notes a division of opinion in the English-language press and a strong anti-European attitude in the French-language press.

38 Quoted in Peter Stursberg, *Lester Pearson and the American Dilemma* (Toronto: Doubleday, 1980), 143.

39 Quoted in ibid., 143-4, 146. Lodge and other Americans were later known to grumble that they and not Pearson should have won the Nobel Peace Prize.

40 A poll showed that only 10 percent of the French thought the Americans treated them as equals. See Frédéric Bozo, *Two Strategies for Europe: De Gaulle, the United States, and the Atlantic Alliance* (Lanham, MD: Rowman and Littlefield, 2001), 2-3.

41 Eayrs, *Canada in World Affairs*, 186n.

42 Paradoxically, Canada's military still sported British-style uniforms and rank insignia, and the Royal Canadian Air Force proudly clung to British nomenclature – squadron leader, wing commander, group captain, etc.

43 Arthur Andrew, *The Rise and Fall of a Middle Power: Canadian Diplomacy from King to Mulroney* (Toronto: James Lorimer, 1993), 31.

44 The Liberal politician was Jack Pickersgill.

Chapter 8: Diefenbaker and the Dwindling British Connection

1 Macmillan, on his first visit to Diefenbaker's Ottawa, in October 1957, remarked on his host's appreciation of "the high plane" of the British prime minister's approach to alliance diplomacy: Macmillan quoted in Alistair Horne, *Harold Macmillan* (New York: Penguin, 1989), 2:57.

2 Basil Robinson, *Diefenbaker's World: A Populist in Foreign Affairs* (Toronto: University of Toronto Press, 1989), 103.

3 Ibid., 98.

4 Rusk to Kennedy, 14 May 1961, *Foreign Relations of the United States, 1961-1963*, vol. 13 (Washington: Government Printing Office, 1994), 1152-3.

5 Robinson, *Diefenbaker's World*, 100, 110.

6 There is a curious lack of consideration for the role of the postwar Commonwealth in contemporary British political history. See, for example, Hugo Young, *This Blessed Plot: Britain and Europe from Churchill to Blair* (London: Papermac, 1999), which barely mentions the subject.

7 Statistics Canada, *Canadian Statistical Review: Historical Summary, 1970* (Ottawa: Statistics Canada, 1972), 123, 125.

8 See David Calleo, *Rethinking Europe's Future* (Princeton, NJ: Princeton University Press, 2001), 22-3.

9 Peter Clarke, *Hope and Glory: Britain, 1900-1990* (London: Allen Lane/Penguin, 1996), 279.

10 Library and Archives Canada (LAC), Privy Council Records, RG 2/1892, Cabinet conclusions, 9 May 1957.

11 Young, *This Blessed Plot*, 70, terms "the official advice ... laughably erroneous."

12 EFTA comprised seven countries around the periphery of Europe, from Portugal to Finland. As a free trade association rather than a customs union, it did not impinge on Canadian exports.

13 Reid was Canadian ambassador to West Germany at the time: Escott Reid, "Western European Integration," 15 January 1959, quoted in Isabel Campbell, "Harmony and Dissonance: A Study of the Influence of Foreign Policy Goals on Military Decision-Making with Respect to the Canadian NATO Brigade in Germany, 1951-1964" (PhD diss., Laval University, 2000), 67-8.

14 LAC, RG2/1892, Cabinet conclusions, 11 April 1957.

15 United Kingdom, National Archives, CAB 35/31, CC 50(57), 9 July 1957; the $625 million estimate was presented to the Cabinet by the president of the Board of Trade on 23 July: ibid., meeting of 23 July 1957.

16 LAC, RG 25, file 50401-40, A.F.W. Plumptre, "UK Proposal for Canada-UK Free Trade Area," 9 September 1957; RG 2, vol. 1893, Cabinet conclusions, 28 November 1957, in which Ellen Fairclough, representing an industrial riding, had to be reassured that the government had never intended to purchase British goods in lieu of Canadian ones.

17 In his history of Canadian trade policy, *A Trading Nation: From Colonialism to Globalization* (Vancouver UBC Press, 2002), Michael Hart notes that "Diefenbaker's impulse smacked of naiveté and nostalgia. He seemed to have little appreciation that trade policy, like all branches of foreign policy, is not solely within the control of a single government" (298).

18 Duplessis was quoted by Pierre Sévigny, a Quebec Conservative MP and later minister: Peter Stursberg, *Diefenbaker: Leadership Gained, 1956-1962* (Toronto: University of Toronto Press, 1975) 57, 77.

19 The British were, as a senior British diplomat put it, "taken aback," because they "did not perceive fully how the Commonwealth would evolve and the reduced political and economic role that [they] ... would play in it." See Sir Nicholas Henderson, "Britain's Decline: Its Causes and Consequences," *Economist*, 2 June 1979, 29-40.

20 The Canadian High Commissioner in London, George Drew, a former premier of Ontario, provided his own unique form of diplomacy, short-circuiting the usual channels of communication between the two capitals.

21 Afrikaans is a variety of Dutch.

22 David Reynolds, *Britannia Overruled: British Policy and World Power in the 20th Century* (London: Longmans, 1991), 219-20.

23 United Kingdom, National Archives, CAB 128/35, CC 22 (61), Cabinet conclusions, 20 April 1961.

24 LAC, Privy Council Records, Cabinet conclusions, 15 July 1961.

25 Public opinion was sharply divided, even among those groups that traditionally favoured the Conservatives, such as business people. Normally Conservative newspapers were also divided as to the government's policy: Peyton Lyon, *Canada in World Affairs, 1961-1963* (Toronto: Oxford University Press, 1968), ch. 8.

26 David Reynolds, *Britannia Overruled*, 219, interprets the Commonwealth reaction as "grudging approval." This seems an exaggeration, not only for Canada but for most other Commonwealth members. On Hees and Fulton, see LAC, Privy Council Records, Cabinet conclusions, 9 and 14 September 1961.

27 United Kingdom, National Archives, 128/36, CC 31(62), Cabinet conclusions, 3 May 1962: "Canadian ministers seemed to be particularly suspicious of the encouragement given by the United States Administration to Britain's application."

28 Macmillan by this point regarded Diefenbaker as "a very crooked man for whom the only thing that mattered" was "the political advantage of himself and his party," quoted in Horne, *Macmillan*, 2:356.

29 See, for example, the analysis by *Maclean's* Ottawa correspondent Blair Fraser, in his *The Search for Identity: Canada, 1945-1967* (New York and Toronto: Doubleday, 1967), 186. Referring to the publicity given to Canadian views on the Common Market issue, "a British civil servant" commented, "[The] public isn't used to hearing this sort of talk. Civil servants and politicians don't mind it, but the British voters were furious." But the politicians apparently *did* mind, while "British voters" didn't.

30 Nigel Lawson, *The View from No. 11* (New York: Doubleday, 1993), 511. Lawson described the Commonwealth as "a largely meaningless relic of Empire."

31 Calleo, *Rethinking Europe's Future*, 156.

32 LAC, RG 59, 611.42/5-362, Merchant to Milton Rewinkel, acting director, Office of BNA, 3 May 1962.

CHAPTER 9: NUCLEAR NIGHTMARES, 1957-1963

1 See *Thin Ice* (New York: Random House, 1997) by Bruce McCall, a *New Yorker* writer, on a Canadian boy's view of the distant and glamorous United States as compared to what he perceived to be his own dull, grey, Ontario upbringing.

2 These were the titles of, respectively, a novel by Sloan Wilson and works of sociology by William Whyte and David Reisman, available in the mid-1950s in the new fashion of American quality paperbacks. The applicability of their descriptions is less important than the fact that Canadians readily accepted these and other critiques of 1950s society as apt diagnoses of their own surroundings.

3 National Archives and Records Administration (NARA), RG 59, 1955-59 series, 742.00/6-1157, Livingston Merchant to Secretary of State, 21 June 1957. There was a run on the British pound and French franc; oil markets, afflicted by an Arab oil boycott, were in chaos; and the Americans refused to help; see also items 742.00/6-1857 and 742.13/6-2457.

4 Diefenbaker did complain to the British about the "tendency of America to treat Canada like Mexico or Brazil." See James Ellison, *Threatening Europe: Britain and the Creation of the European Community* (London: Macmillan, 2000), 130.

5 Blair Fraser, *The Search for Identity: Canada, 1945-1967* (New York and Toronto: Doubleday, 1967), 189-90.

6 Ibid., 190. These views are undoubtedly very close to Pearson's on this issue.

7 Basil Robinson, *Diefenbaker's World: A Populist in Foreign Affairs* (Toronto: University of Toronto Press, 1989), 22-3.

8 David Reynolds, *One World Divisible: A Global History since 1945* (New York: Norton, 2000), 253.

9 See, for example, Patrick Kyba, "Alvin Hamilton and Sino-Canadian Relations," in *Reluctant Adversaries: Canada and the People's Republic of China, 1949-1970*, ed. Paul M. Evans and B. Michael Frolic (Toronto: University of Toronto Press, 1991), 168-86.

10 Robert Bothwell, Ian Drummond, and John English, *Canada since 1945: Power, Politics, and Provincialism*, rev. ed. (Toronto: University of Toronto, 1989), 216-18; *Canada Year Book, 1967* (Ottawa: Queen's Printer, 1967), 973.

11 COCOM, sometimes spelled CoCom, stood for the Coordinating Committee for Mutual Export Control. It restricted those exports of Western countries (basically NATO members) that had military or nuclear applications.

12 Trudy Huskamp Peterson, *Agricultural Exports, Farm Income, and the Eisenhower Administration* (Lincoln: University of Nebraska Press, 1979), 128-9. The sale to Poland took place over strong Canadian objections.

13 Robinson, *Diefenbaker's World*, 92.

14 See on this point the argument in Richard Gid Powers, *Not without Honor: The History of American Anticommunism* (New Haven, CT: Yale University Press, 1998).

15 Eisenhower sent a personal letter to Diefenbaker on 9 July 1960 ("Ike" to "John") suggesting that Secretary of State Christian Herter confer with Minister of External Affairs Howard Green on the subject of Castro. I am indebted to John Dirks for this information.

16 Minutes of 451st meeting of the National Security Council, 15 July 1960, *Foreign Relations of the United States, 1958-1960*, vol. 6 (Washington: State Department, 1991), 1018-19.

17 Minutes of the 464th meeting of the National Security Council, 20 October 1960, ibid., 1098. The quotation is by Douglas Dillon, the undersecretary of state.

18 Michael Hart, *Fifty Years of Canadian Tradecraft: Canada at the GATT, 1947-1997* (Ottawa: Centre for Trade Policy and Law, 1998), 77-8.

19 David Calleo, *Rethinking Europe's Future* (Princeton, NJ: Princeton University Press, 2001), 221-2, stresses the importance of European agricultural interests and notes that the United States is also a world leader in agricultural subsidies. On the other hand, one might observe that European agri-

cultural subsidies benefit mostly agribusinesses and that the accompanying heavy hand of EU regulation is deeply unpopular among smaller farmers, even in France.

20 On this point see Ethan Kapstein, *The Insecure Alliance: Energy Crises and Western Politics since 1944* (New York: Oxford University Press, 1990), 83-5, 139-40. Coordination of oil supplies occurred through a committee of the Organisation for European Economic Co-operation until that organization was replaced by the Organisation for Economic Co-operation and Development (OECD) in 1960.

21 Edward Thrasher (economic officer, Ottawa embassy, 1957-1960), Association for Diplomatic Studies and Training, "Canada Country Collection," Trinity College Library, University of Toronto.

22 Daniel Yergin, *The Prize: The Epic Quest for Oil, Money and Power* (New York: Simon and Schuster, 1991), 512-13.

23 Richard H.K. Vietor, *Energy Policy in America since 1945: A Study in Business-Government Relations* (New York and Cambridge: Cambridge University Press, 1984), 128. The reasoning was that, without a market in the United States, Canada would build new oil pipelines to its eastern provinces, at that time supplied by oil from Venezuela.

24 The number of US nuclear devices grew from 1,200 to almost 24,000 in just eight years in the 1950s: Vojtech Mastny, "Did NATO Win the Cold War? Looking Over the Wall," *Foreign Affairs* 78 (May-June 1999): 183.

25 Freeman Dyson, *Weapons and Hope* (New York: Harper and Row, 1984), 33-4. Dyson adds: "The book and the film created an enduring myth, a myth which entered consciously or subconsciously into all subsequent thinking about nuclear war ... On the fundamental human level, in spite of all the technical inaccuracies, it spoke truth. It told the world, in language that everyone could understand, that nuclear war means death. And the world listened." According to Spencer Weart, the book sold four million copies and was serialized in forty newspapers (Weart, *Nuclear Fear: A History of Images* [Cambridge: Cambridge University Press 1988], 217-18).

26 The play caused great controversy in England when originally broadcast on the BBC, and presumably the CBC anticipated the same kind of vivid reaction in Canada.

27 On pacifism, see Thomas Socknat, *Witness against War: Pacifism in Canada, 1900-1945* (Toronto: University of Toronto Press, 1987); on the postwar history of pacifism, see Patricia McMahon, "The Politics of Canada's Nuclear Policy, 1957-1963" (PhD diss., University of Toronto, 1999), 134-5. McMahon notes the reputation of the Canadian Peace Congress, the largest pacifist group, as communist fellow travellers.

28 BOMARC was an acronym for Boeing Michigan Aeronautic Research Center.

29 Denis Smith, *Rogue Tory: The Life and Legend of John G. Diefenbaker* (Toronto: Macfarlane, Walter and Ross, 1995), 310ff. The BOMARC was recommended by the defence minister, George Pearkes, on the basis of American assessments in the summer of 1958 of the strategic threat to North America. The highly competent Cabinet secretary, R.B. Bryce, to whom Diefenbaker turned for advice, supported Pearkes's recommendation.

30 Diefenbaker had sought to justify the Arrow decision by claiming that the aircraft was not only expensive but obsolete. Expensive it certainly was, but whether it was obsolete was plainly doubtful, especially when the prime minister almost immediately purchased the similar (but cheaper) American F-101 and F-104 fighters.

31 McMahon, "The Politics of Canada's Nuclear Policy," 73-5.

32 Geoffrey Pearson, *Seize the Day: Lester B. Pearson and Crisis Diplomacy* (Ottawa: Carleton University Press, 1993), 101.

33 The original decision, in October 1958, was to acquire the American Lacrosse missile, designed to carry tactical nuclear warheads; later the choice fell on the Honest John system: Jon B. McLin, *Canada's Changing Defense Policy, 1957-1963: The Problems of a Middle Power in Alliance* (Baltimore, MD: Johns Hopkins University Press, 1968), 112-13.

34 Control over warheads was the subject of the black comedy *Dr. Strangelove* (1964), in which a de-
   mented American general, Jack D. Ripper, decides to pre-empt the Soviets by launching his bombers at the USSR. One gets through, and as a result the world is destroyed by a Soviet "doomsday
   machine," triggered by the American attack. The doomsday machine was the ultimate deterrent:
   once triggered by a nuclear attack it could not be defused or otherwise stopped. The Soviets had,
   unfortunately, kept its existence a secret, so that its deterrent effect was nil.

35 John Lewis Gaddis, *We Now Know: Rethinking Cold War History* (New York: Oxford University Press,
   1997), draws attention to armaments as props in an international relations drama: "Nuclear weapons,
   it is now clear, had a remarkably *theatrical* effect upon the course of the high Cold War" (258).

36 Isabel Campbell, "Harmony and Dissonance: A Study of the Influence of Foreign Policy Goals on
   Military Decision-Making with Respect to the Canadian NATO Brigade in Germany, 1951-1964"
   (PhD diss., Laval University, 2000).

37 The US Secretary of Defense, Robert McNamara, recalled answering, "Well, I understand that if we
   don't we are in trouble, but if we do use them, the Soviets will destroy Washington and New York."
   McNamara is quoted in Deborah Shapley, *Promise and Power: The Life and Times of Robert McNamara*
   (Boston: Little, Brown, 1993), 119-20. The situation does not appear to have changed much in the
   next few years: see, for example, US ambassador Llewellyn Thompson to Seymour Weiss, 29 December 1964, in the National Security Archive collection, available at http://www.gwu.edu/~nsarchiv/
   NSAEBB/NSAEBB31/index.html.

38 Quoted in Gaddis, *We Now Know*, 140; according to V. Zubok and C. Pleshakov, *Inside the Kremlin's
   Cold War* (Cambridge, MA: Harvard University Press, 1996), 198-9, Khrushchev took a gamble on
   Berlin and, apart from sowing dissension and discouraging German acquisition of nuclear weapons,
   had no long-term goal in view. The Canadians obliged on the former – becoming dissidents – and
   would have agreed with him on the latter, having themselves no longer-term objective.

39 Jules Léger (NATO ambassador) to External Affairs, 17 December 1958, LAC, RG 25, file 50102 vol.
   40, 1. I am indebted for this and other insights on the Berlin Crisis to Laura Madokoro's "Canada
   and the Berlin Crisis of 1958: A Study in Alliance Politics" (MA essay, University of Toronto, 2000).

40 Davis to Robertson, 19 February 1959, quoted in Madokoro, "Canada and the Berlin Crisis."

41 Quoted in Marc Trachtenberg, *A Constructed Peace: The Making of the European Settlement, 1945-
   1963* (Princeton, NJ: Princeton University Press, 1999), 263.

42 Isabel Campbell, "Harmony and Dissonance," 14-15, notes that "much Canadian commentary on
   German affairs written throughout the late 1940s, 1950s and even into the 1960s contains the underlying assumption that the German character was flawed and that politics in Germany required
   careful monitoring."

43 See on this point, John Lewis Gaddis, *We Now Know: Rethinking Cold War History* (New York:
   Oxford University Press, 1997), 263: Khrushchev's policy was "an old Bolshevik's romantic response,"
   according to a Soviet general.

44 Quoted in Gaddis, *We Now Know*, 265.

45 NARA, State Department Records, Department of State to US embassy in Ottawa, 20 November
   1962. I am indebted to John Dirks for this reference.

46 This may have been the silliest incident in the history of Canadian-American relations, but that
   does not mean that it was not serious. The American ambassador, whom Diefenbaker threatened
   with the secret document in a conversation in May 1962, was appalled by what he described as the
   prime minister's "tirade" and drew it immediately to Kennedy's attention: Livingston Merchant to
   George Ball, 5 May 1962, *Foreign Relations of the United States (FRUS), 1961-1963*, vol. 13 (Washington: Government Printing Office, 1994), 1172-7.

47 Basil Robinson, *Diefenbaker's World: A Populist in Foreign Affairs* (Toronto: University of Toronto
   Press, 1989), 284-7. Robinson debriefed Merchant on 3 December 1962: Merchant to Ball, undated
   memorandum, referring to the 3 December conversation, *FRUS, 1961-1963*, 13:1190-1.

48 Willis Armstrong and McGeorge Bundy quoted in Knowlton Nash, *Kennedy and Diefenbaker: Fear and Loathing across the Undefended Border* (Toronto: McClelland and Stewart, 1990), 209.

49 Willis Armstrong interview with author, Toronto, December 1991.

50 Merchant to Secretary of State Rusk and Undersecretary George Ball, undated but probably 3 December 1962, *FRUS, 1961-1963*, 13:1190-1.

51 National Archives and Records Administration (NARA), RG 59, 611.42/121762, Butterworth to State, 17 December 1962.

52 Patricia McMahon, "The Politics of Canada's Nuclear Policy, 1957-1963" (PhD diss., University of Toronto, 1999), 29.

53 Quoted in John English, *The Worldly Years: The Life of Lester Pearson, 1949-1972* (Toronto: Knopf, 1992), 262.

54 "It was very upsetting to me," Walter Gordon, MP for Davenport (Toronto) and a future finance minister, said; and some Liberals were sufficiently upset to leave the party and cross over to the newly founded New Democratic Party. But politically the sounder judgment was that of Keith Davey, the Liberals' principal backroom strategist: "More important than the issue was the fact that [Pearson] had taken a position in contrast to Diefenbaker's waffling and waffling." Quoted in Nash, *Kennedy and Diefenbaker*, 229; McMahon, "Politics of Canada's Nuclear Policy," 314.

55 William R. Tyler, assistant secretary of state for European affairs, to Undersecretary George Ball, 29 January 1963, *FRUS, 1961-1963*, 13:1193-4.

56 "You son of a bitch," the minister of agriculture is supposed to have said to his colleague, the minister of national defence. "You total, unashamed shit." Et cetera. Quoted in Nash, *Kennedy and Diefenbaker*, 261.

57 Interestingly, in both language groups, young potential voters aged twenty-one to twenty-nine were significantly more inclined to accept nuclear devices than were their elders. Peyton Lyon, *Canada in World Affairs, 1961-1963* (Toronto: Oxford University Press, 1968), 541-2.

58 A point made very early on by one of Diefenbaker's most trenchant critics, Peter C. Newman, in his book, *Renegade in Power* (Toronto: McClelland and Stewart, 1963).

59 Quoted in Deborah Shapley, *Promise and Power: The Life and Times of Robert McNamara* (Boston: Little, Brown, 1993), 381.

60 Willis Armstrong interview.

CHAPTER 10: INNOCENCE AT HOME

1 Pickersgill wrote several volumes of autobiography; the one covering this period is *The Road Back* (Toronto: University of Toronto Press, 1986).

2 Hellyer later wrote an autobiography, *Damn the Torpedoes* (Toronto: McClelland and Stewart, 1990).

3 On Gordon, see Stephen Azzi, *Walter Gordon and the Rise of Canadian Nationalism* (Montreal and Kingston: McGill Queen's University Press, 1999).

4 National Archives and Records Administration (NARA), RG 59, 1967-69 series, box 1949, file POL CAN-US, Memcon, J. Chapman Chester, US State Dept. EUR/CAN, reporting a conversation with Robert Reguly, the *Star*'s Washington correspondent, 16 February 1968; Azzi, *Walter Gordon*, 69.

5 Mitchell Sharp, *Which Reminds Me ... A Memoir* (Toronto: University of Toronto Press, 1994), 53-4, 244-5.

6 Tom Kent, *A Public Purpose: An Experience of Liberal Opposition and Canadian Government* (Montreal and Kingston: McGill-Queen's University Press, 1988), 233; Greg Donaghy, *Tolerant Allies* (Montreal and Kingston: McGill-Queen's University Press, 2002), 23.

7 Pickersgill, *Road Back*, 200-3; Azzi, *Walter Gordon*, 107-10.

8 See Robert Bothwell, Ian Drummond, and John English, *Canada since 1945: Power, Politics, and Provincialism*, rev. ed. (Toronto: University of Toronto, 1989), 294-5.

9 Quoted in Azzi, *Walter Gordon*, 114.

10 See William Kaplan, *Everything that Floats: Pat Sullivan, Hal Banks, and the Seamen's Union of Canada* (Toronto: University of Toronto Press, 1987) for a vivid account of this international labour war.

11 Sharp, *Which Reminds Me*, 143-5. See also David Rockefeller, *Memoirs* (New York: Random House, 2002).

12 Bothwell, Drummond and English, *Canada since 1945*, 214; Michael Hart, *Fifty Years of Canadian Tradecraft: Canada at the GATT, 1947-1997* (Ottawa: Carleton University Press, 1998), 55-6.

13 Frank Stone, *Canada, the GATT and the International Trade System* (Montreal: Institute for Research on Public Policy, 1984), 86-8.

14 Ibid., 95.

15 Hart, *Fifty Years*, 85-6.

16 Ibid., 97.

17 Despite this, Canada also ran a large and apparently perpetual trade deficit with the United States in automotive products, which was the largest part of Canada's overall trade deficit with the Americans.

18 Azzi, *Walter Gordon*, 125; Julius Katz, interview with author, February 1980.

19 Dimitry Anastakis, *Auto Pact: Creating a Borderless North American Auto Industry, 1960-1971* (Toronto: University of Toronto Press, 2005), 88.

20 Georgetown University Library, Foreign Affairs Oral History Program, Canada Country Collection, Julius Katz interview, 1995.

21 Ibid., 347-8.

22 Data from John Holmes, "From Three Industries to One: Towards an Integrated North American Automobile Industry," in *Driving Continentally: National Policies and the North American Auto Industry*, ed. Maureen Molot (Ottawa: Carleton University Press, 1993), 25, 27.

23 Anastakis, *Auto Pact*, 126.

24 Canadian Institute of Public Opinion, press releases, 21 September 1960. The 10 percent figure was down from 18 percent in 1950.

25 Ibid., 29 July 1959, 12 April 1961, 2 December 1961, 10 August 1963. There was a tendency in the polling press releases to use dramatic language. The tenor of US-Canadian relations rose and fell, crises appeared and disappeared, and Canadians answered polling questions that were often both impractical and improbable, in terms of the options put before the pollees.

26 Stephen Azzi discusses the impact of Grant in his *Walter Gordon*, 125-7, although he mistakenly places the date of publication as April 1965. Other commentators were less enthusiastic: for them the "masterpiece" described a Canada that had never existed, populated by figments from Grant's family history.

27 Doug Owram, *Born at the Right Time: A History of the Baby Boom Generation* (Toronto: University of Toronto Press, 1996), 207. As Owram points out, Grant became part of a youth pantheon that included Hermann Hesse, Jean-Paul Sartre, Allen Ginsberg, and Paul Goodman; by extension, the pin-striped and elegantly suited Gordon took his place among the revered hairies of the youth cult.

28 NARA, RG 59, 1964-66 series, CFPF, box 1990, file POL [1 of 2], W.W. Butterworth, "Canada, 1965: Year of Incertitude" [January 1966].

29 Sharp, *Which Reminds Me*, 145-7; Azzi, *Walter Gordon*, 145-7.

Chapter 11: Innocence Abroad

1 Library and Archives Canada (LAC), RG 25/50273-40(3), Pearson to St Laurent, 6 May 1954.

2 David L. Anderson, *Trapped by Success: The Eisenhower Administration and Vietnam, 1953-61* (New York: Columbia University Press, 1991), 59-64. The French had established a semi-independent government in Vietnam during the war; it was that government that appeared in Geneva.

3 CIRUS would soon become the subject of prolonged and sometimes aggravating disputes between Canada and India, for the Canadians had forgotten to specify that the reactor and its product, plutonium, should be used only for peaceful purposes. This issue had not yet arisen in July 1954, and relations with India were unclouded.

4 K.P.S. Menon, *Many Worlds: An Autobiography* (London: Oxford University Press, 1965), 218.

5 The Chinese originally suggested Indonesia, a neutral country, but then came up with Canada: Geoffrey Pearson, *Seize the Day: Lester B. Pearson and Crisis Diplomacy* (Ottawa: Carleton University Press, 1993), 119; LAC, RG 25/50273-40(3), Eden to Foreign Office to Commonwealth Relations Office to High Commissioner in Ottawa, 19 July 1954.

6 LAC, RG 25/4629/50052-A-40(1), Pearson to Sherwood Lett, Canadian commissioner, 22 August 1954. It is a point on which Indian historians of Indian foreign policy tend to agree. On this point see M.S. Rajan's essay "India and the Commonwealth, 1954-56," in *International Relations and Foreign Policy of India*, vol. 5, *Great Britain, Commonwealth, and India's Foreign Policy*, ed. Verinder Grover (New Delhi: Deep and Deep Publications, 1992), 356-77.

7 Two Canadian diplomats, W.T. Delworth and C. Dagg, later put it this way, after reviewing the Vietnam files: "Hanoi's tactics in preventing people from leaving the North were not the aberrations of a new, insecure government; they were the stock-in-trade of a system of government to which Canadians reacted with disbelief and extreme distaste." Quoted in Douglas Ross, *In the Interests of Peace: Canada and Vietnam, 1954-73* (Toronto: University of Toronto Press, 1984), 120.

8 National Archives and Records Administration (NARA), RG 59, 751G.00/7-1655 G. Frederick Reinhardt, Saigon, to State Department, 16 July 1955. Some Canadian staff blamed Brigadier Megill, the senior Canadian officer, for some of the passivity, as the Americans saw it.

9 Mieczyslaw Maneli, *War of the Vanquished* (New York: Harper and Row, 1971), 34-5.

10 LAC, RG 25/4638/50052-40(41), Smith to DEA, "Cambodia – Aid Trade and the Ploy for Asia," 11 June 1956.

11 In Saigon the French assigned a military facility, the Camp des Mares, to the ICC, much to the fury of Diem, who wanted to send the commissioners to the mountain resort of Da Lat, out of sight and out of mind.

12 LAC, RG 25/4629/50052-A-40(1), Léger to Minister, 3 September 1954.

13 It should, however, be noted that Australia over the years helped considerably with Canadian communications.

14 LAC, RG 25/10123/21-13-VIET-ICSC-4, pt. FP.3, "Report of the Liaison Team on Its Visit to the Canadian Delegations to the Commissions for International Supervision and Control in Indo-China" copy 17, Canadian eyes only [September 1964].

15 NARA, RG 59, 751G.00/3-1955, State Department to Saigon embassy, 19 March 1955, signed by Dulles, reflecting his conversations with Pearson in Ottawa on 18 March. (There is no record of this conversation in the 1955 volume of *Documents on Canadian External Relations*.)

16 NARA, RG 59, 751G.00/5-555, Kidder, Saigon, to Secretary of State, 5 May 1955: "No action yet taken by Viet Minh or Vietnamese re discussions preparatory to elections. ICC/Canadians still feel strongly inadvisable ICC act as mediator. Not only is this job not ICC according wording Geneva agreement, but Canadians also feel might be disadvantageous South Vietnam have committee including Poles and Indians attempt mediate (which means find compromises) on such questions as free elections."

17 Escott Reid, *Radical Mandarin: The Memoirs of Escott Reid* (Toronto: University of Toronto Press, 1989), 277. There is good reason to believe that Reid was correct, or at least that the Communist side contemplated a trade-off of Laos and Cambodia for a united (Communist) Vietnam: UK National Archives, FO 371/117160, Saigon embassy (Stephenson) to Foreign Office, 30 March 1955. Ross, *Interests of Peace*, 177-8, speculates that "Canadian diplomatic approaches to Nehru moderated the

Indian stand somewhat," perhaps because of a simultaneous Canadian-Indian agreement to provide a nuclear research reactor to the Indians.

18 NARA, RG 59, 751G.00/7-2055, US embassy, Saigon, to State Department, 20 July 1955: "9. ICC Indians and Canadians with whom we have talked blame government for today's violence because (A) Government has fomented anti-ICC feeling through long press campaign and past week's demonstrations; (B) Despite alarming signals and reported requests from ICC and hotel manager for strong police protection today, none was forthcoming; (C) Police at Majestic made no attempt stop vandals." The US embassy was especially embarrassed because the prominent Washington hostess Pearl Mesta was also staying at the Majestic.

19 Anderson, *Trapped by Success*, 115-19. Anderson notes that "the failure to heed Collins' warning had tragic results ... Diem's ill-fated rule ... substantiated much of Collins' assessment."

20 This was the later opinion of John Holmes, who was responsible in 1955-1956 for Vietnam policy, under the minister, Pearson. Holmes is quoted in John Hilliker and Donald Barry, "Uncomfortably in the Middle: The Department of External Affairs and Canada's Involvement in the International Control Commissions in Vietnam, 1954-73," in *Creating the Peaceable Kingdom and Other Essays on Canada,* ed. Victor Howard (East Lansing: Michigan State University Press, 1998), 170.

21 Qiang Zhai, *China and the Vietnam Wars, 1950-1975* (Chapel Hill: University of North Carolina Press, 2000), 75, 78-9. It was the period of the "peaceful coexistence" doctrine enunciated by Nikita Khrushchev.

22 As William J. Duiker points out, the circumstances of the North Vietnamese decision and its reception in the South matter, because they defined whether and how the subsequent war was an invasion – and hence international – or domestic. As he suggests, it was both, which was an unsatisfactory situation for advocates on both sides: *U.S. Containment Policy and the Conflict in Indochina* (Stanford, CA: Stanford University Press, 1994), 236-7.

23 On Eisenhower and Laos, and especially Eisenhower and nuclear weapons, see David Kaiser, *American Tragedy: Kennedy, Johnson and the Origins of the Vietnam War* (Cambridge, MA: Harvard University Press/Belknap, 2000), 34.

24 The report is quoted in R.B. Smith, *An International History of the Vietnam War*, vol. 2, *The Kennedy Strategy* (New York: St Martin's, 1985), 75-6.

25 United Kingdom, National Archives, FO 371/170088, H.A.F. Hohler, embassy, Saigon, to FO, 2 January 1963.

26 The legal report was ready in December 1963 and was communicated in February 1964: Hilliker and Barry, "Uncomfortably in the Middle," 172.

27 United Kingdom, National Archives, FO 371/175512, Gordon Etherington-Smith to Ted Peck, FO, 25 June 1964.

28 LAC, RG 25/1124/21-13-VIET-ICSC-6 pt. 1, Cox to DEA, 26 February 1964.

29 NARA, RG 59, 1963-66 series, box 2943, file POL 27 VIET S, Lodge to State Department (distributed to White House and Secretary of Defense), 5 June 1964.

30 United Kingdom, National Archives, FO 371/180217, A.S. Fair, British High Commission Ottawa, to C.F. Hill, FO Far East and Pacific Dept, 30 December 1964.

31 United Kingdom, National Archives, FO 371/180550, A.S. Fair (Ottawa) to C.F. Hill, 23 June 1965.

32 LAC, RG 25/10123/21-13-VIET-ICSC-4, pt. 4.2 KG [King Gordon?] to Cadieux, 28.7.65, "Vietnam: Future of the Commission."

33 Ross, *Interests of Peace*, 23.

34 NARA, RG 59, CFPF, box 2922, file POL 27-14, State Dept. to Saigon, 9 September 1964, listed the various sources of intelligence, including Canadians, Indians, British (consulate in Hanoi), and French (delegation in Hanoi): Philip Habib (Saigon) to State, 9 December 1965; dispatch copy of "Canadian colonel" report on Hanoi, 16 September to 19 November 1965.

35 NARA, RG 59, CFPF, box 2922, file POL 27-14, included in Saigon to State Dept., 9 September 1965.

36 LAC, RG 25/10123/21-13-VIET-ICSC-4 pt. 4.2, DEA to Delhi, copies to London, Washington, Paris, Saigon etc. 28 June 1965 (Cadieux interview with Acharya).

CHAPTER 12: VIETNAM AND CANADIAN-AMERICAN RELATIONS

1 Tim O'Brien, *The Things They Carried* (New York: Broadway Books, 1998), 55.

2 Larry Martin, interviewed in Kim Willenson with the correspondents of *Newsweek*, *The Bad War: An Oral History of the Vietnam War* (New York: New American Library, 1987), 259.

3 Estimates run from 25,000 to 100,000, with some (perhaps many) arriving unofficially, never to be counted by Statistics Canada. John Hagan, in his *Northern Passage: American Vietnam War Resisters in Canada* (Cambridge, MA: Harvard University Press, 2001), estimates total male "war resisters" in Canada as almost 26,000. He makes the useful point that there were also females who came north for the same political reasons, even though they were under no threat of being drafted at home, and argues that males and females should be considered part of the same movement. The females he estimates at not quite 27,000: ibid., 241, table B.5.

4 Quoted in Lawrence M. Baskir and William A. Strauss, *Chance and Circumstance: The Draft, The War and the Vietnam Generation* (New York: Vintage, 1978), 175.

5 Hagan, *Northern Passage*, 41-2. Tom Kent, the deputy minister of the Department of Manpower and Immigration, also pointed out that the veterans in the immigration service were most likely to have been non-commissioned officers – from his point of view a rigid and unimaginative group.

6 Quoted in Hagan, *Northern Passage*, 40-1.

7 Peter Kent, "Introduction," in Les D. Brown, *There It Is* (Toronto: McClelland and Stewart, 2000), xi-xii.

8 Seymour Martin Lipset, *Continental Divide: The Values and Institutions of the United States and Canada* (New York: Routledge, 1990), 138-42.

9 John Paul and Jerome Laulicht, *In Your Opinion*, vol. 1, *Leaders' and Voters' Attitudes on Defence and Disarmament* (Clarkson, ON: Canadian Peace Research Institute, 1963), 19, 21.

10 The figures were reported in Blair Fraser, "Our Quiet War over Peace," *Maclean's*, 23 January 1965, 18, and very approvingly cited in Dean Acheson, "Stern Daughter of the Voice of God," in *Neighbors Taken for Granted: Canada and the United States*, ed. Livingston Merchant (New York: Praeger, 1966), 139.

11 National Archives and Records Administration (NARA), RG 59 611.4211-1261, Rufus Z. Smith, counsellor at the US embassy in Ottawa, "United States-Canadian Relations: The Canadian Politician's Dilemma," 11 December 1961.

12 NARA, RG 59, box 1990, file POL 1-3 CAN-US, Butterworth annual report for 1964, enclosed in a letter to Deputy Assistant Secretary Bob Schaetzel, 4 March 1965.

13 Canadian Institute of Public Opinion, "As Presidents Change in US, Our Relations Stay Static," 8 August 1964. This and other polls belie the assertion, common among Quebec nationalists, even moderate nationalists, that they are the most pro-American group in Canada. Lysiane Gagnon wrote in 1985: "[No] matter how French-speaking it is – and maybe precisely for that reason – [Quebec] is the most pro-American province in Canada." Gagnon is quoted in Robert Chodos and Eric Hamovitch, *Quebec and the American Dream* (Toronto: Between the Lines, 1991), 14.

14 Quoted in Chodos and Hamovitch, *Quebec*, 14.

15 Canadian Institute of Public Opinion, "US Intervention in Viet Nam Viewed with Mixed Feelings," 24 July 1965.

16 Martin Goldfarb and Tom Axworthy, *Marching to a Different Drummer: An Essay on the Liberals and Conservatives in Convention* (Toronto: Stoddart, 1988), 143

17 On this point see the interesting book by William Strauss and Neil Howe, *Generations: The History of America's Future, 1584 to 2069* (New York: Quill, 1991), 261-78. Their argument is basically that similar experiences shape a generation, and that the generation that fought the Second World War

was most likely to take a proactive view of foreign relations. Though this theory is based on American data, it is possible to extrapolate their notion for the very similar Canadian age cohort. A cautious historian would also observe that this idea is indicative rather than prescriptive.

18 Martin was actually coequal with the minister of justice, Lionel Chevrier, who had also been elected in 1935, but Chevrier had left Parliament for a few years in the 1950s.

19 Bill Bundy, interview with author, Princeton, NJ, November 1998.

20 John M. Dunn, "Meeting of April 19, 1964," Lyndon B. Johnson Library, National Security File, Country File, Vietnam, vol. 9 (Memos), box 4; a censored version is reproduced as Memorandum of conversation, US embassy, Saigon, 19 April 1964, *Foreign Relations of the United States (FRUS), 1964-1968*, vol. 1 (Washington: Government Printing Office, 1995). The Bundy memorandum, dated 27 April and censored, is in the LBJ Library, National Security File, Vietnam, vol. 7 (Memos), box 3. I am greatly indebted to Andrew Preston of Cambridge University for copies of the memos.

21 LAC, RG 25/10122/21-13-VIET-ICSC-2, R.L. Rogers to Jack Maybee, Personnel, n.d. [1964]; J. Blair Seaborn to author, 4 Sept. 2000.

22 Rusk to Lodge, 1 May 1964, *FRUS, 1964-1968*, 1:281; Fredrik Logevall, *Choosing War: The Lost Chance for Peace and the Escalation of War in Vietnam* (Berkeley: University of California Press, 1999), 156 and 461n4, makes a circumstantial assertion that Lodge mentioned Seaborn as early as the 19 April meeting. In fact Lodge mentioned Geoff Murray, whom he had known at the United Nations in the 1950s. I am grateful to Andrew Preston for this clarification.

23 Rusk to Lodge, 1 May 1964, and Lodge to Rusk, 4 May 1964, *FRUS, 1964-1968*, 1:281-2, 282n.

24 Chester Cooper, *The Lost Crusade: America in Vietnam* (New York: Dodd, Mead, 1970), 326.

25 Memorandum of conversation, 28 May 1964, *FRUS, 1964-1968*, 1:394-6; Logevall, *Choosing War*, 157-8.

26 Conversation as summarized in Logevall, *Choosing War*, 161-2.

27 Qiang Zhai, *China and the Vietnam Wars, 1950-1975* (Chapel Hill: University of North Carolina Press, 2000), 131-2.

28 Quoted in Michael Lind, *Vietnam: The Necessary War* (New York: Free Press, 1999), 190.

29 Logevall, *Choosing War*, 209-10.

30 The process is convincingly analyzed in David Kaiser, *American Tragedy: Kennedy, Johnson and the Origins of the Vietnam War* (Cambridge, MA: Harvard University Press/Belknap, 2000), chs. 12 and 13.

31 Cabinet minutes, 20 January 1965. At the same meeting, National Defence Minister Paul Hellyer raised the announcement of "highly provocative" South Korean aid to South Vietnam. Pearson noted that Canadian protests would do no good.

32 Cabinet minutes, 9 February 1965.

33 Cabinet minutes, 20 January 1965; Kaiser, *American Tragedy*, 407.

34 The prominent Southam columnist Charles Lynch was particularly sceptical of the South Vietnamese government and its links to the Canadian delegation to the ICC: *Ottawa Citizen*, 9 March 1965, extensively quoted in Victor Levant, *Quiet Complicity: Canadian Involvement in the Vietnam War* (Toronto: Between the Lines, 1986), 187-8.

35 Bruce Hutchison, *The Far Side of the Street* (Toronto: Macmillan, 1976), 354. Hutchison adds that Pearson was urged to intervene or speak out by "one Democratic statesman still powerful in Washington today." The reference is almost certainly to Humphrey. On Geoffrey Pearson, see John English, *The Worldly Years: The Life of Lester Pearson, 1949-1972* (Toronto: Knopf, 1992). Family pressure as a factor in Vietnam politics should also not be underestimated. The children of US defense secretary Robert McNamara were also against the war, and his son hung a US flag upside down in his room as a sign of protest: Deborah Shapley, *Promise and Power: The Life and Times of Robert McNamara* (Boston: Little, Brown, 1993), 379-81.

36 Cabinet minutes, 2 March 1965. The issue before the Cabinet was the danger of American magazines displacing or overwhelming Canadian magazines.

37 Johnson approved Rolling Thunder on 10 February: John Carland, *Stemming the Tide* (Washington: Center of Military History, 2000), 15-16; see also William M. Hammond, *Public Affairs: The Military and the Media, 1962-1968* (Washington: Center of Military History, 1988), 139. Paul Kattenburg, *The Vietnam Trauma in American Foreign Policy, 1945-75* (New Brunswick, NJ: Transaction Books, 1980), 123-5, outlines the "refined deterrence" American strategists thought they were implementing with Rolling Thunder.

38 George Herring, *America's Longest War: The United States and Vietnam, 1950-1975*, 3rd ed. (New York: McGraw-Hill, 1996), 144-8.

39 Hammond, *Public Affairs*, 154-6. The source of the report was Peter Arnett.

40 Arthur Sylvester to Fred Friendly, president of CBS News, 12 August 1965, quoted in ibid., 190.

41 LAC, RG 25/10122/21-13-VIET-ICSC-2, Cadieux to Minister, 5 March 1965.

42 English, *Worldly Years*, 362-3.

43 Charles Ritchie, interview with author, Ottawa, May 1990. LAC, RG 25/10122/21-13-VIET-ICSC pt. 2, copy of letter, incomplete with first of three pages missing but signed by Charles Ritchie and probably dated 20 (or 19) June 1965.

44 On this point I agree with the argument of Thomas Schwartz in *Lyndon Johnson and Europe: In the Shadow of Vietnam* (Cambridge, MA: Harvard University Press, 2003).

45 Kattenburg, *Vietnam Trauma*, 217.

46 Cabinet minutes, 5 April 1965.

47 The high commissioner reported: "[Pearson] said that in a way, the meeting with the president was the best that they had had, because they really had something to disagree about and had found that they could do so without ceasing to be friends. The President started off by expressing considerable annoyance about Mr. Pearson's speech, though it appears he had understood Mr. Pearson to have proposed that the Americans should call off their bombing at once, whereas all that he had suggested was that there might come a moment when such a gesture would facilitate the opening of negotiations." Sir Henry Lintott to Sir Neil Pritchard, 20 April 1965, UK National Archives, FO 371/180550.

48 Douglas Ross, *In the Interests of Peace: Canada and Vietnam, 1954-73* (Toronto: University of Toronto Press, 1984), 299.

49 Levant, *Quiet Complicity*.

50 Kattenburg, *Vietnam Trauma*, 218-19.

51 English, *Worldly Years*, 369-70.

52 Arnold Heeney, *The Things That Are Caesar's: The Memoirs of a Canadian Public Servant* (Toronto: University of Toronto Press, 1972), 194-5.

53 Paul Martin, *A Very Public Life*, vol. 2, *So Many Worlds* (Toronto: Deneau, 1985), 493.

54 Ross, *Interests of Peace*, 450n.

55 Goldfarb and Axworthy, *Different Drummer*, 85. The sample was composed of delegates to the Conservative (1967) and Liberal (1968) leadership conventions.

56 The reasoning frequently was that the Saigon regime manifestly did not enjoy popular support and that Ho Chi Minh's government in Hanoi did. According to this line of thought, though a Communist outcome might not be entirely desirable, it was a more democratic solution than continuing to support a hopelessly unpopular cause. See the discussion of the evolution of intellectual opinion on Vietnam in Robert R. Tomes, *Apocalypse Then: American Intellectuals and the Vietnam War, 1954-1975* (New York: New York University Press, 1998).

57 Chester Ronning, *A Memoir of China in War and Revolution, from the Boxer Rebellion to the People's Republic* (New York: Pantheon Books, 1974), 257-8.

58 Chinese aid is described in Qiang, *China and the Vietnam Wars*, 134-8.

59 Ibid., 167-8. Qiang notes: "Mao found the continued confrontation in Indochina useful to reinstill ideological commitment in the population at home and to mobilize domestic Chinese support for his grand ideological enterprise: The Great Cultural Revolution."

60   Canada, Cabinet minutes, 17 March 1966, quoting Pearson; Ronning, however, explicitly denied that he had ever asked to go to China or that there was even a suggestion of it: Ronning interview in Peter Stursberg, *Lester Pearson and the American Dilemma* (Toronto: Doubleday, 1980), 273-4. In the face of very strong testimony to the contrary, and statements to the Cabinet at the time, by both Pearson and Martin, it seems that Ronning was not candid in his denials.

61   Canada, Cabinet minutes, 21 June 1966.

62   NARA, RG 59, Bundy files, lot 85 D 240, file WPB Chron, Bundy memorandum for the record, 22 June 1966 of a dinner with Paul Martin and senior Canadian officials.

63   English, *Worldly Years*, 372.

64   NARA, RG 59, CFPF, box 1949, file POL CAN-US Memcon, 1 May 1967, between Ambassador A.E. (Ed) Ritchie and Rufus Smith.

65   William H. Hammond, *Public Affairs: The Military and the Media, 1962-1968* (Washington: Center of Military History, 1988), especially chapters 1 and 2. Hammond points out that the media managed to create the impression that all that was required was for the efficient Americans instead of the inefficient and corrupt Vietnamese to run the war.

66   NARA, RG 59, CFPF, box 1949, file POL CAN-US, Butterworth to Secretary of State, secret, 23 October 1967.

CHAPTER 13: NATIONAL UNITY AND FOREIGN POLICY

1   On this point, see Gilles Lalande, *The Department of External Affairs and Biculturalism*, Study no. 3 of the Royal Commission on Bilingualism and Biculturalism (Ottawa: Queen's Printer, 1969), 43-4, 27. Lalande's study was criticized at the time and has been since: see John Hilliker and Donald Barry, *Canada's Department of External Affairs*, vol. 2 (Montreal and Kingston: Montreal-Queen's University Press, 1995), 349-50.

2   The international impact of the Algerian war has been analyzed in Matthew Connelly, *A Diplomatic Revolution: Algeria's Fight for Independence and the Origins of the Post-Colonial Era* (New York: Oxford University Press, 2002), especially 278-9.

3   Gérard Pelletier, *Years of Choice, 1960-1968* (Toronto: Methuen, 1987), 76.

4   Ibid., 152-3.

5   *Canada Year Book, 1948-49* (Ottawa: King's Printer, 1949), 860, table 1. Although $242.5 million was authorized as an export credit for France, as of the end of 1947 only $198.4 million had been drawn.

6   De Gaulle later told Georges Vanier, the Canadian envoy to his government, that he had been "very touched" by his reception by government personalities in Ottawa and that he had expounded his approach to international relations to Prime Minister Mackenzie King: Eric Roussel, *De Gaulle* (Paris: Gallimard, 2002), 437.

7   Dale C. Thomson, *Vive le Québec Libre* (Toronto: Deneau, 1988), 27-8.

8   The prominent French diplomatic historian Maurice Vaïsse has argued that de Gaulle's desire to intervene in Quebec can be dated to the year of Algerian independence, 1962. In 1967 de Gaulle told an interlocutor that he had said "Vive le Québec libre" "to restore Algeria to the French." See Vaïsse, *La grandeur: Politique étrangère du général de Gaulle, 1958-1969* (Paris: Fayard, 1998), 652 and note 9.

9   The birth rate declined with the availability of the birth control pill, but also with the erosion of the dominance of the Catholic Church and its anti-contraception doctrine. Nervousness over demography is noted by Martin Sullivan, in his *Mandate '68: The Year of Pierre Elliott Trudeau* (Toronto: Doubleday, 1968), 426.

10 When the Canadian constitution was drawn up as the British North America Act, 1867, Canada was still a British colony and did not manage its own foreign affairs. The BNA Act had a clause that authorized the federal government to enforce *British* treaties on the provinces, but that did not apply to treaties Canada negotiated under its own authority. When Canada acquired formal power

over foreign affairs in 1931, it was unclear whether that applied to federal matters only or included the power to represent the provinces as well.

11 In 1937 the assistant undersecretary for external affairs, Laurent Beaudry, demanded that the department's language be switched to French. His superiors, bureaucratic and political, took this as a sign that Beaudry was unwell: Lita-Rose Betcherman, *Ernest Lapointe: Mackenzie King's Great Quebec Lieutenant* (Toronto: University of Toronto Press, 2002), 380n17.

12 Quoted in Robert Bothwell, *Canada and Quebec: One Country, Two Histories,* 2nd ed. (Vancouver: UBC Press, 1998), 105-6.

13 Evidence on Malraux's view of Quebec separatism is contradictory. He was certainly interested in the topic: Thomson, *Vive le Québec Libre,* 108. The French consul general in Montreal is said to have described him as "a crypto-separatist," but the minister himself also prudently told the Quebec delegate general that he did not think separatism would benefit Quebec: John Bosher, *The Gaullist Attack on Canada, 1967-1997* (Montreal and Kingston: McGill-Queen's University Press, 1999), 70-1.

14 Thomson, *Vive le Québec Libre,* 144-8 deals with the background of the Gérin-Lajoie speech. Thomson argues that Lesage, while aware of the speech, had not necessarily approved it. Given that Lesage had read the document and replied "c'est bon," either the Quebec government was under the insouciant guidance of an indifferent leader or, more plausibly, in my opinion, that Lesage decided to provoke a crisis or to see how far he could get with a statement that was bound to cause trouble.

15 The question was discussed in Cabinet on 26 April 1965, where Pearson made it clear that the federal position was that only the Canadian government had the authority to conclude treaties or agreements with foreign powers, contrary to what Gérin-Lajoie and Lesage had been arguing in recent statements and speeches. The question of Pearson's meeting with Lesage, and what was agreed there, has been clarified by an exchange in the *Globe and Mail* between Allan Gotlieb and Tom Kent, Pearson's principal policy adviser, who was present at the Pearson-Lesage meeting: *Globe and Mail,* 5 and 11 October 2005. The quotation is taken from Kent's letter to the editor, published 11 October.

16 Thomson, *Vive le Québec Libre,* 148-9.

17 Quoted in Ron Graham, *One-Eyed Kings: Promise and Illusion in Canadian Politics* (Toronto: Harper Collins, 1986), 66.

18 *Documents Diplomatiques Français,* vol. 17, *1960 Tome II (1 janvier-30 juin)* (Paris: Imprimerie nationale, 1997), 498-501, "Entretien du général de Gaulle avec M. Diefenbaker à Ottawa le 19 avril 1960," followed by "Entretien du général de Gaulle avec M. Diefenbaker en présence des ministres des Affaires étrangères," 501-4. In these interviews the Canadians fed questions to the French president, who responded at some length on subjects of global concern. No specifically Canadian items were mentioned.

19 Roussel, *De Gaulle,* 832.

20 Planning for the visit went back to the late summer of 1963.

21 The Ball reference is in Roussel, *De Gaulle,* 833, along with a description of the visit.

22 John English, *The Worldly Years: The Life of Lester Pearson, 1949-1972* (Toronto: Knopf, 1992), 320.

23 Pearson told the German chancellor as much in June 1964: LAC, RG2, Privy Council Office, Series A-5-a, vol. 6271, Cabinet minutes, 11 June 1964.

24 The "independence" of the French nuclear force is open to question. The French military continued to cooperate with the Americans and British, and French nuclear warheads were aimed at the Soviet Union. The French, largely on German insistence, maintained liaison between their army in Germany and their erstwhile NATO allies. See David Miller, *The Cold War: A Military History* (London: John Murray, 1998), 33-7, 141-4. Despite some odd lapses in his text, Miller seems well informed on NATO and European issues.

25 There was some basis for this assertion. French diplomats were uncomfortable with the idea of meddling in Canada's internal affairs and let their sentiments be known, if not to Canadians then to

Americans: National Archives and Records Administration (NARA), RG 59 CFPF, box 1990, file POL CAN-D, R.G. Long, US embassy Paris, to State, 12 August 1966: "During conversations in recent weeks on Canadian affairs, the Quai's North American desk officer, Michel de Ladoucette, has tried to play down the importance of France in Canadian affairs ... By the tone and substance of his remarks M. de Ladoucette indicated a feeling of American uneasiness over French involvement in Canada, and at one point he volunteered the statement that the French Government is not trying to foment trouble in Canada since this would not be in France's interest. He qualified this, however, by saying on a personal basis that he could only speak for the Quai d'Orsay (thus excluding General de Gaulle)."

26 Rusk to Johnson, 6 June 1966, *Foreign Relations of the United States, 1964-1968*, vol. 13 (Washington: State Department, 2001), 409-10, and Rusk to Johnson, 11 June 1966, ibid., 410-1.

27 Bosher, *Gaullist Attack*, 94-5; Bosher bases his assessment on a reading of Cadieux's personal papers.

28 NARA, RG 59, CFPF, box 1990, file POL CAN-D, Rufus Smith, memorandum of conversation between himself, Butterworth and Cadieux, 13 May 1966.

29 There was abundant suspicion that the French secret service, SDECE, was active in Canada: Bosher, *Gaullist Attack*, 23-6; Cadieux, among others, shared the suspicion.

30 Roussel, *De Gaulle*, 833-4.

31 Quoted in Graham Fraser, *PQ: René Lévesque and the Parti Québécois in Power* (Toronto: Macmillan, 1984), 38.

32 Pierre Godin, *La Révolution Tranquille*, vol. 1, *La Fin de la grande noirceur* (Montreal: Boréal, 1991), 409-38. Godin notes that Johnson's Irish father was a notable anglophobe who compared the oppression of Ireland to the oppression (by the English) of French Canadians.

33 As Fraser points out, Johnson's position was roughly the same as René Lévesque's later "sovereignty-association" (Fraser, *PQ*, 37).

34 According to Alain Peyrefitte, de Gaulle called Johnson "votre Johnson" when he found him timid, and "mon ami Johnson" when he was pleased with him: *C'était de Gaulle* (Paris: Fayard, 1999), 3:370.

35 Pierre Godin, *Daniel Johnson*, vol. 2, *La difficile recherche de l'égalité* (Montreal: Ed. de l'homme, 1980), 193-200, gives April, but Roussel, *De Gaulle*, 835, citing a letter from the Quebec delegate general, makes it clear that it was in mid-February.

36 Godin, *Daniel Johnson*, vol. 2, ch. 6, describes the visit from a pro-Johnson and anti-Ottawa point of view.

37 Anne Rouanet and Pierre Rouanet, *Les trois derniers chagrins du général de Gaulle* (Paris: Grasset, 1980), translated and quoted in Thomson, *Vive le Québec Libre*, 194-5.

38 Thomson, *Vive le Québec Libre*, 186-7.

39 Roussel, *De Gaulle*, 835-6. Vaïsse, *Grandeur*, 657, notes that the French ambassador from 1965 to 1968, François Leduc, was quite respectful of Canadian sovereignty, though his immediate predecessor had not been.

40 Martin to Pearson, 24 February 1967, quoted in John Hilliker and Donald Barry, *Canada's Department of External Affairs*, vol. 2, *Coming of Age, 1946-1968* (Montreal and Kingston: McGill-Queen's University Press, 1995), 398.

41 De Gaulle told Madame Pauline Vanier, widow of Georges, at a private dinner in April 1967 that Quebec's destiny was to become a sovereign state: Roussel, *De Gaulle*, 836.

42 NARA, RG 59, box 1948, file POL 17 CAN-FR, Maynard Glitman, economic officer, EUR/CAN in the State Department, Memorandum of conversation with Sharp at the Joint US-Canadian committee on trade and economic affairs, held in Montreal, 20 June 1967. Glitman concluded that "Mr. Sharp may have underestimated the current extent of French-Quebec amity."

43 Thomson, *Vive le Québec Libre*, 198; Roussel, *De Gaulle*, 836, concludes that de Gaulle at this stage was being deliberately deceptive. De Gaulle even supplied texts of proposed speeches in Ottawa. Had they been given, they would have contradicted in thought and tone the speeches he actually gave while in Quebec.

44 Nevertheless, the 6 percent that went to the radical Ralliement pour l'Indépendance Nationale (RIN) would have gone to the Liberals in an earlier election and probably made the difference between Lesage's victory and defeat. This point was not lost on the politicians concerned. (Another 2 percent went to other fringe separatists.)

45 Translated in Thomson, *Vive le Québec Libre*, 199.

46 Peyrefitte, *C'était de Gaulle*, 3, 307.

47 Thomson, *Vive le Québec Libre*, 201.

48 Ibid., 203.

49 Roussel, *De Gaulle*, 841. "Connerie" may be translated as "rubbish" or "utter stupidity."

50 André Patry, the Quebec chief of protocol, found the words disconcerting, and later told Roussel that de Gaulle was showing signs of age: Roussel, *De Gaulle*, 840-1.

51 Pierre Berton, *1967: The Last Good Year* (Toronto: Doubleday, 1997), 309.

52 Ibid., 308.

53 Gérard Bergeron, *Du Duplessisme à Trudeau et Bourassa, 1956-1971* (Montreal: Parti pris, 1971), 437-68.

54 Fraser, *PQ*, 41: "Lévesque was, if anything, annoyed."

55 Roussel, *De Gaulle*, 841; Vaïsse, *Grandeur*, 649.

56 France increased its cultural, technical, and scientific aid to Quebec from 5 million to 40 million francs between 1967 and 1970: Vaïsse, *Grandeur*, 665.

57 Godin, *Daniel Johnson*, 2:312.

58 Pierre de Menthon, *Je témoigne: Québec 1967, Chili 1973* (Paris: Editions du Cerf, 1979), 17.

59 When Johnson died in the fall of 1968, de Gaulle was reported to have wanted to attend the funeral, but was dissuaded by Couve de Murville: Vaïsse, *Grandeur*, 668n.80

CHAPTER 14: CHANGING THE MEANING OF DEFENCE

1 Creighton, incidentally, believe that Canada's first century might well be its last because the country had turned its back on its British heritage. On the military tattoo, see Paul Hellyer, *Damn the Torpedoes: My Fight to Unify Canada's Armed Services* (Toronto: McClelland and Stewart, 1990), 233, 238.

2 Alan James, *Keeping the Peace in the Cyprus Crisis of 1963-64* (London: Palgrave, 2002), 107-8, points out that the Canadians, initially hesitant, finally decided to join UNFICYP because they feared being blamed for the failure even to establish a UN force.

3 *The Gallup Report*, 12 October 1968. Incidentally, the percentage of Americans agreeing that the United States was a sick society was almost identical (36 percent) with the figure in Canada, though the percentage disagreeing was far higher.

4 These papers included the *Toronto Star*, the *Edmonton Journal*, the *Globe and Mail*, *La Presse*, *Le Devoir*, and the *Vancouver Sun*. The study was conducted by political scientist Rod Byers and was dated 8 December 1967: cited in John English, "Problems in Middle Life," in *Canada and NATO: Uneasy Past, Uncertain Future*, ed. Margaret MacMillan and David S. Sorenson (Waterloo, ON: University of Waterloo Press, 1990), 65n.31.

5 Quoted in ibid., 8.

6 Quoted in J.L. Granatstein, *Canada, 1957-1967: The Years of Uncertainty and Innovation* (Toronto: McClelland and Stewart, 1986), 226.

7 Isabel Campbell, "Harmony and Dissonance: A Study of the Influence of Foreign Policy Goals on Military Decision-Making with respect to the Canadian NATO Brigade in Germany, 1951-1964" (PhD diss., Laval University, 2000), 147-8. The senior Canadian officer in London, Major General

George Kitching, finally and reluctantly concluded in 1962, in Campbell's words, that "Canadians would do better developing a closer relationship with the Americans." Kitching, who had started off in the British army, had been especially well disposed to the British.

8 Campbell, "Harmony and Dissonance," 150-1.
9 Ibid., 153.
10 David Miller, *The Cold War: A Military History* (London: John Murray, 1998), 306. Miller notes that the CF-105 had "demonstrated a very high performance ... ahead of any contemporary Western aircraft in its field." The Canadians also built 200 F-104s and 240 F-5s (known as the CF-5 in Canada), ibid., 308-9.
11 On Hellyer and his career as minister of national defence, I am greatly indebted to the excellent account in J.L. Granatstein, *Canada, 1957-1967*, ch. 9.
12 The UN figure is 711,000; the Israeli government estimated 400,000.
13 Andrew Boyd, *Fifteen Men on a Powder Keg: A History of the UN Security Council* (London: Methuen, 1971), 192-5.
14 George Ignatieff, *The Making of a Peacemonger* (Toronto: University of Toronto Press, 1985), 220-1.
15 See Hammarskjöld's "secret report" on his negotiations with the Egyptian government in 1957, dated 5 August 1957 and published in the *New York Times* on 19 June 1967 as "Hammarskjöld Memorandum on Mideast Peace Force."
16 Quoted in John English, *The Worldly Years: The Life of Lester Pearson, 1949-1972* (Toronto: Knopf, 1992), 145.
17 Avi Shlaim, *The Iron Wall: Israel and the Arab World* (New York: Norton, 2000), 237. Nasser announced the blockade before U Thant arrived in Cairo, presenting the secretary-general with a fait accompli. On the developing crisis, see Michael K. Carroll, "From Peace (Keeping) to War: The United Nations and the Withdrawal of UNEF," *Middle Eastern Review of International Affairs* 9, 2 (2005): 72-93.
18 Memorandum of conversation, 25 May 1967, *Foreign Relations of the United States* (FRUS), *1964-1968*, vol. 12 (Washington: State Department, 2001), 718.
19 David Taras, "Canada's Jewish Community and Support for Israel," in *The Domestic Battleground: Canada and the Arab-Israeli Conflict*, ed. David Taras (Montreal and Kingston: McGill-Queen's University Press, 1989), 49; Michael Marrus, *Mr. Sam: The Life and Times of Samuel Bronfman* (Toronto: Viking, 1991), 447-50. See also the comments in Nicholas Faith, *The Bronfmans: The Rise and Fall of the House of Seagram* (New York: St Martin's, 2006), 125.
20 So Hellyer told the House of Commons: *Globe and Mail*, 24 May 1967; the late departure was confirmed by General Rikhye, the UNEF commander, on 26 May: *Globe and Mail*, 27 May 1967.
21 Paul Martin, *A Very Public Life* (Toronto: Deneau, 1985), 2:567. Martin argues that the Canadian government felt a need to be circumspect and to hold back from participating in an abortive American plan to establish a maritime force that would maintain peace in the Middle East – presumably by forcing the entrance to the Straits of Tiran and the Gulf of Aqaba. Yet even after the Canadian contingent was evacuated from the Sinai, Canadian reluctance to subscribe to the maritime force continued.
22 Shlaim, *Iron Wall*, 241.
23 Boyd, *Fifteen Men*, 202-3.
24 George Bain, "Misunderstanding Understood," *Globe and Mail*, 30 May 1967, citing an article by Max Frankel in the *New York Times*.
25 Dean Rusk, Johnson's secretary of state, told a Canadian interviewer in 1993 that "We didn't take Canada's views into account. Canada played a very small role in US Middle Eastern policy. We heeded the Arabs and the Israelis." Quoted in Edelgard Mahant and Graeme Mount, *Invisible and Inaudible in Washington* (Vancouver: UBC Press, 1999), 80. On the other hand, virtually no American allies had much influence over US Middle East policy in 1967 – not just Canada.

26 "Businesslike Peacekeeping," editorial, *Globe and Mail*, 30 May 1967.

27 Quoted in Tareq Ismael, "Canada and the Middle East," in *Canada and the Third World* , ed. Peyton Lyon and Tareq Ismael (Toronto: Macmillan, 1976), 267-8.

28 Canada, House of Commons, *Debates*, 11 April 1967.

29 English, "Problems in Middle Life," 61-2. The issue of Canada's NATO commitments was brought before Cabinet in May 1967 but resolved only in September.

30 NARA, RG 59, vol. 4 (2 of 2), J.L. Gawf, first secretary, US embassy, to State Department, 30 March 1966, NSF country file box 166, Canada cables.

31 Quoted in Marc Trachtenberg, *A Constructed Peace: The Making of the European Settlement, 1945-1963* (Princeton, NJ: Princeton University Press, 1999), 398.

32 Ibid.

33 Deborah Shapley, *Promise and Power: The Life and Times of Robert S. McNamara* (Boston: Little Brown, 1993), 401.

34 Paul Martin, *A Very Public Life* (Toronto: Deneau, 1985), 2:479-80.

35 An excellent article by John English captures Canada's uneasiness about NATO under Pearson: "Problems in Middle Life," 47-66.

36 Harlan Cleveland, *NATO: the Transatlantic Bargain* (New York: Harper and Row, 1970,) 143.

37 Frédéric Bozo, *Two Strategies for Europe: De Gaulle, the United States, and the Atlantic Alliance* (Lanham, MD: Rowman and Littlefield, 2001), 192-3.

38 Harmel report: Ministerial Communiqué, The Future Tasks of the Alliance Report of the Council, Brussels, 13-14 December 1967, www.nato.int/docu/comm/49-95.

39 Cleveland, *NATO*, 146.

40 Tom Keating, *Canada and World Order: The Multilateral Tradition in Canadian Foreign Policy* (Toronto: McClelland and Stewart, 1993), 160.

41 As William Hyland observes in his *Mortal Rivals: Superpower Relations from Nixon to Reagan* (New York: Random House, 1987), 16, NATO's new flexible doctrine gave the US administration a reason to keep American troops in Europe. By extension, it also gave Canada such a rationale.

42 Robert Komer to Lyndon B. Johnson, 16 March 1966, quoting Acheson, *FRUS, 1964-1968*, vol. 13 (Washington: US State Department, 1995), 336.

Chapter 15: National Security and Social Security

1 National Archives and Records Administration (NARA), RG 59, box 1527, 1967-69, DEF 4 CAN-US, State Department to US embassy, Ottawa, 9 June 1967.

2 Ibid., Memorandum of conversation between André Bissonnette of the Defence Liaison division of External Affairs and Richard Straus of the State Department at the Calgary meetings of the Permanent Joint Board on Defence, 21 September 1967.

3 Polls showed Trudeau to be the overwhelming favourite of young Canadians: Doug Owram, *Born at the Right Time: A History of the Baby Boom Generation* (Toronto: University of Toronto Press, 1996), 304.

4 "The Style of Canadian Diplomacy," n.d. but late 1967 or early 1968, memorandum enclosed in Gotlieb to author, 29 April 2003.

5 Three decades later American investors still cited Quebec separatism as a major reason for not investing in Canada: Dean Beeby, "East Coast and Quebec Woes Taint Canada for US Investors," *National Post*, 8 July 2002.

6 Quoted in J.L. Granatstein and Robert Bothwell, *Pirouette: Pierre Trudeau and Canadian Foreign Policy* (Toronto: University of Toronto Press, 1990), 8.

7 That was clear even from some of Trudeau's private remarks in the spring and summer of 1968; see ibid., 15. Trudeau told Mitchell Sharp that after studying some of the papers presented by his bureaucrats he understood why Canada would have to remain in NATO.

8 Ivan Head and Pierre Trudeau, *The Canadian Way: Shaping Canada's Foreign Policy, 1968-1984* (Toronto: McClelland and Stewart, 1995), 77. Head and Trudeau misidentify the Centurion tank, used in the 1950s and 1960s by the Canadian brigade in Germany, as a Second World War model. See David Miller, *The Cold War: A Military History* (London: John Murray, 1998), 268.

9 Vojtech Mastny, "Did NATO Win the Cold War? Looking Over the Wall," *Foreign Affairs* 78 (May-June 1999): 180.

10 Quoted in ibid., 11.

11 John Hilliker and Donald Barry, *Canada's Department of External Affairs*, vol. 2, *Coming of Age, 1946-1968* (Montreal and Kingston: McGill-Queen's University Press, 1995), 407-10.

12 Mitchell Sharp, *Which Reminds Me ... A Memoir* (Toronto: University of Toronto Press, 1994), 161-2. As Sharp points out, in 1968 Trudeau was denounced from the pulpits in many Canadian churches as a communist.

13 These assumptions are quite plainly expressed in Head and Trudeau, *The Canadian Way*, 74-5.

14 Poll figures cited in Bruce Thordarson, *Trudeau and Foreign Policy: A Study in Decision-Making* (Toronto: Oxford University Press, 1972), 35.

15 NARA, RG 59, 1967-69 series, file POL 7 CAN, US Mission to NATO to State, 2 March 1969. Costas Melakopides, *Pragmatic Idealism: Canadian Foreign Policy, 1945-1995* (Montreal and Kingston: McGill-Queen's University Press, 1998), 93, sees the same phenomenon as evidence of "the authenticity of Ottawa's commitment to détente."

16 Robert Ford, *Our Man in Moscow: A Diplomat's Reflections on the Soviet Union* (Toronto: University of Toronto Press, 1989), 115.

17 A point actually admitted by one of Trudeau's ministers to an interviewer in 1971, and confirmed by public opinion polls: Thordarson, *Trudeau and Foreign Policy*, 108.

18 Data are from Peyton V. Lyon and Brian Tomlin, *Canada as an International Actor* (Toronto: Macmillan, 1979), 112.

19 Stephen Clarkson, "Conclusion: The Choice to Be Made," in *An Independent Foreign Policy for Canada?* ed. Stephen Clarkson (Toronto: McClelland and Stewart, 1968), 253-69.

20 Thordarson, *Trudeau and Foreign Policy*, 111.

21 Quoted in Eric Kierans with Walter Stewart, *Remembering* (Toronto: Stoddart, 2001), 150.

22 Sharp, *Which Reminds Me ...*, 166.

23 According to Head and Trudeau, Sharp phoned in the middle of a state dinner at the prime minister's residence: *The Canadian Way*, 82.

24 Head and Trudeau are notably coy on this point (see ibid.). The authors refer to "ministers" who opposed existing policies or were unconvinced by the arguments presented by External Affairs and National Defence. Unfortunately they do not identify who took which position, apart from Sharp and Léo Cadieux, who represented their departments' arguments. Robert Ford, *Our Man in Moscow*, 115, refers to "a considerable sentiment among some ministers ... in favour of a semi-neutralist foreign policy for Canada, along the lines of that of Sweden." Eric Kierans, in *Remembering*, 151, notes that Pelletier seldom spoke in Cabinet and Marchand "had little of substance to say about NATO."

25 NARA, RG 59, box 1256, DEF 6 CAN, US embassy, Ottawa, to Secretary of State, 7 July 1969.

26 NARA, RG 59, box 1256, 1967-69, DEF 6 CAN, US embassy, Bonn, to Secretary of State, 23 May 1969.

27 When Léo Cadieux presented the Canadian cuts at a luncheon meeting for NATO defence ministers on 28 May, he "produced an extremely frank and categorically negative reaction from all ministers present," according to the US ambassador, Harlan Cleveland. Healey suggested that there could not be an alliance in which "each ally fights his own private war." NARA, RG 59, Cleveland to Secretary of State, 30 May 1969, State Department Records, DEF 6 CAN.

28 German foreign minister Willy Brandt commented that during his visit to Ottawa his contacts "had been with those who needed no convincing." See NARA, RG 59, US embassy, Bonn, to Secretary of State, 1 May 1969, State Department Records, DEF 6 CAN.

29 NARA, Nixon materials, NSC files, country files, box 670, Canada I, Helmut Sonnenfeldt to Henry Kissinger, 28 May 1969.

30 Lyon and Tomlin, *Canada as an International Actor*, 112.

31 Thordarson, *Trudeau and Foreign Policy*, 44.

32 NARA, RG 59, file POL 7 CAN, US embassy, Oslo, to State Department, 16 June 1969.

33 Head to George Ignatieff, 12 September 1969, quoted in Granatstein and Bothwell, *Pirouette*, 29.

34 Dalton Camp, a close adviser and prominent supporter of Conservative Party leader Robert Stanfield, had characterized alliances as little more than an umbrella for the superpowers: Tom Keating, *Canada and World Order: The Multilateralist Tradition in Canadian Foreign Policy* (Toronto: McClelland and Stewart, 1993), 162.

35 George Ignatieff, *The Making of a Peacemonger: The Memoirs of George Ignatieff* (Toronto: University of Toronto Press, 1985), 245. In 1969 Ignatieff was in transit from being UN ambassador to disarmament ambassador in Geneva.

36 Cadieux note on memorandum by Basil Robinson, 27 June 1969, quoted in Granatstein and Bothwell, *Pirouette*, 30.

37 Quoted in ibid., 31.

38 The hexagon is illustrated in Thordarson, *Trudeau and Foreign Policy*, 180.

39 See Granatstein and Bothwell, *Pirouette*, 31-3.

40 Quoted in ibid., 34.

41 The critic was the American academic Robert Endicott Osgood, testifying before the House of Commons Standing Committee on External Affairs and Defence in February 1971: see Granatstein and Bothwell, *Pirouette,* 39 and 391n.1.

42 Sharp, *Which Reminds Me ...,* 177-8.

43 Lawrence Eagleburger, interview with author, Washington, DC, April 2002.

CHAPTER 16: THE 1970S BEGIN

1 Calgary speech, quoted in Ivan Head and Pierre Trudeau, *The Canadian Way: Shaping Canada's Foreign Policy, 1968-1984* (Toronto: McClelland and Stewart, 1995), 140.

2 The flavour is caught in an External Affairs study of Canadian relations with the Third World at the United Nations in 1966: "We think it is regrettable that a small number of Western countries should be found voting together in opposition to these [African-sponsored] resolutions. Part of our difficulties have arisen from our unwillingness to support recommendations calling for sanctions when we are not convinced that a threat to the peace exists, although we have sometimes disguised this view by objecting to the Assembly making judgments of this kind." Library and Archives Canada (LAC), RG 25, v. 3469, file 6-1966/2; a similar approach may be found in a 1971 document quoted by Linda Freeman, *The Ambiguous Champion: Canada and South Africa in the Trudeau and Mulroney Years* (Toronto: University of Toronto Press, 1997), 62.

3 Head and Trudeau, *The Canadian Way,* 142, makes the interesting point that aid programs in the 1950s and 1960s were seen in light of the very successful Marshall Plan for the reconstruction of Europe in the 1940s. In fact the "self-help" programs that came into fashion in the later 1960s and 1970s were very close to the original Marshall Plan model and practice.

4 LAC, Department of External Affairs (DEA) Records, file 23-1-India, departmental memorandum, "Visit of Prime Minister Indira Gandhi to Canada, June 17 to 24, 1973," 8 June 1973; ibid., Commonwealth Heads of Government Meeting, Kingston, Jamaica, 29 April-6 May 1975, Country Paper, India.

5 On reactor exports, see Robert Bothwell, *Nucleus* (Toronto: University of Toronto Press, 1988), 428-30; on the aftermath, see John Hadwen, "A Foreign Service Officer and Canada's Nuclear Policies," in *"Special Trust and Confidence": Envoy Essays in Canadian Diplomacy*, ed. David Reece (Ottawa: Carleton University Press, 1997), 162-9.

6   DEA Records, file 23-1-India, Jenkins (New Delhi) to DEA, 11 June 1974.

7   Quoted in David R. Morrison, *Aid and Ebb Tide: A History of CIDA and Canadian Development Assistance* (Waterloo, ON: Wilfrid Laurier University Press, 1998), 32.

8   Ibid., 35.

9   See J.L. Granatstein and Robert Bothwell, *Pirouette: Pierre Trudeau and Canadian Foreign Policy* (Toronto: University of Toronto Press, 1990), 288-9.

10 To be fair, there was already considerable interest in the Cabinet and the bureaucracy in aid to francophone Africa: Morrison, *Aid and Ebb Tide*, 49-50.

11 The invitation to Quebec to attend the conference in Gabon was strongly opposed by the French ambassador in Ottawa, François Leduc, and by the Quai d'Orsay: Alain Peyrefitte, *C'était de Gaulle* (Paris: Fayard, 1999), 3:372. On de Gaulle, see ibid., 378.

12 So wrote André François-Poncet, doyen of the French diplomatic corps, in *Le Figaro*, quoted in Anne Rouanet and Pierre Rouanet, *Les trois derniers chagrins du Général de Gaulle* (Paris: Grasset, 1980), 156-8. François-Poncet was not alone; de Gaulle, who read his article, complained bitterly about it in retirement.

13 This process is described in some detail in Granatstein and Bothwell, *Pirouette,* ch. 5.

14 Pierre Duchesne, *Jacques Parizeau,* vol. 1, *Le Croisé* (Montreal: Québec-Amérique, 2001), 599-605; see also William Johnson, "The Money Trail Leads to France," *Globe and Mail*, 19 May 2001, A13.

15 See Granatstein and Bothwell, *Pirouette,* 155.

16 National Archives and Records Administration (NARA), RG 59, CFPF, box 56, file POL 7 CAN, Watson, Paris, to State Department, 1 April 1971.

17 This was a target set by Lester Pearson himself when he headed a World Bank study into foreign aid: Granatstein and Bothwell, *Pirouette,* 305-6.

18 G.K. Helleiner, "Canada and the New International Economic Order," *Canadian Public Policy* 2, 3 (1976): 456.

19 See Granatstein and Bothwell, *Pirouette,* 288-9.

20 Head and Trudeau, *The Canadian Way,* 97.

21 Ibid., 98-9.

22 A point made by Freeman, *Ambiguous Champion,* 35: Trudeau's approach, she writes, put him "to some extent ... at odds with the non-white Commonwealth."

23 J.D.B. Miller, *Survey of Commonwealth Affairs: Problems of Expansion and Attrition* (London: Oxford University Press, 1974), 263.

24 Head and Trudeau, *The Canadian Way,* 110-11: Ivan Head had recently toured African Commonwealth countries and had reported to Trudeau that they were in no mood to be put off. Trudeau so informed Heath when the latter visited Ottawa before the Commonwealth Conference.

25 Canada, Cabinet minutes, 14 January 1971, 10.

26 Trudeau's later relations with Heath seem to have been excellent. When later that year Heath achieved success in negotiations with the European Common Market, Trudeau was the only Commonwealth leader to congratulate him: Head and Trudeau, *The Canadian Way,* 114-15.

27 Harry Carter, "Playing for Time: South Africa, 1969-72," in Reece, *"Special Trust,"* 75. Carter, as ambassador, argued that termination of Canadian trade would only dishearten liberal-minded groups in South Africa that relied on and needed foreign diplomats with some influence over the apartheid regime.

28 Freeman, *Ambiguous Champion,* 55, argues that "official support for full economic and diplomatic relations never wavered." She attributes this to a combination of official opinion and economic interests. Head and Trudeau, *The Canadian Way,* 107ff, understandably argue the contrary.

29 This was an issue where Henry Kissinger played an active part, though he was careful to keep the British out in front. See DEA Records, file 23-1-SNAFR, Washington embassy to DEA, 18 October 1976, describing a working lunch between Allan MacEachen and Kissinger. Kissinger told MacEachen

"that if Cda had no need to get involved in African politics it would be wise to stay out of them. What he had been through recently were quote weirdest negotiations ever seen unquote. Africans were always making statements and asserting they did not mean them."

30 The anti-apartheid groups listed by Freeman, *Ambiguous Champion*, 69, were unlikely to come to the aid of the Liberal Party in any season or for any reason.

31 Quoted in Head and Trudeau, *The Canadian Way*, 103.

32 This is one point on which Granatstein and Bothwell, *Pirouette*, 275-7, and Head and Trudeau, *The Canadian Way*, 101ff, appear to agree.

33 For an overview of Mao and China, see David Reynolds, *One World Divisible: A Global History since 1945* (New York: Norton, 2000), 250-61.

34 In their discussion of Canadian relations with China, Head and Trudeau use the term "dictatorial and brutal" to describe the government of Taiwan but say nothing at all about the character of the Maoist regime on the mainland: *The Canadian Way*, 223.

35 NARA, RG 59, CFPF 67-9, box 1939, file POL 12 CAN, A.B. Moreland, Consul General, Toronto, to State Department, 11 April 1968.

36 James Mann, *About Face: A History of America's Curious Relationship with China, from Nixon to Clinton* (New York: Knopf, 1998), 28.

37 Granatstein and Bothwell, *Pirouette*, 186.

38 He said so in an article in *Foreign Affairs* in 1967 cited in Mann, *About Face*, 16-17.

39 Granatstein and Bothwell, *Pirouette*, 187. The Trudeau voyage is described at some length in Head and Trudeau, *The Canadian Way*, 229-37.

40 See the strongly argued book by William Easterly, *The White Man's Burden: Why the West's Efforts to Aid the Rest Have Done So Much Ill and So Little Good* (New York: Penguin, 2006).

Chapter 17: Parallel Lives

1 The largest number of Canadian-born lived in New England, and were mostly French Canadian (135,900 out of 247,100). In other regions the Canadian-born were overwhelmingly English Canadian.

2 According to Canadian figures, 12.8 percent of Canadians returning from the United States had been in the South Atlantic region, including Florida. The proportion of visits in the first quarter of the year – winter vacationers in part – had been rising steadily.

3 See James T. Patterson, *Grand Expectations: The United States, 1945-1974* (New York: Oxford University Press, 1996), 577-9. A quota of 120,000 was established for the entire Western hemisphere, with no specific national quotas within that number. In addition, 170,000 were to be admitted from the rest of the world, which in the 1960s was expected to be mainly southern and eastern Europe.

4 Lubor J. Zink, "The Unpenetrated Problem of Pierre Trudeau," *National Review*, 25 June 1982, 751-6. In the 1960s Zink had been a columnist for the *Toronto Telegram*.

5 Keith Davey, quoted in J.L. Granatstein and Robert Bothwell, *Pirouette: Pierre Trudeau and Canadian Foreign Policy* (Toronto: University of Toronto Press, 1990), 96. Trudeau's interest in American movies extended to American movie stars: he famously dated Barbra Streisand, among others.

6 Canada, Cabinet minutes, 25 March 1971, 34.

7 Leigh Sarty, "Middle Power in Moscow: Canada and the Soviet Union from Khrushchev to Gorbachev," *Queen's Quarterly* 98, 3 (1991): 562-5.

8 National Archives and Records Administration (NARA), RG 59, CFPF, box 2156, file POL 7 CAN, Memorandum of conversation, 11 June 1971, among Richard T. Davies, Deputy Assistant Secretary for European affairs, Jack Perry, and Frederick Quin on the American side, and Kenneth B. Williamson, minister, Canadian embassy and Alan P. McLaine, counsellor, Canadian embassy.

9 Robert Ford, *Our Man in Moscow: A Diplomat's Reflections on the Soviet Union* (Toronto: University of Toronto Press, 1989), 119.

10 Porter letter to the *Washington Post*, 9 February 1978. Porter and Kissinger had had their differences, and Porter was not alone in the State Department in resenting the secretary's behaviour.

11 Gerald Ford Library, National Security Adviser, Memoranda and Conversations, box 7, Memorandum of conversation, President Gerald Ford, Henry Kissinger, Brent Scowcroft, 3 December 1974.

12 Georgetown University Library, Foreign Affairs Oral History Program, Dwight Mason, political counsellor, US embassy, Ottawa, 1980-1983, 1993 interview.

13 Henry Kissinger, *White House Years* (Boston: Little, Brown, 1979), 383.

14 Kissinger sponsored Canada for membership in the Group of Seven (G7), the elite group of powerful Western leaders. It was also true that on economic matters Canada was, relatively speaking, important, with a large GDP – in the mid-1970s more than Italy's, which with Canada was admitted to the G7.

15 Department of External Affairs (DEA) Records, file 20-1-2-USA, minutes by J.R. McKinney, "Re: Proposals for Joint Meetings of Canada/USA Cabinets," 7 December 1978. McKinney wrote that "my recollection is that it was an extremely unsatisfactory meeting which left hard feelings on both sides that this is really what killed the Committee."

16 Helmut Sonnenfeldt, interview with author, Washington, April 2002.

17 A. Denis Clift, *With Presidents to the Summit* (Fairfax, VA: George Mason University Press, 1993), 200.

18 NARA, Nixon Presidential Materials, NSC files, box 671, file Canada, vol. 3, Sonnenfeldt to Kissinger, 26 October 1971.

19 Kissinger, *White House Years*, 383.

20 John Hilliker and Donald Barry, "Uncomfortably in the Middle: The Department of External Affairs and Canada's Involvement in the International Control Commissions in Vietnam, 1954-73," in *Creating the Peaceable Kingdom and Other Essays on Canada*, ed. Victor Howard (East Lansing: Michigan State University Press, 1998), 181-2.

21 Trudeau was in fact more concerned about the United States than he was about Vietnam: he worried about riots and civil disturbances in American cities and what those might portend for Canada.

22 Canada, Cabinet minutes, 15 January 1970.

23 NARA, RG 59, CFPF, box 1949, file POL CAN-US XL POL 27 VIETS, memorandum of conversation, Secretary Rogers, Kissinger, Joe Scott, Sonnenfeldt etc., Mitchell Sharp, ambassador Ed Ritchie, undersecretary Cadieux, Jake Warren, etc., 24 March 1969. During the meeting, Rogers assured Sharp that when it came to peacekeeping in Vietnam, "we always thought of Canada first." The minutes continued: "The Minister thought it would be useful for the Secretary to say that on Canadian television, since the government was being accused of not being neutral in the conflict by supplying arms to the US and not emphasizing a peacekeeping role for Canada."

24 Public opinion polls cited in Granatstein and Bothwell, *Pirouette*, 41.

25 Gallup Poll, cited in NARA, RG 59, 1967-69 series, file POL CAN-US, Ottawa embassy to State Department, 5 August 1969.

26 Doug Owram, *Born at the Right Time* (Toronto: University of Toronto Press, 1996), 170.

27 NARA, RG 59, CFPF, box 1949, file POL CAN-US, William Macomber [later of Watergate fame] to Congressman Albert Watson, 25 June 1969.

28 During the 1960s the most interesting development in Canadian trade was a rise in commerce with continental Europe and with Japan. Trade with Great Britain decreased as a proportion of Canadian exports and imports: Michael Hart, *A Trading Nation: Canadian Trade Policy from Colonialism to Globalization* (Vancouver: UBC Press, 2002), 246 table 9.1, 259-60.

29 Kissinger in his memoirs commented that Connally's "swaggering self-assurance" produced in Nixon a feeling of "awe"; quoted in Bruce J. Schulman, *The Seventies: The Great Shift in American Culture, Society and Politics* (New York: Free Press, 2001), 40.

30 In a conversation with a senior Japanese diplomat in August 1971, Kissinger said that economics bored him and that in general economic leaders were "political idiots." Editorial note quoting Kissinger, *Foreign Relations of the United States (FRUS), 1969-1972*, vol. 3 (Washington: Government Printing Office, 2002), 169.

31 Quoted in Robert Bothwell, *Canada and the United States: The Politics of Partnership* (Toronto: University of Toronto Press, 1992), 106.

32 David Calleo, *Rethinking Europe's Future* (Princeton, NJ: Princeton University Press, 2001), 158.

33 See John S. Odell, *U.S. International Monetary Policy: Markets, Power and Ideas as Sources of Change* (Princeton, NJ: Princeton University Press, 1982), 255-7, and Richard Parker, *John Kenneth Galbraith: His Life, His Politics, His Economics* (Toronto: HarperCollins, 2005), 491ff.

34 Odell, *U.S. International Monetary Policy,* 254.

35 Quoted in Walter LaFeber, *The American Age: United States Policy at Home and Abroad since 1750* (New York: Norton, 1989), 612.

36 Henry Kissinger, *White House Years* (Boston: Little, Brown, 1979), 962.

37 Quoted in Odell, *U.S. International Monetary Policy,* 260.

38 William Bundy, *A Tangled Web: The Making of Foreign Policy in the Nixon Presidency* (New York: Hill and Wang, 1998), 262-3. Odell, *U.S. International Monetary Policy,* 261, points out that the surcharge would tend to counteract the desired descent in the dollar's exchange rate. But Connally argued that the surcharge was essential, and compared it to a farmer hitting "his donkey on the head with a two-by-four to get his attention."

39 The problem was defined in a memorandum prepared in the Treasury Department in early September 1971: *FRUS, 1969-1972,* 3:179ff: "Requirements for a Secure U.S. Balance of Payments Position," 10 September 1971.

40 There were other grievances, such as government subsidization of a new Michelin tire plant in Nova Scotia.

41 John Holmes, "From Three Industries to One: Towards an Integrated North American Automobile Industry," in *Driving Continentally: National Policies and the North American Auto Industry,* ed. Maureen Appel Molot (Ottawa: Carleton University Press, 1993), 27. In fact the 1970 surplus was the first of three in a row. The auto trade then moved back into deficit for Canada until 1982, when Canada again began running surpluses.

42 Ibid., 35.

43 Bundy, *A Tangled Web*, 268.

44 Canada, Cabinet minutes, 18 August 1971: Sharp as acting prime minister showed his colleagues the draft of a letter to Nixon arguing that the application of the tariff surtax to Canada "was not justified." In discussion both Sharp and Benson predicted that Connally was likely to take a tough line and that the US measures might last some time.

45 Quoted in Granatstein and Bothwell, *Pirouette*, 65.

46 A point made by the Dutch in a conversation with the US embassy in The Hague, Embassy to State Department, 6 December 1971, *FRUS, 1969-1972*, 3:587. The Dutch argued that Canada, given its "weight in U.S. imports," was in a position to set the example in revaluing its currency after which other countries "would have to push their revaluation."

47 "I have never understood Connally," Kissinger later said. "Connally was attempting to use Canada as a key element in breaking up European policy." Memorandum of Conversation, 25 July 1972, among Kissinger, Arthur Burns, and Robert Hormats: *FRUS, 1969-1972,* 3:641.

48 Quoted in Schulman, *The Seventies*, 42.

49 See the minutes of the meeting between Benson and Connally and their staffs, 6 December 1971, *FRUS, 1969-1972*, vol. 3, especially p. 210, where Benson and Connally vigorously disputed whether the United States had a positive or negative balance of trade with Canada.

50 NARA, Nixon Presidential Materials, NSC files, box 671, file: Canada, vol. 3, Sonnenfeldt to Al Haig, 20 October 1971.

51 Head and Trudeau, *The Canadian Way*, 188.

52 NARA, Nixon Presidential Materials, NSC files, box 671, file: Canada, vol. 3, Sonnenfeldt and Robert Hormats to Kissinger, 4 February 1972, "urgent action."

53 Mitchell Sharp said as much in a television interview on 10 April: Canada would not wish to appear to have "knuckled under" to American pressures, especially with a Canadian election coming up. Quoted in Peter Dobell, *Canada in World Affairs*, vol. 17, *1971 to 1973* (Toronto: CIIA, 1985), 41.

54 NARA, Nixon Presidential Materials, NSC files, box 671, file: Canada, vol. 3, Harold A. Scott to Kissinger, 12 April 1972.

55 John Connally with Mickey Herskowitz, *In History's Shadow: An American Odyssey* (New York: Hyperion, 1993), 251-3. Connally's own account places the immediate occasion for his departure as interference with tax policy by John Ehrlichman, one of Nixon's senior aides.

56 H.R. Haldeman, *The Haldeman Diaries: Inside the Nixon White House* (New York: G.P. Putnam's Sons, 1994), 441.

57 Qiang Zhai, *China and the Vietnam Wars, 1950-1975* (Chapel Hill: University of North Carolina Press, 2000), 202-3.

58 Alexander Ross, "One Man Makes Useless Protest on Viet Nam War," *Toronto Star*, 10 May 1972.

59 NARA, Nixon Presidential Materials, NSC files, Country Files-Europe, box 671, file: Canada, vol. 3, September 71-December 72, Secretary Rogers to US embassy in Ottawa, 2 November 1972.

60 Dobell, *Canada in World Affairs*, 289. One note was sent after the bombing was over.

61 Mitchell Sharp, *Which Reminds Me ... A Memoir* (Toronto: University of Toronto Press, 1994), 213.

62 Sonnenfeldt wrote to Kissinger on 17 January 1973, "We now have the attached condolence message. I personally feel it *should be sent* as a civilized gesture. But because of the mood you described yesterday I want to be sure you know this is being done" (emphasis in original). NARA, Nixon Presidential Materials, NSC files, box 750, file: Canada, Trudeau corres.

63 Granatstein and Bothwell, *Pirouette*, 56.

64 Arnold R. Isaacs, *Without Honor: Defeat in Vietnam and Cambodia* (Baltimore, MD: Johns Hopkins University Press, 1983), 97.

65 Head and Trudeau, *The Canadian Way*, 184.

66 Sharp, *Which Reminds Me*, 215-16.

67 Granatstein and Bothwell, *Pirouette*, 218-19.

Chapter 18: The Pursuit of Promises

1 Ivan Head and Pierre Trudeau, *The Canadian Way: Shaping Canada's Foreign Policy, 1968-1984* (Toronto: McClelland and Stewart, 1995), 252.

2 William Bundy, *A Tangled Web: The Making of Foreign Policy in the Nixon Presidency* (New York: Hill and Wang, 1998), 480.

3 Robert Ford, the Canadian ambassador in Moscow, noted that American rapprochement with the Soviet Union meant that Soviet relations with other Western powers such as Canada became less important and certainly less urgent to the Soviets. See Ford, *Our Man in Moscow* (Toronto: University of Toronto Press, 1989), 276.

4 Bundy, *Tangled Web*, 321; Ford, *Our Man in Moscow*, 268, reports that sophisticated Soviet observers such as Georgi Arbatov agreed that *Ostpolitik* was crucial in setting the stage of an improvement in US-USSR relations.

5 Granatstein and Bothwell, *Pirouette: Pierre Trudeau and Canadian Foreign Policy* (Toronto: University of Toronto Press, 1990), 192-3.

6 Ford was contemptuous of Kissinger's frantic grasping for public smiles and chuckles from Brezhnev during Nixon's 1972 visit to Moscow: *Our Man in Moscow*, 268.

7 Ibid.

8 Trudeau visited Cuba in 1976, the first NATO head of government to do so. He had no effect on Cuba's African interventions. The next year, coincidentally, Canada publicly expelled five Cuban diplomats for spying. Trudeau sought good relations with Cuba through most of his time in office, but not at any price. See the discussion in Jorge I. Domínguez, *To Make a World Safe for Revolution: Cuba's Foreign Policy* (Cambridge, MA: Harvard University Press, 1989), 196-7, 272. Canada subsidized Cuban trade and, possibly in return, got some outstanding claims (dating from the expropriation of Canadian business in 1960) paid off.

9 This occurred under both the Ford and Carter administrations: Domínguez, *To Make a World Safe*, 227-8.

10 Thomas M. Nichols, *The Sacred Cause: Civil-Military Conflict over Soviet National Security* (Ithaca, NY: Cornell University Press, 1993), 94.

11 Albert Legault and Michel Fortmann, *A Diplomacy of Hope: Canada and Disarmament, 1945-1988* (Montreal and Kingston: McGill-Queen's University Press, 1992), ch. 11, covers this episode.

12 Mitchell Sharp, *Which Reminds Me ... A Memoir* (Toronto: University of Toronto Press, 1994), 216-17.

13 Quoted in Granatstein and Bothwell, *Pirouette*, 198.

14 Bundy, *A Tangled Web*, 483. The American Central Intelligence Agency (CIA) was especially egregious in overestimating the size of the Soviet economy, but it was not alone.

15 Peter Roberts, interview with author, August 1980.

16 I am greatly indebted to my friend Tom Nichols for clarifying this point. On the other hand, the Soviets poured vast sums, which they could not afford, into Cuba and other distant sinkholes.

17 On stagflation, see Robert Bothwell, Ian Drummond, and John English, *Canada since 1945: Power, Politics, and Provincialism*, rev. ed. (Toronto: University of Toronto, 1989), 351-4. Bruce J. Schulman, *The Seventies: The Great Shift in American Culture, Society and Politics* (New York: Free Press, 2001), 129, defines stagflation as "a virtually inconceivable combination of galloping inflation and tenacious unemployment."

18 J. Rennie Whitehead, "A Brief History of the Club of Rome: A Summary and Personal Reminiscences," available at http://www.cacor.ca/corhis.html.

19 Daniel Yergin, *The Prize: The Epic Quest for Oil, Money and Power* (New York: Simon and Schuster, 1990), 568.

20 Bothwell, Drummond, and English, *Canada since 1945*, 347.

21 National Archives and Records Administration (NARA), Nixon Presidential Materials, WHCF, CO28-EX, fg6-11-1, John Whitaker, Peter Flanigan, memorandum for the files, 24 February 1971.

22 NARA, Nixon Presidential Materials, NSC files, box 671 file Canada vol. 3, Robert Hormats to Kissinger, 15 October 1971.

23 NARA, RG 59, Lot 72D303, briefing books 1958-76, box 99, covering note for Rogers, "Meetings with Sharp," April 1972.

24 Granatstein and Bothwell, *Pirouette*, 84.

25 Avi Shlaim, *The Iron Wall: Israel and the Arab World* (New York: Norton, 2000), 321.

26 Ethan Kapstein, *The Insecure Alliance: Energy Crises and Western Politics since 1944* (New York: Oxford University Press, 1990), 165. Head and Trudeau, *The Canadian Way*, 155, refer to the "harsh reaction of the oil-consuming nations of the North." It is difficult to discern what, at the time, this was.

27 Dobell, *Canada in World Affairs*, vol. 17, *1971-1973* (Toronto: CIIA, 1985), 205.

28 Sharp, *Which Reminds Me ...*, 209; NARA, RG 59, CFPF 67-9, box 1939, file POL 7 CAN, US embassy, Ottawa, to State Department, 26 November 1969.

29 David Taras, "Canada's Jewish Community and Support for Israel," in *The Domestic Battleground: Canada and The Arab-Israeli Conflict*, ed. David Taras and David H. Goldberg (Montreal and Kingston: McGill-Queen's University Press, 1989), 55.

30 NARA, Nixon Presidential Materials, White Central Files, CO28, Willis C. Armstrong, "Consultations with Canada on Oil," 9 October 1973.

31 William Simon Papers, Lafayette College, box 12, microfiche 17, Canada 1973-74, William Johnson to William Simon, 24 October 1973.

32 Kapstein, *Insecure Alliance*, 168.

33 NARA, William Simon Papers, Lafayette College, box 12, microfiche 17, Canada 1973-74, William Johnson to William Simon, 24 October 1973.

34 NARA, RG 59, subject numeric files 1970-73, box 2164, file POL CAN-US, George Springsteen, Eur/Can division of State Department to Secretary Henry Kissinger, 30.10.73, "Possible Pressure Points on Canada."

35 Granatstein and Bothwell, *Pirouette*, 87.

36 See ibid., 401-2n.66.

37 On the pipeline negotiations, see Granatstein and Bothwell, *Pirouette*, 101-5.

38 NARA, RG 59, subject numeric files 1970-73, box 2164, file POL CAN-US, James Carson, Secretariat staff, State, to "Mr. Lissy" 21 April 1972.

39 NARA, NSC Trip Files, box 471, President's Visit (April 17-19/72), folder 1.

40 Michael Hart, *A Trading Nation: Canadian Trade Policy from Colonialism to Globalization* (Vancouver: UBC Press, 2002), 254-6.

41 Hugo Young, *This Blessed Plot: Britain and Europe from Churchill to Blair* (London: Macmillan, 1999), 222; Peter Clarke, *Hope and Glory: Britain, 1900-1990* (London: Penguin, 1996), 342-3.

42 Hart, *A Trading Nation*, 288.

43 Ibid., 290.

44 Quoted in Granatstein and Bothwell, *Pirouette*, 161.

45 Quoted in ibid., 161-2.

46 Allan MacEachen, interview with author, 14 March 1988. "We resisted that," MacEachen said.

47 The process is described in some detail in Granatstein and Bothwell, *Pirouette*, 158-72.

48 Michael Hart, in *Colonialism to Globalism*, takes a somewhat more sanguine view of trade relations with Japan.

49 De Montigny Marchand, interview with author, 11 July 1988. In his opinion Finance Minister John Turner and senior civil servants like Simon Reisman, Jim Grandy, Al Johnson, and Jake Warren did not care much about the Third Option, and they conveyed their attitude to major actors in the economy outside Ottawa.

50 Brent Scowcroft, quoted in Granatstein and Bothwell, *Pirouette*, 93. This attitude of amused tolerance is the American counterpart of the Canadian attitude of pained superiority.

51 Ford Library, NSA Presidential Country Files, box 3, Helmut Sonnenfeldt, memo of conversation with Canadian ambassador Jake Warren, 22 October 1975.

52 Ibid., addendum for US ambassador Rush in Paris.

53 Kissinger, *Years of Renewal* (New York: Simon and Schuster, 1999), 693.

54 Ford Library, NSA Presidential Country Files, box 3, Mack Johnson, US embassy, Ottawa, to State Department, 31 October 1975.

55 Canadian diplomat Si Taylor, in an interview, called the French response to Canadian protests "quite sophistical." It was, he said, "Ah, we need the Italians in because of their weakness; surely you Canadians, out of your strength, can afford to ignore this bauble of summitry." Taylor, interview with author, 30 August 1988.

56 Trudeau had wisely decided not to beg favours directly from Giscard, leaving it to others to make Canada's case. See Head and Trudeau, *The Canadian Way*, 197.

57 Mark MacGuigan, interview with author, 19 January 1988.

58 Confidential interview with author. The same interviewee added that in his opinion Schmidt thought Canadians to be "colonial parvenus."

59 Mark MacGuigan, *An Inside Look at External Affairs: The Memoirs of Mark MacGuigan*, ed. P. Whitney Lackenbauer (Calgary: University of Calgary Press, 2002) 45. He cites Genscher's "quiet wisdom."

60 Head and Trudeau's own foreign policy memoir, *The Canadian Way*, 196-7, is opaque on what actually happened at the early summits, though it furnishes some details on the diplomacy that surrounded Canada's eventual invitation to join the G7.

61 See David Calleo, *Rethinking Europe's Future* (Princeton, NJ: Princeton University Press, 2001), 168. French president Valéry Giscard d'Estaing was especially fond of what was called "rigueur." As Calleo points out, this contributed to his defeat in the 1981 French presidential elections.

62 The Ottawa conference was enlivened by the possibility of the attendance of the dictator of Uganda, Idi Amin, who specialized in anti-British tirades. Amin had just expelled the East Indian population of his country, and many of them had found refuge in Canada. In the event, Amin did not come, though his foreign minister did and was allowed to read out one of his master's effusions, to which nobody listened.

63 Head and Trudeau, *The Canadian Way*, 118-19.

64 Ibid., 214.

65 See the synopsis in David Reynolds, *One World Divisible: A Global History since 1945* (New York: Norton, 2000), 384-5.

66 The Soviets built on the foundation of the tsarist regime's railways and factories, and with the help of homegrown and pre-existing engineers, scientists, and other professionals.

67 An argument repeated in Head and Trudeau, *The Canadian Way*, 149-50.

68 On the question of development, and its treatment by historians, see Nick Cullather, "Development? It's History," *Diplomatic History* 24, 4 (2000): 641-53.

69 Granatstein and Bothwell, *Pirouette*, 301-2.

70 Ibid., 302-3.

71 Head and Trudeau, *The Canadian Way*, 147.

72 Ibid., 152. This understanding, they believed, was greater in Canada and especially inside the Canadian government "than, for example, in the United States."

CHAPTER 19: CANADA FIRST, 1976-1984

1 Arthur Andrew, *Rise and Fall of a Middle Power: Canadian Diplomacy from King to Mulroney* (Toronto: James Lorimer, 1993), 142.

2 The most egregious example was an offer in 1970 to contribute $300,000 to the election war chest of the separatists; it was refused by Lévesque. See Pierre Duchesne, *Jacques Parizeau*, vol. 1, *Le Croisé* (Montreal: Québec Amérique, 2001), 599-605.

3 Quoted in Robert Chodos and Eric Hamovitch, *Quebec and the American Dream* (Toronto: Between the Lines, 1991), 156.

4 See J.L. Granatstein and Robert Bothwell, *Pirouette: Pierre Trudeau and Canadian Foreign Policy* (Toronto: University of Toronto Press, 1990), 346.

5 See Chodos and Hamovitch, *Quebec and the American Dream*, 213-4.

6 National Archives and Records Administration, NARA, Nixon Presidential Materials, NSC files, country files, box 670, file: Canada II, Rogers to Nixon, 24 November 1970.

7 Jean-François Lisée, *Dans l'oeil de l'aigle: Washington face au Québec* (Montreal: Boréal, 1990), 196. Trudeau saw Enders almost immediately in his office; Paul Desmarais of Power Corporation and Ian Sinclair of the CPR were among the early callers.

8 Enders, interview with author, 13 May 1988. It is clear that President Jimmy Carter and Secretary of State Cyrus Vance took a favourable attitude to keeping Canada together. It is less clear where National Security Adviser Zbigniew Brzezinski stood. Brzezinski, the son of an exiled Polish diplomat, grew up in Montreal and attended McGill University before moving to the United States. The

Canadian embassy finally concluded that Brzezinski reflected Carter's positive view of Canada rather than the reverse.

9 The phrase is the Baltimore *Sun*'s, quoted in Granatstein and Bothwell, *Pirouette*, 349.

10 Head was the main drafter of the speech: Ivan Head and Pierre Trudeau, *The Canadian Way* (Toronto: McClelland and Stewart, 1995), 203-4.

11 Allan Gotlieb, interview with author, December 1994.

12 LAC, Department of External Affairs (DEA) Records, file 20-12-USA, Gotlieb to Jamieson, "Canada/ United States Relations," 13 September 1978.

13 Ibid., Towe to DEA, 24 October 1978. Towe added that Congress was nevertheless a very great problem – "more powerful, more parochial and more unpredictable." He added that US public opinion was more informed and better disposed toward Canada because of the national unity question, on which there was sympathy for the federal government's position.

14 Robert Hunter, "Managing the North Atlantic Alliance," in *Activism and (Non) Alignment*, ed. Ann-Sofie Dahl and Norman Hillmer (Stockholm: Swedish Institute of International Affairs, 2002), 3.

15 DEA Records, file 10-1-2-USA, Gotlieb to Jamieson, 13 September 1978.

16 Lawrence Martin, *The Presidents and the Prime Ministers* (Toronto: Doubleday, 1982), 267.

17 Many years later, when Trudeau died in 2000, Jimmy Carter served as pallbearer at the funeral, along with Fidel Castro.

18 The Soviet decisions were the product of a struggle between civilian and military factions inside the government: Thomas Nichols, *The Sacred Cause: Civil-Military Conflict over Soviet National Security, 1917-1992* (Ithaca, NY: Cornell University Press, 1993), 104-6.

19 Brzezinski is cited in Martin Walker, *The Cold War: A History* (Toronto: Stoddart, 1994), 245-6.

20 Boycotts were nothing new in sports: the 1976 Montreal Olympics and the 1978 Commonwealth Games in Edmonton were both marred by boycotts or the threat of boycotts.

21 DEA Records, file 20-1-2-USA. "Report of the SSEA's Discussion with Philip Habib, USA Under-Secretary of State, 9 December 1977," in which Don Jamieson told the American diplomat that "he had told the Israelis that they would undercut support from their friends if their objective was territory rather than security guarantees."

22 Barney Danson with Curtis Fahey, *Not Bad for a Sergeant: The Memoirs of Barney Danson* (Toronto: Dundurn, 2002), 238. Danson, Trudeau's defence minister and a prominent member of the Jewish community, was present at the encounter. On the overall subject of the Jerusalem embassy incident I am greatly indebted to Charles Flicker's graduate paper presented at the London School of Economics in 2002.

23 Mark MacGuigan, interview with author, 19 January 1988. MacGuigan considered that Begin's intervention in Canadian politics was the main source of Trudeau's disposition after 1980 to stress the Arab side of the Middle Eastern crisis.

24 Clark was only thirty-nine, Canada's youngest prime minister, and had acquired a reputation for ill-considered and clumsy pronouncements and actions. Implementing his election promises would demonstrate that he was actually a man of principle and especially a man of his word. On the 1979 election and its aftermath see Granatstein and Bothwell, *Pirouette*, 210-18.

25 Charles Flicker points out that several prominent Jewish leaders considered the promise ill-advised and an unnecessary diversion from more urgent, if less symbolically significant, issues.

26 The one, understandably, was immigration minister Ron Atkey, who had urged the policy and probably benefited from it in winning his St. Paul's constituency in the 1979 election. He would lose it in 1980. I am again indebted to Charles Flicker's account of these events. According to him, the Cabinet discussed the issue on three occasions, but reached no conclusion.

27 *Canadian Annual Review of Politics and Public Affairs, 1979* (Toronto: University of Toronto Press, 1981), 264-5. The term "two-track" appears to be a continuing favourite of NATO's – it was used

again in the 1990s. The ministerial communiqué is less opaque: "Ministers confirmed that their Governments were resolved to take steps to reduce the growing imbalance of forces by improving their military capabilities and thus maintain an adequate level of deterrence and defence across the full spectrum ... Ministers believed that efforts to achieve agreement in fields of arms control, disarmament and confidence-building should go hand in hand with the defence efforts of the Allies." "North Atlantic Council, Final Communiqué, Brussels, 13-14 December 1979," http://www.nato.int/docu/comm/49-95/c791213a.htm.

28 The deployment is described in David Miller, *The Cold War: A Military History* (London: John Murray, 1998), 42-3.

29 The guidance system for the missiles was made by Toronto-based Litton Industries. In a rare example of domestic terrorism, a group of radicals ("anarchists") from British Columbia travelled to Toronto and bombed Litton, to the dismay of less militant peace activists: James Stark, *Cold War Blues: The Operation Dismantle Story* (Hull, QC: Voyageur, 1991), 202-3.

30 Wheat, because of the long history of American subsidies, was a perennial bone of contention between Canada and the United States. Bad feeling was in this area the normal atmosphere.

31 Head and Trudeau, *The Canadian Way*, 209.

32 Quoted in Granatstein and Bothwell, Pirouette, 199-200; Head and Trudeau, *The Canadian Way*, 209-10.

33 Mark MacGuigan, *An Inside Look at External Affairs during the Trudeau Years: The Memoirs of Mark MacGuigan*, ed. P. Whitney Lackenbauer (Calgary: University of Calgary Press 2002), 5-6.

34 On US monetary policy, see Bruce Schulman, *The Seventies* (New York: Free Press, 2001), 141-2. On the recession in Canada, see Robert Bothwell, Ian Drummond, and John English, *Canada since 1945: Power, Politics, and Provincialism*, rev. ed. (Toronto: University of Toronto, 1989), 22-3.

35 NARA, RG 59, subject numeric files 1970-73, box 2164, file POL CAN-US, Calgary Consulate General to State Department 23 August and 14 September 1972.

36 See the discussion of the NEP in Bothwell, Drummond, and English, *Canada since 1945*, 451-5. There were other aspects to Trudeau's nationalist energy policies, such as the purchase of the Canadian assets of Fina, a Belgian oil company, by Petro-Canada, Canada's nationalized oil firm.

37 In an amusing footnote, Senator Jesse Helms, a North Carolina Republican, escorted René Lévesque onto the floor of the US Senate and introduced him around. Plainly if Trudeau would not do, the United States should support the break-up of Canada. Allan Gotlieb, interview with author, December 1994.

38 See Granatstein and Bothwell, *Pirouette*, 339-40.

39 Library and Archives Canada (LAC), Eddie Goldenberg Papers, vol. 16, Michael Kirby to Prime Minister, 26 August 1980, enclosing Roger Tassé to Kirby, 15 August 1980. Tassé advised that "on the legal level, there is very strong authority for the proposition that constitutional conventions do not affect the legal authority of a Parliament."

40 On Thatcher's relations with Trudeau on issues other than the constitution, see below, chapter 20.

41 MacGuigan, *Inside Look*, 92.

42 Ibid., 92-3.

43 LAC, Goldenberg Papers, vol. 16, Pinard to Trudeau, 27 October 1980.

44 A perceptive Canadian report in March 1981 commented "Mrs. Thatcher is in real trouble with her own caucus." Recently forty Conservative MPs had either voted against or abstained on a budget resolution, and it was widely believed that Thatcher might soon be replaced by Francis Pym as party leader and prime minister. Michael Kirby to Prime Minister, 27 March 1981, LAC, Eddie Goldenberg Papers, vol. 16, file Memos for PM. At a meeting with Trudeau in London in June 1981, Thatcher admitted that her legislative program was in trouble and that consequently the prospects for the Canadian package were difficult: confidential source.

45 LAC, MG 32 B 15, vol. 10, Mark MacGuigan to Prime Minister, 28 October 1980.

46 Confidential information.

47 Mark MacGuigan, interview with author; Granatstein and Bothwell, *Pirouette*, 358-9.

CHAPTER 20: RETURNING TO THE CENTRE

1 Arthur Andrew, *The Rise and Fall of a Middle Power: Canadian Diplomacy from King to Mulroney* (Toronto: Lorimer, 1993), xviii.

2 J.A. McCordick to Sandra Gwyn, 29 June 1978, private papers. McCordick was second secretary of the Canadian legation in Belgrade in 1948, and there dealt with Trudeau, who had been arrested for entering Yugoslavia without a visa. Trudeau explained that he did not believe in visas, and McCordick replied that that was not the official Yugoslav point of view and that there was some physical danger in ignoring it. "He was at the time stubborn and a bit irrational," McCordick wrote. In a collective interview in Ottawa on 11 December 2002, Mitchell Sharp argued strongly that Trudeau held a fixed prejudice against the professional foreign service.

3 Trudeau is later reported to have said that he thought making Sharp external affairs minister had been a mistake.

4 Andrew Cooper, *Canadian Foreign Policy: Old Habits and New Directions* (Scarborough, ON: Prentice Hall, 1997), 42-3.

5 Measured both in terms of the proportion of French Canadians and the ability of many of the English-speakers to manage French as well, by the time bilingualism came to be adopted as an essential policy under Trudeau. On the other hand, as in all other Ottawa departments, English was the language of work and routine.

6 Nicole Morgan, in her excellent book *Implosion: An Analysis of the Growth of the Federal Public Service in Canada, 1945-1985* (Montreal: IRPP, 1986), xvi-xvii, notes that the veterans' intake imparted an outlook "shaped by the Hungry Thirties and the war," and adds that "in an era of intensive growth, the civil service ... was modelled on our military."

7 Ibid., 50.

8 There is an affectionate portrait of Cadieux in Andrew, *Rise and Fall*, 18-19. Andrew underlines Cadieux's sense of humour.

9 Christina McCall-Newman, *Grits: An Intimate Portrait of the Liberal Party* (Toronto: Macmillan, 1982), 180-6; Gordon Robertson, *Memoirs of a Very Civil Servant* (Toronto: University of Toronto Press, 2000), 308-10, makes it clear that Pitfield's appointment as clerk of the Privy Council in 1974 was in his opinion premature.

10 McCall-Newman, *Grits*, 215. Marc Lalonde, the head of Trudeau's office and a friend of both the prime minister and Pitfield, was associated with this point of view.

11 Michael Pitfield, interview with author, 20 January 1988. Pitfield pondered the words but decided that "reborning" expressed what he meant.

12 Reeves Haggan, interview with author, 4 February 1988; other departures, not all at the same time, included John Starnes, David Kirkwood, and Blair Seaborn: Andrew, *Rise and Fall*, 107-8.

13 J.L. Granatstein and Robert Bothwell, *Pirouette: Pierre Trudeau and Canadian Foreign Policy* (Toronto: University of Toronto Press, 1990), 223.

14 Confidential interview with author, January 1988.

15 In the State Department, for example, professional diplomats at levels above deputy assistant secretary are relatively rare, though not unheard of. The Ottawa embassy, which from the 1930s to the 1960s was confined almost entirely to professionals, has since 1968 usually been the playground of political appointees. Emerson Brown, counsellor at the US embassy in Ottawa, noted the downside of the Canadian Foreign Service in his day: he had first heard of Trudeau in The Hague, when the Canadian deputy chief of mission simply disappeared, without making any farewells, because of the Trudeau budget cuts.

16 Andrew, *Rise and Fall*, 103.

17 Recent research suggests that the seers at Delphi inhaled a potent aerial cocktail of mind-altering vapours issuing from fissures in the earth.

18 This was something that Trudeau knew: Robertson, *Memoirs*, 258.

19 Paul Martin, interview with author, 10-11 February 1987.

20 On Jamieson, see Granatstein and Bothwell, *Pirouette*, 100.

21 Mark MacGuigan, *An Inside Look at External Affairs during the Trudeau Years: The Memoirs of Mark MacGuigan*, ed. P. Whitney Lackenbauer (Calgary: University of Calgary Press, 2002), 42.

22 Mark MacGuigan, interview with author, 19 January 1988.

23 Reeves Haggan, interview with author, 4 February 1988.

24 This point of view can be associated with the later work of the historian Donald Creighton and with the philosophical polemicist George Grant as well as commentators like James M. Minifie and John Warnock. Kim Nossal, in his *The Politics of Canadian Foreign Policy*, 3rd ed. (Scarborough, ON: Prentice-Hall, 1997), 60-4, ably summarizes the debate. The "assets" phrase belongs to the normally sensible journalist Sandra Gwyn, in her article, "The Decline and Fall of Canada's Foreign Policy," *Saturday Night* (April 1978).

25 Thomas Delworth, interview with author, 20 August 2001.

26 See John Campbell, *Margaret Thatcher*, vol. 2, *The Iron Lady* (London: Jonathan Cape, 2003), 253. Thatcher refused to regard Trudeau as "senior" in the G7, preferring to allocate that position to herself. Ideologically, as her biographer puts it, she "had only to sniff a progressive consensus to be against it" (340).

27 Tom Sharpe, *The Midden* (London: Pan, 1997), 15.

28 This is a point convincingly made by Brooke Jeffery, in her sometimes polemical book, *Hard Right Turn: The New Face of Neo-Conservatism in Canada* (Toronto: HarperCollins, 1999), ch. 1, "Breaking the Liberal Consensus." See also the perceptive analysis of the turn away from government and toward the market in David Calleo, *Rethinking Europe's Future* (Princeton, NJ: Princeton University Press, 2001).

29 On the change of generations, see William Strauss and Neil Howe, *Generations: The History of America's Future, 1584 to 2069* (New York: Quill/William Morrow, 1991), 317. The "thirteenth generation" was, they suggest, a generation "fearful" for its own future, measured in economic and social terms. A representative figure, they suggest, is Michael J. Fox, a Canadian expatriate actor, who in the television series *Family Ties* played the conservative child of liberal, baby boom parents. The authors comment that this generation was the "most Republican" in the history of polling; extrapolating to Canada, we might substitute "Conservative," for which "Republican" in this period seems a reasonable analogy.

30 Norman Tebbitt, quoted in Peter Clark, *Hope and Glory: Britain, 1900-1990* (London: Penguin, 1996), 379.

31 MacGuigan, *An Inside Look at External Affairs*, 43-4.

32 See Campbell, *Thatcher*, 2:318-19.

33 Quoted in Granatstein and Bothwell, *Pirouette*, 270. On an earlier occasion Canada had facilitated the transit of British fighter aircraft to Belize in a border dispute with Guatemala. The question of Canadian nuclear exports to Argentina also arose in 1982, from the reasonable fear that a government as irresponsible as the Argentine military junta might try to develop its own nuclear weapons. See MacGuigan, *Inside Look*, 183n.55.

34 Clark, *Hope and Glory*, 389.

35 Sir Charles Powell, Thatcher's private secretary, argued that the Thatcher-Reagan relationship was so strong because both believed in "the same, basic, quite simple propositions: ... that communism was evil and had to be destroyed; they believed in the free market and low taxes." Powell is quoted in Deborah Strober and Gerald Strober, eds., *Reagan: The Man and His Presidency* (Boston: Houghton Mifflin, 1998), 149.

36 MacGuigan, *Inside Look*, 44.

37 Mark MacGuigan, interview with author, 19 January 1988.

38 Allan Gotlieb, interview with author, December 1994.

39 MacGuigan, *Inside Look*, 10.

40 De Montigny Marchand, interview with author, 11 July 1988, agreed that there was a clear connection between the purchase of the tanks and the desired contractual link with Europe. The Finance Department opposed the purchase.

41 General Donald MacNamara, interview with author, September 1996.

42 There is an obvious connection between those who were anti-military nuclear activists and those opposed to all uses of nuclear power. As the nuclear historian Spencer Weart put it, "the reactor wars reflected a profound division in modern society," with most journalists on the anti-nuclear side of the debate: Weart, *Nuclear Fear: A History of Images* (Cambridge, MA: Harvard University Press, 1988), 365. There is of course also a connection between the anti-nuclear activists of 1970 and those of 1980: see Lawrence S. Wittner, *Resisting the Bomb: A History of the World Nuclear Disarmament Movement* (Stanford, CA: Stanford University Press, 1997).

43 James Stark, *Cold War Blues: The Operation Dismantle Story* (Hull, QC: Voyageur, 1991), 299.

44 Examples of such songs include "Overkill" and "It's a Mistake" by Men at Work, "99 Red Balloons" by Nena, and "Two Tribes" by Frankie Goes to Hollywood. I am indebted to Tom Nichols for this information.

45 See Nuke Pop, "Nuclear War Fiction, 1927-1988," www.wsu.edu/~brians/nukepop/chart.html.

46 Quoted in Edmund Morris, *Dutch: A Memoir of Ronald Reagan* (New York: Random House, 1999), 498. It was, Morris wrote, "the first and only [such] admission I have been able to find in his papers."

47 The exchange appears to have included Trudeau telling his fellow leaders, "We should be busting our asses for peace," to which Thatcher replied, "Pierre, you are such a comfort to the Kremlin." See John Noble, "Getting the Eagle's Attention without Tweaking Its Beak," *Policy Options*, February 2003, 39-44, especially 41.

48 Mark MacGuigan, interview with author, 19 January 1988. There is a slightly different phrasing in MacGuigan's memoirs, *Inside Look*, 44. Trudeau's grudging respect did not earn him especially good treatment from Thatcher. According to MacGuigan's successor, Allan MacEachen, Thatcher treated Trudeau rudely at the latter's final G7 summit, in 1984. Reagan, on the other hand, always dealt with Trudeau with courtesy: Allan MacEachen, interview with author, 14 March 1988. According to De Montigny Marchand, Trudeau's "sherpa" for the 1984 summit, Trudeau and Thatcher got into a tremendous row at the summit over relations between the rich First World and the poor Third World.

49 Thatcher is quoted in Christina McCall and Stephen Clarkson, *Trudeau and Our Times*, vol. 2, *The Heroic Delusion* (Toronto: McClelland and Stewart, 1994), 359. Reagan "really liked Margaret Thatcher; that was a very close relationship," Edwin Meese, the White House counsellor, later stated (quoted in Strober and Strober, *Reagan*, 149). He also noted that Reagan "was much more formal with other leaders – Pierre Trudeau and Mitterrand – because they were formal too." The Reagan diary is quoted in Morris, *Dutch*, 486. Reagan once showed his biographer, Morris, a poster in which Reagan as Clark Gable is carrying Thatcher as Vivien Leigh "upstairs for a night of wild abandon" (*Dutch*, 392).

50 "I think Mitterrand himself felt he had to regain some respect for France in the rest of Canada," De Montigny Marchand, a senior Canadian diplomat, commented (interview with author, 11 July 1988).

51 Mark MacGuigan, interview with author, 19 January 1988; McCall and Clarkson, *Trudeau and Our Times*, 2:375.

52 On Eagleburger's remarks, uttered at a lunch at the Carnegie endowment, see McCall and Clarkson, *Trudeau*, 2:512n. Eagleburger immediately sensed that he had made a gaffe; but it was one of those

gaffes that actually encapsulated a sentiment or an atmosphere; and in any case to wonder, colourfully, what the Canadians thought they were doing was a reasonable and defensible stand: Lawrence Eagleburger, interview with author, Washington, DC, April 2002.

53 Canadian newspapers will show the date as 31 August because of the International Date Line.

54 A lively "conspiracy" literature flourished around this issue in the 1980s. Eventually the International Civil Aviation Organization issued a report that placed the blame squarely on what was by then the former Soviet Union.

55 Walker, *Cold War*, 276, 286.

56 The government of Grenada had recently overthrown and then murdered another Marxist leader, Maurice Bishop.

57 In his foreign policy memoirs, *The Canadian Way*, Trudeau and his co-author Ivan Head were still exercised over the American action: "A military invasion unauthorized by international law was not ... an acceptable means" to depose even an admittedly abusive and tyrannical government. Trudeau would evidently have preferred "a negotiated resolution," though how that could have been achieved is unclear. Ivan Head and Pierre Trudeau, *The Canadian Way* (Toronto: McClelland and Stewart, 1995), 130.

58 Probably the only serious political accomplishment of the German peace movement was the replacement of the Social Democratic chancellor, Helmut Schmidt, with a more conservative chancellor, who was, if possible, even more pro-NATO.

59 Jack Matlock, *Autopsy on an Empire: The American Ambassador's Account of the Fall of the Soviet Union* (New York: Random House, 1995), 74-6, observes that Yakovlev sought reassignment because of discomfort with Brezhnev's cult-like status in Moscow.

60 Ibid., 76, notes that in public Yakovlev demonstrated no flexibility on the content of Soviet foreign policy: in 1984 he was still publishing denunciations of the United States' pursuit of "the sickest idea," namely, world military domination. It is therefore a question how candid or revealing his discussions with Trudeau may have been in substance, even if they were relaxed and congenial in form.

61 Mark MacGuigan, interview with author, 19 January 1988.

Conclusion: Multilateral by Profession, Muddled by Nature

1 Though it is inevitably and excessively schematic, the book *Generations* by William Straus and Neil Howe (New York: Quill, William Morrow, 1991) makes a useful point that chronological divisions in the population do help explain fashions in politics and culture. For our period, they map out two generations that, they argue, have different formations and different characteristics: 1883-1900 and 1901-1924.

2 Lawrence Eagleburger, interview with author, Washington, DC, April 2002.

3 It was still a large sum: $9 billion, for 82,000 military personnel and 37,000 civilians.

4 See figures in Timothy Garton Ash, *Free World: Why a Crisis in the West Reveals the Opportunity of Our Time* (Toronto: Viking Canada, 2004), 68-9.

FURTHER READING AND A NOTE ON SOURCES

The forty years of Canadian history between 1945 and 1984 produced mounds of documents and mountains of books. Almost all sources for the period before 1984 are paper records, but they can be supplemented – and have been, for this volume – by reference to the Canadian Broadcasting Corporation's digital archives. Moreover, records originally in paper, such as the Mackenzie King diary and the minutes of the Canadian and British Cabinets, have been digitized and made accessible through the internet, at present down through the mid-1970s. The efforts of organizations such as the Cold War International History Project (CWIHP) at the Woodrow Wilson Center in Washington DC, or the National Security Archive in the same city, have also greatly facilitated researchers' tasks. In some senses, at least, research has been made easier by advances in technology.

Some archives are better than others, and their relative standing has varied with time. The Public Archives of Canada for many years set the standard in the English-speaking world for ease of access and efficiency. Renamed, successively and ineptly, the National Archives of Canada and then, thanks to a merger, Library and Archives Canada (LAC), the archives and its achievements have latterly been rather more mixed – advanced in digitization and, so to speak, distance access, but, thanks to a tangle of "access" and "privacy" legislation, less useful and frequently disappointing to researchers who have made the trek to Ottawa. In some cases papers that were once open are now closed – for example those of Eldorado, formerly the government's uranium agency.

Official documents can be supplemented by private collections, usually the papers of politicians, bureaucrats, and journalists. The papers of most of the politicians mentioned in this book have been deposited in Ottawa, at LAC – Mackenzie King, Louis St Laurent, John Diefenbaker (in microfilm), Lester B. Pearson, and Pierre Elliott Trudeau, to name only the most prominent.

The manuscript collections are a kind of inert memory, awaiting excavation and interpretation. Historical actors often prefer to take a more direct hand in shaping how they are remembered, through memoirs or authorized biographies, or, in a combination of the two genres, ghost-written accounts – what might be called "very authorized" biographies. Lester B. Pearson set the standard, employing two research assistants to find the documents and background material for his memoirs, but reserving the final interpretation for his own quite elegant prose. But Pearson died partway through, meaning that only the first volume of his three-volume memoirs was his alone. The remainder had to be cobbled together by his assistants. As a result the last two volumes are rather cruder than the first, but less studied and less defensive – and possibly of greater historical interest.

Pearson has been the subject of a number of studies, the most important of which is the elegantly written and perceptive two-volume biography by John English, *Shadow of Heaven, 1897-1948* (Toronto: Lester and Orpen Dennys, 1989) and *The Worldly Years, 1948-1972* (Toronto: Knopf, 1992). Pearson's son Geoffrey wrote a very useful study of his father's career, *Seize the Day: Lester B. Pearson and Crisis Diplomacy* (Ottawa: Carleton University Press, 1993); especially noteworthy are the chapters on atomic weaponry and on Suez. Norman Hillmer produced a collection of essays – *Pearson: The Unlikely Gladiator* (Montreal and Kingston: McGill-Queen's University Press, 1999) – that place foreign policy and domestic politics in tandem.

Finally, Pearson was the principal figure in a collection of interviews published in two volumes by the journalist Peter Stursberg. The volume most relevant to foreign affairs is *Lester Pearson and the American Dilemma* (Toronto: Doubleday, 1980).

Louis St Laurent did not compose his own memoirs and was instead memorialized by his former private secretary, Dale Thomson, in his book *Louis St Laurent: Canadian* (Toronto: Macmillan, 1967). Thomson's book contains more than first meets the eye and is based on the St Laurent papers. But those papers had been winnowed during St Laurent's transition from prime minister to opposition leader in 1957, and as a result they are on many issues either non-existent or sadly incomplete. It remains unclear, therefore, whether a better biography can ever be written about St Laurent.

St Laurent's ministers for the most part did not write memoirs. His most important colleague, C.D. Howe, received an authorized biography, by Robert Bothwell and William Kilbourn, inevitably titled *C.D. Howe: A Biography* (Toronto: McClelland and Stewart, 1979). J.W. Pickersgill, the minister of citizenship and immigration, wrote three memoirs, *My Years with Louis St Laurent* (Toronto: University of Toronto Press, 1975), *The Road Back* (Toronto: University of Toronto Press, 1986) and, later, *Seeing Canada Whole: A Memoir* (Markham: Fitzhenry and Whiteside, 1994). Not content with that, Pickersgill edited four volumes of the Mackenzie King diary, covering 1939 to 1948, *The Mackenzie King Record* (Toronto: University of Toronto Press, 1961-1970); these have now largely been superseded by the electronic version of the diary on the internet. Pickersgill was a Liberal partisan who, though he had his reservations about Mackenzie King, adored St Laurent. "Jack thought St Laurent was his mother," Dale Thomson once quipped.

John Diefenbaker also produced memoirs, and also in three volumes, *One Canada* (Toronto: Macmillan, 1972-1975). They certainly make clear how Diefenbaker wanted to be remembered, but they are not all that reliable as a guide to the history of the man and his times. Much to be preferred is the full and mercifully unauthorized biography by Denis Smith, *Rogue Tory: The Life and Legend of John G. Diefenbaker* (Toronto: Macfarlane, Walter and Ross, 1995). Smith spent many years thinking about his subject, and the result is a study that is both learned and penetrating. There is also an excellent study of Diefenbaker's record in foreign policy by the diplomat Basil Robinson, *Diefenbaker's World: A Populist in Foreign Affairs* (Toronto: University of Toronto Press, 1988). Robinson manages the near-impossible in dealing with Diefenbaker – he is unusually balanced and fair. Robinson's work should be supplemented by a study by the journalist Knowlton Nash, *Kennedy and Diefenbaker: Fear and Loathing across the Undefended Border* (Toronto: McClelland and Stewart, 1990). Curiously, one of the first books produced on Diefenbaker's record in foreign policy remains one of the best: Jon B. McLin, *Canada's Changing Defense Policy, 1957-1963* (Baltimore, MD: Johns Hopkins University Press, 1967).

As with Pearson, there is a two-volume collection of interviews about Diefenbaker by Peter Stursberg, more tightly edited and therefore better than the Pearson collection: *Diefenbaker: Leadership Gained* (Toronto: University of Toronto Press, 1975) and *Diefenbaker: Leadership Lost* (Toronto: University of Toronto Press, 1976).

Pierre Trudeau, prime minister from 1968 to 1979 and 1980 to 1984 did leave a memoir of sorts (*Memoirs*, Toronto: McClelland and Stewart, 1993). It managed to rival Diefenbaker's memoirs for lack of substance and satisfaction; and, coming from someone renowned for his style, that quality was notably absent. Two academics, Jack Granatstein and Robert Bothwell, produced a study entitled *Pirouette: Pierre Trudeau and Foreign Policy* (Toronto: University of Toronto Press, 1990). Based on a combination of interviews and documentary research, it took a moderately sceptical view of Trudeau and his achievements. Trudeau and his foreign policy guru, Ivan Head, responded with a book, *The Canadian Way: Shaping Canada's Foreign Policy* (Toronto: McClelland and Stewart, 1995), which takes a somewhat more favourable view of the former prime minister's record but, at the same time, manages to be vastly more informative than the Trudeau memoirs.

A number of foreign ministers have also left their bookmarks. Pearson we have mentioned. His Conservative successors, Sidney Smith and Howard Green, left no memoirs of their own, though there are persistent rumours of a Green biography in the offing. Pearson's own external affairs minister, Paul Martin Sr., produced three books, a very lengthy two-volume memoir, *A Very Public Life* (Toronto: Deneau, 1983, 1985), and his *London Diaries, 1974-1979* (Ottawa: University of Ottawa Press, 1988), the latter edited by W.R. Young. The memoirs in particular suffer from Martin's desire to justify his career at almost any cost. The career might have been better left to speak for itself, as it will in a future biography.

Three ministers of national defence are the subject of books. Brooke Claxton, minister from 1946 to 1954, is ably and on the whole admiringly dissected by David Bercuson in a biography, *True Patriot* (Toronto: University of Toronto Press, 1993). Paul Hellyer did his own memoir, *Damn the Torpedoes* (Toronto: McClelland and Stewart, 1990); the title pretty accurately sums up Hellyer's career. Barney Danson, a defence minister under Trudeau, wrote (with Curtis Fahey) *Not Bad for a Sergeant: The Memoirs of Barney Danson* (Toronto: Dundurn, 2002).

Mitchell Sharp, minister of external affairs from 1968 to 1974, produced a modest and well-regarded set of memoirs, which he wrote himself: *Which Reminds Me ...* (Toronto: University of Toronto Press, 1994). Much shorter than Martin's, they are more informative. Don Jamieson, external affairs minister in the late 1970s, died early but left a draft memoir, published in two volumes, of which the second, *A World unto Itself* (St John's: Breakwater, 1991), covers some of his service in the Trudeau Cabinet. Mark MacGuigan, minister from 1980 to 1982, also left a draft memoir at his death, subsequently edited by P. Whitney Lackenbauer as *An Inside Look at External Affairs during the Trudeau Years: The Memoirs of Mark MacGuigan* (Calgary: University of Calgary Press, 2002). MacGuigan's memoirs received a rather mixed reception, especially from alumni of External Affairs.

The various undersecretaries (today called strictly deputy ministers) left behind only one published account covering this period. Arnold Heeney, undersecretary under Pearson, penned *The Things That Are Caesar's* (Toronto: University of Toronto Press, 1972), based on his diaries. They are quite informative, especially on Canadian-American relations, though marred by the occasional factual error. Basil Robinson, undersecretary in the mid-1970s, wrote on an earlier period. The dearth of undersecretarial memoirs is almost made up by the prolific Escott Reid: *Time of Fear and Hope* (1977), dealing with the origins of NATO, *Envoy to Nehru* (1981), *On Duty: A Canadian at the Making of the United Nations, Hungary and Suez 1956: A View from New Delhi* (1987) and finally, *Radical Mandarin: The Memoirs of Escott Reid* (Toronto: University of Toronto Press, 1989). Reid followed the maxim, To the scribblers belong the spoils. Much of Reid's detail cannot be found anywhere else; but for Reid as for a number of other figures, the interpretation offered by Jack Granatstein in his *The Ottawa Men: The Civil Service Mandarins, 1935-1957* (Toronto: University of Toronto Press, 1982), is to be preferred. Granatstein also authored an important study on Norman Robertson, twice undersecretary and Pearson's close colleague, *A Man of Influence: Norman Robertson and Canadian Statecraft* (Ottawa: Deneau, 1981). Tangentially connected to foreign affairs is Gordon Robertson, clerk of the Privy Council under Trudeau; his book, *Memories of a Very Civil Servant: Mackenzie King to Pierre Trudeau* (Toronto: University of Toronto Press, 2000), is especially informative on the St Laurent period but also makes plain the author's dislike of Pierre Trudeau.

Among ambassadors, several have left memoirs. The best value and the best read are the several volumes by Charles Ritchie: *The Siren Years: A Canadian Diplomat Abroad* (Toronto: Macmillan, 1974), *Diplomatic Passport* (Toronto: Macmillan, 1981), and *Storm Signals* (Toronto: Macmillan, 1983). There are some odd discrepancies in Ritchie's work, but they are unimportant compared to his wicked insights into the diplomatic world. Much more solemn is the autobiography of Canada's long-serving ambassador to the Soviet Union, Robert Ford, *Our Man in Moscow* (Toronto:

University of Toronto Press, 1989). It should be read in tandem with Peter Roberts, *George Kostakis: A Russian Life in Art* (Ottawa: Carleton University Press, 1994), which deals in part with life in the Moscow embassy. George Ignatieff, born in St Petersburg before the Russian Revolution and a refugee to Canada, became a distinguished Canadian diplomat. His memoirs are called *The Making of a Peacemonger* (Toronto: University of Toronto Press, 1985).

Arnold Smith, a former ambassador to the Soviet Union but more importantly secretary general of the Commonwealth in the 1960s, wrote (with Clyde Sanger) a useful account of the latter experience: *Stitches in Time: The Commonwealth in World Politics* (Don Mills, ON: General, 1981). Another ex-ambassador, Arthur Andrew, published a book that was more a historical essay, perhaps even an elegy, than a memoir: *The Rise and Fall of a Middle Power: Canadian Diplomacy from King to Mulroney* (Toronto: Lorimer, 1993). Chester Ronning, *A Memoir of China in Revolution from the Boxer Rebellion to the People's Republic* (New York: Random House, 1974), is revealing and very informative, though not always in ways its author intended.

Ronning's special study was China, but there are a number of books dealing with Canada's relations with Asia. The standard on Canadian-Chinese relations is Paul Evans and B.M. Frolic, eds., *Reluctant Adversaries: Canada and the People's Republic of China, 1949-1970* (Toronto: University of Toronto Press, 1991). Given the flow of information since its publication, it is likely to be superseded in the foreseeable future.

The Korean War has provoked a number of studies. For our purposes, the most important are Denis Stairs, *The Diplomacy of Constraint: Canada, the Korean War and the United States* (Toronto: University of Toronto Press, 1974); Robert Prince, "The Limits of Constraint: Canadian-American Relations and the Korean War, 1950-51," *Journal of Canadian Studies* 27, 4 (1992-1993): 129-52; and William Johnston, *A War of Patrols: Canadian Army Operations in Korea* (Vancouver: UBC Press, 2003). Steven Hugh Lee, *Outposts of Empire* (Montreal and Kingston: McGill-Queen's University Press, 1995) discusses Canada's approach to imperial decline in Asia. The politics of NATO, mentioned elsewhere under defence policy, are discussed in John Milloy, *The North Atlantic Treaty Organization, 1948-1957: Community or Alliance?* (Montreal and Kingston: McGill-Queen's University Press, 2006).

The Cuban missile crisis of 1962, so important to Canadian-American relations, is mentioned in practically any book covering Canadian politics in the 1960s. Canadian-Cuban relations more particularly are covered by John M. Kirk and Peter McKenna, *Canada-Cuba Relations: The Other Good Neighbor Policy* (Gainesville: University Press of Florida, 1997). Latin America more generally is covered in James Rochlin, *Discovering the Americas: The Evolution of Canadian Foreign Policy towards Latin America* (Vancouver: UBC Press, 1997).

Vietnam, the other main point of political dispute with the United States, was endlessly fascinating to Canadians in the 1960s; readers should check the notes to chapters 12 and 13 for contemporary Vietnam-related material. In terms of academic studies, Douglas Ross's *In the Interests of Peace: Canada and Vietnam, 1954-1973* (Toronto: University of Toronto Press, 1984) is mostly history, though with occasional political science jargon thrown in.

Essential to any study of Canadian foreign policy in this period is the volume by John Hilliker and Donald Barry, *Canada's Department of External Affairs*, vol. 2, *Coming of Age, 1946-1968* (Montreal and Kingston: McGill-Queen's University Press, 1995). It is more than an institutional history, though a sense of the foreign affairs bureaucracy is at its core. Hilliker, for many years the head of history in the Department of External Affairs, was one of the editors of the invaluable *Documents on Canadian External Relations*, covering the evolution of Canadian foreign policy from 1909 forward. The later volumes are now available through the internet.

James Eayrs, a distinguished political scientist at (mostly) the University of Toronto, put out five volumes covering Canadian defence and foreign policy for the period 1919-1954, collectively titled *In Defence of Canada*. For our period, volume 4, covering the late 1940s and based in large part on Brooke Claxton's unpublished memoirs, is invaluable. Sean Maloney, *War without Battles: Canada's NATO Brigade in Germany, 1951-1993* (Toronto: McGraw-Hill Ryerson, 1997), covers Canada's European garrison through its many years of deployment. Isabel Campbell's "Harmony and Dissonance: A Study of the Influence of Foreign Policy Goals on Military Decision-Making with respect to the Canadian NATO Brigade in Germany, 1951-1964" (PhD diss., Laval University, 2000) is self-explanatory. Jack Granatstein, *Canada's Army: Waging War and Keeping the Peace* (Toronto: University of Toronto Press, 2002) is a tour de force on its topic.

Canadian foreign relations were chronicled for many years through the series *Canada and World Affairs*, parcelling out the subject in two- or three-year tranches to various academic authors. Eventually the task got too much for the academics, and the series foundered; the last volume covers 1971-1973. Nevertheless, for its period, the series is a first stop for interested researchers. Beginning in 1960, the *Canadian Annual Review* (later called the *Canadian Annual Review of Politics and Public Affairs*) devoted space in each issue to defence and foreign policy. For statistics and trade for this whole period the *Canada Year Book*, published more or less annually by the Canadian government, is an invaluable source of information, especially after the *Historical Statistics of Canada*, 2nd ed. (Ottawa: Statistics Canada, 1983), now available on the Internet, runs out in the early 1970s. The *Canada Year Book* would later be turned into an ornamental objet de propagande, useless for most scholarly purposes, but down to 1984 (and a few years after) it is essential.

Trade and trade policy are usually special (and all too frequently arcane) studies. Perhaps for that reason much of the literature, which is frequently meritorious, is shunned by students on general principles. For this period the most active historian is Michael Hart, *A Trading Nation: Canadian Trade Policy from Colonialism to Globalization* (Vancouver: UBC Press, 2003); Hart's account is vigorous and readable, though it is clear he raises some misgivings among some economists. Also to be commended is an old book by John Young, *Canadian Commercial Policy,* commissioned as a special study for the Royal Commission on Canada's Economic Prospects and published by the commission in 1957. Young's discussion of tariff theory and policy is as clear as it gets. Perhaps as a result the royal commission disclaimed his work in a paragraph at the beginning of the book. Also on the economic side of things is a book by Douglas LePan, an ex-diplomat and poet. But LePan was in at the beginning of postwar economic policy, in a seminar at Cambridge University chaired by John Maynard Keynes, in 1945. LePan's account of the seminar, part of his memoir *Bright Glass of Memory* (Toronto: McGraw-Hill Ryerson, 1979), makes "the dismal science" anything but. Dimitry Anastakis, *Auto Pact: Creating a Borderless North American Auto Industry, 1960-1971* (Toronto: University of Toronto Press, 2005), is a rare case study of a Canadian trade issue, examined over time.

INDEX

Abbott, Douglas, 36

Acheson, Dean, 93; and atomic bomb, 92; and Canadian reaction to Truman Doctrine, 51; and China, 75; and Gouzenko affair, 44; and Great Britain, 101; and Korea, 80, 82, 83, 86, 92; and NATO, 274, 275; and North Atlantic treaty, 70-1; Pearson and, 101-3, 104; as secretary of state, 69; and Truman, 100, 403n5; and Wrong, 359

Achilles, Theodore, 66, 68

Afghanistan, Soviet invasion of, 360, 362

Africa: aid to, 303, 351; British colonies in, 124, 305; Canadian aid to, 302; Commonwealth and, 305; communism in, 335; decoloniz-ation in, 219; francophone, 300-1, 303; oil prices and, 351; Soviet Union and, 335; white settlement in, 305. *See also names of individual countries*

Agence de Coopération Culturelle et Tech-nique (ACCT), 302-3

aid, 79; for Africa, 303, 351; cost of, 112-13; to former colonies, 299; oil prices and, 351; political dimension of, 112; self-help vs, 300, 303; to Third World, 298; Trudeau and, 302, 303, 310-11

aircraft, 98, 111, 116, 262, 383

Alberta: NEP and, 365-6; oil in, 119, 354, 363-4

Algeria, 105, 124, 199, 238, 239, 240

Amin, Idi, 435n62

Andrew, Arthur, 354

Andropov, Yuri, 385

Anglo-American relations, 50, 122; and Korean War, 92; and nuclear weapons, 170; Suez crisis and, 126, 127, 130; trade, 28, 29

Anglo-Canadian relations, 4-5, 15, 51-2, 54, 61-2, 64, 273; during 1950s, 121-2; atomic energy and, 47-8, 49, 142; Avro Arrow and, 141; and Canada's reduction in European commitments, 288-9; Canada's resem-blance to, 6; Canadian help during Second World War, 13-14; defence, 121-2; Diefenbaker and, 138, 147; and dwindling of British power, 149; and external policy, 50;

and Korean War, 92; nationalism and, 58; and South Africa, 143

Anglo-Canadian trade, 28-9, 34, 121, 138, 139, 430n28; Common Market/EEC and, 144-5, 147, 345; Diefenbaker and, 152, 176; free, 140-1, 176; US-Canadian trade and, 138

anti-Americanism, 77-8, 120, 130-1, 191, 192, 234, 318, 332

anti-communism: aid and, 112, 113; of French Canadians, 398n15; Trudeau and, 313; US, 195-6, 206, 218, 271, 309

anti-imperialism, 105-6

Aquin, François, 256

Argentina, war with Britain, 381

armed forces, Canadian, 95, 261-2; Liberal Party and, 131; reduction in, 287, 291; Trudeau and, 382-3; unification of, 263

Asia: Canadian view of, 73-4, 103; capital investment in, 79; colonies in, 74; poverty in, 79; US and, 132. *See also names of individual countries*

Atherton, Ray, 37

Atkey, Ron, 436n26

Atlanticism, 7

atomic industry, 98-9, 111-12, 142

atomic weapons, 54, 107; ban-the-bomb movement and, 218, 383; Canada and, 42-3, 45, 389-90; as deterrent, 114; hydrogen bomb vs, 160; NATO and, 114; research, 47-8; Soviet Union and, 44, 60; UN and, 45-6; US and, 42, 92, 114; use against Japan, 42, 43, 224, 389-90. *See also* nuclear weapons

Attlee, Clement, 44, 45, 64, 92

Auriol, Vincent, 240

Austin, Warren, 85

Australia: and Indonesia, 228; and Korean War, 87; and South Africa in Commonwealth, 143; and UN veto, 21; and Vietnam War, 228, 317

Auto Pact, 189-90, 193-4, 223, 226, 319, 322-3, 325

automobile industry, 188-90

A.V. Roe, 98, 111, 141